ABYSSINIA

Teusa
Tarash

TURKANA

RATE

Moyale

MAREHAN

Mt. Kulal

Serenli

Marsabit

Maroto

BRITISH EAST AFRICA

Marich

Mt. Elgon

Baringo

Lorian
Swamp

PROTECTORATE

Mumia's
Fort Victoria

0°

Vanti
Kismayu   Gobwen

Kisumu

R. Tana

Kisii

KAVIRONDO

Shirati

NAIROBI

R. Juba

MASAI

LAKE
MAGADI

Witu
Patta Is.
Lamu

LAKE
NATRON

R. Sabaki

Mt. Longido

KILIMANJARO

Mt. Meru

Moshi

Tsavo
Voi

GIRIAMA
Malindi

Arusha   Taveta

USAMBARA

MOMBASA

R. Pangani

EAST   AFRICA

Kondoa Irangi

5°

Korogwe
Tanga   Pemba Id

Handeni
Pangani

matinde

Sadani

Dodoma

Mpwapwa

ZANZIBAR

Bagamoyo

DAR-ES-SALAAM

Kilosa

R. Ruaha

Morogoro

Pugu

Rugaro

Iringa

Kidatu

R. Rufiji

Mafia Id

WAHEHE

Mahenge

Ordnance Survey 1937.

35°   40°

HISTORY OF THE GREAT WAR

BASED ON OFFICIAL DOCUMENTS
BY DIRECTION OF THE HISTORICAL SECTION OF THE
COMMITTEE OF IMPERIAL DEFENCE

MILITARY OPERATIONS
EAST AFRICA

VOLUME I
AUGUST 1914 — SEPTEMBER 1916

COMPILED BY

Lieutenant-Colonel CHARLES HORDERN
Late Royal Engineers and General Staff

FOUNDED ON A DRAFT BY THE LATE

Major H. FitzM. Stacke, M.C., *p.s.c.*
The Worcestershire Regiment

Sketch Maps by the Compiler

THE BATTERY PRESS
Nashville

In Association With
THE IMPERIAL WAR MUSEUM
Department of Printed Books

Published jointly by
The Imperial War Museum, London
Department of Printed Books
ISBN: 0-901627-631
and
The Battery Press
P.O. Box 3107, Uptown Station
Nashville, Tennessee 37219

Eleventh in The Battery Press Great War Series
1990
ISBN: 0-89839-158-X

Printed in the United States of America

INTRODUCTION

By

DR. G. M. BAYLISS

The Keeper, Department of Printed Books, Imperial War Museum

I am pleased to introduce this volume, one of a series of reprints of British official histories of military operations in the First World War. For some time I have hoped to make this invaluable source more widely available to students of the Great War; this has now been made possible by co-operation between the Imperial War Museum and Battery Press.

The original editions in the series were produced by the Historical Section of the Committee of Imperial Defence; the first appearing in 1922 and the last in 1949. Apart from Her Majesty's Stationery Office, two commercial publishers were also involved: Macmillian put their imprint on several volumes and Heinemann was responsible for the account of the Gallipoli Campaign. Due to the number of full-colour maps, costs of production were high and this has served to limit later attempts to reprint the series, which have foundered after the publication of text only volumes.

Battery Press, in conjunction with the Imperial War Museum's Department of Printed Books, have taken up the reprinting challenge. In order to make the project viable, we have also decided not to reprint the expensive map volumes. However, readers who wish to obtain copies of any maps in the series are welcome to contact the Imperial War Museum library for further assistance. Since no complete and accurate list of the series exists, the following represents an attempt to remedy this deficiency.

Constantinople
Edmonds, Brig. Gen. Sir James E.

> The Occupation of Constantinople 1918-1923. (Draft provisional history, prepared in 1944 but not printed. It is the intention of Battery Press to produce an expanded version in cooperation with the Imperial War Museum).

East Africa
Hordern, Lt. Col. Charles

> East Africa: Vol. I. August 1914-September 1916 [based on a draft by Major H. Fitz M. Stacke]. London: H.M.S.O., 1941.
> East Africa: Vol. II. [Never published; draft chapters exist in the Public Record Office, London].

Egypt and Palestine
MacMunn, Lieut. Gen. Sir George and Falls, Captain Cyril

> Egypt and Palestine: [Vol. I] From the outbreak of war with Germany to June 1917. London: H.M.S.O., 1928. Accompanying map case.

Falls, Captain Cyril

> Egypt and Palestine: [Vol. II] From June 1917 to the end of the War. Parts I and II. London: H.M.S.O., 1930. Accompanying map case.

France and Belgium
1914
Edmonds, Brig. Gen. Sir James E.

> France and Belgium 1914: [Vol. I] August-October. Mons, the retreat to the Seine, the Marne and the Aisne, August-October 1914. London: Macmillian, 1922 (2nd. ed. 1925; 3rd. ed. 1934). Accompanying map case. [Addenda and Corrigenda to '1914' Vol. I issued with the '1918' Vol. II]. Text volume only reprinted by Shearer Publications, Woking, Surrey, 1984.

Edmonds, Brig. Gen. Sir James E.

> France and Belgium 1914: [Vol. II] Antwerp, La Bassée, Armentiéres, Messines, and Ypres, October-November 1914. London: Macmillian, 1925. Accompanying map case. [Addenda and Corrigenda issued with '1915' Vol. I and '1915' Vol. II].

1915
Edmonds, Brig. Gen. Sir James E. and Wynne, Capt. G. C.

> France and Belgium 1915: [Vol. I] Winter 1914-15: Battle of Neuve Chapelle: Battle of Ypres. London: Macmillian, 1927 Accompanying map case. [Addenda and Corrigenda issued with '1915' Vol. II and

'1916' Vol. I, '1918' Vols. I and II].

Edmonds, Brig. Gen. Sir James E.
France and Belgium 1915: [Vol. II] Battle of Aubers Ridge, Festubert, and Loos. London: Macmillian, 1928. Accompanying map case.

1916

Edmonds, Brig. Gen. Sir James E.
France and Belgium 1916: [Vol. I] Sir Douglas Haig's command to the 1st July: Battle of the Somme. London: Macmillian, 1932 Accompanying appendices volume and map case. [Addenda and Corrigenda to '1916' Vol. I issued with the '1918' Vol. II]. Text volume only reprinted by Shearer Publications, Woking, Surrey, 1986.

Miles, Captain Wilfrid
France and Belgium 1916: [Vol. II]. 2nd July 1916 to the end of the Battles of the Somme: preface by Brig. Gen. Sir James E. Edmonds. London: Macmillian, 1938. Accompanying maps and appendices volume.

1917

Falls, Captain Cyril
France and Belgium 1917: [Vol. I]. The German retreat to the Hindenburg Line and the Battle of Arras: preface by Brig. Gen. Sir James E. Edmonds. London: Macmillian, 1940.

Edmonds, Brig. Gen. Sir James E.
France and Belgium 1917: [Vol. II] 7th June-10th November: Messines and Third Ypres (Passchendaele). London: H.M.S.O., 1948. [Volume begun by Cyril Falls and G. C. Wynne completed and edited by Edmonds].

Miles, Capt. Wilfrid
France and Belgium, 1917: [Vol. III] The Battle of Cambrai; preface by Brig. Gen. Sir James E. Edmonds. London: H.M.S.O., 1948.

1918

Edmonds, Brig. Gen. Sir James E.
France and Belgium 1918: [Vol. I]. The German March offensive and its preliminaries. London: Macmillian, 1935. Accompanying appendices volume and map case. [Addenda and Corrigenda '1918' Vol. I issued with Vol. II].

Edmonds, Brig. Gen. Sir James E.
France and Belgium 1918: [Vol. II]. March-April: continuation of the German offensives. London: Macmillian, 1937. Accompanying map case. [Special addendum to '1918' Vol. II. Further Addenda and

Corrigenda issued with '1917' Vol. I and '1918' Vol. III].

Edmonds, Brig. Gen. Sir James E.
France and Belgium 1918: [Vol. III]. May-July: the German diversion offensives and the first Allied counter-offensive. London: Macmillian, 1939.

Edmonds, Brig. Gen. Sir James E.
France and Belgium 1918: [Vol. IV]. 8th August-26th September: the Franco-British offensive. London: H.M.S.O., 1947

Edmonds, Brig. Gen. Sir James E.
France and Belgium 1918: [Vol. V]. 26th September-11th November: the advance to victory. London: H.M.S.O., 1947

Gallipoli
Aspinall-Oglander, Brig. Gen. C. F.
Gallipoli: Vol. I: Inception of the campaign to May 1915. London: William Heinemann, 1929. Accompanying maps and appendices volume.

Aspinall-Oglander, Brig. Gen. C. F.
Gallipoli: Vol. II: May 1915 to the evacuation. London: William Heinemann, 1932. Accompanying maps and appendices volume.

Germany
Edmonds, Brig. Gen. Sir James E.
The Occupation of the Rhineland. London: H.M.S.O., 1944 [Limited official printing of 100 copies]. Facsimile edition with introduction by Dr. G. M. Bayliss. London: H.M.S.O. in association with the Imperial War Museum, 1987.

Italy
Edmonds, Brig. Gen. Sir James E. and Davies, H. R.
Italy, 1915-1919. London: H.M.S.O., 1949.

Macedonia
Falls, Captain Cyril
Macedonia: [Vol. I] From the outbreak of war to Spring 1917. London: H.M.S.O., 1933. Accompanying map case.

Falls, Captain Cyril
Macedonia: [Vol. II] From the Spring of 1917 to the end of the war. London: H.M.S.O., 1935. Accompanying map case.

Mesopotamia
Moberly, Brig. Gen. F. J.
The Campaign in Mesopotamia 1914-1918. Vol. I: London: H.M.S.O.,

1923. Vol. II: London: H.M.S.O., 1924. Vol. III: London: H.M.S.O., 1925. Vol. IV: London: H.M.S.O., 1927.

Persia
Moberly, Brig. Gen F. J.
Operations in Persia, 1914-1919. Confidential edition. London: H.M.S.O., 1929. Public edition. London: H.M.S.O., [in association with the Imperial War Museum], 1987.

Rhineland
Edmonds, Brig. Gen. Sir James E.
The Occupation of the Rhineland, 1918-1929. Confidential edition. London: H.M.S.O., 1944. Public edition, with introduction by Dr. G. M. Bayliss. London: H.M.S.O., [in association with the Imperial War Museum], 1987.

Togoland and the Cameroons
Moberly, Brig. Gen F. J.
Togoland and the Cameroons, 1914-1916. London: H.M.S.O., 1931.

OTHER RELATED VOLUMES

Order of Battle of Divisions
Becke, Major A. F.
Order of Battle of Divisions. Part 1: The Regular British Divisions. London: H.M.S.O., 1935. Part 2A: The Territorial Force Mounted Divisions and the 1st-Line Territorial Force Divisions (42-56). London: H.M.S.O., 1936. Part 2B: The 2nd-Line Territorial Force Divisions (57th-69th) with the Home Service Divisions. (71st-73rd) and 74th and 75th Divisions. London: H.M.S.O., 1937. Part 3A: New Army Divisions (9-26). London: H.M.S.O., 1938. Part 3B: New Army Divisions (30-41) and 63rd (R.N.) Division. London: H.M.S.O., 1945. Part 4: The Army Council, G. H. Q's, Army and Corps, 1914-1918 London: H.M.S.O., 1945.

Principal Events
Committee of Imperial Defence, Historical Section
Principal events 1914-1918. London: H.M.S.O., 1922.

Transportation on the Western Front
Henniker, Col. A. M.
Transportation on the Western Front 1914-1918; with introduction by Brig. Gen. Sir James E. Edmonds. London: H.M.S.O., 1937. Accompanying case of maps.

PREFACE

Of all the various subsidiary enterprises of the war of 1914–18, the campaign in East Africa, with the first half of which this volume is concerned, is probably the least known. The scene of operations was far away; those engaged—among whom was only a single Regular battalion of the British service—were almost wholly troops drawn from, and returning to, distant parts of the Empire; of these, a large number were native units of the Indian and African forces. To them, as to the South Africans who for a year played so conspicuous a part, the keeping of war diaries and submission of operation reports—the indispensable raw material for the historian—although prescribed as a normal military duty, can hardly have seemed of real importance under the trying conditions of mobile warfare in one of the most arduous campaigns in British military history. Almost at the outset there came a disastrous failure, the redemption of which, though complete, was but gradual. The distant campaign, moreover, bore no visible fruit in any effects elsewhere.

For all these reasons it is not surprising that the material available for compilation of the history is exceptionally scanty. Notably it is to be deplored that even the official daily war diary kept at G.H.Q. contains but seldom the proceedings of conferences at which important decisions were taken; so that the considerations which influenced the Commander-in-Chief cannot always be known. Many of the non-regular units, moreover, for one reason or another, kept no records at all over considerable periods of time.

Fortunately a very large number of survivors of the campaign have rendered priceless assistance to the compiler by filling in gaps in the story and by supplementing, in their comments on the earlier drafts of the history, the meagre information contained in such official records as there are. Not only in regard to the narrative, but also in the matter of topographical information for the sketch-maps, most grateful acknowledgment is due to all those who have so readily made generous and valuable contributions in aid of the work.

No attempt has been made either to criticize, or to deduce lessons from, the campaign in any detail. Such remark as has seemed to be called for has, wherever possible, been left to be inferred by the reader from the actual words of the contemporary records, more especially of the official despatches and other documents; on the tactical side, the technique of bush warfare must naturally remain a matter for the official publications on the subject. Nor, in this first volume, has it been deemed necessary to deal separately with such matters as the engineer and pioneer work of the campaign—much of which necessarily fell to the fighting units themselves; the signal service, which successfully kept up communication over the immense distances involved; the all-important medical services, already dealt with in the official medical history of the war; the air service afforded by the few available machines of that early epoch, whose work is already recorded in the official air history; and the political aspects of the invasion and occupation of enemy territory. All of these, concerning as they do the campaign as a whole, are, it is felt, matters for a later and final volume.

The present volume is founded, as stated on the title-page, on an earlier draft by the late Major H. FitzM. Stacke, M.C., whose sudden death in November 1935 was a serious set-back to the history. To the use of that draft, which has supplied to a considerable extent the chronological framework on which the story has been built up, the compiler is greatly indebted. The devoted labours of Major Stacke extended considerably beyond the period here covered, and it had at first been intended to publish the history of the campaign as a whole. In the course, however, of the work in continuation of his draft, so much additional information was received which threw an entirely new light on what had already been done, that it became necessary eventually to reconstruct the entire history. This has consequently become a wholly fresh compilation, whose author may perhaps be permitted to express not only his indebtedness and gratitude to his predecessor, but also his lasting regret that a valued colleague should not himself have lived to write, as he undoubtedly would have done, the very different account now presented.

One of the few writers on the campaign has expressed elsewhere his conviction that when the official history appeared it could not fail to be inaccurate, for lack of data. On this it can only be said that no effort has been spared to ensure that this history is as complete and as accurate as it can be made; and that correction in regard to any facts stated will be welcomed with a view to subsequent amendment.

Among the numerous commentators and others to whom collectively acknowledgment is made above, and without whose aid the gloomy forecast just mentioned might well have been fulfilled, the compiler is most especially indebted to the following : The Governments of the Union of South Africa, Uganda, Kenya, Tanganyika Territory, Nyasaland, Northern and Southern Rhodesia ; the Colonial Office, especially in connection with the K.A.R. ; the War Office, especially for the assistance of its Librarian, Mr. Baldry ; the India Office, Admiralty and Foreign Office ; Lieut.-General G. J. Giffard, C.B., D.S.O. ; Major-Generals Sir A. H. M. Edwards, K.B.E., C.B., M.V.O., and S. H. Sheppard, C.B., C.M.G., D.S.O. ; Colonels H. F. L. Grant, D.S.O., and R. Meinertzhagen, D.S.O. ; Lieut.-Colonels C. F. Anderson, D.S.O. ; W. E. Beazley, C.I.E., M.C. ; S. J. Cole, O.B.E. ; Sir M. Crofton, Bart., D.S.O. ; L. M. Davies ; R. L. McClintock, C.M.G., D.S.O. ; H. T. Russell.

His acknowledgments are due also to Major E. Boell, of the German *Kriegsgeschichtliche Forschungsanstalt des Heeres*, by whose courtesy up to the middle of 1939 much useful detail as to the German side of the campaign was received.

There is no member of the Historical Section to whom the compiler is not indebted in greater or less degree for cheerful and unfailing help in all his work.

It remains, finally, to make very special mention of the late Major G. S. F. Middleton, The Royal Inniskilling Fusiliers, who by the kindness of the War Office served from 11111 to 11711 on personal attachment to the successive East African historians. Bringing to the work recent experience with the K.A.R. and an enthusiasm for East Africa, he devoted himself whole-heartedly to the history. No one but the compiler can know with what untiring energy he worked to sift from the unpromising material the last grain of information to be extracted from it, nor how greatly he contributed—especially where the K.A.R. was concerned— to the accuracy and completeness of presentation which were his and the compiler's aim.

January 1941.   C. H.

NOTE ON MAPS

The reader will unavoidably be hampered by the absence of detailed maps. This is due not only to considerations of economy but also to the fact that no very accurate maps exist, and to the dearth of contemporary operation and other sketches. Nevertheless it is hoped that the sketch-maps which accompany the text, and without which it will be found difficult to follow the narrative, will suffice to give a general idea of the operations.

Throughout the campaign the deficiencies of the maps in use gave constant trouble. The German territory and adjacent areas were covered by the German standard map, scale 1/300,000 (about 4¾ miles to 1 inch). This plausible map, fairly well got up and officially printed, was in fact far from accurate and in many places blank, as might be expected in a largely unknown country. The limited supply available was gradually supplemented by the British troops with local road sketches and skeleton road-maps ; but the margin of error in these was even greater than in the German map.[1]

In the matter of place-names, variations of language and native usage were further complications. It was only as time went on that harassed staff officers discovered that, e.g., " Makwele " and " Kwa Konje " (sketch 37) were the same place, that " Kwa Mugwe " appeared sometimes as " Kwa Mberue ", and " Kitovo " as " Kwa Mkomba ". A yet further complication was the existence of places bearing identical or very similar names inconveniently near to one another : e.g., two places named Muyaga (sketch 59) ; two named Nyanza (sketch 59) ; Kiemsambi and Kiasimbi (sketch 8). In addition, the German maps showed invented names, of which the commonest was Porilager (camp in the bush) ; the oral evidence of natives as to topographical information could never be relied upon ; while the linguistic interchangeability of certain letters, notably R and L, made matters worse.

Distances were likewise uncertain : e.g., the map distances of Kwamlere and Makanya from Handeni (sketch 37) were respectively 8 and 18 miles ; on the march they proved to be respectively 11 and 23 miles. On the British road-maps produced during the campaign, distances were usually marked in hours of march.

The many discrepancies led inevitably to confusion in dealing with native informants and guides, and at times to unfounded suspicions of treachery.

---

[1] A survivor claims to have seen against a name in a captured German casualty-list the note : " Lost and shot through using a British map ".
A good example of the confusion caused by the bad maps in use is given at p. 495, f.n. 2.

More serious was what one survivor has described as the "ineradicable optimism" with which commanders were apt to base tactical operations on the German maps because these " were presented in a form which they associated with accuracy ". It is safe to say that no map used in this campaign could be relied upon as accurate by the standards prevailing in the European theatre of war. To this must be added the fact that in the earlier stages many of the commanders engaged, not being trained regular soldiers, were unable to make the fullest use of such maps as there were.

For the present volume, the spellings of place-names given in the lists published by the Royal Geographical Society's Permanent Committee on Geographical Names have been adopted ; others are based on the best authority available.

Where no north-point appears, the sides of the sketch-map are true north and south. Distances given in the text are, generally speaking, as the crow flies.

ABBREVIATIONS.

Besides the usual British military abbreviations the following are used :

Abt.	Abteilung.
B.O.A.	Belgian Official Account.
F.K.	Feld-Kompagnie.
Res.K.	Reserve-Kompagnie.
Sch.K.	Schützen-Kompagnie.

CONTENTS

CHAPTER I

INTRODUCTORY :

Note.—Physical Characteristics of the Theatre of War

CHAPTER II

THE NORTHERN AREA : THE OPENING PHASE :

CHAPTER III

THE NORTHERN AREA : INITIAL MILITARY OPERATIONS :

CHAPTER IV

CHAPTER V

CHAPTER VI

CHAPTER VII

CHAPTER VIII

CHAPTER IX

CHAPTER X

CHAPTER XI

CHAPTER XII

CHAPTER XIII

CHAPTER XIV

CHAPTER XV

CHAPTER XVI

CHAPTER XVII

CHAPTER XVIII

CHAPTER XXI

CHAPTER XXII

CHAPTER XXIII

CHAPTER XXIV

CHAPTER XXIX

APPENDICES

SKETCH–MAPS

All sketch maps, except those against which a page number appears, will be found in numerical order at the end of the volume.

CONTENTS   xvii

xviii   CONTENTS

BIBLIOGRAPHY

Note.—The following list does not purport to be a complete bibliography of the East Africa campaign of 1914–18.

I. GENERAL HISTORIES.

(*a*) BRITISH :

(1) *Official* :
Military Operations, France and Belgium.
  ,,   ,,   Egypt and Palestine.
  ,,   ,,   Mesopotamia.
  ,,   ,,   Gallipoli.
Naval Operations.
The War in the Air.
The Union of South Africa and the Great War, 1914–19 (S. African General Staff).
The South Africans with General Smuts in German East Africa, Collyer (S. African Government Press).

(2) *Unofficial* :
The Empire at War : Vol. IV (Africa), Lucas.
British Campaigns in Africa and the Pacific, Dane.
The East African Field Force, 1915–19, Fendall.
General Smuts's Campaign in East Africa, Crowe.

(*b*) BELGIAN :
Les Campagnes Coloniales Belges, 1914–18 (Belgian Official Account).
Ephémérides des Campagnes Belges en Afrique, 1914–17 (Belgian Official).
L'Armée Belge dans la Guerre Mondiale, Tasnier and van Overstraeten.

(*c*) PORTUGUESE :
A Grande Guerra em Moçambique, Pires.

(*d*) GERMAN :
Der Krieg zur See : die Kämpfe in den Kolonien (Official.)
Marine-archiv : der Kreuzer–Krieg 1914–18, von Waldeyer–Hartz. (Official.)
Berichte der Kaiserlichen Schutztruppe, Aug., Sept., Okt. 1914 (Official).
Der Grosse Krieg, 1914–18, Schwarte.
Deutsch-Ostafrika im Weltkriege, Schnee.
Vier Jahre Weltkrieg in Deutsch–Ostafrika, Arning.
Deutschtum und Ausland, 15. Heft : Entwicklung der D.O., Rupie, v. Wehling.

Note.—Up to 31st December 1940 the German official account of the East Africa campaign, 1914–18, believed to be in course of preparation, has not been available.

II. REGIMENTAL HISTORIES.
BRITISH :
Britain's Sea Soldiers : a History of the Royal Marines, Blumberg.
The Royal Fusiliers in the Great War, O'Neill.
The Loyal North Lancashire Regiment, Wylly.
The 2nd Rhodesia Regiment in East Africa, Capell.
The Star and Crescent (17th Cavalry, I.A.), Yeats-Brown.
The 4/10th Baluch Regiment (129th Baluchis), Thatcher.
K.A.R., Lloyd-Jones.
With the Nigerians in German East Africa, Downes.
The Gold Coast Regiment, Clifford.
The Story of the 1st Cape Corps, Difford.

III. MEMOIRS, ETC.
(i) BRITISH :
Three Years of War in East Africa, Buchanan.
Marching on Tanga, F. Brett Young.
Sketches of the East Africa Campaign, Dolbey.
East Africa by Motor Lorry, Campbell.
The Story of a Lion Hunt, Wienholt.
With Botha and Smuts in Africa, Whittall.
Kenya Chronicles, Cranworth.
Ambush, Wynn.

(ii) GERMAN :
Meine Erinnerungen aus Ost-Afrika, von Lettow-Vorbeck.
My Reminiscences of East Africa (translation of preceding), von Lettow-Vorbeck.
Mit Lettow-Vorbeck durch Afrika, Deppe.
Kumbuki, Hauer.
Der Triumph der deutschen Tropen-Medizin, Hauer.
Kriegs–Safari, Wenig.

WORKS OF REFERENCE :
Handbook of British East Africa, Ward and Milligan.
Handbook of Nyasaland, S. S. Murray.
Handbook of Tanganyika Territory, Sayers.
Handbook of Uganda, Wallis.
Military Report on Rhodesia, General Staff, W.O.
The Map of Africa by Treaty, Hertslet.
South and East African Year-Book, Union-Castle Mail Steamship Co.

MISCELLANEOUS :
Africa, W. Fitzgerald.
Smuts v. Lettow ("Army Quarterly", Jan. 1925), Orr.
The Operations on Lake Tanganyika in 1915 (Journal of R. United Service Institution, Nov. 1934), Spicer-Simson.

CALENDAR OF PRINCIPAL EVENTS

Taken mainly from "Principal Events 1914-1918," compiled by the Historical Section, Committee of Imperial Defence. (H.M. Stationery Office, 1922.)

Date.	East Africa.	France and Belgium.	Other Theatres (excluding Balkans Italian, Eastern).	General Events Political and Naval.
1914 August 4th	—	German troops invade Belgium.	—	**Great Britain declares war on Germany.**
6th	—	—	—	Lord Kitchener becomes Secretary of State for War.
8th	**Dar-es-Salaam bombarded by H.M.S. "Astraea"** (first act of war).	—	—	—
8th/9th	Instructions to India for despatch of troops to East Africa.	—	—	—
9th	—	—	—	Belgian proposal to neutralize African free-trade zone.
13th	German vessel *Hermann v. Wissman* disabled; British command of Lake Nyasa established.	—	—	—

Date.	East Africa.	France and Belgium.	Other Theatres (excluding Balkans, Italian, Eastern).	General Events Political and Naval.
1914 August				
14th	German raid on Uvira (Belgian Congo).	—	—	—
15th	German forces occupy Taveta (see 10th March 1916).	—	—	—
16th	—	Landing of B.E.F. in France completed.	—	—
17th	Tanga raided by H.M.S. *Pegasus*.	—	—	—
19th	I.E.F. "C" sails from India.	—	—	—
20th	—	German forces occupy Brussels.	—	—
21st	—	—	German forces from S.W. Africa enter Union of S. Africa.	—
22nd	German attack on Belgian ship *Alexandre Delcommune*, L. Tanganyika.	—	—	—
23rd/24th	—	**Battle of Mons** ..	—	Belgian proposal to neutralize African free-trade zone accepted by Germany.
23rd/28th	Rising of Giriama tribe ..	—	—	—
26th	—	**Battle of Le Cateau** First units of Indian Expeditionary Force land at Marseilles.	German forces in Togoland capitulate.	—

28th	—			Action of Heligoland.
30th	British forces evacuate Vanga.			
September 1st	**I.E.F. "C" reaches Mombasa.** Br.-Genl. Stewart assumes command in E. Africa.			
5th	German forces enter N. Rhodesia : defence of Abercorn begins. Affair of Tsavo			
6th		Battle of the Marne		
6th–12th	Affair of Karonga.			
9th	German forces retreat from N. Rhodesia : defence of Abercorn. Affair of Kisii			
12th		Battle of the Aisne		
12th–21st	British forces advance to the Kagera.			
14th				
15th	—		Outbreak of Rebellion, Union of South Africa.	
19th	—			British and French Governments guarantee integrity of Belgian Colonies.
20th	H.M.S. *Pegasus* sunk by *Königsberg*.			

Date.	East Africa.	France and Belgium.	Other Theatres (excluding Balkans Italian, Eastern).	General Events Political and Naval.
1914 September				
21st	British forces occupy Schuckmannsburg (Caprivi Zipfel).	—	—	—
24th	German forces seize Kwijwi Island (Belgian).	—	—	—
26th	British coastal forces withdraw to Gazi.	—	—	—
27th	—	Siege of Antwerp and 1st Battle of Artois begin.		—
October 7th		Siege of Antwerp and 1st Battle of Artois end.	—	—
10th	German attack on Gazi	—	—	—
16th	I.E.F. "B" sails from India.	—	—	—
19th	—	**Battles of Ypres 1914** begin.	Luderitzbrucht (Ger. S.W. Africa) occupied by Union of S.A. Forces.	—
27th	Anglo-Belgian conference at Kibati.	—	—	—
30th	Königsberg located by H.M.S. Chatham.	—	—	—

Date			**Action of Coronel**
31st	I.E.F. "B" reaches Mombasa. Maj.-Genl. Aitken assumes command of E. Africa.	—	—
November 1st	—	Hostilities against Turkey begin.	—
2nd	Tanga: I.E.F. "B" arrives.	—	—
3rd	Tanga: First British attack on Longido.	—	Allied squadrons bombard Dardanelles forts.
4th	Tanga: Second British attack.	—	—
5th	Tanga: Re-embarkation of I.E.F. "B". Sybil wrecked (L. Victoria).	—	—
6th	—	Indian Expeditionary Force lands in Mesopotamia.	— —
9th	—	—	Emden destroyed by H.M.A.S. Sydney.
17th	Occupation of Longido...	—	—
20th	German attack on Serembiro (Uganda border).	—	British, French and Belgian Governments withdraw proposals to neutralize African free-trade zone.

Date.	East Africa.	France and Belgium.	Other Theatres (excluding Balkans, Italian, Eastern).	General Events Political and Naval.
1914 November 22nd	War Office assumes control of E. African operations.	**Battles of Ypres 1914** end.	—	—
23rd	—	—	—	Portuguese Government announces prospective co-operation of Portugal with Great Britain.
December 4th	Anglo-Belgian conference at Elizabethville.	—	—	—
	Maj.-Genl. Wapshare assumes command in E. Africa.	—	—	—
6th	British attacks on Gombaizi and Itarra (Uganda border).	—	—	¡
8th	—	—	—	**Battle of the Falklands.**
18th	—	—	—	British protectorate over Egypt proclaimed.
20th	British re-occupy coastal area to Umba river.	1st Battle of Champagne begins.	—	—
25th	Occupation of Jasin (see 18th–19th Jan. 1915).	—	—	—

Date			
28th		End of Rebellion in Union of South Africa	
1915.			
January			
8th	Occupation of Shirati (L. Victoria). Lake Victoria flotilla reorganized as naval force.		
10th–12th	Seizure of Mafia Island ..		
14th		Swakopmund (Ger. S.W. Africa) occupied by Union of S.A. Forces.	
16th	Br.-Genl. Malleson despatched for liaison with Belgian forces.		
18th–19th	Affair of Jasin (see 25th Dec. 1915).		
February			
3rd		Turkish attack on Suez Canal.	
9th	British coastal force withdraw to Gazi.		
13th	Col. H. E. C. Kitchener reaches Nairobi.		
14th	Br.-Genl. Malleson opens Anglo-Belgian discussions at Ruchuru.		Anglo-Belgian agreement as to delimitation of Uganda-Congo boundary.

Date.	East Africa.	France and Belgium.	Other Theatres (excluding Balkans, Italian, Eastern).	General Events Political and Naval
1915 February				
18th	Voi-Maktau railway : construction begun.	—	—	—
19th	—	—	—	Allied naval attack on the Dardanelles.
March 1st	British blockade of E. African coast instituted.	—	—	—
9th	Affair of Mwaika ..	—	—	—
10th–13th		**Battle of Neuve Chapelle**	—	—
17th	—	1st Battle of Champagne ends.	—	—
18th	—	—	—	Allied naval attack on the Narrows (Dardanelles).
23rd	M. Tombeur assumes control of Belgian troops. Ruchuru discussions end.	—	—	—
29th	Affair of Salaita ..	—	—	—
April 11th	Withdrawal from Longido completed	—	—	—
14th	German blockade-runner *Rubens* attacked by H.M.S. *Hyacinth.*	—	—	—

Date	East African operations	Western Front	Other theatres	World events
15th	Maj.-Genl. Tighe assumes command in E. Africa			
22nd		Battles of Ypres, 1915 begin.		
25th			Allied landing on Gallipoli.	
May 15th	Salvage of H.M.S. _—_ (L. Victoria).	2nd Battle of Artois begins.		
15th–25th		Battle of Festubert		
23rd				Italy enters the war on the side of the Allies.
25th		Battles of Ypres, 1915 end.		
30th	Affair of Sphinxhaven .			
June 18th		2nd Battle of Artois ends		
22nd–23rd	Capture of Bukoba and subsequent withdrawal. Voi-Maktau railway reaches Maktau.			
23rd				
27th			British advance up the Euphrates begins.	
28th	Saisi : first German attack			
July 9th			German South-West Africa capitulates to General Botha.	

Date.	East Africa.	France and Belgium.	Other Theatres (excluding Balkans Italian, Eastern).	General Events Political and Naval.
1915 July 11th	"**Königsberg**" **destroyed** in Rufiji delta.	—	—	—
14th	Affair of Mbuyumi ..	—	—	—
15th	—	—	—	National Registration Act becomes law in Great Britain.
25th	Saisi : investment by German forces.	—	—	—
August 2nd	Saisi : retreat of investing German forces.	—	—	—
6th	Rhodesian forces join with Union forces from German S.W. Africa (Caprivi Zipfel).	—	Landing at Suvla ..	—
September 20th	Affair of Longido West	—	—	—
25th	—	**Battle of Loos** begins	—	—
28th	—	—	Battle of Kut ..	—
October 8th	—	**Battle of Loos** ends	—	—

Date		
November 12th	Br.-Genl. Northey appointed to command Nyasaland-Rhodesian border.	
22nd	Genl. Sir H. Smith-Dorrien selected for command in E. Africa.	Occupation of Basra
22nd–24th		Battle of Ctesiphon
December 5th		Defence of Kut begins (see 29th April, 1916).
19th		Evacuation of Gallipoli begins.
23rd	Naval operations on Lake Tanganyika begin.	
26th	German vessel *Kingani* captured (L. Tanganyika)	
1916. January 8th		Evacuation of Gallipoli completed.
21st	Longido re-occupied	
February 6th	Anglo-Belgian conference at Lutobo. Lt.-Genl. Smuts selected to succeed Sir H. Smith-Dorrien.	

Date.	East Africa.	France and Belgium.	Other Theatres (excluding Balkans, Italian, Eastern).	General Events Political and Naval.
1916 February 9th	German vessel *Hedwig v. Wissmann* sunk: **Allied command of L. Tanganyika secured.**	—	—	—
10th	—	—	—	Military Service Act comes into operation in Great Britain.
12th	**Action of Salaita**	—	—	—
18th	Affair of Kachumbe (Uganda border).	—	**Conquest of the Cameroons** by the Allies completed.	—
19th	Lt.-Genl. Smuts reaches Mombasa, assumes command in E. Africa.	—	—	—
21st	—	**Battle of Verdun** begins (see 31st August).	—	—
March 5th	British offensive begins: 1st Divn. starts from Longido.	—	—	—
7th	2nd Divn. starts from Mbuyani.	—	—	—
9th	—	—	—	Germany declares **war** on Portugal.

19th	Taveta re-occupied (see 15th Aug. 1914).		
11th–12th	**Action of Latema Nek.**		
14th	Moshi occupied. 1st Div. reaches Moshi area.		
19th	Advance to the Ruvu begins.		
21st	**Action of Kahe**		
23rd	Halt on the Ruvu		
April 3rd	Advance of 2nd Div. to Kondoa Irangi begins (see 17th–19th).		
4th–5th	Occupation of Lolkisale		
10th	Kionga occupied by Portuguese forces.		
12th	Occupation of Madukani. Belgian forces cross Rusisi river.		
17th–19th	**Capture of Kondoa Irangi** (see 3rd).		Outbreak of rebellion in Ireland.
24th	Belgian forces invade Ruanda.	Capitulation of Kut	
25th			
29th			Rebellion in Ireland ends.
May 1st	Belgian forces occupy Kigali.		
6th			

B

Date.	East Africa.	France and Belgium.	Other Theatres (excluding Balkans Italian, Eastern)	General Events Political and Naval.
1916 May 9th–10th	German attack on Kondoa Irangi. Occupation of Mbulu.	—	—	—
19th	Belgian forces occupy Nyanza.	—	—	—
20th	Nyasaland-Rhodesia force invades German East Africa.	—	—	—
21st	—	German attack on Vimy Ridge.	—	—
22nd	Main British advance from the Ruvu begins.	—	—	—
27th	Portuguese operations on the Ruvuma.	—	—	—
29th	Occupation of Neu Langenburg.	—	—	—
31st	Main British advance reaches Bwiko. Nyasaland-Rhodesia force base established at Mwaya.	—	—	—
31st (1st June)	—		—	**Battle of Jutland.**

June			
1st	Belgian forces invade Urundi.		
5th	—		Death of Lord Kitchener.
7th	Main British advance resumed from Bwikc.		
8th	Occupation of Bismarckburg.		
9th	**Action of Mkalamo.**		
9th–10th	Occupation of Ukerewe Island.		
13th	Occupation of Alt Largenburg (L. Nyasa).		
15th	Occupation of Korogwe.		
17th	Br.-Genl. Crewe assumes command of Lake Force.		
	Belgian forces occupy Kitega.		
18th	Occupation of Handeni.		
23rd	Occupation of Njombe.		
24th	**Action of the Lukigura.**		
	Belgian Forces occupy Biharamulo.		
28th	Occupation of Bukobe.		
30th	Belgian forces occupy Nyamirembe.		
July			
1st	—	**Battles of the Somme begin.**	

Date.	East Africa.	France and Belgium.	Other Theatres (excluding Balkans Italian, Eastern).	General Events Political and Naval.
1916 July				
3rd	Belgian engagement at Kato.	—	—	—
5th	Main British advance halts at the Msiha. General Gil reaches Palmas and assumes command of Portuguese forces.	—	—	—
7th	Occupation of Tanga ..	—	—	—
8th	Belgian forces move south from Kitega.	—	—	—
14th	**Capture of Mwanza** :: Belgian engagement at Djobahika.	—	—	—
15th–23rd	Operations to safeguard main British L. of C.			
17th	Occupation of Nyatembe (L. Victoria).	—	—	—
20th	2nd Divn. moves south from Kondoa Irangi. Anglo-Belgian conference Entebbe.	—	—	—
22nd	Lake Force reaches Ilola			
23rd	Occupation of Pangani	—	—	—

	23rd	Genl. Botha visits main British force at Msila Camp.
	24th	Action at Malangali.
	28th	2nd Divn. occupies Nyangalo. Belgian forces occupy Kigoma.
	29th	**2nd Divn. occupies Dodoma** (Central Railway)
	30th	2nd Divn. occupies Saranda and Kilemto (Central Railway).
	31st	2nd Divn. occupies Kiimatinde (Central Railway).
August	3rd	Belgian forces occupy Ujiji.
	5th	Main British advance resumed from the Mkata.
	10th	Advance of 2nd Divn. from Nyangalo to Kilosa begins (see 22nd). Affair of Matamondo. Belgian forces move eastwards from Kigoma and Ruchugi on Tabora.

Date.	East Africa.	France and Belgium.	Other Theatres (excluding Balkans, Italian, Eastern).	General Events Political and Naval.
1916 **August** 12th	2nd Divn. occupies Mpwapwa. Hawthorn's force (Br.-Genl. Northey) returns to Njombe.	—	—	—
15th	Capture of Bagamoyo ..	—	—	—
17th	**Action of the Wami** ..	—	—	—
19th	Hawthorn occupies Mfirika	—	—	—
22nd	2nd Divn. occupies Kilosa (see 10th). Belgian forces occupy St. Michael.	—	—	—
23rd	Main British advance resumed from the Wami.			
24th–26th	Affair of Mlali	—	—	—
25th	2nd Divn. column leaves Kilosa for Kidodi (see 10th Sept.).			
26th	**Lt.-Genl. Smuts enters Morogoro** (Central Railway). Lake Force advance resumed from Ilola.	—	—	—

29th	Main British advance resumed from Morogoro. Br.-Genl. Northey's force enters Iringa.	—	—	F. M. von Hindenburg becomes Chief of the German General Staff.
30th	Lake Force reaches Iln-yanga.	—	—	
31st	—	Battle of Verdun ends (see 19th February)	—	
September 1st	Belgian engagement at Mabama. Belgian advance from St. Michael on Tabora begins.	—	—	—
4th	Surrender of Dar-es-Salaam.	—	—	—
7th–8th	Affairs near Kisaki. Affair of the Msolwe. Occupation of Kilwa.	—	—	—
9th	Main British advance reaches Tulo. Lake Force reaches Kigu-humo.	—	—	—
10th	2nd Divn. occupies Kidodi (see 25th Aug.).	—	—	—
10th–12th	Affair of the Duturi. Belgian engagement at Lulanguru.	—	—	—
11th	Occupation of Mikindan.	—	—	—

Date.	East Africa.	France and Belgium.	Other Theatres (excluding Balkans, Italian, Eastern).	General Events Political and Naval.
1916 September				
12th	Occupation of Kisaki	—	—	—
14th	Br.-Genl. Northey occupies Hange.	—	—	—
	Belgian engagement at Itaga.	—	—	—
17th	Occupation of Lindi	—	—	—
19th	**Belgian forces occupy Tabora.**	—	—	—
	Portuguese forces cross the Ruvuma.	—	—	—
20th	Occupation of Songea	—	—	—
25th	Lake Force reaches Ndala	—	—	—
28th	Lake Force reaches Igalula (Central Railway).	—	—	—
	Affair of Mkapira			

CHAPTER I
INTRODUCTORY.
EAST AFRICA BEFORE 1914.

WITH the exception of a narrow strip along its coast-line, End Papers East Africa—using the name in the general sense adopted in this history—was one of the last areas of the habitable world to be reached by modern civilization. Partly by reason of its climate, partly owing to the accidents of history, the interior as a whole remained unknown to white men until the middle of the nineteenth century, and it was only within the last twenty years of that period that the country came under the influence of the European Powers.

Only a bare outline can here be given of some of the salient facts in the involved and often turbulent history of what has come to be known as the " Scramble for Africa " : a history now easily accessible, the study of which is necessary to a proper understanding of the African colonial situation to-day.

For over nine hundred years the East African coast was controlled by Arab sultans emanating from Oman.[1] For a time, in the sixteenth and seventeenth centuries, their influence suffered at the hands of the Portuguese ;[2] but the Portuguese settlements at Kilwa, Mombasa and

---

[1] The earliest Arab settlement is supposed to have been founded about the middle of the eighth century at Mogadishu, in what is now Italian Somaliland. Kilwa was founded later by Persians from Shiraz. Subsequent Arab or Persian settlements included Malindi, Mombasa, Patta and Lamu, Pemba and Zanzibar, Mozambique and Sofala, and trading stations in Madagascar and the Comoro Islands. Kilwa was long the predominant centre, but was later surpassed in importance by Mombasa. The Imams of Muscat began to establish an influence in East Africa during the latter half of the seventh century and about 1840 the Imam or Sultan, Seyyid Said, transferred his capital to Zanzibar. After his death (1856) his dominions were divided between his sons, Zanzibar with the African coast becoming independent of Muscat.

[2] The first Portuguese to appear in the Indian Ocean was the explorer Vasco da Gama, who doubled the Cape in 1497. He then touched at Mozambique, Mombasa and Malindi before going on to India. Seven years later a strong expedition under Almeida followed in his track, captured Kilwa and Mombasa, and established a base at the former port. Thereafter the Portuguese subdued the whole coast, and in 1558 they established the seat of government for their East African settlements at Mozambique. During the sixteenth century Portuguese explorers made their way up the Zambezi ; later they were driven back by natives of Zulu stock, and by the end of that century Portugal had only a few forts along the seaboard of East Africa, retaining also control of Tete, inland on the Zambezi. The Portuguese seem to have taken little direct interest in Zanzibar.

1

Malindi were eventually destroyed by the Arabs, who from 1729 onwards dominated the whole coast north of the Ruvuma river.

Arab rule, however, did not extend inland. Apart from intermittent trading, chiefly in ivory, and from periodic raids for slaves, the peoples of the interior were little affected by the Arabs : they remained, as they had been for many centuries, in a state of existence comparable to that of the races of northern Europe before the days of the Romans. For the most part the inhabitants of East Africa were grouped in small tribes scattered over wide tracts of country, most of which was undeveloped and covered by forest or bush. In the more favoured regions round the great lakes certain more highly organized communities had arisen, notably the three considerable native kingdoms, Buganda, Ruanda and Urundi.[1]

Mention must also be made of the remarkable dynasty of the Makanjira, in Nyasaland, whose rule ended with the expulsion of Makanjira V in 1895 and his replacement by a nominee of the British Government. Farther north, nearer the coast, the nomadic Masai had established supremacy over the open steppes between the lakes and Kilimanjaro.

With these exceptions there was but little political organization among the tribes of the East and Central African hinterland. They presented a wide variety of race, language, customs and culture, with mutual antagonisms often leading to armed conflict, so that life and property

---

[1] As none of these peoples had any system of writing, their records are only traditional, but it seems clear that the three principal states are of considerable antiquity. The present Kabaka (king) of Buganda is said to be the 34th of his line, and this State has certainly existed for some 350 years. When the explorer Stanley visited it in 1875 it was credited with an area of 70,000 square miles, and a population of nearly three millions. Mutesa, the king, maintained a fleet of 300 to 400 war-canoes on Lake Victoria and could collect an army of 150,000 warriors. Farther south were the kingdoms of Ruanda and Urundi, with populations respectively of about a million and of perhaps one and a half millions. The great majority of these were lowly tribes of Bantu origin living in a state of serfdom, ruled by a dominant race of Hamitic descent, the Batusi, tall, slender and brown-skinned, said to have conquered the country during the seventeenth century. The numbers of the Batusi were estimated in 1914 at not more than 25,000 in Ruanda and about 75,000 in Urundi. Smaller but similarly constituted States were those of Bunyoro and Ankole, now included in the Uganda Protectorate. It may be noted that the very existence of these semi-civilized States in the heart of Africa was unknown in Europe until they were visited by explorers for the first time between 1860 and 1870. The first Arab traders from the coast reached Uganda during the reign of King Suna, 1832–57.

could seldom be regarded as secure, while their primitive weapons could offer no effective resistance to raiders equipped with firearms. In consequence, they suffered greatly during the first half of the nineteenth century from incursions by the coastal Arabs greedy for the profits of the slave and ivory trades ; and it was in connection with efforts to suppress commerce in human beings that European intervention in East Africa began.[1]

Explorers and missionaries working inland from trading settlements on the coast[2] were followed by individual traders, then by organised trading companies and lastly by the armed forces of European Powers. This penetration was at first haphazard, the representatives of Great Britain, Germany and the " International Association of the Congo"[3]

---

[1] When the Muscat Arabs first concerned themselves with inland Africa, ivory and slaves were the two articles of commercial value produced by the continent. The Arabs dealt in both and made one industry support the other. Ivory was abundant in most parts of the interior, where the ignorant natives would barter it eagerly with the Arabs for cheap and gaudy trade goods. The difficulty, therefore, was not its collection but its transport to the coast. Ivory is the heaviest animal substance in the world, and there would be hundreds of tusks in the Arabs' compounds by the time their stock of beads and calico was exhausted. They therefore adopted the simple if ruthless plan of forcing the unfortunate natives to carry the ivory to the distant coast and of there selling it and them together. In this, however, the Arabs needed confederates, as they were few in number and had little stomach for fighting. Their practice was, therefore, to strike a bargain with local robber tribes, and with the assistance of the latter to raid the weaker villages until they had taken as many slaves as they could conveniently handle..

[2] Among the earliest European explorers were :—
The German missionaries Rebmann and Krapf, who respectively, in 1848 and 1849, first sighted Mounts Kilimanjaro and Kenya ;
the British travellers Burton and Speke, who in 1858 discovered Lakes Tanganyika and Victoria ;
Speke and Grant, who in 1862 discovered the source of the Nile ;
Livingstone, who in 1852-6 explored the Zambezi, discovering the Victoria Falls, and in 1859 made his way from the Zambezi up the river Shire to Lake Nyasa, which previously had only been heard of vaguely from early Portuguese travellers ;
Commander V. Lovett-Cameron, R.N., who between 1872 and 1875 explored Lake Tanganyika, discovered its outlet (the Lukuga) into the Congo basin, and made a remarkable journey over much new ground to Benguela on the Atlantic coast ; and finally
the German officer Hermann von Wissmann, who in 1880-3 made the first crossing of Central Africa from west to east.

[3] Developed from the International African Association, which had resulted directly from the Brussels Conference of 1876. Formed in 1879 as a private company by King Leopold of the Belgians, it established trading posts on the Congo between 1879 and 1884. In February 1885 it was recognized by Belgium as having the rights of an independent state, and became known as the Congo Free State, with King Leopold as its sovereign. In November 1907 King Leopold ceded the Congo Free State to Belgium, the territory thus becoming a Belgian colony.

staking out rival national claims in the northern areas of Central Africa. These claims, which were complicated by the traditional rights of the Sultan of Zanzibar and threatened to lead to serious international difficulties, were considered at a conference of the Powers assembled in Berlin at the invitation of the German Emperor in November 1884. The agreement reached was recorded in a document commonly known as the Berlin Act of 1885, signed at Berlin on the 26th February 1885.

This instrument, the provisions of which were applicable to all territories within a defined area forming a wide belt across Central Africa from the Atlantic to the Indian Ocean, pronounced for freedom of trade and suppression of the slave-trade within the territories in question, [1] and included among other matters a declaration framed with a view to their neutrality in the event of war.[2]

After Lord Salisbury's succession to the Foreign Office in June 1885 a joint British, French and German Commission was appointed to determine the limits of the Sultanate of Zanzibar on the East African mainland, the British Commissioner being the future Lord Kitchener.

Following the report of the Commission in June 1886 an exchange of notes between the British and German governments resulted in an agreement as to the respective spheres of influence of the two Powers.

Four years later, under the Anglo-German Agreement of the 1st July 1890,[3] Great Britain was recognized as having a protectorate over the islands of Zanzibar and Pemba, and over the possessions of the Sultan of Zanzibar north of the river Umba ; the coast-line south of that river was

---

[1] The scope of the Act is indicated by its official title : " General " Act of the Conference of Berlin, relative to the Development of Trade " and Civilization in Africa ; the free Navigation of the rivers Congo, " Niger, &c ; the Suppression of the Slave Trade by Sea and Land ; " the occupation of Territory on the African Coasts, &c."

The signatory Powers were : Great Britain, Germany, Austria-Hungary, Belgium, Denmark, Spain, the United States of America (which did not ratify), France, Italy, Holland, Portugal, Russia, Sweden and Norway, Turkey.

For the full text of the Act see " The Map of Africa by Treaty," Sir E. Hertslet, 3rd Edn., 1909 (H.M. Stationery Office), Vol. II., pp. 468-486.

The International Association of the Congo signified its accession to the Berlin Act by a separate Act of Adhesion of the same date (26th February 1885). See Appendix I.

[2] See Appendix II.

[3] By this Agreement Great Britain ceded Heligoland to Germany.

BEFORE 1914 5

recognized as being in the German sphere of influence. Inland, the frontier arranged between the British and the German spheres was for the most part an arbitrary line drawn on a map with but little reference either to the physical features of the country or to the local African population, for the regions which it traversed were at that time almost unknown. Between the sea and Lake Victoria the new frontier cut through the grazing lands of the Masai, dividing that people between the British and the German protectorates ; west of Lake Victoria most of the ancient kingdom of Ruanda fell to the Germans, while its northern (Kigezi) portion was included in the British zone. Considerations of local administrative convenience being thus ignored, it is hardly surprising that strategic requirements likewise were not taken into account, and the line thus drawn[1] was destined eventually to be a source of difficulties for the British authorities in the War of 1914–18.[2]

Meanwhile to the south a similar process of exploration and annexation had opened up the country between the great lakes and the Zambezi. British missionaries had established settlements on Lake Nyasa in 1874–78, and in 1880 had extended their sphere of work to the southern end of Lake Tanganyika, the " Stevenson's Road "[3] (230 miles in length) to connect these two lakes being then planned and in part constructed. British traders, forming in 1878 an " African Lakes Company " (now " Corporation "), followed the missionaries and came before long into conflict with the Arab slave-traders already established round Lake Nyasa. After some sharp fighting during 1888[4] the British

[1] The frontier was demarcated by successive international Boundary Commissions as follows : Anglo-German, 1897-1900 (Indian Ocean to L. Jipe), 1904-06 (L. Jipe to L. Victoria), 1902-04 (west of L. Victoria to R. Chisinga, near Lutobo), 1911 (R. Chizinga to Mt. Sabinio) ; Anglo-Belgian, 1911 (Mt. Sabinio westwards). See Sketches 2, 3.

[2] Notably in regard to the British salient at Taveta in the early days of the war, and to the fact that the important tribes of the Masai and Batusi were on both sides of the Anglo-German frontier.

[3] So called because it was projected and financed by Mr. James Stevenson, then chairman of the African Lakes Corporation.

[4] Known locally as the " North End War ". The armed forces of the African Lakes Corporation were commanded by Captain Frederick Lugard, D.S.O. (now Lord Lugard), who was destined to be both the founder of the force which later developed into the 4th Bn., King's African Rifles, and the organizer in Northern Nigeria of troops which formed the nucleus of the Royal West African Frontier Force. He left Nyasaland in 1889 for Uganda, where he played a leading part in the events which led to the establishment of the British protectorate.

＞A prominent part in the Nyasaland operations was also taken by Mr. (afterwards Sir Alfred) Sharpe, who later became Governor of Nyasaland.

Government intervened, and in September 1889 a protectorate was proclaimed over the Shire highlands. This was extended in 1891 to include the whole of what is now Nyasaland.[1] The next few years were a period of recurring internal warfare against the warlike slave-trading tribes of this area,[2] but by the end of 1897 these had been subdued, and the development of the Protectorate was thenceforward untroubled.

Still farther south British influence had been extended to Bechuanaland in 1885, and in 1888 a treaty was concluded with the Matabele. The British South Africa Company, which received its charter in 1889, was then organized to administer the vast undeveloped regions lying between the Belgian Congo and German East Africa to the north and the Transvaal to the south.

At this juncture there were threats of a trek from the Transvaal Republic into Mashonaland, while Germany began to support Portugal's claims to the territory which afterwards became Northern Rhodesia. Thereupon, acting with great promptitude and determination, Cecil Rhodes, in his capacity as Managing Director of the Chartered Company, despatched to Mashonaland a force of some 500 so-called " Pioneers "[3] and B.S.A. Police. On the 12th September 1890 the Pioneers founded a settlement at what was then named Fort Salisbury, now Salisbury, and the Company's wide territories became firmly established under the British flag. In April 1898 the country was officially named Rhodesia, and in the same year its government was placed in the hands of the Company's Administrator.

In March 1897 Barotseland came under British influence. Two years later North-Western Rhodesia, including Barotseland, and in 1900 North-Eastern Rhodesia, were placed by Order in Council under the control of the Chartered

---

[1] This area was re-named " British Central Africa " in 1893, and reverted to the name " Nyasaland " in 1907.

[2] " The founding of the Protectorate . . . was hardly more than an " incident in the struggle which Europe in general, and Great Britain " in particular, was at that time waging against the African slave " trade. . . . Our conflicts were almost confined to those with tribes " dominated by ruthless alien chiefs, whether Arab, Yao, or Ngoni . . . " the indigenous population welcomed the English."
Murray, Handbook of Nyasaland, 1932.

[3] The " Pioneers " included many officers and scouts with very wide and varied experience, among them notably Captain F. C. Selous, already a famous name in Africa, who fell in action in German East Africa on 4th January 1917.

Company ; and in May 1911 a further Order amalgamated them under one administrative system as Northern Rhodesia.

By the Anglo-German Agreement of 1890, already mentioned, the southern boundary between the British and German spheres of influence had been defined as a line joining the southern end of Lake Tanganyika and the northern end of Lake Nyasa, following the general course of the Stevenson Road and of the River Songwe, all the land to the north falling within the German sphere.[1]

Thus between 1885 and 1890 Germany acquired in East Africa an area extending for about 700 miles from north to south and about 600 miles from east to west, with a coastline of some 470 miles and a land surface almost as large as that of Germany and France combined.[2]

The neighbouring territories allotted to Great Britain were even more extensive, but were more sparsely populated.[3]

---

[1] This frontier was demarcated by the Anglo-German Boundary Commission of 1898.

[2] The area of German East Africa was estimated at 384,000 square miles. That of the German Empire in Europe in 1914 was 208,780 square miles, and that of France 207,054 square miles.

[3] The figures, as estimated in 1914, are given below, those of 1911 for Southern Rhodesia being also included for convenient reference :

(a) *Populations.*

British territories :		Whites	Indians &c.	Africans
East African Protectorate ..	..	5,000	25,000	4,038,000
Uganda	..	1,017	3,651	2,904,400
Nyasaland	..	800	410	1,060,000
Northern Rhodesia	..	2,250	—	875,000
Southern Rhodesia (1911) ..	..	23,606	870	744,600
German East Africa	..	5,336	14,900	7,660,000
				(includes 3,500,000 in Ruanda and Urundi)

(b) *Areas.*

Density of native population per square mile.

British Territories,
East African Protectorate :
246,822 square miles .. .. 16·36
Uganda :
121,437 square miles (including 16,377 square miles of water) .. .. 27·64
Nyasaland :
39,315 square miles .. .. 26·96
Northern Rhodesia :
290,000 square miles .. .. 3·02
Total above :
697,574 square miles .. .. —
Southern Rhodesia :
150,344 square miles .. .. 4·95
German East Africa :
384,000 square miles .. .. 19·95

It should be remembered that a high proportion of the white population in each of the territories consisted of officials, missionaries and their families.

The great lakes of Tanganyika, Nyasa and Victoria, with the rivers Ruvuma and Russisi, formed convenient limits for most of the frontage of the German protectorate. Within the frontiers thus arbitrarily decided, the British and the Germans proceeded to develop their respective protectorates, with widely differing outlook and methods, but from much the same starting-point. In each case a chartered company was formed to develop the dependency; but, after vicissitudes of fortune, these companies, with one notable exception, handed over their functions to the British and German governments respectively.[1] In Uganda the transfer of power resulted from serious disturbances, including a civil war between native factions of differing Christian sects. Even when the administration of Uganda and British East Africa had been taken over by the Crown (1893–95) the internal difficulties of the country were not ended. Mubarak-bin-Rashid's rebellion in the coastal districts during 1896 was followed by a formidable mutiny of the Sudanese mercenary troops of Uganda in 1897, which took several months to put down ; this had hardly been suppressed when during 1898 a revolt again broke out in Jubaland, to be followed by further serious unrest there at the end of 1900. To deal with these successive emergencies troops were brought from India, for, although some military forces had been raised locally, the use of non-African troops for internal security was at that time preferred. It was not until the 1st January 1902 that the local forces were organized on their present basis as the King's African

---

[1] The German company incorporated by Imperial charter in March 1887, surrendered its rights in October 1889, when the country was proclaimed an Imperial Protectorate after the company had failed to suppress a serious native rising.

The Imperial British East Africa Company, formed in 1888, set out to develop what is now Kenya Colony and extended its operations to Uganda. The latter territory was taken over by the Government of the United Kingdom in 1893, and became a British protectorate in June 1894. On 1st July 1895 the Imperial British East Africa Company was dissolved and British East Africa also became a Crown protectorate.

In Nyasaland the development begun by the African Lakes Corporation was followed between 1889 and 1891 by assumption of control by the United Kingdom Government.

Up to 1904-5 the East African protectorates were administered by the Foreign Office. On 1st April 1904 Nyasaland (then British Central Africa) and on 1st April 1905 British East Africa, Uganda and Somaliland were transferred to the care of the Colonial Office. Northern Rhodesia, however, continued to be administered by the British South Africa Company until 1924, when it passed under the control of the Colonial Office.

Rifles.[1] Similar difficulties attended the establishment of the German protectorate.[2]

In the British territories farther south no serious trouble took place after the quelling of the Matabele rebellion of 1896 and the expeditions against the Ngoni and Nguru in Nyasaland in 1897 and 1898 ;[3] and by the year 1910 both the British and German dependencies were enjoying a general tranquillity and good government previously unknown. In the German protectorate this transition to peaceful conditions was marked in 1906 by the appointment of a civilian minister, Freiherr von Rechenberg, as Governor in place of the former Military Governor. He was succeeded in 1912 by Dr. Heinrich Schnee. In the British territories a similar tendency was marked by a reduction of military expenditure, which resulted in 1911 in the disbandment of one of the four battalions of the King's African Rifles.[4]

The establishment of law and order was followed by rapid economic progress and a consequent development of communications. Immediately after assuming the protectorate over British East Africa, the British Government authorized (July 1895) the construction of a railway from Mombasa to Kisumu as an aid to suppression of the slave trade and in order to open up Uganda.[5]

Termed for this reason the " Uganda Railway,"[6] the line was opened for traffic to Kisumu (587 miles) in

---

[1] To suppress Mubarak's rebellion in 1896 the 24th (Baluchistan, Duchess of Connaught's Own) Bombay Infantry was sent from Bombay ; in 1897 the 27th (1st Baluch Bn.) Bombay (Light) Infantry was sent from India to put down the Sudanese mutiny, followed early in 1900 by the 4th Bombay Infantry (1st Bn. Rifle Regiment), which was diverted to Jubaland. At the end of 1899 a troop outbreak in Jubaland caused the despatch from India of a mountain battery and a half-battalion of the 16th Bombay Infantry, with a camel-troop from Aden. In addition to these units, Indian contingents at this time formed part of the local forces maintained in East Africa, and when the King's African Rifles was constituted (1st January 1902) it included a complete Indian battalion (5th Bn., K.A.R.). See also Appendix II.

[2] See Appendix II.

[3] See Appendix II.

[4] See Appendix IV.

[5] Interesting details of the construction of the Uganda Railway are to be found in " The Man-Eaters of Tsavo ", Lieut.-Colonel J. H. Patterson, 1907.

[6] At that time the Uganda Protectorate included the eastern, as well as the western shores of Lake Victoria ; but in 1902 the Eastern Province, extending from the Sio river to Naivasha, was transferred to the East Africa Protectorate, so that the railway in 1914 no longer terminated in Uganda. Communication between the latter protectorate and Kisumu was afforded by a service of lake steamers. See p. 23.

December 1901. In 1896 the German government began the construction of a railway line from Tanga to Mount Kilimanjaro, which reached Moshi (218 miles) in 1912. In 1904 a concession was granted to a German company to construct a second railway line in the German protectorate. This was begun from Dar-es-Salaam in 1905, reached Morogoro (129 miles) in 1908, Tabora (526 miles) in 1912 and finally Kigoma (787 miles) on Lake Tanganyika in June 1914. In Nyasaland, the Shire Highlands Railway from Port Herald to Blantyre (113 miles) was constructed by a British company between 1902 and 1908.[1] Meanwhile the great Cape-to-Cairo line projected by Cecil Rhodes was taking shape, its railhead reaching the Victoria Falls (1,643 miles from Cape Town) in 1904, Kalomo (1,737 miles) in 1905 and Broken Hill (2,017 miles) in 1906. After a pause, construction was resumed, and before the end of 1909 the line had been carried across the Congo border to Elisabethville (2,308) miles. By the spring of 1914 it extended some 70 miles farther.

The railways brought European colonists. Nairobi, of which the site was marked in 1898 only by a railway construction camp, had become an important settlement by 1903 and developed rapidly as the administrative centre of the British East Africa Protectorate.[2]

The development of the German protectorate differed from that of British East Africa, for the wide areas of healthy upland round Nairobi which made farming possible for Europeans had no counterpart in the German territory; but the mountain slopes of Kilimanjaro and Meru and the highlands about Iringa and farther south in the vicinity of Neu Langenburg were suitable for settlement. About Kilimanjaro some 800 Europeans had settled.[3] Of these some 300 were Boers who had preferred German to British rule after the South African War. On the pleasant heights of the Usambara Mountains, nearer the coast, some 200 Germans had found homes in the vicinity of Wilhelmsthal (now Lushoto). Most of the remaining European population was centred in the two principal seaports, about 1,000

---

[1] An extension to Chindio, on the Zambezi (61 miles), was opened in May 1915 as the Central Africa Railway.

[2] In 1907 the population of Nairobi amounted to 580 Europeans, 3,100 Indians and 10,550 Africans; by 1914 these numbers had risen to about 20,000, including 1,200 Europeans.

[3] About 200 were on the slopes of Kilimanjaro, the remainder being at or near Arusha.

residing at Dar-es-Salaam, the headquarters of the Government, and 300 at Tanga.[1] Of the total white population, which in 1914 included some 3,500 adult males, about 450 were government officials, 260 officers and N.C.Os. of the Defence Force, 450 missionaries, 300 engineers, and 809 planters.

Although both the German and the British protectorates had been generally pacified, certain areas still required special measures, notably the wide steppes west of Kilimanjaro, where the Masai submitted unwillingly to deprivation of their former grazing lands, and the northern British districts, where the tribes along the Abyssinian border were still unsubdued. In Jubaland the Marehan Somalis persisted in raiding their more peaceful neighbours until, in March 1913, action against them was sanctioned by the Colonial Office. The surrender of their weapons was demanded. This was refused and, in December 1913, a series of minor operations began, in which a gradually increasing force of the K.A.R., centred on Serenli, became engaged. Although the fighting was not severe, the work involved many marches by small columns across trackless waste land, often through dense thorn-bush, in great heat. By April 1914 the greater part of the available troops in British East Africa and Uganda had been concentrated in this area, which could only be reached by a sea voyage of 300 miles from Mombasa to Kismayu.[2]

Similar difficulties arose west of Lake Rudolf, where between 1910 and 1913 small detachments of the King's African Rifles were unable to check the raiding propensities of the Turkana tribe. The Turkana country, lying in the Great Rift Valley, was then unmapped, the areas near the Abyssinian border having rarely been visited by white men. Early in 1914 the tribe gave further trouble and in July a punitive expedition, to be carried out by the 4/K.A.R., was in preparation.

These expeditions in the unadministered northern areas of British East Africa and Uganda were thus absorbing the greater part of the slender military resources of the two protectorates when, as a result of events in Europe, East Africa was unexpectedly drawn into the " World War."

---

[1] The population in the ports included a large number of nationals other than German, e.g., over 300 Greeks, about 150 Levantines.

[2] See Appendix IV.

NOTE

PHYSICAL CHARACTERISTICS OF THE THEATRE OF WAR

End Papers   Taking in most of the great plateau which lies between the Indian Ocean and the general line marked by Lakes Kivu, Tanganyika and Nyasa, the East African theatre of war stretches for some 800 miles southwards from the Equator to the river Ruvuma, beyond which again, in 1918, operations extended for a while almost to the mouth of the Zambezi.

The inland plateau is traversed, between Lake Victoria and Kilimanjaro, by the geological fissure which, starting in Northern Syria and continuing along the Jordan valley and the Red Sea, cleaves East Africa from north to south. This gigantic trough, the Great Rift Valley, is most conspicuous in the northern area, forming, where the Uganda railway crosses it, a valley some 40 miles wide and 2,000 feet deep, the walls of which rise to 8,000 feet above sea level. Farther south its course is everywhere unmistakable, though less sharply defined, and is marked by a string of lakes—Natron, Magadi, Manyara and others— now either brackish or evaporated to a sediment of soda, which are virtually useless as water for troops or animals.

Linked geologically with the Great Rift, as a western arm running down to join it, is the far deeper trough in which lie the great lakes—Albert, Edward, Kivu, Tanganyika—west of the central plateau, and finally Lake Nyasa, all of whose surface waters are high above sea-level, but whose depths in some cases are far below it.[1] To the west of these a wide expanse of hill country slopes down to the forest-clad valley of the Congo.

Between the central plateau, with its average elevation of over 3,000 feet, and the seaboard runs a low-lying coastal belt, narrow about Mombasa and Tanga in the north, and widening to the southward until in the basins of the Rufiji and Ruvuma it stretches far inland. Within this area great heat and high humidity combine to produce an unhealthy, malarial climate sorely trying to the white races.

Farther from the coast, as the land rises, day temperatures may be even higher, but nights are comparatively cool, and climatic conditions generally are more endurable by Europeans.

In the north, along the former Anglo-German border, lie on either side of Lake Victoria the more temperate highlands from which the great summits of Kilimanjaro (19,710 feet) and Mount Kenya (16,798 feet) to the east, and Ruwenzori (16,790 feet) to the west, rise up beyond the level of perpetual snow. To the south the vast central stretches of the plateau are bounded

---

[1] Lake Tanganyika, the deepest lake in the world, is about 2,600 feet above sea-level and has a recorded depth of 4,708 feet; Lake Nyasa, 1,600 feet above the sea, has a maximum known depth of over 2,300 feet.

by the less lofty ranges of the Ukinga and Poroto at the head
of Lake Nyasa, which extend north-eastwards towards the
highlands and escarpment of Iringa, and southwards to the
Livingstone range bordering the Lake. South-eastwards from
Kilimanjaro, the Pare and Usambara mountains run down
towards the coast at Tanga.

These and many lesser ranges catch and break the rain
clouds carried by the south-east monsoon from the Indian Ocean
between April and October, so that in general the rainfall of
the wet season,[1] though far from uniform, is heavy and the
soil fertile. In all these areas the climate—described in some
parts as " perpetual spring "—favours white settlement ; there,
accordingly, are to be found the more populous and cultivated
areas.

A wide variation of climate, from the sweltering damp heat
of the coast and the fierce sun of the arid central plateau to
to the chilly mists and often piercing cold of the uplands, was
not the least of the difficulties which beset the conduct of the
campaign now to be described. Transitions from heat to cold, and
vice versa, in a war largely of rapid movement, became familiar
hardships, which affected not only the troops, both white and
black, but also—perhaps even more detrimentally—the local
native carriers on whom ultimately all movement depended.

Sparsely populated,[2] and largely uncultivated except in
the immediate neighbourhood of villages and townships, most
of the theatre of operations is covered by what is generically
termed " bush." This varies from open parkland and savannah
on the high plains to dense, quite often impenetrable, forest
about the lakes, in the river valleys, and on the mountain-sides.
In the north, especially, broad tracts of barren land are covered
with thick thorn-bush, and almost waterless ; the few streams
which descend into these desert areas die away into swamps
and brackish pools, and the passage of troops through such
country is no light undertaking.

Desolate stretches of this sort are less common farther south,
where most of the land surface lies lower. Here, however, swampy
rivers bordered by wide belts of tangled vegetation, which in the
rains become raging floods and at any time form serious obstacles
to movement, are found more often. Elsewhere, the lesser
mountains such as the Pare and Usambara, the Mfumbiro on
the south-western borders of Uganda, the Poroto and Ukinga,
and the Nguru and Uluguru north and south respectively of
Morogoro, present all the difficulties of mountain warfare except

[1] Both the period and the intensity of the rainy season, which as a rule
is much earlier in the southern than in the northern areas, fluctuate considerably from year to year, the date of its onset varying by as much as
one and a half months.

[2] See p. 7.

snow and ice. These steep and broken ranges, densely overgrown with forest and mostly untracked, are passable only through narrow valleys, where advance is restricted and the defence has everything in its favour. Again, in the high veld of the Masai steppe, in the neighbourhood of the Great Rift Valley, while the country is mostly open and free from bush, lack of water is an obstacle to any large-scale movement of troops.

Generally speaking, therefore, the ground throughout the area of operations is unfavourable to the movement and supply of armed forces dependent on lines of communication. On such terrain the Germans, with their less complex organization, had an incalculable advantage.

Apart from physical difficulties, immense distances and the rigours of a tropical climate, some reference must be made to the natural enemies to man with which the scene of war abounds. Encounters with the more dangerous of the greater wild animals—lion or rhinoceros in the bush, hippopotamus and crocodile in the rivers—were all in the day's work ; so, too, though less easy to combat, and more universal, were insect pests. Of these comes first the anopheles mosquito, spreading the germ of malaria. Scarcely less formidable is the tsetse fly, prevalent over the greater part of the country, the carrier of sleeping-sickness which is generally fatal to man and of the disease " nagana," deadly to horses and cattle. Others are the insidious burrowing jigger flea, which may cripple bare-footed men ; the spirillum tick, causing a fever with pernicious after-effects ; the white ant or termite, destructive of most materials ; and in addition to the usual " minor horrors of war," such creatures as scorpions, centipedes, poisonous spiders, exceptionally fierce wild bees, and warrior ants.

To sum up. Many features peculiar to the country differentiate the East African from all other theatres of war. Natural difficulties and obstacles on a huge scale and of every variety, imperfectly or not at all surmounted by man with roads, railways, and bridges ; an enervating and unhealthy tropical climate ; periods of incessant deluges of rain ; animals and insect plagues from which immunity can never be ensured ; all these, in a land of vast distances where Nature is a more relentless enemy than any human adversary, combine to confront a commander in East Africa with problems unlike any elsewhere and often well-nigh insoluble.

CHAPTER II

THE NORTHERN AREA—THE OPENING PHASE.

(Sketches 1, 2, 3, 4.)

LOCAL FORCES AT THE OUTBREAK OF WAR.

THE crisis in Europe attracted little serious notice in East Sketch 1 Africa until the last days of July 1914. The warning telegram from the Colonial Office, ordering precautionary measures to be put into force, was received at Entebbe and Nairobi late on the 29th July. At that date the slender military forces of Uganda and the British East Africa Protectorate were widely scattered. They consisted of the 3rd (British East Africa) and 4th (Uganda) Battalions of the King's African Rifles, together with four companies of the 1st Battalion attached from Nyasaland, making a total of 17 small companies.[1] Six of these, however, were engaged in protracted operations against the Marehan tribe on the Juba river, while others, garrisoning the northern borders or moving northwards for a projected expedition against the Turkana, were out of reach of the telegraph. One company was detached at Zanzibar. In the settled areas there remained only the two companies of the 4/K.A.R. at Bombo and Entebbe and about 1½ companies of the 3/K.A.R. at Nairobi or on their way there.

No organized reserve existed to expand the peace establishment of the K.A.R.[2] Nor were there any European volunteer units, although in Uganda a " Volunteer Reserve," not yet officially recognized, maintained a rifle-club and had given its members some elementary training. In British East Africa the East African Police, not a military force, contributed a detachment 50 strong to the defence of the railway.

Besides these there were in the two protectorates about 3,000 Europeans of military age, many of whom, including a number of retired officers, could shoot and ride ;[3] a very small proportion of the 20,000 Indians among the population had had any military training. None of these were organized;

---

[1] For details see Appendix IV.
[2] At Nairobi about 100 ex-askari of the K.A.R. who at once volunteered were taken back into the ranks as " reservists," so-called.
[3] See also p. 22, f.n. 1.

15

no reserves of arms or ammunition were available ; no supply or transport arrangements existed, except such as had been improvised for the Jubaland expedition. There was no headquarters staff to conduct military operations ; nor had any effective steps been taken to collect information as to the resources and possible action of the armed forces in the adjacent German protectorate.[1]

In short, when war broke out the two British protectorates were in all respects entirely unprepared and gravely at a disadvantage.

Sketch 2   THE SITUATION IN BRITISH EAST AFRICA.

From a military point of view, especially in the complete absence of intelligence data, the situation was disquieting.

The richest and best developed portions of the East Africa Protectorate, which had attracted the bulk of the British colonists, lay in the high plateaux about Nairobi and farther to the north and north-west, more than 300 miles from the coast. Their only link with Mombasa, and through that port with the outer world, was the Uganda Railway. From Nairobi to the sea this vital artery ran parallel to the frontier throughout, and was within 70 miles of it at its nearest point.

The frontier, moreover, for the most part a straight line running north-westwards from the coast to Lake Victoria, diverged midway so as to curve round the Kilimanjaro massif, including the latter in German territory.

Within the salient thus formed, the Germans possessed an admirable advanced base area sited on the high-lying, healthy and already settled slopes of the great mountain. This base was served by the Usambara railway, running back 200 miles to their own coast at Tanga, and by practicable tracks coming from the heart of their territory

---

[1] As early as 1904 Army Headquarters in India, doubtless anticipating the possibility of Indian troops being involved, had suggested that information of military value regarding East Africa should be collected, but nothing came of it. A similar proposal made by the War Office in 1911 was, it is understood, negatived by the Government of the British East Africa Protectorate in the interests of a pacific policy. A few officers of the K.A.R., returning from shooting trips in German territory, had reported what little they had seen. The British consul at Dar-es-Salaam, Mr. Norman King, had of his own initiative collected some general information which was afterwards utilized (see p. 62, f.n. 2).

and its central railway. Forward from it ran several lines
of approach to the Uganda Railway : among them, forming
the principal road-connection between the German and
British protectorates, the ancient caravan-route linking
Moshi, which adjoined the terminus of the Usambara
railway, with Voi, the nearest station on the Uganda
railway

Between Moshi and the sea the frontier was crossed by no
recognized tracks and the country was largely impracticable
for the movement of troops, except to some extent in the
low-lying, unhealthy and tsetse-infested bush of the coastal
belt.

It was therefore to be expected that the Germans would
concentrate their available troops in the Kilimanjaro area,
and that their initial efforts would be made from that area.
Three possible lines of operation presented themselves :—

(i) To the north-west of Kilimanjaro rose abruptly
from the plain the minor eminence of Longido, at the
apex of a roughly equilateral triangle whose base of
50 miles was the made road between Moshi and Arusha.
Well-watered in its southern portion, though lacking
rearward communications and local resources, this area
would allow of the concentration of minor forces, while
from it a known native track led northwards for some
60 miles to the Magadi Soda works near Kajiado,
midway on the branch railway linking the main line with
Lake Magadi.   But since beyond Longido the track
was largely waterless and led to no military objective
short of the main railway, little more than a demon
stration was likely to be attempted in this quarter.

(ii) Between the Magadi line junction and Tsavo
station the Uganda Railway was screened from approach
by the waterless Nyiri desert and the rugged hills of
Chyulu.   The tributary head-streams of the Tsavo
river, however, rising in the eastern foot-hills of
Kilimanjaro, opened up lines of approach to Tsavo
station with its important railway bridge.

(iii) Still more favourable to the enemy was the east- Sketch 4
ward trade-route through the depression between the
south-eastern slopes of Kilimanjaro and the northern
Pare mountains.   The trace of the frontier here
formed a British salient ten to twelve miles in depth,
within which a post at Taveta covered the road-bridge

over the Lumi river,[1] less than five miles from the
nearest German territory. Thence about 65 miles
of road led to the Uganda Railway at Voi, where
again was an important bridge. For 45 miles between
the Lumi and the Bura hills the route was waterless ;
but, assuming this difficulty surmounted, here was the
line of operation most likely to be selected by the
enemy.

The first step to be taken, therefore, was to protect the
Voi-Tsavo section of the Uganda Railway.

Accordingly on the 31st July the infantry half-company
of the 3/K.A.R. from Nairobi, followed by the partially-
trained mounted unit,[2] were sent to Voi ; that station and the
Tsavo bridge were put in a state of defence, and two partly
armoured trains prepared.

News of the British declaration of war against Germany,
coming on the 5th August, brought home to the East Africa
Protectorate the realities of a situation hitherto hardly
apprehended. The Governor, Sir Henry Belfield, proclaimed emergency measures.[3] The formation was announced
of a volunteer force, in two categories : (a) for service anywhere within the Protectorate, (b) for service within local
districts. This was received with enthusiasm and volunteers
poured in.

Command of the combined forces in Uganda and British
East Africa was assumed by the senior British officer,
Lieutenant-Colonel L. E. S. Ward, 4/K.A.R., the O.C.
Sketch 1 Troops in Uganda. In aid of British East Africa the two
companies of the 4/K.A.R. then moving northwards against
the Turkana[4] were recalled to Nairobi and the two companies in Uganda transferred to Kisumu, one of the latter
going on to Nairobi.

Sketch 2   At Nairobi a headquarters staff was improvised. The
collection of intelligence was begun, mainly through the
Assistant District Commissioners at Kisii, Taveta and

---

[1] When the frontier was defined in 1886, the Uganda Railway did not
exist. The inclusion of Taveta within British territory had the effect of
retaining British control of the watering-place at the Lumi river, an
important point in view of the long waterless stretch to the eastward.

[2] Half " D " Coy., 3/K.A.R. (2 offrs., 84 o.r.) ; half "A" Coy. (M.I.
recruits, 1 offr., 35 o.r.), with one m.g.

[3] At the outbreak of war the Governor, by virtue of his letters of
appointment, was Commander-in-Chief, responsible for all operations and
for all measures taken to increase the local forces. See Appendix IV.

[4] Operations against the Turkana, with which this history is not concerned, were afterwards carried out by forces from the Uganda police.

Vanga. In the Masai country Lord Delamere, possessing exceptional knowledge of the Masai and influence with that remarkable tribe, established himself on the river Narossera. Here, in collaboration with the District Commissioner, Mr. R. W. Hemsted, he raised a force of Masai scouts, while a motor-cycle despatch-rider service back to Kijabe station was organized by the newly-formed East Africa Mechanical Transport Corps.[1] To protect the branch line to Lake Magadi a small "Defence Force " was organized from the Magadi Soda Company's employees. By the 12th August arrangements had been made to patrol, by one means or another, the whole length of the frontier.

No coast defences had ever existed. At Mombasa, when war broke out, a few small saluting guns and some muzzle-loaders from the ancient Portuguese fort, manned mainly by volunteer ex-ratings of the Royal Navy, were emplaced to cover the mouth of the harbour. Mines to bar the entrance-channel were improvised locally under Commander F. L. Attenborough, late R.N. A Town Guard, about 150 strong, was formed. A half-company of the 3/K.A.R. sent from Nairobi was soon replaced by the formation of two so-called Reserve Companies, one from ex-K.A.R. askari and one from coastal Arabs.[2] But during the first three weeks or so of August Mombasa had little in the way of protection.

THE SITUATION IN ZANZIBAR.

Even more anxious was the situation in Zanzibar, for that island, with no fixed defences, lay within twenty miles of the German coast, almost in sight of Dar-es-Salaam. A wealthy seaport, the age-old focus of trade for the East African coast, Zanzibar was an obvious objective for the enemy. Its polyglot population could not be counted on for defence ;[3] and a further risk lay in the fact that Sayyid

Sketch 1

---

[1] First raised as a small volunteer unit in Nairobi on 6th August 1914 under Lieutenant (afterwards Major) A. F. Dudgeon.

[2] No. 1 Res. Coy. (ex K.A.R.), Captain A. C. D. Saunders, 3/K.A.R., and No. 2 Res. Coy. (Arabs).
    The latter unit, under Lieutenant A. J. B. Wavell, Welch Regt., ret., who had made the pilgrimage to Mecca and had a remarkable knowledge of and influence among the Moslem population, was usually designated " Wavell's Arabs."

[3] On 4th August the German tug *Helmuth*, the only craft in which enemy nationals could have left the island to join the German forces on the mainland, was seized by the port officer, and the Germans were afterwards interned.

Khaled, deposed from the Sultanate by Great Britain three years earlier, was living at Dar-es-Salaam and could claim many sympathisers in Zanzibar.

The British garrison consisted only of a company of the 3/K.A.R., 115 strong. A few ex-askari of the K.A.R. were re-enrolled, and the local police were armed. Beyond these, Zanzibar's only defence lay in the very limited resources of the Royal Navy : at present, a single cruiser.

Early Naval Operations.

End Paper
(N.)
The naval operations on the East African coast are described elsewhere.[1] They formed only a very small part of an extensive whole covering all the eastern oceans, in which one factor was the presence in East African waters of the German cruiser *Königsberg*. That vessel, faster than the three British cruisers of Admiral King-Hall's Cape Squadron— H.M.Ss. *Hyacinth* (flag), *Astraea* and *Pegasus*—which were seeking her off Zanzibar, put out from Dar-es-Salaam on the 31st July and gave them the slip. The *Hyacinth* then returned to other duties off the Cape, followed on the 13th August by the *Astraea*, Captain A. C. Sykes. The latter had in the meantime, on the 8th August, opened the East African campaign by shelling the important German wireless station at Dar-es-Salaam[2] and by boarding and disabling, unopposed, two potential commerce-raiders there.[3] The Germans themselves having scuttled their survey-ship *Möwe* in the harbour and sunk the floating dock so as to obstruct the entrance, the port of Dar-es-Salaam was thenceforward useless to them as a base for the *Königsberg*.

On the 17th August H.M.S. *Pegasus*, Commander J. A. Ingles, now remaining alone, and far inferior in speed and gun-power to the *Königsberg*, similarly raided Tanga and, unopposed, disabled another German merchant ship (*Markgraf*) there. Six days lated (23rd), at Bagamoyo, a

---

[1] See " Naval Operations," Vol. I (2nd ed.), pp. 152–6, 295–6, 338–40, 374–5.

[2] The first recorded act of war.

[3] Merchant ships *König* and *Feldmarschall*. It does not seem to have been found possible to take away as prizes these ships, nor the *Markgraf* from Tanga (17th August), which might all have been of great use in subsequent British military operations along the coast. At Dar-es-Salaam lay also the German ship *Tabora* which, being found partly equipped as a hospital ship, was not interfered with.

landing party sent off by the *Pegasus* to dismantle the cable-station was turned back by the Germans, and the ship, after shelling the local government buildings, returned to Zanzibar, where an insistent call for naval protection continued. Based on that island, for another month she continued to search the coast, after which, as will presently be seen, her activities came unhappily to an end.[1]

DEFENSIVE MEASURES IN BRITISH EAST AFRICA.

Meanwhile, the organization of defence in the British **Sketch 1** protectorates was proceeding. The return of the six K.A.R. companies from Jubaland was hampered both by the lack of shipping[2] and by fear of its effect on the tribes, still hardly subdued, against whom they had been operating. One company,[3] however, was recalled via Mombasa to Nairobi, whence it was sent back to Voi. Most of the remainder were still about Serenli. Whilst the authorities at Nairobi hesitated,[4] the local commander, Major L. H. Soames, acted on his own initiative. On the 18th August he marched south with three companies of the 1/K.A.R., leaving at Serenli about a company in all of the 3/K.A.R.[5]

At Nairobi the enrolment of volunteers went on with sustained enthusiasm. In many cases settlers, even on distant isolated farms, on hearing of the declaration of war, put in caretakers and left at once for Nairobi to offer their services. No arms had yet become available for these willing recruits

---

[1] Before leaving Dar-es-Salaam on 8th August Captain Sykes made a truce with the German authorities there, on the condition that they should refrain from hostile acts during the war. Similarly at Tanga, on 17th ~~August, Commander Tyrwhitt made a truce on the basis that the German~~ armed strength there should not exceed 50 native police. Neither of these agreements was confirmed by the home authorities. On 30th August the Admiralty cabled to the Senior Naval Office, Mombasa, as follows: " H.M.G. does not ratify terms of truce Dar-es-Salaam and Tanga. You " should inform governors of the two towns of this at a convenient oppor- " tunity shortly before any further offensive action is taken against " either of the towns."

[2] Only the small steamer *Duplex* was available.

[3] " B " Coy., 1/K.A.R., guarding the base at Gobwen and Yonti. Embarked at Kismayu 7th, disembarked Mombasa 9th August.

[4] As late as 13th August, in reply to an enquiry by the Colonial Office whether 500 of the K.A.R. could be furnished to assist future operations against the Germans, the Governor stated that these could be assembled at once, but that he was " of opinion that no material advantage would " be gained by taking the troops who were at present employed in " Jubaland."

[5] Half " E " Coy., 3/K.A.R., and a Camel Corps detachment, recalled from Dolo on the Abyssinian border, made a notable return march of 175 miles to Serenli in seven days under very trying conditions.

except their own sporting rifles. This fact, coupled with the inevitable difficulties of training and supply, compelled the cessation of recruiting at least three times during the first month of war, with resulting discouragement to many who had come far and given up much to join. Nevertheless the defence force grew rapidly.[1] An especially gratifying feature was the loyal enthusiasm of the Boer settlers : these were among the first to volunteer and were a most valuable addition to the forces.

The largest Volunteer unit formed was the East Africa Mounted Rifles. Enrolment for it began on the 5th August ; on the 15th it paraded 335 strong, mounted on ponies and mules, in six squadrons, one of which left two days later for Kijabe to join Lord Delamere. On the 19th August a newly-raised machine gun section was added.

Other units formed were the East African Regiment, comprising two European companies, about 100 in all, and a so-called " Pathan " company of Indians ; a Railway Pioneer Corps from employees of the Uganda Railway ; the East Africa Mechanical Transport Corps already mentioned ; with Town Guards at Nairobi and Mombasa and local detachments to guard vulnerable points.

Outside the armed forces, most of the remaining British inhabitants contributed a variety of valuable services. In particular, at Nairobi a Central Supply Committee of business men dealt with food problems.[2] This body, which received from its subordinate District Supply Committees weekly reports of stores and supplies available, provided for the supply of all material required by the troops.

Mention must also be made of the Indian inhabitants, who, though few among them were of the more martial races of India, responded none the less loyally and whole-heartedly to the needs of the situation.

Among the African population an ardent loyalty and alacrity to serve were equally striking. On all sides offers of help and generous gifts of cattle and food-stuffs came in from the native chiefs. At this time, when it was still hoped that the war would be short, and when it was taken for

---

[1] The census total of the male Europeans over the age of 21 was 3,248. Nearly 1,800 enrolled as volunteers ; a further 500, employed in essential government services, could not be spared ; 250 were rejected, medically unfit ; and of the remainder at least 300 were over military age.

[2] For example, wheat flour ran short, and it became necessary to mix a proportion of maize meal into all bread.

granted that any additional troops needed would come from India, no expansion of the K.A.R. was contemplated ; but it was at once apparent that for a campaign in country widely infested by tsetse fly large numbers of carriers[1] would be required, and steps were soon taken to raise them.

On the 13th August Messrs. O. F. Watkins and J. M. Pearson, of the Civil Service in British East Africa, were selected for this duty and instituted what was soon to become the extensive and indispensable organization known as the Carrier Corps. The organizers' difficulties were many ;[2] nevertheless with the aid of local officials, estate-owners and influential native chiefs, large contingents of carriers enrolled in all parts of the country reached Nairobi to be equipped and distributed. By the 11th September the Carrier Corps consisted of five units each 1,000 strong, in companies of 100 under native head-men. It had been intended that the organization should be a civil department ; but various difficulties made it necessary to give Army rank to the two officers in charge, and the force was put on a military basis.

THE FLOTILLA ON LAKE VICTORIA.

Lake Victoria, about the size of the Irish Sea, with its Sketch 3 shores and islands divided almost equally between the two belligerents, presented a small-scale naval problem in which the advantage was preponderantly British. No armed vessels existed on either side ; but a British flotilla of nine small steamers[3] maintained a goods and passenger service

---

[1] The term " porter " is more usual in East Africa ; but as the organization under which native porters were enlisted was named the " Carrier Corps," and as the terms " carrier " and " porter " were used synonymously in all orders, despatches, etc., the word " carrier " has been adopted.

It is hoped to include in Vol. II a short account of the Carrier Corps, without whose devoted services the campaign could never have been fought at all.

[2] E.g., recruiting was also proceeding for drivers and others for animal transport. Desertions from the one service to the other became frequent.

[3] Steamers :

Usoga	..	..	1,200 tons, 8 knots, launched 1913.
Nyanza	..	..	1,146 tons, 9 knots, launched 1907.
Clement Hill	..	..	1,100 tons, 9 knots, launched 1906.
Sybil	..	..	700 tons, 9 knots, launched 1904.
Winifred	..	..	700 tons, 9 knots, launched 1903.

also, under construction,

Rusinga	..	..	1,200 tons, 8 knots.

Tugs :

Kavirondo	..	..	200 tons, 9 knots, launched 1913.
Percy Anderson	..	..	100 tons, 7 knots, launched 1897.
William Mackinnon	..		70 tons, 7 knots, launched 1900.
Husseni	..	..	50 tons, 7 knots, launched 1913.

between the Uganda Railway terminus at Kisumu (B.E.A.) and the principal ports of Uganda, viz., Jinja, Port Bell (for Kampala), Entebbe and Bukakata. By contrast, the only German vessel on the Lake was the tug *Muansa*, 40 tons.

During the first fortnight of the war, with the exception of occasional patrol voyages,[1] normal peace-time services were continued, it being considered essential to maintain the usual communications. On receipt of a report that the *Muansa* was being armed, the only available gun—a 9-pdr. M.L. saluting piece at Kisumu, with no sights—was mounted, first in the *William Mackinnon*[2] and then, with improvised sights, in the *Kavirondo*, which stood by at Kisumu.

THE SITUATION IN UGANDA.

Sketch 3   On the outbreak of war the immediate danger to Uganda was less than that to the sister Protectorate, for the southern districts were for the most part wild country affording no opportunity for any serious invasion, and it was known that the German posts along the border were few and small. It was therefore unlikely that the enemy would make any considerable effort in that quarter : the greater danger lay east of Lake Victoria. In an appreciation dated the 2nd August Lieut.-Colonel Ward laid special stress on the importance of the railway from Mombasa to Kisumu. Compared with the preservation of this vital line of communication the protection of the frontier districts in Uganda, or even of the whole Uganda Protectorate, was of minor importance.

Accepting this view, the Uganda Government, as has been said,[3] sent all their four available companies of regular troops to the assistance of the British East Africa Protectorate. In replacement, two more companies were recalled from Maroto to Entebbe, leaving only one on the northern border.[4]

---

[1] On 13th August the *Percy Anderson*, Lieutenant C. C. Garrett, R.N.R., landed a reconnoitring party on the eastern German shore, and on 14th she captured the German dhow *Upese*. On 20th August the *Winifred*, Commander H. R. Hatch, R.N.R., reconnoitred Bukoba and Sango Bay.

[2] Originally a " Protectorate armed vessel," of whose armament the 9-pdr. had once formed part. The Goanese steward now volunteered as gunner.

[3] See p. 18.

[4] Later, by agreement between the Uganda and Sudan Governments, at the suggestion of the former, some of the northern posts were taken over by Sudanese troops, the first of whom reached Madial early in October.

At the same time a " Reserve Company " of the 4/K.A.R., 90 strong, was formed from ex-askari. The armed native Uganda Police from all over the Protectorate, about 1,100 in all, were concentrated mainly at Kampala, Masaka and Mbarara. Drawn from this force, an " Active Service Company ", 200 strong under Mr. J. W. Dryden, which was destined to be expanded later into the Uganda Police Service Battalion, was embarked on the 6th August for the southern border. Armed guards were also supplied for the Lake vessels.

Some 300 volunteers were enrolled in the Uganda Volunteer Reserve,[1] and supply and medical[2] services established. Preparations were also made to raise a defence force of native levies organized on a tribal basis, towards which the native chiefs of the various " Saza " or county areas at once offered help. At the outset, as it was desired not to involve natives in a white man's war, this step was deferred ; but more men were soon needed, and units were formed for the defence of the southern frontier. These were eventually expanded into the valuable force named the Baganda Rifles, which did useful work both on the border and later, as will be seen, in the march to Tabora.[3]

On the 6th August Captain E. H. T. Lawrence, Acting Commissioner of Police, was made responsible for all defence measures. As in British East Africa, the civil authorities gave invaluable assistance.[4]

Lieutenant-Colonel Ward was succeeded in command of the troops in Uganda by Major I. H. Hickson, 3/K.A.R. who reached Entebbe on the 17th August. The latter decided to concentrate the bulk of the defensive forces at Masaka, with an advanced post at Sanji. The concentration was delayed by a variety of difficulties, and as late as the 27th August there were at Masaka only 250 armed Police. The

---

[1] Companies at Entebbe (70), Kampala (one British, one Indian, each 100), Jinja (30).

[2] Under Captain G. J. Keane, R.A.M.C. (R. of O.), appointed D.D.M.S., a Uganda field ambulance was formed. Native medical subordinate personnel was enlisted and trained, of which a considerable portion came from the secondary schools, whose pupils volunteered eagerly in any capacity.

[3] See Chaps. XXIV–XXVI.

[4] The Chief Justice (Sir Morris Carter), for example, became Supply and Requisition Officer, responsible for recruitment of labour, for transport and supply of all natives, and eventually for the local manufacture of certain war equipment, in which Uganda was at first deficient.

two companies of the 4/K.A.R. from the northern area reached Entebbe, on their way to Masaka, on the 25th August and 1st September, respectively.

THE SOUTHERN UGANDA BORDER.

Sketch 3 The emergency of war revealed the defects of the arbitrary frontier dividing Uganda from the German protectorate. A mere straight line on the map, it forms the chord to the wide southward-sweeping arc of the Kagera river, which from Lake Victoria to Nsongezi is broad and navigable. In that remote and sparsely-populated area there was no physical obstacle to bar hostile incursion into British territory. Nor was it possible to stop the passage of information.[1]

At its western end the frontier twists along rising mountain crests up to the summit of Mount Sabinio, 12,000 feet above sea-level, the meeting place of the British, Belgian and German boundaries. Though possibly satisfactory as a physical dividing-line, this had the defect, already mentioned, of partitioning the ancient native state of Ruanda, of which a northern portion thus came under British rule as part of the Kigezi district of Uganda, while most of the state lay within the German protectorate.

In the latter the Germans had cultivated good relations with the Sultan Msinga, chief of the Batusi, the proud and virile ruling tribe of Ruanda, and on the outbreak of war Msinga sent emissaries to incite his half-brother Nyindo to revolt. The Batusi tribesmen round Kigezi rose in response and burnt the camp of the British Assistant Commissioner, then on Mt. Sabinio, and for some time it proved impossible to restore ordered government in British Ruanda.

Fortunately in this quarter the Germans showed no inclination to assume the offensive.[2] Farther south, on Lake

---

[1] The Uganda police made good use of this by spreading reports of the imminent arrival of 3,000 or more additional troops.

[2] The 7.F.K., stationed in peace at Bukoba, had been withdrawn on mobilization to Mwanza, and the German units on the Belgian frontier north of Lake Tanganyika had also been withdrawn. (See Chap. III, Note II, p. 53.)

There is reason to think that the Germans were deterred from a contemplated march on Kampala in the middle of August by the reports, mentioned in the preceding footnote, of reinforcements arriving in Uganda.

Tanganyika, they took action which led in due course, as will be seen, to the participation of the Belgians in this campaign.

THE BELGIAN CONGO FRONTIER.

From Mt. Sabinio southwards the German protectorate **End Paper** marched with the Eastern Province of the Belgian Congo **(N.)** territory.[1] Here on the outbreak of war the Belgians, relying on the Berlin Act of 1885,[2] had hoped to maintain neutrality, and the Belgian Government had made every effort to this end.

As early as the 30th July 1914 that Government, in view of the menacing European situation, had cabled to the Governor-General of the Congo directing him, in the event either of Belgian mobilization or of a Franco-German war, to take all measures necessary to safeguard Belgian neutrality. This was followed on the 6th August by a brief telegram which deserves quotation : *Armée allemande envahit territoire belge 4 août. Belgique désire pas porter guerre en Afrique. En conséquence observez attitude strictement défensive sur frontières Congo et colonies allemandes.* It is noteworthy that from the outset and in all its dealings at this time with its Allies[3] the Belgian Government clung to its earnest desire, of which this telegram bears witness, to avert the spread of war to African territory.

Receipt of the instructions of the 6th August was communicated to the Governor of Uganda in a letter sent on the 10th August by M. Malfeyt, the Vice-Governor-General of the Eastern Province. M. Malfeyt added that he had entrusted the defence of his Province to M. Henry, a Belgian Army officer now on his staff as Commissaire-Général, and had directed him to consult with the Governor of Uganda with a view to concerting the necessary measures.

Unfortunately in the absence of the telegraph the only means of communication with Uganda was by runner

---

[1] The southern boundary of the Eastern Province was the parallel of 5° south latitude, which cuts Lake Tanganyika at Simba, opposite Ujiji. South of this the Katanga Province extends southwards to the border of Northern Rhodesia.

[2] See Appendix II.

[3] A formal assurance of full support in East Africa by the British Government, in response to Belgian representations in August, was given on 19th September 1914. By that time, however, the course of events had made neutrality in the Belgian Congo impossible.

along some 150 miles of rough track through the mountains between Ruchuru and Mbarara, a route rendered somewhat unsafe by the unrest among the Kigezi natives. No immediate joint action, therefore, was possible ; but cordial relations were established and the way prepared for future co-operation. Meanwhile the Belgian frontier posts were placed in a state of defence, reservists were called up, and the enlistment of recruits to reinforce the local garrisons was begun.

The Belgian hopes of neutrality were destined to be of short duration. On the night of the 14th/15th August the first violation of the Congo territory took place near Uvira, at the head of Lake Tanganyika, where a party landed by the small German armed steamer *Hedwig von Wissmann* destroyed the telephone line. That vessel then, after sinking a number of native canoes on the pretext of their being " intended for the conveyance of troops," cruised along the Belgian shore in search of the small Belgian steamer *Alexandre Delcommune*, which on the 22nd August she discovered beached near Lukuga and proceeded to disable.[1]

In consequence of these actions the Belgian Government sent orders on the 28th August 1914 to M. Tombeur, then Inspecteur d'Etat officiating as Vice-Governor of the Katanga Province,[2] which amounted to a renunciation of neutrality. M. Tombeur was directed to take all military measures for the defence of Belgian territory ; he was empowered to authorize the entry of British troops, to accept the offer of passage for Belgian troops through Rhodesia, and to undertake either with Belgian troops alone or in co-operation with British troops any offensive action necessary in order to maintain the integrity of Belgian colonial territory. These orders were repeated to the Governor-General, who was similarly authorized to support the French troops on the Cameroons frontier.[3]

---

[1] In a German account of various operations in East Africa between August and October 1914 which was printed, apparently officially, in Tanga about 1915, it is stated that on 21st August the *Hedwig von Wissmann* was warned off by the Belgians on approaching their southern frontier port of Moliro, and that her commander learned the whereabouts of the *Alexandre Delcommune* from the Belgian askari sent with the warning message. It is also stated that on 22nd August the first shot was fired by the Belgians.

[2] See p. 202, f.n. 2.

[3] Belgian Grey Book, p. 14.

Throughout September and October communications continued to be exchanged between the Uganda authorities and the Belgians with a view to co-operation, and on the 27th October a meeting took place at the Belgian head-quarters at Kibati between M. Henry and Captain E. S. Grogan, the Assistant Intelligence Officer in Uganda, who discussed the whole situation and found themselves in cordial agreement, although concerted action was not immediately possible.

For practical purposes Belgian neutrality in Africa thus came to an end. No further clash with the Germans, however, occurred for some weeks longer.[1]

DECISIONS AS TO POLICY.

The problem of the policy to be adopted in regard to East Africa was raised immediately on the outbreak of war by a telegram in which, on the 4th August, the defenceless condition of the East Africa Protectorate was represented to the Colonial Office by Sir Henry Belfield. Up to this time responsibility for all defence matters in the British Protectorates had rested with the Colonial Office, not the War Office ; the part of the latter, except for the provision of officers seconded from the Army to serve with the local native formations, being mainly advisory. In every previous emergency in East Africa, any troops required to supplement the local forces had come from India.

Accordingly the Colonial Office turned first to the India Office, with a request for a brigade of Indian Infantry, and other troops, to be held ready for service in East Africa. The India Office, already called upon for help on a large

---

[1] At the outbreak of war the armed forces of the Belgian Congo amounted to little more than a local gendarmerie charged with the maintenance of internal security. This *Force Publique*, as it was termed, consisted of 26 individual companies scattered throughout the various provinces and districts, together with one company of artillery at Shinkakasa near the mouth of the Congo, each company being commanded by the local civil resident (*Commissaire*) of the district. Only in the southerly province of Katanga were four of these companies organized in military formations. The total strength of the force was about 15,000, but this figure included the local district police. Apart from the four companies in Katanga, which had been re-armed with modern Mauser rifles, the *Force Publique* was armed only with the old Albini rifle. A few machine guns and small field guns were kept in the frontier posts. The supply, transport and medical services required for field operations did not exist.

scale in the main theatre of war, referred the request to the Committee of Imperial Defence.

On the 5th August the Prime Minister approved the formation of a joint naval and military sub-committee of the latter body, " for the consideration of combined opera-" tions in foreign territory ".[1]   This, known as the Offensive Sub-Committee, was to submit its proposals to the Cabinet, and to work out details for any schemes which might be approved.[2]

The same day the sub-committee recommended the despatch of an expedition from India against the port of Dar-es-Salaam, a potential hostile naval base, the capture of which would facilitate the protection of commerce and the defence of neighbouring British possessions.   To this on the following day (6th August) was added a recommendation that " further to the expeditionary force " (i.e., that against Dar-es-Salaam) " should be added, for the purpose of safe-" guarding against possible native unrest, if the Indian " Government could spare them, two battalions "—increased almost at once to three—" to reinforce the King's African " Rifles in the East Africa Protectorate ".[3]

---

[1] See " Military Operations, France and Belgium 1914," Vol. II, pp. 20–21.   The object laid down was " to decide what objectives would " be assigned to joint expeditions with a view to producing a definite " effect on the result of the war."

The Germans, lacking submarine cables, relied largely on powerful wireless stations in their colonies to send orders to their warships and warnings to their merchant ships enabling the latter to avoid capture.

The sub-committee's choice of objectives was therefore mainly influenced by the question whether these possessed wireless stations and harbours.

[2] Consultation with the General Staff was not explicitly laid down.

[3] The same afternoon (6th August) two members of the sub-committee, General Sir Edmund Barrow (Military Secretary, India Office) and Colonel A. R. Hoskins (Inspector General, K.A.R.), deputed to make arrangements, brought to the Admiralty a message from the Secretary of State for India as follows :

" Besides the Dar-es-Salaam expedition, India shall send three " battalions for defence at Zanzibar and British East Africa.   It is " hoped that one of these battalions can be sent off as soon as possible, " without waiting for the expedition.   India is to make all military " arrangements, independently of the War Office."

On 8th August these decisions were cabled to the Viceroy, the defensive force for British East Africa being given as one battalion of Indian regular infantry, two battalions of " Imperial Service " infantry (from the Indian native states).   On 9th August orders were cabled for this force to be prepared for immediate despatch.   The cables of 8th and 9th August also conveyed instructions as to the larger and separate expedition against Dar-es-Salaam, which was afterwards postponed and eventually sent against Tanga. See Chaps. IV. V, VI.

Thus India was to be asked to provide two forces : one to capture and hold the principal German port, and another to reinforce the local formations in British East Africa.[1]

Instructed to this effect on the 8th and 9th August, Army Headquarters in India acted promptly. For the reinforcing expedition, known as Indian Expeditionary Force " C ", the 29th Punjabis,[2] Lieut.-Colonel A. B. H. Drew, were placed under orders on the 12th August ; two Imperial Service battalions were made up by half-battalions from the native states of Bhurtpore, Jind, Kapurthala and Rampur respectively. To these were added the 27th Mountain Battery, R.A., a field battery of Calcutta Volunteer Artillery, a machine gun battery and ancillary units. Brig.-General J. M. Stewart, C.B., A.D.C., was appointed in command.

On the 19th August the first contingent of I.E.F. " C ", viz., Force Headquarters, 29th Punjabis, and a section 120th Field Ambulance, sailed from Karachi in the transport *Nairung* for East Africa. These troops were to come as a welcome reinforcement ; for the enemy had already begun to take the offensive.[3]

---

[1] The lack of any reliable military information regarding the East African theatre has already been mentioned (see p. 16, f.n. 1). It follows that the instructions given were based only upon necessarily vague estimates of the opposition to be encountered. That the tasks with which the Indian forces were to be confronted would demand expert local knowledge of the country and tactics peculiar to East Africa, to be found only in the local forces, and in particular that the enemy would be found to possess an efficient fighting force under a bold and competent commander, would seem hardly to have been realized.

[2] Previously detailed as part of the Indian expeditionary force for Europe. The battalion was brought up to war strength by a draft of 250 men from the 30th Punjabis.

[3] See Chap. III, Note II, p. 53.

CHAPTER III

THE NORTHERN AREA

Initial Military Operations.[1]

(Sketches 1, 2, 3, 4, 5, 6, 7, 8.)

Sketch 4 As was to be expected, the enemy's first move was made in the direction of Taveta. This post, in the small British salient at the south-eastern foot of Kilimanjaro, overlooked from high ground beyond the border and cut off from the Uganda railway by over 50 miles of desert, was virtually indefensible ; but on the outbreak of war it remained, nevertheless, in occupation by a small detachment of armed police under the Assistant District Commissioner, Mr. S. H. La Fontaine.

On the 13th August the German commander at Moshi, Captain von Prince, sent a formal demand—which does not appear to have reached Mr. La Fontaine—that Taveta should be evacuated the following day, and on the night of the 14th/15th August a German patrol fired on the frontier piquet of the police, which fell back on Taveta. Early next morning Taveta was attacked by about 300 of the enemy.[2] In the face of these superior numbers Mr. La Fontaine withdrew his detachment, losing only one man killed, across the desert to Voi, leaving Taveta and the Lumi crossing, where the enemy destroyed the bridge, in German hands. On the news of this incursion reaching Nairobi " F " Company 4/K.A.R. was sent down from Nairobi by way of Voi to Bura. For the time being the Germans made no further move in that direction.

Sketch 5 The German seizure of Taveta was followed by alarming reports from the coastal belt south of Mombasa. In this unhealthy area some 25 miles of practicable motor-road

---

[1] Judged by the standards of the campaigns in France and elsewhere, the minor encounters and movements of small bodies of troops with which the East African campaign began may at first sight appear hardly worth mentioning. It therefore seems necessary to remark that they were of considerable local importance, and that they illustrate the prevailing local conditions. Without some account of them it would be difficult to picture the development of the general situation and later operations.

[2] One *F.K.* under Lieutenant Boell, one *Sch.K.*, and a mounted troop under Lieutenant-Colonel von Bock. The Germans advanced at first in close order, and are believed to have intended sending forward under a white flag a demand for surrender. They were fired upon before any flag was seen, and at once deployed to attack.

ran southward from Mombasa to Gazi ; but between Gazi and the British frontier post at Vanga, 30 miles farther south, the thick bush and swamp were traversed only by native tracks. On the German side a partially made road ran up from Tanga to the German post at Jasin, two miles from Vanga.

When war was declared the Assistant District Commissioner at Vanga, Lieutenant T. Ainsworth Dickson, put his strongly-built Customs House into a state of defence and patrolled the frontier, while the Germans, apprehensive of invasion, kept only patrols in Jasin and established a fortified camp some two miles farther south at Kibirule.

A fortnight later came reports of a hostile concentration at Kibirule, and on the 21st August, in response to a call for reinforcements, a half-company of K.A.R. reservists was despatched by sea from Mombasa to Vanga. At the same time a small mixed force[1] was sent over from Zanzibar, accompanied by H.M.S. *Pegasus*. In the absence of any attack this force returned next day to Zanzibar.

On the 27th August a similar unfounded alarm brought the *Pegasus* and the Zanzibar detachment again to Vanga, where they found the newly-formed " Arab Company " of the K.A.R. under Lieutenant Wavell, which had arrived from Mombasa that day. Again they returned to Zanzibar, leaving Lieutenant Wavell in command of the frontier area.

Vanga, on the southern shore of the Umba river's broad estuary, was badly placed for defence. It being obviously undesirable to remove British authority altogether from this area, it was decided to withdraw some ten miles to Majoreni, behind the River Mwena, whence the Assistant District Commissioner could still supervise his territory and where any hostile advance up the coast could be stopped.

On the 30th August, as a show of force before withdrawal, Wavell crossed the border, drove the enemy out of Jasin, and made a machine gun demonstration against the German defences at Kibirule, which made no reply. He then withdrew, evacuated Vanga that evening, and took up a defensive position at Majoreni with outposts at the crossings over the Mwena. Next day (31st) German patrols entered Vanga, where they later blew up the British Customs House.

---

[1] Three British and 2 Indian officers, with 55 K.A.R., 31 Pathan and Punjabi police, and one m.g., under Captain Davies, K.A.R.

C*

To the north of Mombasa also, in the coastal area about the Sabaki river, some alarm had been caused during the last ten days of August by internal trouble among the Giriama tribe.[1] This was quickly put down ; its importance seems, indeed—perhaps naturally at this time—to have been over-estimated. It had at all events the effect of containing, on what seems in retrospect to have been a matter rather for the police, most of the few available troops much needed elsewhere. Mombasa, in particular, from which, except for a few Indian " reservists " and the Town Guard, all troops had gone either south to Vanga or north against the Giriama, remained for a time defenceless ; nor could H.M.S. *Pegasus*, tied by her orders to the protection of Zanzibar, respond to Mombasa's call for her help.

If, therefore, as was thought at the time, the revolt was engineered by the Germans, its instigators scored a minor success, though they made no use of it.

Sketch 4   Other encounters took place before the arrival of the first contingent from India early in September. From the direction of Kasigao, the conspicuous hill 20 miles south of Maungu station, came two unsuccessful attempts against the railway. On the 24th August a detachment of K.A.R. was sent from Voi to Maungu in an " armoured " train in pursuit of a small German raiding party which, arriving at

---

[1] The Giriama, a primitive and not particularly warlike tribe, given to illicit ivory-trading through Arab intermediaries from German territory, and at this time in a somewhat restless state, seem to have been incited to revolt by these Arabs with the usual type of story that British ascendancy was at an end and that the Germans were about to take over the country.

The murder by Giriama on 18th August of two native policemen of the Assistant District Commissioner's escort in the Mangea hills, an attempt by 150 of them next day to raid his camp, and an attack on the mission station at Jilori on the 23rd led to a call for military assistance. On the 24th most of No. 1 Res. Coy., K.A.R., sent by sea from Mombasa, landed at Kilifi. Coming from Bura via Voi, " F " Coy., 4/K.A.R., marched north from Rabai to join No. 1 Res. Coy. on 27th August in the Mangea hills, where Major G. M. P. Hawthorn assumed command of the area.

Next day (28th) " F " Coy. encountered near Jilori a force of ill-armed Giriama estimated at 1,000 strong, which quickly scattered into the bush, losing 30 killed and being, as an officer present put it, " too terrified to come in " ; the K.A.R. loss was 2 men wounded.

For another month punitive patrolling continued, but the tribe gave no further trouble. (⌐)

" E " Coy., 1/K.A.R., from the Juba river, which was landed at the mouth of the Tana, found the northern section of the tribe friendly. This unit remained, awaiting sea transport to the south, until the end of September.

At Bura " F " Coy. was replaced by " B " Coy., 4/K.A.R., from Nairobi, which sent a section forward to Maktau.

Maungu, had gone down the line without troubling to silence the railway telegraph. This party was captured, asleep, at dawn next day (25th). A week later a patrol of B Coy., 1/K.A.R., from Bura, under Lieutenant C. G. Phillips, trailed another German party for two days in the bush and came upon it, early on the 3rd September, near Maungu. The K.A.R. went in with the bayonet, killed one and captured two German askari, but were unable to prevent three Germans and the remainder from escaping into the bush with the loss of their rifles, kit and dynamite.[1]

Both on the Voi–Taveta road and in the upper Tsavo valley, the enemy's two most probable lines of approach, minor clashes occurred with somewhat less favourable results. On the 29th August a mounted patrol,[2] sent out across country from Bura a week earlier, was ambushed by a dismounted German party whilst moving across difficult broken ground between Mzima and the Rombo river. It withdrew successfully, with trifling loss ; but the incident shook the confidence of the native auxiliaries and of the local tribesmen, whose help became less willing, and it confirmed the risks to which the long line of railway was exposed. The difficulties of the ground and the havoc wrought by tsetse now compelled the mounted patrol to return to Bura, and the watch on the approaches to the Tsavo was taken over by a section of " B " Coy., 1/K.A.R., under Lieutenant R. C. Hardingham, established at Campi-ya-Marabu.

The Voi–Taveta road was patrolled by motor-cyclists of the East Africa Mechanical Transport Corps. A small defensive post at Maktau successfully beat off an attack by a German party on the 25th August ; but the motor cyclists were constantly ambushed, and on the 3rd September a bold German raid surprised their advanced camp at Mbuyuni,[3]

---

[1] Realizing the plight of the Germans, unarmed and without food or water in the bush, Lieutenant Phillips tried vainly by shouts and bugle calls to summon them to surrender. On 8th September the commander of the German party, in the last stages of exhaustion, surrendered at Bura, alone. ()

Lieutenant Phillips's detachment moved up from Maungu to Tsavo, where it took part in the affair of 6th September. (See p. 38).

[2] Twenty-four Abyssinian and Somali M.I. under Lieutenant H. H. Davies, with Masai auxiliaries.

The lower Tsavo was difficult country with thick thorn-bush ; the upper valley, approaching Kilimanjaro, traversed more open country which was believed to be suitable for mounted troops.

[3] Motor cycles were not a particularly good means of reconnaissance ; their speed hardly compensated for the noise which gave away their movement and for their awkwardness on bad ground.

scattering them and capturing some of their machines. The E.A.M.T. Corps was reinforced from Nairobi, and patrolling was continued also by the mounted detachment and by the K.A.R.

Beyond sporadic raiding and reconnaissance, however, the enemy attempted no offensive action either from Taveta or by way of his remaining and less favourable line of advance west and north of Kilimanjaro through Longido. **Sketch 6** Along the Magadi branch railway the Soda Company's local defence force, only 48 in all, was distributed in small posts[1] at the stations and in the gorge descending into the Great Rift Valley ; small mounted patrols were pushed southwards to the frontier and signal stations established, one overlooking Lake Natron and one on the heights of Emombarasha midway between Kajiado and the border ; and on the 24th August the crossing of the Kedongai river, at the northern foot of Oldoinyo Erok, was secured by a party of the East Africa Mounted Rifles. A week later, on receipt of reports that the Germans were holding Longido and moving units up to the frontier, the post at Emombarasha was reinforced, and " B " and " E " Squadrons of the E.A.M.R., each about 50 strong, were sent from Nairobi to Kajiado and Kiu stations respectively. These squadrons, making southwards from the railway so as to converge on the Kedongai crossing, found the country clear of the enemy and joined hands on the 4th September without incident. Further reports of German movements towards Oldoinyo Erok led to the despatch of the remainder of the East Africa Mounted Rifles to the Magadi area. Leaving Nairobi on the 8th September for Kajiado, the unit established camps at the Besil river crossing, the Olekononi Pass, in the Emombarasha hills and at the Kedongai crossing. Two of its small squadrons, as will presently be seen, were to be withdrawn again within a week ; and it was not until the 25th September that the rest of the E.A.M.R. came into any serious contact with the enemy.[2]

Mention may be made here, incidentally, of a factor which to some extent affected the operations of both sides

---

[1] Reported to the Germans by natives as " about 20 English at every " station " : an exaggeration characteristic of intelligence work in East Africa.

[2] On 10th September an E.A.M.R. patrol west of Oldoinyo Erok, drove off a small mounted party of Germans making for the railway, wounding one.

in this area. This was the presence in German territory near Arusha, 50 miles south of Longido, of a number of Boer settlers whose political allegiance was dubious. Hoping to win them over to the British side, the Boers in the British protectorate sent emissaries[1] across the border to them. These efforts were frustrated by the Germans, who impounded the horses and most of the rifles of their own Boer settlers, and the latter, fearing for the safety of their farms and families, could make no move. It seems not unlikely that some part of the German forces was contained by the necessity for their supervision.

REINFORCEMENTS FROM INDIA.

The troopship *Nairung*, carrying the first contingent of Indian Expeditionary Force " C ", with Brigadier-General Stewart and his staff, had left Karachi, it will be remembered, on the 19th August. Originally ordered to Zanzibar, she was met off the Seychelles on the 27th August by H.M.S. *Fox*, which escorted her to Mombasa. The two ships, joined by H.M.S. *Pegasus* as they neared port, arrived on the 1st September. The Indian force[2] was at once sent up country by rail, half of the 29th Punjabis being left in the Voi-Tsavo area and the remainder going on to Nairobi, where Brigadier-General Stewart established his headquarters.

The distribution of the troops in the northern area of operations on the 4th September is given in Note I, page 51.

OPERATIONS ON THE TSAVO.

A threat now came from the direction of the Tsavo river. **Sketch 4** On the 3rd September Lieutenant Hardingham's small outpost on the upper Tsavo was engaged near Mzima with a German force[3] heading eastward, much superior in numbers, before which he was compelled to retreat. On hearing of this next day (4th), Major A. A. James, 29th Punjabis,

---

[1] Notably Lieutenant Joubert, of the Boer contingent of the E.A.M.R., who boldly rode alone across the border to Arusha, returning on 20th September.

[2] Force H.Q., 29th Punjabis and one section 120th Fd. Ambulance; total 17 British officers, about 760 Indian regular troops,.

[3] *13.F.K.*, with 2 m.g. of *1.F.K.*, total strength 11 officers, about 200 o.r., 4 m.g., under Captain Schulz. These left Himo on 31st August with orders to discover the British strength, and, if possible, blow up the railway.

commanding at Voi, concentrated the bulk of his troops at Tsavo, leaving a detachment at Voi, and sending a company of the 4/K.A.R. to protect his northern flank at Mtito Andei and to move out to Killakuni.[1]

That night (4th/5th), learning that the Germans were coming on down the Tsavo Valley, James ordered the troops at Maktau, Bura and Mtito Andei to move in towards the Tsavo in order to cut off the enemy's retreat.

On the following day (5th) he sent out from Tsavo two companies of the 29th Punjabis with about 85 men of the 1/ and 3/K.A.R., under Captain H. T. Skinner of the 29th, who in the afternoon met Hardingham falling back some 15 miles up the valley. There followed a good example of the difficulties of East African warfare, in country covered with impenetrable thorn bush and undergrowth, broken by rocky outcrops and hillocks matted with scrub.

Having failed to gain contact with the Germans by nightfall on the 5th, Skinner formed the opinion that they had slipped past him in the bush. He reported accordingly, and was ordered by Major James during the night to turn and take them in flank and rear, driving them on into the latter's troops, who by about 7 a.m. on the 6th September were in position astride the river five miles west of Tsavo.

Soon after midday Skinner, moving down the Tsavo valley and still five miles short of James's position, discovered that he had been mistaken : the enemy was close behind, not ahead of him, and took his rear-guard unaware with heavy fire at short range from a line of low hills which he had just quitted.[2] A brief fight followed, in which many of the Punjabis, experiencing African warfare for the first time, went astray in the bush. A handful of them, however, under Captain Pottinger, successfully enfiladed the enemy's right while the K.A.R., under Lieutenant C. G. Phillips, crossed the river and equally successfully turned the German left. The raiding force hastily abandoned its position,

---

[1] *Voi :* Half Coy. 29th Punjabis ; Pathan Coy., E. Africa Regt. (Vols.).
Tsavo : Three and a half (single) Coys. 29th Punjabis ; 1 sec. " B " Coy., 1/K.A.R. ; half " D " Coy., 3/K.A.R. ; 1 12-pdr. naval gun ; 1 m.g. *Mtito Andei :* " B " Coy., 4/K.A.R.
In addition, " A " Coy., 4/K.A.R., with 2 m.g. of 29th Punjabis, sent from Nairobi, reached Tsavo late on 5th September.
[2] At this juncture a small mixed detachment under Lieutenant G. C. O. Oldfield, 4/K.A.R., sent forward by Major James, arrived and at once joined in. This party suffered severely, Lieutenant Oldfield being killed.

which Skinner at once re-occupied without further opposition.[1] An immediate pursuit of the retreating Germans, however, could not be undertaken, neither supplies nor carriers being available ; and although Phillips with the K.A.R. moved out next day (7th) and found tracks, the enemy was well on the way back to German territory and could not be overtaken.

Nor did better fortune attend the forces brought in from the flanks to cut off the German retreat. The orders sent to Mtito Andei miscarried altogether ;[2] a force of K.A.R. from Bura reached Tembo on the 7th September in time only to intercept a German ambulance party ; and on the same day a mounted detachment from Maktau, which did intercept the German column, being heavily outnumbered, was unable to prevent its escape.[3]

It may be deplored that more punishment was not inflicted on a raiding party so far afield ; the raid, however, was frustrated, and a useful lesson in the unaccustomed conditions of African warfare was learned at little cost by the Indian troops engaged.

Operations Round Kisii.   Sketch 3

The Tsavo affair was followed by activity on the extreme south-western border of British East Africa near Lake Victoria. Here Kisumu, the administrative centre of the Kavirondo district, was held by a garrison some 300 strong,[4] while at Kisii, 50 miles to the south, was a small police detachment with the District Commissioner, Mr. C. E. Spencer.

On the 9th September a serious threat to Kisumu and the railway arose when a considerable German force, arriving

---

[1] British casualties in this, the first engagement of Indian troops in the war of 1914–18, were : 29th Punjabis killed, 1 N.O., 1 o.r. ; wounded, 9 o.r. ; K.A.R. killed, 1 officer ; wounded, 8 o.r.

[2] On 15th September " B " Coy., 4/K.A.R., which had been holding the gap between the Chyulu and Nyulu Hills, was recalled, and next day (16th) it reached Tembo on its way down the Tsavo valley.

[3] Most unfortunately, after nightfall on 7th September, the M.I. detachment met the German ambulance party already mentioned. Recognizing the German speech and unaware of their non-combatant status, the M.I. fired on them, killing a German surgeon and several others. An apology for this regrettable mischance was sent from British headquarters.

[4] " G " Coy., 4/K.A.R., strength 90 ; E.A. Police, 100 ; Town Guard, 130.

by land and supported by the *Muansa*, occupied the undefended Lake port of Karungu and went on to Kisii, compelling Spencer and his police to withdraw towards Kendu.

All the readily available troops in British East Africa having already been sent to the Tsavo area, a call for help was made from Nairobi to the Uganda Government. The two remaining companies of the 4/K.A.R. were despatched from Uganda at once to Kendu, followed soon afterwards by the Reserve Coy., 4/K.A.R.—the last trained troops in Uganda—and 90 Uganda Police.[1]

Sketch 7　　On the 11th September the 4/K.A.R. company from Kisumu was joined at Wire Hill, half way from Kendu to Kisii, by the two Uganda companies under Captain E. G. M. Thorneycroft, who took command of the combined force,[2] 300 strong, and moved to Oyugis, where he met Spencer. The German force, about equal to his own, was still at Kisii.

Moving off at daybreak on the 12th, Thorneycroft deployed at about 10.30 a.m. along a group of hills over-looking Kisii, from which it was perceived that the enemy was holding a parade in the village, heedless of precaution.

The parade broke up in haste, and by midday a lively fight had developed, which went on during most of the afternoon, mainly in the thick bush on the British left, which the Germans endeavoured to turn. In the meantime on the other flank Thorneycroft pushed forward, crossed the stream outside the village and closed with the enemy in a struggle at point-blank range, in which unhappily he himself was killed and his men driven back with some loss. A small German field-gun was silenced early in the proceedings by the good shooting at extreme range of a machine gun under Lieutenant E. L. Musson.[3] Towards dusk, however, the Police and K.A.R. on the left were compelled by weight of numbers to fall back, followed by the remainder.

---

[1] The movement across the lake was covered by the *Kavirondo*, which between 7th and 13th September patrolled the eastern shore and raided Majita, but was unable to bring the *Muansa* to action.

[2] " C " and " D " (from Uganda), " G " (from Kisumu) Coys., 4/K.A.R. strength 250, with 2 m.g. ; E.A. Police det., 50.

[3] The German account admits that the field-gun, given away by its smoke, had fired only a few rounds when its officer became a casualty and the gun was " overwhelmed with salvo fire."

Under cover of darkness the British force withdrew, unmolested and in good order, to Wire Hill, where the second reinforcement from Uganda joined it.[1]

Early next morning (13th September) it was ascertained that the enemy, whose losses had been severe, had retreated from Kisii. By noon the K.A.R. had re-occupied the place, picking up abandoned German arms and baggage, while the Germans were already back in their own territory, out of reach of the pursuit which followed as far as the border.[2]

For some time to come the enemy remained inactive and the area on the whole was quiet.[3]

PRECAUTIONS IN SOUTHERN UGANDA.

Although the Germans remaining along the southern Sketch 8 border of Uganda were in fact too few to attempt any serious incursion, the anxiety caused by the departure of practically all the available trained troops to Kisii, willingly though they had been sent, was intensified by reports of the approach of German raiders towards Kigarama.

---

[1] British casualties were : killed, 1 officer, 6 o.r. ; wounded, 2 officers, 12 o.r.

German casualties officially reported were : killed, 3 officers, 6 German o.r., 33 o.r. ; wounded or missing, 9 Germans (including the commander), 38 o.r. At Kisii 5 Germans and 16 others, wounded, were left to the care of the British.

The use of black powder ammunition by the field-gun and by many of the German troops undoubtedly conduced to their heavier losses, by giving away their whereabouts.

[2] On 15th September an endeavour to intercept the enemy's retreat was made by two squadrons of the East Africa Mounted Rifles, brought from the Magadi area, which attempted to land from H M S *Winifred* at Karungu. The attempt was repulsed by the small German garrison, assisted by the *Muansa*. But immediately afterwards this force, now isolated, sailed for home in the *Muansa*, and later in the day, when the *Winifred* returned in company with the *Kavirondo*, Karungu was found abandoned. The mounted squadrons then returned to the Magadi area.

[3] The local tribesmen, to whom the German raid and Mr. Spencer's first withdrawal before it had seemed the fulfilment of a seditious native's prophecy not long before, were somewhat restive for a time, and did damage at Homa Bay and Karungu ; but within a short time order was restored.

The German force was the *Abteilung Bock* under Captain Bock von Wülfingen, consisting of 7. *F.K.*, with a European detachment, a " ruga-ruga " (native irregular) company, total strength, 52 Germans, 266 askari, 101 ruga-ruga, with three m.g., one 3·7 cm. gun.

The force reached the Mara river from Mwanza on 5th September.

In the action of 12th September Bock decided at 5 p.m. to break off the fight owing to his heavy losses and lack of reserves, and although aware at dusk that the British were evacuating their position, he kept to his decision to retreat, fearing to be cut off by troops coming from Kisumu. A panic among his carriers had intensified the moral effect of his losses.

In consequence such police as could be spared were concentrated, under Captain R. E. Critchley-Salmonson, 4/K.A.R., about Simba; meanwhile a first contingent of Baganda levies was sent south from Masaka, and further contingents were called up.

By mid-September Critchley-Salmonson had in the Simba hills about 175 police and 300 native levies, while German detachments, said to be each 100 strong, were reported to be at Mitaga and at the Kagera crossing near Kimwa.

On the 14th September, in order to conceal from the enemy the withdrawal of regular troops and to forestall hostile action, the small British forces crossed the border on a wide front about Mtugula, and went forward to the Kagera. Encountering no opposition, they occupied the German post south of the river at Kyaka (Kifumbiro) and secured also the crossing at Kimwa (Keshumero). The German territory as far as the Kagera was taken over, and by the 3rd October was under British administration without further trouble.

Meanwhile on the 28th September the second contingent sent to Kisii (Reserve Coy., 4/K.A.R., and Police detachment, 170 in all) returned to Entebbe. This force was now despatched by way of Sango Bay to take over the eastern sector of the frontier, where a week later (7th October) it was reinforced by a small K.A.R. detachment from the northern border. After their arrival the situation in southern Uganda became reasonably secure.

FURTHER ACTIVITIES ON THE TSAVO.

Sketch 4   After the affair of the 6th September it was decided, in order to ensure early warning of any further German raids, to re-establish the outlying post previously held by Lieutenant Hardingham at Campi-ya-Marabu. Here on the 19th September a small garrison of the 4/K.A.R. under Lieutenant A. C. H. Foster, with a mounted infantry section under Captain C. de S. Isaacson, successfully counter-attacked a raiding party before whose advance it had at first fallen back across the Nolturesh, and compelled the raiders to retreat with loss to the border.[1] The incident showed, however,

---

[1] German casualties, out of an estimated strength of 100, were 11 killed, 6 wounded. Unhappily Lieutenant Foster, who though mortally wounded continued gallantly to direct his men, died of wounds, and 6 o.r. were killed.

that Campi-ya-Marabu was ill-placed to bar the route down the Tsavo, and too far from the support of the nearest British post at Tembo. Two days later (21st), therefore, the K.A.R. detachment was withdrawn to the railway while fresh detachments, under Captain A. C. D. Saunders, 3/K.A.R., came up to establish a post in greater strength[1] just below the river junction near Mzima.

On the 25th September Saunders's outposts drove back very easily another German raiding party on the Nolturesh just above the junction. Next day the Germans, apparently reinforced, crossed that river on a wide front and moved down stream against the main British position. The road here, on the left bank of the Tsavo, ran with the river in a defile between a high hill to the north and a mile-wide stretch of impassable thorn to the south. Covering the defile, the British defences had been well sited, and although in the course of the sharp encounter which ensued the enemy contrived here and there to work forward under cover to within 40 yards, the German advance was effectively stopped,[2] the two K.A.R. machine guns putting in notably good work against the German four. Early in the afternoon the enemy broke off the engagement and withdrew. Pursuit was not immediately undertaken, the Germans being clearly in superior force and their withdrawal being suspected as a trap ; but on the following day (27th) patrols ascertained that the raiding force had, yet again, retired to the German border,[3] leaving the railway still intact.

In its repercussions this gratifying little affair was of value out of proportion to its actual scale ; for its good effect on the local tribes was marked and—even better—the vigorous and successful defence put up by the K.A.R.[4] deterred the enemy for some time to come from any further raiding attempts in this direction.

---

[1] " D " Coy., 3/K.A.R. (less one sec.) ; " B " Coy., 4/K.A.R. ; M.I. det. and Somali Scouts, K.A.R. : total 6 officers, 215 o.r., two m.g.

[2] The German official report lays stress on the excellence of the British defences (. . . *in der ausgezeichnet gedeckten und verschanzten Stellung der Gegner*) and the difficulty of dealing with them (*In vortrefflicher Feuerdisziplin lagen die beiden Züge, ohne dass unsererseits das Feuer wirksam wegen der Unkenntlichkeit der feindlichen Schützen erwidert werden konnte*).

[3] The force was found to have been *4. F.K.*, under Captain Schulz; its strength was estimated at 400, probably an over-estimate.

[4] K.A.R. casualties were 2 wounded. The German official report gave German losses as 1 officer (Schulz), 7 o.r. wounded ; they were certainly higher, for several dead were found by the K.A.R.

ACTIVITIES IN THE MAGADI AREA.

Sketch 6   Apart from patrolling and reconnaissance,[1] and a re-distribution of the five squadrons of the East Africa Mounted Rifles in small camps on the slopes of Oldoinyo Erok, nothing of importance occurred in the Magadi-Longido area until the end of September.

At daybreak on the 25th a German force, strength unknown, which during the previous night had halted near the camp of " C " Squadron on the upper Manga river, was pursued into the Ingito Hills by that squadron, only 30 strong, under Captain P. Chapman.

On coming up with the enemy Chapman's advanced guard was checked, and a sharp fight at close quarters ensued, against an almost overwhelming superiority in numbers. Under the fire of two machine guns, and threatened with bayonet attacks on both flanks, the small British force fell back through the bush to rally on two low hills in rear. It had suffered severely, losing 8 killed and 4 wounded ; but it had given a valiant account of itself, and not only was it not pursued, but the enemy turned and retired across the border. Chapman's messages to other squadrons, sent before starting, had either miscarried or been misunderstood, and only when the fight was over did another squadron come up, in time to see the Germans in the distance retreating southwards, carrying their wounded.[2] Since the enemy had abandoned his enterprise, which had been directed presumably against the Magadi branch railway, the East Africa Mounted Rifles had every reason for satisfaction.

During the next four weeks patrolling continued, camps were enlarged and defences strengthened, but no encounter of any importance took place. Meanwhile the Kajiado–Longido track was surveyed and improved ; a pipe-line for water was put in ; a telegraph line, which was continually broken by giraffes, was built ; and by the end of October,

---

[1] On the night 17th/18th September Mt. Longido, where a German force was reported to have arrived, was reconnoitred with a view to organizing an attack ; but the project was found too formidable for the forces available. Other reconnaissances saw no signs of the enemy.

[2] The German force was the *10. F.K.*, reinforced by a mounted European detachment, total strength 12 officers, 47 other Germans, 158 askari, with two m.g. and some 200 followers, under Captain Tafel. Their casualties are recorded as : killed, 1 officer, 6 other Germans ; 7 dead askari were found by the E.A.M.R. ; wounded, Captain Tafel, 8 other Germans, 12 askari.

with a forward base at Kajiado,[1] the route through Longido could be regarded, at need, as a practicable line of advance into German territory.

THE NYIRI DESERT AREA.

On the German side of the border north and north-east **Sketch 2** of Kilimanjaro the fertile slopes of the mountain afforded suitable ground and ample supplies for exploitation by the enemy, whereas in the arid desert of the British territory no force of any size could be maintained. A system of small native warning patrols was organized among the scattered Masai herdsmen of this area ; but these latter were regularly harassed from the Laitokitok foothills, where a German **Sketch 4** defended post had been established, by armed parties up to 50 strong, with some 300 irregulars, who descended on them and seized their stock.

Little could be done against these forays ; but on the 16th October, in response to an appeal by the Masai, 60 K.A.R. mounted infantry were despatched from Bura to Killakuni, whence they moved westwards to meet a force of 50 East Africa Mounted Rifles coming from Oldoinyo Erok. The two forces met on the Kemana river on the 21st. Although their demonstration somewhat heartened the Masai, they had not been able to intercept the raiders, nor were they in adequate force to attack the German defended post ; consequently, with little result to show, they returned to their respective starting points. The enterprise was not tried again, and along the section of line between Tsavo and the Magadi junction the natural difficulties of the country continued to be the principal safeguard of the railway.

OPERATIONS IN THE COASTAL AREA.

In the first three weeks of September nothing of military **End Paper** importance took place along the coast. On the 20th, **(N)** immediately preceding the operations now to be mentioned, came an unhappy naval setback at Zanzibar, where H.M.S. *Pegasus* was caught and destroyed by the *Königsberg*.[2]

---

[1] One (double) Coy. 29th Punjabis was sent on 16th September from Voi to Kajiado. Store depots, a hospital, and a combined veterinary hospital and remount depot were established at Kajiado.

[2] See " Naval Operations," Vol. I (2nd edition), pp. 295-6. Although the *Pegasus* was lost, her eight 4-inch guns were salved, and afterwards played their part in operations on land.

Making no attempt to exploit this success, even though at the moment there was not another British warship within a thousand miles, the *Königsberg* hastily made off to sea and was no more seen until she was run to ground in the Rufiji delta at the end of October.[1]

Sketch 5 At the time, however, the incident caused alarm not only at Zanzibar but at Mombasa. This was increased next day (21st), when there came news of German troops marching northwards up the coast from Jasin against the force some 200 strong under Lieutenant Wavell which, it will be remembered, was holding Majoreni. Early on the 22nd September that place was attacked. Two German columns approaching by parallel routes forced the passage of the Mwena, driving in the British outposts, which fell back on Wavell's newly-erected fort at Majoreni. Here the attack was firmly checked, and after hammering in vain[2] at the fort for most of the day, the Germans withdrew at nightfall behind the Mwena and retired again to the frontier.[3]

Wavell himself, however, had been severely wounded.[4] The evacuation of casualties along a bush track to Gazi, 20 miles back, where the motor road from Mombasa ended, proved difficult ; and on receipt of reports of a fresh German advance, there being in any case difficulties of supply, it was decided to withdraw to Gazi. On the night of the 25th/26th September Majoreni was evacuated.

The withdrawal was closely followed up by the Germans, who occupied Majoreni on the 26th, and on the 28th overtook and harassed Wavell's rear-guard beyond the Ramisi river.

The apparent threat to Mombasa led to the despatch of a company of K.A.R. from Mombasa on the 26th September to reinforce Gazi, and of two (single) companies of the 29th Punjabis from Nairobi to Mombasa, one of which went on to Gazi.

---

[1] See p. 108.
[2] The defences had been constructed with much ingenuity and included a small land-mine which was exploded with considerable effect. ⁊
[3] The German force consisted of *15.* and *17. F.K.*, total about 300, under Captain von Boemcken, whose orders were to reconnoitre in force across the Mwena.
The enemy lost 1 killed, 1 German officer, and 9 o.r. wounded.
[4] British casualties : killed, 2 o.r. ; wounded, 2 officers, 5 o.r. ; missing, 2 o.r.

FURTHER REINFORCEMENTS FROM INDIA.

Meanwhile the remainder of the Indian reinforcements for East Africa, I.E.F. " C," had reached Mombasa. These consisted of the half battalions of Imperial Service troops from Bharatpur, Jind, Kapurthala and Rampur, together with the 27th Mountain Battery R.A., the Calcutta Volunteer Battery (six 15-pdrs.), and a " battery " of four Maxim machine guns manned by British volunteers. With them came a draft for the 29th Punjabis, and medical and supply units.[1]

Of these troops, the Kapurthala and Rampur Infantry were sent to Kajiado, and the Bharatpur Infantry with one section of the Calcutta Battery to Voi. At Mombasa the Jind Infantry with half the Maxim battery were retained in view of persistent reports indicating a further German thrust along the coast ; most of the remaining units went on to Nairobi.

FURTHER OPERATIONS IN THE COASTAL AREA.

On the 5th October the Jind Infantry and the two **Sketch 5** volunteer Maxims were sent by sea to Gazi, while the company of the 29th Punjabis then guarding the railway just outside Mombasa marched southwards along the coast.[2] By the evening of the 6th, just in time, a total force over 850 strong, with six machine guns,[3] was concentrated at Gazi under the command of Major G. M. P. Hawthorn, 1/K.A.R.

At dawn on the 7th October Gazi was attacked from the south-west by a German force under Baumstark, about 300 strong, which drove in the British outposts on the Kikoneni track. Fighting went on in the plantations and bush outside the village during most of the morning.

---

[1] Total strength approximately 27 B.O., 200 British o.r., 2,000 Indian troops all ranks, 400 followers.

[2] " E " Coy., 29th Punjabis, after a trying march of 48 miles in 28 hours, mostly through thick bush in incessant rain, reached Gazi at noon on 6th October.

[3] Two Coys., 29th Punjabis, 2 B.O., 178 o.r., two m.g.
Jind Infantry, 1 B.O., 450 o.r.
" C " Coy., 1/K.A.R., 2 B.O., 90 o.r., one m.g.
Arab Coy., K.A.R., 1 B.O., 60 o.r.
Half Res. Coy., K.A.R., 1 B.O., 32 o.r.
One sec. volunteer Maxim Bty., 2 B.O., 37 o.r., two m.g.
One m.g., lent from Zanzibar.
Total (including two more officers, K.A.R.), 11 B.O., 37 B.o.r., 628 Indian, all ranks, 182 African o.r., six m.g.

Towards noon a counter-attack by the 1/K.A.R. checked the enemy, but eventually Hawthorn fell back on his main defences. A second counter-attack,[1] launched by the same unit early in the afternoon, broke up the attack, and by 4 p.m. the Germans were in retreat.

In the meantime minor efforts had been made by a smaller German force which during the day engaged, but did not come to grips with, Hawthorn's piquets at the crossing of the Mkurumuji to the south of Gazi, and by a small German party from the west which penetrated for a time to the Gazi-Mombasa main road. Neither, however, achieved anything.

Baumstark, retreating on Kikoneni, was followed up as far as the Mkurumuji by two companies of the 29th Punjabis, which collected much abandoned material, but were unable to overtake him. Both German forces now withdrew towards their own territory, attempting nothing further.[2]

A proposal to re-occupy the British district up to the frontier having been vetoed at Headquarters, Hawthorn's force remained for the next month at Gazi. To the south small German posts were established at Majoreni and Kikoneni ; but except for occasional patrol encounters the quiet of the coastal area was now undisturbed.

UGANDA AND THE BELGIAN NORTHERN ZONE.

End Paper (N) By mid-October the situation along the southern border of Uganda was in hand.[3] The last of the northern garrisons

---

[1] In this counter-attack, all four officers of the 1/K.A.R. having been wounded, the K.A.R. colour-sergeant, Sumani, with great determination led his men forward, reinforced soon afterwards by one and a half companies of the Jind Infantry.

[2] The German forces were: main attack, *16.* and *17. F.K.*, Captain Baumstark, strength about 300, four m.g ; southern force, *15. F.K.* and irregulars, Captain von Boemcken, about 180, two m.g. Boemcken had no casualties ; Baumstark lost 8 killed, 23 wounded.

British casualties were: K.A.R., killed, 2 o.r. ; wounded, 4 officers, 4 o.r. ; 29th Punjabis, wounded, 1 o.r. ; Jind Infantry, 1 I.O., 6 o.r.

[3] On 3rd October 1914 the British forces on the Uganda frontier, under Lieutenant-Colonel L. H. Hickson, were as follows (see sketch 8) :

(*a*) Main force, holding the crossing, over the Kagera from Kifumbiro eastwards to Lake Victoria, 550, under Captain Critchley-Salmonson.

(*b*) Watching the Kagera from Kifumbiro westward to Nsongezi, 25 Uganda Police and levies, under Captain J. E. T. Philipps.

(*c*) At Kumba, in the Kigezi District, 35 Uganda Police, under the Assistant District Commissioner, Mr. C. E. E. Sullivan. These were reinforced during October by 50 additional police.

had returned.[1] Their posts had been taken over by Sudanese troops and, except for the still unsubdued Turkana, all was quiet in that quarter. In the south-west of Uganda the British administration had been compelled to withdraw temporarily from those parts of the Kigezi District where the Batusi tribe was in revolt.[2] That tribe, however, **Sketch 3** remained within its own mountains, and the District Commissioner of the neighbouring province, Ankole, had no difficulty in maintaining his own control. By way of Ankole, communications were kept up with the Belgians.

At the end of September the Belgian garrisons between **End Paper** Lake Edward and the northern end of Lake Tanganyika **(N)** were distributed as follows :—[3]

Ruchuru	360
Bobandana	190
Kwijwi	50
Nya Lukemba	325
Uvira	375
Total	1,300

These numbers, although the fact does not seem to have been realized, far exceeded those of the enemy opposed to them in Ruanda and Urundi. The two German units in this area had been withdrawn soon after the outbreak of the war,[4] leaving only the German native police, less than 200 in all, whose weakness was a source of considerable anxiety to their commanders.[5] It speaks well for the military

---

[1] " E " Coy., 4/K.A.R., strength 116 all ranks, marched south in two detachments. The first, under Captain R. H. Leeke, reached Bombo on 7th October ; the second, under Lieutenant E. B. B. Hawkins, arrived on 17th, after handing over Madial to the Sudanese troops (see p. 24, f.n. 4) ten days before.

[2] See p. 26.

[3] B.O.A., I, p. 160.

[4] See Note II, p. 53.

[5] " . . . As soon as the Belgians discover that we have very weak forces "in Ruanda and Urundi, they will cross the Russisi, and we shall not be "able to prevent them ".

(Zimmer to Col. von Lettow-Vorbeck, commander of the German Defence Force, 21st October 1914).

A document captured later gave figures for October as follows :

	European.	Askari.	M.g.
Kisenyi	5	47	1
Chivitoke (on R. Russisi)	1	25	—
Usumbura	18	80	1
	24	152	2

These were under Korvetten-Kapitän Zimmer (late of the survey-ship *Moewe*) whose headquarters were at Kigoma.

qualities of the latter that, nevertheless, by acting with impudent boldness on Lakes Tanganyika and Kivu, they effectively conveyed an impression of strength[1] which contributed to deter the Belgians from taking the offensive.

Sketch 3 On the 24th September a small Belgian post garrisoning the southern end of the island of Kwijwi, on Lake Kivu, was successfully raided by the enemy.[2]

Against the only Belgian craft on the lake, two unarmed whalers used for carrying supplies, the Germans had a modern motor-boat armed with a 37-mm. gun and a machine gun. On the 18th September the enemy's boat captured the larger of the two whalers, and with superiority thus established the German commander in Ruanda, Captain Wintgens, an able and energetic officer of whom more was afterwards to be heard, proceeded to assemble a force of about 50 men, with a machine gun, which on the evening of the 23rd embarked in canoes near Ishara. At dawn on the 24th September the Belgian detachment on Kwijwi Island spotted some of Wintgens's rearmost boats which had missed their way ; but meanwhile the bulk of the expedition had landed behind the Belgian camp, taking the Belgian detachment in reverse and compelling it, after a creditable resistance, to surrender.

Apart from the loss of this outpost no events of importance occurred in this area. A Belgian attempt, made from Ruchuru on the 4th October, to capture the German post at Kisenyi failed in its object, and the Belgians fell back after an unsuccessful engagement with a German force of approximately equal strength, again commanded by Captain Wintgens.

In the Kigezi district a useful service was rendered by the despatch of a Belgian platoon, 75 strong, to reinforce the Uganda Police posts. Along the line of the Russisi occasional minor skirmishes took place. At no point, however, was either side prepared as yet to undertake any serious offensive.

---

[1] See p. 198.

[2] This island formed part of Ruanda, and since the outbreak of war its natives had been restive. On 23rd September orders were sent to the officer commanding the Belgian post there to arrest and deport a resident German missionary suspected of complicity in their misdeeds.

GENERAL SITUATION, OCTOBER 1914.

The end of October 1914 found the general situation in **End Paper (N)** the northern area of operations little changed from what it had been on the outbreak of war. The Germans had seized a small enclave of British territory at Taveta and a fragment of Belgian territory on Lake Kivu ; but these episodes were merely of local importance.   The reinforcements from India had enabled the defence of the British East Africa Protectorate to be reasonably assured, although the protection of the Uganda Railway against sporadic raids was by no means easy.   Three months of minor operations had given the opposing local troops enough experience of warfare to turn them into efficient fighting men.   Neither side, however, was strong enough to hope for decisive victory without reinforcement, and painful experience had made it clear that the conquest of the German colony would not be achieved until the British forces had been substantially increased.   Since at this time the possibility of raising a large addition to the King's African Rifles had not entered into British calculations any reinforcement required could be effected only from some other part of the British Empire.

NOTE I

NORTHERN AREA.

Distribution of Troops, 4th September 1914.

Location	Unit	Approx. Strength.	Total.
In Uganda ..	1/K.A.R., H.Q., " C," " D," Res. Coys.	250	
	Uganda Police (fighting units)	400	
	Uganda Volunteer Reserve ..	300	
		—	950
In British East Africa—			
Kisumu ..	" G " Coy., 4/K.A.R. ..	80	
	Town Guard (volrs.)	130	
		—	210
Nairobi ..	I.E.F. " C," H.Q.	20	
	29th Punjabis, less 2 coys. ..	400	
	" A " Coy., 4/K.A.R. ..	90	
	1 sec. 3/K.A.R. (M.I.)	20	
	K.A.R. m.g. section (2 m.g.) ..	20	
	E.A. Mtd. Rifles, H.Q., 3 sqdns. (ordered Magadi area) ..	240	
	Town Guard (volrs.)	270	

Continued overleaf.

Distribution of Troops, 4th September 1914—continued.

Location	Note	Approx. Strength	Total
Nairobi— continued.	Railway Pioneers (volrs.) ..	50	
	1 sec. 120th Fd. Amb., I.A. ..	20	
		—	1,130
Masai Reserve	E.A.M.R., det.	22	
		—	22
Magadi area	E.A.M.R., 2 sqdns.	95	
	Magadi defence force	48	
		—	143
Kiu	Half " A " Coy., 3/K.A.R. ..	60	
		—	60
Voi-Tsavo area—			
Mtito Andei	" B " Coy., 4/K.A.R. ..	110	
Tsavo ..	Half " B " Coy , 1/K.A.R. ..	65	
Tsavo river	1 sec. " B " Coy., 1/K.A.R. ..	25	
Voi ..	2 coys., 29th Punjabis.. ..	360	
	Half " B " Coy., 3/K.A.R. ..	95	
	Pathan Coy., E.A. Regt. (volrs.)	80	
	Railway Pioneers (volrs.) ..	20	
	Railway Volunteers	60	
	1 12-pdr. naval gun (E.A. Arty., volrs.)	20	
	Det., E.A. Mech. Trpt. Corps ..	20	
Bura ..	1 sec. " B " Coy., 1/K.A.R. ..	25	
	Half " B " Coy., 3/K A.R. ..	95	
	3/K.A.R., M.I., less det. ..	20	
	2 Coys. E.A. Regt. (European volrs.)	82	
	Somali scouts	20	
	1 Hotchkiss gun, 1 m.g. ..	25	
Maktau ..	3/K.A.R., M.I., det.	20	
		—	1,142
Giriama area..	" F " Coy., 4/K.A.R.	80	
	No. 1 Res. Coy., 3/K.A.R. ..	56	
		—	136
Mombasa ..	" H " Coy., 3/K.A.R., 1 m.g. ..	80	
	Town Guard (volrs.)	176	
		—	256
Frontier District (Gazi-Vanga)	No. 2 Res. Coy., 3/K.A.R.(Arabs)	80	
		—	80
Zanzibar ..	" G " Coy., 3/K.A.R.	104	
		—	104
Outside the theatre of War—			
Jubaland ..	" E " Coy., 1/K.A.R. ..	100	
	Half " E," " F " (Camel) Coys., 3/K.A.R.	100	
Returning from	" A," " C " Coys., 1/K.A.R. ..	200	
Jubaland ..	Half " E " Coy., 3/K.A.R. ..	50	
Moyale ..	Half " D " Coy., 3/K.A.R. ..	50	
Morongole ..	" E " Coy., 4/K.A.R. ..	80	
		—	580
	Total (approx.)		4,813

NOTE II.

THE NORTHERN AREA.

The German Side, August—October 1914[1]

In German East Africa the news from Europe had created alarm during the last week in July 1914, and from the 31st July onwards certain precautionary measures were taken. Officers going on leave were stopped at Dar-es-Salaam ; arms and ammunition were collected and arrangements made for a watch along the coast. The cruiser *Königsberg* put to sea on the evening of the 31st July for an unknown destination. On the 1st August Captain Kraut was appointed to command the troops on the northern border, and the *13.F.K.* was ordered north from Kondoa Irangi to reinforce them.[2]

On the 1st and 2nd August official telegrams from Germany informed the German Governor that " Danger of War " (*Kriegsgefahr*) had been proclaimed in Germany and that mobilization might possibly be ordered, but did not specify the enemy. On the 2nd he was further instructed that the proclamation did not affect German East Africa and he was directed to reassure the German colonists. A further communication was promised, but was not received, and the German protectorate remained without definite information until early on the 5th August, when there came from the German wireless station at Kamina in Togoland the news that Great Britain and Germany were at war.

The declaration of war found German East Africa as little prepared for hostilities as were the British protectorates, and its civil authority even less warlike and more at variance with its military advisers. Both constitutionally and by conviction the Governor, Dr. Heinrich Schnee, was opposed to the strong measures which the commander of the Defence Force, Colonel von Lettow-Vorbeck, wished at once to initiate.

Appreciating that " the fate of the German colonies, as of " all other German possessions, would only be decided on the " battlefields of Europe," but holding that to its decision " every " German, regardless of where he might be at the moment, " must contribute," Lettow was of opinion that his forces in German East Africa, though small, might " prevent considerable " numbers of the enemy from intervening in Europe, or in " other more important theatres."[3] This, however, in his view, could only be accomplished if the Germans " attacked or at

---

[1] See also Appendices V and VI.

[2] These preliminary measures were taken in the absence of Colonel von Lettow-Vorbeck, who was on a tour of inspection in the southern districts, and did not reach Dar-es-Salaam until the 3rd August.

[3] Lettow, " My Reminiscences," pp. 3–4.

"least threatened, the enemy at some sensitive point." For any such effort it was necessary to keep the local forces concentrated, "to grip the enemy by the throat and compel him to "employ his forces in self-defence." The Uganda railway presented itself as a suitable objective for attack; and Lettow therefore urged that the available troops should be concentrated in the Kilimanjaro area with a view to an immediate offensive.

The Governor, appointed from the Colonial Civil Service, no soldier, hating the idea of war and of the disruption of his work for the development of the Colony—work on which for the past two years he had set his heart—was opposed to any such active measures. Under his regime no preparations had been made for war against a European Power. In conformity with the general principles of the Berlin Act of 1885, the two main ports of Dar-es-Salaam and Tanga had no coast defences, and he was anxious to avert the bombardment and destruction of their costly harbour works by British warships. Lettow's predecessor, Lieutenant-Colonel Freiherr von Schleinitz, seems to have suggested that in the unlikely event of war it would be best to withdraw from the ports to the difficult country inland, where defence against invasion would be easier; and when the unwelcome emergency arose, Dr. Schnee preferred this plan, distrusting the bold ideas of Lettow, who was, after all, a newcomer, not yet fully acquainted with local conditions. The first essential, in the Governor's view, was to ensure the internal security of the colony,[1] lest news of war between the white races should lead to a native rising like that of 1905. For some days he hoped that hostilities would not extend to the African colonies.[2] He explicitly forbade any attempt to defend the ports against attack from the sea; only with reluctance did he consent to a concentration of the Defence Force units for collective training, a concentration which, he ruled, must not be on the frontier, but in the south, near the capital. For this a camp site was selected at Pugu, 12 miles inland from Dar-es-Salaam.

Sketch 1   Of the fourteen units existing at the outbreak of war, four were at once moved to Pugu, viz., *4.F.K.* from Kilimatinde, *6.F.K.* from Ujiji, *8.F.K.* from Tabora and *10.F.K.* from Dar-es-Salaam. These were joined soon afterwards by *9.F.K.* from Usumbura and *11.F.K.* from Kisenyi. The withdrawal of the two last-named from the Belgian frontier involved risks, especially that of trouble with the natives; but Msinga, Sultan of Ruanda, supported the local German authorities and no trouble occurred. In the Kilimanjaro area the *1.F.K.* from Arusha and *13.F.K.* from Kondoa Irangi were concentrated near Moshi with an additional company formed from native police and a

---

[1] Schnee, *Deutsch Ost-Afrika im Weltkriege*, p. 36.
[2] Schnee, op. cit., p. 28. As to neutrality, see Appendix II.

body of local European volunteers under Captain von Prince, locally redoubtable as "Bwana Sakarani." Farther west, *7.F.K.* moved from Bukoba to join *14.F.K.* at Mwanza, the principal German settlement on Lake Victoria. In the southern half of the German protectorate units were kept at their peace stations, not merely to guard the Nyasaland and Portuguese frontiers, but also for fear of native risings, especially among the recently subdued Wahehe : a fear which proved groundless.

The "field" units (*F.K.*) were now brought to a more or less uniform establishment.[1] Their lack of modern arms was a serious matter : eight out of the fourteen companies were still armed with the 1871 pattern rifle, firing black powder.

As an addition to the Defence Force, such local German reservists and volunteers as were not required for the cadres of regular companies were grouped to form so-called *Schützen* companies, composed entirely of Europeans. These companies, which varied greatly in strength, were employed as units only during the earlier stages of the campaign ; they were later broken up, as and when needed, to replace losses in the German cadres of regular units.[2]

Supply services and a headquarters staff had also to be improvised. Major-General Wahle, a retired officer who had arrived on the 2nd August on a visit to his son, undertook the organization of the L. of C., a task which was to involve him in constant difficulties with the civil authorities.

At Pugu training was carried on actively for some three weeks ; reservists and recruits were enrolled and new units, *15., 16., 17., 18.F.K.*, were formed.

Scarcely had the companies at Pugu begun their training when, on the 8th August, H.M.S. *Astraea* made her raid on Dar-es-Salaam. Roused by the distant gunfire, Lettow at once ordered his troops to the seaport, only to be told that, without his knowledge, the Governor had negotiated a formal and in his view humiliating truce. Thenceforward his relations with the Governor were strained.

Although Dr. Schnee had forbidden any defence of the seaports, the shores of Lake Tanganyika, which formed most of the German western frontier, were not subject to any such prohibition. The only craft of any size on the lake were the Belgian steamer *Alexandre Delcommune*, 70 tons, and the German *Hedwig von Wissmann*, 60 tons, then under repair at Kigoma.[3]

---

[1] See Appendix V.

[2] *1. Sch. K.* and *2. Sch. K.* were formed during the first week at Pugu. **3.** *Sch. K.* was formed soon afterwards from seamen of the German ships which had been disabled at Dar-es-Salaam.

[3] The *Graf von Götzen*, 1,200 tons, was building at Kigoma. The Germans had also the tug *Kingani*, 25 tons. The latter and the *Hedwig von Wissmann* were eventually disposed of by the Royal Navy ; see p. 193. The small British steamer *Good News* was laid up at Kituta.

To secure command of the lake a detachment of 30 men from the surveying ship *Moewe*, which had been scuttled at Dar-es-Salaam, was sent by rail to Kigoma to man the *Hedwig von Wissmann*. On the 22nd August the latter vessel, now armed with four 3·7 cm. guns, disabled the Belgian steamer (see p. 28).

Meanwhile on the 7th August Captain von Prince at Moshi, who telegraphed for instructions, had been answered : " The " Congo Treaty is not in force. Destruction of Uganda Railway " and telegraph line to take place in several places. Quick " action promises good results ". His command probably numbered at least 500,[1] but he did not act at once.[2] On the 13th August, however, Prince telegraphed that " 220 Europeans " and Lincke's company " (of native police) " with 200 askari " were ready for action, and in reply was ordered to " make a surprise attack and capture Taveta ". This, as we have seen, he did on the 15th August. From the German point of view the Taveta affair was unsatisfactory, since the small defending force escaped; but the seizure of the place had some moral effect on the local tribes.

During the next few days the Governor was persuaded to allow the force assembled at Pugu to be transferred to the northern area. There being no connecting railway, this involved a march through undeveloped country in which supplies were scarce. Moving by several routes, the bulk of the force reached the Usambara district at the end of August. The *15.*, *16.*, and *17.F.K.*, grouped under Captain Baumstark, were sent to Jasin for the coastal area. Most of the remainder concentrated eventually about Kilimanjaro.

West of Kilimanjaro, four small posts were established to watch the border between Lake Natron and the Mara river, while on that river a post was established some five miles inside the German border. On Lake Victoria, forts at Shirati and Musoma were manned by small garrisons, *7.* and *14.F.K.*, with a detachment of European volunteers, being at Mwanza under Captain Bock von Wülfingen.

Before the concentration in the Kilimanjaro area had been effected, Lettow had sent explicit orders to his outlying detachments at Mwanza and Moshi to take the offensive, with the

Sketch 2
Sketch 1
Sketch 2
Sketch 3

---

[1] *1.* and *13. F.K.*, with an additional company (later numbered *19. F.K.*) formed from the native police ; a number of European volunteers who were later formed into *7. Sch.* and *8. Sch. K.* ; and a mounted detachment under a retired officer, Lieutenant-Colonel Freiherr von Bock.

[2] Lettow says : " It took considerable time before we were able to set " the force in motion. Many people believed that on the strength of the " Congo Act we were bound to remain neutral and naturally had little " confidence in the instructions they received from the new Commandant." (" My Reminiscences," p. 29).

Uganda Railway as their objective.[1] Both his subordinates
replied that they were faced by considerable British forces,
Captain Bock at Mwanza adding that he could not attempt the
destruction of the railway unless reinforced. Lettow's answer
was a peremptory telegram directing him to move immediately
and destroy the railway between Nairobi and the lake ; but
it was not until a week later (28th August) that Bock
reported his detachment ready to advance " on or about the
3rd September ".

Captain Schulz, now in command at Moshi, was not quite Sketch 4
so dilatory. He sent out the two raiding parties whose failure
has been related (see p. 34) ; but no move from the Kilimanjaro
area seems to have been made until the 27th August, when a
small detachment under Lieutenant von Oppen left Himo with
orders to " destroy or interrupt the railway and telegraph line
" at Tsavo." This was the party which on the 29th August ambushed Lieutenant Davies's mounted patrol (see p. 35). It had
no casualties, but Oppen halted, asking for reinforcements and a
machine gun. In response Kraut, who had meanwhile assumed
command at Himo, sent Schulz with *13.F.K.*, which joined
Oppen on the 1st September. Schulz then went cautiously
forward, through bush which he found difficult, down the Tsavo
valley, driving in Hardingham's post near Mzima on the 3rd
(see p. 37) and encountering James's force west of Tsavo on
the 6th (see p. 38). In the fight on the 6th he had few casualties,
but on receiving reports that British reinforcements were on the
way Schulz decided to retreat. With sound instinct he went back
as fast as possible, leaving his wounded to follow, and by so doing
just avoided being intercepted by the British forces from Bura
(see p. 39).

The column from Mwanza had no better fortune, its advance Sketch 3
ending in the affair at Kisii (see pp. 40–41), as the outcome of which
it abandoned its venture. Bock's report on the matter justly
claimed success in repulsing Thorneycroft's attack on his left
and partial success for his own attack on the British left, ascrib-
ing his decision to withdraw mainly to his heavy casualties. (55 per
cent. among the Europeans of his force). His retreat to the border
was hastened by news of the attempted British landing in his
rear at Karungu.

Thus when Lettow reached Moshi early in September no Sketch 4
definite success had been gained. The next enterprise was more
limited in scope. On the 12th September *13.F.K.* was again
ordered into the Tsavo valley, this time merely to observe the

---

[1] On 20th August Lettow telegraphed to Schulz at Moshi : " Remember
" to destroy railway line," and on the same day he telegraphed to Bock at
Mwanza : " It should be attempted to destroy the Uganda Railway . . .
" attention is specially directed to the viaducts ".

British advanced forces and to do such damage as might be possible. This move, begun on the 15th, led to the indecisive attack on Campi-ya-Marabu four days later (see p. 42). *13.F.K.* was then reinforced by *4.F.K.* with orders to reconnoitre towards Tsavo and to clear the Nyulu hills. Advancing down the Tsavo valley *4.F.K.*, under Captain Rothert, on the 25th September discovered the new British position at Mzima (see p. 43); upon which Schulz brought up the *13.F.K.* and in command of the combined force attacked next day (see p. 43). Himself severely wounded in this attack, and realizing that it had no chance of success, he withdrew and subsequently reported that there was no possibility of breaking through to Tsavo, on account of the difficulty of the country and the strength of the British defence.

Thenceforward in the Kilimanjaro area serious offensive operations were not attempted again by the Germans for some time ; nor do the German colonists seem to have been enthusiastic for further attacks.[1] At all events subsequent attempts against the Uganda Railway were confined to minor raids, which caused anxiety and did some damage but had no lasting effect.

Sketch 6 Similar raids seem to have been sent against the Magadi branch railway before the end of August ; but these failed to reach their objective. A small mounted party under Lincke, which on the 2nd September was ordered to try again, set out from Longido on the 10th, but was turned back the same afternoon by a British patrol, losing a German N.C.O. wounded. A fortnight later Captain Tafel, commanding at Longido, made yet another attempt, apparently on his own initiative, with most of his available troops, *10.F.K.* and a mounted European volunteer detachment. This was the force which, passing west of Oldoinyo Erok by night and halting in the Ingito hills early on the 25th September, was followed up and attacked by Captain Chapman's small squadron of the E.A.M.R. (see p. 44). Tafel himself was wounded, and Captain Niemayer, on whom the command devolved, returned forthwith to Longido, claiming the repulse of Chapman's thirty mounted riflemen as a success.

Sketch 5 In the coastal area the course of events was much the same. During August activity was limited to minor patrolling, no German forces of any size being available. This period ended with the withdrawal of the British frontier guards from Vanga

---

[1] On 25th September Major-General Wahle noted in his diary that his son, " like all old Afrikaners, complains of the conduct of the campaign " by Colonel von Lettow. He (Lettow) thinks only of attacks, through " which some companies have already suffered heavy losses, and ' German " East '—with native troops only—can't stand it . . . it would be a mistake " on Lettow's part to move forward. . . ."

(see p. 33). To Baumstark's three units which arrived soon afterwards were added the *4.Sch.K.* and a small so-called *Arab Corps.*[1] During the first fortnight in September Baumstark learned that the British opposed to him were now established at Majoremi, and on the 21st he ordered the attack which was made by Boemcken on the following day (see p. 46). Had this been pressed its effect might have been considerable, since, unknown to Baumstark, Wavell had become a casualty ; as it was, the German withdrawal enabled the British force to reorganize before evacuating Majoreni next day.

The next move was Baumstark's unsuccessful attack on Gazi on the 7th October (see p. 47). In the course of this affair he was given good reason to realize that the British force was too strong for him, and with considerable difficulty he withdrew and re-assembled his troops, the last of which did not rejoin him in camp on the Mkurumuji until long after nightfall. From there, apprehensive of being cut off from his base at Jasin by a British advance along the coast, he retreated with all speed by Klkonenl to Samanya. His losses had not been heavy, but his troops had been shaken, the Arabs in particular proving untrustworthy and liable to panic. His report laid stress on the latter point and on the sense of inferiority produced in his men by their obsolete rifles firing black powder against the modern smokeless weapons of their opponents.

It will be seen that the various small actions during this first phase of the campaign all presented much the same features : the advance of a small German force, its encounter with a small British force, a confused fight in thick bush, mutual exaggeration of each other's strength, and an eventual retreat as much for the sake of caring for the wounded as from any tactical necessity.

On the whole, the British protectorates may be accounted fortunate in that during the first few weeks of war the forces of the enemy were neither strong enough nor suitably located to take advantage of the tenuity of the British defence.

---

[1] The Germans, like the British, had decided to make such use as was possible of the warlike proclivities of the coastal Arabs ; the unit raised eventually reached a strength of about 50.

CHAPTER IV
TANGA
THE PROJECT AND ITS INCEPTION
(Sketches 8a, 9)

End Paper (N.) ON the outbreak of war the Government of India, it will be remembered, had been called upon not only to reinforce the local forces in East Africa, but further, and as a matter of greater importance, to send an expedition against the primarily naval objective of Dar-es-Salaam. The reinforcements—I.E.F. " C "—had been sent.[1] The larger project, which was at first known as the " Dar-es-Salaam Expedition," was to result eventually in a lamentable reverse at Tanga, in November 1914.

The genesis and development of this project deserve attention, for its essential features were destined to be reproduced, on a far more important scale and with greatly magnified consequences, at Gallipoli.

In formulating the instructions sent to the Government of India on the 8th and 9th August, the India Office had no adequate military intelligence data on which to base its estimate of requirements. Such information as it possessed, amounting to little more than that given in published works of reference, indicated that in German East Africa there were some 2,000 white colonists with military training and that the peace establishment of native troops and police was about 4,500, as to whose military value nothing reliable was known. It was assumed that no large hostile concentration was likely, in view of the probable danger of withdrawing from outlying stations the forces deemed necessary for maintaining internal order. The German rule was known to be harsh, and it was hoped that native revolts would occur. It was, indeed, even thought possible that the German native troops might refuse to fight.[2]

On the foregoing basis the size of the force to be provided from India for the seizure of Dar-es-Salaam was fixed at

---

[1] See pp. 37, 47.

[2] As an example of the misconceptions prevailing, a responsible senior naval officer wrote to the chairman of the Offensive Sub-committee on 6th August 1914 : " I should like to reiterate that I believe the smallest " inducement would tend to make the whole of the German native troops " desert to us, but in so doing they would probably murder all their officers' " wives and children and quite possibly the Hindu population as well."

" about 8,000 in all," to consist of one infantry brigade of the Indian Army, with two or three battalions of Imperial Service troops provided by the Indian native states, and one or two batteries of artillery. Later, when there came an expectation that work on roads and railways would be needed, the two existing companies of Sappers and Miners trained in railway work, and an Indian Pioneer battalion, were added. The instructions made no mention of transport or first reinforcements, doubtless because at this time only local operations in the immediate vicinity of Dar-es-Salaam were contemplated.

These demands were anything but welcome in India. The provision of the Indian Expeditionary Force for the European theatre had already severely strained India's military resources.[1] Doubts were expressed, moreover, as to the adequacy of the Dar-es-Salaam force to achieve its object : a matter on which Army Headquarters, India, was entitled to put forward expert military opinion but does not seem to have done so. The Indian Government, at all events, loyally accepted the new commitment and acted at once.

The 16th (Poona) Infantry Brigade, of the Indian 6th Division, was placed under orders, and on the 17th August its commander Brigadier-General A. E. Aitken, was designated to command the Expedition, receiving formal instructions and such information as there was regarding German East Africa. Ten days later (27th August) he was summoned to Simla to receive further instructions personally.

By that time the general aspect of the war had been seriously altered by the attitude of the Turkish Government. Although that Government had not yet openly declared its intentions, the Turkish Army was being mobilized and there was every prospect that the Ottoman Empire would join in actively against the Allies. It would then be necessary to safeguard the Suez Canal and to protect the oil supplies at the head of the Persian Gulf. For the latter purpose only Indian troops were available ; others, moreover, would be needed on the Canal.[2]

---

[1] See " Military Operations : France and Belgium, 1914," Vol. II. pp. 8–9.

[2] The situation in regard to Turkey, and its close connection with the army in India, whose East African commitments formed but a subsidiary part of much larger commitments elsewhere, are fully dealt with in " Military Operations : Mesopotamia," Vol. I, Chaps. II–V, and " Egypt and Palestine," Vol. I, pp. 7–15.

Such being the situation, on the 28th August the Secretary of State for India telegraphed to the Viceroy that the expedition against Dar-es-Salaam was postponed until further orders.[1] This news, which greeted Brigadier-General Aitken on his arrival at Simla, was warmly approved there, it being felt that to divert troops to East Africa was unjustifiable at a moment when other theatres, regarded as vital, needed every available man and gun. The expedition was not cancelled, however. Brigadier-General Aitken's selection to command held good ; and he was directed to retain his papers and work out his plans, with the assistance of Mr. Norman King, British consul in Dar-es-Salaam, who had been sent to India to place his local knowledge at the commander's disposal.[2]

There the matter rested for about ten days. At Simla and Bombay all were engrossed in despatching the main Indian Expeditionary Force to Europe, a task in which one complication was the known presence of the German cruiser *Königsberg* in the Indian Ocean. In London attention was concentrated on the German drive through northern France and the battle of the Marne.

By the second week in September the situation in the Western theatre had improved ; but that in Eastern waters was causing increased anxiety. Not only was the *Königsberg* still at large and unlocated, but six other German cruisers which had been in the Pacific or South Atlantic might also at any moment appear in the Indian Ocean. It became essential to deprive the enemy of potential naval bases ; the Dar-es-Salaam project assumed enhanced importance.

On the 9th September orders reached India that the force for East Africa, now known as Indian Expeditionary Force " B," was to be held " intact " and ready. Meanwhile, however, the Poona Infantry Brigade had been assigned to the more important sphere of action in the Persian Gulf.[3]

---

[1] This decision was cabled by the Colonial Office to the Governors of the Protectorates in East Africa on 31st August.

[2] Information supplied by Mr. King was officially printed in India and issued to those concerned as a pamphlet entitled " Field Notes on " German East Africa." This added somewhat to the scanty military information previously available.

[3] On the 30th August instructions were sent from the India Office to despatch the 16th (Poona) Inf. Bde. to Egypt " for temporary garrison duty, " keeping in view the ultimate destination of German East Africa." In default of other good troops, however, of which none could be spared, A.H.Q. in India decided that the Poona Bde. must form the force which on 4th October was ordered to the Persian Gulf. See " Military Operations: " Mesopotamia," Vol. I, p. 99.

Of the nine divisions in which the Indian Army was at this time organized, two were being sent to Europe and two were being depleted by the withdrawal of brigades, first for Egypt and now for the Persian Gulf, while clearly in this time of crisis it was out of the question to weaken the North-West Frontier. It was consequently decided that the brigade for East Africa must be that whose withdrawal would least impair India's strategic security. The choice fell on the brigade farthest from the frontier : the 27th, stationed at Bangalore in southern India. Warning orders for mobilization of this brigade were issued on the 10th September. The 27th (Bangalore) Brigade, now to form the nucleus of India's East African expedition, was thus selected not for the quality of its troops, as the 16th (Poona) Brigade had been, but by reason of the geographical situation of its cantonments.

At the same time it was decided to group the units assigned to I.E.F. " B " from the Indian native states as an " Imperial Service Brigade," strengthened by one regular battalion of the Indian Army, and to add a Pioneer battalion with special knowledge of railway work.[1]

These changes, cabled to England on the 11th September, were agreed to by Lord Kitchener. In conveying the agreement the Secretary of State for India, conscious of the seriousness of the task to be undertaken, enquired particularly as to the selection of the commander. This was regarded at Simla as already settled : Brigadier-General Aitken had been appointed and had studied the available data, and there was no apparent reason for any other choice. He was confirmed in his appointment, the decision was notified to the India Office on the 13th September, and in view of the importance of his command he was given the temporary rank of Major-General.

The need for action on the East African coast became increasingly apparent. Prolonged search of the Eastern oceans had failed to bring to battle any of the German cruisers, others of which besides the *Königsberg* might use the many convenient anchorages along the German littoral. On land the German attempts on the Uganda Railway were also an anxiety. On the 14th September,

---

[1] The 61st (K.G.O.) Pioneers, a Madras unit lately engaged in building tne hill railway to Ootacamund, was accordingly detailed in place of the 48th (Sikh) Pioneers, previously selected.

on receipt of the news that the *Emden* was making successful raids in the Indian Ocean, orders were cabled to India that the start of I.E.F. " B " should be no longer delayed.

Beyond signifying general approval of the proposed organization of the expeditionary force, Lord Kitchener at the War Office had no part in the preparations. Neither the plan of operations nor the instructions to the commander were submitted to him or to the General Staff before issue.[1] There had never, indeed, been any idea that the East African operations should be conducted by the War Office, which under the pre-war system was little concerned with East Africa.[2] For the operation against Dar-es-Salaam the India Office took as appropriate the procedure success-fully followed in the China (" Boxer ") Expedition of 1900, a minor effort during the South Africa campaign. Control of the Expedition was to be undertaken by the India Office in conjunction with the Colonial Office. The commander was to be responsible to the Secretary of State for India for the conduct of all the operations in German East Africa.

These proposals, embodied on the 18th September in a memorandum by General Sir Edmund Barrow, Military Secretary at the India Office, were approved by the Committee of Imperial Defence ; and the India and Colonial Offices, in consultation with the Admiralty, proceeded to work out an outline scheme and to draw up instructions for its execution.

OBJECTIVES AND INSTRUCTIONS

During the weeks which had elapsed since the initial decision to seize Dar-es-Salaam, important factors in the East African situation had altered, and not for the better. The German local forces had revealed themselves as good fighters well led by an enterprising commander. At sea the risks from German warships, if they had not increased, had certainly not diminished. Naval participation in the Dar-es-Salaam venture, beyond a small escort to the

---

[1] When the instructions afterwards became known to the General Staff they caused, unofficially, much apprehension as to the fate of the expedition.

[2] See p. 30. At this time (mid-September) the depleted operations and intelligence branches were more than fully occupied in following the greater events in the European theatre, while the energies of Lord Kitchener and his senior advisers were bent on the tremendous task of creating the new armies. On the " eclipse of the General Staff " see " Military Operations : Gallipoli," Vol. I, pp. 46–7. 51

transports, was not and could not be assured. The numbers assigned to the expeditionary force were unchanged, but the units originally detailed had been replaced by others of less certain fighting quality. Nevertheless the suspended project was revived without material alteration, except in one most important respect : with no corresponding development of the means of execution, its scope was now vastly expanded.

The immediate object, still with an essentially naval purpose, was now not merely to seize Dar-es-Salaam ; it was to deprive the enemy of all potential sea bases on the German East African coast. From that it was but a short step to the prospect of ultimately seizing the whole German protectorate ; and it was on this basis, apparently with no realization of the magnitude of such a task and certainly with no adequate regard to ways and means, that the instructions for Major-General Aitken were drawn up. The extended scheme, evolved in London independently of the War Office, was accepted, seemingly without question, in India.

The 450 miles of German coast-line offered various objectives, and in drafting the instructions it was eventually decided that as a first step, before making any attempt against Dar-es-Salaam, the port of Tanga should be occupied. From Tanga the Usambara railway led northwards to Kilimanjaro. An advance in that direction, co-ordinated with a convergent thrust from British East Africa, would, if successful—an all-important proviso—remove all danger from the British protectorate, secure possession of the richest and healthiest area of the German territory, and pave the way for subsequent operations farther south. It seems to have been realized that this ambitious project, so far beyond that originally intended, might perhaps be found impracticable ; while, therefore, the object of the expedition was defined in the widest terms, the question of the practicability of the operation intended as its first phase was left to the judgment of the commander.

Instructions for Major-General Aitken, approved by the Cabinet, were sent to India accordingly. The wording of the operative paragraphs is important ; it was as follows :–

" 1. The object of the expedition under your com-
" mand is to bring the whole of German East Africa
" under British authority. . . .

D*

" 2. On arrival at Mombasa you will, after conferring
" with the General Officer Commanding Force " C,"
" Sir H. Belfield " [the Governor] " and the Senior
" Naval Officer, make such arrangements as you may
" deem necessary for executing the wishes of His
" Majesty's Government. The Governor will be in-
" structed to put at your disposal for this purpose
" such of the forces in British East Africa, including
" those in Force ' C,' as can be spared with due regard
" to the preservation of order in the Protectorate.

" 3. His Majesty's Government desire that you should
" in the first instance secure the safety of British East
" Africa by occupying the north-eastern portion of
" the German colony, viz., the country between Tanga
" and Kilimanjaro. For this purpose it is suggested
" that you should first occupy Tanga with ' B ' Force
" and that, when this move has had its due moral effect
" on the Germans occupying the hinterland of Tanga,
" Force ' C ' should, if feasible, advance from Tsavo
" and threaten Moshi. It is, however, for you to judge
" whether such an operation is practicable and advisable,
" and whether Force ' C ' should be strengthened by you
" for this object.

" 4. It will be your first duty to establish British
" authority over the whole region above indicated and
" to take such steps as Sir W. Johns[1] may advise for the
" repair of the railway, which presumably will have been
" more or less damaged.

" 5. After the effective control of this region has
" been secured, it will be for you to consider and report
" your plans for the occupation of the Dar-es-Salaam-
" Tabora line, which should be the next object of attack.

" 6. It is possible that the occupation of the Usambara
" country and of Dar-es-Salaam may be sufficient to
" lead the German authorities to endeavour to obtain
" terms, if so, you should make it clear that you are
" not empowered to accept anything short of uncon-
" ditional surrender.

(Here followed seven paragraphs dealing in general
terms with the prospective political administration of
the territory to be occupied.)

*   *   *

---

[1] Director of Railways, I.E.F. " B."

" 14. You will consult freely with the Governor of
" the East Africa Protectorate in all cases where his
" advice or assistance are likely to be of value to you,
" and, in so far as Naval support may be necessary,
" you will act in close co-operation with the Naval
" authorities, who will be instructed by the Admiralty
" to render you every possible assistance."

These instructions were sent by mail[1] on the 1st October,
preceded by a cabled version. In the latter, which was
forwarded from Simla to Major-General Aitken with a covering note to the effect that these instructions were to be
regarded as his orders, there was a slight change in wording
and punctuation. As received by cable, the operative
paragraph 3 read as follows :

" 3. His Majesty's Government desire that you
" should first secure safety of British East Africa by
" occupying country between Tanga and Kilimanjaro.
" For this purpose suggest you should first occupy
" Tanga with ' B ' Force. When this movement has
" had its due moral effect on Germans in hinterland
" of Tanga, Force ' C ' should if possible threaten Moshi
" from the Tsavo side, but it is for you to judge if this
" course is practicable and advisable, also whether
" Force ' C ' should be strengthened by you for this
" object."

In this version the suggestion as to Tanga was in a separate sentence, and the discretion left to the commander
might be read as being restricted to the subject (" this
course ") of a thrust by I.E.F. " C " from the Tsavo
side.

Presumably with this in mind, Major-General Aitken
consulted Army Headquarters at Simla as to the intention
of the paragraph in question.[2] Accepting the interpretation
given by Simla, he thenceforth regarded himself as committed
to a disembarkation at Tanga, whence any further operations
must issue.

---

[1] So far as can now be ascertained, the written version was sent to
Mombasa, and did not reach Major-General Aitken until his arrival there
on 31st October 1914.

[2] " I particularly asked, before leaving India, whether I was bound to
" adhere to this suggestion (of occupying Tanga), and I was clearly and
" precisely told from A.H.Q. that I had better stick to it, as it had in all
" probability been made on the recommendation of the Committee of
" Imperial Defence for good and sufficient reasons." (Report by Major-
General Aitken, 19th September 1915.)

Of the naval truce[1] by which he was to be deprived of such slender chance as there was of effecting surprise he had been told nothing.

COMPOSITION OF THE EXPEDITIONARY FORCE

The units of the expeditionary force,[2] assembled from the length and breadth of India, were for the most part strangers to each other and to their new commanders.[3]

They had had no training together, and indeed Major-General Aitken himself had had no opportunity of seeing them until about a week before they embarked. Their racial composition[4] was very varied. Some came of the hardy races of the north; the majority, however, were drawn from the centre and south of India, and the fighting value of some of the units was doubtful. The quality of the only British battalion, the 2/Loyal North Lancashire, was, of course, unquestionable; the Rajputs of the 13th and the Mahrattas of the 101st Grenadiers had also won good reputations in recent service.[5] But the other three regular battalions—61st, 63rd, 98th—were recruited from the less martial races of the south, and two of them had not seen service in the field for more than a generation.[6]

---

[1] See pp. 21, f.n. 1, 55, 68, 73.

[2] The expeditionary force was composed as follows:

27th (Bangalore) Bde.	Imperial Service Bde.
(Brigadier-General R. Wapshare).	(Brigadier-General M. J. Tighe).
2/Loyal North Lancs. Regt.	13th Rajputs.
63rd Palamcottah Lt. Inf.	2/Kashmir Rifles.
98th Infantry.	Half Bn. 3/Kashmir Rifles.
101st Grenadiers.	Half Bn. 3/Gwalior Inf.

28th Mtn. Bty., R.A.
25th and 26th (Railway) Coys., Sappers & Miners.
61st K.G.O. Pioneers.
Faridkot Sappers (one Coy.).

together with medical, supply, ordnance and civil railway personnel, including that for an armoured train. See also Appendix III.

The 63rd, from Kamptee, and 98th, from Saugor, were brought in to complete the 27th Bde. in replacement of the 108th Infantry, left at Bangalore for reasons of internal security, and of the 61st, now detached to act as divisional troops.

[3] Brigadier-General Wapshare saw the 63rd and 98th for the first time on the day before embarkation; Brigadier-General Tighe met the units of his brigade when they concentrated at Deolali six days before sailing.

[4] See Appendix III.

[5] The 101st had done well in Somaliland and on the N.W. Frontier; the 13th had also served with credit on the Frontier in 1897.

[6] The 63rd and 98th had formed part of the China expedition of 1900 and held the battle honour for that campaign, but had in fact got no farther than Hong Kong. The 61st were also engaged in the same campaign, mainly in road making, in which service they were commended for efficiency.

The units from the Indian native states, though led by Indian officers of untried capacity, included the Gurkhas and Dogras of the Kashmir Rifles and were reported to be efficient. Nevertheless the heterogeneous composition of the whole force and the quality of some of its units were hardly such as to inspire its commander and his staff with confidence.[1]

Mobilization Difficulties

At this time Indian Army battalions were independent numbered units, only linked loosely in pairs or groups for drafting purposes. Each had reservists listed for recall ; but this system was of recent origin, and for some of the units detailed to I.E.F. " B " there were not enough reservists to make up even the reduced war establishment fixed for the force.[2] This was especially the case in the units previously on a low peace establishment,[3] notably the 63rd Palamcottah Light Infantry.[4]

A further grave difficulty arose in regard to arms. Up to the time of mobilization the majority of units in Southern India were still armed with the obsolete converted long M.L.E. rifle ; immediately before embarkation the units of I.E.F. " B " thus equipped were re-armed with the standard short Lee-Enfield, whose sighting and mechanism were unfamiliar. The position with regard to machine guns

---

[1] " My first remark to Major-General Aitken after inspecting our " troops at Bombay was : ' This campaign will either be a walk-over or a " tragedy ' " (Report by Major-General O. II. Cheppard, 11th March 1010.)

[2] On the ground that only fit and seasoned soldiers would stand the East African climate, the total strength of each Indian battalion in I.E.F. " B " was specially fixed at 13 British officers, 753 Indian all ranks. War establishment of the 2/Loyal N. Lancs. was 832. As already remarked, no first reinforcement was provided.

[3] Up to 1914 Indian army units considered unlikely to be needed for field service had a lower peace establishment than the remainder. In Southern India the best recruits went to Sappers & Miners and Pioneers ; the few recruits taken into the Madras infantry units were drawn from those remaining, while older men were kept on to qualify for pension, with resulting dissatisfaction and consequent ill-effects on discipline. The selection of such units for active service was only justifiable on the assumption that no others could possibly be spared.

[4] The 63rd had to be brought up to the prescribed establishment by a large draft from the 83rd Infantry ; similarly the 61st K.G.O. Pioneers were completed by a draft from the 81st Pioneers. For various reasons only seven out of 13 British officers of the 63rd were available ; six officers from other regiments had therefore to be attached, of whom two joined only on the day of embarkation and none had trained with the unit.

was even worse. Of the battalions embarked, only the 101st Grenadiers and 61st K.G.O. Pioneers had possessed machine guns before 1914. The 13th, 63rd and 98th had at the last moment to improvise detachments to man the machine guns with which they were hastily equipped.[1] The battalions from the Indian native states had neither machine guns nor telephones, nor pistols for their Indian officers.

These shortcomings were to some extent accounted for by the fact that India's pre-war policy had been essentially defensive. For that reason, and doubtless also on financial grounds, reserves of warlike stores had been kept to a minimum. Now, the needs of the large force to be sent to Europe had absorbed most of such stores as were available, and defects in the equipment of the smaller expeditions to East Africa and elsewhere followed inevitably.

EMBARKATION

Notwithstanding these difficulties, by the end of September units had received their war equipment[2] and had been brought up to strength. On the 1st October the Imperial Service Brigade concentrated for training at Deolali. By the second week in October the various infantry battalions of the force had all moved to Bombay and been embarked.[3]

Meanwhile preparations for the projected landing on the German East African coast were being made by Commander E. J. Headlam, Royal Indian Marine, who on the 3rd October had reached Mombasa as Marine Transport Officer with the second contingent of I.E.F. " C " and now became Senior M.T.O. to both the Indian expeditionary forces. Lighters and tugs were collected at Kilindini (the port of Mombasa) and Zanzibar, including two large German tugs seized at Zanzibar and Tanga. A body of carriers had also to be collected. The recruiting of a Carrier

---

[1] The m.g. of the 63rd were not issued to the unit until after it had embarked. ◌

[2] Units did not take transport on the normal scale, it being understood that to meet East African conditions carrier transport would be provided on arrival.

[3] The 63rd embarked on 30th September and remained on board for the whole 16 days before sailing. The 28th Mtn. Bty., R.A., 25th and 26th (Rlwy.) Coys. Sappers & Miners, Faridkot Sappers, Ordnance, N.W. Railway armoured train, and other details embarked at Karachi in the *Bharata*, *Homayun* and *Muttra*. The remainder of the force embarked at Bombay.

Corps in East Africa has already been mentioned ;[1] but as its men were now in quarantine owing to small-pox in Uganda, it became necessary to raise 2,000 carriers for I.E.F. " B " from Zanzibar.

During this period the bold and unchecked raids of the German cruiser *Emden*, which on the 22nd September had bombarded Madras, made the provision of strong naval escort indispensable, and although the transports were ready by the end of that month the necessary warships could not be made available until mid-October. Thus the troops, already embarked a week or more earlier, underwent a trying period of inaction, lying out in harbour cramped and uncomfortable on board ship, before sailing.

At last, on the 16th October, the headquarters staff[2] embarked in the transport *Karmala* at Bombay, where the ships carrying I.E.F. " B " formed part of a convoy of 46 transports escorted by the battleships *Swiftsure* and *Goliath* and the R.I.M.S. *Dufferin*. The ships weighed anchor at 5 p.m., and Major-General Aitken set out with his force of 8,000 troops, most of them unknown to him and many of them of doubtful fighting quality, to attempt the conquest of a territory much larger than France.

THE VOYAGE

Two days out from Bombay (18th October) the convoy kept a rendezvous with another convoy from Karachi which included three more ships[3] for I.E.F. " B " escorted by the R.I.M.S. *Hardinge*. From this point the ships diverged, the greater number with the main expeditionary force for Europe making for the Red Sea, others for the Persian Gulf, while the 14 ships carrying Major-General Aitken's force, escorted by H.M.S. *Goliath* and the R.I.M.S. *Hardinge*, headed slowly south-westwards for Mombasa[4].

---

[1] See p. 23.

[2] The staff included Lieutenant-Colonel S. H. Sheppard, D.S.O., R.E. (previously an instructor at the Staff College, Quetta), as G.S.O.1 ; Captain R. Meinertzhagen, R. Fus., p.s.c. (who had served with the K.A.R. 1902–06), as G.S.O.3 (Intelligence) ; Brigadier-General W. Malleson, C.I.E., as Inspector of Communications ; Lieutenant-Colonel C. Bailey, 1st Lrs. (I.A.), as Base and Embarkation Commdt. Mr. Norman King (see p. 62) accompanied the staff. See also Appendix III.

[3] See p. 70, f.n. 3.

[4] The average speed was under eight knots. On 20th October the convoy was delayed 24 hours by turning back for three of its ships which had fallen behind.

For the Indian troops the voyage was a misery. Unused to the sea, and in some cases without their usual food, they suffered considerably from sea-sickness on the days when a slight swell marred otherwise good weather. Their ships were small and crowded, with so little deck space that even physical training was only possible for a few squads at a time.[1] Efforts were made to keep the men fit, and to carry out such military training as was possible ;[2] but as the convoy neared the Line the great heat below decks and the general discomfort became intensified. There can be no doubt that the fortnight's voyage under such conditions told heavily on the whole force, both morally and physically, and was at least a predisposing cause of the failure which was to come.

On the 30th October the convoy was met, 100 miles off Mombasa, by H.M.S. *Fox*. Her commander, Captain F. W. Caulfeild, R.N., together with Commander Headlam and Lieutenant-Colonel J. D. Mackay, just appointed as G.S.O.2 for Intelligence,[3] came aboard the *Karmala* to make preliminary arrangements. With a view to secrecy it was decided to keep the convoy out of sight of land ; meanwhile the *Karmala*, mildly disguised by removal of her Government markings, was to accompany H.M.S. *Fox* to Mombasa, where a conference had been arranged. Captain Caulfeild invited Major-General Aitken to come as his guest on board the *Fox*, but the cruiser could not accommodate the staff also, and the invitation had therefore to be declined : a decision which there was afterwards much reason to regret.

CONFERENCE AT MOMBASA, 31ST OCTOBER 1914

After dark on the 30th October, the *Fox* and the *Karmala* entered the port of Mombasa. Landing early next morning

---

[1] Especially in the *Assouan*, about 1,600 tons, carrying the 63rd. Consequently the loss of condition in this unit was particularly marked.

[2] Among other activities, a detachment of 14 N.C.O.s and men under Captain R. H. Logan, 2/L. North Lancs. Regt., took over two naval 3-pdr. guns on board H.M.S. *Goliath*. These were mounted on extemporised land carriages and under the name of " Logan's Battery " did useful work, first at Tanga from the decks of a transport, and afterwards in land operations.

[3] Major (local Lieutenant-Colonel) Mackay, who had served 14 years in the East African local forces, was appointed direct from London, went thence to India to confer with Major-General Aitken, and had preceded I.E.F. " B " to East Africa. To assist him Mr. Ishmael, also with local knowledge, was sent from London.

(31st) Major-General Aitken and his staff held a conference[1] at Government House with Sir Henry Belfield, Brigadier-General Stewart, commanding I.E.F. " C," and Colonel Ward of the local forces. All agreed that the course of action laid down as a suggestion by the home authorities, and regarded by Major-General Aitken as decided for him,[2] should be followed : the newly-arrived force to land at Tanga and advance thence up the railway towards Kilimanjaro, to meet a convergent advance from British East Africa directed on Longido.

Such little information as there was regarding the enemy indicated that the main German concentration was about Moshi, with outlying detachments along the frontier, and that the coastal districts were not strongly held. The presence of the German force under Baumstark in the frontier area near Vanga was of course known, but Tanga itself was believed to be unoccupied, and had no seaward defences.[3]

Topographical information as to Tanga was very scanty. A plan of the town was available, but there was no accurate map of the surrounding country. From small-scale maps and the Admiralty chart two rough sketch-maps were prepared and reproduced for issue to the troops.[4] These two maps, supplemented by the personal knowledge of the junior intelligence officer, Mr. Ishmael, who had visited Tanga, constituted the whole of the information available for the landing.

From Captain Caulfeild Major-General Aitken had heard for the first time of a factor vitally affecting his plans : the truce which in August had been made at Dar-es-Salaam and Tanga by the British naval commanders.[5] The Admiralty, as has been said, had directed that the unauthorized truce should be denounced, and accordingly on the 22nd October H.M.S. *Chatham* had notified the German authorities at Dar-es-Salaam that it could no longer

---

[1] Unfortunately no written record of the proceedings has been available in compiling this history.

[2] See p. 67, f.n. 2.

[3] Captain Meinertzhagen (G.S.O.3, Intelligence) had submitted a memorandum pointing out that the Germans could easily concentrate troops by rail at Tanga. This appears to have been disregarded.

[4] These sketches were inaccurate, the coastline being distorted and the roads wrongly drawn. They naturally caused confusion.

[5] See pp. 21, f.n. 1, 55 and 68. It will be noted that not even the existence of the truce, much less the important fact that its denunciation was ordered to be timed "shortly before . . . offensive action," was mentioned in the instructions for Major-General Aitken sent to India.

be observed there or at Tanga.[1] Of the delivery of this notification both Captain Caulfeild and Commander Ingles at Zanzibar[2] had been duly informed ; both, however, held that as regards Tanga a separate warning must be given.[3] In vain Major-General Aitken pointed out the disastrous effect any such warning must have on his chances of landing by surprise. The naval officers, punctilious to a fault, insisted that warning must be given[4] and at least an hour's grace allowed. To this, in deference to their views, Major-General Aitken reluctantly agreed.

Assured by all those present at the conference on the 31st October that no opposition was to be expected at Tanga,[5] he decided to proceed with the pre-arranged scheme and, with the agreement of all concerned, including the naval authorities, issued his orders[6] accordingly. The Imperial

---

[1] " Informed acting Governor I considered truce arranged by *Astraea* " and *Pegasus* with Dar-es-Salaam and Tanga was to be disregarded after " sinking of *Pegasus* by *Königsberg*, and also as many reports received " that *Königsberg* had been using the harbour." (H.M.S. *Chatham* to Admiralty, 23rd October 1914.)

Receipt of this warning was recorded in Lettow's personal diary for 22nd October 1914.

[2] Commander Ingles had remained at Zanzibar after the destruction of H.M.S. *Pegasus* (see p. 45).

[3] In reply to a telegram from Captain Caulfeild, sent when Major-General Aitken questioned the need to observe the truce, Commander Ingles said : " By orders from the Admiralty the place will have to be " informed shortly before any hostile act takes place that terms of truce " are not ratified by Home Government."

[4] In this these officers exceeded the requirements of international usage and of the Hague Convention, which lay down no specific period for denunciation of a truce. The wording is (Annexe to Hague Convention, Art. 36) : " If the duration of an armistice is not defined, the belligerent " parties may resume operations at any time, provided always that the " enemy is warned within the time agreed upon." At Tanga no time had been agreed upon.

[5] As a further indication of the easy confidence with which the whole matter was approached, the conference discussed also the subject of civil administration in the German territory after its occupation by the troops : a matter already referred to in Major-General Aitken's instructions from home (see p. 66). Five British territories abutted on German East Africa, and a tentative agreement as to their respective claims was cabled to London for approval. Although not remembered, apparently, when the instructions were first drawn up, nor in the minds of those at the conference,

" The man that once did sell the lion's skin . . . " was promptly quoted in the Colonial Office.

Even more striking is the fact that when Lieutenant-Colonel B. R. Graham, O.C., 3/K.A.R., offered a contingent of his battalion to cover the landing, Major-General Aitken, unaware of the value of African troops in their native bush, refused the offer.

[6] See Appendix III.

Service Brigade, Brigadier-General M. J. Tighe, was to effect the first landing, occupy Tanga and take up a position inland covering the port, leaving the Regular brigade in hand for the subsequent advance. " From reliable informa-" tion received," ran the now historic opening paragraph, " it appears improbable that the enemy will actively oppose " our landing."

With a view to surprise, so far as this was to be had consistently with the naval truce, it was decided that the convoy should go on to Tanga as quickly as possible. The alternative—to establish a base at Mombasa, landing the troops there to rest and recover after their trying voyage —was rejected as being likely to give away useful information to the enemy.[1] At noon on the 1st November, therefore, Major-General Aitken and his staff left Mombasa in the *Karmala* to rejoin the convoy at sea and stand down the coast for Tanga.

Off Mombasa, unhappily, H.M.S. *Goliath* had broken down ; and while the convoy went on its way with only the *Fox* as armed escort, the battleship for the next ten days remained immobile at Mombasa, just when her 12-inch guns might have given invaluable support to the landing. Even without them, however, the force was considered adequate, provided it achieved surprise.

ARRIVAL AT TANGA

During the day and night of the 1st November the convoy, with four tugs towing lighters collected in Mombasa, steamed southwards, coming within distant sight of land,[2] Before dawn on the 2nd it reached an appointed rendezvous 15 miles east of Tanga, where it was joined by the small steamers *Cupid* and *Khalifa* and the tugs *Helmuth* and

---

[1] Attempts to preserve secrecy had not been particularly successful. " The enemy had very fairly accurate intelligence of our resources in " B.E.A. when the war broke out. Every German merchant . . . was a " potential source of information to his country, and on our arrival . . . " after the repulse at Tanga, we found scores of aliens practically at " liberty . . . who had merely been ' put on parole.' Von Lettow told me " that his information was at that time accurate, frequent and reliable. " Nine-tenths of these enemy aliens ought certainly to have been interned " directly war broke out." (Report by Major-General S. H. Sheppard, 10th March 1919.) See also p. 103.

[2] Presumably the shortest course was followed owing to the slow speed of the ships. At several points along the coast columns of smoke, probably warning signals, were seen.

Tanga from Zanzibar, towing lighters packed with the newly-enlisted carriers. At 4.50 a.m. the convoy was stopped, and H.M.S. *Fox* went in alone, to notify the abrogation of the truce.

SKETCH 8ª

MANZA BAY

KWALE

Bagamoyo

Manyungu

Chongoleani   ULENGE

Reef

Amboni   TANGA BAY

R. Zigi   Ras Kasone

TANGA   Niule Reef

Kange

YAMBE

Scale – 6 *Miles to 1 Inch*

0   5   10

Crown Copyright Reserved..

COMPILED BY HISTORICAL SECTION
(MILITARY BRANCH)   *Ordnance Survey 1935.*

Flying a white flag, and proceeding between two reefs by a route which avoided the usual approach known as the Ship Channel, for fear that the latter might be mined, the *Fox* entered Tanga harbour, anchored at 7.5 a.m. and sent a message to the German District Commissioner, Dr. Auracher, to come on board. On reaching the ship, the Commissioner was called upon by Captain Caulfeild to surrender the town under threat of bombardment, and to give information as to any mines laid.[1] Without answering the latter demand, Dr. Auracher pointed out that Tanga, as an open town without defences, was not liable to bombardment, adding that he must refer to superior authority the summons to surrender. At 8.30 a.m. he returned to the shore.[2]

Thereupon Captain Caulfeild wirelessed to Major-General Aitken that an hour's notice had been given, and requested that the convoy should be got into line to enter harbour and that mine-sweeping craft should be sent in.[3]

---

[1] Dr. Auracher apparently understood that he was threatened with death unless he gave accurate information as to mines. His misapprehension seems to have been due to faulty interpreting, and an official reply to this effect was given to a subsequent formal German protest.

[2] On his return to the town Dr. Auracher reported the situation by telegram to Moshi and Tabora, and warned all inhabitants of the impending bombardment. He then, in his capacity as a lieutenant in the reserve, collected the local police and reported for duty with the troops, while the civil population, both German and native, fled inland.

[3] This message was not received till 11.20 a.m. (War Diary, I.E.F. "B").

Nothing further happened for an hour. The German flag still flew from the Government buildings ; otherwise there was no sign of life ashore. At 9.30 a.m. Captain Caulfeild wirelessed that he proposed bringing in three transports[1]—*Karmala, Pentakota, Jeddah*—to the outer anchorage, and the remainder later ; and at 9.40 a.m. followed the message : " No surrender. Rejoining convoy."[2] With no military representative on board his ship, Captain Caulfeild had decided not to bombard the apparently empty town ; meanwhile the convoy was waiting, some 15 miles off shore, and H.M.S. *Fox* steamed cautiously out, to rejoin it about midday. Major-General Aitken's intention to give only one hour's notice before the landing had thus gone by the board, and with it had gone all hope of surprise.

At this stage the fear of mines seems to have been a ruling factor. Captain Caulfeild sent the small craft in to sweep the entrance, and himself went on board the *Karmala*, where a prolonged conference followed.

Captain Caulfeild was unwilling to risk the ships by entering harbour until the sweeping operations had shown it clear of mines ; and since, moreover, the silent houses might prove to be full of troops, it was considered foolhardy to risk a landing on the harbour front unless covered by the guns of H.M.S. *Fox*.[3] Alternative landing-places were therefore now considered. Of these there appeared to **Sketch 9** be three. On the headland of Ras Kasone, at the entrance to the inner harbour, were a conspicuous red house facing the Indian Ocean and a signal-tower facing the channel. Below each of these landmarks a likely beach had been noted from H.M.S. *Fox*, while in the bay inside Ras Kasone, about a mile from the town, a long and narrow strip of sand suggested itself. Outside, a belt of reef lay parallel with the shore, some 300–500 yards out. The seaward face of Ras Kasone was marked by steep cliffs, 40 to 50 feet high, crowned by trees and covered with undergrowth, fringed at their foot by a dense belt of mangroves, in which the only gap was about half a mile south to the headland. Here the cliffs were free of vegetation and an obvious beach indicated a practicable landing. This beach, now

---

[1] Only 3 qualified pilots were available. This message was received at 11.30 a.m. (War Diary, I.E.F. " B ").
[2] Received 10.40 a.m. (War Diary, I.E.F. " B ").
[3] Two 6-inch, eight 4·7-inch.

designated " A," being out of sight of the town and farther from it than the other two beaches " B " and " C," was chosen for the landing, as being that least likely to be defended.[1] It was therefore decided, in keeping with the Operation Order already issued, that the first landing should be made at Beach " A " by the 13th Rajputs, the only regular battalion of the Imperial Service Brigade, under Brigadier-General Tighe. To the latter's command were added the 61st K.G.O. Pioneers for technical work, such as road-making. The task of this force was to occupy the town, holding the approaches on its landward side, and thus to cover the subsequent landing of the whole force in the order already prescribed.[2]

The conference on board the *Karmala* broke up about 2.30 p.m., the officers returned to their respective ships, and in a further Operation Order[3] embodying the decisions made Major-General Aitken laid down that " the town of " Tanga is to be seized to-night."

In the meantime, whilst the British action was being thus slowly organized, the Germans had acted with prompt decision. By 10 a.m. Lettow and his troops from Moshi were on the way,[4] rattling at full speed down the Usambara railway, while his small detachment at Tanga, with police and volunteers, concentrated in the railway cutting east of the town and patrolled the shore.

---

[1] Beach "A" was advocated by H.M.S. *Fox*. Its existence had previously been reported by Lieutenant Ishmael, Intelligence Officer.

[2] See Appendix III.

[3] See Appendix III.

[4] Normally the journey from Moshi to Tanga took about 12–14 hours

CHAPTER V
TANGA
(continued)
THE LANDINGS
(Sketches 9, 10, 11)

RETURNING to H.M.S. *Fox* about 3 p.m. on the 2nd November, Sketch 9 Captain Caulfeild found the marshalling of the convoy unsatisfactory, and delay ensued in manoeuvring the unpractised merchantmen into a formation which he could approve. His small craft were still sweeping for mines, and as the enemy had removed the buoys marking the channel it seemed to him unsafe to take in more than three ships (with his three pilots) at a time. At 4 p.m., however, the *Karmala* with headquarters, and the *Pentakota* and *Jeddah* with the 13th Rajputs and 61st Pioneers, moved in slowly and came eventually to anchor a mile east of Ras Kasone. Accompanying them, the *Fox* anchored off the Red House.

Except for the German flag at the Signal Tower, there was no sign of the enemy until 5.10 p.m., when a patrol was sighted and the *Fox* fired one round of 6-inch, upon which the patrol disappeared. At 5.40 p.m. the sweeping was finished and no mines had been found; lighters came alongside the ships, and just before 6 p.m., as the sun set, disembarkation began.

In the darkness which quickly fell, the unrehearsed loading of the lighters took time, and it was not until about 9 p.m., after further delay caused by counter-orders to the tugs, that the lighters carrying the 13th Rajputs, with machine guns at their bows, assembled under the lee of the *Karmala*.[1] About 10 p.m. the order to move was given, and in a smooth sea, in bright moonlight which must have shown them clearly to German patrols on the cliffs, the tows drew in.

In shallow water about 300 yards off shore the lighters were slipped, drifted shorewards and grounded almost at once. Rifle fire was opened on them from near the Red House, but on this being returned by the machine guns of the 13th Rajputs and the 4·7 inch guns of H.M.S. *Fox*, it ceased, and the landing continued unopposed.

---

[1] A signal detachment here joined the landing party.

The water, though too shallow for the lighters, was breast-deep, too deep for heavily equipped men. But the way was shown by Captain C. R. F. Seymour, 13th Rajputs, who after wading to the beach and back led ashore an advanced party of 50 men from each lighter, carrying only rifles and ammunition. These gained the beach, swarmed up the cliffs to the empty Red House, and established an outpost line round it, meeting no opposition.[1] The Brigade Scouts, under Lieutenant J. A. Ferguson, pushed inland for half a mile, but found no sign of the enemy.

Meanwhile disembarkation went on throughout the night, the troops coming off from the lighters in ships' boats. The 13th Rajputs entrenched a position covering their landing place at the Red House, while a detachment of the 61st K.G.O. Pioneers made its way to the signal-tower, found it deserted and hauled down the German flag.[2] Brigadier-General Tighe landed, together with the Base Commandant, the I.G.C. and other staff officers. Parties of carriers also were landed and set to work. By dawn of the 3rd November the covering force had secured its foothold ; but the men, both of the 13th and of the 61st, debilitated by nearly a month of sea-sickness and cramped quarters, were thoroughly exhausted.

Nevertheless reconnoitring patrols which went forward shortly before daylight discovered the enemy on the alert, and further delay was evidently inadvisable.[3]

ACTION OF THE 3RD NOVEMBER

Sketch 9   At 4.30 a.m. on the 3rd November half a battalion of the 13th Rajputs, with two machine guns, under Lieutenant-Colonel J. A. Stewart, moved off from near the Red House along the line of the so-called " Range " road running south-west into Tanga. The remainder of the battalion, with three (single) companies of the 61st, stood ready to follow. The British vanguard did not reach the outskirts of Tanga until about 5.30 a.m. The German *17. F.K.*, in position

---

[1] Farther along the beach Major F. S. Keen, Brigade Major, and Captain J. M. Colchester-Wemyss, Base Staff, with some signallers, similarly waded ashore.

[2] A signal station established in the tower was in lamp communication with the ships by 2 a.m. and was connected by cable with the Red House.

[3] One patrol under Captain C. R. F. Seymour reached the railway cutting and located two machine guns which fired bursts into the darkness. On its return, however, its report was received with scepticism.

along the railway cutting, held its fire until the leading British·troops had passed the deep ditch which runs parallel with and about 200 yards east of the railway, whereupon it opened rifle and machine gun fire.   The Rajputs deployed and returned the fire, but were unable to cross the open level ground to their front, which was swept effectively by the defence.   The Germans were under good cover, and the machine guns of the 13th Rajputs had difficulty in finding any target.[1]

On hearing the firing Brigadier-General Tighe at Ras Kasone, leaving one (single) company of the 61st to cover the landing place, advanced with the remainder of his force —the other four companies of the 13th, followed by three of the 61st—to join in the attack.[2]

Soon after 6.30 a.m. the second half battalion of the 13th Rajputs came up and was directed by Brigadier-General Tighe to deploy to the left so as to extend the open southern flank of the firing line.   In the thick vegetation the situation to the front was obscure, and Lieutenant-Colonel H. W. Codrington, commanding the 13th, with his adjutant, climbed a small knoll affording a better view. Unhappily their position was given away by an officer who ran up with a message ; a burst of machine gun fire swept the knoll : and all the officers fell, Lieutenant-Colonel Codrington severely wounded and the two others killed.

This unfortunate incident shook the morale of the Indian soldiers, and their dismay was increased when a second officer, Major B. A. Corbett, also fell.   Brigadier-General Tighe now put in his reserve, the three companies of the 61st Pioneers, which made their way with some difficulty through trees and standing crops and came up on the Rajputs' left flank.

As the Pioneers advanced, fresh German troops, newly arrived from Moshi, started an enveloping counter-attack against the British left.

A confused fight at short range ensued.   The leading officer of the Pioneers, Captain B. E. A. Manson, led a section

---

[1] The m.g. of the 13th Rajputs were transported by African carriers ; when the enemy opened fire these bolted, throwing their loads in all directions and disorganizing the detachment.

[2] At about this time the leading German troop train from Moshi reached Kange station, some four miles west of Tanga.   There the German leaders detrained, to avoid bringing the trains under the fire of the British ships, and hurried their men forward by road towards the sound of firing.
See Chap. VI, Note, p. 103.

in a valiant attempt to rush a German machine gun ; he
and all his men were killed. A second attempt to charge at
another point was also beaten back with heavy loss. A
German local counter-attack was then stopped by rapid
fire,[1] and the fight hung in the balance. In response to a
signal for assistance H.M.S. *Fox*, now lying off Beach " C,"
opened fire on the town.[2]

But the German enveloping movement was continued.
The 61st, already exhausted after a night's hard work,
bewildered in the dense vegetation, and startled by their
first experience of machine gun fire, were in no condition to
withstand the onset of the African askari who, with much
cheering and the sound of horns and bugles, could be heard
approaching through the bush against their flank and rear.
The Pioneers fell back for some distance ; the Rajputs, too,
already shaken, had begun to give way. Brigadier-General
Tighe decided that he must retreat ; and his force withdrew,
the surviving British and Indian officers controlling the
retirement as best they could.

The German troops followed up for some distance ;
but a fresh double-company of the 61st Pioneers now came
into action and beat back the pursuit.[3] The firing died away,
and at about 10 a.m. the troops were rallied near the Red
House. The casualties had not been excessive ;[4] but both
the Indian battalions appeared so shaken that Brigadier-
General Tighe could not contemplate using them for further
action that day. His first thought was to renew the attack
at once with the 2/Loyal North Lancashire, who were then
in the act of disembarking at Beach " B " ; but on considering the adverse moral effect if a second weak attack

---

[1] . . . " largely by the individual exertions of Captain Carr-Harris,
" R.E. (who was killed), and Private Lobb . . . ." Despatch, 1st
December 1914.

[2] " 7.40 a.m. Shelled Tanga town. Nine 6-inch, two 4·7-inch
" rounds " (log of H.M.S. *Fox*).

The *Fox* had moved in at 7 a.m. to an anchorage selected with a view
to being clear of the moving transports, not with any tactical object ;
for serious resistance by the enemy was still not expected.

[3] This company had landed at 8.30 a.m. The last double-company
of the 61st, did not get ashore until nearly 10 a.m., owing to the difficulties
in landing already mentioned, its lighters having grounded several hundred
yards off shore on a falling tide.

[4] Total casualties : 13th Rajputs, five out of 12 British officers, 49
out of about 690 o.r. ; 61st K.G.O. Pioneers (five single coys.), two British
officers, 91 o.r., out of about 400. Other officers killed were Captain R. H.
Waller, Staff Captain ; Captain E. D. Carr-Harris, R.E. ; Lieutenant
Ishmael, Intelligence (the only officer with personal knowledge of Tanga.)

were also repulsed, he decided to defer action until assured of ample strength.   He therefore directed the 2/Loyal North Lancashire to take up a position covering the beaches, and reported his situation to Major-General Aitken, stating that the Rajputs and Pioneers could not be relied upon, and that four fresh battalions would be needed to take the town. It did not occur to him, apparently, to reconnoitre the place again in the afternoon.

LANDING OF THE MAIN FORCE

So large a force could not be assembled in time for another attack that day.   Orders were issued, however, for all the fighting units of the force, except the guns and the Sappers & Miners, to be landed as soon as possible ; and in succession, three at a time, the transports were brought in.   During the afternoon, under a downpour of rain, the disembarkation of troops and stores at all three beaches continued.   Beyond the beaches there was no sign of the enemy.   At 5 p.m. Major-General Aitken himself went ashore. By a malevolent irony of chance the town of Tanga now lay deserted save for a few German scouts.[1]   But of this Major-General Aitken and his force, too busy with disembarkation[2] to think of reconnaissance, were unaware.

At sunset, as the last three ships were moving in, the beaches were so congested with troops, stores and undisciplined carriers that it was decided to defer until next morning the landing of the last three units—the 63rd, 98th, and 101st [3]

ACTION OF THE 4TH NOVEMBER

Early on the 4th November these three battalions and Sketch 10 the 27th Brigade Signal Section landed at Beach " C ".[4]

---

[1] See p. 103.

[2] The 2/Kashmir Rifles and the composite battalion (3/Kashmir and 3/Gwalior Rifles), which were ashore by about 4 p.m., with the 2/Loyal North Lancashire established a defensive line across the Ras Kasone peninsula so as to cover the whole area between Beaches "A" and " B," the northern sector being held by the 2/Kashmir Rifles, with outposts at Beach " C," the centre by the composite battalion, and the left by the 2/Loyal North Lancashire with the 13th Rajputs in rear about Beach "A."

[3] As one result the 63rd, who had been standing by all the evening and at 11 p.m. had been transferred into lighters, were then sent back on board ship with orders to be ready to land at 6 a.m.   They thus had little sleep or food before landing to take part in the action of the next day.

[4] The 63rd completed disembarkation by 7 a.m., the 101st by 8 a.m., and the 98th by 9.30 a.m.

The attacking force was now complete, Major-General Aitken having decided that, in view of the dense vegetation and of the difficulty of communication,[1] his guns would co-operate better if used from the deck of a ship in the harbour. The 28th Mountain Battery, R.A., accordingly mounted their guns on the deck of the *Bharata*, which moved up harbour to a position beyond H.M.S. *Fox*.[2]

Major-General Aitken's plan, founded on an infantry drill and tactics not as yet modified by fresh war experience, was simple. Assuming the enemy's position to extend no farther southward than the railway workshops just outside the town, he proposed to advance on a frontage sufficient both to make a direct assault and to turn the German right. His dispositions are shown in Sketch 10 : while the Imperial Service Brigade on the right made a frontal attack, the 27th Brigade on the left would envelop the enemy's open flank and cut off the German retreat. His intention was less definitely stated in his Operation Order[3] No. 3, which was dictated at 10.15 a.m., but it was sufficiently clear.

Direction during the advance was to be given by the 2/Loyal North Lancashire Regt., in the centre ; as will be seen from the sketch, four parallel tracks afforded convenient guiding and dividing lines.[4]

In these dispositions the 63rd, in whom after the previous day's action Major-General Aitken had little confidence, was sandwiched between his two best battalions, the 2/Loyal North Lancashire and the 101st Grenadiers ; and the somewhat shaken units were placed in support, the 13th Rajputs

---

[1] In the course of the action cable was laid forward from the signal tower and Red House (already interconnected) to Force H.Q. and Imperial Service Bde. H.Q., on the central so-called " Range " or "Askari" road near the cemetery, and to 27th Bde. H.Q. on the left flank, respectively. These cables were frequently broken in the course of the action, and in the dense bush the units could only keep in touch by runner. Communication with the ships was by visual signalling from the signal-tower.

[2] Four other ships also moved in (see Sketch 10), in accordance with orders issued before it was realized that the town would be defended. H.M.S. *Fox*, lying off Beach " C," was already within convenient range of the town.

[3] See Appendix III.

[4] Frontages of units, as will be seen, were narrow, e.g., 2/Loyal N. Lancs., 300 yards ; 63rd, 200 yards. The former was formed up with two coys. forward, two coys. in support, each with half the coy. in first line, half in second. The 63rd, also formed up in four lines, with one coy. in each line. The lines in extended order were preceded by ground scouts, but no previous reconnoitring patrols had been sent out.

behind the right brigade and the 98th behind the left, with the equally doubtful 61st Pioneers as a general reserve—an arrangement somewhat open to criticism.[1] The beaches, with their dumps of ammunition and stores, were to be protected by the Gwalior Infantry.

In the thick vegetation covering the whole area, deployment was slow and, although there was no hostile interference, units were barely in position by 12 noon, the hour fixed for the advance. At 12.10 p.m. the order to start was given.

Moving through dense plantations of rubber and sisal under the full heat of the midday sun, the advance was extremely slow, with frequent checks to regain touch.[2] Soon after 2 p.m. the leading companies debouched on to clearer ground, where nevertheless crops prevented a view ahead. By this time a gap had opened between the 2/Loyal North Lancashire and the Kashmir troops to its right, who had edged away towards the shore, and delay ensued whilst the British battalion inclined right-handed to close the gap. The heat was already telling, and straggling had begun, more especially from the 63rd.

About 2.30 p.m. the Kashmir Rifles encountered German patrols,[3] whom they drove back until within sight of the railway cutting, when the enemy's fire increased in violence and the advance was temporarily checked. At the sound of the firing, much farther forward than was expected, the 2/Loyal North Lancashire, inclining still more to its right, pushed rapidly on into the fight, leaving the 63rd far behind. Sending a message to the latter to follow, Lieutenant-Colonel C. E. A. Jourdain, commanding the 2/Loyal North Lancashire, brought up a support company on the right of his line and his battalion was soon hotly engaged.

---

[1] In his subsequent report Major-General Aitken wrote : ". . . I " hoped that the success and good example of my front line might put new " heart into them." The report makes it clear that the disposition of the battalions was decided by Major-General Aitken himself, not by his brigadiers.

[2] The 2/Loyal North Lancashire, in shirtsleeves and with web equipment, moved much faster than the 63rd, who in their heavy leather equipment were also carrying extra ammunition and water-chagals. At 1.45 p.m. the half-battalion of 2/Kashmir Rifles posted about Beach " C " joined the advance in support to the remainder of the unit.

[3] The first shots were fired by the enemy at a boat from the *Assouan*. Its crew at about 2 p.m. was incautiously landing at the jetty to buy food in the town. They fled hastily, several being hit on the way back ; the boat reached the ship towed by three men swimming.

The enemy's greater experience of bush fighting now began to tell,[1] and, while the British battalion and the Kashmir Rifles moved steadily forward the effect of the German fire on the 63rd Palamcottah Light Infantry was soon apparent. The Madrasi troops, like the rest, were suffering much from the tropical heat and consequent thirst. In poor condition as a result of their miserable voyage, and short of sleep during the previous night, the companies of the 63rd began to disintegrate from the moment when the German machine gun fire opened. The officers, both British and Indian, did all that lay in their power ; but too many of the British officers were strangers from other regiments,[2] unable to command the personal loyalty which makes so strong an appeal to the Indian soldier. Nothing could prevent the Madrasi rank and file from pouring back and dispersing into the thick undergrowth of the rubber plantation. By contrast, the newly formed machine gun section fought gallantly, led by Major K. C. T. McCaskill and Captain E. A. Breithaupt ; elsewhere a few stout hearts followed their company officers[3] ; but as a fighting unit the battalion ceased to exist.

Its disappearance left a wide gap between the 2/Loyal North Lancashire and the 101st Grenadiers on the outer flank, with the result that the latter, in turn, were ordered to incline to the right.[4] The whole front of attack was thus closing to the right, in a manner never intended by Major-General Aitken.

As a further result of the collapse of the 63rd, the morale of the 98th Infantry (not yet deployed) seems to have been shaken by the sight of stragglers and the sound of machine gun fire. To complete the discomfiture of this unit, its men

---

[1] In the words of a survivor, " they employed fire tactics certainly " never taught in India . . . controlled bursts of fire, directed by observers " in trees. . . . They ' browned ' the bush, and, if prodigal of s.a.a., it was " often effective and had a demoralizing effect at times on troops who had " never before been under fire."

[2] See p. 69, f.n. 4.

[3] Lieutenant G. N. Proctor, 83rd W.L.I., attached, with Jemadar Abdul Rahman, were followed by 25 men in an attempt to gain a hold on the railway. All the men were shot or fell away ; the two officers got across the cutting, but, being unsupported, had to retreat. In re-crossing the Jemadar was killed.

[4] Brigadier-General Wapshare sent a written order to the 101st to " bring their left shoulders up and march towards this point so as to " envelop the enemy's right."

were then savagely attacked by wild bees.[1] Within a few minutes they were scattered in all directions and they were not reassembled for some time.

On the right flank, however, the attack made progress. The two Kashmir battalions, now partly intermixed with the leading companies of the 2/Loyal North Lancashire and some of the 13th Rajputs, worked steadily forward until they were able to charge in with the bayonet across the railway cutting and reach the town, capturing a machine gun. German reinforcements (parts of *6.* and *17. F.K.*) came up, and in the course of sharp fighting in and among the houses the British reached the Kaiser Hotel, where Captain C. R. F. Seymour, 13th Rajputs, climbed to the roof and brought down two German flags.

On the extreme left the 101st Grenadiers, still isolated in spite of their change of direction, had advanced steadily through the thick vegetation. The (single) company acting as left flank guard was reinforced by another company and, after a short halt to effect this, the battalion pushed on, with four companies in line, past the group of native huts east of the railway workshops. Here the 101st came under heavy fire from *16. F.K.* in the German trenches south of the railway, and suffered severely as they worked their way forward. Major H. Tatum, senior officer of the leading companies, was killed ; led by two Indian officers,[2] the Dekhani Mahrattas of his company made a gallant but vain effort to charge, and, although they were mown down by the two machine guns of the defence, their attempt shook the German askari, some of whom were seen to give way.

Before advantage could be taken of this, however, four more German machine guns (*1.* and *17. F.K.*) came into action, extending the enemy's line southwards, and soon afterwards a counter-attack by fresh German troops (*13. F.K.*) developed **Sketch 11**

---

[1] All units, British and German alike, were thus attacked at various times during the day. One m.g. of the 2/Loyal North Lancashire and several German m.g., were temporarily put out of action by bees. The 3/Kashmir Rifles suffered severely, but used their puggarees as protection and remained in action. Conductor Preston, Signals, who continued taking in a message when attacked, and afterwards in hospital had over 300 stings removed from his head, was awarded the D.C.M.

On various occasions in this campaign it was found that bees, roused by bullets striking among them, were a menace to be taken seriously.

[2] Subadar Siwajirao Kali, Jemadar Dinkanao Jadhao. These officers were specially mentioned for heroic leadership in the battalion commander's report.

against the open left flank of the attack. By this time the leading companies of the 101st had lost half their numbers, and all their British officers had been killed. Putting up a stubborn resistance, they were compelled gradually to fall back. The two companies on the exposed flank, with the two machine guns of the battalion, succeeded in slowing up the enemy's advance to some extent, ably assisted in this by the two machine guns of the 63rd, which continued to be gallantly served by the survivors of their inexperienced detachments. But the superior numbers and bush-craft of the Germans told, and the remnants of the 101st continued to be forced back, breaking up eventually into small groups, still fighting, but scattered in the bush and no longer any protection to the British left, which thus, by about 4 p.m., was dangerously exposed.

Severe street fighting had meanwhile been going on. In an attempt to assist the attack, the guns of the 28th Mountain Battery, R.A., had kept up an intermittent shelling of the town ; but no arrangements for artillery co-operation had been worked out beforehand and no regular system of artillery communication had been arranged, so no messages from the infantry could be received, while from the ship little could be seen of the town owing to the high vegetation. Beyond their moral effect, therefore, the mountain guns were not in a position to contribute to the operation.[1] About 3.45 p.m., at the request of Brigadier-General Tighe, H.M.S. *Fox* opened fire on the town with her 6-inch and 4·7 guns ; but having her view obstructed by the hospital and the bush, and having no method of observation, she too could give no effective assistance. One shell hit a corner of the hospital ;[2] the *Bharata* signalled that others were hitting the British troops ; and after a few rounds the *Fox* ceased fire.

Meantime the 2/Loyal North Lancashire and the Kashmir Rifles, after storming a number of houses and capturing another machine gun, began to encounter stiff opposition.

---

[1] About 150 rounds were fired, mostly unaimed, directed towards the sound of firing in the town. On the ship's iron deck the guns, though partially anchored by coal-bags, bounced unsteadily. Although from the *Bharata*'s position part of the German defensive line lay in enfilade, little but the water-front could be seen even from the mast-head, to which the battery commander had himself hoisted. At this date forward observing officers had hardly been instituted, and the battery commander's suggestion to send an officer ashore was ruled out as unnecessary. The only information as to the situation in the town was brought later by a boat's crew sent ashore for another purpose (see p. 89, f.n. 2).

[2] A German at once ran out and planted a red-cross flag on the lawn.

Further German reinforcements (*7. Sch.* and *8. Sch. K.*) with machine guns came up opposite the left of the North Lancashire ; but no sign of support came to the latter, while the sound of firing could be heard penetrating farther behind the left flank as the 101st were driven back. Among the houses to the right the Kashmir Rifles were visible, but the extent of their success was unknown.[1]

Accordingly, after a brief conference of company commanders, the North Lancashire companies were withdrawn to the railway cutting, suffering heavily in the process from machine guns firing down the straight avenues they had to cross. To this movement the Kashmir Rifles conformed, and along the cutting a defensive line was established by mixed troops of all the units here engaged.[2]

At about 5 p.m. there came a further threat to the already exposed left flank, from a counter-attack delivered by fresh German troops (*4. F. K.*), just arrived. To meet it a defensive flank was hastily formed between the railway and the cemetery by the reserve companies of the North Lancashire, with a few of the 98th, ably supported from the adjoining knoll by the two machine guns of the 61st Pioneers. Near by, some of the 13th Rajputs with their two machine guns held a road-bridge in the defensive line, and three other companies of the 13th were intermingled with the Kashmir Rifles along the cutting.

The rest of the attacking force, unhappily, was either dispersed among the thick vegetation or crowding back to the beaches, which were now covered by a mob of dispirited stragglers and terrified Indian followers and African carriers. Soon after 4 p.m., as the troops began to withdraw from the town and the German counter-attack developed, these unorganized crowds were swept by panic.[3] The stampede

---

[1] Owing to the difference in languages, intercommunication between the 2/Loyal North Lancashire and the Kashmir Rifles was difficult, the latter having only three British officers in all.

[2] In this withdrawal Major F. J. Braithwaite, 2/Loyal North Lancashire Regt., was killed, and Major C. G. Ames, 52nd Sikhs, senior British officer with the Kashmir Rifles, badly wounded. The latter, while unconscious, was stung back to consciousness by bees. He was taken off to the *Laisang* by a boat sent from the *Bharata* in answer to signals by his men : this boat on return to the *Bharata* gave the 28th Mountain Battery, R.A., information as to the situation in the town (see p. 81, f.n. 1).

[3] The panic originated among carriers taking ammunition forward from Beach " C," who came under long-range fire, and at once dropped their loads and ran. Dressed in khaki with tarbooshes, they were mistaken for German askari breaking through.

along the beaches which ensued was with difficulty controlled by the embarkation Staff officers, and the three (single) companies of the 3/Gwalior Infantry posted as guards could give but little help.

Major-General Aitken and his staff had meanwhile thrown themselves into the fight, striving to rally the stragglers and restore the situation.   At 5.13 p.m. an urgent call was made by visual from the signal-tower to H.M.S. *Fox* : " Shell town " as hard as possible, but avoid the railway ". During the next half hour 108 rounds of 6-inch and 4·7-inch were fired into the town, doing immense material damage.   The German troops, apparently, being mainly in the farther part of the town, suffered few casualties ; but, presumably in consequence of the bombardment, no further attack was made, either on the British detachments along the railway or on the exposed left flank.   As darkness fell, the enemy's bugles recalling his troops were heard, and firing died away all along the line.

CHAPTER VI

TANGA

(concluded)

THE WITHDRAWAL

(Sketches 2, 5, 6, 10, 11)

MAJOR-GENERAL AITKEN'S first intention now was to re- Sketch 11
organize his force and to attack with the bayonet the same
night, 4th/5th November, under the tropical full moon.
Brigadier-General Tighe, however, was doubtful, having
regard to the shaken condition of the 13th Rajputs and
61st Pioneers. Meanwhile, there being no water for the
troops near the railway, but a good supply at the hospital,
it was decided to withdraw temporarily to a line with its
right flank resting near the hospital compound[1] and its
left thrown back to cover the approaches to the beaches.

Returning to the White House, Major-General Aitken,
who already knew that the only units still wholly unshaken,[2]
the 2/Loyal North Lancashire and the Kashmir Rifles,
had suffered heavy casualties, met Brigadier-General
Malleson, his I.G.C., and Brigadier-General Wapshare,
commanding the regular brigade, whose reports were not
encouraging. The latter spoke bitterly of the misconduct
of the 63rd and 98th, and of the consequent unavailing
sacrifice of the gallant 101st Grenadiers. The I.G.C. was
equally emphatic as to the " demoralized rabble " collecting
in increasing numbers on the beaches.

All was still silent in Tanga ; but a reconnoitring patrol
under Captain R. Meinertzhagen (G.S.O.3 Intelligence),

---

[1] It must be recorded that the German personnel of the hospital had
worked all day with the utmost devotion, tending British and German
alike. They fortunately had no casualties, though the building was once
hit, as already mentioned, by a shell from H.M.S. *Fox.*

[2] Practically all the other units still had some of their men in the line,
notably the 13th Rajputs, who had fought gallantly in the town. But
considerable numbers, all intermingled, had drifted back, and it was
difficult to estimate how many still had fight in them.

In the 2/Loyal North Lancashire and Kashmir Rifles, in spite of their
heavy losses, there was no thought of defeat. The Brigade-Major, 27th
Brigade, bringing orders to re-embark, met in the darkness an officer of
the 2/Loyal North Lancashire, who at once offered topographical information as to the town with a view to the next attack. The Brigade-Major
replied with regret that " the only information of any value now is that
" which will help us to get out of this . . . place as soon as possible."

91

which in the darkness had pushed forward to the outskirts of the town, had heard German spoken, and exchanged shots with the speakers. It was therefore assumed that the Germans were still in occupation. Their strength was unknown, but there was no reason to assume that the day's fighting had weakened the defence.

After full consideration, Major-General Aitken decided against a night attack. As alternatives, he could either hold the Ras Kasone peninsula or re-embark. The former course would involve difficulties of supply[1] and, if it were adopted, ultimate success must depend on the arrival of reinforcements. None, however, were to be obtained, except by depleting the already slender force guarding the Uganda Railway ; meanwhile, a German counter-attack might drive the shaken troops on Ras Kasone into the sea.

There remained no choice but to re-embark : a course not hitherto contemplated, for which, therefore, no plans had been made. Accordingly the Imperial Service Brigade was withdrawn to a position covering Beaches " A " and " B," Beach " C " being left to the protection of H.M.S. *Fox*. About 8 p.m. a conference of the naval and military commanders was held at the White House to arrange for re-embarkation.

The conference decided that this should be carried out as soon as possible, but must be by daylight : the disorganization of units, and the presence on the beaches of wounded men and of some 2,000 carriers, were complications which were felt to make it undesirable to re-embark by night. By day, however, Beaches " B " and " C " were exposed to view and to fire from the town ; consequently Beach " A " alone could be used. This beach, as will be remembered, was fringed by a reef some hundreds of yards off shore, so that ships' boats would be needed to take the troops off to the lighters. Orders were given accordingly.[2]

Meanwhile a defensive line was taken up across Ras Kasone and patrols were sent out. All remained quiet, and by midnight, behind reasonable defences, the exhausted troops were able to rest.

---

[1] Water-supply in particular was a source of grave anxiety : the supply near the beaches was quite inadequate, and the hospital, where there was a good supply, could not be included in the defensive perimeter.

[2] The naval orders were timed 11 p.m., 4th November.

Next morning (5th November) at about 6 a.m., after a false alarm had caused a general stand-to along the line, a further conference was held to settle details of the embarkation.

For a second time the omission of all previous rehearsal in boat-work was to be seriously felt. Speed in re-embarking appeared essential. This meant, however, not only that the more seriously wounded would have to be left to the care of the enemy, but also that—as the marine transport officer was careful to point out—heavy weights, such as ammunition-boxes, which might hole the boats, could not be salved. Hence, unhappily, came the decision to destroy and abandon all such stores : among them, most of all to be regretted, the machine guns.[1]

Meanwhile from the town the enemy began at dawn to fire on the ships. The *Laisang*, set on fire by hits at short range from two antiquated field guns, was obliged to leave harbour. The mountain guns aboard the *Bharata* were unable to reply, owing to the swing of the ship with the tide ; eventually, after two rounds from H.M.S. *Fox*, fired at random into the town, the German guns ceased fire. A heavy rain-squall then came down, obscuring all targets, incidentally flooding the trenches on Ras Kasone. When it passed, sniping and machine-gun fire began again on the harbour front, and at about 7 a.m. Captain Caulfeild, ordering the *Bharata* up to Ras Kasone to cover the re-embarkation, brought the *Fox* in to a berth near the jetty. Here she was sniped so vigorously that the ship's company was eventually permitted to reply, but no particular damage was done on either side. About 11 a.m. the German guns opened fire again, and were promptly silenced by three rounds of 6-inch from the cruiser, one a direct hit.

Meanwhile at Ras Kasone preparations went on and further stragglers came in.[2] The covering defensive line was held by the 2/Loyal North Lancashire and the Kashmir Rifles, under Brigadier-General Tighe, the former unit taking over six additional machine guns from the 13th,

---

[1] It seems evident that the abandonment of the machine guns in particular, under no molestation by the enemy, tended further to depress confidence.

See p. 94, f.n. 5.

[2] At 6 a.m. a detachment of the 101st Grenadiers, which had been left isolated at nightfall and had held its ground on the far left flank during the night, marched back in good order as a formed body.

61st and 63rd. Off shore lay the *Bharata* with the six guns of the 28th Mountain Battery R.A., and the *Barjora* with Logan's two naval 3-pounders. At the Red House, in an extemporised hospital, were some 130 of the seriously wounded who could not be taken off. Directed by the C.R.E., Lieutenant-Colonel C. B. Collins, the 61st Pioneers cut paths down the cliffs to the beach.[1]

For the re-embarkation, timed to start on a rising tide at 1 p.m., Commander Headlam had assembled 30 ships' boats, manned by volunteers, while H.M.S. *Fox* furnished a strong beach party ; the tugs and lighters were brought close in to the reef, and shortly after noon all was ready.[2]

Re-embarkation then began. First to go were the Indian followers and the 2,000 carriers ; then, in succession, the 61st and 63rd, 98th, 101st and 13th. The need for haste was so strongly felt that no attempt was made to get the troops back to their former ships, and they were put on board haphazard, all units intermixed.[3]

Early in the proceedings shots fired by a German patrol drew a reply all along the defensive line ; fresh and violent panic ensued among the Indian followers on the beach, who fled in chaos into the sea, swimming out to the boats, half swamping them and producing general confusion, out of which order was eventually restored, not without difficulty and violence. In the meantime special parties had been destroying heavy boxes and stores as far as time allowed.[4]

By 3 p.m. all except the battalions holding the covering trenches were off the shore. The Kashmir Rifles were then taken off, followed by the 2/Loyal North Lancashire.[5] The latter, unmolested to the last, filed calmly down to the beach, joined the naval beach parties, and waded out to

---

[1] It is noteworthy that the two companies of Sappers & Miners, highly skilled technical troops, were not disembarked.

[2] Meantime during the morning sham signal messages in clear were ostentatiously sent from the signal tower to the ships, in order to suggest to the enemy that a further attack was imminent.

[3] A large number had to wade out to the boats up to their necks, and many, after remaining all night in the lighters, were not re-sorted to ships until next day (6th November).

[4] Complete destruction was out of the question, and valuable material, including a quantity of ammunition, had to be abandoned intact.

[5] A last appeal by the 2/Loyal North Lancashire, before embarking, to be allowed to take the nine machine guns still in their hands, was refused by Brigadier-General Wapshare. Seven of these had therefore to be abandoned, while two were finally salved.

the boats.   At 3.20 p.m. the evacuation was complete,[1] except for the wounded and the medical personnel left at the Red House.   Throughout, by almost the only piece of good fortune to be recorded anywhere in the melancholy story of the expedition, the withdrawal of the troops was effected without interference by the enemy.   How tragically it might have ended, had the Germans shown even a little of the enterprise that might have been expected of them, will be sufficiently apparent.

During the afternoon Captain Meinertzhagen went ashore under a white flag[2] to arrange for the removal of the wounded.   He was courteously received, on Colonel von Lettow-Vorbeck's behalf, by Captain Freiherr von Hammerstein, with whom it was agreed that the British wounded might be taken off under parole not to serve again in the war.

For the next twenty-four hours an informal truce was maintained whilst the intermingled troops were sorted out and arrangements made to collect the wounded.   On the afternoon of the 6th November, however, a verbal message from the German commander demanded that the convoy should leave Tanga, intimating that at daylight on the 7th any transports within sight would be fired on.   Accordingly, Sketch 8a leaving the *Barjora*, now disarmed of Logan's two guns and flying the Red Cross flag, to embark the wounded, the convoy moved off to an anchorage off Kwale Island. The *Barjora* rejoined next day with 74 British wounded,[3] leaving 49, unfit to be moved, in German hands.   On the 8th November, in all the bitterness of defeat, the expedition returned to Mombasa.

CASUALTIES AT TANGA

During the next ten days the units of I.E.F. " B " were put ashore at Mombasa, while casualties and strengths were worked out, a task complicated by the intermixture

---

[1] The last boat-load reached the ships at 4 p.m.   The total of combatants re-embarked was about 6,200.

[2] Captain Meinertzhagen had earlier walked from Ras Kasone to the hospital, carrying medical comforts for the British wounded and a letter of apology from Major-General Aitken for the damage accidentally done by the shell from H.M.S. *Fox*.

[3] Eight officers, 66 o.r.

A detachment of 50 men of the 2/Loyal North Lancashire, under Lieutenant and Quartermaster R. L. Rowley, unarmed, remained in two lighters off Beach " A " to receive the wounded.   They were courteously treated by the Germans, although their presence was not covered by any agreement and they might legitimately have been made prisoners.

of units on board ship. The casualties[1] were found to have been roughly 820 in all, an eighth of the force, of whom 360 were killed or died of wounds ; about 50 wounded and 30 unwounded were taken prisoner. It will be seen that the gallant 101st Grenadiers suffered far more heavily than any other unit, losing in killed no fewer than 6 British officers, 6 Indian officers, with 38 wounded and missing. The remarkably high proportion of killed to wounded, and the fact that only one officer and 6 other ranks, all severely wounded, became prisoners, both speak eloquently of the fierce fight put up by the 101st on its desperately exposed flank.

Under the conditions which have been described the losses in material and munitions were inevitably very high.[2] Worse, however, than any such material losses was the melancholy loss of morale which thenceforward long afflicted and made useless certain of Major-General Aitken's

---

[1] The casualties at Tanga, including both the 3rd and 4th November, were eventually reported as follows :

	Killed or Died of Wounds				Wounded				Missing			Total
	British		Indian		British		Indian					
	Off.	O.R.	Off.	O.R.	Off.	O.R.	Off.	O.R.	B.O.	I.O.	O.R.	
Staff	4	—	—	—	1	—	—	—	—	—	—	4
2/L. N. Lancs. ..	3	26	—	—	1	62	—	—	1	—	22	115
63rd P.L.I. ..	1	—	3	8	3	—	3	31	—	—	36	85
98th Infantry ..	1	—	—	6	1	—	—	32	—	1	38	79
101st Grenadiers ..	6	—	6	172	—	—	3	28	1	—	6	222
13th Rajputs ..	2	—	2	48	6	—	4	34	—	—	—	96
2nd Kashmir Rif. ..	—	—	—	14	1	—	2	24	—	—	—	41
3rd Kash. R. (½ Bn.)	—	—	—	3	—	—	2	14	—	—	2	21
3rd Gwalior I. (½ Bn.)	—	—	—	1	—	—	—	1	—	—	—	2
61st Pioneers ..	2	—	—	50	3	—	2	52	—	1	38	148
28th Mtn. Bty. R.A.	—	—	—	—	—	—	—	—	—	—	—	nil
Signals	—	—	—	—	—	—	—	—	—	—	1	1
Medical	1	—	—	—	1	—	—	—	1	—	—	3
	20	26	11	302	16	62	16	216	3	2	143*	817

* All Indian except 22 2/Loyal North Lancashire, who were taken prisoner, 18 being wounded. Of the Indians, 30 wounded, 26 unwounded were reported subsequently as prisoners.
These figures do not include casualties among Indian followers and the African carriers, of which no record can be traced.
For German casualties see p. 107.

[2] See p. 94. One m.g. of the 2/Loyal North Lancashire, which broke down in the action of 4th November, was rendered unusable and left on the ground. Two m.g. of other units were left above Beach " A," in addition to the seven m.g. abandoned, by order, by the 2/Loyal North Lancashire.

Several hundreds of rifles were also lost, with much medical, signal and other equipment. No precise figures are available. For German claims see p. 107, f.n. 1.

Indian units. For many months to come, the greater part of I.E.F. " B " was in no condition to resume the offensive.

THE ATTACK ON LONGIDO

An effort which proved equally unlucky and fruitless **Sketch 2** had been made against Longido in aid of the Tanga operation. Major-General Aitken's original instructions had suggested that after the intended occupation of Tanga had had its due moral effect on the enemy, I.E.F. " C " " should, if feasible, advance from Tsavo and threaten " Moshi,"[1] but gave him freedom to use his discretion. At the conference at Mombasa on the 31st October, it had been agreed that, as suggested, Brigadier-General Stewart's forces already in East Africa should make an advance towards the Kilimanjaro area ; but it was decided, first, that the advance should be made simultaneously with the Tanga operation, and, secondly, that it should be directed, not from Tsavo westwards, but from the north by way of Longido.

The latter direction was selected on account of the comparative healthiness of the Longido area, which was, moreover, better suited for employment of the E. Africa Mounted Rifles. Difficulties due to the known lack of water in that area would, it was hoped, be overcome by securing the water supplies existing on Longido mountain.

The enemy holding the mountain was known to have been reinforced after the affair in the Ingito hills at the end of September,[2] and was now estimated to consist of some 200 Germans and 200 to 300 askari.[3] With a view to attacking them a considerably superior British force, some 1,500 in all, with 4 guns,[4] under Lieutenant-Colonel A. B. H. **Sketch 6** Drew, 29th Punjabis, had assembled at Namanga camp (Oldoinyo Erok) at the end of October, and the date of attack was now fixed for the 3rd November.[5]

---

[1] See p. 66.
[2] See p. 44.
[3] An inaccurate estimate. Major Kraut's *Abteilung* at Longido consisted of *10., 11., 21. F.K.* and *9. Sch. K.* (white volunteers), total 86 German, 583 askari, with 6 m.g.
[4] 29th Punjabis, less 2 coys. (total 475) ; half-battalion Kapurthala Infantry (378) ; 5 squadrons E.A. Mtd. Rifles (360) ; 27th Mtn. Bty., R.A., less 1 sect. ; 1 sect. Volunteer Maxim Bty (2 m.g.) ; detachment Masai Scouts.
[5] It will be remembered that the landing at Tanga had been intended for 2nd November.

After reconnoitring Longido, Lieutenant-Colonel Drew decided to make his main attack against the eastern face of the mountain, at the same time making a holding attack on the northern face and sending a small column to skirt the eastern face, seize the water supply known to exist on the southern slopes, and bar the German retreat. His advance across the plain to the foot of Longido was to be made by night, with a view to attack at dawn.

Three squadrons (less one troop) of the East Africa Mounted Rifles, one (single) company of the Kapurthala Infantry and a section of the 27th Mountain Battery, R.A., all under Major Laverton, E.A.M.R., were detailed for the holding attack; the other two squadrons, E.A.M.R., under Captain A. C. Bingley, were to carry out the move round the eastern flank. Preceded by these columns, the remainder of the force left its camp at Namanga at nightfall on the 2nd November, guided by Masai scouts[1] and with a train of 100 mules carrying water in tins.

Neither of the two detached columns was able to contribute any help to the main attack. Laverton, soon after sunrise on the 3rd, was held up near the foot of Longido by a superior force of the enemy; his section of artillery, inexperienced in bush fighting, could give little support, and finding himself unable to make progress he eventually withdrew northwards and returned to Namanga. To the south Bingley's mounted force, about 100 strong, after an unsuccessful search in the darkness for the enemy's water supply, was engaged during the morning of the 3rd by some 300 of the enemy. Being threatened with envelopment and having lost about 15 killed and wounded, Bingley finally fell back to a hillock commanding the German line of retreat to the south, where he remained until dusk. Then, being out of touch and without water, he too made his way back to Namanga. Meantime the main column, after a difficult climb in the dark, found itself at dawn immobilized in thick mist on an unknown ridge some 1,500 feet above the plain. Here its presence was discovered by German patrols, and when the mist lifted it became engaged in a lively action with a considerable German force from a camp visible about one and a half miles away. During

---

[1] The Masai scouts, under Mr. G. J. Orde-Browne, Assistant Com missioner, did particularly good work during these operations.

the morning a counter-attack by the 29th Punjabis stabilized
the situation for the time being ; but the firing stampeded
the mule-train down the mountain-side, a serious mishap
which left the force without water.

About 5 p.m. a determined German attack compelled
withdrawal of the forward companies, and although again
the situation was temporarily restored by a vigorous counter-
attack by the 29th Punjabis, it was evident that little
further success could be expected. Isolated on a mountain
ridge, without water, and with no prospect of support,
Lieutenant-Colonel Drew decided to withdraw under cover
of darkness.

A further German attack at dusk was beaten off. Withdrawal, which then began, was difficult ·owing to rough and
steep ground, and was further hampered by panic among
some of the followers ; but by 7.15 p.m., covered by a rearguard of the 29th Punjabis and the volunteer Maxim Section,[1]
all the wounded and stores had been got away, and soon
after 9 p.m. the last of the troops had disengaged. At
dawn on the 4th November the whole of Drew's forces
were back in camp on Oldoinyo Erok, after 38 hours' marching and fighting.[2]

Described officially as a " reconnaissance in force,"
the Longido operation may be regarded as having achieved
its intended object. In its relation to the landing at Tanga,
however, it was singularly unlucky in its timing. On the
one hand, had it been made a day earlier it might have
deterred Lettow from sending some of his other troops
from about Kilimanjaro to Tanga ; on the other, had it
been made a day later, the *Abteilung Kraut* would have
been absent,[3] giving Drew possession of Longido almost
unopposed and the further prospect of going on to occupy
the whole Kilimanjaro district. It will, of course, also be
seen that if the landing at Tanga had taken place on the

---

[1] The two m.g. of this section did conspicuously well in covering the
withdrawal.

[2] The total casualties were :

29th Punjabis, 8 o.r. killed, 18 o.r. wounded ; E.A.M.R., 1 officer,
9 o.r. killed, 1 officer, 7 o.r. wounded, 1 o.r. missing ; 27th Mtn. Bty. R.A.,
1 officer, 2 o.r. wounded ; other units, 1 o.r. killed, 5 o.r. wounded : total,
1 officer, 18 o.r. killed, 1 officer, 32 o.r. wounded, 1 o.r. missing.

German casualties are given by Dr. Schnee as 5 Germans, 11 askari
killed ; 5 Germans, 19 askari wounded.

[3] As it chanced, the order summoning Kraut to Tanga had been
delayed in transmission : see p. 104.

2nd November, as planned, Longido might equally have been found denuded of Kraut's troops on the 3rd and so might have been easily seized.

RESULTS OF THE OPERATIONS

The news of the failure at Tanga and the withdrawal from Longido was cabled to London on the 5th and 6th November respectively by Major-General Aitken and Sir Henry Belfield. The general situation at the time was gloomy and critical. In Flanders the desperate First Battle of Ypres was still undecided; in the Near East, Turkey had newly come into the war; at sea Admiral Craddock's squadron had just been destroyed by the cruisers of Admiral von Spee. It was felt by the Government that publication of the news of a further reverse would be inadvisable, and accordingly no mention of the events at Tanga was permitted. It was not until several months later that any details of the fighting were given to the public in Great Britain.

Steps were taken also to prevent the news being spread in India. A suggestion by Major-General Aitken that the 63rd and 98th should be sent back to that country in disgrace was discountenanced.[1] On the other hand, in his bitterness over Tanga, Lord Kitchener refused at first to allow any decorations to be awarded to the officers and men recommended for gallantry in the operations.

Inevitably the defeated commander paid the full penalty of failure. After his return to Mombasa, Major-General Aitken set about reorganizing his troops and making dispositions for the defence of British East Africa, to which obviously they must now be devoted. Stricken down some days later by malaria, he was still in hospital when he was ordered by cable, on the 4th December, to hand over command to Brigadier-General Wapshare and return to England. Denied an interview with Lord Kitchener and received with marked disfavour by Sir Edmund Barrow, he was refused any further command, reduced to his substantive rank of Colonel

---

[1] The 63rd and 98th eventually sailed for India from Dar-es-Salaam on 5th January 1917; the 61st K.G.O. Pioneers on 20th February 1918. The 63rd Palamcottah Light Infantry was disbanded in 1922; the 98th has now become the 4th/19th Hyderabad Regt.; the 61st, reconstituted in 1922 as the 1st/1st Madras Pioneers (K.G.O.), amalgamated in 1929 with the 2nd and 10th Bns. Madras Pioneers and with them designated the Corps of Madras Pioneers, was disbanded in 1932.

and relegated to unemployment on half pay until the end of the War. Subsequently, in the more generous atmosphere of 1920 and in the light of fuller knowledge, his case was reviewed ; his difficulties were better appreciated, and some measure of compensation was accorded.[1] He died in 1924, the victim not so much of positive errors as of a combination of adverse circumstances and conditions, originated outside his control, which it had been beyond his power to bend to a successful issue.

On the other hand the fight at Tanga laid the foundations of future fame for his opponent, Colonel von Lettow-Vorbeck. The latter's position had previously been none too easy. A newcomer to the colony, he had been regarded with some distrust by the older settlers, while his uncompromising military outlook had received scant sympathy either from the more cautious and more diplomatic Governor of the colony or from the peace-loving traders of Dar-es-Salaam. Now all was changed. The Governor could not but approve of so resounding a victory, even if won against his orders ; while to the other German inhabitants Lettow became, and remained, the hero of the colony's defence. Thenceforward there was no lack of support for his policy or of confidence in his leadership.

SUMMARY

There can be no doubt that the expedition to Tanga contained from the very beginning all the elements of disaster. Founded upon a plan devised in London, on scanty and far from reliable information, by a committee of officials of the India Office, Colonial Office and Admiralty, its conception was accepted by the Offensive Sub-Committee unquestioningly and without reference to the military experts of the General Staff. In that acceptance lay the root cause of one of the most notable failures in British military history. Other causes, already sufficiently indicated, contributed to make failure doubly certain.

From a military point of view the defects of the project are only too apparent. A scratch force some 8,000 strong, with no knowledge of African warfare, a considerable

---

[1] Major-General Aitken was personally exonerated by a public statement in Parliament. He was allowed to retire with the maximum retired pay of a colonel, Indian Army, and was granted the honorary rank of brigadier-general. Financial compensation for the injury to his career was refused as a matter of principle.

percentage of whose troops was quite unsuited to the purpose, was in the first place to land on a hostile coast as to which little was known, immediately after a fortnight's sea-voyage under debilitating conditions. Devoid of all transport except an unfamiliar carrier service improvised locally to await its arrival, the force was then to make an advance of some 200 miles through difficult and rugged country, up a railway at the head of which stood in considerable strength an efficient and well-led enemy, leaving its flanks and rear open to attack. With a curious blend of optimism and misapprehension of German mentality, it was suggested that the enemy might yield to the moral effect of this advance ; that a large area of his territory might be occupied ; and even that thereafter the force might go on to " occupy " the 500 miles of railway running inland from Dar-es-Salaam, itself 120 miles south of Tanga. Of the possible use of local African troops no mention was made.

The impracticability of these hopeful designs was destined to be finally and cruelly demonstrated at the first attempt to put them into execution. Arriving off Tanga, the expeditionary force was first deprived of all chance of surprise by punctilio as to the naval truce and by careful precaution against the risk of submarine mines. Unpractised in disembarkation and lacking information, it landed slowly and not without confusion. Unversed in bush warfare and insufficiently trained, especially in the use of machine guns, it found itself at a disadvantage in dealing with the German native troops on their own ground. Possessing an overwhelming preponderance of artillery, it suffered nevertheless from the omission to organize adequate artillery support. In actions fought on two successive days at short range in the bush the less reliable units, already dispirited and physically weakened by the voyage, lost morale and gave way. Expecting no resistance, the force met with heavy defeat, and was fortunate in effecting a hasty re-embarkation and departure unmolested. Its failure left lasting ill-effects on the morale alike of the British forces and of the native populations in British territory, and by heartening the enemy did much to prolong a campaign which a better-designed, less ambitious enterprise might well have brought successfully to an earlier end.

As a matter of strange coincidence, Tanga was attacked on the 3rd November 1914. On that same day the historic warning in advance which awoke the Turks was given by the first naval bombardment of the Dardanelles.[1]

NOTE

TANGA : THE GERMAN SIDE

Such attempts as had been made in British East Africa to maintain secrecy[2] had not prevented the Germans from receiving warning of the Tanga expedition some weeks before its arrival. Allusions in the Press, both in East Africa and in India, had reached the Germans ; wireless messages from the Belgian Congo had been intercepted ; natives, with the uncanny African talent for passing news, had brought word from Nairobi and Mombasa. " During October," wrote Lettow, " it became " more and more apparent that with the arrival of 10,000 Indian " troops a hostile offensive was imminent."[3] To his trained eye Tanga was the obvious objective, and towards the end of October he had gone there and discussed the defence of the place with Dr. Auracher, the local Commissioner. The Governor, it is true, had forbidden any action likely to lead to the bombardment of the port ; but Lettow and Auracher had reached cordial agreement, leaving final decisions to await the event.

On the 1st November the only German unit in the Tanga area was the *17. F.K.*, with one of its platoons in the town and the other two a few miles away to the north. Farther north, in the British frontier territory, the other two units (*15.* and *16. F.K.*) of Baumstark's force were at Samanya and Majoreni **Sketch 5** respectively ; along the Usambara railway were small protective detachments of *1. Sch.* and *9. Sch. K.* German headquarters were at New Mochi, the terminus of the railway, 150 miles from Tanga, together with *1.* and *6. F.K.* and *6. Sch. K.* Along the border were distributed three advanced detachments : at Taveta under Captain von Prince, *7. Sch.* and *8. Sch. K.* and *19. F.K.*, with three small guns ; on Kilimanjaro under Major Kepler, *4., 8., 9.,* and *13. F.K.*, with Hering's " battery " of two obsolete field-guns ; at Longido under Major Kraut, *10., 11.,* and *21. F.K.*, *9. Sch. K.*

The bulk of the German defence forces was thus, as the British intelligence had rightly deduced, in the Kilimanjaro area, and the port of Tanga lay virtually empty.

---

[1] See " Military Operations : Gallipoli," Vol. I, pp. 34–5, 43–4.

[2] German and Austrian residents had been interned at Nairobi as early as 9th August, and some measure of martial law had been instituted ; but ineffective censorship and indiscreet talk had had the usual results.

[3] Report, 14th November 1914.

About 9 a.m. on the 2nd November, as has been recounted, Lettow at Moshi received Dr. Auracher's telegram reporting the arrival off Tanga of H.M.S. *Fox* and the convoy. Deciding at once to concentrate at the point of attack, he telegraphed calling in Kraut, Kepler and Prince to Moshi, and ordering Baumstark's two outlying *F.K.* to Tanga by forced marches ; at the same time the troops at Moshi were entrained. Within an hour *6. F.K.* was away, followed an hour later by *6. Sch. K.* with a platoon of *1. F.K.*, down the line to Tanga.

Meanwhile, on the 2nd at Tanga *17. F.K.*, under Adler, with some of Auracher's native police and volunteers, assembled in the railway cutting and sent out the patrols which fired on the first of the British landing parties that evening. Before dawn on the 3rd November this force was in position along the western side of the cutting, where it met the first attack by Brigadier-General Tighe's advanced guard.

The first trains from Moshi, with the units above-named,[1] reached Kange, four miles from Tanga, about 6.30 a.m. on the 3rd. Pushing on at the double, the troops reached Tanga at 7.15 a.m., and after hasty reconnaissance were thrown into the counter-attack which drove back the 61st Pioneers and compelled Brigadier-General Tighe to retreat.[2]

Later in the day Baumstark arrived with *16. F.K.* from Vanga and assumed command. Deciding not to hold the town, he withdrew his forces inland and took up a defensive position at Kange.

Signal communication between Moshi and Kraut's force at Longido having, as it chanced, broken down, the latter did not receive his orders until the 4th November : a delay whose effect on the British subsidiary attack in the north has already been referred to.[3] But with that exception all the German troops from the Kilimanjaro area were on their way to Tanga by the evening of the 3rd November.

End Paper (N.)

At 8 p.m. Lettow with his headquarters reached Korogwe station, where he received first-hand news of the fight from wounded officers and learned that Baumstark had evacuated the town. In his own view the ground about Tanga was well adapted for defence, and accordingly, ignoring a telegraphed order by the Governor not to fight in the vicinity of Tanga,[4] he telegraphed to Baumstark to re-occupy the town. Reaching Kange himself at 3 a.m. (4th November) he hurried forward.

---

[1] Total about 100 Germans and 250 askari, with 4 m.g.
[2] See p. 82.
[3] See p. 99.
[4] *Lettow, den ein Telegramm des Gouverneurs angewiesen sein hätte, ein Gefecht nicht bis in das Weichbild Tangas gelangen zu lassen, trat mit einer Karte dieser Stadt unter die Offiziere und sagte lachelnd : " Sehen Sie, meine " Herren, unter dem Weichbild Tangas verstehe ich dieses ! " und sein Finger fuhr der Demarkationslinie der aüsseren Haüser entlang.* Hauer, *Der Triumph der deutschen Tropen-medizin,* p. 55.

On overtaking Baumstark two miles outside Tanga he ordered strong officers' patrols to be sent out, and bicycled ahead with two staff officers to make a personal reconnaissance.

He has described how he " rode on through the empty " streets " in the moonlight, to see from the harbour's edge " the " transports, a blaze of lights, and full of noise " ; how much he regretted the non-arrival of his two old guns in time to be used against the disembarkation so evidently about to start ; and how, after going on to the beach beyond the hospital, he was even challenged by an Indian sentry who did not fire, before riding back to the town to complete his dispositions.[1]

These are shown in Sketch 10 : the railway cutting held **Sketch 10** by two platoons and a machine gun of 6. *F.K.*, and the native quarter outside the town covered by 16. *F.K.* with two machine guns. Behind the right flank the rest of Baumstark's command— 17. *F.K.*, with composite companies made up from 4. *Sch.* and 6. *Sch. K.* and from a platoon of 1. *F.K.* with Auracher's police— formed a provisional " battalion," while in reserve under Lettow's personal command were Prince's units, 7. *Sch.* and 8. *Sch. K.*, with eight machine guns and three small field guns.[2] The enemy's total strength so far was about 300 Germans, 900 askari, with 13 machine guns.

In addition, 13. *F.K.* arrived during the morning, and 4. *F.K.* was on the way by rail, while Kraut's force—of whose delay Lettow as yet was unaware—might soon be expected.[3]

During the morning of the 4th November the brunt of the fighting fell, therefore, on 6. *F.K.*, and 16. *F.K.*, the former being reinforced, when the 2/Loyal North Lancashire and Kashmir Rifles drove it back into the town, by part of 17. *F.K.* from Baumstark's battalion. About 3.30 p.m., when 16. *F.K.* began to give way before the 101st Grenadiers, Lettow decided to throw in his reserves.

Sending Prince with 7. *Sch.* and 8. *Sch. K.* into the town against the attack by the North Lancashire, he brought the four machine guns of 1. and 17. *F.K.* in on his right flank, at the same time ordering 13. *F.K.* to make the enveloping counter-attack which eventually drove back the 101st.[4]

---

[1] " My Reminiscences," pp. 38–9.

[2] One 47 mm., two 37 mm. In anticipation of a British landing on the harbour front, when the *Laisang* moved in, Prince's force was sent in at 11 a.m. behind the left flank of the defence. It was recalled as soon as it was seen that no landing followed.

[3] Including 4. *F.K.*, 13. *F.K.*, and also 15. *F.K.* which in fact, did not arrive until 5th November, a German return gave the strength present as 352 Germans, 1,319 askari, 5 guns, 21 m.g.

[4] See p. 88.
The four m.g., whose enfilade fire against the left of the 101st greatly assisted 13. *F.K.* in the first stages, were soon afterwards put out of action by bees.

Whilst this proceeded, *4. F.K.*, now detrained at Kange, reached Tanga at about 4.45 p.m. and was at once sent in to make a further counter-attack. But by that time *13 F.K.* was so far ahead that *4. F.K.*, instead of passing wide to the outer (right) flank as ordered, followed up to the left of *13. F.K.*, advancing northwards to deliver the final German stroke which was brought to a standstill before the British centre as darkness fell.

From nightfall until the following afternoon (5th November) Lettow's emotions alternated between hope and disappointment. Having seen the counter-attack of his right wing successfully launched, he spent some time re-organizing Baumstark's force with a view to immediate pursuit towards Ras Kasone. As it became dark he entered the town to organize a similar pursuit on his left flank; but he could find none of his troops, was fired on across the railway cutting, and turned back. From a stray party of askari he learned that the bugles which had been sounded to rally Baumstark's men[1] had been taken up all along the line as a signal to retire, and that his company commanders, giving the signal its usual peace-time meaning, had reassembled their units and marched back to their camps at Kange. For the second time Tanga was empty.

At this juncture Lettow and his small party were again fired on, this time—as we now know—by Captain Meinertzhagen's patrol,[2] and returned the fire. He then sent a runner to Kange with orders recalling the troops to the town, and himself went back to the railway-station.

The German units, somewhat exhausted after their train journey and the subsequent fighting, did not reach Tanga again until dawn (5th November). "It was not now advisable," as Lettow has said,[3] to advance against the British, whose situation was still unknown (they were in fact re-embarking); but the two old field guns which had arrived during the night opened fire on the ships, as has been related.

In the course of the morning *15. F.K.*, of Baumstark's former command, with a small coastal detachment from the south, arrived as reinforcements. Reorganizing his forces into two "battalions," Lettow prepared to meet a fresh attack, sending out patrols towards Ras Kasone. These came up against the British covering troops, drawing as has been narrated, a burst of fire all along the line;[4] and in the meantime H.M.S. *Fox* had moved up harbour and replied to the German guns. Reviewing the general situation, Lettow decided reluctantly that against an enemy in such superior force the defence of Tanga could not be

[1] See p. 90
[2] See p. 91.
[3] " My Reminiscences," p. 43.
[4] See p. 93.

maintained. At 5 p.m. he gave orders to withdraw inland to a position where defence would be easier, where warships could not support a British attack, and where the climate would be less trying.

He was in the act of completing arrangements for this when word came that a British officer had arrived under a white flag, asking for a truce in which to remove the wounded. The British, then, not the Germans, had given up the struggle ; success, not failure, was the outcome of his defence.

The German losses, as officially returned, were : Killed, 5 officers, 11 German other ranks, 55 askari ; wounded, 9 officers, 15 German other ranks, 52 askari. One German N.C.O. was taken prisoner.

Among other unhappy results of the hurried British re-embarkation was, as has been recorded, the loss of a large number of rifles, machine guns, ammunition and stores, all of which were of inestimable value to the enemy.[1] With these the Germans were enabled to re-equip three of their newly-raised companies. Still more important was, of course, the moral effect on the German askari, who from now onwards felt able to meet any troops on equal terms, an effect enhanced by mutual reaction with the notable military qualities of their Commander. " Tanga,' he afterwards wrote,[2] " was the birthday of the soldierly spirit " in our troops."

---

[1] See Lettow, " My Reminiscences," p. 45. Schnee claims the capture of 455 rifles and " half-a-million " rounds of ammunition ; Lettow claims 600,000 rounds. The 10 m.g. captured, of which 8 could be made serviceable, are inflated in some German accounts to 13 and 16. Lettow's Diary, however, records the number as 8, and it is worth noting that he adds : " The fitting of bullet proof shields is in hand "

[2] " *Was mir die Engländer über Ostafrika erzählten*," p. 31.

CHAPTER VII

ON THE DEFENSIVE: The Northern Area

November 1914—January 1915

(Sketches 2, 3, 4, 5, 6, 8, 12, 13, 14)

End Paper
(N.)
On the 6th November the Offensive Sub-Committee met to consider the situation in East Africa. A week earlier the elusive *Königsberg* had at last been located, hidden in the delta of the Rufiji,[1] and an urgent request had been made by the Navy for military help in settling accounts with her. Now there had come, though not as yet in full detail, the news of the reverse at Tanga.

On the recommendation of the Sub-Committee, it was decided that the local authorities—naval, military and civil—in East Africa should confer as to the possibility of renewing the offensive, and that Major-General Aitken should then submit proposals for the further employment of his troops, which meanwhile should be landed at Mombasa. The question of military co-operation against the *Königsberg* would remain in abeyance until the general situation became clearer.

In the exchange of telegrams which followed, Major-General Aitken not only reported unfavourably on many of his troops, but gave far higher figures for the enemy's strength than those previously accepted,[2] stating also that the Germans had been reinforced by reservists from China and Australia.

The last item was hard to believe; but it was soon evident both that previous information as to the enemy's strength had been at fault, and that the troops were in no condition to undertake any early resumption of the offensive.

Accordingly on the 17th November the Secretary of State for India telegraphed to Major-General Aitken: " I " am reluctantly compelled to accept your opinion that we " must temporarily adopt a defensive role, as no reinforce- " ments are available at present." He added a suggestion

---

[1] Naval Operations, Vol. I, p. 338.

[2] Major-General Aitken's estimate was that he was opposed at Tanga by 2,000 Germans with 2,000 askari, and that the total strength of the enemy in East Africa was at least 5,000 Germans, 9,000 askari. See p. 105, f.n. 3, and Chap. III, Note II.

that the two Indian expeditionary forces, I.E.F. " B " and
I.E.F. " C ", should become a single force organised in two
brigades for the defence of the British protectorates.[1]

At the same time the Colonial Secretary, telegraphing to
Sir Henry Belfield that he was " much impressed by the lack
" of accurate information as shown by the result of the
" Tanga operation, " enquired " whether arrangements had
" been made for an intelligence department, and whether the
" results were satisfactory." To this came the prompt reply
that an Intelligence Department " had been most effectively
" organized and conducted . . . but its sphere of action
" had been limited to the vicinity of the German boundary.
" No opportunity had occurred of acquiring any information
" in regard to the strength and distribution of the German
" forces except such as could be deduced from unreliable
" native statements."

It is perhaps hardly surprising that now, in view of the
East African situation as a whole, it was decided by the
Cabinet to make a change in the responsibility for the conduct of the campaign. On the 22nd November 1914 control
of the operations was taken over by the War Office.

REORGANIZATION OF I.E.F. " B "

Meanwhile the various units of I.E.F. " B " had been
landed at Mombasa, re-equipped so far as local resources
would allow, and distributed so as to strengthen the defence
of the East African Protectorate, in order more especially
to ensure the security of the Uganda Railway. On the 8th
November the 2/Loyal North Lancashire and the 98th
Mountain Battery R.A., the units in best condition, were
despatched to Nairobi ; the Faridkot Sappers and half-
battalion 3/Kashmir Rifles to Voi.[2] Added protection to the
railway was given by the 25th and 26th Railway Coys.,
Sappers & Miners, with personnel and armament for the
armoured train, while on the coast the garrison of Gazi was
reinforced by the 2/Kashmir Rifles. The other units of I.E.F.
" B ", in greater need of re-organization, remained at
Mombasa.

---

[1] The telegram was repeated to India and drew a protest against " the
" obvious and complete reversion to the defensive which appeared to be
" contemplated."

[2] At Voi the 3/Kashmir Rifles reinforced the 3/K.A.R., to whose C.O.,
Lieutenant-Colonel B. R. Graham, seconded from the Corps of Guides,
the Kashmir Rifles were indebted for valuable training in bush warfare.

The apprehensions created in adjacent dependencies by the news of the enemy's success at Tanga led to urgent calls for military help from various directions. From Uganda came a request for reinforcements for the southern border there. The Resident at Zanzibar renewed his demands for a stronger garrison. Still more urgent was the Navy's request for aid in dealing with the *Königsberg*, now that she had been found and was penned in.

NAVAL OPERATIONS

The naval aspect of the operations against the *Königsberg* has been described elsewhere.[1] With these the military authorities in East Africa immediately became concerned, in consequence of the request by the Royal Navy for military assistance. H.M.S. *Chatham*, Captain S. R. Drury-Lowe, R.N., which had located the *Königsberg* on the 30th October, was herself too large to approach nearer than five miles from the Simba Uranga mouth of the Rufiji delta, on both banks of which the enemy was reported to have established land defences. Captain Drury-Lowe's proposal to ask for troops to cope with these was warmly endorsed by the Admiralty,[2] and on the 2nd November he reported that he had made a request accordingly. But at this date I.E.F. " B " was off Tanga, where for the next few days that force was fully occupied with the unhappy operations already described. It was not, therefore, until after the return of the force to Mombasa that attention could be given to the problem of the *Königsberg*.[3]

As soon as I.E.F. " B " returned, Brigadier-General Tighe, at Captain Drury-Lowe's request and by order of the India Office, was ordered to report on the Rufiji situation, and late on the 8th November he left Mombasa in H.M.S. *Fox* to join the blockading squadron. He found on his arrival next day that all was in readiness to sink a block-ship in the channel—an operation successfully carried

Sketch 12

---

[1] See " Naval Operations," Vol. I, pp. 374-5.

[2] " Destruction or capture of *Königsberg* is matter of highest import-" ance. . . . Do you require troops ? Ask for whatever you want which is " locally available, but act with promptitude. Keep Admiralty informed " but don't delay action." Admiralty telegram, 1st November 1914.

[3] None of the available papers of I.E.F. " B " record the receipt of any communication on this subject before 7th November. On that date Captain Drury-Lowe informed the Admiralty, and communicated to Major-General Aitken his opinion, that " half a battalion of troops reinforced by " detachments from the ships would be sufficient to deal with the hostile " parties . . . on shore."

out on the 10th November—and that the German collier *Somali*, which had accompanied the *Königsberg*, had been burned out as the result of shell-fire.

The landing of troops, however, whether to eliminate land defences and thus make possible an attack by improvised torpedo-craft, or to establish a spotting-station for co-operation with the two aircraft now due to arrive from South Africa, was a more difficult matter. The extent and strength of the German defences were concealed by dense forest and mangrove swamps. Apart from a captured German chart of the river-channels, no proper maps were available. In the shallows off the coast the ships could not come within effective range of the concealed defences, nor could the light craft alone give sufficient support to the landing party. The grim experience of Tanga only a week earlier was all too vividly in mind. It was evident that experienced troops, and more than a half-battalion, would be necessary. On the 13th November, after careful reconnaissance and consultation with the naval commander, Brigadier-General Tighe reported that not less than 1½ battalions of good troops would be required.

In Major-General Aitken's view this was out of the question. Both to Simla and to London he reported that less than 4,000 of the infantry in East Africa could be considered reliable ; that from these, in view of the German menace to the British protectorates, he could by no means detach so many as 1½ battalions ; and that the proposed operation " might lead to a disaster ".[1]

The lessons of Tanga had sunk in ; and since at this time there was no possibility of sending either reinforcements or additional vessels suitable to support a landing, the project of providing co-operation on land against the *Königsberg* was perforce abandoned. The naval blockade of the delta continued.[2]

---

[1] " . . . I consider it of the first importance that the enemy's trenches, " which are protected by Q.F. guns, maxims and rifle fire, should be shelled " first, and as this cannot be done I feel unable conscientiously to advise " carrying out this operation, which, seeing how unsupported the infantry " would be, would not only be most hazardous, but might lead to a " disaster." Telegram 14th November 1914.

[2] On 28th and 30th November 1914 Dar-es-Salaam was bombarded by H.M.Ss. *Goliath* and *Fox* (see "Naval Operations," Vol. II, pp. 236–7). This operation was of no military value ; the palace of the German governor was among the buildings destroyed, as to which a British officer later wrote : " We bitterly regretted the loss of this large building when we were " at our wits' end for hospital accommodation after we had occupied " Dar-es-Salaam in 1916."

MINOR OPERATIONS INLAND

Inland, between the sea and Lake Victoria, few events of military importance occurred during November and December 1914. On the 17th November, acting on reports received from Masai natives, a detachment of the East Africa Mounted Rifles occupied Longido, which had been evacuated by the enemy on the 6th. It was followed by a force of all arms about 600 strong, which established itself on the mountain, with its line of communication to Kajiado protected by fortified posts at Lone Hill, Kedongai and the Besil river.

Sketch 6

Farther west the barren lands of the Masai, lacking communications and water, were unsuited for military operations. The Masai themselves, intolerant of discipline and with little liking for the white man, afforded no source of recruits to either side, though a few exceptions among them did fine work as scouts and observers. Except for a minor German raid into their territory in mid-December[1] no military events occurred in this area.

Sketch 13

On the eastern shores of Lake Victoria, where the border had been closely watched by scouts and hunters since the affair at Kisii[2] in September, the enemy had begun in October to assemble troops south of the Mara river, with forward posts at Utegi and Mohuru Bay. Early in November, after a clash between a strong patrol of the 4/K.A.R. and a German patrol from the south, a troop of the East Africa Mounted Rifles known as " Ross's Scouts ",[3] 40 strong, under Major C. J. Ross, D.S.O., was sent as an independent force to reinforce the border ; and on the 17th November this troop, together with " E " Coy., 4/K.A.R., under Major R. F. B. Knox, established defended camps in the Suna and Butende

---

[1] To deal with this, on 11th December one coy. 2/Loyal N. Lancs. and one coy. 1/K.A.R., under Major H. A. Robinson, 2/Loyal N. Lancs., left Nairobi for Magadi Lake and made a trying march, in tropical heat with little water, to the western heights of the Great Rift valley. Touch was gained with Lord Delamere, but the raiders avoided action and retreated behind the German border. On 26th December the British force was withdrawn.

[2] See p. 39.   During October this area had been placed under the orders of O.C. Troops, Uganda (Lieutenant-Colonel L. H. Hickson), for purposes of military administration and command.

[3] Major Ross, not a regular officer, resigned his commission in December, 1914. Some of the European volunteers of his troop followed suit, and subsequently the remains of it, under Lieutenant (afterwards Major) J. J. Drought, evolved into what became known as Drought's Scouts or the " Skin Corps."

areas, from which they raided German territory, meeting little opposition.

Eleven days later (28th) Ross rode boldly into the German lake port of Shirati, to find it evacuated, and then to be shelled out of it the same afternoon by a British lake steamer which chanced to select that day for action against the place. Returning next day to Butende, Ross sent out on the 1st December a detachment of K.A.R. and Police, about 50 strong, which had a sharp fight with a small German force at Susuni, losing one officer and two askari killed, before darkness enabled the enemy to disengage and withdraw.

For some weeks thereafter nothing beyond occasional patrol skirmishes took place.[1] Karungu, a place hitherto of no importance, was developed as a base for future operations.

OPERATIONS ON LAKE VICTORIA

After the affair at Karungu on the 15th September,[2] in **Sketch 3** which the *Winifred* had been beaten off mainly by the guns of the German tug *Muansa*, it was decided to arm some of the British flotilla on Lake Victoria, which hitherto had been hampered by lack of armament and by being kept to maintain communications across the head of the lake. By the end of October the *Winifred*, *Kavirondo* and *Sir William Mackinnon* had been equipped each with a 12-pdr. gun manned by naval ratings, and with lighter weapons.

These ships and the *Sybil* then cruised about the lake, searching for the *Muansa* in particular, raiding hostile craft generally, and seeking out German dumps of food and wood fuel. On the 28th October the *Winifred*, which not long before had engaged German troops on shore at Kaienzi Bay, shelled the German wireless station at Bukoba, though with poor success ; three days later a landing party from the *Sybil* destroyed a German gun on Juma island. Unluckily the *Sybil*, on the 5th November, struck a rock off the headland of Majita and had to be beached there. Efforts to salve her proving fruitless, she was disabled and left. Soon afterwards the three armed vessels were recalled to protect the unarmed steamer plying between Entebbe and Kisumu,

---

[1] The British force, under Major Knox, concentrated at Suna Camp ; the main German force remained south of the Mara.

[2] See p. 41, f.n. 2.

an unknown craft having been reported in that part of the lake ; but no enemy was seen. Patrolling of both the eastern and the western shores was then resumed and kept up for some weeks without further incident.[1]

OPERATIONS IN UGANDA

Sketch 8   It will be remembered that by the beginning of October the slender British forces in Uganda had pushed forward to the line of the Kagera.[2] The principal points held were Kifumbiro (Kyaka fort), Kimwa, and the high ground of Kanabulem, the detachment on the latter finding also a guard at Mushenyi Ferry across the mouth of the Kagera, with an advanced post beyond the river, facing Mitaga. Farther west were observation posts at Kiemsambi and Nsongezi. Headquarters remained at Sanji, covered by an entrenched position at Simba.[3]

After the news of the reverse at Tanga it was expected that the Germans at Bukoba, now known to have been reinforced and estimated at 800 strong, would attempt to regain their territory along the Kagera. Of this the first sign was a German force seen opposite Kiemsambi on the 16th November. The post there was reinforced by 75 of the Uganda Police with a machine gun, and in response to a call made to Nairobi for reinforcements a company of the 4/K.A.R. was released from Kisii, while the 13th Rajputs were detached from the main British forces to Uganda.[4]

On the 20th November the enemy attacked the British posts at the river crossings along the line of the Kagera from Kifumbiro to the Lake. The main attack was made, by a force estimated at more than 400 strong, against Kifumbiro, where a temporary bridge had been built and a British garrison established in the former German fort, Kyaka, on the southern bank. At the same time a German

---

[1] A German wireless message decoded on 10th December revealed a plan derived from the British seizures of wood fuel : it was proposed to dump at suitable spots tempting piles of logs, among which one or two were to be hollow and filled with dynamite. There is no record of this having in fact been done.

[2] See p. 16.

[3] The total force available at this time was : K.A.R. Reserve Coy. (at Sanji), 125 ; Uganda Police, 377 ; Baganda levies, about 2,000.

[4] The 13th entrained at Mombasa on 19th November, and on 22nd embarked at Kisumu for passage across the lake.

force about 200 strong with a machine gun moving along the lake shore from Kigarama, drove in the small British outpost on this flank, which fell back to make a successful stand at Mushenyi Ferry. In the centre an attack on Kimwa was also checked.

At Kyaka fort a successful defence was maintained throughout the day. By a pre-arranged plan,[1] however, it had been decided to withdraw from Kyaka, so as to draw an attacking enemy northwards until his retreat could be cut off by a flanking thrust from Kimwa ; and accordingly Kyaka was evacuated after dark, the temporary bridge destroyed, and the garrison withdrawn through Rukuba to Kiasimbi.[2]

The intended counterstroke, unfortunately, could not be made. The posts lower down the river were kept fully engaged by the enemy, and on further German reinforcements being reported the Kimwa detachment was withdrawn to Minziro. Meanwhile the Germans following up the Kyaka garrison pushed as far as the hills about Kabuoba, securing also their right flank at Itarra, where they drove back a reconnoitring patrol from Minziro on the 23rd November.

After the arrival of reinforcements during the ensuing week, the defensive force was reorganized.[3] It had been ascertained that not more than about 400 German troops were north of the Kagera. Lieutenant-Colonel Hickson decided to pass to the offensive, attacking the enemy's main body at Gombaizi with his own main force, and with his detachment from Minziro clearing the enemy off Itarra and intercepting the German retreat. He moved off at midnight 5th/6th December.

---

[1] The plan was laid down in instructions sent from H.Q., Uganda, on 14th October 1914.

[2] British casualties were seven wounded.

The German force engaged appears to have consisted of 25 Germans, 230 trained and 30 recruit askari, 35 Arabs, 160 irregulars, with one gun and three m.g., under Captain Bock von Wülfingen.

A German account speaks of the British having " here, as at other " places, shown themselves masters of the art of holding small defended " localities [*Kleinbefestigungskunst*], so thoroughly that an assault could " not be carried through." (Arning, *Vier Jahre Weltkrieg*, p. 206.)

[3] The main body, concentrated at Kiasimbi, under Lieutenant-Colonel L. H. Hickson, 4/K.A.R., now consisted of " D " Coy., 4/K.A.R. ; two coys. (less detachment at Simba), 13th Rajputs; 150 Uganda Police; one section 28th Mtn. Bty., R.A. ; one " battery " (four m.g.), K.A.R.

At Minziro were the reserve coy., 4/K.A.R. (125 strong), with 40 Uganda Police ; and on the Kanabulem ridge, two coys. 13th Rajputs.

The main attack met no opposition worth mentioning. Taken by surprise, the Germans hastily evacuated Gombaizi and retreated rapidly southwards. The flanking attack was equally successful in driving the enemy off Itarra, and pushed on to Kabakorongo, but was not in time to cut off the retreating Germans, who were able to recross the Kagera and stand at Kyaka fort. On the night of the 6th Hickson encamped at Rukuba.

Advancing next day (7th), he shelled Kyaka, silencing a German gun ; but his artillery made no impression on the thick stone walls of the fort, and he found the enemy also holding a strong position on the northern bank which he considered it inadvisable to attack without better artillery support. He therefore withdrew to Rukuba and established himself strongly there.

No further offensive was attempted on either side. The climate of the Kagera valley seriously affected all except the locally-raised troops, fever and dysentery taking heavy toll of British and Indians alike, while the artillery was immobilized by horse-sickness among the mules. For some months to come, beyond occasional patrol skirmishes, all was at a standstill along the Kagera.[1]

THE VOI-TSAVO AREA

Sketch 4　　Along the two main lines of approach to German territory, the Tsavo valley and the Voi-Taveta road, no particular change of dispositions was made up to about the end of November. Forward defended camps were maintained at Mzima and Maktau, opposed to which were German camps on the lower slopes of Kilimanjaro about Rombo, and positions along the Lumi river, notably one on Salaita Hill. An outlying post farther north, held by Somali M.I. of the K.A.R.,[2] was established at Loosoito, while to the south a K.A.R. detachment watched the border from Kasigao.

---

[1] On 1st December 1914 Major E. H. T. Lawrence left Kampala to assume command of all the Uganda Police in the field, which he organized as a battalion, now to be known as the Uganda Police Service Battalion.

In January 1915 the southern Uganda border was organized for police purposes in three sections, known respectively as the Ankole, Kigezi and Masaka districts.

[2] Mainly to protect Masai herdsmen against German raids. In January 1915 the M.I. were relieved by one Coy., 2/Kashmir Rifles, under Major R. A. Lyall, which soon afterwards moved south to Epiron, where it remained for some weeks undisturbed.

In all this area there were frequent patrol encounters, often at close quarters in thick bush, especially in the Tsavo valley.[1] Despite constant vigilance German raids on the railway increased in frequency and in audacity, piquets being attacked and trains being stopped or derailed by bombs on the line. The total damage was slight, but the effect of constant and often fruitless pursuit in the bush was harassing.[2]

REORGANIZATION

Meanwhile the forces in East Africa were reorganized **Sketch 2** as a whole. The two Indian expeditionary forces were amalgamated and redistributed in two commands known as the Mombasa Area and Nairobi Area, under Brigadier-Generals Tighe and Stewart respectively, the former area extending to Kilimanjaro and the latter including Uganda.

Major-General Aitken, in consultation with the local authorities, decided that the best line for an eventual offensive would be by way of Voi to Taveta and Moshi. On the 23rd November, the War Office having assumed control on the previous day, he telegraphed proposing that as a first step a railway should be built along this line. The local Government saw no commercial value in the proposal, but he stressed its military advantages and on this ground asked to retain the railway material and expert personnel which had accompanied his force from India.[3]

Soon afterwards Major-General Aitken was succeeded in command by Brigadier-General Wapshare.[4] In notifying the latter of his appointment, the Secretary of State for War

---

[1] Regarding these a K.A.R. officer wrote : " . . . patrol activity was " even more hampered by rhinos than by the Germans. . . . On one " occasion . . . a whole K.A.R. company was completely routed by a " charge of three rhinos. Every carrier dropped his load and fled back to " Mzima. . . . The operation was abandoned. . . ."

[2] Attempts were even made to use a privately owned kennel of lion-hunting bloodhounds, but without success, scent usually being cold before they could arrive from Voi. The only effectual counter-measures were found to be (i) to clear the thorn-bush back on both sides of the line, forming a rough abattis, (ii) a continuous line of whitewash along the red earth of the permanent way (which was not ballasted).

[3] On 17th November Lieutenant-Colonel J. Sutherland, Asst. Dir. of Railways, I.E.F. " B," had been directed to reconnoitre for a route to Maktau and beyond. He reported favourably on 20th November, and a detailed survey was then put in hand.

[4] See p. 100.

Major-General Aitken left on 17th December. Brigadier-General Wapshare was then given temporary rank as major-general.

laid down that a defensive attitude must be adopted, it being impossible to foresee a date at which reinforcements could be sent. Minor offensive measures, however, if considered feasible locally, might be undertaken. In reply to further enquiry as to possible alternatives, the new commander gave his views.

A railway forward from Voi would take, he estimated, four months to reach Bura and two more to reach Taveta. Since this line could not be ready in time to enable the offensive to be renewed before the rains began in April, he did not recommend its construction. For a fresh offensive he would require at least two more infantry brigades, a regiment of Indian cavalry and an additional mountain battery; given these, the former plan of a main landing at Tanga combined with an advance inland against the Kilimanjaro area could be carried out.

At this stage of the war, when every available man was needed in more vital theatres, no such reinforcement of East Africa could be considered. The resumption of the offensive was therefore postponed; for the time being all that could be done was to maintain the existing position, and to improve it by means of such minor enterprises as might be found practicable. This having been decided, the troops were redistributed accordingly.[1]

---

[1] At the end of November 1914 the distribution was as follows:
Uganda:
    13th Rajputs; 2 Coys. 4/K.A.R.; 1 sect. 28th Mtn. Bty., R.A.; 350 Uganda Police; 2,500 levies.
Eastern Lake Area:
    Two Coys. 4/K.A.R.; Ross's Scouts, E.A.M.R.
Nairobi:
    G.H.Q.; 2/L. North Lancs. (less 2 Coys.); 98th Infantry (less 2 Coys.); 29th Punjabis and K.A.R., details; 28th Mtn. Bty., R.A. (less 1 section); 25th and 26th (Railway) Coys., S. & M.; 300 Police.
Magadi Area:
    29th Punjabis (less 2 Coys.); 2 Coys. 2/L. North Lancs.; half Bn. Rampur Infantry; half Bn. Kapurthala Infantry; 1 Coy. 1/K.A.R.; 1 Coy. 3/K.A.R.; 4 sqdns. E.A.M.R.; 27th Mtn. Bty., R.A.; Calcutta Volunteer Bty. (less 1 sect.); E.A. Pioneer Coy.
Voi-Tsavo Area:
    2 Coys. 29th Punjabis; 2 Coys. 98th Infantry; 61st (K.G.O.) Pioneers; half Bn. 3/Kashmir Rifles; half Bn. Bharatpur Infantry; 3 Coys. 1/K A.R.; 1 Coy. 3/K.A.R.; 1 Coy. 4/K.A.R.; half Coy. M.I., K.A.R.; one sect. 27th Mtn. Bty., R.A.; 1 sect. Calcutta Volr. Bty.; 1 naval 12-pdr. gun; Faridkot Sappers; Somali Scouts.

Continued at foot of next page.

Concurrently with the redistribution of the troops the duties of the Staff were also reorganized. By contrast with the inadequate intelligence service of the British forces, an elaborate German spy system was discovered. To deal with this, new Martial Law regulations were introduced by the Governor. These and the censorship were administered by Brigadier-General Malleson, the I.G.C.[1] At the same time the intelligence service was taken over by Captain R. Meinertzhagen, whose organization expanded and steadily increased in efficiency as time went on.

A host of difficult problems confronted the administrative staff, compelled as they were to reconcile widely varying regulations, requirements and practice of the British, Indian and Colonial services in such matters as food, munitions, pay and allowances. Many of these problems were never satisfactorily solved;[2] but the defence of the British territories seemed assured, with a margin for more active operations in due time.

Continued from previous page.

Coastal Area :
  2/Kashmir Rifles ; half Bn. Jind Infantry ; 2 Coys. 3/K.A.R. ; Arab Coy. ; Volunteer m.g. Bty.
Giriama Area :
  2 Coys. 3/K.A.R.
Zanzibar :
  1 Coy. 3/K.A.R.
Mombasa (Reserve) :
  63rd P.L.I. ; 101st Grenadiers.

In addition one and a half coys. 3/K.A.R. and police detachments were in posts on the northern frontier of B.E.A. and Uganda, and some companies of Baluchees troops in the Turkana area.

In January 1915, at Major-General Wapshare's request, one sqdn. 17th Cavalry and the 130th Baluchis (Jacob's Rifles) were sent from India, the former intended especially for patrol work in the open country about Longido, which was free from tsetse. One (Pathan) company of the 130th Baluchis having been disbanded for insubordination at Rangoon, the battalion was brought up to strength by attaching one company from the 46th Punjabis. It reached Voi early in February 1915, the cavalry squadron at the same time going to the Longido area.

[1] On 9th December 1914 Major-General Wapshare specially requested that Brigadier-General Malleson should be retained for this purpose.

[2] For example, by February 1916 the Indian Mountain Artillery units had to deal with paymasters in Great Britain, India, East Africa and South Africa. Even so late as 1917 two columns in the field, one mostly Indian troops and one mainly K.A.R., were differently equipped, rationed and maintained.

A further difficulty, less felt at this time than later, lay in the fact that the principal means of communication—the railway—had to serve the needs not only of the troops but of the entire civil population both of B.E.A. and of Uganda.

OPERATIONS IN THE UMBA VALLEY

Sketch 5 In the coastal area the British forces had, it will be remembered, been withdrawn in September to Gazi, with outposts near Kikoneni and on the Ramisi river. South of the latter the Germans had been, since then, free to ravage the evacuated British territory, with the result that the native population had fled northwards in increasing numbers. By the end of November some 5,000 of these fugitives were being sheltered and fed, and Major-General Wapshare decided that the British territory must be freed from the Germans infesting it.

It was known that these were only small detachments, mainly between Majoreni and the Umba river; but behind them larger forces were reported south of Jasin, at Duga and Kilulu. To deal with them it was decided to employ a force about 1,800 strong, with 6 machine guns,[1] under Brigadier-General Tighe. The transport requirements of this force were met entirely by carriers, there being no made roads or tracks south of Gazi, and the whole area being notoriously unhealthy and beset with tsetse fly. In all some 5,500 carriers had to be employed.

By the 16th December the main body of the force was assembled and ready, in the Msambweni area near the coast; inland the Jind Infantry half-battalion went forward to Kikoneni, while the Scout company was at Mwele Mdogo. Further to assist the intended operation, arrangements were made for naval demonstrations along the coast, in particular at Manza Bay and Moa, which it was hoped would keep the enemy from reinforcing his forward posts.

Next day (17th) the force moved off. The advanced guard, under Lieutenant-Colonel H. A. Vallings—two companies of the 3/K.A.R. supported by a half-battalion of the 2/Kashmir Rifles and a machine gun section—crossed the Ramisi river unopposed, halted that night at Kidimu, and on the following afternoon (18th) crossed the Mwena, leaving behind a detachment to re-establish the former defended post at Majoreni. Driving off a few hostile patrols south of the Mwena, the advanced guard halted at Kasiagano, where it remained for twenty-four hours whilst the main body closed up and its own patrols reconnoitred the Umba

---

[1] Composition: 101st Grenadiers; 2/Kashmir Rifles; half Bn. Jind Infantry; " B," " D " Coys. 3/K.A.R.; one Arab coy.; one coy. Scouts (Indian and Arab); two m.g. sections.

valley. It was now joined by the flanking column of the Jind Infantry, which had spent two nights camped on Mrima hill, and later by the Scout company, which had traversed the whole area inland between Mwele Mdogo and Jombo hill, passing through Mwamkuchi, Kengeja and Bandu.

On the 20th December the force went forward to the Umba, driving weak German patrols back across that river. Thanks to the skilful bush tactics and fighting qualities of the two K.A.R. companies in the vanguard[1] the operation had so far gone without a hitch and almost without a casualty. The absence of opposition was largely due to the naval demonstrations farther south, which had most successfully effected their purpose ;[2] no substantial reinforcements reached the German outposts along the Umba. The river was in high flood.

Next day (21st), the advanced guard forced a passage practically unopposed[3] and found Vanga deserted. The southern bank of the river, though elaborately prepared for defence, was also clear of the enemy, whose nearest post was at Jasin,[4] within gun range of the north bank.

Early on Christmas Day Jasin was attacked by the two companies of the 3/K.A.R. with one company of the 101st Grenadiers, all under Captain T. O. FitzGerald, K.A.R. The German outposts, taken by surprise, were rushed with the bayonet, and after a short engagement the garrison was driven out, with little loss on either side.[5]

British territory being now clear of the enemy, Brigadier-General Tighe disposed his force to hold the border. Establishing a base at Moa, so that supplies could be received by sea instead of by carriers overland, he decided to keep the

---

[1] " These K.A.R. companies were invaluable, and were used as a substitute for light cavalry, always in contact with hostile patrols." Report by Brigadier-General Tighe, 3rd January 1915.

[2] On 18th December H.M.S. *Fox*, with the auxiliary cruiser *Kinfauns Castle*, made a demonstration off Tanga. At the same time the transports *Barjora* and *Rheinfels*, under Commander Headlam, R.I.M., carrying one coy. 63rd P.L.I. and a sect. 28th Mtn. Bty. R.A., having made a feint of landing at Moa, went on to Manza Bay, where some small craft were made prizes. Reconnaissance showed that landing at the latter place would be feasible but that at Moa the bush was too thick.

[3] German reports alleged a panic in the German Arab units.

[4] Called by the Germans Jassini. The place, a fair-sized village, was evacuated by the Germans on 23rd December on the approach of a K.A.R. detachment, but was re-occupied next day in somewhat greater strength (reported as 50 men).

[5] British casualties, two o.r. killed, three o.r. wounded ; German, one officer, six o.r. killed.

bulk of his troops encamped on the north bank of the Umba, near its mouth, with advanced posts on the south bank, three companies at Jasin and four at Samanya. Farther inland a half battalion of the 101st, with Wavell's Arabs and two machine guns, was posted at Bwaga Macho, while Lieutenant Jones's scout company patrolled the upper reaches of the Mwena.

On the 27th December these dispositions were completed. Jasin was found to be unoccupied by the enemy, and in its vicinity a strongly defended camp was established among sisal plantations which formed a good natural all-round obstacle. This post, it was considered, was far enough forward to ensure ample warning of any German advance from the south, and Brigadier-General Tighe was directed to go no farther. No events of military importance occurred during the next fortnight ; but in the unhealthy climate of the Umba valley sickness among the troops increased to a disquieting extent, much to the detriment of their fighting value.

OCCUPATION OF MAFIA ISLAND

Sketch 12   As an aid to the Royal Navy in their operations against the *Königsberg*,[1] it was suggested by Captain Drury-Lowe, R.N., in December that Mafia Island, lying some 10 miles off the mouth of the Rufiji, a potential source of help to the German cruiser and well-placed to be of use as a base from which to operate against her, should be occupied as soon as troops could be made available. The German garrison was reported to be only some 30 strong. The proposal was agreed to, and on the 8th January 1915 Lieutenant-Colonel L. E. S. Ward, K.A.R., embarked at Mombasa, with a force, numbering about 500, to carry it into effect.[2]

That night H.M.S. *Fox*, after searching the shores of Mafia Island, anchored in Chole Bay, where she was joined next evening (9th) by the *Kinfauns Castle* with the troops. So far as was known, the German detachment was encamped on high ground near Ngombeni, at the southern end of the island.

---

[1] See " Naval Operations," Vol. II, pp. 237-238.

[2] Composition : four (single) coys. 1/K.A.R., with two m.g., and one coy. 101st Grenadiers. The force was followed next day (9th) by one coy. 63rd P.L.I., detailed as permanent garrison of the island.

On the 10th January the British force landed on the thickly bush-clad cape at Kisimani, some four miles from Ngombeni, while H.M.S. *Weymouth* and small craft watched the remaining coast-line of the island. The landing was unopposed, and reconnoitring parties found the natives friendly. Reconnaissance established that the Germans were in fact entrenched at Ngombeni.

There Lieutenant-Colonel Ward attacked them successfully on the morning of the 11th January, driving the remnants of the defence into the bush and capturing the German commander, Lieutenant Schiller, severely wounded.[1] Early on the 12th Ward's force, supported from the sea by the *Fox*, moved on to Kilindoni, which was occupied by 9 a.m., no resistance being offered. The same afternoon the German Government official in charge of the island made an unconditional surrender.

The company of the 63rd Palamcottah Light Infantry detailed as garrison, under Lieutenant-Colonel J. D. Mackay, was then landed, and the remaining troops re-embarked for Mombasa. These latter, however, while on passage were diverted to Vanga in relief of units affected by the bad climate of the Umba valley.

UMBA VALLEY OPERATIONS : SECOND PHASE

Up to the 11th January 1915 Brigadier-General Tighe's **Sketches, 5, 14** forces in the Jasin area remained undisturbed. The defended camp at Jasin was held by two (single) companies, reinforced during daylight by a third sent out from the camp known as Umba Camp on the Umba river. The enemy, in no great strength, was known to be at Duga and Kilulu, six to eight miles away.[2]

On the 12th January a German force consisting of *4. Sch.K.* and half of *15. F.K.* attacked Jasin, attempting to envelop the place from the north. The attack was held by

---

[1] British casualties were : killed, one o.r. ; wounded, three officers, seven o.r. German losses are given as two killed, five wounded, excluding Lieutenant Schiller. The latter, with his wife, was sent to hospital at Zanzibar, with orders from Major-General Wapshare that on recovery both were to be liberated on parole in return for the release of two British officers captured at Jasin (see p. 127).

[2] It is now known that Lettow had already decided to make an attack in force on the British detachment at Jasin. Six coys. from Kilimanjaro were brought to Tanga by rail, and by the second week of January nine coys. in all were concentrated south of Jasin.

the two companies of the 2/Kashmir Rifles then at the camp, assisted by a company of the 3/K.A.R. from Umba Camp, which stopped the enemy's northern advance at a sisal factory at the ford over the Suba river. Meanwhile, in response to a call for help, two companies of the Jind Infantry and a section of the 28th Mountain Battery, R.A., arrived from Umba Camp. These drove off the enemy from the sisal factory, and the whole German force withdrew towards Duga.[1]

In consequence of this affair Jasin was reinforced by an additional (single) company, from which a detachment 40 strong established a defended post at the sisal factory ; defences generally were strengthened, and additional food and water stored.

Four days later a German force, estimated at three companies, again attacked, and was again driven off by the garrison—now found by the 2/Kashmir Rifles and a company of the 3/K.A.R.—and by reinforcements from Umba Camp.

The climate, however, had by this time affected all the British troops, and the arrival on the 17th January of the *Barjora* with the four companies of the 1/K.A.R. which had taken part in the capture of Mafia Island, to replace the two companies of the 3/K.A.R. which had hitherto borne the brunt in the Umba valley, was a welcome relief. At Jasin the garrison now consisted of one company of the 101st Grenadiers and two of the 2/Kashmir Rifles, the latter finding the post at the sisal factory ; the whole under Colonel Raghbir Singh, commanding 2/Kashmir Rifles, with Captains G. J. G. Hanson and J. Turner.

At daybreak on the 18th January Jasin was heavily attacked. Its S.O.S. rockets gave the alarm at Umba Camp, and fortunately the usual daily detachment from that camp—on this occasion a company of the 101st—arrived as the attack opened, in time to join the garrison.[2] From Umba Camp Lieutenant-Colonel P. H. Cunningham, temporarily in command, at once sent up three companies of

---

[1] British casualties were five o.r. wounded. German casualties were reported as : killed, four o.r. ; wounded and missing, three Germans, three o.r. ; wounded, 14 o.r.

[2] Excluding 40 of the 2/Kashmir Rifles at the sisal factory, the garrison is believed to have consisted of : 101st Grenadiers, 138 ; 2/Kashmir Rif., 144 ; K.A.R. m.g., 9 ; signallers, 5 ; total 296.

K.A.R.[1] under Captain G. J. Giffard, 1/K.A.R., to the Suba river north of Jasin, where they were checked by heavy fire from a low bush-covered ridge overlooking the river. It seemed that the enemy had surrounded both Jasin Camp and the sisal factory, the latter being especially strongly attacked.

Captain Giffard, directing the two companies of the 3/K.A.R. to attack across the river, endeavoured with his own company of the 1/K.A.R. to relieve the sisal factory ; but in the face of considerably superior hostile strength both attempts proved unsuccessful. The 3/K.A.R. companies, which in a determined and well-led rush had gained the southern bank of the Suba, were obliged after two hours' hard fighting to fall back across the river, and Giffard had no option but to reorganize and call for reinforcements. Meanwhile the troops inland, from Samanya and Bwaga Macho, were on the way ; but these were not destined to render any help.[2] After a temporary lull the attack was renewed, both Jasin camp and the sisal factory being subjected to very heavy rifle and machine gun fire. The fire was answered with great spirit by the Indian troops, but their fire discipline was at fault, and by 11 a.m. the Kashmir Rifles at the factory had fired their last round. They had no thought of surrender. Led by Subadar Mardan Ali, they charged out with bayonets and kukris, scattering into the bush, and eventually 29 of the 40 reached Umba Camp.

On receipt of Giffard's report, Lieutenant-Colonel Cunningham sent up the remaining three companies of the 1/K.A.R.,[3] two (single) companies of Jind Infantry, and the

---

[1] " B " Coy. 1/K.A.R., Captain G. J. Giffard ; " B," " D " Coys., 3/K.A.R., Captain T. O. FitzGerald. In addition, "A," " C," " E " Coys. 1/K.A.R. were then still on board the *Barjora*. Disembarkation was hampered by lack of boats, and the track from the improvised pier to the camp lay through mangrove swamps.

[2] One and a half coys., 2/Kashmir Rifles, under Major Haidar Ali Khan, which left Samanya at 7.40 a.m. and drove off a German patrol near Chuini, reached the Suba north of the sisal factory at 9 a.m. Held up by heavy fire here, they turned left to gain touch with the main force, and eventually reached Umba Camp, where they remained.

From Bwaga Macho two coys. 101st Grenadiers, with half the Arab coy., reached Samanya at 9.40 a.m. By some error they then followed the left bank of the Umba, became isolated in the bush, and finally returned to Samanya.

[3] "A" and " C " Coys. reached the fighting line ; " E " Coy., last to disembark, remained in reserve near the Umba river.

At Umba Camp two coys. 101st Grenadiers and two coys. Jind Infantry were retained for defence of the camp.

section of the 28th Mountain Battery R.A.   The latter was
soon engaged at only 300 yards range with German machine
guns which were quickly put out of action, after which it
repulsed with " shrapnel, zero " fire a German attempt to
rush the guns with the bayonet.[1]

Dispositions were then made for a fresh counter-attack,
the 1/K.A.R. companies on the right being directed against
the sisal factory while the Jind Infantry in the centre and
3/K.A.R. on the left were to cross the Suba below the factory
and advance direct on Jasin.   The enemy's fire had again
died down, but the hostile dispositions in the bush along the
farther bank of the Suba could not be made out.

At noon the attack was launched, the Jind companies
firing three preliminary volleys before charging across the
river.   As they reached the farther shore a devastating
cross-fire was opened upon them, and with the loss of nearly
half their numbers[2] they were compelled to retreat to the
northern bank.

On the right the 1/K.A.R. were also brought to a standstill.   On the left the 3/K.A.R., crossing the Suba once more,
held their ground on the southern bank notwithstanding the
withdrawal of the Jind Infantry in the centre ; but no
further progress could be made, and soon these companies
in turn were ordered back across the river.

By this time it was evident that the enemy was in some
strength.   Brigadier-General Tighe, who had now assumed
direction of the operations, decided to renew the attack on
the following day, bringing in meanwhile his outlying units.
He asked also for the two companies of the 101st Grenadiers
then in reserve at Mombasa, and for naval co-operation.
Jasin camp was provisioned for a week, and was believed to
be strong enough to hold out so long as its ammunition
lasted.

Unhappily the ammunition did not last.   By nightfall
of the 18th January most of it[3] had already been expended ;
the one machine gun had become unserviceable ; and from
noon until about 9 p.m. the camp had been shelled by field-
guns at close range.   Colonel Raghbir Singh, commanding
the 2/Kashmir Rifles, a very gallant officer and the inspiration

---

[1] The section fired 40 rounds in five minutes.
[2] Out of a total strength of about 120, casualties were 36 killed, 21
wounded, the latter including the C.O., Major-General Natha Singh, and
the only British officer, Captain MacBrayne.
[3] 300 rounds per man.

of the defence, had been killed, and morale had been badly shaken. The possibility of escape by a sortie was considered by Captain Hanson, now in command; but this, since maintenance of the defence might well be vital to Brigadier-General Tighe's plans, he rejected.

At dawn on the 19th January the enemy's bombardment was resumed with increased intensity. Some few of the 2/Kashmir Rifles continued to reply; but a sixth of their number had become casualties,[1] and the two companies of the 101st, lately filled up with new drafts after their ordeal at Tanga and with many men debilitated by the climate, now proved incapable of further effort. About 7 a.m., with his ammunition almost exhausted and seeing no signs of relief, Captain Hanson decided that the defence could be maintained no longer.

The white flag was hoisted.[2] About 8 a.m. a reconnoitring force from Umba Camp reached the neighbourhood, to learn that Jasin had fallen

In the course of the day H.M.S. *Weymouth* arrived in response to Brigadier-General Tighe's request for naval co-operation, together with the troops from Mombasa and a detachment of the 2/Loyal North Lancashire, 200 strong. During the 20th January the cruiser shelled Jasin, and the Bwaga Macho detachment was recalled; but there was to be no further fighting.

Two days later (22nd) Major General Wapshare, who had gone in person to the Umba valley on hearing of the reverse at Jasin, received from Lord Kitchener a strongly worded telegram forbidding further offensive action[3] Sickness among his troops was rapidly increasing Mightily deciding against any attempt to cling to the border, he gave orders for it to be abandoned, directing that a part of the force[4]

---

[1] Casualties at Jasin camp were: 2/Kashmir Rifles, 12 killed, 13 wounded; 101st Grenadiers, six killed, four wounded.

[2] Captains Hanson and Turner were taken before Colonel von Lettow-Vorbeck, who congratulated them on their defence, returned their swords and released them on parole, under the condition that they should not serve again during the war.

[3] " You are entirely mistaken to suppose that offensive operations " are necessary. The experience at Jasin shows you are not well informed " of the strength of the enemy . . . you should concentrate your forces " and give up risky expeditions . . . in East Africa, where we cannot " reinforce you sufficiently to be sure of success." (Telegram received at Umba Camp 11.30 a.m., 22nd January 1915.)

[4] Four coys. 2/Kashmir Rifles, four coys. 3/K.A.R., with four m.g., under Captain E. F. D. Money.

should continue to hold the healthier area about Gazi and Msambweni, the remainder being withdrawn by sea.

Preliminary orders were issued accordingly by Brigadier-General Tighe on the 29th January. During the next ten days, with every precaution to ensure secrecy, evacuation was begun, covered by the force detailed to remain behind, which maintained constant touch with the German outposts. On the evening of the 8th February the last of the troops were embarked and the covering force marched off northwards, reaching its destination next day (9th). For another two days the *Weymouth* remained off Jasin to deal with any hostile pursuit ; none, however, was attempted.

The operations begun in December had thus ended two months later with the British forces thrown back to the area from which they had started, having suffered nearly 500 casualties.[1] Against this must be set the fact that the enemy had won no easy success,[2] and was by no means disposed to carry matters any further. Nevertheless the morale of the British forces undoubtedly had again been shaken, and they were not likely to be capable of passing to the offensive for some time to come.

---

[1] The first casualty returns were incomplete. In July 1915 revised returns for the Indian units totalled two I.O., 74 o.r., killed ; three B.O., three I.O., 39 o.r. wounded. K.A.R. casualties are stated to have been : 1/K.A.R., wounded, one B.O., 10 o.r. ; 3/K.A.R., killed, 15 o.r. ; wounded, one B.O., 38 o.r. ; prisoners, three o.r., missing one o.r.

At Jasin a total of 276 taken prisoner was made up as follows : 101st, 132 (including four wounded) ; 2/Kashmir Rifles, 131 (including 14 wounded) ; K.A.R. m.g. section, eight ; 31st (Indian) Signal Coy., five.

[2] See Lettow, " My Reminiscences," pp. 56–62. The German force consisted of *1., 6., 9., 11., 13., 15., 17. F.K.* and *4. Sch., 7. Sch.*K. Its casualties appear to have been : killed, 27 Germans, 61 o.r. ; wounded, 36 Germans, about 150 o.r. Colonel von Lettow-Vorbeck was himself wounded, and his staff officer, Freiherr von Hammerstein, died of wounds.

CHAPTER VIII

ON THE DEFENSIVE:

(*continued*)

THE NORTHERN AREA

January—March 1915

(Sketches 3, 4, 6, 12, 13)

LORD KITCHENER'S rebuke to Major-General Wapshare was supplemented a few days later by a further War Office telegram, sent on the 25th January 1915, which restricted him to the defensive and made it quite clear that for the time being nothing more could be done for East Africa.[1] There could, therefore, be no hope of resuming active operations during the few weeks of good weather still remaining before the rains broke.

THE VOI-MAKTAU RAILWAY (i)

The War Office telegram of the 25th January had plainly implied that it was hoped eventually to pass to the offensive : and with this in view it was now possible, since time was no longer of the first importance, to reconsider the evident advantages of building the railway, for which preliminary Sketch 4 surveys had been made, westwards from Voi towards Taveta. Accordingly, on the 6th February, Major-General Wapshare telegraphed a strong recommendation that this work should be undertaken.

He pointed out that, in order to attack the German forces which were known to be strongly established at Taveta, at least a brigade would be required, with powerful artillery support ; a force which could hardly be maintained in the barren tract between Maktau and the Lumi river

---

[1] " After careful consideration of the circumstances it is considered " that for the present you should adopt a definitely defensive attitude " along the Anglo-German frontier from the Lake to the sea, keeping " your forces concentrated at suitable points to enable you to act as " required. . . . Secretary of State desires you to understand that with " heavy calls all over the world it is not practicable to meet requirements " of East Africa at present, and that you must therefore bide your " time."

without a railway. Such a railway, moreover, improving the connection between the rich Kilimanjaro area and Mombasa, might later be of commercial value. Work on it could be begun at once with the 5 miles of permanent way material brought from India by I.E.F. " B " ; an additional 35 miles would be required.

The proposal was approved by the War Office ten days later (16th), and on the 18th February, with the concurrence of the Governor—it being stipulated that the whole cost should be charged to War funds—orders were given to start work. The 25th and 26th (Railway) Companies, Sappers and Miners, 61st (K.G.O.) Pioneers, with 300 Indian railway coolies and a unit of 1,500 African labourers, were assembled at Voi, and by the first week in March the project was well under way.[1]

EFFECTIVES AND MAN POWER

End Paper (N.) The inactivity now imposed on the British forces could not fail further to lower their morale, already depressed by the events which have been recounted. In particular the Indian rank and file, split up into small detachments strung out to guard stations and bridges along the Uganda Railway, were so seriously affected as to neglect even elementary military precautions except in the presence of a British officer. On more than one occasion their posts were surprised and captured without resistance by German raiding parties.

Combined with the factor of inactivity, moreover, was the increasingly detrimental effect on British and Indian troops alike of the climate, not merely in the notoriously unhealthy coastal belt but inland also, both on Lake

---

[1] Conversion of the Voi-Maktau track into a road for wheeled traffic had been begun some weeks earlier by the Faridkot Sappers and 61st Pioneers with large gangs of Africans. This road, 37 miles long, crossiug the Voi river on a fine suspension bridge designed to carry 5 tons, proved of great value in the advance in 1916.

A similar road, also 37 miles long, was made by the same units from Tsavo station to Mzima. This was a much heavier task, in rough bush-clad country, the work including three substantial bridges over the Tsavo. It was completed by Christmas 1915, at great cost in money, labour and sickness, and was not used after February 1916.

The African labourers clearing the bush for the new railway, formed as the African Labour Corps, 1,500 strong, under Major Earley, did excellent work in spite of frequent attacks by German patrols.

Victoria and in the Tsavo valley, where fever and dysentery were rife.[1]

Yet another factor which had some disturbing effect was the enemy's propaganda directed to inciting all Moslems in East Africa to join the Germans against the British. Despite counter-proclamations by the Aga Khan and the Sultan of Zanzibar, a number of desertions took place.[2]

At the same time the first enthusiasm of the volunteers raised locally began to diminish. A considerable number of these were needed to return to their farms for the important early months of the year ;[3] others were permitted to return to England in order to join for service in France ; many fell sick ; and from a variety of causes the strengths of such units as the East Africa Mounted Rifles rapidly decreased,[4] while in some cases discipline tended to become slack.

Meanwhile the general question of the local forces in East Africa had been under consideration at the War Office, and early in January 1915 Lord Kitchener sent

---

[1] Some significant figures for the 2/Loyal North Lancashire are given in Chap. XXIX, Note p. 520.

On 15th April 1915 the Rampur Infantry was reported unfit to march after a few weeks on the coast.

On 22nd June 1915 the Kagera District H.Q. wrote : " A special " report on the health of the Indian troops is being submitted. The health " of the African troops is very satisfactory, but the fighting value of the " Indian troops has been much reduced by African fever developed in " Uganda, where the rains have been abnormal." See also the Note referred to above.

On 31st July 1915, after six months in Uganda, the 10th Rajputs were reported as " almost incapacitated by sickness : and in November 1915 the regimental M.O. reported that 95 per cent. of the unit needed a 3 months treatment for malaria.

[2] In February 1915 a mutiny occurred in a small unit of Somali mounted infantry (K.A.R.) commanded by Captain the Hon. R. B. Cole, which had previously done good work ; whether this was from religious causes, or from dissatisfaction among men of a race by nature unruly, is uncertain. The unit was disbanded, a new M.I. unit being formed under Captain Cole with personnel from the 2/L. North Lancs., into which the loyal remnant of Somalis was absorbed, the whole being then designated " Cole's Scouts."

[3] On the recommendation of the Governor this was approved, subject to military exigencies, as being necessary to ensure food production for the troops in the field.

[4] The E.A.M.R. dwindled from 500 to 250. Even of these not all could be counted on, it being necessary to withdraw a number of Boer troopers for duty with ox transport, work in which they were adepts. The E. African Regiment (see p. 22) shrank to a total of 40, its " Pathan " company disappearing altogether.

out his elder brother, Colonel H. E. C. Kitchener[1] a staff officer of much experience, accompanied by Lord Cranworth, who already was well acquainted with the country, to confer with the authorities on the spot " as to the desirability " of raising irregular corps for service in East Africa." On the 11th January Major-General Wapshare was informed that this mission had sailed and was asked whether in his opinion " a limited number of officers and " selected civilians with East African experience " would be of value.

His enquiries on this point from various local authorities on the subject, including the Chief Secretary (Mr. Bowring) and Lord Delamere, brought no hope of any increase in the number of European volunteers, nor was there any response to a formal public appeal made on the 23rd January for an additional 500 recruits. Enquiring then of Army Headquarters at Simla whether a corps for East Africa could be raised from volunteer units in India, he was told that no promises could be made, especially in regard to officers and arms ; and on the 26th January this suggestion, after reference to the War Office, was negatived.

So far the solution of the man-power problem which was eventually arrived at—the only good solution, expansion of the K.A.R.—had not been suggested. On the 19th January, however, this was put to the War Office by Major-General Wapshare as " the only feasible scheme ". He estimated the minimum period necessary for training at eight months ; adding, a week later, that if this were agreed to and sanction given, he would, as he put it, " commence raising two " battalions, or as many less as I am directed ".

Here the Colonial Office was clearly concerned, and Major-General Wapshare was directed to confer on the subject with the Governor. On the 15th February the latter, in reply to an enquiry by the Colonial Office (3rd February) " as regards immediate enlistments, cost and terms of " enlistment ", submitted detailed proposals. He expressed a wish " to recruit up to 1,200 ; but probably not more than " 600 [were] obtainable ". These were to be enlisted for three years or the duration of the war. He proposed not to form any new units of the K.A.R., but to strengthen those existing, and expected that this increase would " be absorbed by " replacement of losses and discharges ". No new company

---

[1] Afterwards second Earl Kitchener.

commanders would be needed, therefore, and extra subalterns only in the proportion of one per hundred recruits.[1]

The period of training was estimated, as before, at eight months. The question of cost, now taken up at home, was eventually left to be settled later, and on the 25th February the Colonial Office approved an increase of the K.A.R. by 600 men.

Meanwhile Colonel Kitchener and Lord Cranworth, who reached Nairobi on the 13th February, had discussed the whole subject of the local forces with the Governor and Major-General Wapshare, and had visited various parts of the East Africa Protectorate. Their visit was not without its difficulties and misunderstandings, doubtless due in part to the fact that Colonel Kitchener had no knowledge of the country ; in part due also to the very natural inability of the local authorities—unprepared for large-scale war and accustomed to rely on India for any aid needed—to realize either the unsuitability of British and Indian troops for East African warfare or the possibilities of expanding the African units which later experience was to demonstrate.

Colonel Kitchener's conclusions, given in a telegram from Major-General Wapshare to the War Office on the 18th March, were unfavourable.[2] They appear to have convinced

---

[1] The experience of the campaign subsequently showed that a much higher percentage of Europeans was necessary. The early ascendancy of the German askari was undoubtedly due, partly to their better shooting, but largely to their high percentage of white officers and N.C.Os.

The German proportion was about 1 white to 10 natives ; a ratio not nearly reached in the K.A.R. until 1918, and not attained until the end of the campaign (see Appendix IV, table (I)).

[2] " Colonel Kitchener's report as follows : ' I consider it impossible to " ' raise more European volunteers in British East Africa. . . . With the " ' help of the Governor Uganda I could raise 1,000 good Uganda natives. " ' They would, however, take from 8 to 12 months to train, and at the " ' conclusion of the war could only be used to garrison the north western " ' districts [of Uganda] owing to climatic and food conditions. I do not " ' consider that their value would justify the extra expenditure. Suitable " ' British officers [for them] would also be a great difficulty.' "

In a written report, also dated 18th March, Colonel Kitchener attributed the difficulties of raising more European volunteers to (1) divergent views of civil and military authorities, (2) the high pay enjoyed by local officials in " more or less non-combatant duties," (3) reluctance in the Protectorate to add to its expenses for the war. No further reference was made in the report to the possibility of expanding the K.A.R.

Colonel Kitchener's views were not shared by the O.C. 3/K.A.R. nor by the Commandant E. Africa Volunteers.

Lord Cranworth, also dissenting, submitted through Col. Kitchener a recommendation that " the main line to pursue must lie in the most rapid " expansion possible of the existing King's African Rifles." Cranworth. " Kenya Chronicles," p. 186.

the Secretary of State for War that no considerable increase in the local forces was possible.

Nevertheless it was known at G.H.Q. in Nairobi that the German forces were being continuously increased by a flow of African recruits. On this point the Intelligence service, now organized under Captain Meinertzhagen, gave reasonably accurate estimates.[1] This aspect of the situation, however, seems not to have been impressed on the home authorities[2] In regard to the British local forces the administrative difficulties standing in the way of recruiting, training, officers, arms, and finance were evidently considered insuperable, and for the time being nothing further was done.[3]

During the early months of 1915, moreover, a number of minor incidents demonstrated the need for a high standard of training and local knowledge in dealing with the German-led askari in their native bush, and in consequence no suggestion to create new units was viewed with favour.[4]

---

[1] The following table gives the British estimates of German strength at various dates, compared with the actual figures later ascertained :

	Europeans	Askari	R.R.*	Guns	M.G.
Int. Report 31.3.15 ..	2,500	9,153	1,100	47	78
German Return 1.4.15 ..	*2,275*	*7,647*	*1,858*	*32*	*78*
Int. Report 31.5.15 ..	2,111	6,450	4,550	60	62
German Return 6.6.15 ..	*2,201*	*8,598*	*1,976*	*33*	*80*
German Return 15.7.15 ..	*2,217*	*10,093*	*1,586*	*32*	*83*
Int. Report 30.7.15 ..	2,114	8,650	4,170	60	66
German Return 1.9.15 ..	*2,596*	*10,794*	*2,818*	*52*	*88*
Int. Report 23.9.15 ..	2,094	11,100	2,880	47	79

* The column headed " R.R." covers all partially-trained effectives—recruits, armed porters and auxiliaries.

[2] In an appreciation prepared in March 1915 Major-General Wapshare stated as to the German forces that " In the whole of G.E.A. there are " probably about 3,000 white men under arms, all of good quality, and " probably 8,000 black, including levies." These figures were fairly accurate (see f.n. 1 above), but did not bring out the fact that the German askari strength had already doubled since the outbreak of war and was still increasing.

[3] As an exception, an excellent small local unit, the Baganda Rifles, was formed in Uganda during 1915 and did valuable work in the operations in the western area (see Chaps. XXIV—XXVI).

[4] For example, in April 1915, a private offer to raise a battalion of Zulus and one of Swazis was declined on the ground that " only *organized* troops " can hope to carry through the invasion of German East Africa, and we " cannot find rifles, equipment or transport for any ' scratch ' corps . . . " the fighting we have to face here requires troops not only brave but very " highly trained."

Continued at foot of next page.

Newly-raised units, nevertheless, were the only possible source of reinforcements, since no troops could be spared from elsewhere. In February 1915 Major-General Wapshare was informed that a Rhodesian contingent and a battalion raised in England from the Legion of Frontiersmen would be sent to him. The 2nd Rhodesia Regiment,[1] 500 strong, arrived at Mombasa on the 14th March and was sent to Kajiado. It was joined there early in May by the 25th (Service) Battalion, Royal Fusiliers (Frontiersmen), 1,166 strong, raised and commanded by Colonel D. P. Driscoll, D.S.O., the veteran of the South African War.[2] These two units formed a most valuable accession to the British fighting strength.

NAVAL OPERATIONS AND BLOCKADE[3]

As early as the 16th December 1914 the Colonial Secretary had suggested a blockade of the German East African coast. The task was accepted by the Admiralty, but it was not until the 1st March 1915 that the necessary ships could be provided. In the meantime Mafia Island had been seized, but the naval problem of the *Königsberg* had not been solved.

End Paper
(N.)

In the second week of February Major-General Wapshare was called upon for a report on a naval proposal to land 2,000 Royal Marines for a combined operation against that

---

Continued from previous page.

Opinion in South Africa, moreover, was adverse to the employment in a warlike capacity of the formidable Zulu and Swazi peoples, it being felt that any such step might afterwards lead to grave political, social and military problems which would fall entirely on the Union.

[1] Raised in November 1914. See p. 176.

[2] In February 1915 Colonel Driscoll, who had raised and commanded Driscoll's Scouts in the South African War, obtained permission to organize a unit from the Legion of Frontiersmen, a picturesque body of experienced fighters well known in London before the war. Within three weeks he had obtained the necessary numbers, one-third of them from the Legion. They included men of every type from every land, among them the famous hunter F. C. Selous; some who wore French decorations won in the Foreign Legion; W. N. Macmillan, an American of great wealth and corresponding physique; an ex-General from Honduras, and so on. Their average standard of experience and intelligence was so high that it was decided the battalion should carry out its military training in East Africa, and it sailed from Plymouth on 10th April 1915.

On arrival at Kajiado it was found that nearly half the battalion had never fired a British musketry course and on 16th May these men were sent to Nairobi for this purpose.

[3] See " Naval Operations," Vol. II, pp. 236-9.

vessel. He replied unfavourably ;[1] as an alternative he
suggested that he should be reinforced sufficiently to enable
him to take the offensive, clear the Moshi-Tanga area,
capture Dar-es-Salaam, and thence drive southward in
overwhelming strength against the *Königsberg*. There was
no possibility, however, of any such powerful reinforcements
being available, and this project likewise lapsed.

The blockade of the coast was duly instituted as from
the 1st March ; but the *Königsberg* was to absorb most of
the limited naval force available for four months longer.

THE EASTERN LAKE AREA

Sketch 13   At the beginning of January 1915 a recrudescence of
German activity was reported in the area east of Lake
Victoria, where a hostile force 200 strong began raiding
British territory from Susuni and a German detachment had
occupied Taraqueta Hill.   Thereupon the two companies of
the 4/K.A.R. in the vicinity were reinforced from Nairobi
by a company of the 2/Loyal North Lancashire and a section
of the 28th Mountain Battery, R.A.   Control of the combined
British forces was assumed by Brigadier-General J. M.
Stewart, now commanding at Nairobi, who decided to utilize
the British command of the Lake in order to strike at the
German lake-side hamlet of Shirati.

The reinforcements were embarked on the 7th January ;
next day (8th), after the ships' boats had been fired on at
Shirati itself and the place had been shelled in retaliation,

---

[1] Telegram to War Office, 17th February 1915.
" After conference with S.N.O., I am most decidedly of opinion that
" the project of cutting out the *Königsberg* from the sea is impracticable
" from a military point of view for the following reasons " [see sketch 12] :
        " The ship is 12 to 15 miles up the river.   The delta is most intricate,
" with many islands and swamps, and with roads known only to the
" enemy.   There is sea-water right up to her; drinking water is only
" obtainable from wells, situation unknown, which could easily be
" damaged.   It would be impossible to bring water to the troops on
" boats from the ships, owing to difficult water channels.   The climate
" is very bad.   The foreshore is strongly held with many maxims and
" Q.F. guns, whilst, owing to the reefs, the warships cannot materially
" support a landing ; and surprise is impossible.   The water approaches
" may be mined, and the whole area is covered by the *Königsberg's* guns.
" The operations would probably last a considerable time, and the Germans
" can be heavily reinforced from the Central Railway in four or five days ...
" I consider that, were this proposal to cut out the *Königsberg* attempted,
" it would probably end in failure, if not worse ; and the bad effect of this,
" considering the present state of feeling among the Arab and Mohammedan
" population, can hardly be estimated."

a landing was successfully effected without opposition in the bay close by, the enemy's small garrison meanwhile hastily making good its escape. Thus abandoned, Shirati was occupied by the British force, with Major T. McG. Bridges, 2/Loyal North Lancashire, in command, while Brigadier-General Stewart went on to Uganda to examine the situation there.

Meanwhile " G " Company, 4/K.A.R., from Karungu, had reinforced " E " Company of that unit at Suna, and on the 11th January these two companies joined Bridges at Shirati. On the 12th the whole force moved out against a German detachment reported at Utegi, but found no signs of the enemy ; and four days later, detaching " E " Coy., 4/K.A.R., under Captain R. F. B. Knox, to make a sweep southwards before returning to its former camp at Butende, the remainder of the force returned to Shirati.

Learning at noon on the 16th January that a German force, 100 strong, was occupying Gurribe hill, Knox made for the border and at dawn next day, leaving his baggage in the bush, attacked. After a confused fight on the steep and broken hill-side Knox's company gained the crest, capturing a small gun and all the German baggage ; but his own baggage-train, meanwhile, its whereabouts betrayed by local natives, had also been attacked and over-whelmed. The affair thus ended with each side in possession of the other's baggage,[1] and with the enemy in retreat. Resuming his march, Knox went on to Butende.

News of this affair brought Major Bridges from Shirati with most of the remainder of his force, which joined Knox on the 21st January and pushed on to the frontier at Shirari ;[2] but no further signs of the enemy were found, and on the 23rd, leaving the two K.A.R. companies to fall back and take up a defensive position at Niasoku, Bridges returned to Shirati.

Soon afterwards the reverse at Jasin led to the recall of Major Bridges with his company of the 2/Loyal North

---

[1] 4/K.A.R. casualties were 4 killed, 5 wounded ; a medical officer with the baggage was taken prisoner. German losses were estimated at 3 Germans, 15 askari killed.

The captured German gun, too heavy to remove, was disabled and left.

[2] Not to be confused with Shirati, which is on the lake, 35 miles to the westward.

Lancashire and the mountain guns, which left on the 29th January for Nairobi. For the next month the Eastern Lake border remained quiet.

Sketch 3   At the end of February the quiet was broken again. Considerable German forces under an energetic commander, Captain Hexthausen, had assembled near Ikoma, the enemy had re-entered Shirati, and hostile patrols had pushed up to the frontier. In response to a request by the O.C. Troops, Uganda, Lieutenant-Colonel L. H. Hickson, who had now himself taken control in the eastern Lake area, the two K.A.R. companies there were once more reinforced, this time by a mixed force about 250 strong.[1] On the 2nd **Sketch 13**   March, on which day German raiding parties burned villages about Butende, the whole force was concentrated at Niasoku.

On the 4th March Hickson crossed the frontier, driving off small parties of the enemy from Ekoma Hill on that day and from Susuni on the 5th, and reaching the vicinity of Tonuno on the 8th. Early next morning he resumed his march, heading westwards towards Ikoria.

At about 8.30 a.m. his leading troops, the K.A.R. mounted infantry under Lieutenant H. H. Davies, preceded by Ross's Scouts, encountered near Mwaika the advanced guard of a German force approaching from the south. At this point the route ahead crossed two roughly parallel ridges, with a shallow valley between, on the nearer and higher of which the Scouts were halted at the moment of encounter.

The mounted infantry galloped forward, coming into action on the right of the Scouts and securing the crest line.[2] Following up, the Reserve Coy., 3/K.A.R., with the two mountain guns, came up into line in the centre on the highest portion of the ridge, with the remainder in prolongation to the left flank. At the same time the enemy made a dash for the lower ridge, and over the rocky intervening ground a sharp fight developed. One of the mountain guns, under the personal direction of Major A. M. Colvile, R.A., the artillery commander, was man-handled to within 200 yards of a German machine gun, which was silenced by a direct hit.

---

[1] Reserve Coy., 3/K.A.R. ; K.A.R., M.I. Coy. (80 strong) ; the remains of Ross's Scouts, 16 in all, under Lieutenant Drought ; one sect. 28th Mtn. Bty., R.A.

[2] " Somalis and Abyssinians were competing that day and they at " once made good that flank." (Note by an officer present.)

Each side then endeavoured to turn the flank of the other. On the British right the enemy was held ; Lieutenant-Colonel Hickson, seeing that the ground behind the enemy was suitable for mounted action and wishing to discover the German strength, pulled in his M.I. from his own right flank in order to send them in a wide turning movement round the right of the enemy. Meanwhile on the British left a German bayonet charge drove off a party which had also attempted to turn the enemy's right and had gained a knoll on the opposing ridge. Neither a K.A.R. half-company which again effected a lodgment on the knoll, nor the M.I., which successfully reached a position in rear of it, were able to evict the enemy. So matters remained, both sides clinging doggedly to their ground, until nightfall, when the Germans disengaged and withdrew. Reconnaissance next day (10th March) showed that they had retired behind the Mara river.[1] In the words of a survivor, " the hopes of a "round-up were not fulfilled"; but a notable blow had been dealt against the enemy. As one of the most successful small engagements for some months, the affair was salutary in its effect upon the local tribes and, above all, welcome as a tonic to the spirits of the troops in general.

From Mwaika Lieutenant-Colonel Hickson moved westwards, established a defended camp near Utegi, and sent an urgent call for further reinforcement. In response, one company of the 2/Loyal North Lancashire from Nairobi and " A " Coy., 4/K.A.R., from Mzima, together with " Logan's battery "[2] of two naval 3-pounders, were sent to join him at Utegi, where they arrived on the 15th March. The move proved unnecessary the Germans attempted no further offensive, and a week later the detachments of the 2/Loyal North Lancashire and 4/K.A.R., together with the section of the 28th Mountain Battery, R.A., were recalled to Nairobi.

TRANSPORT

It will be remembered that the two expeditionary forces from India brought with them very little transport, it being known that in East Africa transport would for the most

[1] K.A.R. casualties were : killed, 3 officers, 1 British N.C.O., 9 o.r.
The enemy's strength appears to have been 18 Germans, 204 askari, with 1 m.g. German losses have been given as : killed, 1 German, 10 askari ; wounded, 3 Germans, 25 askari ; missing 2 askari.
[2] See p. 72, f.n. 2.

part have to take the form of carrriers, recruited locally. A Carrier Corps had been raised ;[1] but when, at the end of 1914, the forces in East Africa were re-distributed and re-organised, the question of their transport called for further consideration.

On the 16th February 1915 Major-General Wapshare gave orders for the formation of a mule corps on Indian lines, and for the raising of a corps of 200 African machine gun porters.[2] Difficulty was experienced with both these measures. A suggestion that a mule corps should be supplied from India was negatived, Indian resources having already been depleted by the requirements of the Indian forces elsewhere.[3] It remained only to organize such animal transport as could be obtained locally ; remount depots were formed at Nairobi and Nakuru, the latter chosen as being the best spot in the country for horses and mules. Fortunately the rains in March were good, and ample grazing was available as the new transport units took shape.

In the light of the later experience of the campaign, in the course of which over 200,000 carriers were raised, without whom it could never have been carried on, the difficulty in regard to carrier transport which was undoubtedly experienced at this time is remarkable.[4]

On the return of I.E.F. " B " from Tanga the carrier contingents already raised were re-organized and reduced in numbers. The Zanzibar contingent specially raised for

---

[1] See pp. 22–23.

[2] An attempt was also made to train oxen for pack work, and in May 1915 one section of 28th Mtn. Bty., R.A., was supplied with óxen for this purpose. The attempt was not a success.

[3] " It would greatly increase our chances of success if India would " earmark a mule corps for use in British East Africa when the general " offensive is resumed after the completion of the railway. . . ." (Telegram to W.O., 24th February 1915). The proposal was negatived on 15th March.

[4] Extracfs from Major-General Wapshare's telegrams to War Office :
(i) " Porters are very expensive and are never dependable, whilst water " difficulties preclude their use for large bodies of troops." (24th February 1915).
(ii) " The transport problem is serious. . . . Mules exist only in small " numbers. Oxen are more plentiful, but . . . civil authorities consider " the drain on cattle even up to now will react most seriously. . . . Donkeys " are only a make-shift. . . .
" Porters suitable for military transport cannot be obtained in large " numbers without compulsion. The coast Swahilis are good . . . but " few . . . and require high pay. A few of the Uganda tribes are useful, " but . . . rapidly lose health when out of their own country. . . . The " largest numbers available are Kavirondo and Wa-Kikuyu . . . can " carry only light loads. I am trying to raise 200 machine gun porters but " so far entirely without success." (About 10th March 1915).

Tanga was disbanded for financial reasons.[1] Between January and May 1915 the carriers recruited in Uganda were repatriated, a separate Uganda Transport Corps being formed in April ; those remaining in British East Africa were reorganized as the Carrier Section, East Africa Transport Corps,[2] distributed along the whole front of operations, with recruiting depots at Nairobi, Kisumu and Mombasa.[3]

As the needs of the troops increased the number of carriers obtainable on a voluntary basis proved insufficient, with increasingly inconvenient consequences to the movements and supply of units ; and by agreement with the civil authorities compulsion was introduced. Training camps were instituted, and it was soon seen that the service was far from unpopular with the natives.[4]

During the first month of 1915 the expansion of supply and transport services continued. Two ammunition columns were formed, for the Voi area and the Longido area respectively. In May the amount of transport required for the whole of the forces was worked out afresh,[5] including consideration of the use of light motor transport, for which in the dry season reasonably good tracks could be cleared through the bush in most parts of the country.[6]

THE MAGADI-LONGIDO AREA

The subject of transport was of special importance in Sketch 6 regard to the fifty miles of rough track which linked up the forward posts on Longido and Oldoinyo Erok with the

---

[1] The Zanzibar carriers were paid Rs.25 per month, as against East African ~~carriers, Rs.10.~~

[?] Captain O. F. Watkins, who had raised them, now became D.A.D. Transport, E.A.T.C.

[2] Some difficulties arose from the parallel formation of an African Labour Corps for the Voi-Maktau railway (see p. 130, f.n. 1), owing to desertions from one corps to the other.

[4] On 20th April 1915 it was noted at G.H.Q. that " thanks to a little " compulsion by the civil authorities, we have got some 200 gun-porters " of good class. As soon as they came here, saw their uniforms, and heard " that they were to be drilled like askari, they were delighted ; we shall " probably get another hundred."

The gun porters were first allotted to the mountain batteries, R.A., but were afterwards withdrawn, and distributed to infantry units for service as m.g. carriers.

[5] Details are unfortunately not available.

[6] Solid-tyred Napier and Daimler 30 cwt. and 3-ton lorries, possibly the only types then available at home, were at first sent out. The unsuitability of these for East Africa was soon seen, and confirmed the recommendations of the D.A.D.M.T. (Major Dudgeon), who had early advocated light pneumatic-tyred vehicles of the box-car types such as were afterwards provided.

Magadi railway.   To keep these supplied had not been easy
even in the dry season, and it was to be expected that the
heavy rains of April and May would make the use of wagon
transport impossible.   In any case these outlying posts, not
vitally necessary, entailed an undue dispersal of force.   On
the 9th March, therefore, with the rainy season imminent,
preliminary orders were issued to withdraw the forward
troops to the Besil river, where a defended camp was to be
established.   Soon afterwards the rains broke, washing away
many bridges and in some places obliterating all tracks.

The withdrawal began on the 1st April.   Through the
downpour the troops and their ox-wagons struggled along
in small columns, the last details leaving Longido on the
8th April.   By the 11th the rear parties had reached Besil
Camp, which was occupied as an outpost while the remainder
of the troops returned to Kajiado.   Beyond occasional
patrol skirmishes, no attempt was made by the enemy to
interfere with the withdrawal.

Its effect, however, was naturally to embolden the
German raiding parties in the area, enabled now to operate
from posts pushed out to the Kedongai river and the Ingito
hills.[1]   These gave trouble periodically.

On the 7th May a party of mounted Germans rode up
the Rift Valley and blew up the Magadi Railway near Neuki
station ;   a week later an E.A.M.R. patrol was ambushed
north of the Ingito Hills ;[2] and during the next three months
a variety of such incidents occurred to test the constant
alertness of the troops.

THE VOI-TSAVO AREA

Sketch 4   In the area east of Kilimanjaro, between the mountain
and the Uganda Railway, generally termed the Voi-Tsavo
area, patrolling by the British and raiding by the Germans
continued into the early months of 1915.   During February

---

[1] German accounts claim that the Germans re-occupied Longido on
13th April, Oldoinyo Erok on 17th April, and Kedongai and Ingito on
20th April. British intelligence in the area, whose local native agents
were discouraged by the withdrawal, was for a while somewhat at a loss.
It reported on 4th May that Longido had not been re-occupied.   The water
supply at these places was at this time an attraction for patrols of both
sides, which clashed occasionally.

[2] As an example of the many peculiar conditions of the campaign,
several men of this patrol, wounded and captured, whom their captors
felt obliged to leave disarmed in the bush, spent an uneasy night in hiding
from lions which could be heard close by devouring dead mules.

reports of increasing German strength on the north-eastern slopes of Kilimanjaro caused some anxiety for the British post at Epiron,[1] and on the 3rd March a small column[2] from Tsavo, under Major P. H. Dyke, 130th Baluchis, left Campi-ya-Marabu to visit the camps of the Kashmir Rifles at Loosoito and Epiron. Turning south-eastwards along the frontier, and thence past Rombo and Mzima, it returned to Tsavo on the 19th March without any incident beyond one minor skirmish. Its progress, " marked by much signalling "and increased activity of hostile patrols" as it traversed the frontier, while leaving Epiron no better protected, apparently attracted the enemy's attention ; for on the 10th March, Major Lyall's detachment of Kashmir Rifles at Epiron was surprised and scattered in the bush by a German raiding party, losing 11 killed or captured.

The Masai, for whose protection Epiron had been occupied, being now on the move in their seasonal migra-tion, the detachment was withdrawn to Loosoito. News of a further threat to it by a strong German force was received on the 22nd March, and a week later (29th) two companies of the 3/Kashmir Rifles and one of the 1/K.A.R., under Captain E. F. D. Money, left Mzima to go to its assistance.

The attention of the enemy was at the same time diverted by a demonstration made from Maktau against the German position on Salaita Hill. Under Major G. Newcome, 130th Baluchis, a column some 300 strong[3] which left Maktau on the 28th moved off from Mbuyuni at midnight 28th/29th towards Salaita. It was accompanied by 16 cars of the East Africa M.T. Company, which carried ammunition and water and towed its 12-pdr. gun.[4]

At 7 a.m. on the 29th March the force moved to the attack of Salaita Hill, to be met by vigorous rifle-fire and the sending up of S.O.S. rockets, and pushed in to close range. For the next four hours a lively exchange of fire was maintained.

---

[1] See p. 116, f.n. 2.

[2] Two coys. 130th Baluchis, 1 coy. K.A.R., strength 5 B.O., 113 Indian and 50 African o.r., with 2 m.g.   As an example of transport requirements, the force had with it 98 donkeys, 158 carriers.

[3] 1 coy. 130th Baluchis with 2 m.g. ; 1 coy. 1/K.A.R. ; Calcutta Vol. Bty., one 12-pdr.

[4] The first employment of mechanized first-line transport in the campaign.

Unluckily, as the result of a heavy downpour of rain which converted the track into deep mud, the gun became bogged and had to be sent back to Maktau.

About 11.15 a.m. Major Newcome, having decided that the demonstration must by now have successfully attracted German reserves, had just issued orders to retire when a message was received that his right was seriously threatened. Heavy rifle and machine gun fire was opened by the enemy on that flank as the two companies began a steady retirement.

Unhappily the two machine guns, in the centre of the line, also came under intense fire as the withdrawal began. In the high grass their plight was not observed by the companies retiring on either side ; their carriers, new to war, fled panic-stricken, abandoning the guns, which it became impossible to bring away. Only after his force had reassembled out of range did Major Newcome become aware of their loss.

Apart from this the demonstration had succeeded at relatively little cost.[1] It was learned later that it had, as intended, drawn the enemy's forces all along this sector of the frontier, thus effectively diverting pressure from Lyall's threatened detachment at Loosoito.

It was not, however, in time to spare Lyall all molestation. On the same day (29th March) a hostile force 300 strong moved against him. Abandoning his camp by the Metigangu river for a covered position on Loosoito Hill, he watched the enemy encircle and shell his empty camp, the hostile force being so far superior in number to his own that he kept his detachment concealed until the enemy eventually withdrew. Deciding then to evacuate Loosoito, he made a circuitous three days' march to Eidalal, where he joined hands with the force under Captain Money which was on its way to his support. After retrieving stores left at Loosoito the whole force then withdrew to Mzima.

---

[1] Total casualties, 6 killed, 10 wounded, 5 missing.

CHAPTER IX

ON THE DEFENSIVE

(continued)

THE NORTHERN AREA

April—September 1915

(Sketches 2, 3, 4, 5, 6, 8, 12, 13, 15, 16, 17)

DURING the first half of 1915 the general situation in other Sketch 15 theatres of war continued to make it impossible to depart from the policy of a strict defensive in East Africa. Mesopotamia, in particular, was an ever-increasing drain on Indian resources, not only absorbing all available munitions but also demanding additional technical troops.[1] Early in April Major-General Wapshare was himself ordered to that theatre of war, and on the 15th April he left Nairobi, handing over the command to Brigadier-General (afterwards Major-General) M. J. Tighe.

The new commander, called upon by the War Office for his views on the situation, replied on the 20th April. Expressing agreement with his predecessor in regard to the building of the railway forward from Voi towards the German frontier, he gave his opinion that, if " at least 1½ brigades of good " troops " were provided, he would be able to take the offensive in the Kilimanjaro and Tanga areas. He proposed also a preliminary operation against Dukoba and Mwanza, to be co-ordinated, he hoped, with a Belgian advance into Ruanda.[2]

Lord Kitchener's reply, now as in January, was uncompromisingly unfavourable. " The impossibility of promising " further reinforcements cannot be too strongly impressed " on you ", he said ; " we have grave doubts as to the " wisdom of undertaking any serious offensive ".[3] The

---

[1] The two regular Bde. Signal Sections, 31st Signal Coy., R.E., in East Africa were transferred to Mesopotamia, sailing from Mombasa for Basra on 3rd April 1915.

[2] See Chaps. XII, XXIV.

[3] Telegram, 4th May 1915. See also p. 129, f.n. 1.

project of operations on Lake Victoria was discouraged, and in a further telegram Major-General Tighe was restricted to " protection of our own possessions ".[1]

Even this, however, now began to be difficult of execution. Under cover of the heavy rains, the enemy's activities were extended ; his askari, immune to fever and now taught by war, were excellent scouts and stalkers, against whose raids it became increasingly difficult to protect the British outposts and the Uganda Railway.

PROTECTION OF THE UGANDA RAILWAY

Sketch 4　On the 1st May Brigadier-General Malleson was appointed to command the Voi area, with special instructions both as to the guarding of the Uganda Railway and as to the necessity of conserving the troops with a view to an eventual offensive.

It was hoped at first that such strong advanced posts as those at Maktau and Mzima would ensure the safety of the railway, and early in April Mzima had been reinforced by a company of the 130th Baluchis under Major W. A. S. Walker. These excellent Indian troops, however, were still often at a loss in the bush ; and as early as the 11th April a small party of them ran into a strong German patrol, Major Walker being killed.

Sketch 2　Ten days later (20th April) the railway service was disorganized for several days by the blowing up of a bridge between Makindu and Simba by a German raiding party.[2] This incident and another on the 27th April[3] led a further dispersal of the British forces in railway protection, and on the 10th May Colonel H. E. C. Kitchener was appointed Sketch 4 Inspector of Railway Defences. Soon afterwards, as a

---

[1] " My view is that you have not sufficient forces to undertake offensive " operations beyond your border. . . . It is unwise with the existing " forces . . . to embark on projects involving occupation of German " territory, and you should limit your endeavours to protection of our own " possessions. Any co-operation which you are able to afford to the " Belgian troops should be limited to that which is compatible with the " foregoing instructions." W.O. telegram, 14th May 1915.

[2] The Germans, 14 strong, surprised and captured the bridge guard of one N.C.O. and four men of the 98th Infantry, afterwards releasing them in the bush. The German commander appears to have posed successfully as a British officer.

[3] The line was blown up near Kibwezi and a train which came up was fired on by some 50 Germans, who caused seven casualties.

further reinforcement, the newly-arrived 2/Rhodesia Regiment was transferred from the Magadi area to Maktau and the Tsavo valley.[1]

In the meantime, information having been received that the German raiders of the 20th and 27th April had been based on Loosoito, which was reported strongly held by the enemy, a mixed column some 300 strong,[2] under Lieutenant-Colonel Jourdain, 2/Loyal North Lancashire, was assembled at Simba. To mislead the enemy and contain his detachments, Sketch 2 similar columns were at the same time assembled at Mzima and Maktau.

Jourdain's force, leaving Simba on the 10th May and approaching Loosoito after a long final night march in order to surprise the German camp at dawn on the 14th, drew blank. The site was found evacuated and the column returned to Simba, covering 36 miles in $22\frac{1}{2}$ hours in very bad weather. The strain of this expedition proved too great for the white troops, many of whom went sick on return to Nairobi.

The subsidiary column from Maktau, making a reconnaissance in force towards Salaita, did not become engaged. The Mzima column,[3] however, under Major R. Cashel, Sketch 4 2/Rhodesia Regiment, which on the 13th May made a sweep southwards from Campi-ya-Marabu following the left bank of the Tsavo, had a sharp fight that afternoon with some 200 Germans who attacked it whilst it was in search of a crossing-place. Hampered by its experimental donkey transport,[4] the column was in some difficulty, but eventually drove off the attack, crossed the Tsavo and made its way back to Mzima.

The bush enclosing the upper reaches of the Tsavo afforded the enemy such opportunities of concealed approach that a week later (20th May) the 2nd Rhodesia Regiment was ordered to concentrate at Mzima. There its C.O., Lieutenant-Colonel Capell, re-organized the defences and introduced a new system of patrolling under which the size

---

[1] One coy. to Maktau ; one coy. to Mzima ; one coy. to Crater Hill and the Tsavo valley l. of c. ; one coy. in reserve at Tsavo.

[2] Composition : one coy. 2/Loyal North Lancs. ; one coy. 3/K.A.R. ; Cole's Scouts ; K.A.R.M.I. ; one section 27th Mtn. Bty., R.A.

[3] A mixed detachment of 2/Rhodesia Regt. and 130th Baluchis, total strength 207, with two m.g.

[4] The experiment went to confirm that donkeys were unsuitable for work in the bush, being noisy and intractable.

of a patrol was decided by its mission : the " fighting patrol,"
at least 100 strong with machine guns, capable of attacking
or of resisting any probable attack, and the " reconnoitring
patrol," normally one officer or British N.C.O. with two
askari, small enough to escape observation. This common-
sense arrangement, which corresponded with the German
practice,[1] proved very successful. Whereas hitherto patrols
had in many cases been discomfited by the enemy, during
the ensuing months the Rhodesians more than held their
own in bush fighting. Unhappily the climate of the Tsavo
valley proved deadly to them.[2]

As the British units decreased in strength through
sickness the enemy's boldness increased. In spite of constant
patrolling, it was impossible to watch every mile· of line
continuously.[3] Raiders with the choice of direction and
time could always find some spot momentarily unguarded,
where a charge could be laid beneath a rail.[4] With increasing
Sketch 2 frequency the line was attacked all along the 200 miles
between Simba and Samburu ; train services were interrupted, and locomotives—for the better of which few
spare parts were to be had—derailed or damaged.[5] As the
weeks went by and the German patrols became ever more
enterprising, the problem of railway defence gave rise to
increasing anxiety.

[1] With the exception of the demolition parties (*Sprengpatrouillen*),
which were generally two or three Germans, 8 to 20 askari, with a few
carriers for the explosives.

[2] Rheumatism, fever, dysentery and veld-sores were prevalent. By
15th June 111 of all ranks (i.e., over 25 per cent. of strength) were in hospital
and many others sick or on light duty.

[3] On the single line of rail in a narrow clearing through the bush,
patrols moving singly or in pairs were in great danger from lions. On
14th December 1915 a sepoy of the 3/Kashmir Rifles was killed and eaten
by a lion close to Tsavo station.

[4] It was eventually discovered that the enemy, with creditable guile,
had for some time had a camp on the Athi river, about 15 miles east of
Mtito Andei. Some raiding parties were undoubtedly based on this
camp, the existence of which was not suspected, it being naturally assumed
that the enemy would approach the railway from the west. The camp
was not found until after it had been evacuated.

[5] (i) The Mallet articulated compound engines, with large L.P. cylinders
in front, were especially liable to damage. The old South African device
of pushing a truck ahead of the engine was adopted ; and when the enemy
countered with a detonating mechanism set to delay until a predetermined
number of wheels had passed over, the engines were put still further back.

(ii) The Voi-Mombasa section of the railway depended for water
chiefly on a pipe-line running alongside the track. Fortunately, although
marked by frequent man-holes, the pipe-line was never discovered by the
enemy. The German permanent-way inspector previously in charge of
that section had left for German East Africa before the pipe was laid.

OPERATIONS ON LAKE VICTORIA

At the end of 1914 it was decided that the small armed **Sketch 3**
vessels on Lake Victoria[1] should be organized as a naval
force. Commander G. S. Thornley, R.N., who arrived from
England in January 1915, assumed command of a flotilla
consisting of the *Winifred, Nyanza, Kavirondo, William
Mackinnon* and *Percy Anderson*. The ships were authorized
to fly the White Ensign, their R.N.R. officers were formally
called up for service and their remaining officers were
granted temporary commissions. Their armament also was
improved, three 4-inch guns salved from H.M.S. *Pegasus,*
with naval personnel, being sent up from the coast.

During February H.M.S. *Winifred,* now armed with one
of these guns, scoured the southern waters of the Lake for
the *Muansa,* which was eventually found on the 11th
March, and after an unequal fight was driven ashore near
Rusenye. Six days later the German craft was refloated and,
evading the vigilance of the *William Mackinnon* which had
been left on watch, was towed into Mwanza for repairs. She
was to remain a potential menace for some months to
come.[2]

The refloating of the *Muansa* made it the more necessary
to make sure that the enemy should not similarly salve the
stranded British *Sybil,* lying since the previous October at
Majita. As a first step, on the 30th March the *Winifred*
made 19 direct hits on the *Sybil* with 4-inch and 12-pounder.
The *Sybil,* however, was still a possible asset to the enemy
and, after a proposal to blow her up had fallen through for
lack of explosives, it was decided to attempt salvage.

Accordingly on the 11th May the flotilla left Karungu,
conveying a landing force of two companies of the 2/Loyal
North Lancashire and one of the 3/K.A.R. under Major
R. E. Berkeley of the former unit. Next morning the
troops landed unopposed at Majita and took up a covering position, driving off in so doing a small hostile party
without loss to themselves, while the ships' crews tackled
the *Sybil.*

The repairs were completed by the night of the 13th/
14th, when a violent storm again filled the *Sybil* with

---

[1] See p. 23, f.n. 2.
[2] There is some evidence to show that the *Muansa* was merely scuttled
in shallow water in order to make it appear that she was badly
damaged.

water, and it was not until the morning of the 16th that she
was refloated. The covering troops were then withdrawn
to Karungu.[1]

Sketch 13   The salvage of the *Sybil* had fortunately not been interfered with by a considerable German force which was known
to be on the Mara river, not 50 miles to the northward. This
force camped near Mwaika on the 11th May, sending patrols
into Shirati and raiding across the border. Once again
Lieutenant-Colonel Hickson, at Karungu, was reinforced,
this time by two companies of the 3/K.A.R. from Nairobi,
and on the 30th May he moved with his K.A.R. and 2/Loyal
North Lancashire companies to Niasoku. At his approach
the Germans once more retired. With the exception of a
minor skirmish on the 5th June and of occasional small
raids, the area remained quiet for some months longer.

Farther east, between the Mara and Lake Natron, small
mobile bands of mounted German irregulars continued at
intervals to harry the unwarlike Sonjo natives. Fantastic
stories of their deeds, and even of a mythical German woman
addicted to inflicting indescribable cruelties on prisoners,
were symptomatic of the effects on morale of inaction, a
bad climate, and an enterprising enemy.

BUKOBA, 22ND–23RD JUNE 1915

Sketch 3   Notwithstanding the orders restricting him to the
defensive, Major-General Tighe considered it advisable to
undertake at least some minor offensive enterprise, if only
to restore the self-confidence of the troops. For this the
most promising area seemed to be Lake Victoria, since his
now established command of the Lake would facilitate
surprise. His previous proposal to attack Bukoba or Mwanza,
or both, had been rejected ; but after further representations
to the War Office, and on the strict understanding that
nothing should be undertaken which could lead to subsequent
complications—as had happened at Jasin—consent to an
operation on the Lake was obtained. It remained to decide
on the objective.

Mwanza, the main German base, was known to be too
strong to promise an easy success; the eastern shores of

---

[1] The nature of the climate is indicated by the fact that, although the
troops were only three nights on outpost duty, within a fortnight every
officer and man of the 2/Loyal North Lancs. detachment was down with
fever.

the Lake offered no suitable alternative.   On the southern Uganda border, however, the enemy was reported to have increased his forces ; and to forestall a possible hostile offensive in this quarter it was decided to attack Bukoba, the German administrative centre for the district south of the Kagera, where incidentally a powerful wireless station formed an important link in the enemy's communications.

Bukoba was known to have been fortified, with German troops estimated at a total of about 1,500 within three days' march ; a considerable force would therefore be required. Arrangements were made for the main operation to be coupled with a series of diversions to be carried out along the line of the Kagera by the forces in Uganda.[1]

The force detailed for the main operation comprised some of the best troops available in British East Africa, to a total fighting strength of about 1,600, with 2 guns and 12 machine guns,[2] under Brigadier-General J. M. Stewart. Assembling at Kisumu, its units embarked on the ships of the Lake flotilla[3] on the 20th June, and at about 10 p.m. on the following evening (21st) arrived off the western Sketch 16 shore to the north of Bukoba.   In the bright moonlight their arrival was observed from Busira Island, where flares and rocket signals went up.

At dawn on the 22nd the *Nyanza* moved in on Bukoba, threatening the township, while the other vessels began disembarkation of the troops at a convenient landing-place some 3½ miles north of the town.

First to land were the half battalion of the 25/Royal Fusiliers, under Lieutenant-Colonel Driscoll, with the Faridkot Sappers and the machine guns of the East Africa

---

[1] Between 16th and 25th June a detachment of the Uganda Police Service Bn., 100 strong, starting from Ngarama, demonstrated against German posts between Nsongezi and Mitai Aiyu.   A show of force was also made on occasion by a body of some 1,000 porters who manoeuvred conspicuously in extended order within view of the enemy.   On 21st June the main Kagera mobile column, 400 strong, made a feint towards Kyaka ; next day smaller detachments from Kakindu and Minziro made similar movements towards the river crossings near those places.   (See sketch 8.)

[2] Detail (approximate total strengths in brackets) : 2/Loyal North Lancs. Regt., less two coys. (274) ; 25/Royal Fus., less two coys. (462) ; three coys., 3/K.A.R. ; one coy., 29th Punjabis (198) ; m.g. section, E. Africa Regt. (37) ; Volunteers, 4 m.g. ; one sect. 28th Mtn. Bty., R.A. (94) ; Faridkot Sappers (91) ; medical and supply units.

[3] H.M.Ss. *Winifred* (flag), *Usoga, Nyanza, Rusinga, Kavirondo, Percy Anderson.*

Regiment. Meeting no opposition, the Fusiliers took up
a defensive line covering the landing-place, where they
were joined by the remainder of the force, except the
3/K.A.R., and local command was assumed by Lieutenant-
Colonel Jourdain, 2/Loyal North Lancashire Regiment.

At this juncture fire was opened on the ships by a gun
sited near the Customs house south of the town. The fire
was returned by the ships, but the German gun, although
its position was marked by the smoke of its black powder,
was difficult to silence. In consequence the K.A.R. companies, which it had been intended to land near the Customs,
were diverted to the north of the town, landing about a mile
south of the main beach and taking up a position with their
right in touch with the Fusiliers.

Inland from the latter the 2/Loyal North Lancashire
were held up for some time by a force of some 200 Germans
with a machine gun on a rocky ridge (" Arab Ridge ").
About noon the mountain guns engaged the German field
gun, after which, having compelled it to move to a better-
covered position inland, they engaged and presently knocked
out the machine gun on Arab Ridge. The infantry then
made its way forward and by about 5.30 p.m. had gained
the ridge, the Fusiliers meanwhile moving up to " Fusilier
Knoll " at the southern end of the enemy's position, the
whole of which was evacuated. During the remaining
daylight the force pushed forward, bivouacking on the high
ground for the night.

At daylight on the 23rd June the enemy could be seen
digging in along the northern outskirts of Bukoba. Orders
were issued for the 25/Royal Fusiliers, who pushed on at
dawn, to advance direct on the town, the 2/Loyal North
Lancashire working round it from the north-west, with the
3/K.A.R. and 29th Punjabis in reserve. Progress was
delayed between 7 a.m. and 8 a.m. by hostile machine gun
fire and by an abortive German local counter-attack, and
was further held up by torrential rain during the next hour;
but soon after 9 a.m., the rain having ceased, the 2/Loyal
North Lancashire went forward, followed by the 29th
Punjabis and supported by the mountain guns. The defence,
greatly inferior in numbers, gave way.

Towards 11 a.m., as the German field-gun was being
withdrawn past the Protestant Mission, two direct hits
destroyed its bullock-team, and the fire of the British guns,

continuing, frustrated all efforts to rescue it.[1]   The gun was
eventually secured by the advancing British troops.   About
1.30 p.m. the Fusiliers and the K.A.R. entered the town,
where they were joined by the 2/Loyal North Lancashire
coming in from the westward.   By 3 p.m. the enemy, scattering in retreat to the north-west and south-west, was out of
touch and the affair was over.

Brigadier-General Stewart had then to destroy the
wireless station and the fort.   This having been done, and
everything of military value having been wrecked or
removed, the force re-embarked, leaving Bukoba empty and
a prey to the surrounding tribes, who joyfully completed
what was sometimes called the " Sack of Bukoba ".[2]

Though not far-reaching, the success of this well-planned
operation, gained at slight cost in casualties,[3] did much to
restore and revive the morale of the British forces.   In the
Lake area generally, moreover, following as it did on
Hickson's blow struck in the smaller affair at Mwaika two
months earlier, it made a considerable and valuable impression on the native population.

THE END OF THE *KÖNIGSBERG*

Success at Bukoba was quickly followed by the cheering Sketch 12
news that the Royal Navy had at last disposed of the
Königsberg.   The story has already been told elsewhere.[4]
On the 11th July 1915 the career of the German cruiser came
to an end ;   but although the ship now lay battered and
wrecked, her guns and most of her crew were still in the
enemy's service,[5] available now to swell his land forces.
Her guns in particular ten 4·1-inch and two 3·5-inch—
were a priceless acquisition to Colonel von Lettow, as events
were to show ;   nor were they his only windfall.

---

[1] The section of the 28th Mtn. Bty. R.A., was the same which had previously done good work at Jasin (see p. 126).

[2] Sixty-seven rifles and 32,000 rounds of S.A.A. were captured, and
many other weapons with much ammunition were destroyed.   The captured German 2·9-inch gun was unfortunately lost, slipping from a lighter
into the lake during re-embarkation.

[3] Total casualties were :   killed, seven o.r. ;   wounded, two officers,
23 o.r.   German casualties were estimated at about 50.

[4] See " Naval Operations," Vol. III, pp. 63–7.

[5] The original complement of the *Königsberg* was 322 (*Krieg zur See :
Kreuzerkrieg, Band II*, p. 134).

In May 1915 118 of the crew were landed to join the field units.   In the
final action 19 were killed, 45 wounded, leaving a further 140 to be similarly
transferred.

GERMAN MUNITION REPLENISHMENTS

Sketch 5

At G.H.Q. elation over the Bukoba success was quickly chastened by startling information received from a British subject, Mr. Munro, interned by the Germans in Bukoba and released when the place was captured.

On the 14th April 1915 H.M.S. *Hyacinth*, it was known, had chased into Manza Bay (ten miles north of Tanga) and there destroyed—as she believed—by shell-fire the British ship *Rubens*, suspected of attempting to run the blockade in aid of the *Königsberg*. From Mr. Munro it was learned that the supposed destruction of the *Rubens* with all her cargo, far from having been complete, had been ineffective. All the arms and munitions on board had been salved, and with them the Germans were equipping more troops.

Received at first with incredulity, the story was soon corroborated by prisoners, deserters and spies. German empty cartridge-cases brought in were found to bear the date-stamp 1915 ; and in spite of suggestions that these had been smuggled through Portuguese territory the Intelligence staff gradually collected ample evidence of the truth of Mr. Munro's statement.[1]

THE VOI MAKTAU RAILWAY

Sketch 4

Under the general direction of Sir William Johns and Lieutenant-Colonel J. Sutherland,[2] the work of pushing out the new railway westward from Voi, with a pipe-line for

---

[1] See " Naval Operations," Vol. III, pp. 6–8. The adventurous story of the *Rubens* has been told at length by her commander, Kapitan-Leutnant Christiansen, in his book *Durch* ! *Mit Kriegsmaterial zu Lettow-Vorbeck.* He describes how, when shelled, her decks were intentionally covered with inflammable material, the burning of which successfully deceived H.M.S. *Hyacinth.*

News that the *Rubens* was on the way seems to have been conveyed somehow to Captain Looff of the *Königsberg*, besides whom only Lettow himself knew of it.

The munitions carried are stated to have included : 1,800 rifles ; 4½ million rounds S.A.A. ; two 6-cm. guns ; 4 m.g. ; 1,000 rounds 10.5-cm. (4.1-inch) ; 500 rounds 8.8-cm. ; 3,000 rounds 6-cm. ; 3,000 rounds 3·7-cm.; one ton explosive (Trinitroanysol) ; 200 tents ; telegraph and telephone material.

There is little doubt that these munitions, especially the S.A.A., even though somewhat damaged by sea water, were of incalculable value in enabling Lettow to remain in action. See also Lettow, " My Reminiscences," p. 67.

[2] Director and Deputy Director of Railways respectively.

water,[1] had been proceeding actively since its inception in February. By the end of March five miles of track had been laid, a month later 6½ miles more, and at the end of May railhead was approaching Bura ; on the 23rd June the line had reached Maktau.

Up to the middle of May the work was little interfered with by the enemy, whose nearest advanced post was at Salaita. But as the rains died down there were frequent German raids and patrol encounters, in one of the first of which, on the 5th May, the Area Commander (Brigadier-General Malleson)[2] was attacked whilst making a personal reconnaissance near Mbuyuni and escaped only through the devotion of his escort of the 130th Baluchis.[3]

During the first week in June a German force from Salaita, estimated at 400 strong, pushed forward to Mbuyuni, within a day's march of Maktau, and established a post from which constant raids were either made on working parties or attempted on the new railway.[4] These did no serious material damage, but their effect was harassing and Brigadier-General Malleson decided that the Germans must be dislodged from Mbuyuni.

AFFAIR OF MBUYUNI, 14TH JULY 1915

The British force at the Maktau railhead had been **Sketch 4** strengthened early in July by the addition of the 2/Loyal North Lancashire from Nairobi and by Cole's Scouts. The

---

[1] The pipe-line was necessary to supply not only the railway itself but also the garrisons at Maktau and elsewhere, and later the large force assembled for the advance in 1916. The supply was derived from the Bura Hills (1,800 feet high) and was conveyed eventually to Mbuyuni, a distance of 37 miles. Some 20 miles of 2½-inch pipe were luckily obtained from the Uganda Railway, and 17 miles of 4-inch, 3½-inch and 3-inch from India.

The work was carried out by the E. African Pioneers, a small corps of skilled white engineers and mechanics, with large gangs of Africans. This corps did a very great amount of invaluable work throughout the campaign.

A survivor records that the work " was interfered with more by " elephants than by enemy patrols."

[2] On 1st May Brigadier-General Malleson assumed command of the Mombasa Area (afterwards designated the Voi Area), which extended from the coast to Kilimanjaro, including the railway as far as Simba. Beyond this the Nairobi Area extended westwards, including Uganda, under Brigadier-General Stewart.

[3] Subadar Ghulam Haidar, 130th, who covered the retreat of Brigadier-General Malleson's car and who fell whilst gallantly attacking the on-coming Germans, was recommended for a posthumous V.C.

[4] On 14th June the line was blown up between Voi and Bura ; other attempts were made on 27th June west of Bura, and on 6th July close to Maktau camp.

remaining units on the Voi-Maktau line were now concentrated at Maktau, and on the afternoon of the 13th July Brigadier-General Malleson moved off with his force organized in two columns, at a total strength of about 1,200, with 3 guns and 11 machine guns,[1] against the Germans at Mbuyuni.

The strength of the enemy there, variously estimated, was believed to be about 600. Other German forces were known to be at Salaita, Mwarusa, Taveta, Lake Chala, and Ziwani; but the nearest of them, at Salaita, was fully 12 miles beyond Mbuyuni.

Sketch 17   From previous reconnaissance it had been ascertained that at Mbuyuni the enemy was holding the farther, i.e., the western, of two parallel ridges, at right angles to the main Voi-Taveta road, separated by an open valley about two miles wide where the road crossed them and converging farther north into one.

Brigadier-General Malleson's plan was simple: his main column was to make a frontal attack at daylight; the flanking column, after a night march, was to envelop the enemy's left, while Cole's Scouts were detailed to work round to the enemy's rear and gain command of the Taveta road beyond.

The main body bivouacked for the night about 8 miles from Maktau, covered by the troop of K.A.R. M.I. and the 3/K.A.R. with a machine gun of the 29th Punjabis. At about 3 a.m. on the 14th July this machine gun opened on a German patrol that approached the outposts, so that the advantage of surprise was lost from the outset.[2] Moving off at dawn, and somewhat delayed at first by a small German outlying detachment, the advanced guard gained the crest of the eastern ridge about 7.30 a.m. and pushed on, reinforced a little later by the 29th Punjabis, who came up on the right of the K.A.R. The advance across the open grassland

---

[1] *Main Column :* Two coys. 2/Loyal N. Lancs ; 29th Punjabis, less four (single) coys. ; two coys. 1/K.A.R. ; one troop M.I., 3/K.A.R. ; one section 27th Mtn. Bty., R.A. ; one 12-pdr. (naval) gun ; total, all ranks, 762, with three guns, eight m.g.

Flanking Column : 130th Baluchis, less four (single) coys. ; two coys. 4/K.A.R. ; two coys. 2/Rhodesia Regt. ; Cole's Scouts (M.I.) ; total, 461, with three m.g.

[2] The Punjabi m.g. team and K.A.R. had no language in common. Captain C. G. Phillips, commanding the K.A.R., had given orders that hostile patrols should be captured, preferably without firing. British patrols did not normally take out m.g., and the m.g. fire therefore indicated the presence of a larger force.

of the valley was checked by the enemy's rifle and machine gun fire on a line some 300 to 500 yards from the German trenches, which were well concealed in thick scrub on the lower slopes of the western ridge. The three guns, meanwhile, escorted by the 2/Loyal North Lancashire, came into action on the eastern ridge.

To the north the flanking column, under Lieutenant-Colonel C. U. Price, 130th Baluchis, had made a well-timed circuitous night march, led by Cole's Scouts and the 4/K.A.R., which brought it on to the enemy's left flank at daybreak. Here too a small outlying piquet of the enemy was early encountered, but gave little trouble.[1] As Lieutenant-Colonel Price's column came up, its outer (right) flank now covered by Cole's Scouts, who successfully posted their machine gun in rear of the German camp, the 4/K.A.R. and Rhodesians worked forward, with the 130th Baluchis on their left. Towards 8 a.m. they were checked, the enemy's fire holding up the 130th, and it became necessary to await the progress of the main attack visible to the south.

Having to cross badly exposed ground, however, the main attack could make little headway, and by about 10.30 a.m., when the 29th Punjabis had lost their commanding officer (Lieutenant-Colonel H. A. Vallings) killed and adjutant wounded, it came to a standstill. Intercommunication between the two columns appears to have been difficult, and it seems likely that this, indirectly, was the cause of Brigadier-General Malleson's decision, when he learned at about 11.30 a.m. that Price was likewise held up, to break off the attack.

Orders to this effect had not yet reached Lieutenant-Colonel Price when, about 1 p.m., a message from Cole informed him that a German force was approaching from the north-west. Thereupon he withdrew his forward companies a short distance, after which he held his ground for the next hour under a lively hostile fire. The Germans reported by Cole's Scouts seem to have done nothing ; but, on receipt of Brigadier-General Malleson's order, Price disengaged and brought away his force in a steady and well-executed withdrawal, with slight loss, the enemy making little attempt to follow up.

---

[1] An officer of Cole's Scouts, whose mount bolted with him into the German lines before he could turn it, has recorded that on the enemy's extreme left there was only one line of lightly held trenches.

The withdrawal of the main column, covered by the 1/K.A.R. under heavy fire, was less fortunate, a panic among the African porters causing the loss of much equipment, including many ammunition boxes of the 29th Punjabis and a machine gun of the 2/Loyal North Lancashire.[1] No pursuit was attempted by the Germans, and soon after 2 p.m. the engagement was at an end, greatly to the disappointment of those units of Price's column which had realized the great weakness of the enemy's extreme left flank.[2]

The force returned to Maktau the same evening.[3] For several weeks longer it remained on the defensive, while German patrols continued to harass the British posts and raid the railway. British patrols reconnoitring towards Mbuyuni had little success, the German strength there remaining unknown.[4]

FURTHER GERMAN RAIDS

Sketch 4   A month after the action at Mbuyuni there came a further reverse at the isolated hill of Kasigao, 30 miles south of Voi, where an observation post of the 130th Baluchis, 87 strong, under Captain H. G. Sealy, was attacked on the 13th August by a strong German detachment. On taking over the post early in August Captain Sealy, dissatisfied with its defences, had begun the construction of a new defended camp, planning to use material from the old works, which thus were in a partly-dismantled state when the attack was made.

Timely warning was given by the British outposts, but the Germans succeeded in climbing to a point overlooking the camp, from which their fire raked the half-made defences. After about two hours the enemy rushed the camp, capturing

---

[1] The 1/K.A.R. reported with justifiable satisfaction that they had lost no equipment and had even brought away their dead.

[2] The m.g. officer of Cole's Scouts, waiting behind the German camp, recorded that as soon as the main attack began " there was a hurried " retreat down the road of mixed porters and askari," with which his gun dealt effectively.

[3] Total British casualties were : killed, two officers, 31 o.r. ; wounded, eight officers, 157 o.r. ; missing, one officer, 12 o.r.

[4] It is now known that on 14th July 1915 the German units at Mbuyuni were *1., 6.* and *10. F.K.*, total 45 Germans, 600 askari, 69 irregulars, with six m.g. The outflanking threat which caused Price to begin withdrawal was made by *6. F.K.*, which at first was in reserve. German casualties, as officially reported, were : killed, five askari ; wounded, four Germans, 17 askari, nine others. The wounded included Captain Vorberg, commanding the force, who was succeeded in command by Lieutenant Merensky.

Captain Sealy and 38 of his men, of whom 5 others were killed ; the remainder escaped into the bush, through which they eventually reached Voi and other posts.[1]

A strong column from Voi at once re-occupied Kasigao. Doubt was felt as to retaining this isolated post, whose sole useful function was to transmit by helio the information brought by natives regarding German patrol movements in the vicinity ; eventually it was decided to maintain it with a K.A.R. garrison, 40 strong.   It seemed likely, however, that the enemy's easy success was attributable to help from the local tribesmen, who could neither give proofs of good faith nor explain their failure to give warning, and were thought possibly to have been terrorised by the German reputation for harsh treatment of natives.   Accordingly, as a punishment and a warning to others, the hillmen of the Wa-Kasigao, some 600 in all, were deported from their villages on the mountain to the less congenial area along the coast.[2]

In the neighbourhood of Maktau the enemy displayed increasing boldness.   On the 3rd September German raiders who had attacked a train were pursued into the bush by a mobile force, 67 strong, of European mounted infantry under Captain J. S. Woodruffe, followed by a detachment of the 130th Baluchis.   Woodruffe, having successfully gained a hill on the enemy's line of retreat, was heavily attacked ; he himself was wounded, many of his men were hit, and his outnumbered M.I. had to gallop for it.[3]

A counter-success was gained on the 14th September, when the Mounted Infantry force moved south from Maktau in co-operation with some 100 men of the 130th Baluchis who had taken up an ambush the previous evening on a known German route.   A German patrol 60 strong fell into

---

[1] The enemy had two Germans, three askari wounded.

[2] Other punitive measures had meanwhile already been instituted along the Uganda Railway, which during the last week of July alone was blown up at five separate points.   " No native community in Africa," wrote the principal staff officer at Nairobi, " could be ignorant of the " passage of strangers through their district, and it is more than probable " that our natives are more afraid of the enemy than of us."   A system of fines and punishments, instituted for tribes and communities in whose districts the railway might be damaged, was only partially successful ; for example, on 29th August a serious explosion almost destroyed one of the best locomotives.

[3] The incident is memorable for the heroism of Lieut. Wilbur Dartnell, Royal Fusiliers, who, although severely wounded and helpless, insisted on being left behind, hoping his presence might save the lives of seven other wounded men near by.   His devotion was in vain, all being killed by the German askari as they rushed the hill.   He was awarded a posthumous V.C.

the trap, losing 32 killed.[1] The episode restored to some extent the confidence of the troops at Maktau, but elsewhere things were going none too well.

AFFAIR OF LONGIDO WEST

Sketch 6   A further British reverse occurred on the 20th September, when a mixed force some 450 strong[2] was led by Lieutenant-Colonel Jollie, 28th Cavalry, Indian Army, now commanding the Magadi area, against a German detachment occupying the former British camp at Longido West. Leaving Besil Camp on the 16th, and halting for two nights on Oldoinyo Erok for reconnaissance, the force reached Longido at dawn on the 20th.

The enemy's camp, sited at the foot of a ridge running roughly north and south down the southern face of the mountain, was flanked on either side, east and west, by open ground well prepared for defence. The plan of attack was for " A " Company, 3/K.A.R., to rush the camp from above, down the ridge, in conjunction with subsidiary holding attacks by " B " Company, 3/K.A.R., from the west and by the K.A.R. M.I. and the East Africa Mounted Rifles from commanding ground to the east, the cavalry being meanwhile posted in the plain below to intercept the enemy's retreat. The German strength was believed to be not more than about 80.

The plan miscarried from the first. " A " Company, after an exhausting night march ending in dense forest on the upper slopes, debouched from the forest at dawn and duly began its descent ; but on coming under fire its askari swerved off the ridge right-handed towards " B " Company, instead of taking to a watercourse down the eastern side, which offered cover to within a few yards of the enemy. Neither " B " Company nor the M.I. could hope to cross the cleared ground on the enemy's flanks.[3]

---

[1] British casualties were : killed, one officer, two o.r. ; wounded eight o.r.   Unhappily the officer killed was the O.C. of the Baluchi detachment, Lieutenant A. H. Wildman.   In this affair notably good work was done by an Indian officer and several men of the 130th who had been at Kasigao, and who here showed that they needed only a fair chance to prove their worth.

[2] Composition : one sqdn. 17th Cav., I.A. ; E.A.M.R., 135 strong; M.I., 3/K.A.R. ; "A," " B " Coys., 3/K.A.R.

[3] In the words of an officer present, " the situation then was that rifle " fire was being directed from both sides on the German ridge, ineffective " so far as the Germans were concerned as they had a well prepared strong- " hold among the rocks, but unfortunately resulting in casualties to our " own men on both sides ; while our snipers above were apparently firing ' on friend and foe alike."

By 10 a.m. the attack had come to a standstill. Casualties, partly from our own cross fire, were mounting ;[1] the troops were suffering from thirst, the water near by being held by the enemy. Lieutenant-Colonel Jollie broke off the attack and withdrew. Next day the German camp was found evacuated, but no further operations were attempted.

Contemporary accounts show that the cause of failure, here as at Mbuyuni, was almost certainly the omission to ensure good intercommunication between the various units engaged, and that the German force, though stronger than had been expected, well dug in and on the alert, only narrowly escaped capture.

The Coastal Area and the Railway

After the evacuation of the Umba valley in February there **Sketch 5** was little activity in the coastal area, where the only troops remaining between April and August were Wavell's Arabs and the half-battalion of Bharatpur Infantry. The latter, much affected by the climate, was relieved on the 21st August by the half-battalion of the Kapurthala Infantry, under Major-General Pooran Singh of Kapurthala State.

Six days later (27th), a detachment of this unit, 70 strong, which had been sent south across the Ramisi river in an effort to assist refugees from villages raided by the enemy, lost 15 killed in an engagement at Mzima Hill and had hastily to return to Msambweni.

The health of the Kapurthala Infantry had already suffered, and some stiffening was clearly required. The event brought out, however, the dangerous weakness of the British forces, the greater part of which was tied to the protection of the Uganda Railway. The only units available to reinforce the coastal area were a company of the 4/K.A.R., **Sketch 2** which was brought from Karungu and, from Kajiado, a detachment of the 25/Royal Fusiliers. The latter in turn soon went down with fever, and by mid-October was capable of little beyond passive defence. So threatening did the situation on the coast then appear, that the Mombasa Town Guard was called out and work begun on a new defensive line to cover Mombasa harbour in the event of the troops being driven in from Msambweni.

---

[1] Total British casualties : killed, 13 o.r. ; wounded, two officers, 33 o.r. ; missing, six o.r.

G*

Nevertheless, grave as might be concern for Mombasa, the potential menace in that direction remained secondary to the disquieting realities of the situation in the Voi-Tsavo area. Here, assisted by the full moon of the latter half of September, the enemy's raiding parties became even more active ; demolitions on the railway were almost of nightly occurrence,[1] the troops along its length became worn out in patrolling and futile pursuits in the bush, while the number of locomotives remaining undamaged steadily diminished. Morale continued to suffer. As the strength of the British forces wasted from sickness, that of the Germans increased, while the aggressive attitude of the enemy's advanced troops seemed even to point to the possibility of a German invasion.[2]

GENERAL SITUATION, AUGUST-SEPTEMBER 1915

On the 2nd August 1915 Major-General Tighe telegraphed to the War Office pointing out that, thanks to the supply of munitions landed by the German blockade-runner, the enemy's forces might well be raised to 20,000 men, and contrasting this figure with the progressive decline in his own force. On the 14th he supplemented this message with a telegraphed summary of the situation.

After mentioning the receipt of information that the enemy had already salved four and might shortly salve others of the *Königsberg* guns, and that the Admiralty had been asked to verify the rumoured arrival of a second store-ship at or near Tanga,[3] he went on as follows : " If " this is true it radically alters the whole situation. The " Germans have an unlimited recruiting area. Evidently " the two store-ships were expected, and recruits have been " trained in anticipation of arms being available. The " Germans may therefore now have 20,000 reliable troops " under arms and may be equally superior to ourselves in " field guns and machine guns ; but for the last three weeks " Mbuyuni and Taveta have been so strongly piqueted " that I have been unable to obtain any information about " enemy movements there.

---

[1] On 20th September the armoured train was derailed by a land-mine near Mtito Andei ; on 23rd and 25th near Tsavo, and on 24th near Makindu, other demolitions occurred. (Sketches 2, 4.)

[2] See also p. 164, f.n. 1.

[3] The rumour, though widely credited, was without foundation.

"Owing to ever-increasing sickness among my European
"and Indian troops my reliable infantry now totals 4,000
"men, of whom not more than 3,000 can be concentrated on
"the Maktau and Mzima lines. Should the enemy make
"a determined advance on those two lines, a contingency
"which I regard as quite possible, the situation will be
"serious. . . ."

It was not the military command alone that was anxious.
On the 24th August the naval Commander-in-Chief telegraphed to the Admiralty repeating the information given
above. He reported that the Royal Navy had already assisted
the troops by landing two of the aeroplanes used against
the *Königsberg* and two 4-inch guns with naval crews ;
that in an emergency he could also land up to 150 men for
the defence of Mombasa ; but that the general situation was
"very serious." "If submarines arrive," he added, "as is
"generally expected, there is no naval force capable of dealing
"with the situation."

To these pessimistic views no definite answer was returned
for several weeks. Indeed, at this juncture it was impossible
for Ministers in London to decide upon a policy in regard to
East Africa, for in the principal theatres of war tremendous
issues were in the balance. On the Western Front the Allies
were about to launch in Artois and Champagne the long-
projected offensive which ended, so far as the British Army
was concerned, at Loos. In the Mediterranean the renewed
attack in Gallipoli had been brought to a standstill at Suvla
Bay ; in the Balkans the imbroglio destined to necessitate
the expedition to Salonika was beginning to take shape ;
in Mesopotamia events had made it possible to visualize an
early advance on Baghdad. On the Eastern front the
Austro-German offensive had forced the Russians back from
Warsaw and the eventual outcome was uncertain. Thus in
the decisive theatres the ultimate issue depended on events
then in progress ; and therefore as yet no policy could
definitely be shaped for East Africa, nor any assistance from
home be proffered. From a different quarter, however,
some help could now possibly be expected.

At the outbreak of war, events in the Union of South
Africa had occasioned no little anxiety. But before long it
became evident that the overwhelming majority of the South
African peoples were loyal to the Allied cause, and it had
been possible to withdraw the British troops from the Union.

Early in 1915 General Botha had taken the field against the German protectorate of South-West Africa in the arduous campaign which he brought to its victorious conclusion with the German capitulation on the 9th July.

The question of assistance from the Union to the forces in East Africa was then taken up, at first demi-officially. At the outset it was complicated by two factors : General Botha desired a General Election, to ascertain the extent of his backing, before undertaking any fresh commitment ; and the British Government was naturally unwilling to divert to East Africa any resources which might be of value in the decisive theatres of war.[1]

Early in August, following on Major-General Tighe's representations in regard to his situation, further consideration was given at home to the question whether South Africa could provide the assistance which he so badly needed. On the 10th August he learned that the Union Government was preparing to send to Europe, at the request of the British Government, ten batteries of artillery which had been used in the conquest of the German south-western colony. These the Union did not feel justified in transferring to East Africa without the British Government's consent ; but at the same time, as some measure of assistance, an offer was made to open recruiting in South Africa in order to raise to a total of 800 the strength of the 2/Rhodesia Regiment, now in East Africa and already much depleted by sickness.

The offer was gratefully accepted. So also was a subsequent offer of two 5-inch howitzers not required in Europe.[2] No decision could be arrived at, however, in regard to a

---

[1] The Germans were early aware of the possibility that help might come from South Africa. Lettow mentions " news received at the end of " June 1915 that General Botha was coming to the East African theatre " from South Africa with 15,000 Boers." (" My Reminiscences," p. 72). The progress westwards of the Voi-Maktau railway seems to have been regarded by him as a particularly strong confirmation of this expectation, long before any decision as to the sending of South African troops had in fact been arrived at : " The construction of this military line proved that " an attack with large forces was in preparation, and that it was to be " directed on this particular part of the Kilimanjaro country. The " anticipated intervention of the South Africans was therefore imminent." With shrewd military insight he goes on to say : " It was important to " encourage the enemy in this intention, in order that the South Africans " should really come, and . . . in the greatest strength possible, and thus " be diverted from other and more important theatres of war. With the " greatest energy, therefore, we continued our enterprises against the " Uganda Railway." (Op. cit., pp. 74-75.)

[2] Designated No. 4 South African Howitzer Bty., and re-named in February 1916 the 12th (Howitzer) Bty. See Chap. XIII, Note I, p. 219.

more extensive South African participation in the East
African campaign until the political situation in the Union
had been cleared up by the then impending General Election.
It was agreed, nevertheless, on the 30th September that, as
a first step, two South African staff officers[1] should be sent
to East Africa to study on the spot the possibilities of co-
operation.   From this time onwards, notwithstanding various changes of plan, it was reasonably certain that South
African troops in considerable numbers would arrive in the
near future.

The struggle in East Africa thus entered upon a new
phase.

---

[1] Lieutenant-Colonel A. M. Hughes, D.S.O. ; Lieutenant-Colonel Dirk
van Deventer.

It would seem that these officers were shown the relatively open country
of the two proposed lines of advance, Voi-Maktau and Kajiado-Longido
(Sketch 2), and that, under the impression that the whole campaign would
be conducted in similar country, they recommended the sending of a considerable number of mounted troops—in whose use in guerrilla warfare
South Africa excelled—with animal transport, all unsuited to the tsetse-
infested country in which most of the subsequent fighting was to take place.
Had they been over, e.g., the Tsavo-Mzima country as a sample resembling
the probable theatre of war, they would very possibly have recommended
differently.

CHAPTER X

ON THE DEFENSIVE:

(continued)

THE SOUTHERN AREA

August 1914—May 1915

(Sketches 18, 19, 19A)

End Papers, To the south of the German colony the outbreak of war
Sketch 18 found Nyasaland and Northern Rhodesia even less prepared
than the British protectorates to the north. They had
known less than a generation of settled government ; their
white populations[1] were small and scattered ; their territories along the Anglo-German border between Lakes
Nyasa and Tanganyika were undeveloped and weakly
defended. On the German side the border districts, only
recently subdued and with no considerable white population, were equally undeveloped. The Germans had, however, the initial advantages of coming under a single political
administration and of possessing a few trained troops near
the border,[2] while their command of Lake Tanganyika
enabled them, so far as limited transport resources allowed,
to bring up reinforcements from the Central Railway
terminus at Kigoma.

Facilities for communication on either side were few.
No railway approached the border. The Stevenson Road,
which had never been properly completed, had fallen into
disrepair. In the south of Nyasaland metalled roads connected Zomba with Liwonde and Blantyre, but in the
northern districts of the two British dependencies few roads
fit for wheeled traffic existed. In the German territory
Bismarckburg was connected by road with the hill-station
of Neu Langenburg (now Tukuyu), from which a good road
went down to Mwaya. Other roads in fair condition joined
Neu Langenburg to the headquarters of neighbouring
districts at Iringa, Mahenge and Songea.

---

[1] See p. 7, f.n. 1.
[2] *5. F.K.* at Masoko ; one *Zug* (about **55**) of *6. F.K.*, detached from
Ujiji, at Bismarckburg. The latter detachment was withdrawn just
after the outbreak of war to proceed with its unit to the training camp
at Pugu (see p. 54), leaving 50 Police at Bismarckburg.

Through Nyasaland and along the border ran the African trans-continental telegraph, linking Blantyre, Zomba and Karonga with Fife and Abercorn.[1] In the German districts there was no telegraph, the quickest means of inter-communication being by heliograph through Iringa.[2]

BRITISH FORCES AUGUST 1914

(i) *Nyasaland.*—The only regular troops near the Anglo-German border were the 1/K.A.R., which normally garrisoned Nyasaland. When war broke out, however, more than half of that unit was away on service in Jubaland; of its four remaining (single) companies two were dispersed on leave and the others, recently raised, consisted mainly of recruits and were stationed in the south of the protectorate.[3] The northern border was merely patrolled by small bodies of armed police.

On receipt of the warning telegram from England on the 30th July 1914 active mobilization measures were at once taken by the Governor, Sir George Smith. Within three days the men of the 1/K.A.R. companies on leave had been recalled to Zomba ; over 100 ex-askari responded to a call to rejoin,[4] forming an addition of two " Reserve " companies ; a unit of European volunteers was formed from the Nyasaland Volunteer Reserve ;[5] the organization of a headquarters staff and of supply, transport and medical services was taken in hand.[6] In all this the ten available officers of the 1/K.A.R. received invaluable help from the

---

[1] The telegraph started from Umtali, S. Rhodesia, crossing Portuguese territory. A branch telegraph line connected Blantyre with Fort Jameson. See also p. 185, f.n. 2.

[2] The telegraph line from Kilosa to Iringa was extended to Neu Langenburg in November 1914 : " A work which was from a military point of view extremely urgent." (Lettow, " My Reminiscences," p. 95).

[3] See Appendix IV. " D " Coy. (80 strong), on return from British East Africa, and " F " Coy. (100), awaiting embarkation for Jubaland, were on leave. " G " Coy. (70), was stationed at Mangoche, " H " Coy. (50), at Bn. H.Q. at Zomba. The regular officers available were in all 1 captain, 4 lieutenants (temporary Captains), 5 lieutenants.

[4] Termed " reservists," as in Uganda and B.E.A. In all 158 rejoined, forming " A." R. and " B." R. (i.e., Reserve) Coys. 57 Police also transferred to the 1/K.A.R.

[5] Raised in 1901 as the Central Africa Rifles and reconstituted in 1908, mainly to organize the European residents for defence in case of internal trouble. Its members had formed local rifle clubs and attended lectures by the (Regular) Staff Officer to the force. Many were Government officials who could not be spared, but 70 out of a total strength of 175 were serving by 5th September. See also Appendix IV.

[6] In particular, a useful medical unit was formed under Dr. H. Stannus.

numbers (including two officers on leave from India) who hastened to offer themselves : retired officers, civilian officials, planters and traders, most of whom, including many with specialist knowledge, were given temporary commissions.

By the 10th August 1914 the 1/K.A.R. had been re-organized in three double companies,[1] which with an improvised artillery unit of four 7-pdr. M.L. guns were assembled at Fort Johnston as the Nyasaland Field Force, under Captain C. W. Barton, 1/K.A.R.

(ii) *Rhodesia.*—By the terms of its Charter the British South Africa Company was responsible for maintaining law and order within its territories and had organized military forces for the purpose, necessarily differentiating between Northern and Southern Rhodesia.

In September 1912 the Company, at the suggestion of the Committee of Imperial Defence and with the concurrence of the War Office and Colonial Office, had appointed Colonel A. H. M. (afterwards Major-General Sir Alfred) Edwards as Commandant-General of the Rhodesian forces,[2] it being arranged that in the event of war he and they would come under the orders of the High Commissioner for the Union of South Africa.

Southern Rhodesia, with its comparatively large white population[3] and longer history, possessed in the British South Africa Police a famous armed force, mainly of British personnel and for the most part mounted, about 550 strong, with a section of artillery and some 20 machine guns. This was backed by an organized body of Active Volunteers, over 850 strong, and by a number of " Rifle Companies " numbering about 1,100. On the outbreak of war the question of expanding these forces, which is dealt with hereafter, was at once vigorously taken up, and a small reinforce-ment was soon sent north to the adjoining territory.[4] As

---

[1] From "D" and "F", "G" and "A" R., "H" and "B" R. Coys. respectively.

[2] Colonel Edwards, after much service in the 1st and 5th Dragoon Guards, commanded the Imperial Light Horse and " A " Division, South African Constabulary, in the South African War, 1899–1902, and thereafter the Transvaal Volunteers. After becoming Military Secretary to the Viceroy in 1905, he retired in 1906. From 1906 to 1912 he was an Assistant Commissioner of the Metropolitan Police.

His appointment as Commandant-General (a colonial, not an army appointment) was gazetted in February 1913.

[3] See p. 7.

[4] See Chap. XI, Note II, p. 194.

yet, however, the northern border attracted less attention than the questions of service overseas and nearer home.

In Northern Rhodesia the British population was so much smaller[1] and so scattered that to maintain European units in time of peace was out of the question. The Company's force here was the Northern Rhodesia Police, of Africans under British officers, the military branch of which was about 450 strong, organized on the general lines of a battalion of the K.A.R.[2] Of its five companies, one at headquarters at Livingstone was formed as a mobile column to move wherever required, the remainder being distributed at out-stations.[3] Apart from the Police, some 300 British settlers were members of local rifle clubs; they and others were prompt in offering their services, which were gladly accepted.

As a first step, the Police posts at Abercorn and Fife were reinforced to enable patrolling to be carried out; but the weakness of the border, even after everything possible had been done to reinforce it, was to remain an anxiety throughout 1914 and 1915.

INITIAL OPERATIONS IN NYASALAND

The southern districts in which the Nyasaland Field Force End Paper (3) was assembled were in no danger, being separated from the German colony east of Lake Nyasa by a wide belt of neutral Portuguese territory. The danger point was the North Nyasa district lying west of the Lake, some 400 miles away, where the Anglo-German border followed the Songwe river for about 70 miles. To convey the Field Force thither by land over unmade tracks was obviously too long a business when quick transit could be effected by way of the Lake, the command of which it was therefore essential to secure.

A British flotilla of seven small vessels was available as transport, one of which, the *Guendolen*, was armed.[4] The

---

[1] See p. 7.
[2] Many of the men were ex-askari of the K.A.R.
[3] Distribution: H.Q. and " A " Coy., Livingstone; " B," " C," " D," " E " Coys. at Mongu, Kasempa, Kasama and Fort Jameson respectively; small detachments of " D " Coy. at Abercorn, Fife, Mporokoso, Luwingu and Fort Rosebery (sketch 18). Each company had two m.g.
[4] Three Nyasaland Government vessels, including the *Guendolen*, 350 tons, Commander E. L. Rhoades, R.N.R., armed with one 3-pdr., two 6-pdr. guns; 2 vessels of the African Lakes Corporation; 2 vessels of the Universities Mission, including the *Chauncey Maples*, 320 tons; all with speed about 9 knots.

only German vessel on the Lake was the *Hermann von Wissmann* (not to be confused with the *Hedwig von Wissmann* on Lake Tanganyika), about 90 tons, which was reported to be undergoing repairs at Sphinxhaven, a small sheltered bay on the German (eastern) shore.[1]

Early on the 13th August the *Guendolen*, carrying 25 men of the 1/K.A.R. under Captain H. G. Collins, with a demolitions expert, located the German vessel high and dry at Sphinxhaven and summoned her to surrender, to the consternation of her captain and crew, who were unaware of the outbreak of war. The captain, engineer, and mechanics having been made prisoners, the vessel was disabled by removal of essential parts of her engines, and the *Guendolen* returned to Fort Johnston.

Having thus gained command of the Lake, the Field Force, strength about 500,[2] embarked at Fort Johnston on the 16th and 17th August for Vua and by the 22nd was concentrated at Karonga, the principal British township at the head of Lake Nyasa.

Up to the 20th August no activity was shown by the enemy, whose District Commissioner at Neu Langenburg was apparently unaware that war had broken out.[3]   On that **Sketch 18** day a small German force crossed the Songwe, fired on a British patrol and occupied Kapora, three miles inside British territory.   Two days later (22nd), just as the British force was arriving, a message was received at Karonga from Captain von Langenn-Steinkeller, commanding the German troops, warning the British authorities to evacuate the place with all Europeans, especially women and children, " to avert a massacre ", since they would shortly be set upon by African troops. To this, naturally, no reply was sent.

---

[1] Sphinxhaven, so named by the Germans, consisted only of a few repair sheds and native huts, with no telegraph.

[2] Eighteen officers, 9 British volunteers, 478 o.r., with 3 m.g., 4 7-pdr. and 2 9-pdr. M.L. guns.

[3] Neu Langenburg being out of touch with the German headquarters (see p. 166), the local commander had a free hand. On 17th August a letter from the German District Commissioner at Neu Langenburg, dated 15th, enquiring whether Great Britain was at war with Germany, was received and answered by the British Resident at Karonga. Meanwhile on the 15th Lettow had telegraphed to Neu Langenburg : " Make full " use of any opportunity offered and secure the initiative by attacking " wherever possible. You can call up the police and any men fit for " service, also native auxiliaries. More precise instructions cannot be " given." The telegram, sent via Bismarckburg, took several days on the way.

During the next fortnight the Field Force collected a considerable train of carriers—a matter of some difficulty, the local natives proving unsuitable—and supply arrangements, both by land and by way of the Lake, were organized. Meanwhile reconnaissances by the *Guendolen* and the 1/K.A.R. established that about 40 of the enemy were at Kapora ; the German main force, estimated at about 570 strong with native irregulars and a field-gun, was said to be approaching from Mwaya.[1]

By the 7th September the preparations of the British force were complete.

AFFAIR OF KARONGA

9th September 1914

The country about Karonga was level, thickly covered Sketch 18 with thorn bush and high grass to a distance of five to ten miles from the shores of the Lake ; farther inland, low barren foot-hills led to a range of rocky hills. The nineteen miles of bush between Karonga and the Songwe were traversed by some few native tracks, with a rough semblance of a road running northwards from Karonga through Kirapura and Kapora, over a bridge near the mouth of the Songwe river, to the village of Songwe just inside German territory.

Having detailed a garrison, under Lieutenant P. D. Bishop, 1/K.A.R., to remain at Karonga,[2] Captain Barton planned first to dispose of Kapora. In order to obtain surprise, he decided to attack from the west instead of Sketch 19 frontally. At 2 p.m. on the 9th September his force moved off along the Mambande track, his intention being to camp for the night on the Lufira river, about midway between Mambande and Kirapura, and to attack Kapora early next morning. Soon after starting, however, he received a native's report that a party of some 40 Germans was in Mambande. To deal with these he ordered a detachment of the 1/K.A.R. forward to cross the Lufira two miles east of

---

[1] In fact 5. *F.K.* with two previously separate detachments, a small artillery unit, and native auxiliaries. A German source gives the strength as 22 Germans, 270 askari, 40 ruga-ruga, with two 3·7 cm. guns, 4 m.g., and some 500 native spearmen. Farther west a small force, mainly Wahehe irregulars, under Lieutenant Falkenstein, was operating from Itaka towards Fife. Reinforcements were said to be on the way from Iringa.

[2] Eleven British, 43 o.r., 1/K.A.R., 30 Police, 2 9-pdr. and 2 7-pdr. M.L. guns.

Mambande, turn west, and cut the German line of retreat, while with his main force he proposed to move more slowly and attack from the south and west.

At 4.45 p.m. his scouts reported parties of the enemy on the Kirapura–Karonga road, adding that Langenn's main force, moving south, had reached the Songwe. Passing on this information to Bishop at Karonga, Barton gave up his projected attack on Mambande and decided to camp, as he had originally intended, on the Lufira. Eventually, much delayed by the difficulty of the country, his force camped in the bush, a mile short of its destination, about 10 p.m. So far, except for the reports already mentioned, he had had no definite information regarding the enemy.[1]

Continuing northwards at dawn on the 9th September, Barton's leading troops reached the Lufira at 6 a.m. and became engaged with German patrols across the river. At 8.30 a.m., while this affair was still going on, the sound of gunfire from the south coincided with the arrival of a message, confirmed by natives who came up soon afterwards, to the effect that a German force was on the point of attacking Karonga, nine miles to his rear.

Hampered by his carriers and realizing the need of prompt action, Barton detached one company of the 1/K.A.R. under Captain A. H. D. Griffiths, which left at 9 a.m. to return in all haste to Karonga, while with the remainder of his force he moved across to the Kirapura–Karonga road to cut the German line of retreat.

At Karonga, where the strongly-built Residency and trading offices and compound were well suited for defence, the small garrison[2] had been attacked early on the 9th September. It put up a stout resistance until about 11 a.m., when Griffiths' company, hurrying to the sound of the firing, arrived. The attacking Germans, deployed round the

---

[1] On the evening of 8th September reports by scouts of the rearguard, corroborated by natives, that there were Germans between the Field Force and Karonga, were regarded as unlikely to be correct. In fact some of Langenn's scouts may well have been there.

[2] A British field hospital and nursing staff, also a large number of non-combatant natives, were in the compound, which was about 100 yds. square, enclosed by a loopholed five-foot brick wall.

Shortly before the attack developed a tug towing a barge with supplies for the Field Force had started from Karonga northwards along the coast. It was fired on after passing the Rukuru ; the barge broke loose, drifted ashore and was captured. The episode fortunately delayed the German guns from coming into action against the compound wall.

compound, who had already suffered considerably from the fire of the defence,[1] were totally unprepared for a sudden attack from the rear. Griffiths men fell upon them with a will; both German machine guns were surprised at short range and knocked out; and very quickly Langenn's force, broken up and straggling through the bush, was in hurried and disorderly retreat across the Rukuru. Unfortunately Griffiths' company, after its forced march and subsequent fight, was too exhausted to take up an immediate pursuit.

Meanwhile Barton with the main body encountered the first of the retreating Germans near the Kasoa stream. A party of German native spearmen was surrounded and disarmed before it realized that the oncomers were British, and a number of stray German askari were put to flight with the bayonet. About 1.30 p.m., however, in the thick bush beyond the southern bank of the Kasoa, the British force became heavily engaged with what was evidently the German main body, which had been successfully intercepted. A violent fight at short range ensued, both sides making the usual attempts to outflank each other, with guns and machine guns brought up into the line to gain a better view.[2]

About 2.30 p.m. the enemy's fire slackened and Barton charged in with the bayonet, driving back the Germans and rushing one of their guns. Rallying in the bush, however, the enemy counter-attacked, and a sudden burst of fire caused considerable loss among the 1/K.A.R. as they were re-forming. But the K.A.R. were not to be denied; they deployed and attacked again, and after some further confused fighting they drove the Germans off into the bush.[3]

---

[1] Langenn himself had been seriously wounded and temporarily blinded.

[2] British casualties so far were few, the German fire being wild and high. Cordite ammunition gave the British troops a great advantage over the Germans, the smoke of whose black powder both obscured their aim and gave away their whereabouts.

[3] Casualties were as follows. British: killed, three officers, two British volunteers, eight askari; wounded, three officers, four British volunteers, 42 askari.

German: killed (buried by the British force), seven Europeans, 51 natives; captured, three officers, 31 askari, 42 spearmen. According to a German source, the totals were: killed, six Europeans, 27 askari, six porters, 35 auxiliaries; missing 26 askari, four porters, six auxiliaries (evidently excluding the Wassungu spearmen); wounded, three officers, four Europeans, 37 askari, seven porters, four auxiliaries. An official return of 5. F.K., afterwards found, gave a total of 102 killed, wounded and missing out of a total strength of 148.

Two German guns, two m.g., many rifles and much ammunition were captured.

In a situation which was still obscure the British force was not in a position to turn and pursue the scattered Germans trickling away northwards. Early in the fight Captain Barton had himself been wounded ; he had insisted on remaining in command until sure of success, but was obliged now to hand over to Captain H. W. Stevens, who took the force back to Karonga.

There, from prisoners and collected reports, it became clear that the British and German forces had passed each other in opposite directions in the bush on the previous afternoon, and that the invaders, committed to action so far afield on inadequate information, had been lucky to escape destruction.[1]

From Karonga the Field Force, reorganized and replenished after this gratifying initial success, went forward through Kapora to the Songwe, meeting no opposition. So far as could be ascertained the German force had reassembled near Ipiana, a small post midway between the river and Mwaya.

It would have been possible now for the British force to occupy a position along the border or to take the offensive beyond it. But whereas the enemy was able to reinforce his troops from other parts of his territory, the Field Force comprised the whole available military strength of the Nyasaland Protectorate and could not afford to take risks. It was decided, therefore, to establish the Force at Karonga, fortifying that place so as to ensure successful resistance to any

---

[1] On 7th September Langenn's main force occupied Kapora. He had as yet no information as to the strength of the British forces in Karonga, but the absence of resistance by British patrols led him to under-estimate his opponent's numbers. Next day (8th), sending Lieutenant Aumann with 30 askari and 500 Wassungu auxiliaries to West Ngerenge as a flank guard, he moved south to Kirapura. At noon two different native sources gave him fairly accurately the British strength at Karonga. Unconvinced, he decided to go forward with a " reconnaissance in force " to ascertain the British strength and if possible capture Karonga. Accordingly he ordered his main body to march after dark so as to reach the mouth of the Rukuru at dawn, there to meet a detachment 50 strong to be sent by water, directing Aumann meanwhile, from West Ngerenge, to approach Karonga from the west.

Langenn heard nothing of the movements of Barton's force. Leaving his baggage north of the Lufira, he moved off at first down the direct road and then along a bush track between the road and the lake, and did not reach the Rukuru mouth until 5.45 a.m. (9th).

further hostile incursion, and maintaining patrols up to the border.[1]

The Germans made no further move. From this time until the heavy rains set in in December only occasional clashes of patrols took place. With the arrival of the wet season the state of the ground made military operations impossible, and for some time to come the Nyasaland border remained quiet.

On the 29th December 1914 command of the Nyasaland forces was assumed by Lieutenant-Colonel G. M. P. Hawthorn, 1/K.A.R.

EXPANSION OF THE RHODESIAN FORCES

The internal rebellion which broke out in the union of South Africa in September 1914 not only brought the Union's newly-started campaign in German South-West Africa to a temporary standstill, but had repercussions in Southern Rhodesia. From the outset every able-bodied man of British extraction clamoured to serve overseas ; but since no law existed to make this possible, and no force could be raised without the permission of the High Commissioner in South Africa, all that could at first be done was to draw up a register, on which over 3,000 men volunteered for overseas service. Assured of its numbers, the Administration offered a first contingent of 500 men to the Imperial Government on the 16th September. The view at home at this time being that local requirements should come first, the offer was transferred to the Union and, after consultation between Lieutenant-General Smuts and Colonel Edwards, was accepted on the 9th October. On the 15th recruiting was opened, and within a week a contingent 525 strong, including 1 officer and 25 men from Northern Rhodesia, had been raised as the 1st Rhodesia Regiment, which on the 14th November left for the Union.[2]

End Papers (S.)

---

[1] Karonga was preferable to the border area by reason both of its climate and of its supply resources. Cattle, fresh milk, vegetables and fresh fish were to be had at most seasons of the year. With the wet season (in this area from about November to May) at hand an even more important military consideration was its rainfall, about 30 inches instead of nearly 150 inches along the Songwe. " This difference favoured our forces very " greatly as compared with the enemy in the matter of health. This in itself " thoroughly justified the selection of Karonga as our defensive position." (Lieutenant-Colonel G. M. P. Hawthorn, Despatch, 11th October 1915).

[2] After garrisoning Bloemfontein during the rebellion, the 1/Rhodesia Regt. took part in the subsequent operations in German S.W. Africa, and at the conclusion of these was disbanded at Capetown.

Meanwhile, on the 22nd October the Legislative Council requested the Administration to " recruit and train forth- " with in Southern Rhodesia 1,000 men to be placed at the " disposal of the Imperial Government for active service in " this territory or elsewhere." The resulting offer was accepted on the 16th November and a further contingent, the 2nd Rhodesia Regiment, was at once raised and trained at Salisbury, eventually to form, as already recorded, a welcome reinforcement in British East Africa. Drawn from the ardently loyal British population, these fine units were in the main composed of men new to soldiering who, accepting United Kingdom rates of pay which were meagre in Colonial eyes, took quickly to arms and to Regular Army standards of discipline. They were not, however, available for the Rhodesian northern border.

To strengthen the defences there a small volunteer force was raised in Northern Rhodesia, largely by the efforts of Major R. Gordon, late Gordon Highlanders, which was named the Northern Rhodesia Rifles. In the various units of this force, some formed for local defence and some for service in the field, every able-bodied man of Northern Rhodesia's small white population hastened to enrol.

The local situation, nevertheless, gave no ground for complacency ; the watch on the Caprivi Zipfel[1] was containing a considerable portion of the available force, and on the border anything beyond a strictly defensive attitude was out of the question.

THE RHODESIAN BORDER

Sketch 18

During the first three weeks of war nothing occurred along the Rhodesian section of the border except sporadic raids by German native auxiliaries who on occasion cut the telegraph line between Abercorn and Fife. At the beginning of September Abercorn was threatened by a German force from Bismarckburg, about 100 strong,[2] with a light gun, which was accompanied by some 250 irregulars who ravaged the country, looting and committing rape, incidentally again cutting the telegraph.

On the 5th September the Abercorn garrison, 40 Northern Rhodesia Police under Lieutenant J. J. McCarthy,

---

[1] See Chap. XI, Note II, p. 194.
[2] A German return gave the strength as 4 Germans, 52 askari, 60 armed carriers, under the command of a medical man, Oberarzt Westhofen.

which had placed the only suitable building (the prison) in a state of defence, drove off a first attack by the German force.

Meanwhile the mobile column of the Northern Rhodesia Police, about 100 strong under Major H. M. Stennett, which had left Livingstone on the 8th August, was on its way to Kasama, where it arrived on the 5th September.[1] Its arrival coincided with that of a message from the Resident Magistrate at Abercorn asking for help ; the column at once pushed on, and after a march of 99 miles in 66 hours it reached Abercorn at 3 a.m. on the 9th September, meeting no opposition.

Three hours later the Germans again attacked, bringing their gun into action, and again were driven off. Next day (10th) they struck their camp and withdrew, followed up by Lieutenant McCarthy with a Police detachment which came up with them early on the 11th and chased them back across the frontier.[2]

The news of the first attack on Abercorn, coupled with the fact that the British reinforcements expected there had not yet arrived, led Mr. Lyons, the District Commissioner at Kawambwa, near the western Anglo-Belgian border, on his own initiative to send a pressing request for help to the nearest Belgian authorities, at Pweto. **End Papers (S.)**

At this time the Belgian 2nd Battalion was guarding the western shore of Lake Tanganyika, with headquarters at Lukuga (Albertville), the principal Belgian township on the Lake, and with a detached company at Baudouinville. Between Lakes Tanganyika and Mweru the 1st Battalion was being assembled at Kitope and the 3rd at Pweto. Their assembly was still in progress when on the 11th September Major Olsen,[3] commanding the troops in the Katanga province, received and acted on Mr. Lyons's message. On the 13th Lieutenant Leleux, then temporarily commanding the 1st Battalion, moved off with one company by way of Mporokoso for Abercorn, where he arrived on the 22nd.

---

[1] Formed from " A " Coy., N.R.P., which then began the formation of a second mobile column. See p. 169.

[2] British casualties at Abercorn were 3 killed. An enemy return gave the German loss as 2 irregulars killed ; the British estimate was 8 enemy killed.

[3] An officer of Danish birth with a distinguished record of service with the Belgian Congo forces, exercising his command under the Vice-Governor General of the province (at this time M. Tombeur), to whom he was Chief of Staff. (See p. 202, f.n. 2 ; B.O.A., I, pp. 24, 85).

His march was arduous owing both to lack of water and to the attitude of the local natives, who at his approach fled into the bush, leaving their villages bare of supplies. He was followed by Major Olsen himself, with the remainder of the 1st Battalion, who reached Abercorn on the 25th. The Belgians proceeded to strengthen the defences, but, in conformity with the defensive role prescribed by the Government of the Belgian Congo, made no attempt to move into German territory. Nothing further of military significance took place for some weeks,[1] and in November, the danger to Abercorn having apparently passed, the Belgian troops were recalled to their own territory. They were on the point of departure when, on the 17th and 19th November, armed parties landed from the German craft on Lake Tanganyika, Sketch 18 raided the lakeside villages of Kituta and Kasakalawe respectively.[2] In response to a request by Major Stennett, the first of the Belgian companies to depart, which had left on the 19th for Mporokoso, was recalled by Major Olsen. At the same time the latter detached from Abercorn a force about 150 strong which co-operated in driving off the raiders, who made off up the Lake. Thereafter all was quiet. On the 26th November the Belgian troops left Abercorn to return to Katanga ; in view, however, of the raids just mentioned, this was countermanded by the Belgian authorities, and the 1st Battalion remained at Mporokoso for the time being. From Mporokoso, where for a while the troops came down to half rations owing to lack of local supplies, the unit eventually returned to Abercorn, arriving at the beginning of February 1915. During the ensuing eight months the 50-mile sector between the Saisi river and Lake Tanganyika was held by the combined Rhodesian and Belgian forces.[3]

---

[1] On 27th September a German force was reported to have crossed the border and to have withdrawn on learning of the presence of the Belgian troops.

[2] At Kituta (17th November) the raiders destroyed British property, damaging the small steamer *Cecil Rhodes* which lay hauled up on the beach, and re-embarked before a Belgian party sent from Abercorn could interfere. On 19th November they seized a quantity of telegraph material at Kasakalawe and set about further destruction, but were engaged next day (20th) by 50 N.R. Police and the Belgians mentioned in the text, who with some difficulty reached the shore, fired on the German ships' boats and compelled the raiders to re-embark. No further raids from the Lake were attempted.

[3] The Belgians would have preferred to hold a separate, all-Belgian sector. (B.O.A., I, p. 96).

Meanwhile, in Northern Rhodesia mobile units of the newly-raised Northern Rhodesia Rifles, each consisting of one officer and 25 men, had been training, and in December 1914 the border was further reinforced by a column of these, under Major A. Boyd-Cunninghame, which made a notable march northwards to join the garrison of Fife.[1]

By this time the rains had set in along the border, and for the next few months the only activity was that of patrols, which from time to time were engaged in minor but often hard-fought encounters with the enemy.[2]

UNREST IN NYASALAND

In January 1915 a complication, unconnected with the war, arose in the form of a native rising in the Chiradzulu district, midway between Zomba and Blantyre. The possibility of serious trouble was averted by the prompt action of the K.A.R. depot at Zomba and of the local Europeans, and by the despatch from Karonga of a double company ("F" and "H"), 1/K.A.R., with a machine gun and a 7-pdr. M.L. gun, under Captain H. G. Collins,

End Paper (S.)

---

[1] Four units formed and trained at Broken Hill, about 100 in all, under Major Boyd-Cunninghame, left the railway at Kashitu (50 miles north of Broken Hill) to march about 320 miles across country to Kasama with 30,000 lb. of supplies in 16 ox-wagons. The Northern Rhodesia Administration has recorded that this force, having no native assistance worth mentioning, for most of the way "chopped this first wagon-road "through the fly and drove the wagons themselves: an heroic under-"taking during a period of exceptionally heavy rain."

At Kasama another unit joined from Fort Jameson. Leaving the wagons at Kasama (where all the oxen eventually died from fly), the column marched with carriers another 100 miles to Saisi, whence it went on two weeks later to Fife.

[2] On 6th and on 27th December 1914 German raiding parties near Fife were driven off by the N.R. Police. On 26th January 1915 a patrol under Captain J. J. McCarthy, N.R.P., was engaged with a small raiding party; on 17th March a Belgian platoon fought a successful minor action on the river Samfu, capturing a German officer. Near Fife, on 10th April, a German patrol was captured, and a week later (17th) a strong patrol under Major Boyd-Cunninghame successfully attacked a stockaded position at Mwenengamba, 5½ hours march east of Fife, killing or capturing 40 German askari and irregulars. In this affair unhappily Lieutenant S. Irvine, leading the attack, was killed. A month later a patrol of 40 men of the N. Rhodesia Rifles under Major Boyd-Cunninghame was heavily attacked at night, losing 2 killed, 3 wounded. On 18th April a Belgian patrol was engaged against a German post on the Kalambo river. Another Belgian detachment, established in March on the Samfu river to check hostile raids on frontier villages, had a lively action on 21st May in co-operation with a patrol of the N.R.P. under Captain McCarthy, driving off a German force. (B.O.A., I, pp. 99–103).

which was landed at Fort Johnston and made a remarkable march of 86 miles in 47 hours. The force arrived on the 29th January to find only small isolated parties left to round up, the rebels having meanwhile been defeated and scattered by some 40 British volunteers and 100 K.A.R. recruits under Captain L. E. L. Triscott, 1/K.A.R.; but the rising caused some alarm and depleted for a time the already scanty numbers of troops available to defend and patrol the border.[1]

THE ATTACK ON SPHINXHAVEN, 30TH MAY 1915[2]

End Paper (S.) In March 1915 a detachment of the Royal Navy from H.M.S. *Fox*, 3 officers and 6 ratings with five 6-pdr. Hotchkiss guns,[3] under Lieutenant-Commander G. H. Dennistoun, R.N., reached Nyasaland and took charge of the flotilla on Lake Nyasa. British command of the lake was undisputed; but in May reports were received that the Germans at Sphinxhaven were attempting to repair the damage done to the *Hermann von Wissmann* by the *Guendolen* in August 1914. It was decided to send an expedition to Sphinxhaven, with the object either of cutting out the vessel or of completing her destruction where she lay.

On the 20th May 1915 the same company of the 1/K.A.R. which had dealt with the native rising in the Chiradzulu district four months earlier, about 180 strong with two machine guns, under Captain H. G. Collins, embarked at Fort Johnston in the armed steamers *Guendolen* and *Chauncey Maples*. Having picked up medical personnel at Nkata Bay, the ships sailed for Sphinxhaven after dark on the 29th May and anchored off the German shore before dawn next morning.

---

[1] The rising was instigated by a religious fanatic named John Chilembwe of the so-called " Watch-Tower " sect. Three Europeans were murdered, and the intention was to start similar risings elsewhere in the protectorate. There is no evidence that the Germans had any hand in the matter, although messages from Chilembwe to the German authorities were intercepted. About a fortnight after the rising was quelled Chilembwe was killed by the police whilst attempting flight into Portuguese East Africa.

A German officer, Lieutenant von Veltheim, wounded and captured at Karonga in September 1914, who was at Mlanje, placed his services at the disposal of the British magistrate there, organized the defence and virtually assumed military command of the station.

[2] No account of this affair is given in " Naval Operations."

[3] Of these, two were mounted in the *Guendolen* and three, on field mountings made in Zanzibar, were later sent to Karonga. Two 12-pdr. naval guns arrived in August 1915.

The coast-line near Sphinxhaven is deeply indented, with successive small bays separated by rocky headlands. The landing place selected was a bay about a mile south of the " haven " itself, having a sandy beach on which by 4.15 a.m. on the 30th May the landing had been completed without opposition. Less than half a mile from the landing-place, whilst moving along a rough track through high grass and

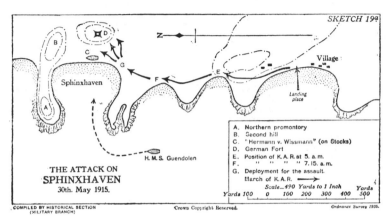

SKETCH 19a

Village

Sphinxhaven

Landing place

H. M. S. Guendolen

THE ATTACK ON
SPHINXHAVEN
30th. May 1915.

A. Northern promontory
B. Second hill
C. " Hermann v. Wissmann" (on Stocks)
D. German Fort
E. Position of K.A.R. at 5. a.m.
F.   "   "   "   " 7.15. a.m.
G. Deployment for the assault.
       March of K.A.R. ━━▶
Scale—490 Yards to 1 Inch   Yards
Yards 100   0   100 200 300 400 500

COMPILED BY HISTORICAL SECTION
(MILITARY BRANCH)   Crown Copyright Reserved.   Ordnance Survey 1935.

dense scrub, the vanguard was met by heavy rifle-fire and opened rapid fire in reply, before which the enemy retired. At daylight the advance was resumed through a stretch of very difficult bush under intermittent sniping, the *Guendolen* meanwhile shelling the northern promontory of Sphinxhaven, where German troops had been observed. Soon afterwards machine gun fire was opened from a small stone fort on a hill behind the haven. The *Guendolen's* guns then switched to this target while the two companies, supported by her fire, worked forward. At about 11 a.m. the *Guendolen* ceased fire, the charge was sounded and the German fort was rushed with the bayonet. Not standing to await the charge, the garrison disappeared into the bush and the haven was occupied.

The *Hermann von Wissmann* was found beached, with the damage done in 1914 still unrepaired, and as it was evidently impossible to tow her away, she was further disabled.[1]

---

[1] Two holes were blown in the ship's bottom with dynamite, wrecking her propeller and boilers. The slipway blocks were also wrecked.
The ship remained disabled until March 1918, when she was repaired and taken into the British service, re-named *King George*.

182   MAY 1915

About 2.30 p.m. the force re-embarked, unmolested until some of the enemy returned to open machine gun fire on the rear party.[1]

Disembarking at Vua, the troops marched to Karonga, where they rejoined the Field Force on the 1st June.[2]

---

[1] The last party, under a native N.C.O., was brought off from the northern promontory by a boat from the *Guendolen*, under Captain J. E. E. Galbraith, 1/K.A.R., covered by rapid fire from the ships.

[2] The only British casualty was Volunteer J. Sutherlànd (afterwards intelligence officer to Brigadier-General Northey), wounded.

Known German casualties were 1 killed, 5 wounded ; the fire of the ships is believed to have inflicted others. About 7,000 rounds of ammunition were captured, together with a German flag and a green flag with crescent and star.

Well-deserved tribute to the good work of the flotilla was paid in the despatch sent by the Governor of Nyasaland to the Colonial Secretary, dated 1st November 1915.

Lieutenant-Commander G. H. Dennistoun, R.N., was awarded the D.S.O. for his services on this occasion.

CHAPTER XI

ON THE DEFENSIVE:
(concluded)

THE SOUTHERN AREA

June 1915—April 1916

(Sketches 18, 20, 20A)

THE DEFENCE OF SAISI

IN the interests of British prestige among the warlike tribes **Sketch 18**
on the northern border of North-Eastern Rhodesia it was
imperative that the Germans should not be permitted to
penetrate into Rhodesian territory. Early in 1915 it was
realized that, owing to the increased strength and activity
of the enemy, the garrisons of Fife and Abercorn which
had sufficed to patrol the border in the early days of
the war were no longer able effectively to defend it. An
additional post, now essential, was therefore established
some 30 miles east of Abercorn, at a point where the valley
of the river Saisi offered the enemy a favourable line of
approach.

Known to the British as Saisi and to the Germans as **Sketch 20**
Jericho Farm, the post was sited in the angle between the
Saisi and its tributary the Mambala, on a rocky knoll overlooking the bridge by which the Stevenson road crosses the
Saisi. Consisting of an outer ring of trenches surrounding
a central fort on which much labour and ingenuity had been
expended,[1], it was garrisoned by a combined Anglo-Belgian
force some 400 strong, under Lieutenant-Colonel F. A.
Hodson, Northern Rhodesia Police, commanding the troops
on this section of the border.[2]

---

[1] The ground was mostly solid rock which, for lack of explosives, had
to be broken by the primitive expedient of lighting fires on it and then
cooling it suddenly with water.

[2] Lieutenant-Colonel Hodson assumed command on 13th December
1914. The garrison consisted of :
British : six officers, 14 British volunteers, 208 o.r., N. Rhodesia Police,
with one 7-pdr. M.L. gun, manned by B.S.A. Police, and two m.g.
Belgian : 1st Bn., six officers, 200 o.r., with one 4·7 cm. Nordenfelt
gun, one m.g.

The establishment of this post within a mile of the frontier led to increased patrolling by both sides and consequently to occasional minor encounters.[1] During June 1915, when evidence accumulated that the enemy was being considerably reinforced,[2] reconnaissance activity was intensified, patrols pushing out into German territory as far as the Mozi river, and it became apparent that an attack on the Saisi post was impending.

Early on the 28th June, under cover of thick mist along the rivers, German forces attempted to close on the post, first from the north-west and soon afterwards from the south and east. During most of the morning and part of the afternoon the garrison, supported by its two small guns from the knoll, was engaged in confused and indecisive fighting over the relatively open ground south and west of the fort. The attack was not pressed home and at nightfall the enemy withdrew.[3]

Nothing further happened at Saisi during the next four weeks, the enemy, as was learned later, awaiting reinforcements, including artillery. Command of the garrison was meanwhile taken over by Major J. J. O'Sullevan, N.R.P.[4]

On the 25th July a German force numbering about 800, with two guns, under Major-General Wahle, arrived to make a second attempt.[5] About 3.30 a.m. on the 26th July German troops were reported by the piquet on the Saisi bridge to be entrenching west of the river. Before dawn a considerable force of the enemy had occupied Lobb's Farm, about 1½ miles west of the Allied position, and by 7.40 a.m.,

---

[1] On 24th April 1915 a raiding force 130 strong under Lieutenant G. P. Burton, penetrating 34 miles into German territory, attacked a German transport column near Mwazye, dispersing its escort and capturing many carriers with their loads. On 20th June a party under Major J. J. O'Sullevan, scattered a German patrol; four days later (24th) a stronger force under Lieutenant-Colonel Hodson, attempting to surprise one German party which retreated at his approach, captured another.

[2] See Note III, p. 196.

[3] Allied casualties were : Killed, one British volunteer, two o.r., N.R.P. ; wounded, Belgian 1st Bn., six o.r.   The German losses, according to Lettow (" My Reminiscences," p. 97) were : killed, three Germans, four askari ; wounded, two Germans, 22 askari.

The attack appears to have been made by *24.* and *29. F.K.* (see Note III).

The reason given by Lettow (op. cit.) for the withdrawal is lack of artillery.

[4] Changes made in the garrison brought the totals (see p. 183, f.n. 2. above) to : British, three officers, 11 volunteers, 160 o.r. ; Belgian, six officers, 282 o.r. ; guns and m.g. unchanged.

[5] Presumably *18., 23., 24., 29. F.K.* (see Note III).

when, on the usual mist lifting, a German gun opened fire from the high ground north of the Saisi, the enemy was seen to have pushed across both the Saisi and the Mambala and to be dug in as shown on Sketch 20, investing the post.

During the 26th and 27th an intermittent shelling by the two German guns produced little effect either on the fort or its surrounding trenches, and no infantry assault was attempted. The garrison began, however, to run short of food ; it suffered also from thirst, there being no well in the fort and the river not being accessible, except at considerable risk after dark. Nevertheless the defence was maintained, the accurate fire of the Allied guns keeping down the fire of the old-pattern German pieces.[1]

On the 28th July the sound of firing to the westward indicated the approach of an attempt at relief made from Abercorn by the remainder, about 350 in all, of the Belgian 1st Battalion. A detachment, 34 strong, of that unit made its way through the investing Germans to join the garrison ; but the greater part of it was unable to get through and the investment went on.

A German summons to surrender received on the 31st July was peremptorily refused.[2] The same evening, about 7.30 p.m., a violent fire was opened by the enemy, some of whom attempted to advance to the assault, but were at once checked and drew off.[3] The attempt was not repeated.

The investment ended, with no further incident, on the night of the 2nd/3rd August, when the Germans raised the siege and withdrew

---

[1] One lucky shot by the British 7-pdr. apparently scored a direct hit on the muzzle of a German gun.
The range to the German trenches (600–1,400 yards) was somewhat long for the British rifles, most of the troops being armed with the single-loading ·303 Martini-Enfield, while some still had the ·450 Martini-Henry.

[2] By a grave mischance the British officers who went out to meet the white flag were fired upon, and a formal apology was received the same day from the German commander. In the words of a survivor of the campaign, " the conduct of the war in this sector was courteous." As an example, the telegraph line between Abercorn and Bismarckburg remained in operation until Brigadier-General Northey's arrival in February 1916, a daily test signal being exchanged between the respective postmasters.

[3] " Officers could be distinctly heard encouraging the men, but they " never came nearer than the outer thorn fence, from 200 yards to 60 yards " from the trenches. The darkness was too great to attempt a sortie or " pursuit." Major J. J. O'Sullevan, report, 5th August 1915.

The total casualties were few.[1] The relieving column, under Major de Koninck, marched in next day. It had been engaged on the 28th and 29th July with part of the investing force, crossing the Saisi on the 29th in an attempt to take the enemy in rear from the south, and its approach must certainly have contributed to Wahle's decision to abandon his enterprise.[2] In due time the thanks of His Majesty's Government were conveyed to the Belgian Government for the promptness with which the Belgian troops had been recalled to meet the emergency at Saisi and for their valiant assistance in dealing with it.

The successful defence of Saisi did much to enhance not only British but Allied prestige among the local natives, whose sympathies the Germans had made great efforts to detach, and went far to secure the border against further attack.

MOVEMENTS OF BELGIAN TROOPS

Sketch 18   The affair of Saisi had repercussions on the plans which at this time were under consideration by the Belgians for their forces as a whole. Colonel Tombeur, as we shall see,[3] after ordering the withdrawal of his three southern battalions from Katanga to the northern front, had left for the north early in June and was now out of reach. Of these battalions the 1st was at Abercorn and Saisi ; the 2nd had started northwards from Lukuga ; and the 3rd, at Pweto, where Major Olsen was still completing his many preparations for the move, was on the point of following.

On hearing of the second attack on Saisi Major de Koninck, commanding the 1st Battalion at Abercorn, at once moved to the assistance of Saisi as has just been described, reporting his action to Major Olsen. Receiving this report on the 1st August, Olsen equally promptly set out himself with the 3rd Battalion from Pweto to Abercorn. The relief

---

[1] British, one o.r. wounded ; Belgian, five killed, three wounded, one missing.

The German losses were reported by Major O'Sullevan as five Germans, 28 askari killed.

Major J. J. O'Sullevan was awarded the D.S.O. for his conduct of the defence. ʲ

[2] A report by Wahle gave as his reasons (i) that his artillery had produced little effect and (ii) that he did not feel justified in risking an assault with the bayonet " in view of the present situation in the Protectorate."

[3] See pp. 206–7.

of Saisi two days later ended the emergency, but in the existing situation Olsen decided to remain on the Rhodesian border for the time being. At the end of August the 3rd Battalion took over Saisi, the 1st returning to Abercorn, and during the next two months these units kept up reconnaissance and patrolling with the object, in the words of the Belgian official account, of attracting the enemy's forces southwards and thus, by dividing them, compensating for their own defection from the attacking forces in the north.[1]

The modification in Belgian plans resulting from Olsen's independent action led in September to discussion between the British and Belgian authorities, both locally and at home, as to the continuance of Belgian co-operation on the Rhodesian border. The High Commissioner in South Africa, called upon for his opinion, telegraphed on the 16th September to the Colonial Secretary that the Belgian troops should remain, at any rate until the new South African contingent arrived and command of Lake Tanganyika—which he expected by mid-November—had been secured ; their withdrawal might lead to a serious German incursion, endangering both British and Belgian territory, the effect of which would offset any Belgian offensive farther north. This view did not prevail, however ; on the 29th October the 3rd Battalion, and on the 3rd November the 1st Battalion, left Rhodesia.

REORGANIZATION OF THE FORCES

Meanwhile, the news of the investment of Saisi had given Emd Paper a sharp stimulus to recruiting throughout both Rhodesia (S.) and the Union of South Africa. The campaign in German South West Africa had come to its victorious close and was no longer a pre-occupation. But the need to reinforce the northern borders of Nyasaland and Rhodesia, already recognized, became more insistent.

For Nyasaland arrangements had been made in July to raise a contingent, ultimately 264 strong, mainly departmental units, in South Africa. A suggestion made on the 9th August by the Commandant General in Rhodesia that, in addition to the raising of another 300 men locally, a further contingent should be raised in the Union was commended

---

[1] B.O.A., I, p. 121.

by Lord Buxton to the Colonial Office.[1]   On the 16th August Mr. Bonar Law replied that His Majesty's Government would be grateful if a contingent of 1,000 men from South Africa for service on the border could be recruited at South African rates of pay.[2] This was at once agreed to by the Union and the additional contingent,[3] which like its immediate predecessor was to play its part in Brigadier-General Northey's operations in 1916, was raised without delay.

In the meantime the additional 300 men raised in Southern Rhodesia were enrolled in the B.S.A. Police.[4] By the 18th October 1915 they had reached their destination, arriving in good time to replace the Belgian troops.

Notwithstanding their arrival, however, the departure of the Belgians so far depleted the fighting strength on the border that Lieutenant-Colonel Hodson deemed it necessary to dispense with the post at Saisi, which was evacuated and **Sketch 18** demolished at the end of October. In its place a new post was established by the Nyasaland authorities at Fort Hill, mid-way between Karonga and Fife.[5]

In November 1915 the Commandant General proposed that in Southern Rhodesia, which hitherto had drawn only

---

[1] ". . . Commandant-General . . . proposes to raise 300 men locally " and to despatch latter to border via Broken Hill, but owing to the " immense difficulty connected with . . . transport . . . any force . . " sent this way must be comparatively small, whereas eventually a con- " siderable force may be necessary not only to deal with the enemy but in " view of possible native trouble in Nyasaland, which would be aggravated " presumably by a British reverse, and . . . might spread elsewhere. . . . " [Administrator] considers . . . defence [of the] line Tanganyika to " Nyasaland affects Nyasaland and Imperial interests as much as " Rhodesian and that the retirement of the Rhodesian forces from the " border would seriously increase the danger of native trouble in Nyasa- " land." (Telegram, Lord Buxton to S. of S. for the Colonies, 10th August 1915.)

[2] The financial aspect of this matter appears to have been one of the factors which led eventually to the War Office taking over the control of the operations in the southern area, where at this time the military organization was still controlled by the Colonial Office.

[3] 1st and 2nd South African Rifles.

[4] These men were recruited to form two " Special Service Companies," partly from serving police but mainly from Rhodesian volunteers, with a few ex-soldiers of the 1/Rhodesia Regt. who had served with that unit in the German S.W. Africa campaign.

"A" Special Service Coy., with one 12-pdr. gun, leaving Livingstone on 18th August, went by road from Broken Hill to Abercorn ; " B " Coy., to minimise transport and supply difficulties, moved via Beira, Chinde and Fort Johnston to Fife.

[5] German raids into British territory near Fife led to sharp encounters on 20th October and 22nd December 1915.

on its white population, a unit of native troops, preferably Matabele, should also be formed. This proposal, however, which resulted eventually in the raising of the Rhodesia Native Regiment, was not finally approved until April 1916.[1]

APPOINTMENT OF BRIGADIER-GENERAL NORTHEY

The High Commissioner in South Africa, after giving his views in September 1915 in regard to Belgian co-operation on the Rhodesian border, had urged that on the arrival of reinforcements a more active defence should be undertaken. The continued passive defence, he said, was " having a " demoralizing effect on our troops and the opposite effect " on the enemy's morale ", and he feared that British prestige among the natives was being impaired.

Lord Buxton's recommendation of increased activity was approved on the 27th September, " if local military " authorities concur ". As the logical outcome he cabled on the 9th October a further suggestion that, in view of the increasing importance of the military situation on the border, a senior British Regular officer should be appointed to the command of all the Allied forces operating on it.[2] In this he was strongly supported by Colonel Edwards, who was himself eligible for the suggested appointment but more valuable in his own ; and early in November, when the departure of the Belgian troops had simplified the matter into one solely for British decision, Lord Buxton's proposal was approved.

On the 12th November 1915 Brigadier-General E. Northey was appointed as Commander of the Combined " Forces on the Rhodesia-Nyasaland Frontier of German " East Africa ", and on the 4th December he sailed for Capetown on the way to take up his command.[3] His

---

[1] See Chap. XXVIII.

[2] In a further telegram (13th October) Lord Buxton stated that the total number of troops, including 1,200 Belgians, would be about 4,500 men. These figures appear to be exclusive of the reinforcements then being raised in the Union.

[3] Brigadier-General Northey had previously seen active service in India (1891–2) and in South Africa (1899–1902). In 1914 he had commanded his battalion (1/K.R.R.C.) from Mons to Ypres and later he had commanded the 15th Infantry Bde. in the battles of Ypres, 1915, where he was wounded.

Accompanied by his principal staff officer (Captain W. A. C. Saunders-Knox-Gore, D.S.O., K.R.R.C.), he reached Capetown on 24th December, and four days later went on to Pretoria.

On arrival in Africa he came under the orders of the Colonial Office.

appointment marked the opening of a new phase of the campaign in the southern area of operations.

Although decided upon to meet a local situation, the new appointment chanced to come about at a moment when British policy with regard to the campaign as a whole was under special consideration by the Government.[1] No very precise instructions, therefore, could be laid down for Brigadier-General Northey either by the War Office, which had selected him, or by the Colonial Office, under which he was to serve. All that the former could tell him was that his task would be to ensure the security of the Nyasaland–Rhodesia border and that his forces would be too small to attempt an invasion of German territory; his rôle, in short, must be defensive.[2] Anything more definite than this would, it is evident, have been premature and, since the situation might alter before his arrival, might have proved impossible of execution. He had, however, ample opportunity before leaving England to confer with General Sir Horace Smith-Dorrien, newly designated to command in East Africa.

Reaching Pretoria on the 30th December 1915, Brigadier-General Northey discussed the situation with the High Commissioner and with Generals Botha and Smuts. Agreement was quickly reached on a vigorous policy of driving back the Germans from the border as soon as the strength of the forces and the conditions of climate would permit, and three days later he continued his journey. At Bulawayo, Livingstone and Salisbury in succession he went fully into local conditions and administrative problems, in particular " the very difficult question of supply and transport over

---

[1] See p. 213.

[2] These instructions were given verbally by the Director of Military Operations (Major-General C. E. Callwell) and do not appear to have been put on record. The War Office views, as conveyed by letter to the Colonial Office, may be summarised as follows : No serious offensive on the border was likely to be possible until the arrival of the South African reinforcements. Combined operation by British and Belgian flotillas on Lake Tanganyika, with a view to a Belgian landing at Kigoma and an advance on Tabora, were projected for December. A main offensive by Sir Horace Smith-Dorrien might be expected in January. It was therefore likely that the enemy's pressure on the southern border would shortly be sensibly decreased. Brigadier-General Northey would be kept informed of any contemplated movements in order that he might, " as far as possible, " arrange co-operative offensive action." The War Office letter continued : " His primary function is to secure the British territory in " Rhodesia, but he should also take such measures as will facilitate the " proposed operations mentioned above and as are within the power of the " forces at his disposal to carry out with reasonable prospect of success." (W.O. letter 22nd November, 1915.)

" the Rhodesian Railway to the north-eastern border ",[1] with the Commandant General and other Rhodesian authorities. Going on through Beira and Chinde and thence up the Zambezi, he reached Zomba on the 29th January and, after a fortnight spent there in a thorough reorganization and co-ordination of transport, medical and supply arrangements in Nyasaland, he finally reached the border at Karonga on the 16th February 1916.

It remained now for him to inspect the 250 miles of frontier for which he had become responsible, from Karonga through Fort Hill and Fife (Ikawa) to Abercorn. This he at once proceeded to do, reconstituting and modernizing the old-fashioned defences at these places, arranging for carriers and supplies, road-making, and preparing generally for the more active policy now to be followed.[2] The journey from Karonga to Abercorn and back took up seven weeks ; but on his return early in April to Karonga, where he established his headquarters, he was able to write in his War Diary :
" I am now quite satisfied of the security of the border, " and that it will be defended in the best way, that is, by " no opportunity being lost of fighting the enemy . . .".[3]

THE GENERAL SITUATION, APRIL 1916

By the beginning of April 1916 the general situation in the southern area of the theatre of war had greatly improved. The arrival of South African and Rhodesian reinforcements had ensured at least the security of the border ; the appointment of Brigadier General Northey had established a unified

---

[1] War Diary, Brigadier-General Northey.

[2] Most of the border defences were conspicuous high-command works of a pre-machine-gun era, requiring such large garrisons for their extensive perimeter that no troops remained to form a striking force. By constructing smaller works laid out on up-to-date lines Brigadier General Northey was able to release the troops necessary for his fighting columns.

His report brought out the need for howitzers and rifle-grenades, since the enemy's defences likewise were high-command works, mostly sited on hill-tops.

The number of carriers available had hitherto been only sufficient to convey supplies up to the frontier ; much organization was therefore required to enable mobile forces to get forward.

There had also for some time been a serious shortage of native food, reserves of which had to be built up.

[3] On 25th February 1916 the C.I.G.S. telegraphed to Lieutenant-General Smuts informing him of Brigadier-General Northey's primary function in terms identical with those of the War Office letter of 22nd November 1915 already quoted, preceding these with the words " whilst " conforming as far as local circumstances permit to your instructions."

command ; the reorganization of defences was actively proceeding, while preparations for carrying out the more vigorous policy now decided upon were well advanced. Meanwhile the success of the British flotilla on Lake Tanganyika[1] had endowed the Belgians with a new freedom of movement, and had thereby contributed materially to the planning of inter-allied co-operation.

During the rainy season, of which only a few more weeks remained, patrolling of the border was kept up, although with the small forces available it was impossible to obtain full information as to the enemy's strength and distribution. New German posts had been established at Luwiwa, thirteen miles north-east of Fife, and Namema, eleven miles north of Saisi. But even though reinforcements might conceivably reach the enemy from the interior of the German territory, there could be little doubt that the British forces distributed along the border now outnumbered considerably those opposed to them.[2]

It was therefore possible to look forward with confidence to the near future, and to envisage a welcome prospect of activity, on however small a scale, co-ordinated with that of the forces of Lieutenant-General Smuts in the main theatre of war.

NOTE I

THE TANGANYIKA NAVAL EXPEDITION[3]

End Papers　　On Lake Tanganyika, where within a fortnight of the outbreak of war the Germans had disabled the solitary Belgian vessel,[4] the enemy's command of the Lake waters remained throughout 1915 undisputed and to all appearance indisputable. Thus the German western frontier was protected, while considerable number of Belgian troops were immobilized in the passive defence of the Belgian shores : a situation obviously bearing on the question of Belgian co-operation in general.[5]

In April 1915 it was suggested to the Admiralty by Mr. J. R. Lee, a big-game hunter with both knowledge of the country and naval experience, that a naval detachment with light motorboats should be sent out to deal with the German craft on the Lake. His suggestion was reinforced almost immediately by a

---

[1] See Note I, p. 193.
[2] See Note III, p. 196.
[3] See " Naval Operations," Vol. IV, pp. 81–5
[4] See p. 28.
[5] See Chap XII.

similar proposal made independently through the War Office, as a result of Brigadier-General Malleson's discussions with the Belgians at Ruchuru.[1] Accordingly the Admiralty " determined to treat these waters as an outlying sea within the " sphere of British naval power."[2]

Early in June 1915 two motor-boats, christened *Mimi* and *Toutou*, each armed with a 3-pdr. gun and a machine gun, with a detachment of the Royal Navy under Commander G. B. Spicer-Simson, R.N.,[3] were despatched in the utmost secrecy from England. The story of their epic journey of over 8,000 miles, transported by sea to the Cape, thence by train to the Belgian Congo territory, then by tractors and oxen through untracked forests and over high hills to the Lualaba river and so by way of the Kabalo-Lukuga railway to Lake Tanganyika, has been told elsewhere.[4]

The expedition reached the Lake at the end of October 1915 and spent the next two months in building a safe harbour, named by it Kalemie.[5]. Its operations now came under the control of the Commandant General in Rhodesia, he being the nearest British military commander.

On the 23rd December the boats were launched and three days later (26th) they fought what their commander called " a " naval action in miniature ", in which within eleven minutes of opening fire the *Mimi* disabled the German armed steamboat *Kingani*, which hauled down her colours.[6] Ordered into the British harbour, the *Kingani* was so badly damaged that she sank just after reaching it ; but within three days she was refloated and repaired. A 12-pdr. gun was added to her armament[7] and on the 15th January 1916, being the first German warship to be brought in as a prize and transferred to the Royal Navy, she hoisted the White Ensign as H.M.S. *Fifi* of the British flotilla.

No further action took place until the 8th February 1916 (the *Toutou* having meanwhile been sunk in a storm), when the German vessel *Hedwig von Wissmann* (not to be confused with the *Hermann von Wissmann* on Lake Nyasa) was brought to action and sunk in flames. In neither this nor the previous action were there any British casualties.

---

[1] See pp. 198–202.
[2] " Naval Operations," Vol. IV, p. 81.
[3] Director of the Gambia Survey, 1910–14.
[4] In addition to the official account, a full account by Commander Spicer-Simson is given in the Journal of the Royal United Service Institution for November 1934.
[5] Under the prevailing strong S.E. wind, blowing straight up the lake, heavy seas dangerous to small craft at times arise.
[6] *Mimi* scored 12 hits in 13 rounds. The German crew lost both officers and three out of four seamen killed.
[7] " The ship . . . was only 56 feet long, while the gun was 12 feet " long ; when we fired it right ahead, the recoil stopped the way, even . . . " at full speed." (Commander Spicer-Simson, op. cit.)

Of the two German vessels remaining, one, a small craft similar to the *Kingani*, was later chased on to the coast and wrecked ; the other, the newly-built *Graf von Götzen*, about 1,000 tons, believed to be armed with some of the *Königsberg's* guns, caused some anxiety by her presence but remained inactive in harbour at Kigoma, where Belgian aircraft bombed her from time to time.[1]

Meanwhile, however, the successful action of the British naval craft had completely reversed the previous situation on Lake Tanganyika. With the disappearance of the *Hedwig von Wissmann* the command of that inland sea passed finally to the Allies.

NOTE II

THE CAPRIVI ZIPFEL

End Paper (S.) At the outbreak of war the defence of Northern Rhodesia was complicated by the fact that the south-western corner of that dependency marched with the projecting tip (in German, *Zipfel*) of a narrow strip of German territory which extended eastwards from German South-West Africa to within thirty miles of the Victoria Falls. This, known as the Caprivi Zipfel or Strip, had originally been acquired for Germany in 1890 by the Chancellor after whom it was named, in order to afford a trade outlet to the waters of the Zambezi.

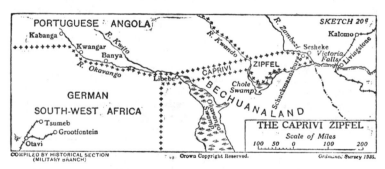

To meet possible attack from this direction against the Victoria Falls bridge, a point of vital importance[2] on the railway running from the Cape through the Rhodesias to the Belgian

---

[1] The *Graf von Götzen* was eventually scuttled by the Germans in July 1916.

[2] Had the bridge been destroyed it could hardly have been rebuilt in war time, being 650 feet long, with a central span of 500 feet, across a gorge some 400 feet deep.

Congo, two troops of the B.S.A. Police were sent from Southern Rhodesia in the early days of the war to reinforce the Northern Rhodesia Police, and on the 21st September 1914 a combined column of the two Police forces, under Major A. E. Capell, B.S.A. Police, occupied Schuckmannsburg, the only place of any importance in the area, unopposed.

To the west the country is a desert. Nevertheless, it being still possible that German troops from the south-west might attempt to break across in order to join those in German East Africa, the Police detachments remained in the vicinity, the B.S.A. Police being eventually replaced by the second of the two mobile columns formed by the Northern Rhodesia Police (see p. 177). Reconnaissance westwards, however, was restricted both by the difficulties of the country and the lack of troops, and the situation was met by enrolling a small group of expert lion-hunters as special-service scouts in the B.S.A. Police, who pushed westwards across the Kwando river to Libebe on the Okavango and thence north-westwards up the River Kwito, meeting a variety of adventures and maintaining an effective watch.[1] They ascertained that the Germans, having destroyed the Portuguese posts at Kwangar and elsewhere, had a clear road in that direction if they could surmount the difficulties of the country.

During May and June 1915, as General Botha's forces operating in German South-West Africa drove the enemy before them, it began to seem more likely that the Germans, and in particular the Boer rebels led by Maritz who had gone over to them, might attempt to break away north-eastwards. Detachments of the N. Rhodesia Police were accordingly sent forward from Kasempa, Mongu and Livingstone to the line of the Zambezi north of Sesheke.[2]

On the 8th July 1915—the day before the enemy's capitulation near Tsumeb to General Botha—information was received by the Government of Southern Rhodesia that a large party including Maritz, with a considerable train of wagons and animals, pursued by the Union forces, was in flight and might make for the Victoria Falls. A reinforcement of 100 B.S.A. Police, with two machine guns, under Major A. J. Tomlinson, was sent up and a combined force concentrated at Sesheke under Lieutenant-Colonel H. M. Stennett, while Major R. Gordon[3] was sent westwards into German territory to take command of the scouts working there and to gain touch with the South Africans.

---

[1] See Wienholt, " The Story of a Lion Hunt."
[2] Including a N.R.P. post at Sioma, 100 miles N.W. of Sesheke, where it was thought wagons could cross.
[3] See p. 176.

At the end of August 1915 Gordon's men joined hands with Union troops sent forward from Grootfontein (G.S.W.A.) by General Botha after the German surrender.' Maritz and his party, however, succeeded in escaping into Portuguese territory, which was still neutral, and were interned. Gordon then turned to pursue another party including 8 Germans, trailed them across the wilderness for 135 miles in eight days, rounded them up on the 17th September and brought them back some 700 miles to Livingstone.

The last of the enemy in German South West Africa having now been disposed of, the Rhodesian forces were withdrawn and towards the end of 1915 reinforced the northern border about Fife and Abercorn.

Note III

SOUTHERN AREA

German Reinforcements

April–July 1915

During the early months of 1915 German troops gradually concentrated at Bismarckburg, movement being restricted by the inadequacy of lake transport (the steamer *Graf von Götzen*, completing at Kigoma, was not ready until June).

In April, *22. F.K.* from Kigoma, with *18.* and *23. F.K.* from Dar-es-Salaam, were ·ordered to Bismarckburg, where also a local detachment was expanded by recruits from Kigoma to form the *29.F.K.* Command of this force was assigned to Major von Langenn, but in May this officer with *18., 22.,* and *23.F.K.* was sent on to Neu Langenburg. On 25th May Major-General Wahle assumed command of the southern area, bringing with him *24.F.K.* and part of *10.Sch.K.*, the latter being soon afterwards divided up between the other units. On 17th June Wahle sailed from Kigoma in the *Graf von Götzen* for Bismarckburg, whence he marched on 21st June towards Saisi. His strength on 15th July 1915 was given as :

	German	Askari	
24.F.K.	19	222	2 m.g.
29.F.K.	33	128	2 m.g.
Staff and details	4		2 field guns, old pattern, (C/73).
Total	56	350	2 guns, 4 m.g.

To these were later added, from Neu Langenburg area :

	German	Askari	
18.F.K.	18	152	2 m.g.
23.F.K.	15	178	2 m.g.
Total	33	330	4 m.g.

Leaving at Neu Langenburg :

	German	Askari	
5.F.K. and details ..	57	599	1 4·1-in. gun.
22.F.K.	16	207	6 m.g.
Staff	5		
Total	78	806	1 gun., 6 m.g.
Inclusive Total ..	167	1,486	3 guns, 14 m.g.

CHAPTER XII
PLANS FOR BELGIAN CO-OPERATION
October 1914—April 1916
(Sketch 3)

End Paper (N.) AT the meeting at Kibati in October 1914 between Captain Grogan and M. Henry[1] the latter had stated that he now had about 1,000 men north of lake Kivu and 700 between that lake and Lake Tanganyika, and had offered, in the event of a British attack, either to take the offensive in German territory or to assist the British forces with such troops as could be spared.

He over-estimated, however, the German strength opposed to him,[2] putting this at 2,000 men, mainly about Lake Tanganyika. On this basis he feared that any Belgian offensive north of Lake Kivu would expose Uvira, or even the railway then under construction towards Lukuga, to considerable danger, unless carried out in conjunction with a British offensive from Uganda. The Belgian policy, therefore, he said, was to stand on the defensive until the British desired Belgian co-operation ; and here the matter rested for the time being.

At the beginning of January 1915, in prompt response to a request by the British commander in Uganda, a Belgian force of 500 men, with 2 guns, took over the defence of the Sketch 3 Uganda border in the Kigezi district. Their arrival had a good effect on the hitherto unruly Batusi in this area, and the civil administration was soon afterwards restored to normal.

Meanwhile, as the outcome of discussion between the British and Belgian Governments, the principle of full cooperation along the whole of the Belgian Congo border had been accepted. Its acceptance coincided with a suggestion made to the War Office on the 8th January 1915 by Major-General Wapshare that Brigadier-General Malleson, whom he was sending to confer with the Governor of Uganda, should go on from Uganda to gain touch with the Belgians and ascertain their general situation, since a threat from their direction might materially assist an attack elsewhere by dispersing the enemy's forces. He added that, as no

---

[1] See p. 29.
[2] See p. 49, f.n. 3.

198

official sanction for co-operation had yet been received, it was intended that Brigadier-General Malleson's mission should be "on purely non-committal lines."

On the 10th January a War Office memorandum on the military situation in East Africa, drawn up for transmission to the Belgian Government, was sent to the Foreign Office with a letter confirming the Army Council's advocacy of full co-operation. Brigadier-General Malleson's mission was approved by the War Office, with the intimation that there was "no need that it should be on non-committal lines" and that Major-General Wapshare should "endeavour to "arrange the fullest possible co-operation" between his own and the Belgian forces.[1] Brigadier-General Malleson accordingly left Nairobi on the 16th January and, after a difficult journey, reached Ruchuru on the 14th February.[2]

He had with him an appreciation, drawn up at G.H.Q. on the 13th January 1915, which showed that Major-General Wapshare, having but scanty information regarding either the Belgian forces or the Germans opposed to them, had not yet been able to come to a decision in regard to co-operation between the Allies along the northern half of the Congo border, but could not reinforce to any appreciable extent his small force in Uganda. On the 20th January Brigadier-General Malleson, after conferring with the Governor of Uganda, had suggested to G.H.Q. an endeavour to attract German forces into Ruanda by a British advance from Uganda against Kigali, and an effort to isolate them there, both by a Belgian advance through Usumbura and by the capture of Bukoba and Mwanza. No details, however, had been worked out, and the difficulties of communication—even a telegram took six to ten days between Ruchuru and Nairobi—were an insuperable obstacle to any rapid concerting of plans.[3]

---

[1] W.O. telegram, 11th January 1915.

[2] By car from Nairobi via Entebbe and Kampala to Fort Portal, on foot across the slopes of Ruwenzori towards Lake George, and so to the Belgian frontier post at Kisindi. Continuing by canoe for five days down Lake Edward, in danger from hippopotamus and crocodile, Brigadier-General Malleson reached Kibale, whence with a Belgian escort he marched to Ruchuru. (Sketch 3).

[3] As the records now available do not bear the dates of receipt, it is impossible to reconstruct the exact sequence of events, although it is evident that a number of mutually conflicting telegrams crossed each other.

The difficulty of Brigadier-General Malleson's mission in this respect suggests the utility in East African warfare of wireless in any such mission hereafter. The need for very precise instructions and full information is markedly brought out in the various documents examined.

Major-General Wapshare had been ordered, it will be remembered, to restrict himself to the defensive. In a telegram dated the 29th January, which must have over-taken Brigadier-General Malleson, the latter was informed of this decision and, in reply to his suggestions, was instructed that all proposals for co-operation with the Belgians or for operations from Uganda would have to be submitted to the War Office. Major-General Wapshare added that, although unwilling to send a column to Kigali and unable to do so before the rains, he was prepared " to " co-operate during March by operations on the Lake and " threatening or capturing Bukoba or Mwanza, or both," and called for the views of the Belgian authorities.

End Paper (N.) In the meantime the British Government, approving the War Office memorandum advocating co-operation, communicated it to the Belgian Government on the 27th January. Its arrival had been anticipated by the Belgian Minister for the Colonies, who on the 20th January telegraphed to the Governor-General of the Congo not only informing him of the acceptance of co-operation but adding that an offensive by the Belgians was envisaged for the month of April.[1] The Minister supplemented this telegram by a letter dated 23rd January, giving it as his Government's view that the action to be taken would probably consist of an Anglo-Belgian advance from Abercorn against Bismarckburg ; a Belgian offensive in the north, directed first against Kisenyi and the Ruanda district and later against Usumbura ; and organization of the defensive along Lake Tanganyika and the river Russisi. With this in view the Governor-General was called upon to bring his forces north of Uvira up to a total of 5,000 men, possibly to be increased to 7,000, by drawing on reserves and garrisons in the interior of the Congo colony.

This plan, which seems to have been formulated independently by the Belgian Government as its interpretation of the agreement on co-operation, was communicated by M. Henry to Brigadier-General Malleson immediately on the latter's arrival at Ruchuru in February. It conveyed to him, not unnaturally, the impression of a change of inter-allied policy of which he had no knowledge, and thus, although he was received with the utmost cordiality, he felt himself from the outset somewhat at a disadvantage.

---

[1] B.O.A., I, p. 173.

The Belgians were, moreover, in serious straits with regard to transport and munitions, and several of their frontier posts were short of food. Emphasizing that they could undertake no serious operations until their ammunition needs in particular were made good, M. Henry asked that these requirements should be transported via Mombasa and Uganda, a request which added considerably to the demands already being made on the British transport system.[1]

During the next six weeks a variety of plans were discussed. It was soon apparent that, while the Belgians at Ruchuru assumed both the possibility and the necessity of large-scale British operations in co-operation with their own, Major-General Wapshare was in no position to undertake more than minor local activities. Sanction to the construction of the Voi-Maktau railway had led him to assume that on its completion he would be reinforced for an invasion of German East Africa in which the Belgians would collaborate ; but on the 11th March, in keeping with his previous instructions to remain on the defensive, he was informed that this assumption was unwarranted. Any co-operation with the Belgians must be effected with the troops already at his disposal and would be subject to War Office approval.

His intimation of this to Brigadier-General Malleson crossed a proposal by the latter that the Belgians, whose numbers were now definitely to be increased to 7,000, of whom some 5,000 would be available for the offensive, should traverse Uganda and concentrate at Masaka ; they would then eventually strike southwards through Mwanza against Tabora and the Central Railway concurrently with a British offensive on a large scale against the German colony. This proposal is of interest as being the first suggestion of Tabora as an objective.[2]

But it did not commend itself to M. Henry ; and Major-General Wapshare, in view of his orders from home, could not accept it. The utmost he could offer was to attack Mwanza in conjunction with a Belgian advance on Kigali ; moreover, even if a large-scale offensive were eventually sanctioned, he could not promise any assistance to the

---

[1] A detachment of 2 officers and 50 men of the 4/K.A.R. was sent at the end of March to Fort Portal to act as escort from that point onwards for various Belgian consignments of arms and ammunition which arrived via Nairobi, Kisumu and Kampala during the ensuing weeks.

[2] See Chaps. XXV, XXVI.

Belgians in the way of supplies or transport : " their co-
" operation must be self-contained and made from their
" own base."[1]

End Paper
(S.) On the 23rd March Brigadier-General Malleson was
informed by M. Henry that control of the whole of the
Belgian operations was to be taken over by M. Tombeur,
the acting Governor of the Katanga Province.[2] As M.
Tombeur was at this time at Elisabethville, completely
out of touch, and as M. Henry now regarded himself as
divested of authority, Brigadier-General Malleson had no
option but to return to Nairobi.

Although his mission had achieved little practical result
and a combined offensive seemed indefinitely postponed,
he had gained a useful insight into both the Belgian point of
view and the practical difficulties inherent in co-operation.
As a minor outcome it was agreed that the Belgian force in
the Kigezi district, already mentioned, should remain,
affording valuable assistance to the scattered British forces.

Before leaving Ruchuru Brigadier-General Malleson
wrote at some length to M. Tombeur on the situation
generally, again urging the strategic value of his suggestion
that Tabora should be the Belgian objective. In this connection he touched also on the German command of Lake
Tanganyika,[3] which continued for some months to be the
governing factor in the Belgian Congo situation.

Meanwhile in the south co-operation between the British
forces in Rhodesia and the Belgians in Katanga had also
been for some time under discussion. As early as the
beginning of September 1914,[4] Belgian troops had been
sent to the assistance of the small British garrison of
Abercorn. At the end of November 1914 the Administrator

---

[1] Telegram, 16th March. Proposals for action on Lake Victoria were
renewed in April and May by Major-General Tighe after Brigadier-General
Malleson's return, and led ultimately to the attack on Bukoba in June
(see pp. 150–153), which was made independently of Belgian co-operation.

[2] On the outbreak of war M. Charles-Ernest Tombeur, Inspecteur
d'Etat, acting Vice-Governor-General of Katanga Province, exercised
command of the troops in that area. He was subsequently commissioned
(see p. 203, f.n. 2). (B.O.A., I, p. 85).

[3] Brigadier-General Malleson had discussed at Ruchuru the possibility
of bringing light craft of the Royal Navy to Lake Tanganyika to end
the German supremacy on those waters. Proposals to this effect were
eventually telegraphed to the War Office on 26th April 1915, after his
return to Nairobi. By a curious coincidence these had been anticipated
by similar proposals sent independently to the Admiralty and received
only a few days earlier. See Chap. XI, Note I, p. 192.

[4] See p. 177.

of Northern Rhodesia, Mr. L. A. Wallace, with the Commandant General of the Rhodesian forces, Colonel A. H. M. Edwards, had visited Elisabethville to confer with M. Tombeur. Full agreement was reached, on the basis that so long as Belgian troops remained in Northern Rhodesia these should be under the orders of the senior British officer, and that the British should guard the border between Fife and Abercorn while the Belgians, based on Abercorn, should cover the southern shores of Lake Tanganyika.

For several months discussions on policy between the British and Belgian Governments continued, not without considerable divergences of view. Matters were not made easier by the fact that the Rhodesian forces were local troops, administered by the Colonial Office, over whom the War Office had no official control : a feature of British administration which, seeming incomprehensibly anomalous to the Belgian Government, led at times to complaint and undoubtedly hampered negotiations for co-operation in the campaign as a whole.[1]

Among those who took part in discussions in London in January 1915 was Lieutenant-Colonel Molitor, who at the outbreak of war had been in command of the Belgian Force Publique in the Eastern Province.[2] Returning at the

---

[1] For example, the Belgian note of May 1915 (see p. 205) refers to " the " multiplicity of British authorities "—British East Africa, Uganda, Rhodesia, South Africa, Nyasaland—and observes, with some show of reason, that on the British side " unity of command does not seem to " have been realized."

[2] Lieutenant-Colonel Molitor, on deputation to Europe, had been designated for the command of all the Belgian Congo forces, and in January had conferred with the War Office, on his way through London back to the Congo. His selection had been notified by the War Office to Major-General Wapshare and by the latter to Brigadier-General Malleson.

On 23rd February 1915 the Belgian Government, in view of the expansion of their forces (the Belgian note of May 1915 gives the reason as *L'importance croissante des effectifs*), appointed M. Tombeur to assume the direction of the Belgian operations as a whole (*prendre la direction de l'ensemble des opérations*), with Lieutenant-Colonel Molitor as his Chief of Staff, local command being assumed in the Eastern and Katanga Provinces respectively by M. Henry, then at Kibati, and by Major Olsen, hitherto Chief of Staff in Katanga, at Pweto.

As the B.O.A. points out, Pweto and Kibati are 500 miles apart, and having regard to the distances involved it is not surprising that M. Tombeur's control could only be established gradually. It took a month for news of his appointment to reach M. Henry. (B.O.A., I, p. 176, f.n. 1).

On 3rd July 1915 M. Tombeur and M. Henry were commissioned respectively as colonel and lieutenant-colonel in the Force Publique. (B.O.A., I, p. 273).

end of February, this officer passed through Salisbury (Southern Rhodesia) on his way to Elisabethville, and good use was made of the opportunity for further consultation.

His visit coincided with the receipt by Colonel Edwards of a letter from M. Tombeur, whose insistent advocacy of a general inter-allied offensive against the German colony had already been transmitted to the High Commissioner in South Africa.[1] M. Tombeur urged that an offensive from the Rhodesian border was an indispensable concomitant to a concerted Anglo-Belgian offensive which, he said, had been agreed upon to take place, at a date as yet undecided, on the frontiers of Uganda and the Belgian Eastern Province. He envisaged in very general terms a methodical and encircling penetration of the German territory.[2]

Accordingly at Salisbury Lieutenant-Colonel Molitor suggested a combined advance on Bismarckburg, to divert German attention from the offensive in the north. The Germans, however, retaining command of Lake Tanganyika, were in a position not merely to reinforce Bismarckburg but to land troops in flank and rear of any columns committed to such an operation. It was extremely doubtful, too, whether the Allied forces in that area could obtain either carriers or supplies in sufficient quantity ; nor was any motor transport available, even from South Africa.[3] The

---

[1] " The offensive is certainly possible and should result in a complete " success . . . if all the frontiers are attacked at the same time : on the " coast line, the British East Africa frontier, Uganda, the Belgian Congo, " Rhodesia, Nyasaland and Mozambique." (M. Tombeur, 1st February 1915).

[2] " In a general way the march of all existing columns should have " as their objective the railway from Dar-es-Salaam to Tanganyika. It " is no doubt on some point of the line that the Germans have organized " the base of their defence. This point will be either Kilosa or Tabora. " It will only become known by passing through the country. It is " evident that all the Allied forces should converge on this point. . . ." (M. Tombeur, 18th February 1915).

[3] All available M.T. in South Africa had been taken for the operations then still in progress against German South-West Africa.

A calculation dated 15th April by the Administrator of Northern Rhodesia showed that to supply a force of, say, 2,000 Belgians and 1,000 British operating from Abercorn for 14 days would necessitate raising and feeding a total of 6,000 carriers for carrying food alone. There was little prospect of living on the country ; nor could a force be supported from resources to be found in German territory, if occupied, until June when the new crops would have ripened.

scantily-populated country between Abercorn and Bismarck-burg was barren, and from the supply point of view a far preferable, and probably essential, first objective would be the fertile area about Neu Langenburg.[1]

These objections could hardly be contested. In due course, after referring them to London, the High Commissioner for South Africa was instructed by the Colonial Office that when the time came—probably not before May or June—for the Anglo-Belgian operations contemplated in the north, Rhodesian forces might " be able to make a " diversion by adopting a less passive attitude " ; but that it seemed undesirable that they should adopt " any seriously " aggressive measures such as attack on Bismarckburg or " Neu Langenburg."[2]

Meanwhile, M. Tombeur had nevertheless continued to press on his Government during March his own very different policy. As a first pre-requisite he rightly stressed the necessity, already referred to, of gaining command of Lake Tanganyika, observing that this should be a task for the Belgians, who had river and rail access to the lake, rather than for the British. He proceeded to reiterate his advocacy of a converging attack by the British, the Belgians, and the Portuguese, " so that the Germans would " have to confront seven or eight attacks among which " they would find it awkward to distinguish the most " important."[3]

End Paper (N.)

His views were endorsed by the Belgian Government, which, early in May, propounded them to the Foreign Office as affording the only plan likely to lead to a decision. The strength of the Belgian forces was given as 10,000 men, of whom 6,000 were in the north for the proposed main attack, 2,000 in the south for a demonstration against Bismarck-burg, and 2,000 maintaining the defensive along the western shore of Lake Tanganyika. Stating that these would reach their maximum efficiency by the 1st July, the Belgian Government dealt at some length with the situation generally, urging that a combined general offensive should be undertaken by that date. If, on the other hand, the proposal for an advance against Bismarckburg were not accepted, the

---

[1] This was borne out in 1916. See Chap. XXVII.
[2] Telegram, 8th April. The War Office telegraphed to the High Commissioner in the same sense on 10th.
[3] B.O.A., I., pp. 178–181.

Belgian Government proposed to withdraw immediately for use elsewhere their troops now in Rhodesia, rather than leave them there inactive.[1]

Unfortunately, as the War Office had already indicated to Major-General Tighe,[2] it was quite impossible for the British Government to give a favourable answer. In a formal reply on the 24th June Sir Edward Grey, while re-affirming the general principle of full Anglo-Belgian co-operation along the frontiers of the German colony, in the south no less than in the north, made it clear that no general offensive could at present be undertaken. His Majesty's Government, he said, being committed to most arduous operations in Europe and being obliged to devote all its resources to these, could assume no new burdens in Africa ; its forces in that theatre of war, therefore, must remain on the defensive. With regard to the Belgian decision to withdraw in that case from Rhodesia, he could but point out that such a withdrawal might leave open the whole southern coast of Lake Tanganyika, thereby not only endangering Belgian territory but also inevitably imperilling the success of the forthcoming naval expedition[3] to that lake. He suggested that withdrawal should at any rate be postponed until the result of the naval expedition should be known.

Meanwhile, having become aware early in June of the British views, the Belgian Government had on the 12th June authorized M. Tombeur to withdraw from Rhodesia if he deemed it safe to do so, and to use his troops in Katanga as he thought best;[4] and on the 7th July the British Government was informed to this effect.

Monsieur—now Colonel—Tombeur had indeed already made his decision. Since his three battalions in Katanga

---

[1] Replying on 22nd April 1915 to M. Tombeur, the Belgian Minister for the Colonies laid down, as the three-fold aim of military effort on the Congo frontier :

    (1) To gain command of Lake Tanganyika,

    (2) To deter the enemy from invading Belgian territory by compelling him to defend his own,

    (3) To occupy, as a pledge, part of the German territory, viz., Ruanda and Urundi, seeking if possible to extend that occupation as far as Lake Victoria.

The first of these appeared difficult and could not be the first step. M. Tombeur was to be the sole judge as to dispositions to be made and operations to be undertaken. (B.O.A., I., pp. 192-4 ; II., p. 125).

[2] See p. 146, f.n. 1.

[3] See Chap. XI, Note I, p. 192.

[4] B.O.A., I., p. 200.

were not to be used in the south he destined them for an offensive eastwards from the line of the Russisi, to be made in conjunction with his main thrust from Lake Kivu into Ruanda, in August or September.[1] He gave orders accordingly ; but his own movements[2] carried him ever farther out of touch, and the course of events on the Rhodesian border[3] compelled his local subordinate, Major Olsen, not merely to defer the withdrawal ordered but, on the contrary, to reinforce the battalion already in Rhodesia.

This combination of circumstances was held by the Belgian authorities to have vitiated Colonel Tombeur's plan of campaign, drawn up at the end of July, in which participation by the Katanga troops was an integral factor.[4] In any case at this time the situation along the Congo border was such that there could be no question of an early Belgian offensive. With the exception of minor local operations, Belgian activities for some months to come were restricted, like those of the British, to re-organization and preparation.

The Belgian aims, however—the conquest of Ruanda and the command of Lake Tanganyika—remained unchanged. Colonel Tombeur, on reaching the northern zone of operations early in November 1915, proceeded at once to reorganize with this object in view. Apart from the **End Paper (S.)**

---

[1] B.O.A., I., p. 201. A suggestion made by Colonel Tombeur in a letter dated 10th June, that the Katanga troops could best be used by bringing them round through Beira and Mombasa to participate by surprise in the suggested advance from Mwanza on Tabora was not followed up. B.O.A., I., p. 106.

[2] Colonel Tombeur with his staff left Pweto on 6th June for the north on a five months' journey, inspecting and re-organizing as he went, and eventually reached Kibati on 11th November. B.O.A., I., p. 191, footnote.

[3] See pp. 186–7.

[4] Colonel Tombeur's plan, dated 31st July, envisaged a Belgian conquest of Ruanda without British assistance. (*Il n'est guère désirable pour nous que les troupes de l'Uganda participent à la conquête du Ruanda*). It included, however, establishment of a Belgian flotilla to regain command of Lake Tanganyika and the suggestion that operations there would be assisted by a British naval demonstration on the sea coast, having regard to the importance attached by the Germans to the Central Railway. The time needed for the transfer of the Katanga troops and for preparation for the flotilla would necessitate postponement of the operations until the end of September. (B.O.A., I, pp. 203–211).

The suggestion of a naval demonstration, which was conveyed to the British Government in August, was found unacceptable, since no troops were available to make an effective landing, without which it was felt that such a demonstration would be worse than useless. Though no mention of it was made, the Tanga failure can hardly have been forgotten.

units still in the southern province of Katanga[1] and distributed for defence along the shores of Lake Tanganyika,
his forces then totalled some 9,000 fighting troops, organized
in eight battalions.[2] Since, however, his supply, transport
and communication services were as yet incomplete, and the
heavy rains of the winter months would impede movement,
Colonel Tombeur decided to remain for the time being on
the defensive, meanwhile completing preparations for an
eventual advance.

One essential factor in these preparations was the problem of the command of Lake Tanganyika.   The early
successes of the Germans had been ended by the British
naval expedition, which by wresting from them the control
of those waters had secured the flank of any Belgian advance
north of the lake.[3] The news of the successful engagement
with the *Hedwig von Wissmann* was received at British
headquarters in Nairobi on the 15th February 1916, and
active co-operation by the Belgian forces now became a
practical possibility.

As a first step, early in January 1916, Major-General
Tighe despatched Major E. S. Grogan as liaison officer
with the Belgian forces. On the way to take up his appointment Major Grogan conferred on the 20th January at
Masaka with the Governor of Uganda and the principal
military officers of that area. A meeting was then arranged
between Major-General Tombeur[4] and the Governor of
Uganda, Sir Frederick Jackson, with their respective staffs,
who met on the 6th February at Lutobo. As the outcome of
the conference the Belgian authorities agreed to take the
offensive as soon as certain additional transport facilities[5]
and the necessary medical services for them could be
furnished from British resources, stipulating also that British

---

[1] See pp. 186–7. The 1st and 3rd Battalions, marching by inland routes
did not reach the Russisi front until the end of January 1916.   By contrast
it may be noted that the same journey is normally made by steamer up
Lake Tanganyika in four days.

[2] Increased by April 1916 to 12 battalions, forming four 3-battalion
regiments.   The subsequent operations of the Belgians are narrated in
Chap. XXVI.

[3] See Chap. XI, Note I, p. 192.

[4] Colonel Tombeur was promoted Major-General on 23rd January
1916.   B.O.A., I, p. 219.

[5] They asked for 5,000 carriers, organized under British officers, and
an ox-train of 100 wagons, agreeing that the cost should be defrayed
by the Belgian Government.   Ratification by the Belgian Government
was received during March.

troops should take over the outpost line in the Kigezi hills
which they had maintained since the early days of the
war.[1]   The difficulty, however, of obtaining the carriers
indispensable to any military operation made delay inevitable ; the transport problems confronting the British
forces were already grave enough.   Consequently it was
found necessary in the end to defer the Belgian offensive,
first until the end of March, then to the middle of April
1916.[2]

---

[1] See pp. 50, 198.
[2] See Chap. XXVI.

CHAPTER XIII

PREPARATIONS FOR THE OFFENSIVE

THE NORTHERN AREA

September 1915—February 1916

(Sketch 2)

End Paper
(N) THROUGHOUT British East Africa the prospective arrival of South African help had from the first had a stimulant effect, reviving energies which during the long period of enforced inaction had tended to become dormant, notwithstanding the patriotic enthusiasm with which so many had earlier sprung to arms. Mention has been made of the legitimate claims, both of agriculture and of commerce, which in the earlier months of 1915 had diminished the strength of the volunteer units.[1] The German menace, however, had continued to increase; compulsory service was already in sight in Great Britain; and nothing less, it was felt, was appropriate in East Africa.

On the 6th September 1915 a mass meeting of settlers held at Nairobi adopted unanimously a resolution to this effect, which was accepted by Sir Henry Belfield and was acted upon without delay. A central War Council[2] of civil and military authorities, presided over by Mr. (afterwards Sir Charles) Bowring, was set up and returns were prepared of all the white population.

British East Africa was thus not only the first of the overseas dependencies to adopt the principle of compulsory military service, but was the only one to do so on the initiative of its own popular representatives outside the Administration.

The result, however, was rather to emphasize the considerable effort already made than to tap any important

---

[1] See p. 131.

[2] "A vital necessity in the establishment of confidence between the "local government, the military authorities and the settlers . . ." Its resolutions . . . "were adopted in every case." (Sir C. Bowring).

In this connection generally, notable service was given by Major E. S. Grogan, who played a large part in the meeting of 6th September.

new source of man-power.[1] It was obvious that the only
profitable course would be to concentrate upon the expansion of the King's African Rifles, towards which the first
steps had already been taken.[2] Nevertheless the renewed
sense of general participation in the war effort of the Empire
had an inspiring effect on all concerned.

POLICY AND COMMAND

Meanwhile, the subject of future policy in regard to the
East Africa campaign was under discussion both in London
and at Nairobi. Major-General Tighe's somewhat depressing
summary, cabled on the 14th August,[3] was supplemented
in due time by a previously-written appreciation sent on
the 31st July, which reached the War Office on the 30th
August. With these before him the C.I.G.S., Lieutenant-
General Sir Archibald Murray, prepared for Lord Kitchener
a memorandum on the situation, dated the 8th October.
In it he emphasized the strategic advantages held by the
enemy, the possibility of a German offensive against British
East Africa, and the adverse effects which would result if
such an offensive were successful. To provide for the security
of the British protectorate, he said, reinforcements of " at
" least one brigade of reliable infantry " would be required ;
but " in order to render our position permanently secure
" and to restore our damaged prestige in that theatre of
" war " offensive action would be necessary, for which, he
estimated, " about 10,000 men " would be needed in all.

Concurrently with the problem of military reinforcements, there had arisen as a separate matter the Belgian
Government's proposal, made at the end of August, that
German attention should be diverted from Lake Tanganyika
by a British naval demonstration on the German seaboard,
preferably against Dar-es-Salaam.[4] This proposition was

---

[1] Three months later, telegrams (23rd and 29th December 1915) from
the G.O.C. to the War Office gave the following figures : 850 settlers and
270 government officials were serving in some military capacity (E.A.M.R.,
town guards, etc.). Of 1,437 other " whites " fit for service, 193 were
aliens or missionaries or otherwise unavailable ; 453 could not be released
from government or railway employ. Of the 791 remaining, no more than
99 could be taken without grave interference with the economy of the
protectorate, vital alike to the civil population and to the military forces.

[2] See Appx. IV.

[3] See pp. 162–3.

[4] See p. 207, f.n. 4. It was known that guns from the *Königsberg* had
been mounted at Dar-es-Salaam.

unfavourably received by the British authorities both at home and on the spot.

On the 8th November their opposition was confirmed by an inter-departmental conference, held in London at the instance of the Foreign Office, under the chairmanship of Vice-Admiral Sir D. A. Gamble. Endorsing the professional view that a naval demonstration without an effective landing would be useless, the conference expressed the opinion that neither this nor any offensive operation should be undertaken unless a brigade, in addition to the force which had been promised on the 1st November by the Union Government,[1] could take part. It further recommended that " the question of entire control of operations in " Rhodesia, Nyasaland and German East Africa should " receive the consideration of the War Council."

Resulting from this, a special sub-committee of the Committee of Imperial Defence, assembled by direction of the Prime Minister, recommended on the 12th November as follows :

(*a*) that steps should be taken " to ensure the con- " quest of this German colony with as little delay as " possible " ;

(*b*) that, accepting the general figure of 10,000 already suggested by the C.I.G.S. for the reinforcements necessary, a New Army brigade[2] should be sent to East Africa to make up two complete brigades of white troops which, with the others already arranged for, would bring the total to 12,600 ;

(*c*) that an adequate staff for the large numbers involved should be furnished from home.

It also recorded its opinion that :

(*a*) since the transport of troops must take time and the rains in the area affected would begin about April, it was " desirable to move the Union Government to " proffer further assistance to make sure of success " during the few weeks available " ;

(*b*) Belgian co-operation was desirable and could only be secured " by placing a definite and consistent military " policy before the Belgian military authorities ". On

---

[1] See p. 215.
[2] The 1st S. African Inf. Bde., then in England, having been specially enlisted for service elsewhere, was not available to be diverted to East Africa, as had been suggested by the Union Government.

this point it was suggested that, when a plan of campaign had been decided upon, the Belgians should be informed of its main features and be invited to co-operate.

These conclusions were accepted by the British Government, which on the 22nd November 1915 selected General Sir Horace Smith-Dorrien for the command of the new expedition against German East Africa.

Sir Horace proceeded to draw up a detailed memorandum on the situation as he saw it. He pointed out that offensive operations would call for considerable numbers of heavy guns, aeroplanes and transport vehicles. He proposed, as his general plan, to engage the main German forces in the Kilimanjaro area by convergent movements westwards from **Sketch 2** Maktau and southwards from Kajiado, the Rhodesian and Belgian forces meanwhile containing the outlying German detachments. A separate force was then to make a surprise landing, preferably at Dar-es-Salaam, to strike at the enemy's rear and line of communication. Given sufficient strength to carry out this enveloping movement, General Smith-Dorrien hoped that the campaign might be quickly brought to an end ; but he saw no promise of a decision before the rains of April and wished to defer the decisive general attack until the drier months later in the year.

The whole scheme was strongly opposed by Lord Kitchener.[1] He had been out of England, visiting the Dardanelles, when the matter was under discussion. On his return he protested strongly against any such diversion of force from the principal theatres of war. In a formal minute of dissent, dated 14th December 1915, he expressed his fear that the proposed reinforcements would prove inadequate despite expectation, and characterized the whole idea of an offensive in East Africa as " a dangerous project in the " present state of the war, when we require to concentrate " all our efforts on defeating the Germans in Europe ".

Lord Kitchener's protest was over-ruled by the Government. On the 18th December Sir Horace Smith-Dorrien was formally appointed to the command, and on the 24th he sailed for East Africa by way of the Cape, where he had been directed to confer with the Union authorities as to the raising and equipment of the reinforcements from South Africa.[2]

---

[1] Lord Kitchener, having visited German East Africa in 1885 (see p. 4), had some personal knowledge of the local conditions.

[2] For the formal instructions given to General Sir H. Smith-Dorrien on his appointment see Note II, p. 222.

Unhappily he fell ill on the first day of the voyage and developed pneumonia. Having recovered to some extent by the time of his arrival in South Africa, he was able to begin making his arrangements for the coming campaign, but further ill-health compelled him reluctantly to resign his appointment and return to England.

On the 6th February 1916 South Africa's famous leader, Lieutenant-General Jan C. Smuts, became Commander-in-Chief of the forces in East Africa.

RE-ORGANIZATION OF THE EAST AFRICAN FORCES

At Nairobi an intimation that the Union of South Africa might be able to provide assistance on a larger scale than had been expected had led Major-General Tighe to issue on the 2nd November 1915 to his subordinate commanders a plan for convergent movements against the Kilimanjaro **End Paper** area from Maktau and Kajiado respectively. At the same **(S)** time he asked the naval authorities to consider making raids on Kilwa, Lindi, and Mikindani in order to divert the German reserves in that direction and arouse unrest among the native population.

On the 24th November 1915 he was informed of General Sir H. Smith-Dorrien's selection for the command. Five days later (29th) his proposals for the preliminary grouping of his troops were approved by the War Office, subject to Sir H. Smith-Dorrien's final decision, and he was directed to improve facilities for movement and supply, especially water-supply, along the proposed lines of advance.

The prospect of a transition to the offensive necessitated in any case considerable re-organization. The arrangement by which throughout 1915 the troops, whilst pinned to a passive defensive, had been administered under the Mombasa and Nairobi Area commands respectively[1] in no way corresponded to the requirements of an offensive. In December, therefore, the bulk of the troops in the Nairobi area were **Sketch 2** ear-marked to form a " Magadi Division ", which in January 1916 became the 1st Division, destined for the Kajiado–Longido line of advance ; the troops about Lake Victoria were allotted to an independent area command ; and the nucleus of a 2nd Division was organized from the units in the Voi-Tsavo area, where much preliminary hard work had

---

[1] See p. 117.

already been done on road and rail communications, including preparations to extend the Maktau branch railway westwards.[1]

THE SOUTH AFRICAN EXPEDITIONARY FORCE

In the meantime the extent and nature of the aid to be provided by the Union of South Africa were taking shape. To an early proposal by the Union to send five batteries of artillery the British Government demurred, having already asked for the despatch of all available artillerymen to Europe. Cavalry, on the other hand, were not needed on the Western Front, consequently the South African mounted units were available. Eventually the War Office, requested that the Union should send to East Africa one infantry brigade and five batteries of artillery, with the necessary supply and medical units. On the 19th October 1915 the British headquarters in East Africa was empowered to correspond direct with the South African authorities on matters of detail, and in conformity with an offer cabled by the Union Government on the 1st November it was arranged that South Africa should furnish one infantry brigade, one battalion designated the Cape Corps (coloured troops, " Cape boys "), one reserve battalion and two mounted regiments. Soon afterwards three field batteries were added. The provision of two additional mounted regiments was also foreshadowed, with a view to forming a mounted brigade.

Recruiting, which opened in South Africa in November, was so successful that the projected establishment of the contingent for East Africa was substantially increased. By the 13th the Union was able to announce the raising of five mounted regiments, six infantry battalions and five batteries of artillery, with the necessary services and a large amount of transport. Soon afterwards the promise of infantry was raised to two full brigades (eight battalions) in addition to the Cape Corps.[2] By the beginning of December most of

---

[1] See p. 130, f.n. 1.

[2] The principal units formed were :

1st South African Mounted Brigade .. (unbrigaded)	1st, 2nd, 3rd S.A. Horse. 4th S.A. Horse.
2nd South African Infantry Brigade	5/, 6/, 7/, 8/S.A. Infantry.
3rd South African Infantry Brigade .. (unbrigaded)	9/, 10/, 11/, 12/S.A. Infantry. Cape Corps (one bn.).
South African Field Artillery ..	1st, 2nd, 3rd, 4th, 5th Batteries.
Medical units	2nd S.A. Field Ambulance, 2nd S.A. General Hospital.

Continued at foot of next page.

the units were up to establishment and it had been decided that they should proceed to East Africa between the 15th December 1915 and the end of January 1916. At last the coming of these eagerly-awaited reinforcements was a certainty, and it had become possible seriously to make plans for passing to the offensive. The prospect restored confidence and aroused elation throughout the East African command.

Early in December the distribution to be taken up by the South African units on their arrival was worked out in an exchange of telegrams between Major-General Tighe and the War Office. During January and February 1916 the new units arriving were moved into camps sited in accordance with the general plan, and by the end of February their dispositions were for all practical purposes complete.[1]

OTHER REINFORCEMENTS

In addition to the reinforcements from South Africa, the 40th Pathans and 129th (D.C.O.) Baluchis from the Indian Corps, which was being withdrawn from France, were transferred to East Africa, reaching Mombasa early in January 1916.

In December two batteries of 5-inch howitzers, one battery of 4-inch naval guns, and one battery of 12-pdr. (18 cwt. naval) guns were allotted from England.[2] In addition three sections of armoured cars and the 570th (M.T.) Coy., R.A.S.C., were sent from home, the latter reaching Mombasa on 27th November.

Another welcome addition to the forces was a detachment of the Royal Naval Air Service under Flight-Commander J. T. Cull, R.N.A.S., 15 strong, with two Caudron aeroplanes, which had taken part in the *Königsberg* operations ; they reached Maktau on the 9th September 1915. They had many difficulties to overcome,[3] and coupled with these the breaking of the monsoon temporarily put a stop to flying.

Continued from previous page.

On 24th December 1915 two regiments of the 1st Mtd. Bde. embarked at Durban, followed a week later by the remaining regiment. The 2nd S. Afr. Inf. Bde., 4th S. Afr. Horse, S. Afr. Fd. Arty., and medical units embarked during January 1916 ; 3rd S. Afr. Inf. Bde. and Cape Corps followed in February.(•)

The total of the original South African Expeditionary Force for E. Africa, despatched up to 31st March 1916, was about 18,700.

[1] See p. 219. The first South Africans (1st S.A. Mtd. Bde.) landed at Mombasa on 30th December 1915.

[2] See Note I, p. 219.

[3] See " The War in the Air," Vol. III, pp. 21 *et seq.*

By the end of December, however, when a third machine and additional pilots had arrived, routine air reconnaissance and photography were possible, and even in the bush useful information was being obtained. The R.N.A.S. further contributed four Rolls-Royce armoured cars, previously used in the German S.W. Africa campaign, which did valuable work against hostile patrols in the Maktau area and later were to prove their tactical utility in battle.

LABOUR

Behind the fighting troops a large and increasing number of native carriers was employed by the supply and transport services.

Construction of the Voi-Maktau railway and its accessory works had absorbed such large numbers of the locally-recruited carriers that by the end of 1915 the Carrier Section of the East African Transport Corps had come to resemble a labour rather than a transport organization. Consequently in February 1916 a Military Labour Bureau was formed to take over the staff and duties of the former Carrier Section, thus becoming the controlling authority for all native labour and transport personnel.[1]

SUPPLY

Supply requirements were calculated on the basis of maintaining in East Africa 90 days' supplies for the whole force, the needs of Indian units being furnished from India and those of British, Rhodesia and South African troops from South Africa. Ammunition was provided on a basis of 1,000 rounds per rifle, 1,500 rounds per field gun, and 750 to 1,000 rounds per howitzer and heavy gun. To replace wastage in arms some 11,000 rifles were sent from Hong Kong.[2]

---

[1] Major O. F. Watkins, head of the Carrier Section, now became Director of Military Labour. A special branch of the E.A. Pay Corps, formed in March 1916 to deal with enlisted African labour, was transferred in July 1916 to the Military Labour Bureau, and thereafter was responsible for the pay of all African personnel with the forces, other than fighting troops. In April 1916 the M.L.B. became responsible for the equipment of carriers and labour units, for which previously there had been no prescribed source of supply.

The European establishment for native labour and transport units was fixed at the figure found best from experience, viz., two officers, four British N.C.O.s, per 1,000 Africans.

[2] These rifles had originally been bought in China for the Russian Government. Whilst on the way to East Africa, 5,000 of them were diverted to Arabia for the use of the Sherif of Mecca.

In the forward areas the problems of supply became ever more formidable as the new troops assembled.[1] The 2½-inch pipe-line laid forward from Bura to Mbuyuni could supply 40,000 gallons of water a day, while tanks carried by rail could add a further 20,000 gallons, and storage was provided in the forward camps. The daily requirement of the force, however, was of the order of 100,000 gallons, and it was therefore necessary to hold back a proportion of the troops until the last moment at Maktau and Mashoti. Even so, water-supply was a constant anxiety.[2]

THE FORCES AS A WHOLE

Although during the period here under review the first substantial increase in the K.A.R. was in progress, administrative problems of finance, training and provision of officers were as yet obstacles to any large-scale expansion. The outstanding value of these troops for African bush warfare was fully realized;[3] but it was still widely taken for granted that the campaign could be concluded quickly by the forces available from other parts of the Empire, and in the large assemblage of units for the projected offensive the proportion of combatant native African troops was small.

The forces as a whole, however, were imposing, at any rate in point of numbers. On the 3rd February 1916 the total strength of the combatant units in the country and on their way was estimated at 27,350, with 71 guns and 123

---

[1] The volume of traffic handled on the Maktau branch railway is indicated by the following figures :

October 1915	.. ..	15,146 train-miles.
November 1915	.. ..	21,983 train-miles.
December 1915	.. ..	25,478 train-miles.
January 1916 ..	.. ..	32,064 train-miles.
February 1916	.. ..	38,206 train-miles.

[2] On 26th February 1916 the head works of the water supply in the hills above Bura were damaged by a raiding party of English-speaking Germans who posed as English and bluffed the official in charge. On their return journey they were captured. Though liable to be dealt with as spies, they were treated as ordinary prisoners of war.

[3] In August 1915 Major-General Tighe's G.S.O.1 (Lieutenant-Colonel, afterwards Major-General, S. H. Sheppard) wrote : " . . . the more " African troops we have, the better." A month later he wrote : " . . . " The K.A.R. . . . hardly ever lose a rifle. . . . The conclusion is the " same that every thinking soldier in the force has arrived at after a year " in British East Africa, namely that only the best and most highly trained " troops, British or Indian, are or can hope to be a match for the trained " Africans of a fighting tribe in the bush . . ."

machine guns.[1] Of these by far the greater part consisted of British, South African and Indian units, of whom more than half were entirely new to the country, unacclimatized, and inexperienced in the conditions of warfare peculiar to it.

NOTE I

ARTILLERY UNITS IN EAST AFRICA

The artillery units and formations of the British force at the beginning of the offensive in 1916 were :

(i) *4th Indian Mountain Artillery Brigade :* 27th and 28th (Indian) Mountain Batteries, R.A., each six 10-pdr. guns, with pack mule transport.[2] These two batteries had arrived in October and November 1914 with I.E.F. "C" and "B" respectively. A Brigade Headquarters was lacking until formed on the 1st December 1915 at Maktau under Lieutenant-Colonel C. E. Forestier-Walker, R.A. In fact, however, the two batteries did not serve together as a brigade, and the Brigade Headquarters extended its command to include various other units. At Salaita (12th February 1916), for example, the command consisted of the 28th Mountain Battery R.A., the Calcutta Volunteer Battery (afterwards No. 8 Battery) and the 1st Light Battery (afterwards No. 6 Battery). At this time the 27th Mountain Battery, R.A., was in the Longido-Magadi area. Later No. 9 Battery (Royal Marines) was included.

(ii) *South African Field Artillery* (arrived January 1916) : Five four-gun batteries, 13-pdr. Q.F., with horse and mule transport and ammunition columns. These batteries were numbered 1 to 5, Nos. 1 and 3 batteries forming the 1st Brigade and Nos. 2, 4 and 5 the 2nd Brigade.

---

[1] The distribution generally of the principal units was decided upon as follows :
  Maktau Striking Force : Force H.Q. ; two S. Afr. Infantry Bdes. ; Voi Bde. (25/R. Fus., 2/Rhodesia Regt., 130th Baluchis, five coys. 3/K.A.R.) ; 4th S. Afr. Horse ; Belfield's Scouts ; four armoured cars ; three bties. S. Afr. Fd. Arty. ; 28th Mtn. Bty., R.A. ; remaining British artillery.
  Tsavo-Mzima : 2/Kashmir Rif. ; four coys. 4/K.A.R.
  Longido area : S. Afr. Mtd. Bde. ; E.A.M.R. ; one sqn. 17th Cav. ; 29th Punjabis ; 129th Baluchis ; half-bn. 3/Kashmir Rif. ; four coys. 1/K.A.R. ; Cape Corps (one bn.) ; two bties. S. Afr. Fd. Arty. ; one composite Field Bty. ; 27th Mtn. Bty., R.A.

[2] At the end of 1915 one section of each mountain battery was equipped experimentally with carrier-transport in place of pack mules in areas infested by tsetse fly. The original gun-shields were replaced at the end of 1915 by a lighter pattern, manufactured from specially hardened steel in the Nairobi ordnance workshops.

(iii) *No. 6 Battery* (previously No. 1 Light Battery): two naval 12-pdr. 8 cwt. (originally two naval 3-pdr.), manned by personnel from the 2/Loyal North Lancashire under Major R. H. Logan. Drawn by M.T. (at first Hupmobiles, later Reo lorries).

(iv) *No. 7 Battery :* four 15-pdr. B.L., used during 1915 for local defence at Maktau and Besil (then known as Nos. 2 and 6 Light Batteries and manned by details of Indian Infantry and Royal Fusiliers). Constituted early in February 1916 as a mobile battery, manned largely by R.G.A. personnel from Mauritius, under Captain H. N. J. Keene, R.G.A. Drawn by ox transport.[1]

(v) *No. 8 Battery* (arrived October 1914) : The Calcutta Volunteer Battery, six 12-pdr. B.L. (6 cwt.) with ox transport. Manned by the Calcutta Volunteers, under Major G. Kinloch.

(vi) *No. 9 Battery* (landed 10th February 1916) : Four 12-pdr. 18 cwt. (naval) guns at first with ox transport, afterwards with Napier lorries. Manned by Royal Marine personnel, under Major G. E. Russell, R.M.A.

(vii) *No. 10 Battery* (before February 1916 called No. 3 Heavy Battery) : Originally two naval 4-inch Mark III from H.M.S. *Pegasus* on improvised field carriages, manned by R.N.R. personnel, commanded by Captain G. St. J. Orde-Browne, R.A., ret.[2] A third gun was added on the 11th February 1916. The guns were drawn by Packard lorries, with six Reos for ammunition.

(viii) *No. 11 Battery* (landed February 1916) : Four naval 4-inch Mark VII guns, manned by Royal Marine Artillery personnel, under Captain H. R. Purser, R.M.A. Drawn by special M.T., which arrived later. Renumbered No. 15 Battery in April 1916. These guns each weighed, with carriage, 4½ tons.

(ix) *No. 12 (How.) Battery* (before February 1916 called No. 4 S. African Howitzer Battery) (arrived 6th October

---

[1] This was probably the most heterogeneous of all the units which served in East Africa, its personnel consisting of :
R.G.A. from Mauritius.
Cape Garrison Artillery from Cape Town.
Details from 25/Royal Fusiliers.
African gun-boys for ammunition duties.
Indian drivers for A.T. carts.
An East African Dutchman as teamster.
Apart from the regular battery commander, the officers were volunteers from India, one from the N.W. Railway, one from Calcutta, one from Madras.
[2] Assistant District Commissioner in B.E.A. on outbreak of war

1915) : Two 5-inch B.L. howitzers from South Africa, manned by R.G.A. personnel stationed at the Cape, under Captain C. de C. Hamilton, R.A. Mule draught. (See p. 164).

(x) *No. 134 (Cornwall) (How.) Battery* (T.F.) : Personnel sent from England, arrived Mombasa 1st February 1916 and took over four 5·4-inch B.L. howitzers sent from India. Arrived Maktau 4th February 1916 and there equipped with ox draught.

(xi) *38th Howitzer Brigade R.G.A.* : Formed at Denham 17th January 1916 from the 11th (Hull) Heavy Battery R.G.A. which had been raised as a unit of the new armies by the East Riding T.F. Association. Comprised :—

11th and *158th Batteries :* each four 5-inch B.L. howitzers, sent complete from England, arrived Mombasa 14th March 1916, but not sent up to the front until May. See also p. 285, f.n. 2.

(xii) *Nos. 130, 131, 132 Trench Mortar Batteries* were en route from England when the offensive began, having left on 26th January, 1916.

The higher organization of units was as follows :—

No. 1 R.A. Group (1st Divisional Artillery) (Lieutenant-Colonel C. E. Forestier-Walker, R.A.).
    1st South African Field Brigade (Nos. 1 & 3 Field Batteries).
    No. 7 Field Battery.
    No. 27 Mountain Battery, R.A.

No. 2 R.A. Group (2nd Divisional Artillery) (Lieutenant-Colonel O. K. Tancock, R.A.).
    4th Indian Mountain Artillery Brigade.
    No. 10 Heavy Battery.
    2nd S. African Field Brigade.
    No. 9 Field Battery (joined 6th March 1916, then attached to the 4th Ind. Mtn. Arty. Bde.).
    No. 2 Ammunition Column.

Army Artillery
    Heavy Brigade—Nos. 10 & 11 Heavy Batteries.
    Howitzer Brigade—No. 12 Howitzer Battery.
        No. 134 Howitzer Battery.
        38th Howitzer Brigade.
        Heavy Artillery Ammunition Column.

Lieutenant-Colonel Tancock acted as C.R.A. from 29th March 1915 until, on 27th January, 1916, Brigadier-General J. H. V. Crowe arrived at Nairobi and assumed command of all artillery in British East Africa.

NOTE II

INSTRUCTIONS TO GENERAL SIR H. SMITH-DORRIEN

General Sir Horace Smith-Dorrien.

In accordance with the terms of the subjoined decision of the War Committee, you are appointed to command the troops in British East Africa :—

" General Sir Horace Smith-Dorrien to receive instruc-
" tions in the sense that, prior to the next rainy season in
" East Africa, he is to undertake an offensive defensive
" with the object of expelling the enemy from British
" territory and safeguarding it against further incursions.
" The decision as to the ultimate scope of the offensive
" operations to be undertaken against German East Africa
" after the rainy season should be postponed until General
" Sir Horace Smith-Dorrien has reported in the light of the
" experience gained before the rainy season."

As you are aware, the South African Government are preparing a considerable contingent for service in British East Africa. You should, therefore, proceed as soon as possible to South Africa to confer with the Governor-General and the Union Government as to the enlistment, equipment, and organization of those forces. You should be careful to refer any important questions, particularly those having a financial bearing, to the War Office for decision.

From South Africa you will proceed to British East Africa, where you will take what steps you consider necessary to carry out the above decision of the War Committee. In planning and in carrying out any operations you should always remember that the present state of the war in Europe will not allow of your being supplied with any additional forces beyond those now assembled in, or about to be sent to, British East Africa.

Communications have been made through the Belgian Government to the Belgian forces in the Congo to co-operate with you in any plans you may make, and the British forces in Rhodesia should also be communicated with in case their co-operation may be advisable. Neither of these forces, however, will be under your command. On all points connected with the combined operations of the Naval and Military forces you will confer with the Admiral in command of the Naval Forces in those waters.

Although the Colony of British East Africa has been placed under martial law, the Governor of that Colony will continue to perform the functions of his office, but he has been instructed by the Colonial Office to give every possible assistance to the military authorities, and to take no steps that might in any way affect the military operations without first securing your approbation. In case of any difference of opinion arising, the matter should be referred to the Home Government for decision, a report being made by you to the War Office.

In case of it being possible to raise locally any contingents of white or black troops, you should, where considerable numbers are involved, obtain the sanction of the War Office before taking action.

On arrival in British East Africa, and after fully examining the state of affairs on the spot, you should telegraph to the War Office your plans of operations.

During the tenure of your command, you are authorised to confer direct with the Commander-in-Chief in India and with the Governor-General of South Africa on all points of detail, not policy, connected with the Indian or South African troops under your command.

(Signed) KITCHENER.

The War Office.
18th December 1915.

CHAPTER XIV

THE PERIOD OF PREPARATION

SUBSIDIARY OPERATIONS

October 1915—February 1916

(Sketches 2, 4, 5, 6, 8, 21)

End Paper (N)

WHILST assembly for the coming offensive was proceeding, little had occurred in the western half of British East Africa beyond occasional raids in the Longido–Magadi area and periodical reconnaissances by the Lake Victoria flotilla. In Southern Uganda nothing of importance took place until December 1915. At the request of the Belgian Congo authorities a demonstration, designed to prevent German reserves from moving to the Ruanda area, was then arranged.

Sketch 8

This was to take the form of a raid across the Kagera near Nsongezi—a district in which so far no great military activity had been shown—combined with a minor attack from Dwargandi against the German post at Kanyonza. At the same time a feint was to be made against Kimwa, to divert the enemy's attention to the eastern end of the Kagera line, while on Lake Victoria the flotilla was to stage a feint of landing in force near Bukoba.

According to the information available, the enemy near Nsongezi had some 175 men at Katamba, piqueting the river crossings, and a post of 40 men at Kanyonza ; but considerable German reinforcements were within two or three days' march. Surprise, therefore, was essential.[1] On the 5th December a force some 500 strong,[2] with two guns, under Lieutenant-Colonel W. F. S. Edwards, Inspector-General of Police for Uganda and British East Africa, was assembled north of Nsongezi. At dawn on the following day its advanced guard, crossing the river unopposed at " Kiboko " " Ferry " near by, found that the German post, complete and intact, had been abandoned. A bridge-head was

---

[1] The indispensable preliminary reconnaissance, carried out by Lieutenant E. B. B. Hawkins, 4/K.A.R., and an Intelligence agent (Mr. Lenon), took 10 days and nights in all.

[2] Composition : Three coys. 4/K.A.R. ; 250 Uganda Police Service Bn. ; 1 sect. 27th Mtn. Bty., R.A. The section R.A. had reached Mbarara, from Kajiado, on 15th November.

established and a light floating bridge, brought up in sections, was thrown across the Kagera.[1] In the ancillary operation against Kanyonza the enemy's camp was similarly found abandoned. No casualties were sustained in either affair.

Concurrently with these raids three ships of the Lake flotilla, after shelling German trenches in Kemondo Bay, 12 miles south of Bukoba, landed a detachment of about 100 men of the 98th Infantry early on the 5th December at Lubembe Point. This force held its ground for some hours against three successive German attacks, after which, having effected its purpose, it was withdrawn, under increasing hostile pressure and not without loss.[2] The affair was magnified by the enemy into a German " victory ".

After these operations the Uganda border was quiet for some weeks. On the 8th December 1915 command in the Kagera district was handed over by Lieutenant-Colonel Edwards to Lieutenant-Colonel H. E. Towse. The bridgehead at Kiboko Ferry was consolidated as a starting-point from which the whole Kagera line might eventually be turned. With this crossing secured, the situation of the British troops—hitherto necessarily on the defensive, for lack of boats—was vastly improved : reconnaissance to the southward was facilitated, and a menace to the enemy set up.[3]

The Nsongezi bridge-head consisted eventually of a strongly defended camp on high ground at Dwenkuba, some two miles south of the river, with defences at either end of the bridge itself and support from a flanking position north of the river at Nkurungu, all based on a camp at Ngarama. Between these and the next British post to the eastward, Kachumbe, were 35 miles of unoccupied country, to cover which an observation post was established in January 1916 on the high ground at Kabuer.

Patrolling from the British posts, at times far into hostile

---

[1] The river was here 80 yards wide, with steep banks 50 feet high in places, the current running 8 knots.

[2] British casualties were : Killed, 5 o.r. ; wounded, 2 B.O., 38 o.r.

[3] For the purpose of any effective southward movement across the Kagera it would obviously be necessary to regain possession of the important crossing at Kifumbiro (Kyaka) held by the enemy since December 1914 (see p. 115). With this in view a crossing farther east than Nsongezi, say at Kabuer, would have been preferable ; Nsongezi, however, was selected as fitting better with the Belgians' desire to have pressure on their front relieved.

territory, was regularly maintained.[1] The Germans for their part attacked Dwenkuba on the 17th January 1916, losing 6 killed, 11 wounded and captured out of their force of 100 men ; anothèr abortive attack came on the 22nd, and yet another, with a field-gun in support, on the 25th.[2] For the next few months, with the exception of one further local German attack, described hereafter, there was no activity on either side along the Kagera.

DEFENCE OF THE UGANDA RAILWAY.

Along the Uganda Railway the aggressive attitude of the enemy's patrols had been maintained during October and November.[3] The British railway patrols were supplemented by an " outer fringe " of K.A.R. detachments on the more likely lines of approach ; but even the K.A.R. felt the strain of constant outpost duty and frequent fruitless pursuit, so that eventually native irregulars[4] were substituted for them, all the regular troops being retained near the railway itself. Even then the vital main line, along much of its great length, was so exposed to German attack that the British command was more than ever anxious lest it should be interrupted before the South African reinforcements materialized.[5]

These apprehensions were increased when, on the 20th November, a considerable German force[6] approached, but failed to locate, the mixed detachment of the 3/K.A.R. and irregulars which in August, under Lieutenant N. A. Kenyon-Slaney, had re-occupied Kasigao. On the 6th December, however, part of the German force, numbering about 250, with three guns and several machine guns, attacked the

Sketch 4

---

[1] At the end of December a patrol of the Uganda Police Service Bn., under Captain L. Handley, made a five-day journey southwards into German territory to Kageye Ferry, 75 miles inside the border, to destroy ferry-boats. Extricating themselves from an encounter there with the enemy, who had removed the boats, they returned without loss and with 80 head of German cattle.

[2] The section, 27th Mtn. Bty., R.A., had left on 22nd January to return to British East Africa. In the affair of 25th January the German gun was silenced by a 15-pdr. manned by Uganda Police.

[3] In the third week of November five German raids were made on the line on successive nights.

[4] Notably the Wakamba tribe, armed only with bows and arrows.

[5] On 8th November the Uganda Railway, then still under civil management, had 35 locomotives awaiting repair, most of them damaged by German land-mines. On 14th November the railway was placed under military management.

[6] *3. F.K.*; two *Züge, 21. F.K.*; 35 men of *7. Sch. K.*; *Batterie Sternheim*, all under Captain Doering.

detachment, which put up a stout resistance. After two hours' fighting a German summons to surrender[1] was rejected ; but after a further German assault had been repulsed the garrison's ammunition ran out. It was then ordered to evacuate its defences and escaped in small parties, down precipitous slopes and through the bush below, to Buguda and Mackinnon Road station, having lost 8 killed in the 3/K.A.R. and 14 irregulars captured.

The German occupation of Kasigao, within easy striking distance both of the main railway line and of the Maktau branch, still further intensified the anxieties at G.H.Q. The immediate impulse to retake the place was restrained, however, largely by the views of Brigadier-General Malleson. Such an operation, he pointed out, would need a considerable force, with artillery support ; provision of such a force would denude the already inadequate posts along the railway ; supply and water difficulties, more especially the latter, would be very great ; and finally, the opening of the projected British offensive would of itself compel the enemy's withdrawal. These views prevailed. An " inner screen " of defended posts was established on the hills of Pusa, Goya and Pika Pika and the posts on the railway were reinforced. In all, the equivalent of some eight battalions was disposed round Kasigao in a semi-circle from Mashoti to Samburu.[2] Thus, as an example on a minor scale of a

---

[1] The *parlementaire* was an Abyssinian N.C.O., who in conversation with fellow tribesmen in the 3/K.A.R. detachment indicated the German dispositions. His information greatly assisted the garrison in its subsequent escape. It may here be noted that the Abyssinians in the II.A.R. made excellent soldiers, of a high standard of intelligence.

[2] The distribution on 31st December 1915 was as follows :—

Mashoti	2/Loyal N. Lancs. (less 350) ; 6 guns.
Bura	25/R. Fus. (less 300) ; 4 guns.
Mwatate	1 Coy. 101st Grenadiers ; 1 (Rlwy.) Coy. S. & M.
Voi River	1 Coy. 101st Grenadiers.
Voi	Half Bn. Bharatpur Inf. (less 200) ; 1 Coy. 63rd P.L.I. ; 1 (Rlw.) Coy. S. & M. ; 4 guns.
Maungu	350 2/Loyal N. Lancs. ; 300 25/R. Fus. ; 275 130th Baluchis ; 4 Coys. 61st Pioneers ; 1 Coy. 3/K.A.R.
Mackinnon Road	2 Coys. 29th Punjabis ; 200 Bharatpur Inf.
Samburu	H.Q. Railway Defences ; H.Q. 63rd P.L.I. ; 125 130th Baluchis.
Railway patrols :	
Voi-Mackinnon Road ..	3 Coys. 3/K.A.R.
Pusa	1 Coy. 1/K.A.R. ; 1 m.g.
Goya	1 Coy. 4/K.A.R. ; 1 m.g.
Pika Pika	1 Coy. 3/K.A.R. ; 1 m.g.

strategic detachment, some 5,000 British fighting troops were contained by the German force at Kasigao, about 650 strong (*3., 4., 21.F.K.*).

Apart from further raids on the railway[1] the enemy undertook no serious enterprise, doubtless expecting not to remain long himself unmolested.

MINOR OPERATIONS IN THE COASTAL AREA

Sketch 5   Early in January 1916 fresh trouble developed in the coastal area. On the 9th Wavell's Arabs, about 80 in all, stationed 12 miles west of Gazi at Mwele Mdogo, marched westwards to meet a German force reported to be approaching from Ngurungani, some 25 miles west of Mwele Mdogo. Encountering the enemy at Mkongani, the Arab company suffered a heavy reverse at the hands of what proved to be a much superior German force, Major Wavell and 30 of his men being killed.

Sketch 2   On the 10th January two German *F.K.* were driven off from Ngurungani, after several hours' fighting, by a British column some 600 strong sent from Samburu (on the railway, 20 miles to the northward) under Lieutenant-Colonel B. R. Graham, 3/K.A.R.[2]   Prevented from pursuit by lack of water, the column returned to Samburu.

In that neighbourhood all was now quiet. But on the coast itself the disaster to the Arab Company, a unit created and inspired by Wavell's unique personality, and now deprived of its leader, seriously affected its fighting value and necessitated its reinforcement.

Most opportunely, the 40th Pathans had disembarked at Mombasa on the 9th January. Two companies of this unit were sent to Mwele Mdogo, the remainder of the battalion being retained for the defence of the port.[3]   This accession of strength sufficed to restore the situation along the coast, where for some time to come the enemy attempted nothing further.

---

[1] On the night 25/26th December 1915 a determined German attack on Ndi station was beaten off. An attempt next day (26th) by a detachment of 3/Kashmir Rifles to head off the raiders failed, the C.O. of that unit, Major Gandarb Singh, being killed.

[2] Composition : 280 2/Loyal N. Lancs. ; 200 25/R. Fus. ; half Bn. Bharatpur Inf. ; 1 Coy. 3/K.A.R. ; 1 sect. 28th Mtn. Bty., R.A.

[3] On 9th January 1915 the 40th Pathans entrained for Kajiado, less 1 coy. sent to Mwele Mdogo. Next day (10th) the unit was recalled to Mombasa, and a second company was sent to Mwele Mdogo.

An additional line of defended posts was at this time constructed to strengthen Mombasa harbour defences.

THE LONGIDO-MAGADI AREA

The new divisional organization had come into being on Sketch 6 the 16th December. In the Longido-Magadi area preparations were now made to re-occupy Longido, as a necessary preliminary to the impending offensive. Reconnaissance had shown that the mountain was held only by small German detachments, unlikely to offer serious resistance. By the 15th January 1915 the British force detailed for their expulsion, totalling about 600, with 4 guns, was assembled at Besil Camp.[1] Moving out on the 16th and camping successively at Olekononi and Kedongai, the force occupied Longido on the 21st January, meeting no opposition more serious than a skirmish between the opposing mounted troops. Work was at once begun on the improvement of communications back to Kajiado.[2]

No further signs were found of the enemy, who was reported by the Masai to have retreated far to the southward across the desert. Contact was eventually made by mounted patrols which located German advanced posts Sketch 2 25 miles away at Nagaseni, under the shadow of Kilimanjaro. Apart from a few such encounters no further activity took place in this sector for some weeks.[3] The troops meanwhile concentrated at Longido, Namanga and Kedongai. Sketch 6

THE VOI-TSAVO AREA

In the Voi-Tsavo area the formation of the 2nd Division Sketch 4 was in progress. On the 11th January 1916 Major-General Tighe left Nairobi to establish Divisional Headquarters in the Voi area, where Brigadier-General Malleson had already made preparations to move forward. A week later (18th January), covered by the advancing troops, the railway and pipe-line were pushed on towards Mbuyuni, which had been evacuated by the enemy and was occupied on the 22nd

---

[1] Composition: One sqdn. 17th Cav.; E.A.M.R.; 29th Punjabis; 27th Mtn. Bty., R.A. (less 1 sect.); Faridkot Sappers; with some scouts of the S. African Mtd. Bde.

[2] Reconnaissance was carried out for a branch railway from Kajiado to Longido, but the project came to nothing.

A seemingly small but important matter was the provision of 24-foot poles for the telegraph as a precaution against damage by giraffes, which had constantly interrupted the line.

[3] On 6th February a patrol of 17th Cav. was surprised near Nagaseni by a German mounted patrol and suffered severely, losing both its British officers killed.

January.[1]   Serengeti, six miles on, was reached on the 24th,
the M.I. and armoured cars having meanwhile dispersed
some 200 Germans in the vicinity.   After some days' halt
here to allow the rail-head and water to come up, the advance
was resumed, unopposed, continuing until in the first week
Sketch 21 of February the advanced troops and rail-head were established near the Nyoro nullah, three miles short of the
prominent hill of Salaita, known to the Germans as Oldorobo,
on which patrols had located a German force in position.

As Brigadier-General Malleson had foretold, an immediate
consequence of this advance was the enemy's abandonment
of Kasigao, whose German garrison was located, marching
westward, by patrols south of Mbuyuni on the 31st January.
A few days later a British signals post was re-established at
Kasigao.

On the 3rd February, the enemy's strength and dispositions on Salaita having proved to be too well screened by
the bush to be ascertained by patrols, a reconnaissance in
force was made by the 2/Rhodesia Regiment and the 130th
Baluchis, with the 28th Mountain Battery, R.A., and the
Calcutta Volunteer Battery.   The Germans were found to
be in considerable strength, and in fact threatened a turning
counter-stroke round the British northern flank.   This,
however, was not pressed and the British force withdrew
with trifling loss.   To a cabled enquiry next day (4th) by
Sir H. Smith-Dorrien, Major-General Tighe replied on the
7th February that he proposed to capture Salaita between
the 12th and 14th, and expected the railway to come up
four days later.   He proposed to make no move by way of
Sketch 4 Mzima, but to use the troops there to co-operate with his
main advance.

Air reconnaissance now began for the first time to play
its part, a fuller account of which has already been given
elsewhere.[2]   In the early days of February 1916 the small
R.N.A.S. detachment at Maktau was reinforced by the
newly-formed 26th (South African) Squadron of the Royal
Flying Corps.   Formed in England on a nucleus of South
African personnel who had served in German South-West
Africa, the squadron reached Mombasa on the 31st January
1916 and made its first flight on the 9th February.   Previous

---

[1] On this date, incidentally, the armoured train was blown up by a
German mine at Maktau.
[2] See " The War in the Air," Vol. III.

flights by the R.N.A.S., however, had taught the enemy concealment ; the first report by the R.F.C. pilots was that, while able easily to locate our own men, they could see no trace of the Germans. Nevertheless their eight B.E.2.c machines were a welcome addition to the sole surviving Caudron of the R.N.A.S. and afforded further encouragement to the troops.

ACTION OF SALAITA

On the 11th February 1916 Brigadier-General Malleson, **Sketch 21** commanding the 2nd Division, drew up Operation Orders for the attack on Salaita.   From ground reconnaissance and air reports the enemy's strength was estimated at about 300 with machine guns but without artillery.[1]   The troops detailed for the operation comprised most of those available, totalling about 6,000 men, with 18 guns and 41 machine guns.[2]

In the previous action at Salaita on the 29th March 1915[3] a British frontal attack had been met by a counter-attack on its right flank, and at Mbuyuni on the 14th July 1915[4] the main attack had been similarly held.   This time, Brigadier-General Malleson decided that his main attack should be a turning movement from the north, to be made by the newly-arrived and fresh 2nd South African Brigade, under Brigadier-General P. S. Beves, while frontally the 1st East African Brigade, whose troops had borne most of the brunt of the campaign hitherto, was to contain the enemy.   The general dispositions are shown in Sketch 21.

The two brigades left Serengeti camp independently at dawn on the 12th February, the South Africans moving north-westward across country and the remainder along the

---

[1] The German force consisted in fact of *1., 14., 15., 18., 30. F.K.* and *6. Sch. K.*, total about 120 Germans, 1,200 askari, with 12 m.g. and 2 small guns, under Major Kraut.   In rear were the *Abteilung Schulz (6., 9., 24. F.K.)* about 600 strong, between Taveta and Salaita, and *3., 10., 13. F.K.* about Taveta.

[2] Detail : 1st East African Inf. Bde. (2/Loyal N. Lancs., 2/Rhodesia Regt., 130th Baluchis).
2nd South African Inf. Bde. (5/, 6/, 7/S.A. Infantry).
Divisional Troops : M.I. Coy. ;   Belfield's Scouts (mounted) ;   **4th** Indian Mtn. Arty. Bde., less 27th Mtn. Bty., R.A. (i.e., 28th Mtn. Bty., R.A.) ;   No. 1 Light Bty. (two 12-pdr.) ;   Calcutta Volr. Bty. (six 12-pdr.) ;. No. 3 Heavy Bty. (two naval 4-inch) ;   No. 4 Heavy Bty. (two 5-inch how.) ;   four armoured cars, R.N.A.S. ;   Volr. Maxim (m.g.) " battery " ; 61st Pioneers.

[3] See pp. 143–4.

[4] See pp. 155–8.

main Taveta road. Both forces reached the Nyoro nullah, about 1½ miles apart, at about 6.45 a.m. Soon afterwards two co-operating aircraft reported newly-dug German trenches extending northwards from Salaita hill.[1]

On the right flank the South Africans continued their march, the 7/S. African Infantry leading, until 8 a.m., when at about 1,000 yards from the objective that battalion deployed, with the 6/S.A.I. and 5/S.A.I. (less two companies in reserve) echeloned back on its right and left respectively. Meantime the two naval 4-inch guns opened from the Nyoro nullah, the 1st East African Brigade with the remaining artillery moving up to within 3,000 yards of Salaita, where the guns came into action at 9 a.m.

Before long the 7/S. African Infantry, although closely supported by a section of the 28th Mountain Battery, R.A., which eventually brought its guns up into the firing line, was held up by the enemy's fire some 500 yards short of the foot of the hill. Brigadier-General Beves now sent the 6/S.A.I. on to extend the enveloping movement, keeping the 5/S.A.I. and his four remaining mountain guns in reserve ; his mounted troops (Belfield's Scouts), unhappily, had disappeared out of touch to the north.

About 10.45 a.m. the 1st East African Brigade was sent forward, the Rhodesians leading, to assist the South Africans by direct attack on the eastern face of the hill. Towards noon its advance brought it, with the 2/Loyal North Lancashire in the centre, flanked by the Rhodesians on the left and by the 130th Baluchis held back on the right rear, to the edge of the bush about 1,000 yards from the German trenches. Here it came under heavy fire across comparatively open ground and could make little further progress.

Meantime to the north Beves had ordered the 7/S. African Infantry, whose casualties were mounting, to fall back. As it did so, a counter-attack by 15.F.K. developed against the 6/S.A.I. farther to the right. To cover his exposed wing Beves despatched the bulk of the 5/S. African Infantry to form a defensive flank ; but touch was not easily maintained in the bush, and warning sent by Belfield's Scouts of a new counter-attack now launched from farther north by Schulz's

---

[1] Subsequent examination suggested that these and other works seen on the higher slopes of Salaita were dummies. The trenches manned by the enemy encircled the foot of the hill.

three *F.K.* (*6.*, *9.*, *24.*) arrived too late to prevent the onset of this force from taking the South Africans by surprise.

Pressed from three sides and exhausted also by thirst, in conditions similar to those which had been the undoing of the Indian units at Tanga, the South Africans, as yet inexperienced in East African warfare, were compelled to yield more ground. Their retirement was well covered by the 28th Mountain Battery, R.A., assisted by No. 1 Light Battery (Logan's), the Volunteer machine gun battery and the machine guns of the 2/Loyal North Lancashire, while on the right of the latter the 130th Baluchis came up in support. The steadiness of these units, especially at a moment when German askari pushed in with the bayonet between the Baluchis and the 2/Loyal North Lancashire and stampeded their transport mules, successfully held the German counter-attack. The Baluchis, in particular, under Major P. H. Dyke, heavily attacked in front and flank, refused all offers of assistance, keeping off the enemy until a covering line had been formed along the Nyoro nullah. The whole force was then withdrawn to Serengeti.

The casualties in the 2nd South African Brigade amounted to 138 in all.[1] In the other units they were slight.

Attributable fundamentally to an unduly optimistic plan, the repulse at Salaita was undoubtedly a setback to the revived morale of the British forces, and in its effect on that of the German askari its results were even more serious. Its lessons, however, were salutary. It brought out once again, as at Mbuyuni, the cardinal error of not ensuring adequate intercommunication and co-ordination between the two separated brigades.[2] It gave the South Africans their first experience of bush fighting. It exemplified the unreliability of estimates of the enemy's strength not arrived at from good intelligence or close reconnaissance;[3] it showed the difficulties of air reconnaissance in bush country;

---

[1] The 7/S. African Infantry lost 6 o.r. killed ; 5 officers, 42 o.r. wounded 1 officer, 29 o.r. missing.
German casualties are given by Schnee as : 9 killed ; 4 Germans, 30 o.r. wounded.

[2] From the artillery point of view the action was of importance, being the first in this theatre of war in which F.O.Os. with the infantry were employed by all batteries. The procedure did not work perfectly on this occasion, telephone lines being frequently broken. Much ammunition was wasted on the dummy trenches, the real defences at the foot of the hill being invisible. Nevertheless the experience gained proved valuable later.

[3] See p. 231.

and above all it demonstrated once again the fighting spirit and abilities of the enemy, impressing upon the South Africans a much-needed realization of the formidable qualities alike of Indian troops and of well-led askari whom there had been at first a tendency to regard as "only "native troops."[1]

ARRIVAL OF LIEUTENANT-GENERAL SMUTS

On the 19th February 1916 Lieutenant-General Smuts landed at Mombasa. He was met by Major-General Tighe, who explained the general situation, after which the Commander-in-Chief proceeded at once to make a personal reconnaissance, from Mbuyuni and Longido respectively, of the proposed lines of advance. He decided that an immediate offensive was both possible and desirable, cabled this opinion to England when he reached Nairobi on the 23rd February, and two days later received the sanction of H.M. Government for his contemplated operations.[2]

He decided to adhere in principle to the plan already prepared, for the execution of which the existing dispositions had been made.[3] There would be a convergent advance on Kilimanjaro from the north and east ; but the repulse at Salaita had shown that strong opposition was certain on that line and that it would be wise to avoid direct attacks against German entrenched positions in the bush. Prompt and decisive action was essential, moreover, if success were to be gained within the time-limit set by

---

[1] See " The South Africans with General Smuts," pp. 58–9. A contrasting attitude, in the mutual admiration which grew up between the 2/Rhodesia Regt. and the 130th Baluchis, especially after the fine performance of the latter at Salaita, is deserving of record. The following message was sent on 13th February 1916 : " To the officers, rank and file " of the 2nd Rhodesia Regiment, we, the Indian officers, rank and file " of the 130th Baluchis, having come to know this morning from our " Officer Commanding that all the officers, rank and file of your Regiment " requested heartedly to the G.O.C. for [leave to go to] our help when " yesterday we were surrounded by the enemies ; pay our best and hearty " thanks for this sympathetic kindness and militarism. We hope for the " future that we all will [fight] side by side to each other. We pray to " our Heavenly Father for the victory of our Government. . . . We are, " your best sympathetic, Indian officers, rank and file of 130th Baluchis.",

[2] The decision threw a heavy burden on the Transport directorate which had been busily equipping the new units with first line transport on their arrival, and providing transport echelons in rear.

[3] The idea of a subsidiary attack in the vicinity of Dar-es-Salaam, to which Sir H. Smith-Dorrien had attached some importance, was not considered further at this stage.

the coming of the rains. For these reasons he decided to transfer the South African Mounted Brigade from the northern to the eastern line of advance, where it would act directly under his own orders in a turning movement to the north of Salaita and Taveta.[1]

In the meanwhile the 3rd South African Infantry Brigade reached Mombasa and was concentrated at Mashoti. With its arrival and that of the Cape Corps battalion the South African Expeditionary Force was complete. By the 4th March 1916 all minor moves had been carried out. All was in readiness for the advance.

---

[1] The transfer of the S. Afr. Mtd. Bde. from Kajiado to Mbuyuni brought a heavy additional demand, not provided for, on the already scanty water-supply on the Maktau-Mbuyuni line of advance.

CHAPTER XV

KILIMANJARO, 1916:

THE FIRST PHASE

5th–14th March

(Sketches 2, 4, 22, 23, 24, 25)

Sketch 2 At the beginning of March 1916 the strength of the German forces in the northern area of operations, excluding the detachments, roughly 1,000 strong in all, in the coastal area, was estimated by British headquarters at a total of about 6,000 (including 700 Germans), with 16 guns and 37 machine guns.[1] These, it was known, were concentrated, on ground particularly well suited for defence, mainly in the district about the southern and western foothills of Kilimanjaro.

Sketches 4, 22 Below the impassable massif of Kilimanjaro itself, the strip of country traversed by the road from Mbuyuni to Moshi is bounded on the south by the steep slopes of the Pare mountains, themselves flanked to the eastward by Lake Jipe and the unhealthy swamps surrounding it. From Lake Jipe the marshy, unfordable and crocodile-infested river Ruvu flows westwards round the northern end of the Pare range, to be joined near its crossing of the Usambara railway by the rivers Himo and Rau and eventually to unite with the rapid Pangani, which runs south-eastward past the Pare and Usambara ranges to the sea.

The combination of hills, lake, marshes and river constituted to the south of the Taveta-Moshi road a natural obstacle almost as formidable as Kilimanjaro to the north ; nor was there any practicable break in the Pare chain short of the Ngulu valley, twenty miles farther south, which was known to be naturally difficult and already prepared for defence, and was accessible only across a waterless desert. No movement, therefore, could be undertaken in that direction : the only possible line of advance from the east was by way of Taveta.

Along this line resistance was to be expected successively at Salaita, already the scene of two unsuccessful efforts ;[2] at the Lumi river ; and in the gap, some 15 miles wide,

---

[1] See Chap. XVI, Note I (ii), p. 260.
[2] See pp. 143, 231.

between Kilimanjaro and the Pare range.   Here the ground
was commanded from the north by the heights of Chala,
a spur of the mountain 600 feet above Taveta, and by the
twin hills of Latema-Reata, rising 700 feet above the plain,
while to the south of these hills an unbroken stretch of bush
and swamp extended to the Ruvu.   Any movement beyond
Taveta was thus practically restricted to the alternatives
of the Moshi road, north of Latema, and the Taveta-Kahe
track passing between Latema and Reata.[1]

West of Kilimanjaro the country, though it was expected Sketch 2
to present less physical difficulty than that to the south-
east, was little known.   It was certain, however, that the
size of the force to operate from the direction of Longido
would be restricted both by the difficulties of supply between
Kajiado and Longido and by the lack of water in the 25-mile
stretch between Longido and Ngaseni.   Any thrust from the
west, therefore, must be subsidiary to the advance from the
east, and clearly the success of the combined movement on
exterior lines would depend on careful co-ordination and
timing.

LIEUT.-GENERAL SMUTS'S PLAN

Lieut.-General Smut's plan, briefly summarised in the Sketch 22
previous chapter,[2] now stood as follows.

The 1st Division, under Major-General J. M. Stewart,
starting two days before the eastern advance, was to march
south from Longido, as shown on Sketch 22, to cut the
enemy's line of communication.[3]

From the east the South African Mounted Brigade and
the 3rd South African Infantry Brigade, both under Brig.-
General J. L. van Deventer, were to seize the Chala heights
as the first stage of the turning movement planned against
Taveta.   A day later the 2nd Division, under Major-General
M. J. Tighe, was to move against Salaita ; meanwhile the
Force Reserve was to follow van Deventer to a central
position on the Lumi river, in readiness to reinforce either

---

[1] Throughout the Kilimanjaro operations the Germans, holding all
the high ground, had every advantage in the matter of observation.
They had, in addition, a thorough knowledge of the country, which to the
British was unfamiliar.

[2] See pp. 234–5.

[3] Some difference of opinion existed as to the number of days' start
which should be given ; the matter was settled by Lieut.-General Smuts.

the 2nd Division or van Deventer as required.   Advanced
G.H.Q. accompanied the Force Reserve.   Operation Orders
to this effect were issued on the 1st March 1916.[1]

THE MARCH OF THE FIRST DIVISION

Sketch 23   The enemy's strength on the western side of Kilimanjaro
was estimated at five *F.K.*, totalling about 800 rifles.[2]   Three
of these were believed to be between Mt. Meru and Kilimanjaro, at Lolgorain and Geraragua, with outposts at Ngaserai,
Ngaseni and Osseki ; one was located on Mt. Meru near
Kampfontein, one at Boma Ngombe.

On the morning of the 5th March 1916 the 1st Division,
whose concentration had been completed two days earlier,
moved off from Longido to the Sheep Hills,[3] and after a
halt there, to avoid crossing the waterless area in the heat
of the day, resumed its march southwards at dusk.   Meanwhile during daylight Major-General Stewart had sent out
a small mounted column of the 17th Cavalry and E.A.
Mounted Rifles, under Lieut.-Colonel F. Jollie, towards
Kampfontein, to divert the enemy's attention from his own
route and then to turn eastward and rejoin the Division
during the night.   Under cover of darkness he also detached
to his left flank two companies of the 29th Punjabis and a
section of the 27th Mountain Battery, R.A., which, early
next morning (6th), drove off the German detachment at
Ngaserai.

At 8 a.m. on the 6th March the main body reached the
Engare Nanyuki, where it halted for the day.   Jollie's
column was now ordered to seize the hill of Ngaseni ; but
his men and animals badly needed rest and water, and it
was not until 3 p.m. that, supported by a detachment of the
1/K.A.R. under Captain G. J. Giffard, the mounted troops
occupied the hill.

During the 7th the Division concentrated at Ngaseni,
sending out reconnaisance patrols to Osseki and Kampfontein, while a flanking column composed of the 129th
Baluchis and the Cape Corps, under Lieut.-Colonel J. A.
Hannyngton, moved out eastwards to establish a post

---

[1] The Order of Battle is given in Note I, p. 248.
[2] The German strength was, in fact, about 1,200.
[3] Up to this point, from which at dawn on 5th March an advanced
detachment of the 29th Punjabis drove off a small German outpost, the
road was screened from the enemy's view.

between the two streams of Engare Nairobi, in order to cover the 1st Division's line of communication.

Geraragua, at the head of the Sanya river, was reached on the 8th March.[1] Here, close under the steep wooded slopes of Kilimanjaro and looking across a wide expanse of bush to the west and south, the force was in unknown country. So far no opposition had been encountered. Local natives, however, asserted that the main route between Geraragua and Bomba Ngombe, through the dense forests and ravines of the foot-hills, had been prepared for defence, bridges being blown up and defiles blocked. Major-General Stewart accordingly decided to make a detour west of the river Sanya.

Early on the 9th he sent forward his mounted troops under Lieut.-Colonel Jollie to reconnoitre the line of advance to the river Mbiriri. Intermittent communication was being maintained by wireless[2] with G.H.Q. at Mbuyuni ; but the general situation was obscure, and lacking information as to the enemy Major-General Stewart was unwilling to commit himself to a blind advance through the bush. His anxieties were increased by difficulties of supply consequent on heavy rainstorms—precursors of the rainy season— which had swamped the tracks behind him.[3]

At 3 p.m. on the 9th March a telegram was received from the Commander-in-Chief urging the 1st Division forward with all speed. No word had come back from the mounted column, which did not return until after dark, when it arrived with its horses exhausted and reported that no way could be found through the bush. Realising then that in such country mounted men were of little more use for reconnaissance than men on foot, Major-General Stewart decided to go on at daylight with his dismounted units, leaving Jollie to rest his horses and follow.

Next day (10th March), preceded at dawn by an advanced guard of a company of the 1/K.A.R. supported

---

[1] The 129th Baluchis rejoined the 1st Division at Geraragua.

[2] From 6th to 10th March communication was possible only via Longido ; from 11th onwards, when the great mass of Kilimanjaro no longer intervened between the two H.Q., it was possible to communicate direct. Other means of communication were all unsatisfactory. Cable and air-line laid during the advance were broken, by wheeled traffic and giraffes respectively. Visual signalling was only occasionally practicable. Motor cyclists did useful work, but were hampered by lack of roads.

[3] The supply columns were in such difficulties that the Faridkot Sappers were sent back, on all available M.T. vehicles, to repair the road.

by a half-battalion of the 29th Punjabis and a section of mountain artillery, the Division moved off at noon due south through the bush. Three miles short of the Mbiriri it halted for the night. At 7.45 a.m. on the 11th a further message urging haste came from Lieut-General Smuts. With no information yet regarding the enemy, Major-General Stewart pushed on, without waiting for his mounted troops, making for the road bridge over the Sanya river three miles west of Boma Ngombe. Still unopposed, he reached the bridge that evening and found it intact.[1]

In the meantime Jollie's mounted units,[2] which with most of the artillery and wheeled transport eventually left camp at Geraragua about 4 p.m. on the 10th March to follow the main column, unexpectedly came up against a German force holding a wooded ridge over which the bulk of the 1st Division had passed a few hours earlier. The Germans, apparently in considerable strength, put up a vigorous fight during the brief daylight remaining, and when, towards dusk, they were reported to have outflanked the left of the line, Lieut.-Colonel Jollie withdrew for the night, with trifling loss, to a defensive position in the bush covering the guns and transport. Next morning (11th), finding the enemy still in position, and being out of touch with the Division, Jollie decided to return to Geraragua until forward communication could be established,[3] and by 11 a.m. his troops were back in camp. No news of all this reached Major-General Stewart until the evening, when he was nearing the Sanya bridge. A company of the 29th Punjabis, sent back early on the 12th March, met and guided Jollie's

---

[1] On 11th March, 1916, intercommunication by air was attempted for the first time, an aircraft being sent from Mbuyuni to discover the where-abouts of the 1st Division. It passed within sight of the main column, but failed to spot the troops, despite all their efforts to attract its attention. Later it sighted the mounted column and baggage near Geraragua and on its return to G.H.Q. reported that " General Stewart's troops were about 14 miles north of Boma Ngombe ".

[2] No records of the mounted column for this period are traceable.

[3] The enemy was apparently as much at a loss to understand the situation as were our mounted troops. The German force under Major Fischer seems to have consisted of 8. Sch. and 9. Sch.K., which, having realized that the British movement on 5th March towards Kampfontein had been a feint, were marching across to occupy the prepared positions east of the Sanya. Had the British main body been aware of Fischer's arrival, his position would have been serious ; had Fischer appreciated the true state of affairs, Jollie's force with most of the guns and transport of the Division might have been in considerable danger. The incident typifies the uncertainties of bush warfare.

column to rejoin the Division. The affair had delayed by at least an extra day, the already overdue arrival of the 1st Division on the scene of action.

THE ADVANCE FROM THE EAST

Between the 3rd and 5th March Lieut.-General Smuts's **Sketch 23** forces, excluding the 1st Division, concentrated about Mbuyuni and Serengeti. Leaving Mbuyuni on the evening of the 7th March, Brig.-General van Deventer with his own South African Mounted Brigade and the 2nd and 4th Batteries, South African Field Artillery, followed by the 10/ and 11/S.A. Infantry of the 3rd South African Infantry Brigade (Brig.-General C. Berrangé) and the 61st Pioneers, reached the Lumi river near the southern end of the Ziwani swamp at 6 a.m. on the 8th. The remainder of Berrangé's brigade (11/ and 12/ S.A. Infantry) with the 28th Mountain Battery, R.A., marched at the same time from Serengeti by a parallel route passing north of Salaita, and was followed by the Force Reserve, consisting mainly of the 2nd S. African Infantry Brigade (Brig.-General P. L. Beves), which was accompanied by Lieut.-General Smuts.[1]

By 6 a.m. on the 8th March both columns had reached the Lumi. While Berrangé secured a crossing opposite Lake Chala, van Deventer, pushing his mounted brigade across,[2] detached a squadron to seize Kilimari Hill and himself moved with the 1st and 2nd S. African Horse and the 2nd Battery, S.A.F.A., against the northern wall of the extinct crater within which lies Lake Chala At his approach a German detachment holding the crater at once retreated southwards on Taveta, after which, the heights having been occupied and reconnaissance having shown that Taveta was held by the enemy in some strength, van Deventer concentrated the bulk of his mounted units at Chala for the night.[3]

Meanwhile Berrangé, who was joined in the course of the day by the Force Reserve, had been engaged during most of the 8th March in minor operations to clear the vicinity

---

[1] The C.-in-C. took with him his B.G., G.S. (Brig.-General J. J. Collyer), and G.S.O.2. The remainder of advanced G.H.Q. remained at Mbuyuni.

[2] The 61st Pioneers meanwhile bridged the Lumi, which by noon had been crossed by most of the S. African artillery.

[3] The 3rd S. Afr. Horse, 10/ and 11/S.A. Inf. and 4th Bty. S.A.F.A. were held up for a time near the Lumi crossing by a German force from Rombo which threatened their line of communication.

of his crossing-place of small bodies of the enemy, one of which had attacked his transport east of the Lumi.

Whilst the flanking forces were thus occupied the heavy artillery and the 2nd Divisional artillery, covered by the 1st East African Brigade, carried out a bombardment of Salaita which, as events were to show, was unnecessary. It was followed at 2.30 p.m. next day (9th March) by a general advance of the division and the occupation, unopposed, of Salaita, which had been abandoned by the Germans at the first sign of the British move.[1] To the westward the bush prevented observation and, therefore, lacking information about the enemy and unwilling to risk his troops in an advance by night without reconnaissance, Major-General Tighe left two battalions to hold Salaita and brought the rest of his force back to railhead some three miles in rear.

During the 9th March Berrangé, who had sent forward the 9/S.A. Infantry and the 28th Mountain Battery, R.A., to the vicinity of Lake Chala, sent the 12/S.A. Infantry to seize Warombo hill and the Lumi bridge on the main road, gaining these without opposition, but not in time to intercept the German withdrawal from Salaita. In the meantime van Deventer, continuing his advance south-westwards from Chala, secured the high ground north of the main road ·in rear of Taveta. Next morning (10th March) the 2nd S. African Horse drove the enemy out of Taveta after a sharp skirmish, following up as far as the hills Latema and Reata, after which the unit was recalled to Taveta.[2]

On the same day the infantry of the 2nd Division, detaching garrisons at Serengeti and Salaita, went forward past Salaita to Taveta, where it was rejoined in the course of the following evening (11th) by the bulk of the artillery and mechanical transport, which had had to await completion of a bridge over the Lumi.[3] By the afternoon of the 10th

---

[1] " It was evident that this " [van Deventer's] " enveloping move-" ment . . . rendered the Oldorobo position . . . untenable." Lettow, " My Reminiscences ", p. 110.

[2] The total casualties of the mounted force from 8th to 10th March were 2 killed, 19 wounded, 8 wounded and captured.

[3] The existing bridge was found unfit for heavy traffic. The stream, flowing between steep banks, was 12 feet below ground level. It was forded with difficulty by the ox-drawn guns and vehicles of No. 8 (Calcutta Volr.) Bty. and 134th How. Bty. and ambulances.

A transportable lattice girder bridge specially made by the Bombay S. & M. Bridging Train was found of unnecessarily large span (36 ft.) and in place of it a wooden trestle bridge was built.

Latema and Reata were strongly held by the enemy, and British aircraft reported considerable movement between them and the German camps farther west.

In the words of Lieut.-General Smuts, " it was now clear " that the enemy had withdrawn . . . in two directions, " along the Taveta-Moshi road . . . and along the Taveta- " Kahe road between Reata and Latema Hills . . . but " the exact line of retirement of his main forces was un- " certain . . . an enemy force of unknown strength was in " position on the Latema-Reata nek.   It was essential to " discover whether this was only a covering force, or whether " the enemy was in such strength as to threaten a counter- " attack towards Taveta.   In either case it was necessary " to drive him from the nek before I could advance beyond " Taveta."[1]

After making a personal reconnaissance on the 10th March Lieut.-General Smuts decided to attack Latema-Reata next day.

ACTION OF LATEMA NEK
11th–12th March 1916

The two hills stood, as will be seen on the sketch, at an Sketch 25 oblique angle to the general westward line of advance.   To turn them from the north, round the greater mass of Latema, would therefore be difficult ; a turning movement from the south was impracticable owing to the nature of the country.[2] Accordingly Lieut.-General Smuts decided on a frontal attack by the 2nd Division, to whose support he ordered the Force Reserve from Lumi to Taveta, while the Mounted Brigade was to push on westwards past Mamba Mission towards Moshi.

The troops available to deliver the attack were the 130th Baluchis, 2/Rhodesia Regt., and 3/K.A.R., total about 1,500, of Brig.-General Malleson's 1st E. African Brigade, supported at first by only 12 guns.[3]

Reconnaissance during the morning of the 11th March Sketch 24 by the mounted infantry of the 2/Loyal North Lancashire and Belfield's Scouts brought little information as to the enemy's defences concealed in the scrub along the crest

---

[1] Despatch, 30th April, 1916 (" London Gazette ", 20th June, 1916).
[2] See p. 236.
[3] No. 8 Bty., six 12-pdr. ; No. 6 (Logan's) Bty., two 12-pdr. ; 134th (How.) Bty., four 5·4-in. how.
  About 5.30 p.m. on 11th March, No. 9 Bty., four 12-pdr., and No. 5 Bty. S.A.F.A., four 13-pdr., arrived from the Lumi river.

of the two hills. At noon the 130th Baluchis and the 3/K.A.R. advanced to the attack, and on reaching the foot of the slopes both were held up by the enemy's fire.

News of this took some time to come back, owing to the difficulties of communication in the bush, and unhappily at this juncture Brig.-General Malleson, who had been suffering from dysentery all day, found himself compelled to report sick. Command was taken over, at about 4 p.m., by Major-General Tighe, who ordered forward the 2/Rhodesia Regt., that unit's place in reserve being taken by the 5/S. African Infantry, the leading battalion of the 2nd S. African Brigade (Force Reserve), which was now arriving from Chala.

About 5 p.m. the Rhodesians moved off.[1] By this time the 130th and 3/K.A.R., after nearly five hours under fire at close range, were somewhat exhausted ; local German counter-attacks had compelled the 130th to yield ground, and the 3/K.A.R., whose commanding officer, Lieut.-Colonel B. R. Graham, had been killed, had also fallen back. Passing through them the Rhodesians attacked, some reaching the crest, where they held on ; but the unit lost formation in the thick scrub and when, at about 6 p.m. a strong German counter-attack was launched from Latema nek on the British left, the greater part of it fell back. With the bulk of the other two battalions it was then withdrawn to the lower ground, where the 5/S. African Infantry had meanwhile arrived and was digging in. A German attempt to rush the new alignment was beaten back about 6.30 p.m.

Towards 8 p.m. the 7/South African Infantry, sent up by Lieut.-General Smuts, reached the scene. Major-General Tighe, judging that the Germans were in no great strength and could best be dislodged by means of a night attack with the bayonet, now assigned this task to the 5/ and 7/South African Infantry.[2] The attack was planned and gallantly led by Lieut.-Colonel the Hon. J. J. Byron, commanding the 5/S.A.I., but was met near the crest of the two hills by a

---

[1] The sun was now setting behind Latema, dazzling the Rhodesians as they crossed the plain, while the hillsides were in deep shadow and so densely covered with vegetation that the infantry ascending could not be seen from the guns. Some British casualties were caused through this and through one battery setting a wrong range.

[2] " This operation was . . . fraught with considerable risk, as there was " no opportunity of reconnoitring the ground . . . nor was it certain the " enemy was not . . . in large numbers. On the other hand the moon " was in the first quarter and so facilitated movement up to midnight . . . " Despatch, 30th April, 1916.

fierce German counter-attack which forced most of the South Africans back. Nevertheless, although touch between the various groups was lost, detachments of the 7/S. African Infantry, which had formed the first wave, succeeded in gaining the ridges on either side of the nek, where they held on until daylight. Unknown to them, a party of the 2/Rhodesia Regt. still clung determinedly to a point farther along the Latema ridge, where they had been since the previous evening. Byron himself, however, who reached the nek by way of the road, came under heavy cross fire from three machine guns at short range and, after his party had been reduced from 40 to 20 men and he himself had been wounded, withdrew. He rejoined the main force at 1.30 a.m. (12th March), in time to cause an advance by the 130th Baluchis, who were on the point of being sent forward, to be countermanded.

The bayonet attack having thus apparently failed, and **Sketch 25** no reinforcements being at his disposal,[1] Major-General Tighe could do little more during the night than report his uncertain situation. Neither he nor the Commander-in-Chief was aware that the South African and Rhodesian detachments still stood fast on the ridge ; reports, moreover, doubtful but not impossible, of a German movement towards the Lumi round the British left had been received at G.H.Q. Accordingly at 4.30 a.m. on the 12th March Lieut.-General Smuts, preferring to await the effect of the turning movement initiated by his mounted troops[2] rather than renew the attack on Latema-Reata, ordered Major-General Tighe to withdraw his whole force before daybreak.

The withdrawal was unmolested. Unexpectedly, as day broke, it was seen from the plain that British troops— the detachments which had not come in and had regretfully been set down as missing—were still on the ridge. Lieut.-General Smuts immediately sent up the 8/S. African Infantry

---

[1] Maj.-Gen. Tighe's requests for reinforcements were refused by the C.-in-C., who had only the 6/ and 8/S.A.I. available.

[2] On 11th March the 4th S.A. Horse (2nd Divnl. troops) and 12/S.A. Infy. (Flanking Force), temporarily detached, moving along the Moshi road, had a brisk skirmish with a small German force on the northern slopes of Latema. Farther north the 9/ and 10/S.A.I., with the 28th Mtn. Bty. R.A., moved from near Chala to Spitz Hill, the 11/S.A.I. remaining at Chala as escort to artillery and baggage. The S.A. Mtd. Bde. was concentrated about Chala during the day (11th) and moved to Spitz Hill that evening.)The action of the S.A. Mtd. Bde. during 11th March is not mentioned in the records available.

and No. 9 Field Battery from Taveta in every motor vehicle
that could be collected, to re-occupy the two hills, which it
was found that the enemy had just abandoned. On reaching
the nek No. 9 Battery endeavoured to shell the retreating
Germans, but little in the way of targets could be seen in the
bush. Pursuit was out of the question, the British units
in the vicinity being still in process of re-assembling and
re-forming.[1]

With Latema and Reata in British hands a resumption
of the general advance became possible. On the 12th March
Brig.-General van Deventer, detaching the 9/S.African Infantry and the 28th Mountain Battery, R.A.,[2] which moved
unopposed to Mamba Mission, went forward to the Himo
river, where after overcoming slight opposition by a German
rearguard he secured the crossing.[3]

ARRIVAL OF THE 1ST DIVISION

Sketch 25   On the 12th March, whilst waiting at the Sanya bridge
for his lagging mounted troops, Major-General Stewart
reconnoitred eastwards along the direct Moshi road to a
point some three miles beyond Boma Ngombe. No signs
of the enemy were seen ;[4] but the bush country lent itself
to ambush, and until the situation became clearer Major-
General Stewart considered further movement in this

---

[1] British casualties amounted to about 270 in all. Detailed returns
gave the following :

	Killed.	Wounded.	Missing.	Total.
2/Rhodesia Regt.	15	43	2	60
130th Baluchis	3	25	—	28
3/K.A.R.	14	58	9	81

No details are traceable for the 5/ and 7/S.A.I.
German losses, according to Dr. Schnee, were : killed, 5 Germans,
12 askari ; wounded, 10 Germans, 57 askari ; missing, 2 Germans, 37
askari ; total 123. The figures are certainly under-stated ; at least 40 dead
were found.

[2] This detachment moved down the Himo river on 13th March, crossed
it, and remained on the western bank until 18th, when it went on to
Kifumbu hill accompanied by the 12/S.A.I. Its losses in animals from
tsetse were heavy.

[3] At the Himo river, which was about 40 feet wide with steep banks
20 feet high, the bridge had been destroyed by the enemy, leaving only
the remains of the stone abutments. Ox-drawn traffic was able to ford
the stream ; a wooden trestle bridge was built, and during the next few
days the girder bridge originally intended for the Lumi (see p. 242, f.n. 3)
was brought up and erected on new abutments.

[4] The Germans under Major Fischer, falling back from Geraragua,
were at this time concentrating behind the Kikafu river.

direction inadvisable. In the afternoon he received yet another telegram from G.H.Q. urging him forward ; but it was not until after nightfall that the Division was completed by the return of Jollie's mounted units.

At 8.30 a.m. on the 13th March these, now under Lieut.-Colonel Laverton, E.A.M.R., were despatched south-eastwards in the direction of Marago-ya-Tembo with a view to acting against the Usambara railway. The remainder of the Division moved eastwards to Boma Ngombe, whence in the afternoon Major-General Stewart despatched a column some 1,500 strong drawn from the 2nd East African Brigade, with a section of the 27th Mountain Battery, R.A., under Brig.-General S. H. Sheppard, to march by the southerly Moshi road as far as the Kikafu and then strike through the bush towards Masai Kraal, in order to intercept the German retreat on Kahe.

At the East Kware river, an awkward obstacle, Sheppard was obliged to leave his guns and transport, and about 1.30 a.m. on the 14th March, when very heavy rain came down, he halted for the night near the Kikafu.[1]

In the meantime Lieut.-General Smut's main forces approaching from the eastward met only negligible opposition. At nightfall on the 13th March van Deventer's mounted troops, although their wheeled transport was delayed by extensive obstructions on the roads, were in the vicinity of Moshi. The 2nd and 3rd South African Brigades meanwhile had moved to Himo Bridge, the 2nd Division remaining about Taveta.

Early on the 14th March was Deventer's force reached Moshi and New Moshi station, which were found deserted, with no rolling stock on the line. It was evident that the Germans had retired southwards down the railway. At 9.30 a.m. a motor-cyclist sent forward to Boma Ngombe established the first direct contact with the 1st Division.

---

[1] Brig.-General Sheppard's column eventually went on towards New Moshi. Caution was needed as the forces from the west and east drew together. Some of Sheppard's advanced guard, of the 1/K.A.R., whose uniforms were not unlike those of the German askari, were fired on near the railway by the South Africans, who were unaware of their approach. The 129th Baluchis were at once sent forward, and an unpleasant incident was narrowly averted. A survivor, remarking that in the bush " the " rule of ' safety first ' tended to make one shoot first and apologize after ", adds : . . . " two Union Jacks were sent out in front . . . the bearers of " the flags deserve a passing tribute."

NOTE I.
ORDER OF BATTLE, 5TH MARCH, 1916.

	1st Division (Major-Gen. Stewart)	2nd Division (Maj.-Gen. Tighe)	Force Reserve (Brig.-Gen. Beves)	Flanking Force (Brig.-Gen. van Deventer)
Mounted Troops	E.A. Mtd. Rifles Sqdn. 17th Cavalry K.A.R. M.I. Coy.	4th S.A. Horse Belfield's Scouts M.I. Coy. (L.N. Lancs.) No. 10 (R.N.) Armd. Car Bty.		1st S.A. Mounted Brigade 1st S.A. Horse 2nd S.A. Horse 3rd S.A. Horse
Infantry	2nd East African Brigade 25/Royal Fusiliers 29th Punjabis 129th Baluchis Cape Corps Battn. Attached: 1/K.A.R. (4 Coys.) E.A.M.G. Coy.	1st East African Brigade 2/L. North Lancashire 2nd Rhodesia Regt. 130th Baluchis 3/K.A.R. (5 Coys.) Attached: Kashmir Rifles (composite Bn.) Volr. M.G. Coy.	2nd South African Brigade 5th S.A. Infantry 6th S.A. „ 7th S.A. „ 8th S.A. „	3rd South African Brigade 9th S.A. Infantry 10th S.A. „ 11th S.A. „ 12th S.A. „
Artillery	No. 1 Group R.A. 1st S.A. Field Bde. (Nos. 1 and 3 Btys.) No. 7 Field Bty. 27th Mtn. Bty., R.A. 1st Div. Ammn. Column	No. 2 Group R.A. 4th Ind. Mtn. Arty. Bde. No. 6 Field Bty. No. 8　„　„ No. 9　„　„ No. 10 Heavy Bty.* 134th How. Bty.* 2nd Div. Ammn. Column	No. 5 S.A. Field Bty. No. 12 How. Bty.*	2nd S.A. Field Bde. (Nos. 2 and 4 Btys.) 28th Mtn. Bty., R.A. S.A. Div. Ammn. Column.
Other Units	Div. Signal Coy. Half Coy. Faridkot S. and M.	Div. Signal Coy. Half Coy. Faridkot S. and M. One Sec. E.A. Pioneers	Under G.H.Q. No. 26 Sqn. R.F.C.* 61st Pioneers	
Fighting Strength (approx.)	1,000 British† 1,750 Indian 1,250 African — 4,000 18 guns 22 m.g.	6,100 British† 1,500 Indian 900 — 8,500 25 guns 61 m.g.	Total 13,000 British† 3,250 Indian 2,150 African — 18,400　57 guns, 99 m.g.	2,100 Mounted 3,800 Infantry — 5,900 14 guns 16 m.g.

† "British" here includes S. African, Rhodesian, etc.
* Army Troops

In addition, the following units were in the theatre of war :—

Lines of Communication :—

Mombasa	Gwalior Infantry ($\frac{1}{2}$ Bn.) ; Mombasa Defence Force.
Coast District · Mwele:	$\frac{1}{2}$ Coy. 40th Pathans ; one Coy. 4/K.A.R.
Msambweni:	Jind Inf. ($\frac{1}{2}$ Bn.).
No. 1 Sec. L. of C. .. (Mile 4 to Voi, incl. Kasigao).	40th Pathans (less $\frac{1}{2}$ Coy.). 63rd P.L.I. (less one Coy.).
No. 2 Sec. L. of C. .. (Voi to Mile 218).	101st Grenadiers (less one Coy.).
No. 3 Sec. L. of C. .. (Mile 218 to Nairobi).	Kapurthala Inf. ($\frac{1}{2}$ Bn.). Details, 1/K.A.R., 3/K.A.R. Det. 61st Pioneers. Nairobi Defence Force.
No. 4 Sec. L. of C. .. (Nairobi to Kisumu).	Two Coys. 17th Infantry.
Kisumu	One Coy. 63rd P.L.I.
Voi to Mbuyuni	25th, 26th (Rly.) Coys., S. & M. 2nd Kashmir Rifles ($\frac{1}{2}$ Bn.) Bharatpur Infantry ($\frac{1}{2}$ Bn.). One Coy. 101st Grenadiers.
Kajiado to Longido ..	17th Infantry (less two Coys.) Rampur Infantry ($\frac{1}{2}$ Bn.).
Lake Area :	
Karungu	98th Infantry (less one Coy.).
Uganda :	
Kagera Line	H.Q., 2 Coys. 4/K.A.R. One Coy., 98th Infantry. Baganda Rifles. Nandi Scouts. Volunteer M.G. Section. One Sec. Volr. Field Arty. (15-pdrs.). Det. East African Pioneers.
Reserve	Five Coys, 4/K.A.R.
Total Fighting Strength (approx.)	7,000 Indian. 2,000 African.
	$\overline{9,000}$
	9 guns. 25 m.g.

Remarks.—1. *Transport:* (i) *1st Divn.*—Units' 1st line transport was completed just in time for the advance. A supply column (ox-transport) marched one day in rear of the troops.

(ii) *2nd Divn.*—1st line transport of several units was brought up to strength by temporarily denuding Force Reserve.

2. The Mzima line of operations was closed down, under orders issued on 29th February. The troops at Mzima were transferred to the Voi–Mbuyuni line.

NOTE II

LATEMA NEK, 11TH-12TH MARCH, 1916: THE GERMAN SIDE.[1]

The German units at first engaged at Latema Nek were the *Abteilung Kraut* (*18., 30.F.K., Wangoni* K.) with *Sternheim's Bty.*, total about 550, with three 6-cm. guns, 4 m.g. These were reinforced during the action by *16.F.K.* (from *Abt. Adler*) and *6.Sch. K.* (from *Abt. Schulz*), bringing the totals to about 1,000 rifles, 3 guns, 8 m.g. Their distribution is shown in Sketch 25.

Sketch 25   The night of 11th/12th March 1916 was, as it turned out, a landmark in the opening phase of Lieut.-General Smuts's operations. Throughout the 11th Lettow had held his reserve (*Abt. Adler*) at Himo Bridge ready either to reinforce Kraut on Latema or to oppose van Deventer. In the evening, considering Kraut secure, he decided to strike at van Deventer. Including the *Abt. Schulz* (five *F.K.*) and *Abt. Stemmermann* (four *F.K.*), he could concentrate at least 2,300 rifles, with 25 m.g., against van Deventer's total of about 3,500 : odds at which he considered his trained askari could take on the then inexperienced South Africans in the difficult forest country of the Kilimanjaro foot-hills. His forces were on the point of starting, with a view to a surprise attack at dawn, when at 10.30 p.m. Sternheim, commanding the artillery at Latema, reported by telephone the renewal by the South Africans of the attack, " which had pene-"trated into the Reata position in great force ". The fall of Latema would endanger Lettow's communications through Kahe ; so, cancelling his previous orders, he ordered his troops east of Himo to withdraw southwards to the Taveta-Kahe route and himself set out across country, reaching the vicinity of Latema at daybreak on the 12th March. Some of Kraut's troops had already withdrawn, and in any case Lettow's hope of surprising van Deventer had gone. Before the greatly superior numbers of the British main force Lettow had no course open but to retreat towards Kahe.

(Lettow: *Was mir die Engländer über Ostafrika erzählten*, pp. 39–41 ; " My Reminiscences ", pp. 114–5.)

The German withdrawal thus resulted directly from the tenacity of the few hardy Rhodesians and South Africans whose " penetration " during the night had so impressed the enemy, and who at daylight on the 12th March made the most of their presence on the crest of Latema. It was doubtless influenced also by the threat of envelopment by van Deventer, then already well past the left flank of the Latema position.

---

[1] See also Chap. XVI, Note I, p. 259.

CHAPTER XVI
KILIMANJARO, 1916—(concluded)
THE ADVANCE TO THE RUVU
15th–23rd March
(Sketches 4, 26, 27)

THE hopes of decisive success, founded by Lieut.-General Smuts on his convergent manoeuvre from the north and east, having been frustrated by the belated arrival of the 1st Division, fresh plans had now to be made.[1]

Although the Germans had fallen back, they had not been effectively brought to battle, much less suffered tactical defeat. They were still in a position to strike from a flank at the main British line of communication through Taveta, which it was essential to make secure before the forces were immobilized by the onset of the rains.[2]

A few days were spent in reconnaissance and redistribution of units, while supplies were brought up, roads and bridges repaired and preparations made to extend the railway westwards from the railhead near Serengeti.[3] The reports received pointed to the line of the Ruvu as the next which the Germans might hold ; in the words of the C.-in-C.'s subsequent despatch, " it was of vital importance for

---

[1] The causes of Maj.-General Stewart's late arrival—Boma Ngombe is only 60 miles from Longido—may be sought not so much in any excess of caution in difficult, unknown, and unmapped country, as in the experience of himself and most of his troops in African warfare. His supply anxieties, though natural, would have been less had he realized that even on short rations (as happened so often afterwards) his men could and would push on. The delay caused by Jollie's encounter with Fischer was an added misfortune. A more mobile force with only mountain artillery, and light transport would certainly have got through more quickly. Nevertheless the one vital necessity was that the 1st Divn. should arrive in time ; and it is difficult to avoid the impression that this was not appreciated quite soon enough.

[2] On the L. of C. the enemy's patrols were at this time boldly sniping British camps at night from the bush.

[3] Extension of the railway began on 14th March, and by 23rd March railhead was at Taveta. In 8½ working days the 25th and 26th (Rlwy.) Coys., S. & M., laid 10½ miles of line, including survey, earthwork, plate-laying and a 3-span bridge over the Lumi.

A particularly useful reconnaissance by the 1/K.A.R. (1st Div.) from New Moshi on 16th and 17th March reported on the German defences at Kahe ; South African mounted patrols also reconnoitred Kahe and Arusha Chini. A small detached force of the 1st S.A. Mtd. Bde., under Major H. de Jager, usually known as the Bde. Scouts, occupied Arusha unopposed, the enemy retiring at its approach.

251

"purposes of railway extension and future advance that
"the enemy should be driven south of this river before the
"rains commenced."[1]

Sketch 26   The plan now decided upon by Lieut.-General Smuts
is shown on Sketch 26. Its effect, as will be seen, would
be not merely to drive the enemy behind the Ruvu but to
cut off his retreat along the railway, leaving no line of escape
except the unlikely one round the northern end of the Pare
range, which could be blocked by the 2nd Division from
Taveta.

By the 17th March all was in readiness.

THE ADVANCE TO THE RUVU

About midday on the 18th March the advance to the
Ruvu began.[2] The hills of Kifumbu, Euphorbien, and
Unterer Himo were carried without difficulty, the two
former by the 3rd S. African Brigade (Brig.-General Berrangé)
and the latter by the 2nd S. African Brigade (Brig.-General
Beves), assisted by two battalions of the 1st East African
Brigade from Latema, supported respectively by the 28th
Mountain Battery R.A. and the 5th S.A.F.A. and 9th
Batteries. On the right flank, however, Laverton with the
mounted troops of the 1st Division encountered strong
opposition at Masai Kraal and at dusk withdrew; Sheppard's
2nd East African Brigade, which had bivouacked about
Moshi, being meanwhile ordered forward to Kile in support.

On the 19th March, by which time it was evident that the
bulk of the enemy's forces was concentrated in the thickly
overgrown tract of country extending ahead to the Ruvu,
the advance was resumed.

Near Masai Kraal Laverton was again held up; but on
the arrival of the 129th Baluchis, sent up early in the afternoon by Sheppard, the enemy was driven off without
difficulty,[3] falling back beyond the "Store" on the Kahe
road, about which point and Masai Kraal the 2nd East

---

[1] Despatch, 30th April, 1916.

[2] On the night 17th/18th March, Belfield's Scouts (2nd Divl. troops)
seized Unterer Himo hill, but they were driven off by superior numbers of
the enemy at dawn on the 18th.

[3] The 129th, with experience of the Western Front, made light of the
enemy's fire and progressed well through difficult bush until checked by
wild bees. These, wrote an officer present, "were everywhere, and so,
" shortly, were the machine-gun ranks". The Brigadier's comment is
said to have been: "Bees have stopped them; I thought the Germans
" could not have."

African Brigade dug in for the night. On either side of the Himo river progress was hampered by dense tangled thorn bush. Through this the 3rd S. African Brigade made its way until at about 4.30 p.m. it came upon the *Abteilung Otto* (*9., 24. F.K.*), holding a cleared area about 1½ miles south of Euphorbien Hill, where a hot fight continued until nightfall and further progress, despite invaluable close support by the 28th Mountain Battery, R.A., was impossible. East of the Himo the 2nd S. African Brigade and the two co-operating battalions moving south from Unterer Himo were brought to an early standstill by even thicker bush. As a result of these checks and of the evident difficulty of the country, Lieut.-General Smuts recalled both brigades to their starting points of the morning and re-cast his plans, abandoning the attempt to advance along the Himo and deciding to strike at Kahe.

Directing the 130th Baluchis and 2/Rhodesia Regt. (2nd Divn.) to take over Unterer Himo, he ordered three battalions of the 2nd S. African Brigade to reinforce Sheppard's brigade on the Kile–Kahe road. Brig.-General van Deventer was at the same time ordered with the Mounted Brigade, the 4th S. African Horse and Nos. 2 and 4 Batteries, S.A.F.A., to make a wide turning movement southwards from New Moshi against the German left at Kahe.

At this juncture Major-General Stewart relinquished command of the 1st Division prior to returning to India. The Division was placed under the command of Brig.-General Sheppard, who remained with his brigade at Store while the other units moved up from New Moshi to Mue Camp near Kile Bridge.

Most of the 20th March was devoted to reconnaissance. **Sketch 26** At 4.30 p.m. Brig.-General van Deventer moved off from New Moshi. At about the same time Brig.-General Beves sent off from Himo the 6th, 5th and 8th S.A.I., his freshest battalions, which bivouacked that night a mile north of Sheppard's camp at Store.

Meanwhile Sheppard's patrols reconnoitred the banks of the Defu (or Mue) and Soko Nassai rivers, to find them so swampy and so thickly overgrown as to be almost impassable.[1]

---

[1] Nevertheless a patrol of the 129th Baluchis located the left flank of Stemmermann's position near the junction of the two rivers (Sketch 27). " With considerable skill," says Lettow, " patrols worked close up . . . . " and so concealed the movements of the enemy." (" My Reminiscences ", pp. 120–1.)

At Store the defences of the 2nd East African Brigade's perimeter camp were strengthened, and a company of the 29th Punjabis was put out as outposts. In the evening the famous scout Pretorius brought warning that the enemy was massing for attack.

About 10 p.m., to the accompaniment of bugles and cheering, a violent German onslaught was launched on the outpost line, which Brig.-General Sheppard at once reinforced with 1½ companies of the 129th Baluchis and details which brought the defences up to about the strength of a battalion, with three machine guns. During the next two hours the Germans charged no less than five times across the cleared field of fire, 100 yards wide, one rush coming within ten yards of the line, in a manner which evoked admiration from the British troops ; but each attempt was broken by the unshaken steadiness of the defence, and towards 1 a.m. the enemy drew off.[1]

Meanwhile, under a full moon, van Deventer's mounted column, following the cross-country route shown in Sketch 26, successfully completed its 25-mile march, encountering no enemy and obstructed only by the difficulties of thick scrub and an occasional meeting with rhinoceros. Two hours before daybreak the column halted at a point some two miles west of the Pangani opposite Baumann Hill.

ACTION OF KAHE

21st March 1916

Sketch 27 Early on the 21st March, after an unsuccessful reconnaissance at daylight for crossings over the Pangani, van

---

[1] British casualties were 33 in all. German casualties are not known in detail, but 18 dead were buried next day. (See also p. 257, f.n. 2.) Lettow has stated that two *F.K.* commanders died of wounds and another was wounded. He considered that " . . . the very severe " action . . . proved that we had come up against the enemy's main " position ; to assault it seemed hopeless." (" My Reminiscences ", p. 121.)

It is not known which German units were engaged, but Stemmermann and Bock had at least eight *F.K.* at hand with which to attack (see Note III and Sketch 27). The C.-in-C.'s despatch (30th April, 1916) quotes prisoners as stating that the German force was 500 strong, with another 500 in reserve, and that German casualties were from 70 to 100. It seems certain that the enemy was in greater strength than was realized at the time.

H.Q. 1st Divn. arrived at Brig.-General Sheppard's camp while the attack was in progress.

Deventer moved off northwards.[1] On sighting German troops holding Kahe Hill, he detached a squadron each from the 1st and 3rd S. African Horse, which after a difficult and dangerous passage of the river[2] seized the hill about 11 a.m., a small force of the enemy evacuating it as they came up.

In the meantime the rest of the column, given away by its dust, had come under fire from a *Königsberg* gun, while German units were seen moving out from Kahe station to oppose its advance. To meet them three squadrons of the 1st with two troops of the 3rd Horse were sent forward at 7.30 a.m., followed by two squadrons of the 2nd and one of the 4th Horse and supported by Nos. 2 and 4 Batteries, S.A.F.A. The Germans were found well posted, with their left resting on the river, and progress was gradual.

At Kahe Hill German reinforcements arriving from the northward made vigorous but abortive attempts between noon and 2.30 p.m. to recapture the hill, to which at about 11 a.m. the remainder of the 3rd Horse had been sent up, covered by No. 2 Battery, S.A.F.A., west of the river.[3]

By 11.30 a.m. Kahe station had been taken and the Germans driven back to the railway bridge, which they crossed and blew up, their line then following at first the left bank of the river and passing thence to the east of Kahe Hill. During the afternoon both sides made vain efforts to work round the southern flank; but van Deventer no longer had enough troops in hand to justify any serious endeavour to reach the railway from this direction, and an opportunity to inflict at least considerable losses on Lettow, if not to capture or disperse his forces, was lost.[4]

Meanwhile the main British attack had been proceeding. As soon as he knew that van Deventer was approaching Kahe station Lieut.-General Smuts ordered the 1st Division forward.

Brig.-General Sheppard's dispositions, shown diagrammatically in Sketch 27, were as follows. Between the Defu and the main road the 6/ and 8/S. African Infantry were

---

[1] The first information to reach G.H.Q. as to the mounted column was a report received at 7.53 a.m. from an aircraft which had seen it opposite Kahe Hill about 6 a.m. The two W/T sets of the S.A.Mtd.Bde. had for some unknown reason been left at New Moshi.

[2] The stream was deep and rapid, with swampy banks, and the swimming horses were swept down against overhanging trees.

[3] Aircraft reported the 3rd S.A.H. as crossing the river at 11.30 a.m The F.O.O. of No. 2 Bty., S.A.F.A., also swam the river, to observe from Kahe Hill.

[4] Casualties in the Mtd. Bde. were 1 killed, 12 wounded, 4 missing.

deployed, each on a two-platoon frontage, with the 7/S.A.I. in support. From the road to the Soko Nassai the 29th Punjabis were in front, supported by the 129th Baluchis. In reserve were the 25/Royal Fusiliers and 1/K.A.R. of the 1st Division, with the 5/S. African Infantry. Artillery support was given by Nos. 1 and 3 Batteries, S.A.F.A. and No. 12 (How.) Battery, with the 27th Mountain Battery, R.A., moving in close support of the infantry. Two armoured cars took the main road.

Sketch 27　　The enemy's position had been well chosen. The well-nigh impassable Soko Nassai protected its eastern flank, the almost equally difficult Defu the western. Immediately in front was a belt of relatively open ground from 800 to 1,600 yards wide, covered by machine guns sited both frontally and on the nearer bank of the Soko Nassai on the right flank.[1] The attacking troops were thus confined in a narrowing tongue of ground bounded by rivers which were not only wider and deeper than was expected, but full of crocodiles. Beyond the open belt just mentioned the bush was exceptionally thick, and movement correspondingly slow.

At 11.30 a.m. Sheppard's forces moved off, meeting at first no opposition, though a shell or two from a *Königsberg* gun passed overhead. About 12.40 p.m. the leading troops debouched into the open grass-land, beyond which was dense undergrowth evidently fringing a river and strongly held. This was totally unexpected, it having been assumed that the enemy was holding the right bank of the Ruvu.[2]

Heavy fire was at once opened by the Germans, against which, in spite of valiant efforts by the 29th Punjabis and the 8/S. African Infantry, assisted by guns of the 27th Mountain Battery, R.A.[3], brought up into the firing line, it was found impossible to cross the open ground.

---

[1] Machine guns and snipers were also boldly placed in clumps of trees and grass well in front of the main position. Most skilfully concealed, they inflicted a considerable proportion of the casualties suffered.

[2] By an unlucky combination of events, patrols had reported that the enemy's position was " on the banks of a large river ", while information given by natives had suggested that the Soko Nassai did not, as the map indicated, run into the Defu, but died away, like many other rivers hereabouts, into a dry watercourse. The serious obstacle of the Soko Nassai, solidly held by the enemy, thus came as an unpleasant surprise.

All available maps were unreliable.

[3] Little help could be given by the artillery. Few targets were visible in the vegetation along the Soko Nassai ; the field batteries for a time over-estimated the range, in the belief that the enemy was along the Ruvu ; the howitzers meanwhile became engaged at long range with the *Königsberg* gun.

Deciding, therefore, on a flank movement, Brig.-General Sheppard ordered a double company of the 29th Punjabis to pass the Soko Nassai to its left in an attempt to turn the German position. The passage was effected with great difficulty, and on the eastern bank the Punjabis were held up by a machine gun and by heavy rifle fire. A company of the 129th Baluchis with a machine gun, which was then sent across to their support, silenced the enemy ; unluckily its own gun jammed during the bold attempt to rush the Germans which followed, and here too the advance came to a standstill.

Towards 4 p.m., by which time casualties had mounted up, the enemy's fire increased in intensity, and Brig.-General Sheppard, in anticipation of a hostile counter-attack, brought in from reserve the 25/Royal Fusiliers and the 5/S. African Infantry, recalling also the two companies from beyond the Soko Nassai. Shortly afterwards Lieut.-General Smuts informed him of the progress of van Deventer, with whom, however, touch had not been gained. Nor was there contact so far with the 3rd South African Brigade, which during the day had been in readiness independently at Euphorbien Hill.[1]

At 4.45 p.m. Brig.-General Sheppard was ordered to dig in for the night on the ground he held. Intense German fire broke out again as the British fire slackened, but nothing followed, and the British troops settled down for the night undisturbed except by occasional sniping. In the bright moonlight the wounded were brought in,[2] but patrolling across the open was out of the question.

[1] Throughout 21st March, Borrange (3rd S.A. Bde.) at Euphorbien Hill, and the 2/Rhodesia Regt. and 130th Baluchis (1st E.A. Bde.) at Unterer Himo, had awaited orders to move southwards against Otto and Adler ; but owing to the obscurity of the situation and the difficulty of the country they did not move till late in the day and were soon afterwards recalled.

Farther east, the 2/Kashmir Rifles and a section of No. 8 Bty. S.A.F.A. (2nd Divn.), sent from Taveta, occupied Kingarunga unopposed.

[2] Total British casualties on 21st March were about 290, mostly in 1st Divn., whose return was :

	European.	Indian.	Total.
Killed	24	13	37
Wounded	144	77	221
Missing	—	3	3
	168	93	261

Gun ammunition expended : 27th Mtn. Bty., R.A., 292 ; Nos. 1 and 3 Bties., S.A.F.A., about 300 ; No. 12 (How.) Bty., not known.

German casualties from 18th to 21st March (almost certainly underestimated) are given by Dr. Schnee as : killed, 5 Germans, 25 askari ; wounded, 10 German, 80 askari ; missing, 6 Germans, 45 askari.

K*

For the following day (22nd March) Brig.-General Sheppard now planned to hold his front line with his attached South Africans and to turn the enemy's right with the 2nd East African Brigade. But at dawn on the 22nd March his patrols met with no opposition : the German defences everywhere had been abandoned. The 1/K.A.R., brought up from reserve along the main road through Kahe, established a bridgehead on the south bank of the Ruvu. The road-bridge was found demolished ; between it and the railway a *Königsberg* gun had been left behind unserviceable ; many signs were seen of a hasty German evacuation ; but the enemy had retreated some miles along the road and railway, and was out of touch.

Farther north Berrangé's brigade and the two battalions from Unterer Himo similarly made their way southwards unopposed.[1] During the 22nd and 23rd March the British forces went forward to the line of the Ruvu.

Sketch 4. Reconnaissance showed that the Germans had withdrawn to Lembeni, where they established a defensive position. That the Mounted Brigade had not been fortunate enough to intercept them was a matter doubtless for regret ; but the fact remained that its approach, which made the Kahe position untenable, was a prime cause of Lettow's general retreat.[2]

GENERAL SITUATION, 23RD MARCH 1916

The action at Kahe thus brought the first phase of the offensive to an end. True, the German resistance had not been broken ; but the enemy had been ousted from the most precious corner of his territory, the seizure of which relieved British East Africa from all fear of further hostile enterprise based upon it.

---

[1] The scouts of the 2/Rhodesia Regt., approaching the Rasthaus, were in brief contact with the last of a German rear party hurrying away. They " found an almost impregnable position just evacuated ; hot meals, " porridge and stores were still in the beautifully-constructed trenches ". (Capell, " The 2nd Rhodesia Regiment in East Africa ", p. 59.)

[2] See also Note II, p. 261. Lettow has stated (" My Reminiscences ", pp. 122–3) that he thought it necessary to remain himself at Kahe village, where he was unable to control his reserves at Kahe, and that the report that the British were moving in his rear towards Kisangire compelled him to order withdrawal.

He recounts his astonishment at discovering, when he reached Kisangire just after midnight 21st-22nd March, that the report had been erroneous.

It will be noticed that his withdrawal on a previous occasion (Latema, see Note II) is also attributed to a misleading report.

The pause which was now to be imposed by the rainy season came opportunely. Time and work were needed to build up the line of communication, to reorganize and refit and to make the preparations without which no further general advance could be attempted. But henceforward the Germans, not the British, would be on the defensive, and it was possible to look forward to the conquest of the whole German colony.

NOTE I

THE STRENGTHS OF THE OPPOSING FORCES, MARCH 1916.

(i) *British Forces*

The first complete Return of Ration Strength for the British Forces was cabled by G.H.Q. to the War Office on the 22nd March 1916, with the reservation that, " owing to difficulties and many omissions and inaccuracies ", the figures were only " approximately correct ". Summarized, the figures were :

	Officers			*Other Ranks*		
	British*	Indian	African	British*	Indian	African
Main Field Army :						
G.H.Q., 1st and 2nd Divns. (including Flanking Force and Force Reserve), with attached troops.	892	123	3	17,166	6,150	1,374
Lake Area :						
Military	71	6	1	51	221**	1,622
Naval	19	—				
Coast Area :						
Military	16	15	1	6	329	302
Naval..	7	—	—	9	52	83
L. of C., etc. :						
Combatant units	86	161	4	91	5,571**	745
Supply and Administration (excluding Field Formations).	351	53	—	2,386	651	131
Base Depot	21	—	2	959	136	587
In transit	63	—	—	1,912	—	—
In Hospital	124	15	—	1,313	820	219
Total	1,653	373	11	23,922	13,930	5,063

---

* " British " includes South African, Rhodesian, etc.
** Includes one company, 98th Infantry, on the Kagera Line, remainder of this unit (in the East Lake Area) being included under L. of C.

(i) *British Forces* (*contd.*)

Followers :						Indian	African
Serving	..	..	..	..	..	3,137	18,910
In Hospital	..	..	..	..	..	427	541
						3,564	19,451

				Animals			
				Horses	Mules	Donkeys	Bullocks
Main Field Army	..	..	..	5,484	841	—	—
Remounts	..	..	..	351	230	—	—
Transport	..	..	..	—	4,126	564	12,310
				5,835	5,197	564	12,310

Remarks

Figures given for field formations, include medical, transport, supply and clerical personnel. Fighting strengths on 3rd March 1916 are given in Chap. XV, Note I, p. 248. Between 3rd and 22nd March 1916 the following additional units arrived :

5th Light Infantry (Indian Army ; strength 9 B.O., 9 I.O., 508 o.r.

38th How. Brigade R.G.A. See Chap. XIII, Note I, p. 219).

Nos. 1, 4, 5 Light Batteries Armoured Cars. Landed on 14th/15th March 1916, but were not in time to take part in the Kilimanjaro operations.

(ii) *German Forces*

1. The most complete available detailed return of the German forces is contained in a report by Lettow to the Governor dated 1st January 1916, giving the composition and armament of each unit. The total effective force in the German Colony is given as 2,712 Europreans ; 11,367 askari ; 2,531 irregulars and armed porters ; 50 guns ; 95 machine guns.

The ration strength of the troops then in the Kilimanjaro area is given as 1,100 Europeans ; 4,659 askari ; 13,571 other enlisted natives (irregulars, armed " company porters," and carriers) ; 1,870 native followers (" boys ").

2. Between 1st January and 5th March 1916 the number of trained askari presumably increased. In this period *18., 28.,* and *30. F.K.* were transferred to the Kilimanjaro area.

3. Certain changes made during 1915 may also be noted : *4., 5.,* and *6. Sch. K.* were reorganized on the same lines as *F.K. ; 1.* and *10. Sch. K.* were broken up, the personnel being transferred to other units ; a new *1. Sch. K.* (81 Germans, 45 aksari) was formed at Dar-es-Salaam ; *8.* and *9. Sch. K.* became mounted.

4. The distribution of units in the German Colony on the 5th March 1916 was as follows :[1]

---

[1] These figures were obtained in April 1939 through the courtesy of the official German *Kriegsgeshichtliche Forschungsanstalt des Heeres.*

Area	Commander	Equivalent Total	Detail
Tanga ..	Major Baunstark ..	3	*17.F.K., 4.Sch.K., Ldst. Abt. Tanga.*
Kilimanjaro ..	Major Kraut	3	*18., 27. F.K., W.K.*
	Hauptm. Stemmermann	3	*11., 16. F.K., 5.Sch.K.*
	„ Schulz ..	5	*6., 9., 15., 24., 30. F.K.*
	„ Demuth ..	5	*1., 10., 19. F.K., 6., 7.Sch.K.*
	„ Augar ..	3	*3., 13., 14. F.K.*
	Major Fischer	5	*8., 28. F.K., 8. & 9. Sch.K.* (mounted) *Abt. Aruscha.*
	Hauptm. Döring ..	2	*4., 21 F.K.*
Mwanza and	„ v. Chappuis	5	*A, B, D, E, F.K.*
E. Lake.			
Bukoba ..	„ Gudowius ..	3	*7.R.K., C.K., Abt. Bukoba.*
L. Kivu ..	„ Wintgens ..	6	*7., 23., 25., 26.F.K., Ruanda A. & B.K.*
R. Russisi ..	Major v. Langenn-Sterinkeller.	2	*14. R.K., Abt. Urundi.*
Kigoma ..	Korvettenkapitän Zimmer.	2	*22.*Stammkomp., *Abt. Möwe.*
Bismarckbg.	Oberltnt. Francken ..	1	*29.F.K.*
N. Langenbg.	Hauptm. Falkenstein	2	*5.F.K., L.K.*
Iringa ..	„ Styx	1	*2.F.K.*
Mahenge	Major v. Grawert ..	1	*12.F.K.*
Lindi	Kapitän. Hinrichs ..	1	*20.F.K.*
Mohoro ..	Hauptm. v. Bomsdorff	1	*Abt. Delta.*
Dar-es-Sal. ..	Kapitän z.S. Looff ..	6	*22.F.K., 1., 2., 3.Sch.K., Abt. Königsberg, Ldst. Abt. Dar-es-Salaam.*
	Total ..	60	

Remarks

Small local units, e.g., the *Rombo, Songea, Pangani,* etc., detachments, which considerably below the strength of a *F.K.,* are not included.

7.Sch.K. consisted of about 100 Europeans, 60 askari, 3 m.g. ; *8. Sch.* and *9.Sch. K.* (mounted) together totalled about 130 Europeans, 120 askari ; *13.F.K.* had 4 m.g.

On 6th March 1916, *17.F.K.* was transferred to the Kilimanjaro area.

NOTE II

THE GERMAN FORCES, KILIMANJARO, 5TH–21ST MARCH, 1916.

The German units in the Kilimanjaro area on the 5th March Sketches 25, 1916 (to which must be added *17.F.K.* from Tanga), totalling 27 27 companies, are enumerated in the preceding Note. With these were the light field batteries of *Fromme* and *Sternheim,* 7 guns in all, and 11 guns in various local defences.

The successive confusing changes in the allocation of units to *Abteilungen* in the course of the operations from 5th to 21st

March need not be given in detail, The following is an outline of the German distribution and movements on 21st March 1916, when the action at Kahe concluded the opening phase of the British offensive.

At dawn on 21st March the German forces confronting Lieut.-General. Smuts were distributed as shown in Sketch 27, the composition of the various groupings being as follows :

Abteilung	*Units*	*Equivalent* *F.K.*
Adler ..	*15., 16., 17.*	3
Bock	*1., 8., 8.Sch., 9.Sch., Rombo det.*	4
Kornatzki ..	*18., 30.*	2
Kraut ..	*27., " W."*	2
Otto	*9., 24.*	2
Schulz ..	*4., 6., 13., 19., 21., 6.Sch., 7.Sch.*	7
Stemmermann	*3., 10., 11., 14.*	4
	Total ..	24

In addition, *5.Sch. K.* remained near Lake Jipe, *28.F.K.* about Kampfontein and the *Arusha Det.* at Arusha.

It will be noted that Fischer no longer commanded a group. Of the *Abteilung Bock*, one *F.K.*, and one *Sch.K.* had been bivouacked at Kahe station, the remainder at the confluence of the Defu and Rau. During the morning of 21st March Bock was reinforced by Kornatzki's two *F.K.*, and by *19.F.K.*, *6.Sch.K.* from Schulz, so that by 10 a.m. he had the equivalent of eight *F.K.* under his command. With these he made three successive attempts to dislodge van Deventer's squadrons from Kahe hill (see p. 255) ; but the efforts failed for want of adequate preparation and by reason of an erroneous report that British mounted forces were approaching Kisangire, which led to a hurried retreat (see p. 258, f.n. 2). In the course of the afternoon Bock's force gradually became strung out in its withdrawal, until at 5 p.m. it stood as follows :—

Lt.-Col. Bock, two *F.K.*, Kahe bridge (south bank) ;
Capt. Kohl, two *F.K.*, Baumann Hill ;
Capt. Kornatzki, two *F.K.*, retiring along railway to Kisangire. *1.F.K.*, *4.Sch.* and *8.Sch.K.* had also been sent back to Kisangire.

During the afternoon the *Abteilung Schulz* (now five companies) was transferred to the westward and was put in to counter-attack round Stemmermann's right flank. The group was delayed, however, by the difficult bush on the east bank of the Soko Nassai, and its effort came to nothing.

The *Abteilung Adler* was brought back to Kahe village, where it remained in reserve until nightfall.

The *Abteilungen* of Otto and Kraut did not move and were not engaged.

CHAPTER XVII

THE ADVANCE FROM KILIMANJARO

MAJOR-GENERAL VAN DEVENTER'S ADVANCE TO KONDOA IRANGI

Sketches 28, 28a, 29, 30)

FORTUNATELY for the Kilimanjaro operations the rainy Sketch 28 season, which in that area normally brings all movement of wheeled traffic to a standstill early in March, had set in late in 1916. Before it began in earnest Lieut.-General Smuts, behind his outpost line along the Ruvu, had first to dispose his troops with a view to their well-being during the period of waiting and then to consider his future plans.

As a preliminary he decided to re-organize his forces " not only for the vigorous prosecution of the coming " campaign, but also to secure the smooth and harmonious " working of a most heterogeneous army, drawn from almost " all continents and speaking a babel of languages."[1] Concurrently with this, work on roads, bridges and blockhouses, survey, patrolling and reconnaissance went on unceasingly.[2] Most of the infantry of the force was redistributed into camps on high ground at Moshi, Himo and Mbuyuni, while the mounted troops were concentrated about Arusha, an area reputed to be healthy for horses.

In place of the two divisions in which the troops had hitherto been organized Lieut.-General Smuts now formed three divisions, two of South African troops under South African commanders, and one comprising the Indian units together with the United Kingdom, East African and Rhodesian troops. With a view to mobility he decided to

---

[1] Despatch, 27th October, 1916, " London Gazette ", 17th January, 1917.

[2] Reconnaissance was welcomed by the troops as a change from the arduous work in back areas. In one typical incident a havildar of the 129th Baluchis, who volunteered to reconnoitre 15 miles down the railway to Kisangire (Sk. 4) and whose first report was received with some reserve, returned from a second reconnaissance with evidence of a German outpost's presence : officer's pistol, sentry's rifle, corporal's stripes and a bugle.

263

include a mounted brigade with each South African Division, and to this end the raising of a second mounted brigade was at once begun in the Union.[1]

At this juncture Major-General Tighe, whose services were required in India, relinquished command of the former 2nd Division, and the vacant divisional command—now to be the 1st Division—fell to Major-General A. R. Hoskins.[2]

The field army as now reconstituted stood as follows :[3]

1st Division (Major-General A. R. Hoskins) : 1st East African Brigade (Brig.-General S. H. Sheppard) ; 2nd East African Brigade (Brig.-General J. A. Hannyngton).

2nd Division (Major-General J. L. van Deventer) : 1st South African Mounted Brigade (Brig.-General Manie Botha) ; 3rd South African Infantry Brigade (Brig.-General C. A. L. Berrangé).

3rd Division (Major-General C. J. Brits, to come from South Africa) : 2nd South African Mounted Brigade (Brig.-General B. G. L. Enslin) ;[4] 2nd South African Infantry Brigade (Brig.-General P. S. Beves).

In South Africa, besides the 2nd South African Mounted Brigade, two unbrigaded mounted regiments and a motorcyclist corps were raised for East Africa, together with substantial reinforcing drafts.[5] Another accession to the

---

[1] " . . . to secure the necessary mobility to enable us to cope more " expeditiously with the enemy askari army of fleet-footed Africans." (Despatch, op. cit.)

The decision was a natural one for any South African unfamiliar with East African conditions ; but in the outcome, by reason of the difficulties of maintenance and animal mortality experienced in this campaign, and of the consequent strain on transport resources, the mobility of the force as a whole was hardly benefited.

[2] Brig.-General Hoskins had been Inspector-General of the K.A.R. at the outbreak of war. He then served in France and early in 1916 was selected to be Lieut.-General Smuts's principal staff officer. He reached G.H.Q. on 23rd March, 1916, to find that that appointment had been filled by Brig.-General J. J. Collyer and that he himself was to command the new 1st Division, which he took over on 1st April.

[3] For details of Inf. Bdes. see p. 248.

Artillery was redistributed as follows :

1st Divn. : *Group* 1 : 5th (S.A.), 6th, 7th Fd. Bties. ; 27th Mtn. Bty., R.A. ; one sect. 38th How. Bde.

2nd Divn. : *Group 2* : 2nd and 4th Bties., S.A.F.A. ; 28th Mtn. Bty., R.A. ; 12th How. Bde.

3rd Divn. : *Group 3* : 1st and 3rd Bties., S.A.F.A. ; 8th Fd. Bty. ; one sect. 38th How. Bde.

For details of artillery units see Chap. XIII, Note I, p. 219.

[4] Arrived in May 1916. Major-General Brits arrived in June 1916.

[5] In April and May 1916 some 4,500 reinforcements were sent and over 3,000 were under training.

East African forces was the 5th Light Infantry, Indian Army,[1] from the recently concluded campaign in the Cameroons.

The question of drawing on West Africa for further reinforcements was now considered. The Nigerian units which had served in the Cameroons were still in need of rest ; but the Gold Coast troops had suffered less, and in May, there being no further need for any considerable forces either on the Gold Coast or in Sierra Leone, it was decided to transfer to East Africa the 2/West India Regiment, which had formed the garrison of Freetown, and a battalion of the Gold Coast Regiment.[2]

Meanwhile events had led at last to the initiation of that large-scale expansion of the K.A.R. which was destined to contribute so greatly to the successful outcome of the campaign.[3] Practical experience had quickly shown the inestimable worth of these troops in the peculiar conditions of East African warfare, and the addition of three new K.A.R. battalions which was sanctioned in April, although it could not make itself felt for some months, in effect doubled the establishment of K.A.R. in the northern theatre of operations.

A considerable increase in the number of irregular auxiliaries was also sanctioned. An organization of " Intelli-" gence Scouts," both armed and unarmed, built up during the preceding twelve months by Major R. Meinertzhagen, General Staff Officer (Intelligence), had proved of the utmost value, more especially in the Kilimanjaro operations, and the subsequent advance through unknown and ill-mapped country would hardly have been possible without them.[4] Native irregulars were also increasingly used, as the danger to the Uganda Railway diminished, to replace troops in protecting the quieter sections of the line.[5]

A further small addition to the forces at the end of 1915 were the small units raised as African Rifles in Zanzibar and Mafia Island, which began as constabulary and later

---

[1] See pp. 260, 312.
[2] A Nigerian brigade formed later in the year reached East Africa in December 1916. See Vol. II.
[3] See Appx. IV.
[4] Attachment of a few of these scouts, who never lost their way, to patrols of Indian and other units unused to the bush, was found especially useful. Their exploits under Pretorius and others, particularly in the Lake area (see Chap. XXIV) under Capt. J. J. Drought, became almost legendary. Their numbers eventually exceeded 3,000.
[5] See p. 226, f.n. 5.

furnished landing parties on the coast from time to time as required.[1]

In March 1916 four Voisin aircraft and four Short seaplanes, with a detachment of the Royal Naval Air Service, arrived from home. The Voisin machines were sent to Mbuyuni in relief of the original R.N.A.S. detachment, which was transferred to Zanzibar.[2] They were very welcome, casualties having reduced the eight B.E.2.C. machines of the 26th Squadron, R.F.C., to four. Eight more aircraft (Henri Farman) arrived early in May.

LIEUT.-GENERAL SMUTS'S PLANS

End Paper (N) At the end of March 1916 Lieut.-General Smuts established G.H.Q. at Old Moshi, on the slopes of Kilimanjaro, 4,800 feet above sea level. Assured of an ample superiority of force, he proceeded to plan the further development of the campaign.

The considerations which led him to the strategy which he decided to adopt, given at some length in his subsequent despatch,[3] may be summarized as follows.

The occupation of the Kilimanjaro–Arusha area had followed logically from the situation which he had found on his arrival in East Africa. The enemy's territory which he had now just entered was of vast extent, practically devoid of roads. It contained no vital points, no cities or important centres, and its only dominant features were its two lines of railway, both still in the enemy's hands. All available information indicated that the Germans intended to offer for as long as possible an obstinate resistance in the Pare and Usambara mountains, but to avoid a decisive encounter there by eventual retirement into the Tabora area, their principal source both of recruits and of supplies, which was linked by the Central Railway to their seat of government at Dar-es-Salaam.

In such circumstances, as Lieut.-General Smuts put it, a faulty initial strategy " might lead to months of futile " marching and wasted effort." His study of the situation brought him to consider three alternative courses of action.

---

[1] These units were amalgamated as the Zanzibar African Rifles at the end of 1916 and, although racially distinct, became part of the 1/7 K.A.R. (See Appendix IV.)

[2] All R.N.A.S. personnel on the mainland were now grouped to form No. 7 (Naval) Squadron, under Sqdn. Commdr. E. R. C. Nanson.

[3] Despatch, 27th October 1916.

Of these the first, naturally occurring to him with the strategy recently successful in German South-West Africa fresh in his mind, was an advance inland from the coast along the railways from Tanga and Dar-es-Salaam. This he at once rejected. Tanga, now that he had gained the other end of the Tanga railway, he regarded as of no importance. Dar-es-Salaam would, as he observed, " have great political " and military importance and would much facilitate the " transport and supply arrangements for the campaign into " the interior ". But at Dar-es-Salaam the heavy seas of the prevailing monsoon would, he saw, make a landing on any large scale extremely hazardous, while in the unhealthy coastal climate after the rains his troops would be very seriously depleted by sickness.[1]

A second alternative, more promising superficially, was to strike south from Lake Victoria through Mwanza against Tabora. Its obvious advantages—a relatively short line of advance from the Lake onwards and a threat to the enemy's best recruiting area, with the possibility that the loyalty of the German askari might weaken in consequence—were far outweighed by its equally obvious disadvantages, at once revealed by the map. To transfer a large force and maintain it along an extended line of communication through British East Africa, with that line exposed once more to short-range attack by an enemy concentrated on interior lines in the Pare mountains, was out of the question. Lieut.-General Smuts's main objection to such a course, moreover, was that " to occupy so huge a territory as German East Africa " within a reasonable time a simultaneous advance from " different points along different routes was essential." On the German border east and west of Lake Victoria he had already some 2,000 rifles, while a considerable Belgian force about Lake Kivu was prepared to co-operate. The western portion of the German colony therefore, could safely be left to these forces : it was only necessary to set them " simultaneously in sympathetic motion."

The third and simplest alternative was to operate south- **End Paper** wards from the existing positions in the Kilimanjaro–Arusha **(N)**

---

[1] Although the point is not mentioned in the C.-in-C.'s despatch, presumably recollection of the failure at Tanga would also weigh against any contemplated landing operation.

It is understood that much information as to the Gallipoli landing was available at G.H.Q., and that although the project of a landing at Dar-es-Salaam had been shelved (see p. 234, f.n. 3), it had not hitherto been ruled out entirely.

area.   Here Lieut.-General Smuts perceived two choices :
a move down the line of the Usambara railway, and an
invasion of the interior of the colony from Arusha directed
to gain the Central Railway.   His grave objection to moving
down the Usambara railway was that this was clearly what
the enemy expected and desired, as was shown by the

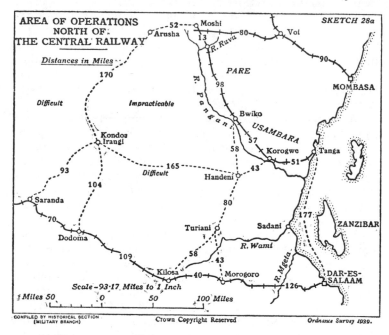

massing of the greater part of his forces in that area " which
" nature and art had prepared admirably " for defence,
with the railway behind it as an excellent line of communication.   Another objection was geographical : to restrict the
campaign to this area would leave the greater part of the
German colony untouched.

On the other hand, to advance from Arusha into the
interior with a view to permanent occupation would require
a force strong enough to resist any attack which might be
brought against it.   For the purpose of such an attack the
Germans, on interior lines and with the two railways, could
move troops more rapidly than their assailants ; or, if the
British forces in the Pare–Usambara area were unduly

weakened, the enemy might from that direction again endanger British communications with both the interior and the coast.[1]

While fully appreciating the risks just mentioned, Lieut.- **Sketch 28** General Smuts decided on the third alternative. He was confirmed in his decision by the information given to him by local Afrikaner settlers : " that the violence of the coming " rainy season would be mostly confined to the Kilimanjaro " area " and that farther west and south the rains " would " not markedly interfere with military operations ". If that were so—unhappily the information was totally incorrect[2]—by moving towards the interior he would avoid a complete standstill during the wet months of April, and May. The enemy had helped him, moreover, by concentrating about the Usambara railway, and " the door to the " interior stood wide open and unguarded ".[3]

He resolved accordingly, while the greater part of his force would have to stand fast along the Ruvu during the rains, to detach the new 2nd Division, under Major-General J. L. van Deventer, which was to move south-westwards towards Kondoa Irangi and the Central Railway. He would thus occupy a considerable tract of the enemy's country within the next two months. If, as he expected, this move induced the enemy to transfer forces from the Pare–Usambara area to meet it, the opposition to an eventual advance by the main British force down the Pangani would be correspondingly weakened.[4]

By this strategy Lieut.-General Smuts expected to make the most of all his forces, while the role allotted to the 2nd Division in particular promised to be one especially suited to the natural qualities and tactical predilections of

---

[1] Had Dar-es-Salaam been in British hands these advantages would evidently have been neutralized.

[2] " The statement, however, came from shrewd judges of . . . movement " of mounted men and transport . . . Indeed it was not often that " information came from a source so well able to provide sound intelli- " gence." (" *The South Africans with General Smuts* ", p. 101.) From this it would seem that at this early stage the value of the British Intelligence service was under-rated.

[3] Despatch, op. cit. In fact *28.F.K.* had retreated south-westwards from Arusha to the vicinity of Lolkisale ; farther west there was a German military station at Mbulu.

[4] The section of the despatch from which the foregoing summary of the Commander-in-Chief's view of the general situation is taken, while dealing with occupation of the German territory, makes no direct mention of plans for bringing the enemy's forces decisively to battle.

the South African troops, inured as they were to long marches and veld warfare and led by commanders accustomed to exercise initiative and resource.

Sketch 28a. Moreover, since the waterless area between the Arusha–Kondoa route and the Pangani was practically impassable to troops, German forces from the Usambara railway could only move to oppose the 2nd Division by a long circuit southwards through Handeni and along the Central Railway. Van Deventer, therefore, need have little fear for his flank and line of communication.[1]

OCCUPATION OF LOLKISALE

Sketch 29. Accordingly the 1st South African Mounted Brigade, numbering about 1,200, after an arduous march in continual heavy rain, concentrated at Arusha during the last week of March. Its patrols located a German force, estimated as 500 strong and apparently isolated, holding the prominent solitary hill of Lolkisale, 35 miles to the south-west, and in possession of the only springs anywhere in the neighbourhood.

The capture of Lolkisale, evidently an essential preliminary in the task allotted to Major-General van Deventer, was just the type of operation suited to the South African mounted force. After two days' very thorough reconnaissance, the Mounted Brigade (less one squadron 2nd S. African Horse) with the 2nd and 4th Batteries, S.A.F.A., moved off from Arusha at noon on the 3rd April, the 2nd Horse being ordered to ride on independently and make a detour round Lolkisale during the night so as to be in position by dawn to cut off the enemy's retreat. The remainder of the force, after a halt some ten miles out, made a difficult night march which brought it within 12 miles of Lolkisale, to a point from which at 4 a.m. on the 4th April it continued on its way.

---

[1] The strategic importance of Kondoa Irangi, with practicable lines of advance radiating to points on the 180-mile stretch of railway between Saranda and Kilosa, will be noted. It will also be seen that the line of advance down the Usambara railway forms a kind of narrow *couloir*, 100 miles long, from the Ruvu to Bwiko, well adapted for the step-by-step retirement contemplated by the enemy. On the restricted frontage between the deep and rapid stream of the Pangani and the mountains, divided by a belt of bush between river and railway, it would be difficult in the face of resolute opposition for an attacking force to develop its superior strength or to make any wide outflanking movement.

Had either the present-day railway between Mwanza and Tabora, or a line (now surveyed) linking the Usambara and Central Railways between Korogwe and Kimamba, or both, been in existence in 1916, both British and German strategy might well have been very different.

Lolkisale, rising 1,500 feet above the plain and some six miles in circumference, proved to be steep and rugged, its slopes covered with large boulders, trees and scrub. At 9 a.m. the troops dismounted, about 3,000 yards from the mountain, and by 9.30 a.m. they were hotly engaged. The 2nd Horse, which meanwhile had covered nearly 50 miles during the night, joined in from the west and south, two troops of the 3rd Horse moving round to meet them.

In the course of the 4th and 5th April, using the traditional Boer tactics of working uphill from boulder to boulder and firing at each puff of smoke, the South Africans gained ground, well supported by their artillery. The issue, nevertheless, remained undecided, and the severe thirst from which men and horses were suffering began to be serious.

About 4 p.m. on the 5th April the Germans fell back from the right flank of their position, giving up a spring of water which for the moment was the saving of the situation, and by dusk the 2nd Horse had gained the crest, a small detachment under Major J. Wilkens making its way to within thirty yards of the German trenches.

Already, however, the local lack of water had told so heavily on the horses that Major-General van Deventer seriously considered sending them back to Arusha ; many of them were dying of horse-sickness ; rations were exhausted, and the tracks in rear were so swamped that supplies were inevitably delayed—a foretaste of what was to come A quick decision was essential, and a general assault was ordered for dawn next day (6th).

During the night 5th/6th April the South Africans closed up on their advanced detachments, and at dawn intensive fire was opened in preparation for the assault. But the previous day's artillery and rifle fire had done their work, and as the order to charge was given a white flag was put up and the Germans surrendered.

The enemy's force proved to be the *28.F.K.*, less its commander, who had been wounded and evacuated on the previous day.[1] The South African casualties, thanks to skilful tactics and effective artillery support, were trivial.

---

[1] The capture included 2 officers, 15 other Germans, 114 askari, 300 company porters, with 2 m.g. and a considerable amount of ammunition and stores. The German casualties are not known.

The German surrender is attributed by Lettow (" My Reminiscences ", p. 126) to the fact that after the commander, Capt. Rothert, had been wounded the garrison failed to realise the difficulties of the South Africans in regard to water.

The successful seizure of Lolkisale opened the way for the 2nd Division. Captured documents and other evidence indicated that the enemy intended reinforcing Kondoa Irangi and Ufiome ; but this would take time, and Major-General van Deventer was ordered to press on, followed by the infantry of the division.

OCCUPATION OF MADUKANI

Concurrently with the operations against Lolkisale, Major-General van Deventer decided on a subsidiary movement wide to the western flank, towards Lake Manyara. Accordingly on the 2nd April, preceded by a patrol on the 1st, a squadron of the 2nd S. African Horse under Captain E. P. W. Green was detached to proceed to Madukani.[1] On the 7th this move was justified by a telegram in which the Commander-in-Chief informed Major-General van Deventer of the probability that small numbers of the enemy were at Mbugwe (Madukani), Mbulu, Ufiome and Kondoa Irangi, and directed him to occupy those places before the enemy's reinforcements could come up.[2] The " Brigade Scouts " under Major H. de Jager,[3] 50 strong, were at once sent after Green's squadron, followed next day (8th) by three squadrons of the 4th S. African Horse under Lieut.-Colonel F. A. H. Eliott with a convoy of supplies. On the 10th April, learning that Green had occupied Madukani after a brief skirmish[4] and that some 200 of the enemy were holding Mbulu, Major-General van Deventer sent orders to Eliott to push on in order to cut off their retreat, and to the 3rd S. African Infantry Brigade (Berrangé) to despatch a battalion and the 28th Mountain Battery R.A., to Madukani ; the remainder of the Brigade with the 12th (How.)

---

[1] Also variously known as Maduk, Mbugwe, Mudikani, and Köthersheim.

[2] On 10th April G.H.Q. Intelligence calculated that by the 20th April at latest considerable opposition might be expected at Kondoa Irangi, on the assumption that after the Lolkisale affair German troops would be hurried from the Usambara railway round to Kondoa through Morogoro and Dodoma (Sketch 28).

[3] See p. 251, f.n. 3.

[4] It is now known that after this encounter the German forces near Madukani divided, a detachment under Lieut. Kämpfe marching to Ufiome to bar an advance from Lolkisale towards Kondoa Irangi, and the remainder taking up positions to cover Mbulu on the western wall of the Great Rift Valley. By a fortunate chance helio communication was, after much difficulty, established between Madukani and Lolkisale just in time for the former move to be reported by Capt. Green on 11th April.

Battery, R.A. and an attached machine gun company to move south through Lolkisale and Ufiome on Kondoa Irangi.

On the 11th April, therefore, orders were sent by Brig.-General Berrangé to the 10/S. African Infantry (less one company left at Arusha) and 28th Mountain Battery, R.A., to move to Madukani.[1] Early on the 13th April these units, under Major (local Lieut.-Colonel) L. M. Davies, R.A., left Kumbulin to follow the mounted squadrons.

On the 12th April, acting on Captain Green's report of the previous day that most of the enemy's force at Mbulu had moved off towards Ufiome, Major-General van Deventer recalled the detached mounted troops to the latter place, Captain Green forthwith, and Lieut.-Colonel Eliott with Major H. de Jager to follow him on the arrival of the composite column at Madukani.

THE MARCH TO KONDOA IRANGI

Meanwhile the Mounted Brigade moved on from Lolki- Sketch 29
sale, notwithstanding the wastage among its horses and the ever-increasing difficulties of communication and supply along tracks rapidly becoming a quagmire under the rains.

Starting on the 7th April, a picked detachment 200 strong, under Lieut.-Colonel P. L. de Jager, reached the Tarangire river on the evening of the 8th to establish a camp there and reconnoitre towards Ufiome, incidentally rounding up a small German party which had escaped from Lolkisale. Water and grazing being good, they were joined next day (9th) by all the remaining mounted troops whose horses were fit to march, and here they remained for some days of much-needed rest.

[1] No copies of these orders can now be traced. It would appear that the only order issued to the column of the 10/S.A.I. and 28th Mtn. Bty., R.A. was to proceed to Madukani and that it was not known exactly where the place was. It may well be held that the objective of the column should have been more definitely specified. But it must be remembered that the information available was of the scantiest, there were no proper maps, and time was pressing. Commanders and staffs alike were not trained soldiers, but learning as they went, under every kind of difficulty ; and it was probably inevitable that the troops successively despatched in the direction of Lake Manyara should have been sent off more or less at a venture.

On 10th April, 3rd S.A.Inf.Bde.H.Q. was at Lolkisale, 9/ and 12/S.A.I. on the march from Moshi to Arusha, 11/S.A.I. moving from Kumbulin to Lolkisale, and 10/S.A.I. with the 28th Mtn. Bty., R.A., at Kumbulin. The only means of communication was by motor-cycle, and the prevailing road and weather conditions doubtless account for the lapse of time between Major-General van Deventer's order of 10th and the departure of the column on 13th April.

Behind them the 3rd S. African Infantry Brigade (less the 10/S.A. Infantry) was on its way, toiling through mud and torrents of rain in a poisoned air.[1] Transport problems became daily more acute : more and more lorries became bogged, needing teams of mules and oxen to release them. For a week no transport vehicles got through from Arusha to Lolkisale. To add to the difficulties, the wireless at Kumbulin broke down ; despatch-riders found it impossible to force their machines through the mud ; the weather made visual signalling impossible ; and the sole means of communication left to the Divisional Commander was by mounted orderlies stationed at intervals of ten miles.

Without waiting for the labouring infantry, Major-General van Deventer pushed forward his mounted troops, now reduced to 800 men, on the 12th April through the sodden bush to Ufiome. A small German force[2] encountered that day was chased next morning (13th) from the Ufiome heights, beyond which the bush gives place to the open grass-land of the Masai Steppe, country ideal for cavalry were it not for tsetse fly. Across this for twenty miles a running fight in the rain continued, until at nightfall the South Africans reached Salanga, where, whilst waiting for supplies to come up, they lost numbers of their unfortunate horses from fly.[3] On the 16th April the Mounted Brigade, now only 650 strong, went on to within 7 miles of Kondoa Irangi. The hills north of that place appeared to be held in some force, and after minor skirmishing during the 17th van Deventer attacked on the following day, supported by effective artillery cross-fire at no more than 3,000 yards. Attempted counter-attacks on his flanks were beaten off ;

---

[1] " Up to this date 250 horses and 60 mules had died, and owing to the " fact that spades and picks were not available and the bush was too green " to burn, the position is better imagined than described." War Diary, 2nd Divn., 8th April, 1916.

[2] This was Kämpfe's detachment (see p. 272, f.n. 4), reinforced by *1.Sch.K.*, a mounted unit about 80 strong from Kondoa Irangi, and by stragglers from Lolkisale, probably about 200 in all.

On receiving news of the British move against Lolkisale Lettow had ordered a concentration at Kondoa Irangi as follows :—*13.F.K.* (whose peace station had been Kondoa Irangi) from the Usambara area, by road from Handeni ; *23.* and *25.F.K.* from Kigoma (on 12th April) by rail to Saranda ; *2.Sch.K.* (mounted) from Saranda.

Captain Klinghardt, from Kigoma, was placed in command of this force on 10th April.

[3] Between Lolkisale and Salanga the 1st S.A. Mtd. Bde. lost 140 horses and 50 mules dead and many more incapacitated.

the Germans fell back in the evening to the low hills covering Kondoa Irangi, and on the 19th evacuated the place, leaving some of the houses in flames.

After pursuing the retreating enemy for some five miles and capturing 5 Germans and some 60 other stragglers, the exhausted troops were recalled and establishment of a permanent camp was begun.[1] No great amount of supplies was found,[2] and as the surrounding country had been practically denuded of food-stuffs by the enemy the troops had to eke out their scanty rations mainly with local fruit— green guavas, paw-paws and ground nuts—until supplies arrived, while the horses had little chance to recover condition.

For the time being the 1st S. African Mounted Brigade, its strength now below 600, was completely immobilized. Nevertheless its achievement, towards which its attached field batteries had made an effective contribution, had been notable. In the teeth of every adverse circumstance it had attained its objective, depriving the enemy of an important locality.[3]

During the period of enforced inaction before his infantry **Sketch 28** came up Major-General van Deventer consolidated his position, sending patrols southwards to Chambalo and Kwa Mtoro and collecting what supplies there were within a radius of some thirty miles. The native headmen were summoned and informed that, British authority having been established, they were guaranteed protection and must furnish assistance. Through them large numbers of carriers were obtained and used to bring up rations and stores from Salanga and Ufiome.

The situation of the Mounted Brigade, isolated in German territory and nearly two hundred miles by road from the main body of the field force, might well seem precarious.

---

[1] The ground was so saturated that in places the gun-teams sank trace-deep in the mud, and the horses of the mounted units were brought to a standstill.

[2] Some 800 head of cattle—in which the district is rich—and 200 donkeys, formed a useful acquisition.

, [3] The German strength at Kondoa Irangi at this time was given in one estimate as ten companies, totalling 1,400. In fact the German units present were *13.F.K.*, which arrived after a forced march by the difficult road from Handeni on 18th April, and part of *2.F.K.* and *23.Sch.K.*, then arriving. Remnants of *28.F.K.* and *Kämpfe's detachment* in the vicinity were reported as valueless by Capt. Klinghardt who had now assumed command.

The German troops engaged therefore probably did not exceed 400 all told.

To the eastward, however, the barren waste stretching for over a hundred miles to the Pangani was crossed only by the single road to Handeni, while a similar arid stretch extended westwards towards Tabora. It was unlikely in the extreme that any considerable hostile force could cross either area, and although the German detachment at Mbulu was a minor menace to the line of communication it could do little in face of the detached force now at Madukani.[1] Only from the direction of the Central Railway was any serious German attack to be apprehended, and Major-General van Deventer, whilst awaiting the arrival of his infantry, made his dispositions accordingly.

ARRIVAL OF THE 3RD S.A. INFANTRY BRIGADE

The 3rd South African Infantry Brigade, marching doggedly southward from Arusha in the downpour, fording swollen rivers and struggling through quagmires along the unmetalled tracks, took more than a fortnight to reach Kondoa Irangi, the 11/S.A. Infantry arriving on the 30th April and the remainder of the brigade (less 10/S.A. Infantry), with the 12th (How.) Battery, R.A. and the East Africa Volunteer Machine Gun Company, on the 1st May.

The severity of the march told heavily on the health of the troops. Supply columns were so delayed by mortality among animals that units were often on half rations and devoid of essential replacements of clothing and equipment.[2] Under such conditions the effective strength of the brigade fell rapidly, so that on arrival the three battalions together mustered only 1,844 of all ranks.[3] These, however, encouraged by the initial success at Lolkisale, were fit and confident. Their arrival brought Major-General van Deventer's total fighting strength to about 3,000.[4]

---

[1] See p. 272.

[2] Many men whose boots were worn out had to remain on the L. of C. until re-equipped ; others marched on nearly barefoot ; some, it is said even bartered their worn-out boots with natives for food.

[3] 9/S.A.I., 27 officers, 472 o.r. ; 11/S.A.I., 27 officers, 746 o.r. ; 12/S.A.I. 22 officers, 550 o.r.

In addition, 12(How.)Bty., R.A., 1 officer, 25 o.r., 25 Cape Boys ; E.A.M.G. Coy. started 62 strong, with 4 m.g. (strength on arrival is not known).

[4] Including the 4th S.A. Horse, arrived from Madukani 28th April. No detailed figures for the mounted units are available.

EFFECT OF THE RAINY SEASON

The forecast made to Lieut.-General Smuts by the local experts was falsified, as has been described, by the onset of the heaviest rainy season known for many years. So bad, indeed, was the state of the Arusha-Lolkisale section of the road that a new route to avoid it had been made early in May direct from the Sanya river crossing to Lolkisale,[1] shortening the line of supply by some twenty miles ; but the needs of the 2nd Division continued to make heavy demands on the transport and supply services as a whole. It seems likely that if the paralyzing effect of the rains on all movement[2] had been foreseen the move of the division would have been deferred until the country dried again, even at the cost of giving the enemy more time for counter-measures.

Had this policy been adopted, and had the movement of van Deventer on Kondoa Irangi been deferred to synchronise with that of the main force down the railway, certainly the 2nd Division would have suffered far less and moved more quickly ; the strategic situation of the enemy would have been more difficult in consequence, and it may be that the combined movement would have resulted in an earlier and more decisive conclusion of the campaign.

[1] Much work was also done on the road through the hills about Ufiome, in order to avoid the black cotton soil and the tsetse-infested route skirting them to the south-east.

From Moshi to the Sanya, M.T. could be used ; from the Sanya to Ufiome light cars and ambulances in convoy could be got through with difficulty, but supplies were carried by ox- and mule-wagon ; from Ufiome to Kondoa Irangi light Reo lorries and box-cars were used. So heavy, however, was the toll taken of animals by fly, of all M.T. by becoming either bogged or held fast in loose sand, and of transport personnel by the arduousness of their work, that Major-General van Deventer was often left dependent on the scanty supplies obtainable locally.

The protection of his L. of C. was taken over by the 17th Infantry and Bharatpur Infantry, released from the Mombasa–Nairobi railway, total about 1½ battalions. It may be noted that not one vehicle was lost by enemy action.

[2] For example : the 4th Light Armoured Car Bty. (4 naval cars) under Lt.-Commdr. W. Whittall left Mbuyuni on 7th April to join the 2nd Divn. On the 11th, just after the rains began, the cars crossed the Sanya ; but they became deeply bogged every few miles and did not reach Arusha until four weeks later, by which time 40 per cent. of the personnel were down with fever or dysentery. They did not reach Kondoa Irangi till the last week in May.

Of the Moshi–Arusha road a survivor, writing of " the hopeless task " of making this swamp passable for wheels ", says : " Its state was " indescribable, wet black cotton soil poached to a morass. It was hard " work for an unladen man to go two miles an hour . . . I saw a telegraph " lorry do 800 yards in 4 hours, laying out an anchorage ahead and then " warping up to it with a steel cable."

On the other hand, in all probability not even the experts of Moshi and Arusha could have foretold that so exceptional a rainy season was to neutralize the advantages which the Commander-in-Chief might justifiably expect from the earlier move of the 2nd Division, his reasons for which have already been given.[1]

About Kilimanjaro and the Usambara railway the rains had likewise been of surpassing violence.[2] All low-lying areas became lakes ; the numerous rivers and streams in flood swept away almost every bridge ; roads became impassable stretches of deep mud. By the devoted exertions of the technical troops the railway from Voi had been pushed up by the 23rd March to a railhead at Taveta, and was being energetically extended to join the Usambara line at Kahe.[3] On the 25th April, the first through train from Voi reached Moshi.

The difficulties and restrictions due to the rains were intensified by the fact that by the nature of the operations the various headquarters had of necessity been scattered in widely-separated localities.[4] A heavy strain was thus thrown on the ancillary services, signals in particular (visual signalling being largely out of the question) ;[5] but these, each in its own sphere—medical, ordnance, transport, supplies—were maintained with undaunted determination in the face of the most trying difficulties and hardship. Thanks to these services the troops were fed and cared for ; nevertheless the health of the force inevitably suffered

---

[1] See pp. 268–70.

[2] The rainfall at Moshi from 14th–30th April, 1916, was 17.86 inches. On occasion as much as 4 inches fell in one day.

[3] To ensure rapid progress and quick repair in the event of damage the line was laid as a surface one, and many stretches of it were consequently under mud and water, at times axle-deep. Its bridges stood up to the floods well, but much extra labour was needed to supplement construction gangs.

In May and June an extension from Kahe towards Arusha was taken as far as the Sanya river, which was reached on 2nd July. This went no farther during the war, but was eventually extended to Arusha in 1929.

See also Chap. XIX, Note II, p. 326, f.n. 1.

[4] The Administrative and Intelligence branches of G.H.Q., for example, were partly at Moshi and partly at Nairobi ; Railways branch between Nairobi, Voi, Kilindini, Mbuyuni, Moshi ; I.G.C., Nairobi, Moshi, Arusha ; 1st Divn., Moshi and Mbuyuni ; 2nd Divn., Arusha, Lolkisale, Ufiome, Kondoa Irangi ; 3rd Divn., Himo.

[5] At this time (April–May) over 2,500 miles of telegraph line were being worked, handling some 5,000 messages a day.

and some units had to be withdrawn from the fronts to recuperate.[1]

THE DEFENCE OF KONDOA IRANGI

Although the British troops were immobilized by the rains, the Germans, whose movements could be made, at least in part, by rail and who travelled lighter, were not crippled to the same extent. By the 29th April information received at G.H.Q. showed that a succession of German units was passing southward through Handeni towards the Central Railway, obviously directed against the 2nd Division,[2] and by the same date van Deventer's patrols south of Kondoa Irangi were reporting indications of their appioach from Dodoma and Saranda. Natives reported five German companies advancing from Saranda, and on the 30th April a patrol of the 2nd South African Horse was in contact with the enemy near Kwa Mtoro.

The menace from the southward made it necessary to **Sketch 29** eliminate the small German detachment on the flank of the line of communication at Mbulu. Accordingly, whilst his troops at Kondoa Irangi were preparing positions for defence, Major-General van Deventer directed his detached force at Madukani to drive the enemy out of Mbulu. To reinforce it he sent a composite squadron, mainly from the 2/S.African Horse, under Major J. C. Carroll, which moved up the Bubu river to Masogoloda and the escarpment wall of the Great Rift valley.

The positions taken up at Kondoa Irangi are shown **Sketch 30** generally in Sketch 30. The township itself lies in the shallow valley of the Mkonda stream, in a region of rocky hills. One of the largest of these, lying south of the town and flanked on the east by a lake, was the obvious position to take up and was held by the three infantry battalions, with the four mounted units disposed on outlying heights to the flanks and rear.

---

[1] The 2/Rhodesia Regt. went back at the end of March into rest in the good climate of Kabete, near Nairobi. The 2/Loyal North Lancashire Regt. was so depleted by dysentery and malaria that early in April it was sent to South Africa for convalescence. This unit embarked from Mombasa on 8th May with 537 all ranks, leaving behind its m.g. coy. reinforced by all fit men of the battalion to a total of 170, plus a small mounted infantry detachment and " Logan's battery " (see Chap. XIII, Note I (iii), p. 220.

[2] Lettow had now decided to transfer the bulk of his force from the Pangani area to oppose van Deventer at Kondoa Irangi, assuming that the main British effort would be made on this line of operation. His decision is stated by Arning to have been made on 21st April.

South of the heights thus occupied, on the far side of a valley about two miles wide, lay a parallel line of hills of which two, " Range Rock Hill " and " South Hill ", overtopped the British ridges by some 500 feet. Midway between, on a rise known as " Rock Rabbit Ridge ", outposts were established.

Sketch 28

During the first week in May signs of the enemy's approach in force multiplied. On the 4th May, after a patrol encounter on the Saranda road, a German force estimated at six to eight companies approached from Mponde, driving in a British post at Kwa Mtoro. On the 6th a number of German units passed through Chambalo, and by the following day the enemy's presence about six miles from Kondoa Irangi was confirmed by streams of native fugitives claiming the promised British protection, from whose reports the German strength was estimated as probably more than 20 companies.

Sketch 30

By the evening of the 8th May the enemy approaching along the Dodoma and Handeni roads was within five miles, and on the afternoon of the 9th a German gun[1] opened from South Hill, compelling withdrawal of the outposts on Rock Rabbit Ridge.

About 7.30 p.m. on the 9th May the enemy launched an attack in force on the south and east faces of the main position, the brunt falling on the 11/S. African Infantry. Under a quarter moon giving light enough to move freely, the German askari charged gallantly up the slopes with the usual bugling and cheering ; but they had little cover, the flares and star shell of the defence lit up the ground, and each attempt to assault was stopped by the South African rifle and machine gun fire. A German machine gun near the southern end of the lake was rushed and captured by the 11th, while the 12/ S. African Infantry counter-attacked the enemy's right. Fighting went on until about 2.15 a.m., when the Germans fell back and did not renew the attack.[2]

---

[1] Gun ammunition had apparently run low ; a *Königsberg* 4·1-inch gun used at Kondoa Irangi was firing home-made iron shell filled with black powder.

[2] British casualties were : 11/S.A.I., killed, 2 officers, 2 o.r. ; wounded, 12 o.r. ; 12/S.A.I., killed, 2 o.r. ; wounded, 1 officer, 4 o.r.

German casualties are given by Dr. Schnee as : killed, 2 officers, 3 other Germans, 50 askari ; wounded, 5 Germans, 66 askari ; missing, 2 Germans, 19 askari. The German losses included Capt. von Kornatzki killed, Lt.-Col. von Bock severely wounded.

The successful repulse of the German attack was followed by a month's deadlock. The German forces present were evidently considerable, certainly much in excess of the British ;[1] but their initial failure " immediately to take pos-" session of the low hills now held by the enemy "[2] had clearly had a deterrent effect. Major-General van Deventer for his part, in accordance with orders from G.H.Q., remained on the defensive. His troops had little rest : constant alarms, daily shelling and nightly patrol encounters kept both sides on the alert. Both sides, too, endeavoured as usual to envelop each other by extension of the flanks, especially to the eastward. Thus on the day after the attack (10th May) infantry detachments moved out to " Middle " Hill " and " Battery Hill " ;[3] soon afterwards mounted troops occupied " Koen's Kop ", which was later held by the infantry ; and in the same way the enemy occupied successively " Beacon Hill ", and later " Black Rock ", and other heights beyond. Little, however, was destined to come of these manoeuvres.

---

[1] A fairly close estimate of their total numbers made after the attack was 20 companies, say 4,000 men. This was arrived at on the spot by Major Meinertzhagen, who by a most fortunate chance was on a visit to the 2nd Divn., with two other Regular staff officers from G.H.Q., when the attack took place. Their visit proved extremely useful, not only to the organization of the defence generally, but in the expert interrogation of prisoners, the value of which had hardly been sufficiently recognized.

At G.H.Q. Maj. Meinertzhagen's estimate, indicating as it did the extensive transfer of German troops away from the Pangani, was not willingly accepted until the weakness of the opposition eventually en-confirmed by the main force in the subsequent advance proved its correctness. (See p. 287.)

It it now known that the attack was delivered by :
Abteilung Otto (*9.*, *14.*, *24.F.K.*),
Abteilung Bock (*15.*, *19.F.K.* *6.Sch.K.*),
Abteilung Kornatzki (*18.*, *22.*, *27.F.K.*).
Total, about 1,800.

These units deployed for attack in the valley between South Hill and Range Rock Hill.

In addition the following were present in support : on South Hill—*Abteilung Stemmermann* (*8.*, *11.*, *21.F.K.*), *Abteilung Klinghardt* (*13.*, *23.*, *25.F.K.*) ; on Range Rock Hill—*Abteilung Chappuis* (*4.*, *10.F.K.*, *14.Res.K.*) ; on eastern flank (near Malatu), *Abteilung Meyer* (*8.*, *9.Sch.K.*, *Arusha Det.*).

The total German force present was, according to Dr. Schnee, about 4,000 rifles, with about 20 machine guns, three heavy and several lighter guns. On the L. of C. were : *6.F.K.*, *1.* and *2.Sch.K.* and *Rombo Detachment*.

[2] Lettow, " My Reminiscences ", p. 135.

[3] Battery Hill afforded covered positions for the field batteries engaging Range Rock Hill ; later, " North Hill " was used by the heavier artillery. *Continued at foot of next page.*

OCCUPATION OF MBULU

Sketch 29 Lieut.-Colonel Davies's small column from Arusha, after a grim march in the universal mud and rain, reached Madukani on the 17th April, upon which Eliott and de Jager with their mounted troops withdrew to Ufiome as ordered.[1] At Madukani, described by a survivor as " the one island " standing out of the marsh," Davies remained for the next three weeks, without orders, completely out of touch[2] and under conditions of severe hardship : on short rations, in an unhealthy climate telling on men and animals alike, with his Indian artillery personnel in particular suffering as much in spirit as in body from lack of their native food-stuffs.[3]

On the 2nd May Major-General van Deventer's order to attack Mbulu was received, together with the information that Major Carroll's squadron was on its way.[4] At the same time command of the force at Madukani passed to Lieut.-Colonel J. W. V. Montgomery, commanding the 10/S. African Infantry, it having been found that he was in fact senior to Lieut.-Colonel Davies.

Montgomery's preparations for attack took time, and it was not until the 7th May that the force moved off, through swamps, mud and a swollen river to the foothills beyond.[5] On the 8th, after reconnaissance, attack was ordered for

Continued from previous page.

To enable German accounts of the operations to be followed the names given to the various hills by both sides are appended :

British.	German.
(main position)	Schanzenberg.
Bosch Kop.	Stuhrberg.
Spitz Kop.	Flussberg.
Observation Hill.	—
Middle Hill.	Euphorbien Berg.
North Hill.	Fünfkoppen Berg.
Battery Hill.	—
Koen's Kop.	Höhe G.
Versveld's Kop.	Sattel Höhe.
Beacon Hill.	Buechsel Höhe.
Range Rock Hill.	Königsberg Höhe (Höhe E.).
South Hill.	Höhe C. & D.
Black Rock	Kidunda.

[1] Eliott had reached Madukani on 12th April.

[2] All attempts to communicate by helio failed. The first communication received was from Divn. H.Q. on 2nd May as narrated.

[3] A point in connection with Indian troops which constantly stood out in this campaign.

[4] See p. 279.

[5] Owing to losses in animals one section, 28th Mtn. Bty., R.A., had to remain at Madukani. The remaining four guns crossed the river on improvised rafts.

noon next day. Considering a direct ascent of the escarpment impracticable if opposed, Montgomery detailed Davies, with a company of the 10th, a section of his battery and two machine guns, to make a holding attack in that direction whilst the remainder of the force made a wide detour to the south in order to cut off the enemy's retreat.

Accordingly during the afternoon of the 9th and the following night Lieut.-Colonel Davies led his small force in a stiff climb up the steep, rocky and wooded escarpment, his advance being at first opposed by some 60 of the enemy well posted in trenches overlooking his line of ascent. These were effectively shelled at short range by his two guns, and by nightfall the enemy's fire had died down. At 9.30 p.m. the advance was resumed by moonlight, but on difficult slopes and in a thick mist made slow progress ; and although by 1.30 a.m. on the 10th the advanced party reached the top and found the ground evacuated, it was not till daylight that the whole force was assembled on the plateau. Here the troops were given a rest pending arrival of the main force. Their casualties were 1 killed, 1 wounded (both in the 10/S. African Infantry).

Montgomery's turning movement proved long, arduous and unnecessary. Meeting no opposition, his force made its way up through steep rock-strewn forest, taking 13 hours to reach the plateau above, along which it returned to rejoin Davies's detachment at 12.30 p.m. on the 10th May. Learning that Mbulu had been evacuated, Montgomery decided to rest his troops after their exhausting all-night march, and occupied Mbulu on the following day. In his view Lieut.-Colonel Davies had advanced too fast, thereby depriving him of a chance of cutting off the enemy ; but it seems more probable that the Germans, aware of Carroll's force coming up in their rear, had had no intention of standing, so that Montgomery's flanking movement was destined from the outset to missfire.

Of Carroll, meanwhile, there had been no sign beyond a message received on the 8th May via Ufiome, to which Montgomery had replied declining to postpone his own operation. Carroll reached Masogoloda on the 9th and next day climbed some 2,400 feet to Monumanaga. Leaving the latter place late on the 10th, he joined forces with Montgomery at Mbulu at 11.30 p.m. on the 11th. As ill-luck would have it, he had missed by only about six hours the

Sketch 29

Sketch 28 retreating Mbulu garrison as it passed through Dungobesh on its way south-westwards to Mkalama. As his horses were rapidly falling sick, some from tsetse and some from the sudden change to the cold of the high ground, he remained at Mbulu.[1]

Montgomery's force was now ordered to Kondoa Irangi, where every available man and gun were needed, and moved **Sketch 29** off on the 14th May by way of Monumananga (17th) to Masogoloda, where he arrived late on the 18th. An increasing number of his men were suffering from malaria and all were short of food, the villages on the way having been already denuded and there being hardly any vehicles or pack animals to collect supplies farther afield. From Masogoloda Davies with his faster-moving battery[2] went ahead to reach Kondoa Irangi on the evening of the 20th May, followed by the remainder of the column on the 22nd.

REINFORCEMENT OF THE 2ND DIVISION

Sketch 30 At Kondoa Irangi both sides still restricted themselves to patrol activity and intermittent shelling. The South African troops, at first careless in regard to cover from artillery fire, soon learned wisdom, and their losses were slight ; but the wide frontage held meant constant duty in the front line, rations arrived short and intermittently, so that the troops were often half starved, while heat by day and cold by night weakened their resistance to fever. The sick rate mounted alarmingly.[3] Constant patrolling and reliefs of squadrons in the line allowed the horses no rest, and the effective mobile strength of the 1st Mounted Brigade steadily dwindled.[4] Since, moreover, the move of the newly-formed 2nd Mounted Brigade from South Africa was still engaging all suitable shipping, no remounts were available.

The mobility of the 2nd Division was consequently much impaired ; but its fighting strength was gradually increasing. On the 22nd May, concurrently with the start of the main advance down the Pangani[5], the whole defensive line from

---

[1] Whilst at Mbulu Maj. Carroll was for a time fully occupied in dealing with unrest and cattle-raiding among the native tribes.

[2] Less 1 sect. left at Mbulu.

[3] On 25th May about 100 were sick in Kondoa Irangi ; by 19th June the number had risen to 1,200.

[4] A return on 23rd May showed that out of 3,894 horses issued to the 1st S.A.Mtd.Bde. up to that date 1,639 had died since the beginning of operations in March ; 718 had been sent back to hospital, and only 1,123 fit horses were with the Bde.

[5] See Chap. XVIII.

Spitzkop to Koen's Kop was taken over by the 3rd S. African Infantry Brigade, the mounted troops being freed for use farther afield.

Following the arrival of the 10/S. African Infantry and **Sketch 29** the 28th Mountain Battery, R.A., from Mbulu, the 7/ and 8/S. African Infantry, detached from the 2nd S. African Infantry Brigade, arrived from Arusha and formed a general reserve. They in turn were followed by a newly-raised South African Motor Cyclist Corps, 300 strong, the 1st Field Battery, S.A.F.A., the (Indian) Volunteer Machine Gun Company and two armoured cars of the 4th Light Armoured Battery.[1] One of the two howitzers of the 12th Battery having been wrecked by a premature burst on the 15th May, the loss was made good by a section of the 11th (How.) Battery, R.A.,[2] which arrived at the beginning of June. The divisional artillery was further reinforced by the 10th (Heavy) Battery, which was brought into action on North Hill ; and thus, in the heart of the African continent, the guns of the sunken *Pegasus*[3] answered those of the derelict *Königsberg* once more. Finally, two aircraft, after many adventures and mishaps, arrived on the 5th June.[4]

Strengthened by these reinforcements, Major-General van Deventer made his preparations for a further advance. Apart from patrol actions, no engagement of any importance took place until the second week in June. By that time the rains had ceased, roads were fast drying up and freedom of movement was in sight.

---

[1] See p. 277, f n 2. Out of four armoured cars one had broken down at Lolkisale, another at Ufiome ; a third broke down on arrival at Kondoa Irangi Three days after arrival the m.g. were taken out of the cars for use in the line.

[2] See Chap. XIII, Note I (xi), p. 221. The 11th (How.) Bty. (38th (How.). Bde., R.G.A.) had been divided into two independent sections. The Right Secn., re-named " No. 13 Bty.", joined the 1st Divn. The Left Secn., as " No. 11 Bty.", was sent to the 2nd Divn. and on reaching Kondoa Irangi was grouped for tactical purposes with No. 12 Bty.

[3] See Chap. XIII, Note I (vii), p. 220.

[4] The aircraft were sighted from Kondoa Irangi on 31st May, but, having failed to recognize their destination, turned back and made a forced landing in the open country to the north, for want of petrol. Fortunately they were not attacked. The aerodrome constructed for them at Kondoa Irangi was shelled by a *Königsberg* gun and the aircraft had to move out 12 miles to the northward.

CHAPTER XVIII

THE ADVANCE FROM KILIMANJARO—*(continued)*

LIEUT.-GENERAL SMUTS'S ADVANCE TO THE MSIHA

(Sketches 28, 31, 32, 33, 34, 35, 36)

SITUATION OF THE MAIN FORCE

Sketch 28 IN the Kilimanjaro area the rains had begun to abate by the second week in May, and Lieut.-General Smuts determined to move at the earliest possible moment. " The " direction of that movement was settled for me," he wrote, " by the necessity of clearing the enemy from the Pare and " Usambara mountains before the further invasion of " German East Africa could safely proceed."[1]

The situation of the 2nd Division at Kondoa Irangi had given rise to some anxiety, but on the return to G.H.Q., on the 16th May, of the staff officers who had visited the division[2] there was reassurance on that point. Their estimate of the German strength now opposing van Deventer was at first received with some reserve ; nevertheless all the evidence since the end of April had indicated that considerable forces of the enemy had left the Usambara railway for Kondoa Irangi, and that consequently an advance southwards from the Ruvu would be opposed by relatively small numbers. On the other hand it was known that a succession of points along the railway had been **Sketch 31** prepared for defence, and it was calculated that the enemy might conceivably be able to bring back a great part of his forces from Kondoa Irangi to the Usambara within about **Sketch 28** fifteen days. In the words of the Commander-in-Chief, " it was therefore advisable for my advance to reach the " Western Usambara in a fortnight ; further, if it could " reach Handeni before the arrival of strong enemy rein- " forcements . . . it would be impossible for the enemy " to make effective resistance to the simultaneous advance " of both columns 170 miles apart."[3] There was thus every reason for an early move.

---

[1] Despatch, 27th October 1916.
[2] See p. 281, f.n. 1.
[3] Despatch, op. cit.

The mountains themselves were high and for all practical purposes impassable. On their eastern side were fertile cultivated valleys, but the western slopes fell sheer to the railway and main road, overlooking a waterless belt of level country some twenty miles wide, covered with dense thorn bush, between the mountains and the Pangani river.[1] The river was wide, rapid and unfordable ; but along its eastern (left) bank ran a strip of open ground varying in width from a few hundred yards to nearly a' mile, offering an easy route, with unlimited water, apparently undefended except by small hostile observation posts.

THE ENEMY'S FORCES

Excluding the units assumed to be at Kondoa Irangi, the enemy's numbers remaining were estimated as being between 1,200 and 2,000.[2] Even during the rains occasional enemy raids had continued to be made against both the Uganda Railway and the new line from Voi to Kahe.[3] It was to be presumed, also, that the enemy had made such use as he could of the period of inactivity to increase his fighting power, and on this point the unwelcome news was received at G.H.Q. early in May that a second blockade-runner had succeeded in landing supplies on the southern coast of the German territory.[4]

---

[1] The only good track crossing the thorn belt was that between Marago Opuni and Same.

[2] G.H.Q. Intelligence figures on 24th May were Usambara, 200 Germans, 800 askari, 6 guns, 14 m.g. ; Tanga and coast, 20 Germans, 350 askari, 1 gun, 2 m.g.

A German account (April) gives the total as 3,000, in 12 units of varying strength, only 4 of which were armed with modern weapons, and 12 guns.

The detail of the force in the Usambara, under Major Kraut, appears to have been : *1., 3., 16., 17., 30.F.K.* ; *5, 7.Sch.K.* ; *Rombo det.* ; *Batterien Sternheim* (3 guns), *Fromme* (4 guns).

[3] The Uganda Railway was blown up near Maungu on 11th April and near Mackinnon Road on 17th May. At the end of May the line was threatened for a time by a German force, said to be 300 strong, near Ngurungani.

[4] The *Marie* reached Sudi on 16th March. Reports of her arrival were received by the naval authorities on 10th April. She was located up a creek next day by whalers accompanying H.M.S. *Hyacinth*, which shelled her reported position. After four days intervening bad weather the locality was again shelled by H.M.Ss. *Vengeance, Hyacinth*, and *Challenger* ; unfortunately no air spotting was available. On 26th April kite-balloon observation reported that no sign of the ship could be seen, and it was learned later that she had made good her escape.

The *Marie's* cargo included four 10·5 cm. howitzers, two 7·5 cm. mountain guns, several m.g., a considerable quantity of S.A.A. and ammunition for the *Königsberg* guns, clothing, stores, tobacco, sweets, *Continued at foot of next page.*

LIEUT.-GENERAL SMUTS'S PLANS (i)

Sketch 31 On the 19th May Lieut.-General Smuts telegraphed to the C.I.G.S. his intention to start a general advance with his main force, adding an appreciation of the difficulties which, from the nature of the country, he foresaw and did not underrate.

Realizing that his advance " was expected to follow " the railway, which had been fortified at all convenient " points for a hundred miles "[1]—a somewhat pessimistic picture—he decided that the greater part of his force should follow the line of the Pangani ; a second portion would at the same time work down the railway, while a small third force, moving from Mbuyuni up the valley of the Ngulu, would co-operate from the eastward.

The movement of these columns was expected to outflank and envelop any position in which a stand might be attempted in the northern Pare range. Failing this, Lieut.-General Smuts envisaged a vigorous pursuit by which the enemy's forces opposed to him, under Major Kraut, were to be cut off from all retreat southwards out of the mountains, and to be brought to surrender there before he resumed his march to strike at the Central Railway and Dar-es-Salaam.[2]

RE-DISTRIBUTION OF THE 1ST AND 2ND DIVISIONS

For the purpose of his intended operations, which he proposed to direct in person, the Commander-in-Chief resolved to abandon for the time being the normal divisional

---

Continued from previous page.
and a selection of Iron Crosses including " enough of the 2nd Class to enable " half of . . . the [*Königsberg's*] company to have one each " (Lettow, " My Reminiscences ", p. 118). She also landed some trained artillery personnel who were afterwards of great value to the enemy.

The arrival of all these, after the interval of some weeks required for their conveyance by carrier to Dar-es-Salaam, had both a material and a considerable moral effect, encouraging the enemy and impressing the natives. A detailed account is given in *Krieg zur See, die Kämpfe in den Kolonien, Band II*, pp. 198–204. The affair is not referred to in " Naval " Operations ".

[1] Despatch, op. cit.

[2] " If enemy makes a stand . . . object will be to cut off his retreat " to Usambara mountains. If he escapes in time, then to follow up " rapidly to Usambara mountains. After arrival at Mkomazi river . . . " I shall first endeavour to cut off enemy's retreat from Usambara to " Central Railway and then attack both from the Mkomazi river and the " coast at or south of Tanga to compel his surrender. When this has " been accomplished next objective will be possession of Central Railway " and Dar-es-Salaam for operations in south and far west . . ."
Telegram, C.-in-C. to C.I.G.S., 19th May 1916.

and brigade organization—1st and 3rd Divisions—of his forces on the Ruvu.[1] These he now re-grouped as follows, retaining only the Force Reserve under his own hand and placing the whole of the remainder under the command of Major-General A. R. Hoskins, G.O.C. 1st Division.

River Column	Centre Column	Eastern Column.
(Brig.-Genl.	(Brig.-Genl.	(Lieut.-Col.
S. H. Sheppard)	J. A. Hannyngton)	T. O. FitzGerald)
Sqdn. 17th Cavalry.	E. African Mtd. Rifles	One Coy. K.A.R. M.I.
2/Rhodesia Regt.	(det.).	3/K.A.R.
130th Baluchis.	40th Pathans.	One Section 27th Mtn.
Composite Bn. Kashmir	129th Baluchis.	Bty., R.A.
Rifles.	Half-Bn. 2nd Kashmir	One Section Indian
No. 5 Bty. S.A.F.A.	Rifles.	Field Ambulance.
27th Mtn. Bty., R.A.	No. 6 Field Bty.	Ammunition and Supply
(less one section).	No. 7 Field Bty.	Columns.
One (double) Coy. 61st	One Section E.A.	
Pioneers.	Pioneers.	
One British Field	Two Sections Indian	
Ambulance.	Field Ambulance.	
Two Sections Indian	Ammunition and Sup-	
Field Ambulance.	ply Columns.	
Ammunition and		
Supply Columns.		

Divisional Reserve
(Maj.-Genl. A. R. Hoskins)

H.Q., 1st Division.
M.I. Coy. (L.N. Lancs., 25/R. Fus.).
E.A. Mtd. Rifles.
25/Royal Fusiliers.
29th Punjabis.
L.N. Lancs., M.G. Coy.
No. 1 Armoured Car Bty.
One Section E.A. Pioneers.
One Section British Field
Ambulance.
B.A. Field Ambulance
Ammunition and Supply
Columns.

Force Reserve
(2nd S.A. Inf. Bde., less 2 Bns.
(Brig.-Genl. P. S. Beves).
Belfield's Scouts.
5/S.A. Infantry.
6/S.A. Infantry.
No. 8 Field Bty.
134th (How.) Bty.

THE ADVANCE FROM THE RUVU TO BWIKO   Sketch 31

Between the 18th and 21st May the River and Centre Columns, with the Divisional Reserve, concentrated about Kahe, while the Eastern Column assembled at Mbuyuni and the Force Reserve at Himo. The successive stages of the march of all three columns are shown in Sketch 31.

---

[1] See pp. 248, 264. The 3rd Divn., which had not yet been joined either by the 2nd S. Afr. Mtd. Bde. or by its divisional commander, and which had detached two battalions to Kondoa Irangi, at present consisted only of H.Q., 2nd S.Afr.Inf.Bde., with the 5/ and 6/S.A.I. See also p. 293, f.n. 3.

On the afternoon of the 22nd scouts reported Kisangire station evacuated ; from the Centre Column a company of the 129th Baluchis went forward and occupied it, the remainder of the Column moving off at 6 p.m. and reaching the station unopposed early on the 23rd. During the previous night the River Column, followed by the Divisional Reserve, began its march down the left bank of the Pangani. Meanwhile on the other flank the Eastern Column, which had left Mbuyuni after dark on the 20th May, occupied Nyata Hill, overlooking the so-called Ngulu Gap at the head of the Ngulu valley, on the morning of the 23rd. Its scouts found strong entrenchments, unoccupied, on Kandaro Hill. In the course of the 23rd the Centre Column occupied Lembeni, still unopposed, where it found defences similarly abandoned.

On the 26th May, when the Centre and Eastern Columns were at Same and Maji-ya-Njuu respectively, with the River Column abreast of them, it became evident from the map that there would be no opposition short of the point, some forty miles on, where the Pangani sweeps in close under the mountains between Mabirioni and Mikocheni. Any hostile position there could, however, be turned from the eastward by way of the Mkomazi valley. Intelligence reports indicated that this route was undefended. Lieut.- General Smuts therefore diverted the greater part of the Centre Column[1] eastwards from Same through the hills, and in the afternoon of the 27th May[2] Brig.-General Hannyngton effecting a junction with FitzGerald's Eastern Column near Mandi Hill, assumed command of the two forces as a combined column which went on towards Gonja.

The River Column, in the meantime, had continued its march down the Pangani, meeting no opposition worth

---

[1] The Centre Column, which had been hampered by lack of vehicles and the slowness of ox transport, left most of its transport at Same together with No. 7 Bty. and the (ox-drawn) ammunition column. The only guns accompanying the march through the hills were the two 12-pdrs. of No. 6 Bty.

[2] On this day the C.-in-C., riding ahead to reconnoitre for himself in disregard of personal danger, narrowly escaped capture by a German patrol ('' Crowe, General Smuts's Campaign '', p. 133).
This practice, entirely in keeping with his earlier training on the veld, was frequently the cause of great anxiety to his staff.
G.H.Q. War Diary records :
'' 13th June :   C.-in-C. rode out 10 miles west from Luchomo . . . to find water and road.
'' 17th June.   C.-in-C. rode out ahead of force to hill 3½ miles S. of Sangeni.''
Similar entries occur on each of nine successive days at this period alone.

mentioning,[1] but under conditions of considerable hardship[2] and with constant difficulties of transport and supply. On the evening of the 29th May, having covered 112 miles from his starting point, Brig.-General Sheppard camped in the vicinity of Mabirioni, his camp and the dust of his transport drawing some desultory fire from a *Königsberg* gun and light artillery.[3]

Ahead, air reconnaissance had reported small formed bodies of German troops near Mikocheni and defences covering a half-completed bridge, which became known as " German Bridge," crossing the Pangani at that point. Since Hannyngton, delayed by the difficulties of his route, had only reached Gonja and therefore was not yet in a position to play his part in turning the German defences confronting Sheppard, the latter made his dispositions for attack on the following day (30th May). Ordering the 2/Rhodesia Regiment to push forward along the river, he directed the remainder of his force towards the mountains in order to turn the German northern flank.

The plan was completely successful. Moving off early on the 30th, the Rhodesians, now reduced by sickness to a fighting strength of about 300, but with six machine guns, in the course of an admirably conducted, almost " sealed pattern " engagement across the open ground during the morning, drove the enemy in disorder from his trenches. Meanwhile the 130th Baluchis, followed by the 27th Mountain Battery, R.A., crossed the railway and soon after mid-day, after an arduous climb, established themselves on the foothills overlooking the bridge. An attempted counter-attack against the Rhodesians' left flank was quickly broken up with the co-operation of the mountain guns, which silenced also a German field gun in the plain, and the enemy fell back on Bwiko. The British troops bivouacked

---

[1] An advanced guard of the 17th Cav. captured a small German patrol near Marago Opuni.

[2] Wider tracks through the bush had continually to be hacked out by the troops, who carried heavy loads of water and extra S.A.A. under a tropical sun, often on short rations and—a matter especially affecting Indian units—with insufficient time for cooking. On one occasion the Kashmir Rifles had to be brought up from the rearguard to clear a track with *kukris*. The march throughout taxed the skill and resource of the technical troops, whose work merits special mention. A vivid account is given in " Marching on Tanga " (F. Brett Young).

[3] Since the column must have presented a fine target to the Germans holding the heights, the weakness of the hostile gunfire was in itself an indication that no serious opposition was likely to be encountered.

Sketches 31, 32

for the night where they stood, those on the high ground suffering considerably from the cold.

Next morning (31st) it was found that the Germans had withdrawn, evacuating Bwiko without so much as cutting the telegraph lines.[1]

Sketch 31 Whilst the enemy was thus in retreat, Hannyngton's column moved down the Mkomazi valley. Beyond Gonja a good road had been known to exist ; but the German demolitions had been thorough, and the bridge at Shegulu, which the column had been ordered to secure on the 30th May, was found to be beyond any repair within Hannyngton's resources. He continued his march, therefore, east of the river past Makokani, encountering some opposition near Lasa Hill on the 31st, and finally, without further encounter with the enemy, made contact with mounted scouts of Sheppard's column at Mkomazi station on the 1st June.

PAUSE AT BWIKO

Sketch 32 At Bwiko, even though the forward movement had nowhere been seriously opposed, the re-united force could look back with satisfaction on its achievement. " The " rapidity of our advance ", in the words of Lieut.-General Smuts, " had exceeded my best expectations. We had " reached the Usambara in ten days, covering a distance " of about 130 miles over trackless country . . . "[2] The force had, however, outrun its means of supply, and a pause was now enforced by the necessity of repairs to roads and the railway,[3] and of replenishing supplies. The damage to the railway had involved over-working all road transport,

---

[1] British casualties, all in the 2/Rhodesia Regt., were one native scout killed ; 2 officers, 8 o.r., wounded.

A German account (Arning) states that four German *F.K.* were engaged.

[2] Despatch, op. cit.

[3] The line was metre-gauge, with rails slotted into steel sleepers. It had been thoroughly and skilfully damaged by the enemy, bridge girders wrecked, abutments blown down, points and crossings destroyed or hidden in the bush, and fittings removed.

The technical units engaged on reconstruction, viz., 25th, 26th, 28th (Rlwy.) Coys., S. & M., were among the hardest-worked of Lieut.-General Smuts's troops and rendered inestimable service under very difficult and trying conditions. Throughout the operations the railway was carrying both repair material and the many requirements of the force. Nevertheless re-laying and repairs were effected at from one to two miles a day, a rate seldom exceeded even in straightforward new construction under favourable conditions in peace. ⌠

At the time, this fine performance was hardly appreciated at its full worth, dissatisfaction being expressed in some quarters with what was

Continued at foot of next page.

with consequent heavy wastage in vehicles[1] and resulting shortage and hardship. Supply arrangements, in fact, had virtually broken down ; the troops were already on half-rations or less, and might well have run out of ammunition if heavy fighting had been necessary. For four days the force at Bwiko and Mkomazi was at a standstill, as much isolated as that at Kondoa Irangi. Its situation, indeed, foreshadowed already the effects of the ever-increasing strain on men, animals and material alike which the driving operations of the next few months were destined to impose.

During the pause Lieut.-General Smuts, having established G.H.Q. at Bwiko on the 31st May, took the opportunity to visit the 2nd Division.[2] In the meantime Major-General Hoskins completed preparations to continue the advance : road, rail and bridge repairs—in particular the completion of German Bridge and of crossings over the Pangani near Bwiko—were hurried on, supplies replenished and minor changes made in the composition and designations of the columns.[3] On the 5th June he was directed to move on when ready, without awaiting the return of the Commander-in-Chief.

Continued from previous page.
regarded as slow progress. This, however, was quickly disposed of by an explanation of the technical aspects involved.

" While operations lasted there was never a day when the railhead " dump was short of supplies for the road transport to remove. Nor do " I know of any occasion when military operations were delayed through " failure of the railway in bringing up men or materials ; though naturally " occasions arose when the army could have advanced more rapidly had " it been possible to push on railhead at a greater speed. This is specially " true of the repairs of the Tanga line." (Report by Dir. of Railways, 10th Feb. 1917.)

[1] Repairs to vehicles were hampered by a general lack of spares, provision of which was one of the major difficulties of the campaign : one that was never fully overcome even by the ingenuity in improvisation which it engendered.

[2] Leaving Bwiko on 2nd June, the C.-in-C. returned to Moshi and went thence by car to Kondoa Irangi (222 miles), where he arrived on 5th June. He left on 7th, reached Moshi next day, and rejoined the main force on 10th June.

[3] On 3rd June the two Kashmir units were reconstituted. The " Composite Bn." was broken up, the 2/Kashmir Rifles (one bn.) being included in Brig.-General Sheppard's command and the 3/Kashmir Rifles (half bn.) in that of Brig.-General Hannyngton.

Hannyngton's force, combined with FitzGerald's (" No. 1 Col."), now designated No. 2 Column, comprised : K.A.R.M.I., 40th Pathans, 129th. Baluchis, 3/Kashmir Rifles, 3/K.A.R., one secn. 27th Mtn. Bty., R.A., Nos. 6 and 7 Bties., one secn. E.A. Pioneers, with medical and supply units.

Sheppard's " River Column " now became No. 3 Column.

The ordinary divisional organization was resumed early in August (see pp. 335, 348).

LIEUT.-GENERAL SMUTS'S PLANS (ii)

Sketch 32 So far as was known, Kraut's force had retired down the railway towards Mombo. Its link with the main German forces under Lettow, however, was a trolley-line running from Mombo south-westwards to the important nodal point, Handeni.[1] A move from Bwiko against Mkalamo, where the trolley-line crossed the Pangani, would therefore either isolate Kraut in the Usambara range or compel him to retreat on Handeni. On the other hand, the only good road followed the railway.

Air reconnaissance had reported trenches under construction covering Mkalamo bridge, while hostile detachments were known to be in position at Mkumbala, with a *Königsberg* gun, and at Hill 620, five miles farther west.

Having little other definite information, Lieut.-General Smuts now decided to send Hannyngton's force along the railway and with the remainder of his troops, crossing to the western (right) bank of the Pangani, to proceed direct by way of Mkalamo.

Sketch 28 Informing the C.I.G.S. of this, he explained that Handeni and Kondoa Irangi were each about 100 miles from the Central Railway at Morogoro and Dodoma respectively, adding : " if Central Railway is occupied at Morogoro and " Dodoma, enemy force could be pressed together on Central " Railway and brought to battle or surrender. Occupation " of Morogoro should also enable portion of force to " operate . . . against Dar-es-Salaam, which would give " us new sea base and render unnecessary . . . lines of " communication . . . from north ".[2]

THE ADVANCE RESUMED

Sketch 32 On the 4th June Hannyngton sent forward the 129th Baluchis with the K.A.R. M.I. to establish an advanced camp near the Ngoha river. Encountering stiff opposition along the river from some 300 of the enemy, and having orders not to become committed too deeply, the force withdrew after some hours to the Langata ridge, where it remained and was later reinforced by two companies of the 3/K.A.R. and a section of the 27th Mountain Battery, R.A.

---

[1] The German trolley-line (gauge 1 ft. 11½ in.) was to become of great value to the British force, despite its shortage of rolling stock. A proposal to extend the metre gauge line from Mombo to Mkalamo was found impracticable on survey being made.

[2] Telegram, 9th June, 1916.

Three days later (7th) these units went forward again, this time as advanced guard to the remainder of Hannyngton's column, which occupied Mazinde next morning with little opposition and continued its march at dawn on the 9th. On approaching Mombo the advanced guard—now the 40th Pathans, with a vanguard of K.A.R. M.I.—was held up for a time by machine gun fire; this was soon silenced by the mountain guns[1], and after some further skirmishing Mombo was occupied at 4 p.m. Two trains seen leaving for Korogwe were shelled at long range, but the enemy was not overtaken in time to prevent him from destroying the railway bridge, water-tanks and workshops. Whether the opposing Germans had retired on Korogwe or Handeni was uncertain; it seemed evident, however, that they were little more than a rearguard[2] intended to delay any advance down the Mkomazi whilst Kraut withdrew down the trolley-line to Handeni.

On the 10th June a German district official came in from the hill-station of Wilhelmsthal, north of Mombo, to report that he had in his charge there some 500 women and children, with about 70 male non-combatants, whom the Germans had decided to leave behind rather than expose them to the unhealthy climate farther south. These were assured of their safety and left where they were, under British care. No papers of any military value were found.

Meanwhile, in preparation for the move of the remainder of the British force, Brig.-General Sheppard's column encamped on the western bank of the Pangani.[3] During the first week of June four aircraft of the 26th Squadron R.F.C. bombed the bridge at Mkalamo and reconnoitred ahead, but without much result, since little was visible in the bush.

In the course of the 7th and 8th June Sheppard's column,[4] marching in two echelons by the densely overgrown and

---

[1] A direct hit was scored on one m.g., which was afterwards picked up.

[2] Later found to have consisted of *17.F.K.* and *Wangoni K.* (*Abteilung Kempner*), about 300 strong with 2 m.g.

[3] At Bwiko the Pangani, described as " like a canal ", 100 ft. wide, 14 ft. deep, with a 4-knot current, was crossed by a footbridge for troops in single file and two flying ferries for vehicles. In addition to the usual difficulty with nervous animals, the river abounded with crocodiles. These could always be stunned by bombs in the stream, but it was found necessary to cage in all watering places, and cases occurred of animals whilst watering being seized by the head and dragged under.

[4] Less the sqdn. 17th Cavalry, 5th Bty. S.A.F.A., and ammunition column.

often swampy and difficult track which was the only route, reached a point about half way to Mkalamo. His advanced troops, consisting of the 29th Punjabis (previously in Divisional Reserve) and 130th Baluchis, with a company of the 61st Pioneers and a section of the 27th Mountain Battery, R.A., under Lieut.-Colonel P. H. Dyke, camped on the evening of the 8th some three miles ahead of the main body, with orders to push on to the trolley-line next day.

ACTION OF MKALAMO, 9TH JUNE, 1916

Sketch 32   Informed on the 8th June of the resumption of the British advance, Kraut, who had already withdrawn his heavier artillery down the trolley-line towards Handeni, had concentrated about Mkalamo, leaving his rearguard in the Usambara to fend for itself.[1] His force was posted as shown in Sketch 32, a detachment on Mafi Hill and the remainder, grouped as the *Abteilung Döring*,[2] on the west bank of the Pangani covering the bridge.

Dyke's force, marching at 5 a.m. on the 9th through relatively open bush, was unopposed until 11.15 a.m., when a British aircraft drew fire from Mafi Hill and two light guns opened from the hill against the column. No casualties were caused, but Dyke diverged away from the river into a belt of dense and trackless thorn through which progress was very slow.

Sketch 33   About 1 p.m. the two leading companies of the 130th, under Major H. D. Moore, came up against the enemy well dug in, and the usual bush fight ensued at short range. The two companies suffered somewhat heavily, losing three British officers, but held their ground and were reinforced by the remainder of the battalion. Adopting the standard outflanking tactics, Dyke sent up two companies of the 29th Punjabis on the right of the 130th, followed by the remainder of the 29th to the left, in an endeavour to ascertain the extent of the enemy's position. His mountain guns came into action, but could find no target in the bush.

As the British companies came up, German units extended their line correspondingly. About 2.30 p.m. Brig.-General Sheppard arrived to direct operations in person,

---

[1] Kraut was eventually rejoined at Handeni by Kempner, from Korogwe, on 15th June.
[2] *1., 3., 16.F.K.* and one platoon *5.F.K.* See also p. 305, f.n. 1.

followed by the 2/Rhodesia Regiment and the remainder of his column. On the scene of action, where visibility was only a few yards, he found it impossible to ascertain his exact whereabouts, beyond correctly estimating that Mkalamo was about a mile away. The fight continued with fluctuations of advance and retreat until, at about 3.15 p.m., a German counter-attack round the British left struck the rear of the column, including the dressing-stations, driving medical officers and wounded alike into cover in the bush.[1] Still holding the Rhodesians and the 2/Kashmir Rifles in reserve, Brig.-General Sheppard sent in a company of the latter battalion which repulsed the German counter-attack ; but, as by this time little more than an hour of daylight remained, a decision could hardly be forced by dusk, and the forward troops were therefore ordered to fall back a short distance and dig in for the night. This was success-fully effected and the night was quiet.

Casualties, despite the closeness of the fighting and great expenditure of ammunition, were few.[2]

Next morning (10th June), patrols sent out at dawn discovered immediately that, once again, the Germans had retreated. It then became clear, too, that Brig.-General Sheppard, believing that he was working round the enemy's right flank, had in reality come up against the German centre and left.[3] Mkalamo village, fired before the German departure, was deserted and smouldering. The trolley-line

---

[1] A more detailed account is given in " Marching on Tanga " (F. Brett Young).

[2] 15 killed, 33 wounded, mainly in the 130th Baluchis, which lost : killed 2 B.O. 7 o.r. ; wounded 1 B.O. 1 I.O. 17 o.r.

German losses are not known, but certainly exceeded the figures— 3 killed, 11 wounded—given by Dr. Schnee. 18 enemy dead were counted ; 1 German, 4 askari were captured.

As an example of ammunition expenditure, the 130th Baluchis, about 400 strong, expended 18,176 rounds, including 5,400 from m.g. The German units exhausted most of their ammunition.

" The bush was so thick that aimed fire was out of the question, and " the bulk of it was very high and did little damage. . . . Troops there " might as well have been . . . in continued night operations . . cohesion " could so easily be lost irretrievably by units diverging fifty yards from " the line of direction." Capell, " The 2/Rhodesia Regt. in East Africa ", p. 71.

[3] See Sketch 33. The British attack first struck the left of 3.F.K.'s trenches, whose right rested on the river. 16.F.K. then came up, followed by 1.F.K., but a gap between these units was penetrated by a British detachment, presumably of the 130th, and was only closed by a local counter-attack by the last German reserve, the platoon of 5.F.K. The German counter-attack on the British left was made by 3.F.K.

and trolleys—but fortunately not the bridge—had been extensively damaged[1] and it was obvious that Kraut had fallen back towards Handeni.

Sketch 32   In pursuit, the 2/Rhodesia Regiment with the squadron of the 17th Cavalry, pushed on the same evening to Mseni and Luchomo. Behind Sheppard the Force Reserve—Beves with his two South African battalions—closed up to Mkalamo.

Movements of Hannyngton's Column

Hannyngton's next object was to secure Korogwe and the two railway bridges over the Pangani. Leaving most of his baggage at Mombo, he resumed his march on the 11th June. Delayed by bad roads and the necessity of bridging the Vuruni river, he reached Makuyani late on the 12th and, after a day's halt there, went forward on the 14th. After a brief vanguard skirmish, he reached the Pangani at Mauri by mid-day, to find the railway bridge effectively demolished, but no further sign of the enemy.

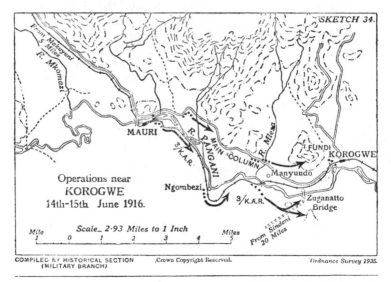

SKETCH 34.

Operations near
KOROGWE
14th-15th June 1916.

Scale— 2·93 Miles to 1 Inch

---

[1] A first estimate of repair material required was 4,000 sleepers, 10,000 fish-plates, 20,000 bolts : quantities quite unprocurable. But within three weeks the Bridging Train, 3rd (Bombay) S. & M., and Faridkot Sappers had the line in fair order, even making wooden fish-plates to which the rails were wired.

Here natives reported that the road bridge at Zuganatto, near Korogwe, nine miles on, was still intact, and it was decided to seize it during the night. The 3/K.A.R., under Lieut.-Colonel T. O. FitzGerald, were detailed to carry out this operation, crossing the Pangani at 10 p.m. by a native bridge which was reported to exist a mile below the railway bridge, and following the southern bank.

The enterprise was not as easy as it looked on the map. The " native bridge " proved to be no more than a few tree trunks across successive stretches of torrent in a deep gorge, and by 3 a.m. only two companies had succeeded in crossing. With these FitzGerald made a difficult march through the bush, noting as he went that the second railway bridge—at Manyundo—had also been demolished. At daylight on the 15th June the two companies rushed a hill commanding the Zuganatto bridge at about 400 yards range, and became engaged with a German force entrenched on both banks.[1] On the arrival of a third company of the K.A.R. about 7 a.m. the Germans abandoned the southern bank, and before long they retreated to Korogwe. The bridge, which was of wood and had been prepared for burning, was found intact.

This success, on which the 3/K.A.R. was warmly and deservedly congratulated, was a good example of the speed and skill with which, under resolute leadership, the African troops were able to work in the bush by night. It was, moreover, of the utmost value, there being no other crossing **Sketch 32** for many miles on either side by which Hannyngton's force could rejoin the main force at Handeni.

At dawn on the 15th June, whilst the K.A.R. were thus engaged, the remainder of Hannyngton's column went forward by the main Korogwe road. At the crossing over the river Mlesa the advanced guard (3/Kashmir Rifles) was temporarily checked by hostile fire which was soon silenced by the mountain guns, and after a further short-lived attempt at resistance from the high ground at Fundi, covering Korogwe, the Germans, whose numbers were evidently small, gave way. At 11 a.m. the advanced guard entered Korogwe without further opposition.

The place was found abandoned in disorder ; the station and engine-sheds, with three locomotives, had been wrecked

---

[1] Two German m.g. were knocked out by a m.g. under Lieut. von Otter, 3/K.A.R.

by explosives. There was no object in going farther, it being now clear that Kraut's forces had been withdrawn to the southward, and in the course of the day (15th) Hannyngton received orders to rejoin at Handeni at the earliest opportunity. Having made arrangements to guard the railway[1] and detached about 200 men[2] to hold Korogwe and the Zuganatto bridge, he marched with the remainder of his force on the 17th June and two days later made contact with the main force near Handeni.

FROM MKALAMO TO HANDENI

Once past Luchomo, where the abundant water of the Pangani was left behind, the route to Handeni traversed thirty miles of barren and almost waterless malarial country in which the rare water-holes had to be located in advance, and progress could not be rapid. From Mkalamo, therefore, where on the 10th June the Commander-in-Chief resumed personal control of the operations, the main force went forward by short stages. Beyond occasional skirmishes with Kraut's patrols no sign of the enemy was seen until, on the 15th June, Sheppard's advanced troops reached the village of Kilimanjaro. Patrols and aircraft now located German defences covering Handeni, in which a stand by the enemy seemed likely.

Deciding against a frontal attack, Lieut.-General Smuts directed Brig.-General Beves's two battalions (Force Reserve) to diverge south-westwards from Mbagwe through Gitu to Sangeni and so round the German western flank. At the same time, screening this movement, Brig.-General Sheppard was to move westwards across the enemy's front to Ngugwini.[3]

These movements resulted in the immediate withdrawal of Kraut to his stores depot at Pongwe, 12 miles in rear. Beves, who reached Sangeni on the 17th, sent on the 5/ and 6/S. African Infantry next day, the former towards Pongwe and the latter between that place and Handeni,

---

[1] The line was raided and blown up north of Mombo on 15th June.
[2] 100 each, 129th Baluchis, 40th Pathans, with 2 m.g.
[3] To cover his own movement, Brig.-General Sheppard sent forward two coys. of the 29th Punjabis to make a feint towards Handeni. This unit then remained for some days at Kilimanjaro to protect the camp and field hospital established there.

in the hope of cutting off the enemy's retreat, and both battalions had sharp skirmishes with retiring German units, on which they inflicted casualties.[1] Kraut, however, had had timely warning of Beves's flank manoeuvre, and as Sheppard, restricted by Lieut.-General Smuts's orders to a covering role, had not pinned the enemy frontally, the German withdrawal was practically unhindered. At 10.30 a.m. on the 18th June Sheppard entered Handeni unopposed.[2]

General Situation, 18th June, 1916

Handeni, a road centre of importance, was of some size, containing a strongly-built boma and a number of European houses amid farms and plantations, with fairly plentiful if indifferent water. It was, however, unhealthy ; the Germans had left behind many Africans suffering from typhoid, and among the British troops, whose powers of resistance under-nourishment had already diminished, dysentery and malaria spread rapidly.[3]

The general situation nevertheless seemed promising. The 2nd S. African Mounted Brigade, which had landed at Mombasa and was on its way up by way of Mbuyuni and the Ngulu Gap, would shortly form a welcome re-inforcement of mobile troops for the main force. In the west the Belgians were about to launch their offensive into Ruanda, in conjunction with British troops under Brig.-General Crewe on Lake Victoria.[4] In the south Brig.-General Northey had already penetrated successfully into German territory.[5] On the 12th June the Commander-in-Chief had ordered Major-General van Deventer, as soon as the reinforcements sent to him were complete,[6] to advance " with a view to " cutting off the enemy's retreat to Iringa. By that " time," he had added, " it is hoped that the Pangani

End Paper (N)

---

[1] The 6/S.A.I. counted 27 enemy dead and captured 4 askari. The 5/S.A.I. captured 3 Germans near Pongwe.

[2] Some useful rolling-stock was found at the trolley terminus at Nderema ; otherwise the enemy left little of any value.

[3] H.Q. 1st Divn. recorded on 15th June (before Handeni) that the effective strengths of all units were down by about 15 per cent., adding : " This is probably due to the hardships to which the troops are now " exposed, bringing out latent fever." Beyond Handeni the percentage quickly increased.

[4] See Chap. XXIV.

[5] See Chap. XXVII.

[6] See pp. 284-5.

" force will be able to cut the railway east of Kondoa,
" and then all forces are to co-operate and decide the
" final issue."[1]

The advance was therefore to be pressed on.

FROM HANDENI TO KANGATA

As the South Africans approached Pongwe the Germans
had continued to retreat. On the morning of the 20th June
the two battalions concentrated at Pongwe prior to resuming

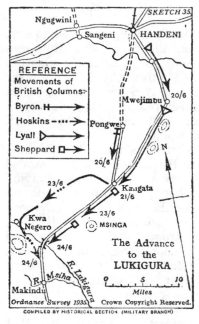

REFERENCE
Movements of
British Columns:
Byron. H——▶
Hoskins —•••▶
Lyall ▷——▶
Sheppard ▢—▶

The Advance
to the
LUKIGURA

0   5   10
Miles

Ordnance Survey 1935 Crown Copyright Reserved.
COMPILED BY HISTORICAL SECTION (MILITARY BRANCH)

their march southwards as
the advanced guard to the
British forces. At Handeni
Sheppard's column de-
tached a force under Lieut.-
Colonel R. A. Lyall, consisting of the 2/Kashmir Rifles,
with the squadron of the
17th Cavalry, a section of
the 27th Mountain Battery,
R.A., two armoured cars
and an ambulance section,
to move in their support.

South of Handeni it
was found that the route
through Pongwe to Kan-
gata, shown as a mere
track on the only available
maps, had been improved
by the Germans and that,
in order to avoid difficult
ground by this route, a
motor road also existed,
making a detour through Mwejimbu. The latter route was
followed by Lyall.

Leaving Pongwe at 2 p.m. on the 20th, the 5/S. African
Infantry, under Lieut.-Colonel the Hon. J. J. Byron, with
a detachment of Belfield's Scouts, became heavily engaged
with the enemy in some strength holding an open valley
about six miles out, and were held up until the evening.
The Germans were well handled, succeeding at one time in
working a machine gun round Byron's right against his

---

[1] It would seem that at this stage it was expected that the enemy's
resistance would collapse when the Central Railway was in British hands.

congested transport, and making a determined though unsuccessful attack on his left towards 6 p.m. Two companies of the 6/S. African Infantry which arrived about 9.30 p.m. restored the situation, and at dawn on the 21st there was no further sign of the enemy.

Meanwhile Lyall, whose route proved longer than had been expected, camped for the night of the 20th/21st at Mwejimbu. The distant firing to the south-west had been heard, but he was out of touch with Byron,[1] and it was not until about·2 a.m. on the 21st that orders reached him to push on to the latter's assistance. Marching at once, he reached the road junction near Kangata about 11 a.m. Here he found, evacuated, a strong German defensive position which suggested that at least four *F.K.* had been engaged, and soon afterwards his cavalry and armoured cars made contact with the South Africans.

The 5/South African Infantry, not yet experienced in bush fighting, had suffered heavily, losing about 20 per cent. of their fighting strength.[2]

ACTION OF THE LUKIGURA,[3] 24TH JUNE 1916

All ground and air reports now agreed that the enemy Sketch 35 had withdrawn to a defensive position on the river Lukigura, 13 miles beyond Kangata. Lieut.-General Smuts therefore, in his own words, " divided [his] force in the hope of getting " round [the enemy's] position with a flying column and " compelling him to stand and fight."[4] For this purpose he formed a special mobile column under Major-General Hoskins, lightly equipped and with pack transport only, consisting of the 25/Royal Fusiliers, 2/Kashmir Rifles, 5/ and 6/S. African Infantry, with the E. Africa Mounted Rifles, 27th Mountain Battery, R.A. (less one section), and the machine gun company of the 2/Loyal North Lancashire Regiment.

---

[1] A patrol of the 17th Cavalry sent to gain touch had not returned.
[2] The effective strength of the 5/S.A.I. was below 500. One platoon had been left with baggage at Pongwe. Casualties were : killed, 1 officer, 19 o.r. ; wounded, 1 officer, 64 o.r.
The German troops engaged were *3., 16.* and *30.F.K.*, grouped as the *Abteilung Boedecker.*
Arning's account states that their retreat was caused by the threat to their flank from Lyall's force ; their casualties are not stated.
[3] This engagement is also known as Kwa Derema, after the ridge on which the principal fighting took place.
[4] Despatch, op. cit.

This force was to turn the enemy's left, while at the same time Sheppard's column, comprising the 29th Punjabis, 130th Baluchis and 2/Rhodesia Regiment, with the squadron of the 17th Cavalry, K.A.R. M.I., Nos. 5 and 8 Field Batteries and two cars of No. 1 Light Battery, was to demonstrate frontally.

Most of these units were by now very weak ; the 25/Royal Fusiliers were about 200 strong, the Rhodesians down to about 170, and Sheppard's Indian battalions each about 350 ; the Kashmir Rifles, however, were still 450 strong, and the South African battalions each about 450.

Sheppard's force, which had bivouacked at Mwejimbu on the night of the 22nd/23rd June, reached Msinga Hill at 5.45 p.m. on the 23rd, halted there, and resumed its march at 3.30 a.m. on the 24th. In the meantime Major-General Hoskins, leaving Kangata at 4 p.m. on the 23rd, made a wide detour west of the main road which brought him, after a halt from midnight until 3 a.m., to the banks of the Lukigura near Kwa Negero as dawn was breaking. Here in the early morning his troops crossed the river, unopposed but considerably exhausted by their night march.

Sketch 36 Towards 7 a.m. on the 24th Sheppard, approaching the Lukigura, became engaged with a German outpost on the high ground in the angle between his road and the river. His armoured cars, pushing on towards the bridge, were suddenly met by close range rifle, machine gun and pom-pom fire which disabled one of them ;[1] his advanced guard deployed and his guns came into action. His role, however, was not to push on but to attract attention, and at 7.45 a.m. he received orders from the Commander-in-Chief to " go " slow," Major-General Hoskins's column being still some distance away.

It was not until nearly noon that the leading platoon of Hoskins's advanced guard, the 2/Kashmir Rifles, forcing its way south-eastwards along a difficult bush track, sighted the enemy on a ridge ahead. Captain A. N. Kerr, commanding the advanced guard, being ordered to make good the ridge, which was flanked on either side by the bush and masked half way up by a strip of cultivation, came under heavy fire as he approached the crops, and was reinforced by the remainder of the battalion. The sound of firing put new life into the troops in rear. " I have never

---

[1] Gallant work by the personnel brought the car back into safety.

" seen men more utterly tired and woebegone than our
" men . . . " wrote an officer of the Fusiliers afterwards.
" They had been marching twenty-four-and-a-half hours,
" kit-laden and without substantial food ; and yet when
" they went into battle all fatigue was forgotten, . . . they
" were careless of further physical trial ".[1]

As reinforcements came up the Germans fell back to
a higher ridge beyond. Reorganizing, the Kashmir Rifles
followed up, with the Fusiliers and two of the Loyal North
Lancashire machine guns in support, while the mountain
guns, vainly seeking targets in the scrub and trees, moved
forward into the infantry firing line.

The Kashmir Rifles, headed by Kerr and valiantly
commanded by Lieut.-Colonel Haidar Ali Khan, pushed in
to close range, preparing to charge. The companies
extended in the bush were somewhat difficult to control,
and the assault had not been launched when three companies
of the 25/Royal Fusiliers under Major H. H. R. White,
in all perhaps 150 strong, came up on the left flank, grasped
the situation instantly, fixed bayonets and rushed forward,
cheering. The Gurkhas and Dogras of the Kashmir Rifles
took up the cheering and charged in alongside the Fusiliers,
sweeping over all opposition. Charging with them went
the mountain battery, in the spirit, as an officer afterwards
justly said, of Norman Ramsay's battery at Fuentes
d'Onoro.

For once—rarest of occurrences in this campaign—the
assault got home with the bayonet. The German machine
guns and a field gun were carried, their detachments
bayoneted and the weapons captured undamaged. The
defending force was driven in utter rout from the ridge
and down to the neighbourhood of the bridge, where it
came under the fire of the 29th Punjabis, which Sheppard
had pushed forward across the river, and its remnants
scattered into the bush.

Except for some shelling of the captured ridge during Sketch 35
the afternoon at about 12,000 yards by a German naval
8·8 cm. gun from beyond the Msiha river, firing had ceased
by 3.30 p.m.

Casualties had been light.[2]

---

[1] Buchanan, " Three Years of War in East Africa ", pp. 109–10.
[2] Total, Hoskins's force, 6 killed, 26 wounded (including 3 killed,
15 wounded, in the 25/R. Fus.) ; Sheppard's force, 4 killed, 10 wounded.

Continued at foot of next page.

This action, the most notable success yet achieved by the 1st Division, fought to its successful issue by Major-General Hoskins with troops whose spirit no physical exhaustion could daunt, was one of the few engagements of the campaign in which the British troops enjoyed the elation of actual victory in battle. Hitherto, the enemy in each of his successive rearguard positions, had escaped punishment. At German Bridge he had evaded envelopment ; at Mkalamo he had resisted attack and withdrawn unmolested ; at Handeni there had been only skirmishes ; at Kangata he had effectively checked pursuit. But at the Lukigura, however small the scale of the action, he had been outwitted and defeated ; the outflanking manoeuvre, so often attempted, had succeeded ; and the whole force gained new confidence in itself and its commander.[1]

FROM THE LUKIGURA TO THE MSIHA

Sketch 28   For some days after the action on the Lukigura the troops remained halted whilst the ground ahead was reconnoitred. To the south-west, beyond the Msiha, high ridges were in sight, obviously suitable for delaying action by the enemy, and beyond them rose the wooded Nguru Mountains. Intelligence reports began to indicate that Lettow was bringing back some at least of his forces from Kondoa Irangi.[2]

Now, however, Lieut.-General Smuts's forces, carried thus far only by the indomitable spirit of his men and the heroic efforts of the transport, supply and medical services, were brought by sheer attrition to a standstill. In little

---

Continued from previous page.
The 5/ and 6/S.A.I. were not engaged.
The enemy's losses included : 4 Germans, 30 askari found killed ; 14 Germans, 20 askari captured, by Hoskins's force ; 7 Germans, 12 askari captured by Sheppard.
The German units present, under *Hauptmann Döring*, were *1.F.K.*, *5.* and *7.Sch.K.*, probably 500 in all. Some amusement was caused by the capture of a German wearing part of the *Königsberg's* ensign made up as an under-garment.
    [1] The British success was fully recognized by the enemy.
" *Hauptmann Döring wurde . . . völlig überraschend . . . angegriffen . . .*
" *Es war dies eine der schneidigsten Unternehmungen der Engländer im*
" *ganzen Verlauf des Feldzuges. Ohne sich um die Verluste zu kümmern,*
" *gingen sie darauf ; unsere Linie wurde von der grossen Übermacht überrannt.*
" *Sie eroberten hier das einzige Feldgeschütz, das wir im offenen Gefecht*
" *verloren, ohne es, wegen Trägermangel aufgegeben, zerstört zu haben. . . .*"
    Arning, *Vier Jahre Weltkrieg*, p. 173.
    [2] Pretorius, with a few Intelligence scouts, was already ranging the mountains some 20 miles to the westward.

over a month his columns had marched considerably over two hundred miles; Bwiko, the nearest point of the Usambara railway, was nearly ninety miles behind. Evacuation of the ever-increasing number of sick was as formidable a task as that of bringing up supplies and meeting even the most pressing requirements of the fighting troops.[1] The absence of such minor luxuries as soap, cleaning materials and tobacco, and of all recreation for troops off duty, tended further to depress the exhausted and hungry men in tattered clothing who had nevertheless responded so unflinchingly to the heavy calls made on their endurance.

Such considerations might well suggest doubt whether the strategic advantages gained by pressing on from Handeni[2] were not too dearly bought. In any case, however, the vital matter of water-supply had made it necessary to go on at least to the Lukigura.[3]

On arrival there it was found that better camping ground existed along the river Msiha, eight miles ahead, and on the 5th July an advance was made, unopposed, to establish at the crossing of that river a standing camp, officially named Makindu or Msiha Camp.[4] Meanwhile the 2nd S. African Cavalry Brigade, accompanied by Major-General Brits, had arrived at Luchomo on its way to the front, and the 1/Cape Corps reached the Lukigura.

While Major-General Hoskins went forward to the

---

[1] A medical officer afterwards wrote: "the numerical strength of the "forces defeated its own object, establishing a vicious circle. It was "impossible to feed the large number of troops, so that . . . sickness "was increased by partial starvation, and the sick troops coming down . . . "blocked the transport and consumed the supplies intended for those "at the front."

[2] At Handeni the enemy "would be well placed for far more dangerous "and effective action against the communications than he was able to "take from 10 miles south of the Msiha." "The South Africans with General Smuts", p. 147.

[3] The transport and supply situation at this time is described in Vol. II of the History of the Royal Army Service Corps: "There were, quite "apart from the conditions of the country, too many troops for the trans-"port at the disposal of the army." At Handeni "no white flour had been "issued for some time, hard biscuit eked out with mealie flour being "provided in lieu. The only meat available was the fly-stricken trek "ox, which had to be eaten at once as it would not keep." At Msiha Camp: "it was impossible further to extend the communications, and "numbers of sick required evacuation. Towards this . . . and . . bringing "up of supplies every vehicle was . . . employed without ceasing." A private account mentions "surprise and delight of the troops on the "arrival of one small tin of jam per six men."

[4] Named by the Germans Mlembule. See also p. 334, f.n. 1.

Msiha the Commander-in-Chief, leaving G.H.Q. on the 26th June, went back to Luchomo intending to inspect his line of communication, which was still exposed to attack from the eastward—an increasing risk which he had knowingly accepted during his southward march, but had been keeping much in mind. At Luchomo, where he saw his I.G.C., Brig.-General W. F. S. Edwards, he was prevented by fever from going farther, and on the 5th July he returned to Msiha Camp.

Here the bulk of his main force remained concentrated until the 1st August to recuperate, replenish supplies and await progress by van Deventer, Crewe, Northey and the Belgians.

In the course of this period the Commander-in-Chief received a welcome visit from General Louis Botha, who with a small entourage from South Africa spent the 23rd and 24th July at Msiha Camp and, before returning to the Union, also visited Major-General van Deventer at Kondoa Irangi. Among the South African troops in particular, most of whom had taken part in the campaign in German South-West Africa, " the sight of their former Commander- " in-Chief produced the extraordinary effect of encourage- " ment and confidence which his presence never failed to " arouse ".[1]

---

[1] Collyer, " The South Africans with General Smuts ", p. 162. As a matter of interest, on his journey to the camp General Botha's motor-cyclist escort was commanded by Sir John Willoughby, who had taken part in the Jameson Raid. His guard at the camp was furnished by the 25/Royal Fusiliers (Lieut.-Colonel Driscoll, see p. 135, f.n. 2.)

CHAPTER XIX

THE ADVANCE FROM KILIMANJARO—*(concluded)*

SUBSIDIARY OPERATIONS, JUNE-JULY 1916

(Sketches 5, 28, 30, 32, 34, 37)

OPERATIONS OF THE 2ND DIVISION

THE deadlock at Kondoa Irangi lasted until the first week Sketch 28 in June. West of the river Bubu the country was fairly open, and mounted patrols had been sent out as far as Kwa Mtoro ; but in that direction the enemy held high ground overlooking all approaches, and in any case, to fit in with the Commander in-Chief's general plan, the direction of the further advance for which the 2nd Division was preparing must rather be south-eastwards.

The rugged hills east of the township, however, lent them- Sketch 30 selves to concealed movement by British and German patrols feeling for each other's flanks. On the 4th June it was discovered that the enemy, after occupying Dalai Hill east of the river Karema,[1] had pushed forward, threatening the British left, on to Versfeld's Kop. Against the latter position the 3rd/S. African Horse moved next morning, but, although reinforced by the 4th/S. African Horse, supported by a section of the 28th Mountain Battery, R.A., that after-noon the mounted troops were effectively held up by the German machine gun fire. During the night of the 5th/6th June the 8/S. African Infantry, from divisional reserve, and a second section of the 28th Battery were sent up, and early next day the attack was renewed. Again the South Africans were stopped by machine gun fire. On the southern flank, however, a deep ravine running down into the Karema offered a covered approach to the south-eastern end of the enemy's ridge, which was reported by natives to be easier ground. By this route a detachment of the 8/S. African Infantry about 150 strong, under Major J. A. Warwick, supported by the 4th Horse, worked round on the following afternoon (6th) through difficult bush and at times under

---

[1] Occupied on 28th May by the *Abteilung Schulz, 8., 11.,* and *21.F.K.,* reinforced on 6th June by *13.F.K.*

heavy machine gun fire, in readiness to attack northwards next day. The 4th Horse, unfortunately, lost touch and eventually withdrew, leaving Warwick isolated.

On the 7th, when this became known at Divisional Headquarters, detachments of the 12/ and 7/S. African Infantry were sent out to Warwick's assistance. After coming under heavy fire from high ground on both flanks, and beating off a German counter-attack made from Black Rock,[1] the 7/S.A.I. under Major F. Haselden gained touch with Warwick, whose detachment, exhausted by two days and nights in a narrow valley under fire from three directions, was withdrawn during the night.

During the 8th the fighting died down, neither side being prepared to face heavy casualties in pushing home an attack;[2] but the efforts to outflank each other continued for three more days. Nongai Hill had already been occupied by the enemy on the 3rd June. On the 9th the Germans extended their line to Italoa ; but their attempt to thrust northwards on the 11th was frustrated by the mounted troops, which on the previous day had occupied Aria and Inda, and at last, with both sides strung out on a frontage totally unwarranted by their strength, these manoeuvres came to an end.

Lieut.-General Smuts, as we have seen, had been at Kondoa Irangi on the 5th and 6th June.[3] He had made it clear that, since the result of his own advance down the Pangani would almost certainly compel the enemy to weaken the forces opposed to the 2nd Division, no serious attack should be attempted by Major-General van Deventer for the time being. During the next fortnight, therefore, nothing occurred beyond the usual patrolling and occasional shelling.[4]

Sketch 28   The situation of the 2nd Division, however, was far from happy, isolated as it was in hostile territory over two hundred miles from its railhead. Mention has already been made of

---

[1] By *Abteilung Otto, 4., 9., 24.F.K.*

[2] Total British casualties were only 4 killed, 15 wounded. German casualties were reported by Schulz as 4 killed ; 3 officers, 12 askari wounded. He estimated British killed at 41.

[3] See p. 293, f.n.2.

[4] On 13th June a *Pegasus* gun of the 10th Heavy Battery put a shell into the German headquarters camp at South Hill, slightly wounding Colonel von Lettow-Vorbeck himself. (Lettow, " My Reminiscences ", p. 138.)

the increasing incidence of sickness among the troops.[1] In the matter of transport and supplies the division was even worse off than the main force, whose plight has already been described.[2] The horses of the mounted troops, continuing to diminish in numbers, were by now all in very poor condition.

At this time, too, information regarding the enemy was scanty and difficult to obtain. The two aircraft recently received had already developed defects and, while still able to furnish a general idea of the unknown surrounding country, were of little value for detailed reconnaissance.[3] Mounted patrols were restricted by the condition of men and horses ; native information was unreliable. On the 19th June Major-General van Deventer reported that a fresh attack on him seemed probable.[4] Events were soon to show that the enemy's intentions were very different.

By the third week in June G.H.Q. was already receiving reports of German troop movements from west to east along the Central Railway. Air reconnaissance from Kondoa Irangi failed to confirm these until the 24th June, when natives reported a German withdrawal.[5] That afternoon the 2nd Division's aircraft bombed hostile columns marching south near Chambalo ; patrols were sent out from Kondoa Irangi round the enemy's flanks and preparations made to attack.

Early on the 25th June the 3rd S. African Infantry **Sketch 30** Brigade moved out against the whole front of the German positions. Only small rearguards were encountered, which

---

[1] See p. 284. The field hospitals had several times to be moved in consequence of damage by shell fire.

[2] See pp. 306-7. The extension of the railway from Kahe to the Sanya (see p. 278) made some, but no considerable, improvement for the 2nd Divn.

[3] For some time past Major-General van Deventer had been pressing for more aircraft, but none could be spared. The early types of machine in use at this period were much affected by the climate.

[4] " Big gun which was at Dodoma was seen at Haneti a week ago. " Several explosions heard this morning which I assume is road-making. " If this is correct I consider it strongly probable that Germans have " decided to make another big attack here . . . "
Telegram, 2nd Divn. to C.-in-C., 19th June.

[5] Begun, according to Arning, on 22nd June. But on 20th the *Abteilung Schulz* has been ordered back from the eastern flank, relieved only by Otto's smaller *Abteilung*.
Kraut had just been pushed out of Handeni. It was probably at this time that Lettow, concluding that the main British advance was coming by that line, contrary to his previous expectation, decided to transfer his troops away from Kondoa Irangi to meet it.

retreated at once. By noon South Hill was occupied, and by 3 p.m. the dominating Range Rock Hill also. Beacon Hill was defended by the enemy until dusk and evacuated **Sketch 28** under cover of darkness. Next day an advanced detachment of the South Africans found German forces retreating by the Dodoma road ; these were engaged on the 27th at Barei, which was cleared and occupied. On the 1st July German camps were seen from the air at Haneti and Meia Meia.

The 2nd Division, on paper nearly 10,000 strong, but with over ten per cent of its numbers in hospital and many more men fit only for light duty, was unhappily in no condition to follow up this unexpected withdrawal, the available transport in particular being wholly insufficient.[1] For another fortnight it remained immobile at Kondoa Irangi, the administrative staff labouring heroically to improve matters on the line of communication and to assemble enough transport to make forward movement possible, while Major-General van Deventer paid a brief visit to G.H.Q.

COASTAL AREA : OPERATIONS IN THE UMBA VALLEY

Sketch 5 During the early months of 1916 the coastal district north of the Umba and east of the Usambara mountains, the scene of much minor activity in the first year of war, remained quiet. In March 1916 the newly-arrived 5th Light Infantry, Indian Army,[2] fresh and fit, took over the British posts at Mwele Mdogo (12 miles west of Gazi) and in the Msambweni area along the coast. Early in May, as soon as the rains ended, strong patrols were pushed southwards, which found hostile defended camps near Jasin and at Mwakijembe, and had minor skirmishes with the enemy. Towards the end of May, as the result of the advance down the Pangani—a hundred miles away—the German troops were reduced to mere outposts, of which that at Mwakijembe was reported to consist of no more than 30 men.

---

[1] See Note I, p. 324.
[2] See p. 265. The unit landed at Mombasa on 4th March, 1916. About 500 strong, it was composed of seasoned soldiers with recent bush experience. These men had a special incentive to good work, the battalion being that which, soon after the outbreak of war, had mutinied at Singapore. The loyal elements had petitioned to be sent anywhere overseas on active service, in order to re-establish the good name of the regiment : as, in fact, they effectively did.

On the 12th June, therefore, the I.G.C. gave orders that the 5th Light Infantry, which had two strong patrols on the frontier under Captains W. D. Hall and C. S. Thane, should take possession of Mwakijembe. These patrols, joined at Lushanga by a reinforcement 200 strong, with two machine guns, under Captain L. P. Ball, which brought the total strength to 400, occupied Mwakijembe accordingly on the 16th June, the weak German detachment beating a hasty retreat.

On the following day the British column marched eastward, parallel to the frontier, on Duga and Jasin. Here, too, the German details left in occupation made no effective resistance. Having demolished the German defences, the 5th Light Infantry returned to its posts at Mwele Mdogo and Msambweni. Its casualties in action had been negligible, but already its numbers had begun to dwindle from sickness. No further fighting took place in this area.

OCCUPATION OF TANGA

After the disastrous repulse of November 1914 Tanga Sketch 8a remained practically undisturbed, except for minor naval demonstrations in December 1914 and August 1915[1]. In March 1916 the naval Commander-in-Chief, now Rear-Admiral E. F. B. Charlton,[2] after conferring with Lieut.-General Smuts at Mbuyuni, decided in agreement with him to defer action by the Royal Navy until the impending Kilimanjaro operations had produced results. On the 19th March Lieut.-General Smuts telegraphed concurring with a suggestion by the Admiral that a naval bombardment of Tanga might indirectly assist the British advance on Kahe already described ; on the same day a landing party from H.M.S. *Severn* occupied Yambe Island unopposed. Three days later (22nd) the *Severn* and *Thistle* landed a naval detachment, together with 80 Zanzibar African Rifles under a N.C.O. of the Royal Marines, on Ulenge Island, which was found deserted. At the same time the *Vengeance* and *Hyacinth* shelled Tanga, the latter firing on a reported emplacement

---

[1] On 20th August, 1915, H.M.S. *Severn*, with two whalers, shelled shipping at Tanga, destroying a lighter laden with a large number of locally-manufactured mines which by a fortunate chance had been brought in for examination on the previous day. The enemy did not lay mines at Tanga again.

[2] Rear-Adml. Charlton relieved Vice-Adml. H. G. King-Hall on 11th February, 1916.

of a *Königsberg* gun, and the battleship putting 74 rounds of 12-inch into the railway station. There was no reply and no sign of life in the place.

Next morning the *Severn*, after shelling Ras Kasone, lowered boats to simulate an intended landing ; still no sign of life was seen ; but as there was no force to land the performance was terminated.

Meanwhile reports that the German ship *Tabora*[1] was being fitted out as a commerce-raider drew the British squadron to Dar-es-Salaam,[2] after which for some weeks the ships were engaged in various 'minor enterprises farther south[3] and Tanga was left alone.

By the third week in June, however, when the British forces had reached Handeni, secured the Usambara railway as far as Korogwe and cleared the Umba river area, the time had come to occupy Tanga. On the 21st June, by way of preliminary reconnaissance, two companies of irregular scouts under Captain T. A. Dickson, with a detachment of Royal Marines 40 strong, landed on Ulenge and waded to the mainland, while the *Talbot* shelled Chongoleani, where German troops had been reported. No opposition was encountered and it seemed plain that no more than small forces of the enemy could be in the area.

During the next week the *Talbot*, *Thistle* and *Severn* shelled various points in the vicinity, and on the night of the 3rd/4th July a force under Lieut.-Colonel C. U. Price, the Deputy I.G.C., consisting of the 5th Light Infantry with a company of the 101st Grenadiers, in all about 500 strong,[4] was embarked at Mombasa to join the squadron.

On the 5th July, the force, covered by the ships, landed unopposed on the southern shore of Manza Bay and moved inland towards Amboni, which was reached next day after disposing of some slight resistance on the way. At dawn

---

[1] See p. 20, f.n. 3.

[2] On 23rd March the *Vengeance* (flag), *Hyacinth* and *Pioneer*, on the Admiral's demand to inspect the *Tabora* being refused, shelled the vessel until she was seen to be on fire and sinking. No damage was done to the town.

[3] Including the unsuccessful attempts against the *Marie* at Sudi (see p. 287, f.n.4). On 25th April trenches near the coast at Dar-es-Salaam were shelled ; on 5th May the *Severn* and two whalers landed a naval party and 60 Mafia African Rifles, under Major W. B. Brook, at the mouth of the Rufiji, unopposed ; on 18th May, Kilwa Kisiwani was reconnoitred by seaplane, supported by the *Vengeance*.

[4] Strengths : 5th L.I. : 7 B.O., 9 I.O., 323 o.r., with 4 m.g. ; 101st Grenadiers : 2 B.O., 201 o.r.

Sketch 28

Sketch 8a

End Papers

on the 7th the Zigi river was crossed, unopposed ; at the same time the ships moved in, the *Severn* landed a party of armed scouts at " Beach A " of unhappy memory, and as the Indian troops entered Tanga from the west these met them from the east.

The town was found evacuated by the Germans and its buildings for the most part undamaged. The landing-stage and railway had, however, been extensively demolished and the hospital stripped of its equipment ; a thousand or more of the Indian inhabitants remained, with a small number of the African population.

Contrary to expectation, the Germans withdrawn from the town remained in the surrounding bush, sniping the British troops, including on one occasion the ship's band of H.M.S. *Vengeance* which was playing in the main square. Patrols were held up by the enemy on the railway near Kange and for the time being Lieut.-Colonel Price contented himself with patrolling and searching the town.[1]

It may perhaps seem surprising that, once the main advance was under way down the Usambara railway, Lieut-General Smuts made no use of his complete command of the sea to establish a base at Tanga early enough to make that port and the railway serve his main force as it moved south from Bwiko.[2] Such an operation, however, would have involved detaching completely a considerable force, for at all costs a repetition of the defeat with which the name of Tanga was (and still is) associated had to be avoided. The port was useless without the railway, repair of which must take time. The extensive preparations and organisation that would have been required would have thrown a heavy additional load on an already heavily-burdened Staff, few of whom had been well grounded in Staff training or were " sea-minded ".

These considerations, at any rate, prevailed. From the outset, as has been shown, the Commander-in-Chief considered Tanga " of no importance after the Tanga railway

---

[1] A plan was found of the very elaborate local defences, including caves in the face of the cliffs designed as m.g. emplacements to oppose a landing. Two *Königsberg* guns on trolley mountings, it was learned, had been sent south. Numbers of improvised mines littered the quays, abandoned since the visit of H.M.S. *Severn* in August 1915 (see p. 313, f.n. 1). See also p. 321, f.n. 2.

[2] As a previous chapter has shown (see p. 288, f.n. 2), Lt.-General. Smuts had in May envisaged the possibility of operating from the coast in the vicinity of Tanga ; but no preparations for this appear to have been made.

had been reached farther north."[1] Yet it may well seem that during the grim famine period between June and September 1916 much suffering and privation among the troops of the main British force might have been minimised, had earlier and fuller use been made of Tanga, now at last in British hands.

OPERATIONS TO SAFEGUARD THE LINE OF COMMUNICATION

Sketch 37   The main British force on the Msiha, weakened though its units were by sickness, was well able to meet any forces which the enemy might concentrate against it from the south. Hitherto Lieut.-General Smuts " had deliberately left the " East Usambara area alone while pushing the enemy . . . " back as fast and as far as possible," satisfied that between his left flank and the sea " the situation . . . would either " clear itself up by retirement of the small enemy forces in " that area or, if necessary, they could be dealt with at a " more convenient time ".[2] The time had now come, however, to deal with the continued menace to the line of communication impending from the eastward, to which reference has been made.[3]

Small garrisons at Handeni and Korogwe, and defensive posts at intervals, gave the line some measure of security, but all along it the enemy had been keeping up an active guerilla warfare, which by the end of June had become a serious matter.[4] Supply lorries were fired on, motor ambulances blown up by mines, telegraph and telephone wires cut, and all who used the road were liable anywhere at any time to be sniped from the bush. The motor-road between Korogwe and Handeni, which was indispensable until the trolley-line service through Mkalamo could be fully re-established, was especially vulnerable. The troops at the I.G.C.'s disposal, strung out along the communications not only of the main force but of the 2nd Division also, were beginning to be insufficient and to feel the strain.

---

[1] Despatch, op. cit.   See also p. 267.
[2] Despatch, op. cit.
[3] See p. 308.
[4] On 24th June, Lettow telegraphed orders to the commander of the small German forces remaining in the Tanga area to " attempt to interrupt " the motor traffic Korogwe–Handeni by patrols."

The enemy was known to have detachments near Korogwe.[1] A report received on the 12th July—but found later to have been inaccurate—from a usually reliable source stated that a hostile force whose strength was put as high as 2,000, including 200 Germans, was entrenching at Mzundu ; this was within 20 miles of Handeni, where the British garrison consisted mainly of unfit men dropped as the advance moved on. On the 13th July an attack on Zuganatto Bridge by a German force from Segera, about 170 strong with a light gun, was beaten off by the bridge guard of 100 men of the Jind Infantry.[2]

Lieut.-General Smuts had already acted. On the 12th July he telegraphed to Brig.-General Edwards orders to " use the forces at [I.G.C.'s] disposal to drive all enemy " parties over the Pangani " ; to destroy all bridges and boats which would make the enemy's return possible ; to send agents to reconnoitre the small seaport of Pangani ; and to move to Hale and pursue the enemy southwards as far as Manga, within reach of the main British force. At the same time he ordered Brig.-General Hannyngton, whose brigade (2nd E. African) was now at Makindu, back to Handeni in order to thrust eastwards against the German force reported near Mzundu.[3]

So limited were Brig.-General Edwards's resources in men and so definite his orders, that he decided to utilize as fighting troops the 25th and 26th (Railway) Companies, Sappers and Miners, then engaged in repairing the Usambara railway. This decision, duly reported by him to G.H.Q. on the 13th July,[4] was a grave one from a point of view which does not seem to have occurred either to him or to the Commander-in-Chief and to which separate reference is made in Note II (page 326).

---

[1] Estimated by I.G.C. on 13th July as follows :

Derema,	3 Germans,	150 askari,	2 m.g.
Hale,	30 ,,	250 ,,	4 ,,
Mfumbili,	8 ,,	150 ,,	2 ,,
Segera,	3 ,,	100 ,,	2 ,,

[2] The Jind Infantry, which had remained in the coastal area until March 1916 and was then dispersed along the L. of C., was reassembled (strength 3 B.O., 14 I.O., 375 o.r.) on 27th June at German Bridge and moved to Korogwe, where on 5th July it relieved a mixed detachment of the 2nd E.A. Inf. Bde. On the morning of 13th July the post of 50 men at Zuganatto Bridge was doubled.

[3] Posts on the L. of C. between Handeni and the Lukigura were now found by the 1/Cape Corps at Kangata.

[4] The Director of Railways does not appear to have been consulted, the units being under I.G.C.'s command.

Including the two technical units, the I.G.C. assembled at Korogwe a force about 500 strong, under Lieut.-Colonel C. W. Wilkinson, R.E., the commander of the Sapper and Miner companies,[1] which moved out after dark on the 13th July with orders to attack the German posts at Segera and Mfumbile.

Turning off the main Handeni road near Msala, Wilkinson worked round so as to approach Segera Hill from the south-west, finding progress difficult, and eventually reached his objective about midnight of the 14th/15th. A detachment of the Jind Infantry which climbed from the south bolted a German signal party from the top of the hill; at the same time the 25th Company, S. & M., ascending a northern spur, came upon a gun detachment coming into action, shot the German N.C.O. on his refusal to surrender, and captured the gun intact.

At daylight on the 15th July the British troops on Segera Hill were attacked from a large German camp on the plain between the hill and the Pangani. After a short and lively engagement, in which a second German gun was located and silenced by the British machine guns, the enemy was driven off and, though reinforced from Hale, was compelled to abandon his camp, which Wilkinson occupied in the course of the morning.[2]

From Segera the column went on to Lerengwa, where no opposition was encountered. On the 17th July the force was on the point of moving off to deal with German troops believed to be at Hale, across the Pangani, when two enemy porters were captured from whom it was learned that the enemy, said to be three companies in all, had left Hale during the previous night and slipped past Lerengwa towards Kwa Mugwe. Acting on this, Wilkinson, following up, at

---

[1] Detail of this column was as under :—

Unit				B.O.	I.O.	B.O.R.	I.O.R.	M.G.
25th, 26th (Rlwy.) Coys.								
S. & M.	..	..	..	5	6	—	300	—
Det. Jind. Infy.	..	..	2	5	—	100	1
British details	..	..	—	—	50	—	3*
Indian „	..	..	—	—	—	100	—
	Total..	..	7	11	50	500	4

* Drawn from armoured cars.

[2] British casualties were 1 killed, 2 wounded. From 10 captured German askari it was learned that the enemy had been the 4.Sch.K. 3 Germans and 3 askari were buried and others were found next day to have been buried at Hale.

about mid-day occupied Kwa Mugwe after driving off a German rearguard. Here in the afternoon the enemy made a brief but determined attack, which was broken up and not renewed.

In the absence of information as to either the enemy or the movements of Hannyngton's brigade farther south,[1] the guns of which were heard about 7 p.m., Wilkinson stood fast at Kwa Mugwe.

In the meantime Brig.-General Hannyngton, having reached Handeni from the Msiha on the 14th July and arranged for the local defence of the place,[2] marched on the 15th to Kwamlere and on the 16th to Makanya. Here began a complex of movements involving much arduous marching but little fighting. Rapid progress was impossible ; the column was of necessity accompanied by a large train of porters, the whole country was bush, little was known regarding the enemy except from vague reports by native agents, and the maps available were inaccurate and often wholly misleading.

Hannyngton's effective fighting units now consisted of the 40th Pathans, 3/K.A.R., and 3rd Kashmir Rifles, with a section of the 27th Mountain Battery R.A. On the 17th July he sent out from Makanya a company of the 40th Pathans to round up any Germans to the north at Mhomoro, and the remainder of that battalion, with his two mountain guns, under Lieut.-Colonel W. J. Mitchell, eastwards to reconnoitre Mzundu, where, as will be remembered,[3] the enemy had been reported to have assembled. Mitchell returned the same afternoon with 3 prisoners, having found no signs of any considerable force of the enemy at Mzundu ; and on the 19th the detached company rejoined, bringing with it the baggage of a small hostile detachment which it had dispersed at Mhomero.

Meanwhile on the evening of the 17th, news having been received of a German force said to be at Kwa Konje, 20 miles to the south, Hannyngton sent the 3/K.A.R., under Lieut.-Colonel FitzGerald, in that direction, together with

---

[1] During the German attack at Kwa Mugwe Wilkinson had been, in fact, in some anxiety lest his opponents, hardly visible in the extremely dense bush, might prove to be Hannyngton's men.

[2] The garrison available consisted of 200 of the 129th Baluchis, mainly unfit, and 300 of the 101st Grenadiers, just arrived from the L. of C. In addition, 100 of the 101st were posted at Sonyo.

[3] See p. 317.

the section of the 27th Mountain Battery, R.A., which on
its return from Mzundu had volunteered to accompany the
K.A.R.

At daybreak on the 18th July FitzGerald's advanced
guard, crossing the Kwa Konje—Mgambo Kadodo track—
encountered a German outpost which at once retreated to
Kwa Konje. Assuming that the Germans there would withdraw eastwards to Ruguzi, he pressed forward to cut them
off, and on the Ruguzi road he duly met an unescorted
German baggage column whose porters hastily dropped their
loads and fled. The baggage was that of the Tanga *Land-
sturm* unit, which was stated by natives to be still in Kwa
Konje ; but on reaching that place FitzGerald found it
empty. The Germans, warned of his approach by their
outpost earlier in the day, had made off north-eastwards,
passing behind his rearguard and cutting his field cable.
They had six hours' start, and the 3/K.A.R. returned
disappointed to Mzundu.

On the same day (18th) a wireless message from the I.G.C.,
informing Hannyngton of Wilkinson's operations farther
north, directed him to move on Kwa Mugwe to meet the
enemy retiring from Hale. Hannyngton, however, lacking
information regarding the enemy in his own vicinity, felt
debarred from acting on this at once, and it was not until
the following day that he had word from FitzGerald of the
German retreat from Kwa Konje towards Mgambo Kadodo.
Thereupon he sent off the 3rd Kashmir Rifles to intercept
the Germans from Kwa Konje ; but it was too late.

FitzGerald rejoined at Mzundu on the afternoon of the
19th. At dawn next day Hannyngton with his whole force
moved east to Mumbwe, whence he despatched to Mgambo
Kadodo a column under Major E. F. D. Money, 3rd Kashmir
Rifles, consisting of that unit and a company of the
3/K.A.R. together with the mountain guns, a machine gun
section of the 129th Baluchis, and a dozen of the K.A.R.M.I.

Outside Mgambo Kadodo that evening Money, learning
from a captured askari that the place was held by a hostile
force, probably at least equal to his own, established himself
on a hill commanding the southward track to Kisaza, where
he was engaged until nightfall by considerable numbers of
the enemy, but held his ground during the night.

The same evening Hannyngton received a report of a
German force of unspecified strength approaching Mumbwe

from Kisaza, which he prepared to meet with his whole remaining force early on the 21st. He thus just missed the retreat of the Germans opposed to Money, who during the night of the 20th/21st evacuated Mgambo Kadodo, abandoning most of their baggage. It was found later that they had divided, one party heading for the coast at Mkwaja, another making a detour southwards round Kisaza towards Ruguzi, some fifty of the latter being the force whose movement had been magnified to Hannyngton.

On the 21st July Hannyngton occupied Mgambo Kadodo, detaching the 40th Pathans to Kisaza, and despatched the 3/K.A.R. towards Kwa Mugwe to gain touch with Wilkinson. This was effected on the 23rd. It could now be assumed that all the Germans were well to the southward.

At this juncture there arrived from Egypt the 57th Wilde's Rifles (Frontier Force), Indian Army,[1] which Lieut.-General Smuts had placed at the disposal of the I.G.C. to clear the hill country north of the River Pangani. Leaving Korogwe on the 19th July, one company making a detour northwards and the remainder following the railway, the 57th met at Muheza next day the 5th Light Infantry from Tanga, neither having encountered any opposition.[2] It was now believed that the Germans, who had clearly abandoned the area about the railway, had retreated towards the coast, and the 57th proceeded therefore towards the port of Pangani, where it arrived on the 23rd July.

On the previous day H.M.S. *Talbot*, sent by Rear-Admiral Charlton on his learning that the land forces were approaching, had shelled what appeared to be a German defensive position so effectively that when, early on the 23rd, she came in to renew the attack, white flags were shown at once. A landing party learned that the German troops had left before dawn, and as naval parties rowed shoreward the 57th entered the town.

---

[1] On 14th June, 1916, the C.-in-C. accepted an offer by A.H.Q. India of the 57th in exchange for the 29th Punjabis, to enable the latter to recuperate. The 57th landed at Mombasa on 12th July and reached Korogwe on 18th.

The 101st Grenadiers eventually went to Egypt in place of the 29th Punjabis, embarking on 28th August.

[2] From Tanga, Col. Price (see p. 315) occupied Kange on 17th July, practically unopposed. The 5th L.I., which reached Pongwe on 18th and Ngomeni on 19th July, was very weak owing to sickness, and returned from Muheza to Tanga for embarkation to Mombasa to recuperate.

Thenceforward the Royal Navy hastened the retreating Germans through successive coastal villages,[1] while small columns continued to harass them inland. Once south of the River Msangazi, however, the scattered parties of the enemy constituted little further danger to the line of communication. The object of the operations having been achieved, Lieut.-General Smuts recalled Hannyngton's force, allotting to his brigade the 57th Rifles, who were fresh, in place of the 40th Pathans, whose numbers were now sadly depleted.[2]

While the 57th marched inland from Pangani, the 40th took up the further pursuit southwards from Mgambo Kadodo, reaching Manga on the 3rd August without incident. Here, reinforced for a time by a detachment of the 1/Cape Corps, under Major C. N. Hoy, which was relieved soon afterwards by the Jind Infantry, the 40th Pathans stood fast for ten days, patrolling the surrounding country.

Wilkinson's force, meanwhile, had been recalled to Korogwe, where the Sappers and Miners resumed their normal technical duties.[3]

GENERAL SITUATION, JULY 1916

By the middle of July 1916 the second phase of the offensive conceived by Lieut.-General Smuts in March and April had come to a close. Great numerical and technical superiority had made it possible to attempt strategic envelopment of the enemy by the bold adoption of double lines of

---

[1] Naval landings are shown on Sketch 37. On 25th July, a German party being reported at Kipumbwe, the place was shelled by H.M.S. *Talbot* until a white flag was shown. After shelling Mkwaja on 26th, the *Talbot* returned to Kipumbwe to find that the Germans had fired the native huts in reprisal for the showing of the white flag.

On 26th July the *Mersey* shelled Sadani and seaplane reconnaissance was carried out.

On 27th a landing party from the *Talbot* drove off a German detachment which approached Mkwaja. On 29th, the *Talbot* shelled Bagamoyo before returning to Mkwaja to re-embark her landing party.

On 1st August the *Vengeance, Talbot, Severn,* and *Mersey* occupied Sadani, unopposed, with a landing force of naval ratings, Royal Marines, 100 armed scouts, and 50 Zanzibar African Rifles. A few casualties were incurred in subsequent skirmishes outside the town.

[2] On 30th July, out of a total strength of 1,089, the 40th Pathans had only 470 fit men.

[3] See Note II, p. 326.

The 27th (Rlwy.) Coy., S. & M., from Kahe, reached Tanga by sea from Mombasa on 30th July and started work on the railway next day. The first train left Tanga on 17th August and linked up with the other S. & M. companies working from Korogwe two days later.

operation issuing from the advanced base at Kilimanjaro : the only course by which that superiority could be fully exploited.

Lieut.-General Smuts's strategy had misled his opponent[1] into a withdrawal which enabled the main British force to shepherd the weak forces left to oppose it out of a succession of prepared positions, at small expense, by astute and prudent turning movements. In consequence an extensive tract of hostile territory, abandoned of necessity by the enemy, could fairly be claimed as being in British hands : a result which in a campaign of this special kind might well be regarded as being of particular value.[2]

The enemy, it is true, had·suffered no tactical defeat of any importance. He had, however, been driven into a situation where, with better subsequent fortune, there should have been a good prospect of eventual tactical envelopment and of his defeat in a decisive encounter. Nevertheless so far, out-numbered and out-manoeuvred, outclassed in regard to all material and incapable alike either of effective offence or prolonged defence, Colonel von Lettow-Vorbeck had successfully avoided being brought to battle. He had rightly appreciated the military value to his country of keeping diverted from the European theatre of war the considerable man-power and extensive resources brought against him, and by a leadership and personality matching those of his British adversary he had kept his limited forces not only in being but in good heart.[3]

The British commander, on the other hand, realized to the full the nccoooity, from tho ctandpoint of both British and Allied policy, of an early successful conclusion of the campaign. Whether this object could have been gained sooner and more certainly if he had deferred the move of the 2nd Division to Kondoa Irangi until after the rains can only be a matter of conjecture ; but subject to this reservation neither the conception nor—within the limitations set by his

---

[1] " At the time " [mid-April], " therefore, the enemy was evidently " directing his principal effort towards Kondoa Irangi." (Lettow, " My Reminiscences ", p. 127.) See also p. 279, f.n. 2.

[2] See p. 269, f.n. 1. The occupation of territory postulated naturally that sufficient garrisons could be left to hold each area as soon as it was cleared.

[3] In particular the German askari were better acclimatized than most of the British forces, far better acquainted with the country and with local conditions and requirements, and were also accustomed to travel much lighter.

resources—the execution of his plans was at fault. With a keen eye for strategic possibilities, at times seemingly to the point of disregard for such fetters as the problems of movement and supply, and retaining in his own hands much that might well have devolved upon a trained General Staff and subordinate leaders, he had driven forward to the very limit of his army's ability. As yet, however, in a campaign necessarily conducted with a variety of troops differing in race, temperament, training and experience, whose material requirements were so diverse as to impose an almost unmanageable complexity on the rearward services, he had been deprived of the success which he might have expected by factors inherent in the nature of warfare in tropical Africa, of which he had no previous experience.

Both at Makindu and Kondoa Irangi Lieut.-General Smuts's forces, willing and undaunted, had been brought to a standstill by exhaustion, sickness, and those enemies to man and beast the tsetse fly and mosquito. It was essential now to restore and improve the lines of communication as well as to give a breathing-space to the troops. A pause was unavoidable ; but it was becoming apparent that the South African units, at present the mainstay of the force, would not be able to stand the climate indefinitely.

Everything pointed, therefore, to an early renewal of the struggle.

NOTE I

ADMINISTRATIVE SITUATION OF THE 2ND DIVISION,
3RD JUNE, 1916.

Copy of telegram from H.Q. 2nd Division, Kondoa Irangi, to C.-in-C., Advanced G.H.Q., repeated Adminstaff, Old Moshi.

G.O.C. 77 30th June. Following is present situation in my division. To-day 711 sick in hospital and 320 in convalescent camp. Lack of strengthening foods such as oatmeal, bacon, jam, cheese, milk, etc., renders it almost hopeless to expect convalescents to get fit for active service. This is also the cause of great amount of debilitation amongst troops. Every effort has been made during the last two months to get forward these essentials and there are now *en route* seven days' rations of which the greater part will go to hospitals. Empty motor lorries returning is the only means of evacuating our sick. The majority of men are lying on the ground in tent hospitals as there are no stretchers available. Infantry regiments for the most part arrived here without blankets—dearth of boots, clothing, soap—the very poor rations are the cause of the heavy sick rate. The nearest receiving hospital is at Ufiome. As it has no transport, it cannot come forward. In my opinion and that of my A.D.M.S. it is most imperative that a stationary hospital with proper equipment and stores be established immediately at Kondoa. If immediate steps are not taken, the situation will daily become worse. The L. of C. only transports as far as Lolkisale and I have to bring everything forward from there with my Divisional Transport and have even to feed L. of C. troops stationed between Salimo and Lolkisale. All ox and mule transport is greatly reduced. The animals are weak and wagons all need overhauling —150 tons in addition to supplies including 9 tons of equipment for L. of C. troops have been carried during past three weeks. 7th and 8th Infantry reached here with only 11 wagons of which 7 are now effective to move. I shall have to take all transport off the Kondoa–Lolkisale road and will then only be able to carry on regimental and supply line transport 7 days' rations. Daily requirements are 30,000 lbs., reckoning 2 lbs. Arrangements will collapse unless I.G.C. takes immediate steps to take over all transport to this place.

The division is at present rationed up to the 10th July. There were 1,130 fit horses in Mounted Brigade on 8th May. On 30th June the returns show 1,376 fit animals. Between these two dates 1,227 remounts were received. Excessive patrol work and lack of horse food are the causes of this condition. At present there are 750 reinforcements en route, 324 on L. of C. transport and remainder on divisional. 500 mules will be at Lolkisale on the 3rd instant. I have to send back troops to that place to bring these on.

Addressed Gensmuts, Advanced G.H.Q., repeated Adminstaff.

Copies for information to :—

> Adminstaff, Nairobi.
> I.G.C., New Moshi.
> Genstaff } Old Moshi.
> D.S. & T. }

Copy of telegram from Adminstaff, G.H.Q., Old Moshi, to B.G., G.S., Luchomo.

Q.C.–366 1st July. Reference G.O.C. II Division No. 77 30th June. D.M.S. has already arranged for hospital at Kondoa and I.G.C. taken over transport same place. Am going into transport question with I.G.C. and will wire further particulars to you tomorrow after consulting heads services concerned and Genstaff here. Meantime L. of C. transport is going forward from railhead now opened at Sanya.

NOTE II

Use of Technical Units as Fighting Troops.

Sketch 28   In July 1916, when the I.G.C. made use of the 25th and 26th (Rlwy.) Coys., S. & M., as fighting troops, restoration of the Usambara railway was vitally important for the supply of the main force ; so much so that on 12th July the C.-in-C. ordered work to be stopped on the line then under construction from Kahe to Sanya " in order to admit of repair of Korogwe–Tanga line **Sketch 34** as well as extension of the line from Mauri to Ngombezi as railhead for supply to Handeni ".[1]

To take specialist railway troops off their technical work for use as infantry, at a time when the fighting troops in front were stationary and short of supplies, was a drastic measure, justifiable only by emergency. It involved more than a mere delay in the railway work whose evident importance is emphasised by the order just quoted : for these units constituted half of the organized military plate-layers and railway bridge-builders in the country, replaceable only by small drafts from India, if at all. They would, moreover, be needed later for work on the Central Railway. Their employment as infantry—combatant troops though they were—involved the risk of battle casualties, to the detriment, if not worse, of essential railway services during the remainder of the campaign.

Seen in retrospect, at all events, the situation at the time hardly seems to have been serious enough to call for such a diversion of highly skilled specialists from their proper technical role.[2]

---

[1] War Diary, Advanced G.H.Q. Railhead reached Mauri on 4th July, and the bridge there was restored by 12th July. Of the four railway units, S. & M., in East Africa, 26th and 28th Coys. were at work on the Usambara line ; 27th Coy. on the Kahe–Sanya extension (see pp. 278 f.n. 3, 322, f.n. 3) ; 25th Coy. having worked on the Mombo–Handeni tramway since 1st July, had reached Ngombezi on 10th July to prepare formation for a branch line thence to a point on the Korogwe–Handeni road.

[2] Instances of the employment of engineers as infantry in France in 1914, notably at Neuve Chapelle, where two companies of Sappers and Miners so used lost all their officers and over a third of their rank and file, led to the issue by Sir John French of a memorandum " calling attention " to the misuse and waste of highly-skilled specialists ". Official History, Military Operations, France and Belgium, 1914, Vol. II, p. 218.

" Engineer units may be regarded as a reserve of fighting men, but will " be used to fight only in an emergency, as a last resource." Field Service Regulations, 1935, Vol. II, 75(4).

This aspect of the matter is not referred to either in the C.-in-C.'s despatch or in any of the contemporary official documents available, nor does it seem to have been mentioned to the I.G.C. by G.H.Q. in reply to his report of his intention.

CHAPTER XX

PROGRESS TO THE CENTRAL RAILWAY

(Sketches 28, 29, 38, 39, 40, 41, 42)

THE 2ND DIVISION REACHES THE CENTRAL RAILWAY

By mid-July the supply and transport difficulties which Sketch 38
had held up the 2nd Division at Kondoa Irangi had been
overcome sufficiently to make a further advance possible.[1]
Reinforcement had been completed.[2] Major-General van
Deventer had returned from his visit to G.H.Q. fully
informed as to the views and wishes of the Commander-in-
Chief and was now in a position to put them into effect.

They were " . . . to clear his right flank towards Singida,
" to move a small column along the Saranda road towards
" Kilimatinde, and to move his main force towards Dodoma
" and farther east on the road to Mpwapwa ". The object
of Lieut.-General Smuts, in his own words, was " . . . not
" only the occupation of the Central Railway, but more
" especially the movement of van Deventer's force to the
" east so as to get into closer co-operation with the force

---

[1] Fourteen days' supplies had been accumulated, half of which were
carried in 1st line transport. Among other preparations, many additional
carriers were enrolled ; 400 oxen and numerous donkeys were impressed
and trained.

The demands made on the divisional M.T. are indicated by the figures
for the period 23rd May to 30th June :—

Cars employed	56
Mileage per car	2,108
Total weight carried, over average of 62 miles	2,380,000 lbs.

During July well over 3,000,000 lbs. of supplies were transported.
Lack of petrol was a constant handicap.

One special difficulty was that for units attached from 3rd Divn., which
had been sent up in motor-lorries, battalion transport had to be improvised
at Kondoa Irangi.

[2] On 7th July the newly-landed 9th S.A. Horse, under Lt.-Col. M. M.
Hartigan, reached Kondoa Irangi.

The 2nd Divn. now consisted of :

1st S.A. Mtd. Bde.	1st, 2nd, 3rd, 4th, 9th S.A. Horse.
3rd S.A. Inf. Bde.	9/, 10/, 11/, 12/S.A. Inf. ; E.A. Vol. M.G. Coy.
Attached from 3rd Division	7/, 8/S.A. Inf. ; Vol. M.G. Coy.
Divl. Arty.	1st, 2nd, 4th Bties., S.A.F.A. ; 28th Mtn. Bty., R.A.
Divl. Troops	S.A. Motor Cycle Corps ; 4th Light Armoured Bty. (armoured cars) ; det. R.N.A.S.

Sketch 28 " at the Nguru mountains " [i.e., the main British force, now preparing to move south from the Msiha] " in dealing " with the main enemy forces as they fell back to the " Central Railway ".[1]

Major-General van Deventer's information regarding the Sketch 38 enemy was somewhat indefinite. Both from his aircraft and from native sources came reports of German camps and defensive positions, indicating that the bulk of the German forces opposed to him was covering the roads leading south and south-east to Dodoma and Mpwapwa respectively, notably at Halingoti, Haneti, Itiso-kwa-Meda and Chenene, with small scattered detachments to the south-westward.[2] The country ahead was known to be difficult and favourable for hostile delaying action.

After the German retreat on the 24th June, patrols had been sent southwards and eastwards from Kondoa Irangi,[3] followed by detachments which by the 12th July had occupied Chambalo and Tumba. In accordance with his instructions, Major-General van Deventer now decided to use the 1st S. African Mounted Brigade to clear the road south-eastward to Mpwapwa while his infantry moved on Dodoma. At the same time two small columns, whose movements will presently be narrated,[4] were organized to clear the roads south-westwards to Singida and Saranda respectively. Operation orders were issued to this effect on the 17th July, and two days later the main advance began.

On the 20th July the scouts of the mounted brigade, followed by the 11/S. African Infantry, occupied Haneti unopposed, while the 3rd S. African Horse drove off the German detachment at Halingoti. From these places the two mounted units converged on Itiso-kwa-Meda, whence

---

[1] Despatch, op. cit.
[2] The distribution of the German units at this date was as follows :—
  (a) On the road to Mpwapwa,
    under Klinghardt   *14. Res.K., 1.Sch.K.*
  (b) On the road to Dodoma,
    Abteilung Lincke   *15., 19., 25.F.K.* ; *8., 9.*(Mtd.)*Sch.K.*
  (c) On the road to Saranda,   *2.Sch.K.*
  (d) Covering Singida,   a small detachment.
These dispositions were gradually ascertained as the operations progressed. The points at which German detachments were reported on 10th–17th July are indicated in Sketch 38.
[3] On 3rd July a patrol 25 strong of the S.A. Motor Cycle Corps reconnoitred eastwards to Neganga Hill and Mbareni. It reported that the route was practically impassable to motor traffic. This was the first use of an independent mechanized detachment in East Africa.
[4] See pp. 331–2.

after a brief encounter on the 22nd the Germans were again driven off south-eastwards.[1] The next two days were devoted to reconnaissance both by the infantry at Haneti and by the mounted troops at Itiso. Chenene, the next objective of the infantry, was reported to be strongly defended. During the afternoon of the 25th July the 11/S. African Infantry, preceded by mounted scouts and armoured cars,[2] drove in the German outposts north of Chenene, but was held up at about 5 p.m. on reaching the enemy's main defences. During the short hour of daylight remaining, little progress was made ; but, as had happened elsewhere so often before, the enemy evacuated the place during the night, and early on the 26th Chenene was occupied.[3] Next day the column, after a sharp little encounter with the *9.Sch.K.*,[4] went on to Meia-Meia, where it was reinforced by the 10/S. African Infantry, S. African Motor Cycle Corps, 12th (How.) Battery and a section of the 28th Mountain Battery, R.A. On the 29th July, Kitunda-kwa-Meda having been occupied without opposition, the armoured cars and a detachment of the Motor Cycle Corps pushed on into Dodoma, which was found evacuated, with a white flag flying from its boma. Van Deventer had reached the Central Railway.

---

[1] At Itiso-kwa-Meda the 1st S.A. Mtd. Bde. was rejoined by the 2nd S.A. Horse (less 1 troop at Mbulu, see p. 284) and 9th S.A. Horse, with the 4th Bty., S.A.F.A., attached. Of the remaining unit of the Mtd. Bde. (4th S.A. Horse), two sqdns. were with the two detached columns (see pp. 331–2) ; the remainder was left for escort duties at Kondoa Irangi.

Brig.-General Manie Botha, comdg the Mtd. Bde., was recalled to the Union at this juncture, being succeeded by Col. (temp. Brig.-General) A. H. M. Nussey on 24th July.

Three armoured cars of No. 4 Light Bty. sent up to join the Mtd. Bde. at Itiso were returned to Haneti to co-operate with the infantry, the country beyond Itiso being considered unsuitable for their use.

[2] Despite land-mines and booby-traps in the road, the armoured cars proved valuable and the crews were afterwards congratulated on their work. They were untouched, though greatly affected by the heat inside the closed cars. The unprotected petrol-tanks, however, were badly holed.

[3] British losses were 2 killed, 4 wounded. The German units engaged were *15.F.K.*, *6.Sch.K.*, *8.(Mtd.)Sch.K.*, under Captain Lincke. From Chenene, Lincke fell back on Kitunda-kwa-Meda, leaving *8.* and *9.Sch.K.* as rearguard at Meia-Meia. Meanwhile Captain Klinghardt, now commanding the German forces in this area, had ordered a general retreat to the line Kongwa–Msagali, covering Mpwapwa, and had been directed to concentrate his rearguard at Nyangalo. On 27th July, Klinghardt went down with typhoid and was succeeded by Captain Otto.

[4] British casualties *nil* ; enemy, 4 killed, 9 Germans and 3 askari captured.

Meanwhile the 1st S. African Mounted Brigade[1] and 4th Battery, S.A.F.A., under Brig.-General A. H. M. Nussey, moving off south-westwards from Itiso-kwa-Meda on the afternoon of the 25th July and continuing its march from Mayu early on the 27th, encountered at Membe the *1.Sch.K.*, which was dislodged by a combined frontal and turning movement and was pursued for some six miles. After a brief halt, the march was resumed, with the intention of attacking next morning a strong German rearguard which was reported to be at Nyangalo. Towards nightfall of the 27th Nussey's leading unit, the 9th Horse, met with vigorous opposition from a German outpost on the road, which again was dislodged by a turning movement ; but a pursuit in darkness over difficult ground well adapted for ambuscade was out of the question.

Early on the 28th July Nussey moved out against Nyangalo. Detaching a squadron of the 1st Horse to deal with a small hostile force reported to be threatening his left rear from Igaga, on the east bank of the Kinyasungwe river, and sending the 9th Horse to get astride the Nyangalo-Mpwapwa road in rear of the enemy, he went forward on a wide front with the 1st Horse (less one squadron) on the right and the 3rd in the centre, retaining the 2nd Horse in reserve.

Of the eight hours' confused fighting which ensued in the bush against the considerable and well-posted German force covering Nyangalo few details are now available. In the course of it, after quickly gaining possession of the enemy's water-holes and cattle, the 1st and 3rd Horse —the former by a bold and well-led series of flank movements turning the German left, and the latter heavily engaged at point-blank range in the centre—drove the enemy in rout and confusion from his position, each capturing a machine gun.[2] Unluckily the threat from Igaga had caused the 9th Horse, waiting to intercept the enemy's retreat, to be diverted at midday to that place, so that the disorganized German units were able to make good their escape.[3]

[1] Less 4th S.A. Horse, brigade scouts, and 1 trp. 2nd S.A. Horse. See p. 329, f.n. 1.
[2] Major J. Wilkens, 1st S.A.H., was specially mentioned for his personal part in capturing one of these m.g.
[3] The German force at Igaga was the *25.F.K.* This unit retreated on the approach of the 9th Horse, which occupied Igaga in the afternoon and rejoined the Mtd. Bde. at Nyangalo next day (29th). The main German force consisted of the *19.*, *23.F.K.* and *1.Sch.K.* German documents found later admitted that the German troops were " forced to retreat " in disorder " with the loss of 2 m.g.

The horses of the Mounted Brigade, which had suffered much from shortage of water all the way from Itiso, were now so exhausted that Brig.-General Nussey, though able to send on the 3rd S. African Horse to secure the railway line at Kikombo, was obliged to stand fast with the remainder of his force at Nyangalo. The 3rd Horse reached the railway unopposed at dawn on the 30th July, by which time it was evident that the bulk of the enemy's forces in this area had retreated eastwards.

It remains to recount the movements of the two detached columns from Kondoa Irangi.[1] The first of these, under Lieut.-Colonel H. J. Kirkpatrick, consisting of the 9/S. African Infantry, one squadron of the 4th S. African Horse, a section of the 28th Mountain Battery, R.A., and a wireless detachment, starting on the 15th July, moved south-westwards as shown in Sketch 38. Its progress, with ox-drawn transport, was inevitably slow ; much work was needed to make the track passable for vehicles, and water was scarce. No serious opposition was met until the 27th July, when the column reached Mponde. Here, in bush too dense for the usual outflanking manoeuvre, it encountered the *2.Sch.K.* holding a prepared position astride the road, from which after some hours' fighting the enemy was driven off.[2]

During the 28th and 29th Kirkpatrick remained at Mponde. Deciding now to push on with his fighting units, leaving his slow ox-transport to follow, he sent forward his mounted squadron on the night of the 29th/30th July to cut the railway west of Saranda. Early next day he followed with the remainder of his force, covered 21 miles unopposed, and at dusk reached the railway. Saranda was found evacuated, and on the 31st July Kirkpatrick went on unchecked to Kilimatinde, which also had been abandoned by the enemy. Here he remained until the 4th August, on which day, leaving his mounted squadron to garrison Kilimatinde, he moved off with the remainder of his column to rejoin the 2nd Division at Nyangalo on the 12th August.

The second detached column, consisting of the 8/S. African Infantry, one squadron of the 4th S. African Horse, one section 1st Battery, S.A.F.A. and a wireless section, under Lieut.-Colonel A. J. Taylor, left Kondoa

---

[1] See p. 328.
[2] British casualties, 8 killed, 9 wounded.

Irangi on the 26th July. Taylor's orders were to " clear " the enemy out of the Singida area ", part of his force making a detour northwards through Masogoloda, where the detached troop of the 2nd Horse which had gone with Carroll to Mbulu[1] was to rejoin. Sending half his mounted squadron, with a machine-gun detachment, under Major J. A. Warwick to Masogoloda, he moved with the remainder of his column westwards, as shown in Sketch 38, through Mkora to Mgari, where he arrived without incident on the 31st July.

Above Mgari a German detachment was found holding a small stone fort commanding the track, which here mounts the escarpment of the Great Rift Valley. By 2 a.m. on the 1st August Taylor had surrounded this work, which he attacked at daylight. He was met by a stout resistance, but when, about midday, he was able to get a gun into action, the enemy—a party of 16 askari, whose German N.C.O. had escaped[2]—surrendered. Next day (2nd August), pushing on without his transport,[3] Taylor reached Singida without further opposition.

Meanwhile Warwick, who on reaching Masogoloda received word of a German force said to be near Lake Basotu, 35 miles to the westward, set off in pursuit without waiting for the mounted detachment from Mbulu, which overtook him near Lake Balangida on the 1st August. His pursuit proved vain, and four days later, after a sweep through uninhabited country to Jumbe Machengo, where he learned that the German party had made off to Usure, he rejoined Taylor's force at Singida.

On the 6th August Taylor, satisfied that the surrounding area was clear of the enemy, left a garrison at Singida[4] and marched south with the remainder of his force to Saranda and Kilimatinde, reaching the latter place on the 12th August. Here for the time being his force remained as an outlying detachment, protecting the railway against any menace by the German forces under Wahle in the west.

Thus by the second week in August Major-General van Deventer had secured possession of the Central Railway from Saranda to Kikombo. The country to the westward

Sketch 29

Sketch 38

---

[1] See p. 284.

[2] Schnee, *Deutsch-Ostafrika im Weltkriege*, p. 190.

[3] The escarpment above Mgari could only be crossed by double-spanning the empty wagons and man-handling the loads.

[4] 112 S.A. Horse, 244 8/S.A.I., with 2 m.g.

had been cleared far enough to safeguard his line of communication—extended now by another 100 miles—and his division was concentrated about Nyangalo ready to move eastwards along the railway.

ADVANCE OF THE MAIN FORCE TO THE WAMI
SITUATION, 1ST AUGUST 1916

Whilst the 2nd Division was pushing forward to the Central Railway in the operations just described, the main British force on the Msiha, whose further operations Lieut.-General Smuts proposed still to control and direct in person as hitherto, was completing preparations to resume its parallel advance southwards through the Nguru mountains. By the beginning of August the troops had been rested and re-equipped ; the line of communication was no longer threatened ; supply and transport difficulties had been largely overcome.[1]

The time had arrived when the Commander-in-Chief might well hope that his strategy would shortly bring about a decisive result. His movement from the Pangani to the Msiha had attracted the bulk of the German forces away from Kondoa Irangi, enabling van Deventer to place himself on their flank, so that at least a convergent attack by the combined British forces, and possibly envelopment of the enemy, might now be looked for. Meanwhile to the west- End Paper ward, south of Lake Victoria, British and Belgian forces (N) acting in concert were pushing the Germans back to Tabora, while in the enemy's rear Brig.-General Northey was penetrating successfully into the German colony from the south.[2]

The country now to be traversed by the main British Sketch 39 force was full of difficulties. Six miles south of Msiha Camp the main southward route, which for some thirty miles skirts the eastern edge of the Nguru mountains, reaches the first foothills. Here it is overlooked by the steep spur of Ruhungu, descending from the outlying mountain mass of Kanga, which is separated from the main Nguru range to the westward by the broad valley of the Mjonga river,

Sketch 28

---

[1] Nevertheless for some weeks to come full rations could seldom be counted on. 1st line vehicles had often to be drawn upon to supplement those of the rear services.

[2] See Chaps. XXVI, XXVIII, respectively.

a tributary of the Wami. Along the lower slopes of Ruhungu the enemy held a strong defensive position barring the road, its front covered by the swampy river Komanziro (which becomes the Rukwenzi lower down), its left flank by sheer mountain and its right by an expanse of bush and swamp stretching eastward to the Lukigura. All available information indicated that this position was strongly held.

The high ridges of Kanga, extending some ten miles from north to south, while affording the enemy valuable observation,[1] were too rugged and overgrown to allow of movement on any large scale. From them any action against the Ruhungu position by day would at once be spotted by the enemy, while to move by night in such difficult country with a large force of troops unaccustomed to night work in the bush would involve difficulties of preparation and hazards in operation which could not be contemplated.

Direct attack was therefore considered out of the question. Moreover, in the words of Lieut.-General Smuts, " if we forced our way down the road against these formidable " obstacles or moved by our left flank through the bush " and tall elephant-grass, part of the enemy force on our " right would get behind us and endanger our communica- " tions. It was therefore essential to advance by way of " the mountains themselves and to clear them as the advance " proceeded southward. This could best be done by wide " turning movements through the mountains which would " have the effect of cutting off the enemy's retreat if he " delayed his retirement unduly ".[2]

Thus, fitting well with the South African aptitude and predilection for outflanking tactics, the best move seemed to be to find a way round. The Intelligence scouts were accordingly sent to explore further the main Nguru range to

[1] The fire of two *Königsberg* guns, also of a 3·5 inch gun brought up on 22nd July, was directed from O.P.'s on these heights with considerable accuracy at long range against Msiha Camp, which in consequence became known unofficially as " Shell Camp ". The guns could not be located from the air, and in any case none of the British artillery had sufficient range to reply, the long-range naval guns of No. 15 (previously No. 11 Heavy) Bty. being held up at Korogwe for lack of M.T. capable of hauling them over unmade roads. (See also Chap. XIII, Note I (viii), p. 220). The German harassing fire caused about 60 casualties between 9th July and 8th August, for about 570 rounds fired, and had some temporary moral effect on the natives. For an account of the emplacing and use of the *Königsberg* guns on Kanga see Arning, *Vier Jahre Weltkrieg* pp. 178–82.

[2] Despatch, op. cit

the westward, where some of them were already at work.[1] They reported not only that the Mjonga valley route was practicable, but that two other routes led through the mountains farther west, one from Wiadigwa through Kwa Chengo to Matamondo in the Mjonga valley and one by way of the Boruma and Lwale valleys to Turiani.

On this information Lieut.-General Smuts decided, while demonstrating against Ruhungu in order to pin the enemy there, to move the greater part of his forces by a wide turning movement round the German western flank so as to come down on Turiani, across the enemy's line of retreat.

The enemy's force in the Nguru area was estimated at 18 or 19 companies, amounting in all to a fighting strength of about 3,000 to 3,500.[2]

The British 1st and 3rd Divisions, the latter including the newly arrived 2nd South African Mounted Brigade, comprised in all eleven infantry battalions, each about 500 strong, and four mounted regiments, each about 400, a total fighting strength of roughly 7,000,[3] with a considerable numerical superiority in artillery.[4] With such preponderance of force it might well seem that Lieut.-General Smuts's

[1] See p. 306, f.n. 2. Doutless for reasons of secrecy, no technical reconnaissance was made by trained officers of the administrative staff. The lack of this was felt acutely when the movements of troops were made.
" The intelligence scouts had, in the light of events, evidently not taken " transport into consideration when they reported the several lines of " advance as ' practicable ' . . . considerable time and damage might " have been saved if the scouts had been accompanied by competent " administrative staff officers " " The South Africans with General Smuts ", p. 173
[2] War Diary, Advanced G.H.Q., 4th August 1916.
The German distribution on 6th August is now known to have been as follows :

Location.	Commander.	Units.
Ruhungu	..Kraut	1., 3., 17., 30.F.K.; 5.Sch., 7.Sch.K.
Massimbani	..Stemmermann	14., 18., 22.F.K.
Kwa Chengo (Mjonga valley) ..	..Poppe.	6.F.K.
Kihumbwi (position uncertain) ..	—	Rombo det.
Dakawa (Sketch 41)	..Schulz	4., 9., 13., 16., 21.F.K. " W " K.
Omari (25 m. S.E. of Dakawa) ..	..Goetz	27.F.K.
Kidete (Sketch 28)	..Kämpfe	Arusha det.

On 11th August the Rombo det. was absorbed into the Arusha det.
[3] See Note p. 348.
[4] But see p. 334, f.n. 1, as to the longer range of the enemy's Königsberg guns.

plan afforded the prospect of a decision at last, could it but be carried through swiftly enough to forestall withdrawal by the enemy : a proviso whose importance subsequent events were to make only too plain.

START OF LIEUT.-GENERAL SMUTS'S OFFENSIVE

Sketch 39   Secrecy being vital, Lieut.-General Smuts decided that the march of his forces should start, not from the Msiha, under the enemy's direct observation, but from new camps in rear, along the Lukigura, notwithstanding the additional distance to be traversed through the bush. In these camps the 3rd Division and 2nd E. African Brigade were concentrated between the 1st and 4th August.[1]

With regard to the enemy's dispositions it was now known that, besides the main body holding Ruhungu, about three companies were in or west of the Mjonga valley, with outlying detachments in the vicinity of Msunga, Kimbe, Mahasi and Hesapo. It seemed unlikely, however, that these could offer any serious resistance.

From the summit of Msansha the general line of advance had been studied personally by the Commander-in-Chief with his divisional and brigade commanders. It was then decided that the 2nd S. African Mounted Brigade, under Brgi.-General B. G. L. Enslin, after capturing the German outlying posts near Kimbe and Msunga, should wheel southwards through the mountains to the Lwale valley, to seize Turiani ; the remainder of the 3rd Division (Major-General Brits) was to follow Enslin to Turiani, while from the 1st Division (Major-General Hoskins) the 2nd East African Brigade under Brig.-General Hannyngton was to move down the Mjonga, driving off the German detachment at Kwa Chengo. At the same time the necessary demonstration against Ruhungu was entrusted to the 1st E. African Brigade under Brig.-General Sheppard. Operation orders[2] were issued on the 3rd and 4th August, and early on the 5th the advance began.

MOVEMENTS OF THE 3RD DIVISION

Sketch 40   Detaching the 7th S. African Horse to deal with the German post near Msunga and the 5th Horse as escort to

---

[1] These movements, observed by the enemy from Kanga, were attributed to the effect of the *Königsberg* guns.

[2] Unfortunately no copy of these important operation orders can now be traced.

his transport, Brig.-General Enslin marched on the 5th August with the 6th and 8th Horse westwards past Kimbe, where the German outpost evaded his attempt to capture it and retreated southwards. Turning south-west, he crossed the Mjonga at Pembe on the 6th and went on unopposed through the mountains to reach the head of the Lwale valley next day and the mission-station at Mhonda early on the 8th. Here, in the gap through which the Lwale descends into the plain, he met strong opposition by the *17.F.K.* and was held up.[1]

Meanwhile the 7th S. African Horse had failed to cut off the Germans near Msunga, had lost touch with its brigade and, in uncertainty as to the route taken by Enslin, had wandered off among the mountains.

In Enslin's wake the 3rd Division H.Q. with Beves's two South African battalions and the divisional transport followed the difficult bush track past Msansha and Kimbe ; but less than three miles out the heavy M.T., blocked by rough ground, tree-stumps and long grass, had to be left behind. By the evening of the 6th August Advanced G.H.Q., with the 1st and 3rd Division H.Q., were abreast of Kimbe, with the three battalions of the 1st Division's reserve some miles in rear and Beves toiling ahead towards Pembe. The difficulties of the route were by now only too apparent, while reports came in from Enslin that matters were even worse farther on. On the 7th, therefore, while G.H.Q. went on to Pembe, the 1st Division H.Q. and reserve battalions returned to the Lukigura. Next day, when Brits's infantry reached Wiadigwa intending to ascend the Boruma valley, the Commander-in-Chief intervened, ordering all heavy transport and wheeled artillery back to the Lukigura and directing Brits to turn south-east, with light transport only, in aid of Hannyngton, who meanwhile had reached the vicinity of Kwa Chengo.

MOVEMENTS OF THE 2ND E.A. BRIGADE

(1ST DIVISION)

Concurrently with the movements just described, **Sketch 40** Brig.-General Hannyngton with the 2nd E. African Brigade made an equally difficult march south-westwards from Kwa Negero through Hesapo to Mahasi, where he scattered a

---

[1] No details of the fighting can now be traced. The casualties of 2nd Mtd. Bde. are recorded as 10 killed, 15 wounded.

German detachment on the 6th August. This route, however, like that to Pembe, proved too difficult for his transport, which was therefore ordered back, its escort of the E. African Mounted Rifles and the machine guns of the 2/Loyal North Lancashire going forward to reinforce his infantry.

On the 7th August the brigade moved southwards across rough hill country to Fagiri Hill, near Kwa Chengo, meeting only trifling opposition. Here, unluckily, there was no water, and as his men had with them only the remains of the previous day's rations, Hannyngton left the 3rd Kashmir Rifles to hold the hill and withdrew his other two battalions to the Mjonga, three miles in rear, to await supplies, for which all his available animals had been sent back to the starting point.[1] These did not return until late on the 8th and it was not until daybreak on the 9th that the brigade was able to move. Two priceless days, when time was all-important, were thus lost.

Firing having been heard to the south-westward during the night of the 8th/9th, Hannyngton moved next in that direction, to fall in soon afterwards with the 7th South African Horse, now making its way south to rejoin Enslin, which reported having encountered during the night a strong German party which had made off towards Matamondo. Together with the 7th Horse Hannyngton took the Matamondo track and, after a minor skirmish in the afternoon of the 9th August, halted near the Mjonga crossing, under cover of rising ground on which he posted the 3/K.A.R. and 57th Wilde's Rifles. Here he had word of the approach from behind him of Major-General Brits with the two battalions of the 3rd Division, which reached Kongo the same evening.

THE AFFAIR OF MATAMONDO, 10TH AUGUST 1916

Sketch 40　　Early on the 10th August strong patrols of the 57th and the 3/K.A.R. advanced on either side of the Matamondo road, over rough ground covered with high elephant-grass, against a line of low hills held by the enemy beyond the Mjonga, and soon became heavily engaged. In the hand-to-hand fighting which ensued one of three German machine

---

[1] On 7th and 8th August the E.A.M.R., 50 strong with 2 m.g., were used as an extemporized supply column, the animals being led with supplies loaded across the saddles. Some of the troops at this time had only dates to eat.

guns was captured,[1] but the two battalions suffered considerable loss and were eventually obliged to fall back, carrying off the captured machine gun. Hannyngton's four mountain guns now came into action, and at about 11 a.m. Major-General Brits, with the 5/ and 6/S. African Infantry under Brig.-General Beves, came on the scene and took command. These battalions, prolonging the line eastwards, drove in the enemy's right flank, but no decisive result had been gained by nightfall, when the firing died down.[2]

Next morning (11th) it was found that the German position had been evacuated and the road to the south was clear. The enemy, however, having made excellent use of difficult ground affording every advantage for delaying action, had gained an additional day for his withdrawal from elsewhere.

The Demonstration Against Ruhungu

Meanwhile to the east of the Kanga massif Brig.-General Sketch 40 Sheppard, with the 1st E. African Brigade of the 1st Division, had been ordered on the 4th August to " demonstrate against " the Ruhungu position in such a way as to prevent the " enemy detaching troops from that area to oppose our " columns operating farther to the west ".[3] He arranged therefore to move through the bush east of the main road to a point on the Rukwenzi river, the course of which was believed to run well clear of the enemy's position, and thence to threaten and harass the position with his artillery.

Accordingly on the 7th August—two days after the western turning movements had started the brigade (less the 29th Punjabis, who took the main road), together with the squadron of the 17th Cavalry, one section of the 27th Mountain Battery, R.A., and the 5th Battery, S.A.F.A., moved to the point selected. On arrival it was found that the river ran close under the Ruhungu position and was so

---

[1] The German m.g. were fitted with shields, the great value of which was brought out on this and similar occasions.

[2] "It was extremely difficult to see the movement of our troops, and the " position of the S. Africans could only be judged by . . . their firing " and by their singing ' Rule, Britannia' whenever they successfully " assaulted a hill." (War Diary, 27th Mtn. Bty., R.A.)
Existing records of this affair are far from complete and in some respects mutually at variance.
British casualties are given as : 57th, killed, 1 N.O., 5 o.r. ; wounded 25. 5/ and 6/S.A.I., killed, 2 offrs., 4 o.r. ; wounded 25. Other units, killed, 2 ; wounded, 7.

[3] Brig.-General Sheppard's report.

overgrown along its western bank as to afford little hope of a successful attack ; it was so commanded that even watering of animals was only possible by night ; the bush was virtually impassable to wheeled traffic ; while to move southward down the river in search of easier ground would expose the line of communication to a counter-stroke from Ruhungu. The troops, moreover, like the rest of the British forces, were suffering from the climate. Brig.-General Sheppard decided, therefore, that his only course was to return to Msiha Camp. To this momentous decision, notwithstanding orders from the 1st Division during the night of the 7th/8th August and early next morning to " make his presence felt ", he adhered, and by 11 a.m. on the 8th he was back on the Msiha.

Reconnaissance whilst on the Rukwenzi had suggested to him that it would be better to move against the left (northern) flank of the Ruhungu defences. But after consultation with Major-General Hoskins on the 8th Brig.-General Sheppard started afresh with his brigade on the 9th, this time in a flanking movement wider to the eastward, where the country was reported to be more open,[1] with Massimbani as his objective for the 11th August. From this, however, he was recalled on the afternoon of the 10th by orders to return to the main road in rear of Ruhungu and to make for its crossing over the River Russonge, which he reached next day (11th).

SITUATION, 10TH-11TH AUGUST 1916

Thus, by the evening of the 10th August, Lieut.-General Smuts's forces were split into four widely separated groups. The principal group (six battalions and a mounted regiment) under Major-General Brits had reached Matamondo, but had gained no definite success and was short of supplies. Some fifteen miles away, in the bush and separated from Brits by the high ridges of Kanga, Sheppard's column (three battalions) was as yet uncertain of the situation on its own front. Back on the Msiha the 1st Division reserve (three battalions), with most of the artillery, remained at a standstill. To the southward the 2nd South African Mounted Brigade was still held up at Mhonda.

---

[1] The country was found, in fact, to be difficult, and on 10th August the wheeled transport, together with the 17th Cavalry and 5th Bty., S.A.F.A., returned to Msiha camp.

At the latter place Enslin, ever since his approach on the 7th August, had been engaged more or less continuously, but indecisively, with increasing numbers of the enemy. These, now supported by artillery, attempted no attack in force, but were strong enough to hold the Mounted Brigade in check effectually. Restricted by the lack of wheeled transport[1] to the scanty rations carried on the saddle, and with no artillery, Enslin found himself able only to hold his ground, at a moment when nothing but a vigorous thrust down to Turiani could have achieved the Commander- **Sketch 40** in-Chief's purpose. Meanwhile, however, Brits was approaching down the Mjonga valley, and on the 11th August Enslin gained touch with him by heliograph. That night Brits reached Diongoja, and next day (12th) the two forces joined hands near Mhonda.[2]

By that time, unfortunately, the Germans had slipped away from the Ruhungu position and no hope of cutting off their retreat remained.[3] Lieut.-General Smuts's plan had required speed of movement and vigorous action by

---

[1] The Mtd. Bde. transport had been diverted to Matamondo owing to the difficulties of the route to Mhonda.

[2] Up to this moment the 2nd Mtd. Bde., without wireless, had been completely out of touch. Since 7th August continuous efforts to locate it from the air had failed. On 10th August, Brits's two battalions, on their way to Matamondo, were incorrectly reported from the air as being the missing brigade, which was not, in fact, sighted until after its junction with Brits on the 12th : yet another example of the difficulty of air observation in such country.

[3] The movements of the German forces at this time (see p. 335, f.n. 1) have since been ascertained as follows :—Hearing of Enslin's opening move (against Kimbe) from Poppé at Ruhungu, who asked for help, Major Kraut had ordered a thousand men from Massimbani to the threatened area. Stemmermann, leaving 18.F.K. under Döring to hold Massimbani, moved at once with 14. and 22.F.K. and reached the vicinity of Matamondo on the evening of 7th August. The approach of the mounted troops to Mhonda was then reported, and on the 8th, after reference to Lettow at Morogoro, Kraut withdrew four F.K. and all available artillery from Ruhungu to Turiani, arriving there on 9th. Two of these F.K. were sent north to reinforce Stemmermann near Matamondo ; meanwhile three more F.K. under Schulz arrived from Dakawa. By 10th August, Kraut thus had at Turiani at least six F.K., roughly 1,200 men, a force about equal to Enslin's famished brigade at Mhonda. Fortunately, however, the fog of war prevented Kraut from realizing his opportunity of dealing with the British forces in detail. Uncertain of their strengths, in the absence of his superior he would not risk offensive action, but contented himself with delaying tactics to give time for the Germans farther north to get away. On the 9th the three F.K. still in the Ruhungu position and the one at Massimbani were withdrawn, reaching Turiani next day (10th). On the 11th, Poppe and Stemmermann arrived from Matamondo, and Kraut was able to report that the whole German force was out of immediate danger of being surrounded.

his flanking columns; but the natural difficulties of the
Nguru mountains had proved too formidable, while the
German delaying tactics both at Matamondo and at Mhonda
had successfully gained the short time needed for the enemy's
withdrawal by the easy line of the road. On the 10th August
scouts of the 25/Royal Fusiliers from Msiha Camp found the
Ruhungu position abandoned, and on the 11th the position
was occupied by a small column from the 1st Divisional
reserve, composed mainly of that battalion. Once again,
however, the enemy had used to the full his advantages of
ground and tactical situation. He had, it is true, been
manoeuvred out of an impregnable position; but he had
withdrawn unmolested with two days to spare, and was
still undefeated.

Viewing the operations in retrospect it is impossible not
to deplore the fact that the intended demonstration by
Brig.-General Sheppard against Ruhungu ordered on the 4th,
was not carried out on the 7th or 8th August as planned,
or even earlier, however slight its chances of inflicting any
serious damage on the enemy. The threat from that quarter
was a vital factor in the general plan.[1] That this was
recognized is shown by the orders to Brig.-General Sheppard,
quoted above; but its importance, particularly in this
instance where the out-flanking columns were to move
through unknown and difficult country, appears hardly to
have been sufficiently appreciated at the time. It seems
now very plain that the failure of Lieut.-General Smuts's
plan was in large measure due to the absence of any show
of attack on the Ruhungu position.

ARRIVAL ON THE WAMI

Sketch 40   By the 11th August the way was open to Turiani. On
the 12th Sheppard's brigade crossed the Russonge and
reached Mafleta, moving on next day southwards to Kipera,
where the crossing of the Wami was secured and a bridge-
head established. At the same time the units left in reserve
on the Msiha, including the artillery, marched by the main
road through the abandoned Ruhungu position to Turiani.
Sketch 41   Beyond Turiani some resistance was offered by German
rearguards, but the main obstacle was the enemy's

---

1 " It will usually be necessary to engage the enemy on his front in
" order to distract his attention and resources from the flank attack."
Field Service Regulations, Vol. III, 1935, Sec. 17(2).

demolition of all bridges over the succession of torrential streams pouring from the mountains into the Wami, repairs taking considerable time. It was evident that the Germans were in retreat, but whether they were moving southwards to Morogoro or south-westwards by way of Kilosa towards Mahenge was as yet uncertain.

The road junction at Kwediombo, where the Kilosa and Morogoro roads diverge, was believed to be strongly held. In order to outflank any position here Enslin with the 2nd Mounted Brigade made a detour to the east through Ngulu-kwa-Boga, where on the 14th August he was reinforced from Sheppard's brigade by the 130th Baluchis and a section of the 27th Mountain Battery, R.A. On the 15th the combined column came in against Kwediombo from the east ; little opposition was encountered and the withdrawal of the enemy's forces was confirmed.[1]

The weather was now unfavourable for air reconnaissance, and in the absence of definite information as to the direction of the German retreat the 2nd East African Brigade (Hannyngton) was ordered forward along the Kilosa road, while Enslin with the 2nd Mounted Brigade and Beves with the 5/ and 6/S. African Infantry (2nd S.A. Brigade) took the route towards Morogoro.

ACTION OF THE WAMI, 17TH AUGUST 1916

Reconnaissance by the South Africans along the **Sketch 41** Morogoro road suggested that the crossing of the Wami at Dakawa was held by the enemy in some strength. In order to turn the German defence, Brig. General Sheppard's brigade

---

[1] After the withdrawal from Turiani, Colonel von Lettow Vorbeck reorganised his forces as follows :—

Abteilung Kraut	..	..	1., 16.F.K., with Bty. Sternheim (one 8·8 cm., one 7·3 cm., one 6 cm.), Bty. Fromme (several 3·7 cms.), one Königsberg gun.
Abteilung Schulz	..	..	4., 9., 13., 21.F.K., with one Königsberg gun.
Abteilung Stemmermann	..	14., 18., 22.F.K.
Abteilung Heyden-Linden	..	17., 30.F.K.

He then despatched Kraut to Kilosa, to take over from Otto, who was brought back into reserve at Morogoro, with 11., 23., 27.F.K., 14. Res.K., 1. (Mtd.) Sch.K., 6.Sch.K., and one 8·8 cm. gun, leaving Lincke with 15., 19., 25.F.K., 8. (Mtd.) Sch.K., 9.(Mtd.)Sch.K. at Kilosa to come under Kraut's command. The units under Otto were then set to evacuating stores from Morogoro to the southward, covered by the Abteilung Schulz (to which Stemmermann was attached) at the crossing over the Wami near Dakawa.

(less the battalion and guns detached to Enslin, as already narrated) moved from Kipera on the 15th August up the right bank of the Wami, halting on the following evening, after a toilsome and difficult march, about six miles short of the crossing.

At the same time Enslin's reinforced brigade, followed by Beves with the 5/ and 6/S. African Infantry, moved up to Dakawa. On the afternoon of the 16th the 130th Baluchis established themselves at the crossing, driving off German snipers from the northern bank and coming under heavy rifle and machine-gun fire which confirmed the presence of a considerable German force on the farther side.[1]

The plan now was that the enemy should be contained by the three infantry battalions while the mounted troops crossed the river farther up-stream (south-westward) to turn his left, Sheppard meanwhile coming in behind the German right.

Sketch 42 Early on the 17th August the two South African battalions, with the 6th Horse, came up on the left of the Baluchis, supported by the 3rd Battery, S.A.F.A. and, later, also by the 13th (How.) Battery. No attempt was made to cross the river,[2] but the troops maintained their position throughout the day, with periodical bursts of heavy fire to which the enemy replied with vigour. Three German machine guns, located about 11 a.m., were silenced by a gun of the 27th Mountain Battery, R.A., which was skilfully brought into the front line by Captain Haskard, R.A.[3]

In the meantime Sheppard's brigade, now reduced to little more than two weak battalions,[4] had resumed its march at 5 a.m. on the 17th, having by that time heard by

---

[1] *Abteilung Schulz (4., 9., 21.F.K.).* In reserve were *13.F.K.* and the Wangoni unit (" *W.*" *K.*).

[2] The Wami was about 30 yards wide, 4 to 5 feet deep. After the German withdrawal it was bridged, the work being completed on 20th August. During the 17th the troops suffered much from thirst, no approach to the river being possible.

[3] The gun was enabled to remain at close range, despite lack of cover, owing mainly to its being fitted with one of the improvised shields adopted locally by the Mtn. Btys.

[4] 29th Punjabis, 2/Kashmir Rifles, one coy. 2/Rhodesia Regt. with 4 m.g., squadron 17th Cavalry, 5th Bty., S.A.F.A.

A detachment 100 strong had been left to guard the crossing at Kipera and others were escorting convoys. Including 200 in reserve, the available rifle strength was about 700.

wireless of the opposition at Dakawa. Towards 9 a.m. the advanced guard, two companies of the 29th Punjabis, came up against a strong and well-prepared flanking position, sited in the bend of a small tributary stream and extending some 500 yards on either side of the line of advance.[1] An hour later the remainder of the 29th were sent up, followed at 11 a.m. by the solitary company of the 2/Rhodesia Regt., but little further progress could be made. Every attempt to extend to a flank was met by a similar counter-move ; the guns could find no targets in the thick elephant-grass and scrub ; the troops, short of food and water, were becoming exhausted.

About 3 p.m. the 2/Kashmir Rifles relieved the 29th Punjabis. Soon afterwards the enemy's fire slackened and gradually died down, and towards 5 p.m. scouts reported the German position abandoned. Firing which had been heard in the direction of the main crossing had also ceased, and as a message from Major-General Brits had reported that the 2nd Mounted Brigade had crossed the river 1½ miles above Dakawa at 2.30 p.m., Sheppard rightly concluded that the enemy had retreated all along the line. His patrols having failed to hit off the Morogoro road before dark, he camped for the night and moved up to the Dakawa crossing next day (18th August).

Meanwhile the 2nd Mounted Brigade (less the 6th Horse) had moved upstream early on the 17th. No details of its operations are now available,[2] but apparently, after crossing the Wami as stated in Major-General Brits's message just mentioned, it took most of the afternoon to work down towards the flank of the German position, which it did not succeed in turning. Doubtless its approach, coupled with the threat by Sheppard from the east, decided the enemy to abandon his dispute of the Dakawa crossing ; but once again the opportunity of cutting off the German retreat appears to have escaped Enslin's grasp.[3]

---

[1] Held by *Abteilung Stemmermann* (*14., 18., 22.F.K.*).

[2] No copy of the orders given to the 2nd Mtd. Bde. can be traced. The war diary reads : " 17th Aug. Cross Wami river and attack enemy " forces on their left flank. Germans retire during night. Our losses " 1 killed, 5 wounded".

[3] Prisoners taken by Sheppard stated that, when the mounted troops appeared to be threatening the German line of retreat, orders were given to prepare to destroy all rifles and ammunition prior to surrender ; but that when the threat failed to develop the order was countermanded. The enemy withdrew unmolested.

The night of the 17th/18th August was quiet. Reconnaissance at dawn on the 18th showed that the enemy was in full retreat towards Morogoro.[1] Pursuit, however, was out of the question ; supplies had run short and the river had still to be bridged[2] in order to get them forward. For the next three days the force remained halted at Dakawa. Air reconnaissance was continued,[3] and from this and other indications it became apparent that the enemy intended continuing his retreat southwards across the Central Railway.

After a conference at G.H.Q. on the 19th August,[4] the 2nd E. Africa Brigade (Hannyngton) was recalled from the Kilosa road to rejoin at Dakawa, while from the 1st Divisional reserve the Cape Corps, 300 strong, was sent on from Turiani towards Kilosa.[5]

SITUATION, 19TH AUGUST 1916

Sketch 28   It was hardly to be expected that Lettow would now do otherwise than retreat to the south of the railway. " When " the advance through the Nguru mountains began ", wrote Lieut.-General Smuts, " the available information tended " strongly to show that, if the enemy retired from the railway, End Paper " Mahenge "—for which Kilosa was the most convenient (N). point of departure—" would be his next objective ". The British commander had therefore " entertained some hope " that, even if we failed in cornering the enemy in those " mountains, he might still be brought to bay at Kilosa . . ."[6] Now, however, whether as the result of van Deventer's move on Kilosa described in the following chapter, or otherwise,

---

[1] British casualties on the Wami, about 120 in all, included the following : 29th Punjabis, killed, 10 ; wounded, 2 B.O., 42 o.r. ; 2/Rhodesia Regt., killed, 1 offr., 4 o.r. ; wounded, 13 ; 130th Baluchis, killed, 3 ; wounded, 1 B.O., 20 o.r.

[2] See p. 344, f.n. 2.

[3] During the days immediately preceding the Wami action, flying had been stopped by bad weather. The opportunity was used to shift the aerodrome from Mbagwe, north of Handeni (Sketch 37) to Komsanga, near Kipera (Sketch 41) whence it was moved soon afterwards to Dakawa. Morogoro was bombed from the air on 21st August.

[4] No record of proceedings has survived. The conference is mentioned only in the war diary of the 2nd E.A.Bde.

[5] On 19th August the Cape Corps started for Kimamba (on the railway), 12 miles east of Kilosa ; (see Sketch 28), where it effected a junction with the 2nd Divn. on 27th August.

[6] Despatch, op. cit.

there was no longer any doubt at G.H.Q. that the bulk of the German forces had retreated to Morogoro.

Doubtless if it had been possible for Lieut.-General Smuts to overtake and come to grips with Lettow before Morogoro, and to hold him there by fighting whilst van Deventer drove forward through Kilosa to take him in flank and rear, the campaign might conceivably have been brought to an early and successful conclusion. But of this, given the German advantages of smaller numbers, knowledge of the country and, above all, mobility and lack of impedimenta, there was never any prospect. While the main British force was temporarily immobile on the Wami, van Deventer, though he was approaching along the railway, was still over sixty miles away ; and Lettow, with a clear start and well served by the delaying action both of Otto ietreating before van Deventer and of Schulz at Dakawa, was not the man to allow himself to be thus cornered.[1]

Nevertheless in the mind of the Commander-in-Chief there was still hope that in the neighbourhood of Morogoro the long pursuit might be brought to a decisive end.

---

[1] " The enemy ", writes Lettow, " expected us to stand and fight "a final decisive engagement near Morogoro . . . To me, this idea was " never altogether intelligible. Being so very much the weaker party, " it was surely madness to await at this place the junction of the hostile " columns, of which each one individually was already superior to us in " numbers, and then to fight with our back to the steep and rocky moun- ' tains, of which the passes were easy to close, and which deprived us of " all freedom of movement in our rear. I thought it sounder so to conduct "our operations that we should only have to deal with a part of the enemy." " My Reminiscences ", p. 149.

NOTE

MAIN BRITISH FORCE, ORDER OF BATTLE, 5TH AUGUST 1916

1st Division (Major-General A. R. Hoskins)

1st E.A. Bde. (Sheppard)	2nd E.A. Bde. (Hannyngton)	Divnl. Troops
29th Punjabis.	57th Wilde's Rifles.	E.A.M.R.
130th Baluchis.	3/Kashmir Rifles.	25/Royal Fusiliers.
2/Kashmir Rifles.	3/K.A.R.	2/Rhodesia Regt.
Attached:	Attached:	Cape Corps Bn.
*Sqdn. 17th Cavalry.	K.A.R. M.I.	No. 7 Field Bty.
One Sec. 27th Mtn. Bty., R.A.	27th Mtn. Bty., R.A. (less one sec.).	L. N. Lancs. M.G. Coy.
No. 5 Bty., S.A.F.A.	M.G. det. 129th Baluchis.	One Sec. E.A. Pioneers.
No. 6 Field Bty.		
*134th (How.) Bty.		
*No. 1 L.A.M. Bty.		
M.G. det. 2/Rhodesia Regt.		
One Coy. 61st Pioneers.		
One Sec. E.A. Pioneers.		

3rd Division (Major-General C. J. Brits)

2nd S.A. Mtd. Bde. (Enslin)	2nd S.A. Inf. Bde. (Beves)	Divnl. Troops
5th S.A. Horse.	5th S.A. Inf.	No. 1 Bty., S.A.F.A.
6th " " "	6th " " "	†No. 3 Bty., S.A.F.A.
7th " " "		No. 8 Field Bty.
8th " " "		*No. 13 How. Bty.
		*No. 5 L.A.M. Bty.
		Vol. M.G. Coy.

Army Troops

134th (How.) Bty.

* Army Troops attached.

† No. 3 Bty., S.A.F.A., was attached to 2nd Mtd. Bde., but went only to Pembe, whence it returned to the Lukigura.

CHAPTER XXI

PROGRESS TO THE CENTRAL RAILWAY—*(concluded)*

(Sketches 38, 43, 44, 45, 46)

ADVANCE OF THE 2ND DIVISION TO KILOSA

THE movements of the 2nd Division to Kitunda-kwa- **Sketch 38** Meda and Nyangalo had taxed the supply and transport services[1] to the utmost, and it was not until the 8th August, when a telegram from the Commander-in-Chief urged it forward " with the least possible delay " to co-operate with his main force, that the division was able to move. By that time its units were for the most part concentrated about Nyangalo ready to move south-eastwards along the railway.[2]

The enemy, so far as was known, was holding the hilly **Sketch 43** area between Msagali station and Kongwa, separated from Nyangalo by twenty miles of waterless country. Information as to his strength was still indefinite, but it might reasonably be assumed that the opposing force consisted of from six to ten companies, which would doubtless adopt the now usual rearguard tactics in a withdrawal south-eastwards on Kilosa, ninety miles away.[3]

---

[1] An advanced supply depot was first established at Cypherkuil, near Chambalo, from which 7 days' rations, in addition to those in 1st line transport (see p. 327, f.n. 1) were issued. A new depot established at Haneti fed the columns from that point through Chenene and Itiso respectively as far as the railway. Work was then started to transfer the advanced supply depot to Nyangalo, but this had not been completed and rations had not been issued in full when the forward move was resumed.

[2] Units reached the Nyangalo area as follows (Sketch 10) ·
28th July :	S.A. Mtd. Bde. (less 4th S.A. Horse) ; No. 4 Bty., S.A.F.A.
(30th July :	3rd S.A. Horse to Kikombo, see p. 331.)
31st July :	4th S.A. Horse ; No. 2 Bty., S.A.F.A.
2nd Aug. :	12/S.A.I. ; 1 sect. (i.e., 1 How.), 12th (How.) Bty., from Meia-Meia.
5th Aug. :	11/S.A.I. ; 28th Mtn. Bty., R.A. (less 1 sect.).
7th Aug. :	4 aircraft (to Dodoma).
8th Aug. :	10/S.A.I. (from Dodoma) ; 12th (How.) Bty. (less 1 sect., i.e. 2 How., formerly 11th Bty.).
9th Aug. :	No. 4 Lt. Armoured (car) Bty. (from Dodoma).

The 7/S.A.I. and 10th (heavy) Bty., from Kondoa Irangi, arrived later (see p. 353, f.n. 2, as to 10th and 11th Bties).

[3] The German units, all under Otto, appear to have been distributed as follows :
Kongwa, *23.F.K.* ; Chunyu, *1.Sch.*, *9.Sch.K.* (small mounted units) ; between Chunyu and Msagali, *19.*, *24.*, *25.F.K.* ; on the railway, under Lincke, *15.F.K.*, *6.Sch.K.* ; at Mpwapwa, recruit and police detachments.

On the 9th August operation orders were issued, and at dawn on the 10th the advance of the 2nd Division began.

Directing the 3rd Horse at Kikombo to follow the railway, with a squadron making a wide sweep southwards, while the 9th Horse detached two patrols (each two troops) to push out from Nyangalo wide to the northern flank,[1] Major-General van Deventer moved by the direct route south-eastwards through Chunyu and Mpwapwa to strike the railway at Gode Gode.

With the remainder of the 9th Horse and three armoured cars as vanguard, his main body now consisted of the 10/ and 12/S. African Infantry (3rd S. African Brigade) under Brig.-General Berrangé, with the 28th Mountain Battery, R.A. (less 1 section), the 2nd Battery, S.A.F.A., and the 12th (How.) Battery, this column being followed and presently overtaken by the remainder of the 1st Mounted Brigade (1st, 2nd, 4th Horse). At the same time the 11/S. African Infantry under Lieut.-Colonel N. H. M. Burne, which, with a section of the 28th Mountain Battery, R.A., had been sent to Kikombo on the 9th August, closed in as a flanking column from that place on Chunyu and followed the division, eventually reaching Mpwapwa on the 14th and rejoining its brigade at Kidete on the 17th.

Nearing Chunyu about 5 p.m. on the 10th August, after a trying march, Brig.-General Berrangé at once sent in the 10th Infantry to attack a German force which held the hills covering the approaches and the only available water.

By nightfall he was in possession of the lower slopes, the 9th Horse working round the enemy's flanks and pushing forward during the night to the crest of the hills, from which the Germans retreated before daylight.[2]

During the 11th August mounted patrols regained contact with the enemy ten miles on, near Mpwawpa. Here somewhat stiffer resistance was encountered, the German rearguard holding the steep heights commanding the road beyond the township, which was evacuated as the column came up. The going was difficult, the country being rugged and thickly overgrown ; but by 5.15 p.m., when the 10/ and 12/S. African Infantry attacked—now supported by the 4th Battery, S.A.F.A. in addition to the 2nd Battery and the mountain

---

[1] The movements of these mounted troops, which met no opposition worth mentioning, are shown in Sketch 43.

[2] Casualties : 9th S.A.H., 2 killed, 5 wounded ; 10/S.A.I., 1 offr., 8 o.r. wounded.

guns—the 9th Horse on the British left and the remaining mounted troops to the right were well round the enemy's flanks. The infantry had little difficulty. But between the 1st Horse, which worked round to the German rear, and the 2nd and 4th, which in an effort to cut off the German retreat met considerable opposition, a gap of nearly a mile was left, which Brig.-General Nussey endeavoured personally to close with some 50 of his men, calling in also the 9th Horse from the other flank. The 9th, unfortunately, were diverted by the intervention of the divisional commander and consequently did not come up until after dark. As often before, the Germans withdrew during the night, succeeding, under cover of darkness and the bush, in filtering through Nussey's cordon and making good their retreat.[1]

During the 12th and 13th August van Deventer's troops remained halted at Mpwapwa. Famished and exhausted after marching nearly forty miles in 32 hours through difficult country[2] on short rations and with little water, they had been twice in action and had outrun their supplies. Air reconnaissance indicated that the Germans had fallen back to Kidete.

On the 14th supplies reached Mpwapwa, and that evening the 9th Horse and the two infantry battalions, with the 28th Mountain and 2nd South African batteries, reached the railway at Gode Gode. Early on the 15th this force was held up by machine-gun fire from the hills west of Kidete, on which the Germans were strongly posted, supported by two guns near the station. One of these was promptly silenced by the 28th Mountain Battery ; the other, on a railway truck which was located with some difficulty, was put out of action by the South African gunners soon afterwards.

As before, while the 9th Horse endeavoured to turn both the enemy's flanks—no easy matter on the rugged bush-clad hills—Berrangé's battalions attacked. Still exhausted by their previous exertions, they met determined opposition. On the right a squadron and part of the 12th Infantry which

---

[1] The German units here appear to have been *14.Res.K.* and *1.Sch.K.*, with part of *23.* and *25.F.K.*   These rallied at Gode Gode, where they were joined by *15.*, *24.F.K.*, *6.Sch.*, *8.Sch.K.* from Gulwe.

British casualties were : 4th S.A.H., 1 killed, 1 wounded ; 10/S.A.I., 1 offr., 7 o.r. wounded ; 12/S.A.I., 1 offr. killed, 1 o.r. died of wounds, 5 o.r. wounded.

The enemy left over 20 dead ; 5 Germans were captured.

[2] Beyond Chunyu the track was so bad that the armoured cars were unable to reach Mpwapwa in time and subsequently had little part in the operations.

established themselves across the railway found the bush well-nigh impenetrable ; the 10th gained ground gradually along the road, the flanking squadron on the left also working its way forward. About 4 p.m. a German counter-attack on the 12th Infantry was easily beaten off ; but in prepared positions on such difficult ground the enemy had everything in his favour and when night fell the advance, despite valiant efforts, was still checked.[1]

As before, however, Otto, the German commander, had no intention of making any prolonged stand. At midnight (15th/16th) the remainder of the 1st Mounted Brigade, which had left Mpwapwa at 3 p.m. on the 15th, came up, and early next morning its patrols found that the enemy had once more slipped away during the night. Derailed trucks and a number of dead were evidence of a serious railway accident in the course of the German withdrawal.

By the evening of the 16th August Nussey, pushing on with only the 1st Horse,[2] now numbering less than 300, found the Germans holding their next rearguard position near Msagara and himself bivouacked at Kirasa. The remainder of the force moved up to the Kidete river to await supplies, which did not arrive until the 18th. On the afternoon of that day Berrangé, whose brigade had been rejoined by the 11/S. African Infantry on the 17th,[3] went forward towards Msagara.

From Kidete to Kilosa for some 25 miles the road, railway and river run together through a winding defile in a wild, hilly and bush-covered country, much of it impassable even on foot : conditions even better suited for German rearguard

---

[1] Casualties, mostly in the 10/S.A.I., were : killed, 3 o.r. ; wounded, 3 offrs., 36 o.r.
Enemy losses are not known.
German units engaged at Kidete were : Right flank (von Chappuis), *14.*, *19.F.K.*, *1. Sch.K.*, one 6 cm. gun ; centre (von Liebermann), *11.*, *7.F.K.* ; left flank (S. of railway, Lincke), *15.*, *25.F.K.*, *6.Sch.K.*, one 8.8 cm. gun ; reserve (Vorberg), *22.*, *24.F.K.*, *8.Sch.*, *9.Sch.K.*
2.Sch.K., driven out of Saranda by Kirkpatrick (see p. 331), rejoined at Kidete after a long detour southwards which gave rise to native reports of large reinforcements arriving from Iringa (see End Paper, N.).
Otto ordered evacuation of Kidete at 2 a.m., 16th August.
It was at this juncture that Lettow ordered Kraut with his two *F.K.* to Kilosa, recalling Otto to Morogoro (see p. 343, f.n. 1). Kraut marched on 16th August from near Kwediombo (Sketch 44) to Kimamba, moving thence by rail to Kilosa.
[2] On 16th August the 2nd S.A.H. was left as escort to the artillery ; the 3rd S.A.H. was patrolling south of the railway ; the 4th and 9th remained about Kidete. These units rejoined the 1st Mtd. Bde. during 17th and 18th August.
[3] See p. 350.

action than those of the arduous route already traversed. Nevertheless at Msagara, where Berrangé attacked at 3 a.m. on the 19th August, the British tactics were entirely successful. So steep and overgrown were the hills flanking the road that the Germans apparently expected attack only down the valley; consequently, when the heights were scaled, on the right by the 11/S. African Infantry and the 28th Mountain Battery, R.A., and on the left by the 12/S. African Infantry, no opposition was met and the enemy's trenches on the road below were hastily evacuated. A deep side-valley barred further progress to the right, but the 12th pushed on and the German retreat became a rout. Msagara station was occupied in the afternoon. There were no British casualties.[1]

Next day (20th) the 1st Mounted Brigade drove the German rearguards off the hills some five miles west of Kilosa. It was shelled in the afternoon at long range by a *Königsberg* gun, the first sign of the approach from the eastward of Kraut, who with two companies had been sent to take over from Otto, the latter having, as we now know, been recalled with two-thirds of his command to Morogoro.[2]

Led by this fire to assume that determined opposition might be encountered on reaching the heights overlooking Kilosa, Major-General van Deventer pushed forward all his available artillery.[3] During the 21st August the 10/ and 12/S. African Infantry relieved the 2nd and 9th Horse, which with the other mounted troops drove ahead and wide to the flanks both north and south of the railway. These movements were enough for the enemy; the same evening natives reported that the Germans were in retreat.[4]

The news was confirmed at daybreak on the 22nd August, when the 9/ and 10/ S. African Infantry[5] found the enemy's defences abandoned and, looking down on Kilosa, saw that

---

[1] The German units engaged were *15.*, *19.*, *25.F.K.*

[2] See p. 343, f.n. 1, and p. 352, f.n. 1.

[3] The 10th (Heavy) Bty. and 11th (How.) Bty., which reached Mpwapwa on 18th August, were held up there by shortage of petrol and by damage to their transport due to bad roads.

[4] Apparently Kraut, uneasy as to his left flank, sent *6.F.K.* (Poppe) to hold a track leading from Msagara through the hills to the plain south of Kilosa. On the evening of 21st August a British mounted patrol encountered Poppe's outposts, and on hearing of this Kraut ordered retreat to Myombo. Arning, *Vier Jahre Weltkrieg*, p. 191.

[5] The 9/S.A.I., which had formed Kirkpatrick's column sent from Kondoa Irangi to Saranda and on to Kilimatinde (see p. 331) rejoined to complete the 3rd S. African Bde. on 20th August.

N*

the rugged hills through which they had forced their way here came to an end. At 7 a.m. the first of the mounted troops entered Kilosa, and in the course of the day Major-General van Deventer with the greater part of his division was established there.

A gruelling phase of the operations was over. By dint of hard, dogged marching, climbing and fighting the South Africans of the 2nd Division, under conditions of steadily increasing hardship as the line of communication lengthened, had pushed back the opposing Germans through the sixty miles of difficult hill country between Chunyu and Kilosa, suffering a minimum of battle casualties,[1] but at the cost of reducing men and horses alike to utter exhaustion.[2]

At Kilosa, therefore, the worn-out infantry remained for the time being. There was no respite, however, for the mounted troops ; their patrols went on to regain touch with the Germans, who were found to be retreating south-eastwards towards Myombo,[3] and almost immediately afterwards a fresh demand was made upon them.

PLANS FOR USE OF THE MOUNTED TROOPS

End Paper
(N)

The approach of van Deventer to Kilosa brought within sight the moment when Lieut.-General Smuts would be able to co-ordinate more closely the operations of the 2nd Division with those of the main force moving on from the Wami. His hopes of bringing about a decision remained undimmed.

---

[1] " The slight casualties sustained over an enormous tract of country, " bristling with dongas and difficulties at every point, were mainly due " to the advance being carried out by avoiding as far as possible frontal " attacks." (Maj.-Genl. van Deventer, quoted in C.-in-C.'s despatch, op. cit.)

[2] " Owing to bad roads, shortage of transport and the rapidity of " advance, the adequate rationing of the troops was not possible. The " under-feeding and over-working are sadly reflected in their state of " health . . . the advance from Mpwapwa to Kilosa was through one " continual fly-belt, where practically all the animals were infected." (Maj.-Genl. van Deventer, op. cit.)
" Horses and transport utterly exhausted . . . my men are not in fit " condition [for] any heavy marching . . . without serious results unless " they are given at least six days' rest. My supply and transport arrange- " ments will not be in order before the 28th . . . " (Telegram, 2nd Divn. to G.H.Q., 22nd August, 1916.)
The line of communication, over 200 miles from Moshi to Kondoa Irangi, was lengthened by almost as much again from Kondoa Irangi to Kilosa.

[3] " . . . enemy retiring slowly but maintaining very strong rearguard. " Owing to the extreme exhaustion of my animals and men it was quite " impossible to deal with the situation in any strength . . . " War Diary, 1st S.A. Mtd. Bde., 23rd August, 1916.

The greater part of the German forces, as we have seen, had been withdrawn to the neighbourhood of Morogoro. From there they might still attempt retreat south-westwards towards the healthy uplands of Mahenge ; but with van Deventer at Kilosa it was more probable that they would aim more directly southwards, towards the Rufiji. Due south of Morogoro, however, and within a few miles of the town, the rugged mass of the Uluguru mountains presented a formidable barrier to movement. If the two southward routes, passing east and west respectively of the mountains, could be blocked quickly enough, it seemed that the elusive enemy might be pinned against the impassable mountain mass and brought at last to bay.

Sketch 44

Telegraphing in this sense on the 20th August, the Commander-in-Chief informed Major-General van Deventer that, to make effective a rapid move by the main British force against the eastern route, it was necessary that the mounted troops of the 2nd Division should bar the western route at Mlali. He asked how soon this could be done, explaining that, if it were done by the mounted troops of the main force, the infantry of the latter acting alone would be too slow to forestall the enemy on the eastern route.

Next day (21st) van Deventer—not yet realizing that within twenty-four hours he would be in Kilosa himself— replied that the enemy was still in strength west of that place and that until the situation cleared it would be impossible for him to carry out the move to Mlali.

On this the Commander-in-Chief at once (21st) sent off the 2nd S. African Mounted Brigade (5th, 6th, 7th, 8th Horse), with the 3rd Battery, S.A.F.A., under Brig.-General Enslin, from Dakawa to the railway at Mkata, with orders to operate against the rear of the Germans at Kilosa. His intention was to recall this force for his eastern advance as soon as Nussey's mounted brigade from the 2nd Division could push forward to take its place. But on the 22nd August, when—unexpectedly soon—Kilosa fell to van Deventer, he decided to send Enslin on from Mkata to Mlali, at the same time informing the 2nd Division of this and adding : " you must pursue enemy . . . as far south " as possible and move your mounted brigade so as to " support Enslin against attack in rear by enemy retreating " before you to Kisaki " (south of the Uluguru range).

His plan, in short, now was that the two mounted brigades, combined under Enslin, should take up the role, previously in his mind for the 2nd Division, of cutting the German line of retreat west of the Uluguru mountains.

Sketch 45 Accordingly on the 24th August, after unsuccessfully representing the plight of his men and horses to the Commander-in-Chief, Major-General van Deventer despatched Nussey with the 1st Mounted Brigade (less the 1st S. African Horse), the 4th Battery, S.A.F.A., a signal troop and a field ambulance, by night march to Mkata, 33 miles away, where this force arrived at 8 a.m. on the 25th, three days behind Enslin. At Mkata Nussey was obliged to leave over a third of his force behind,[1] and that afternoon his jaded and depleted command, totalling barely 900, moved off after Enslin to Mlali.

THE AFFAIR OF MLALI, 24TH–26TH AUGUST 1916[2]

Sketch 46 Enslin, on reaching the neighbourhood of Mlali about 7.30 a.m. on the 24th August, sent forward the 5th, 6th and 7th South African Horse to occupy Kisagale Hill, which overlooked from the west a bend of the Mlali river and the enemy's western route. German outposts on the hill fell back across the river, leaving several prisoners. The South Africans, pushing on, and taking possession of a useful dump of German gun ammunition[3] and food on their way, were then fired on from a farm east of the river. With a view to enveloping this post a crossing was effected some two miles farther upstream by a part of the brigade, headed by the 5th Horse, which was supported by the 3rd Battery, S.A.F.A., from the river bank. The advanced troops were checked, however, on reaching the edge of a small tributary valley, by heavy fire from the higher ground beyond it. Soon afterwards two enemy guns came into action behind the defended farm, and on the arrival of German reinforcements and the development of a threat to his extended right flank Enslin recalled the 5th Horse and withdrew his battery northwards, the better to cover his left.

---

[1] Nussey started from Kilosa with 1,177 mounted, 236 dismounted of all ranks. On the march to Mkata 249 horses broke down. At Mkata all dismounted men were left.

The 1st S.A.H., left at Kilosa, went south to Uleia on 25th (see p. 374; Sketch 44).

[2] Contemporary records are incomplete and few details are available.

[3] About 500 rounds of 4·1 inch ammunition were captured.

Led by the enemy's heavy fire and evident accession of strength to believe that the main German forces were upon him, and already short of ammunition, he fell back on Kisagale hill, to await the arrival of Nussey.[1] During the remainder of the day the enemy maintained a harassing but ineffectual cross-fire.

In the course of the next day (25th) hostile artillery fire continued intermittently, two light guns opening from a fresh position on Enslin's right flank, which the enemy again threatened with envelopment, doubtless to cover the withdrawal southwards of the bulk of the German force. The 3rd Battery, being ill-placed to deal with this, was moved that evening to the southern end of the Kisagale ridge.

Early on the 26th August the Germans were found to have evacuated their positions, abandoning two naval guns, and to have withdrawn to rearguard positions covering their southward route past Mgeta mission-station and through the mountains to Kisaki.[2]

Sketches 44, 45

At this juncture Nussey, with the 1st Mounted Brigade, reached Mlali and came under Brig.-General Enslin's command. The brigade was so exhausted, however, and so short of food, that a day's rest was imperative. Enslin, therefore, with the 2nd Mounted Brigade only, moved out into the hills between Mlali and Mgeta.

On the 27th Nussey's brigade came up on Enslin's left, following up the retreating Germans with considerable difficulty in steep and difficult country, and that afternoon Enslin decided on a flanking movement to the westward with his own brigade while Nussey went forward towards Mgeta.[3] During the 28th and 29th the movement was carried out, meeting little opposition; but owing to the difficulty of the ground its progress was slow. On the afternoon of the 29th Nussey reached Mgeta, whence the last of the Germans had departed that morning, still retreating to the south. Enslin, meanwhile, with the 2nd Mounted Brigade, returned to Mlali.

---

[1] Brig.-General Enslin's subsequent report records that he was obliged to refuse a request by the 5th Horse for reinforcements, his reserve (8th S.A.H.) being needed in case of attack on his left flank " which was " my only way of retreat in case my force was overwhelmed."

[2] Casualties in the 2nd S.A. Mtd. Bde. were 1 killed, 7 wounded.

[3] The positions reached by units made it convenient, with a view to their movement, to allocate temporarily the 5th S.A.H. (Enslin) to Nussey and the 9th S.A.H. (Nussey) to Enslin. The two units remained exchanged until the brigades met again outside Kisaki (see Chap. XXII).

Here he was visited by the Commander-in-Chief, with Major-Generals van Deventer and Brits. As the outcome of this visit, Lieut.-General Smuts ordered Nussey with the 1st Mounted Brigade to continue in pursuit of the enemy from Mgeta mission, while Enslin with the 2nd Mounted Brigade was to make a wide detour to the westward through Msongosi and Mahalaka, away from the mountains, and to be followed by the remainder of Brits's 3rd Division, the two columns converging on Kisaki.

We turn now to the operations of Lieut.-General Smuts's main force, directed on Morogoro.[1]

THE MAIN FORCE REACHES THE CENTRAL RAILWAY

Sketch 45 By the 23rd August the supply situation of the main British force at Dakawa had been restored ; the troops had had a rest and were ready to go forward ; Enslin's mounted brigade, followed by that of Nussey from Kilosa, was approaching Mlali, where the enemy's line of retreat south-westwards from Morogoro would, it was hoped, be effectively blocked. It remained for Lieut.-General Smuts to close the exit south-eastwards, " and thus ", in the words of his subsequent despatch, " to bottle the enemy up in Morogoro ".[2]

" I was not then aware," he wrote, " that a track went " due south from Morogoro through the mountains to " Kisaki, and that the capture of the flanks of the mountains " would not achieve the end in view."[3] As the preceding section of the narrative shows, however, it was not the existence of that unexpected route, taken by only a small portion of the German troops, but the impossibility of placing sufficient force in time at Mlali, which was to prevent fulfilment of the Commander-in-Chief's plan.

---

[1] The German force at Mlali on 24th August consisted at first of three *F.K.* under Otto, sent there the previous day on receipt of the news of Enslin's movement. Lettow has stated (" My Reminiscences ", p. 150) that he had at first intended to concentrate the whole of his forces against Enslin. With this object Otto was reinforced, first by two *F.K.* under Heyden-Linden, then by all the remaining units from Morogoro except the *Abteilung Stemmermann* (three *F.K.*) which was ordered to escort the heavy artillery by the better route east of the Uluguru range. Owing to the difficulty of the country beyond Mlali and the obvious danger of delay, the affair with Enslin was broken off and the Germans continued their retreat southwards through the mountains towards Kisaki.

[2] Op. cit.

[3] Presumably the track referred to is that followed by the small German force under Stemmermann (see f.n. 1 above) across the northern end of the Uluguru range, as shown in Sketch 45.

From Dakawa eighteen miles of tsetse-ridden and water-less country extended southwards to the high hills of Nguru-ya-Ndege and Kihonda covering Morogoro, which were known to have been strongly entrenched. To avoid direct attack on these, with its attendant difficulties of water-supply, Lieut.-General Smuts determined to turn them from the eastward.[1]

On the 23rd August his force left Dakawa, moving first for about nine miles north-eastward down the right (south) bank of the Wami, so as to shorten the distance to be traversed without water, then south-eastward towards the river Ngerengere, which was reached on the evening of the 24th near Msungulu. Among the many hardships of the campaign this march of over 30 miles in as many hours stands out as one of the most trying. The heat was over-whelming, the country broken and difficult, water non-existent between the rivers,[2] and from time to time extensive grass fires[3] added to the difficulties.

Beyond the Ngerengere the advanced guard mounted troops, led by Lieut.-Colonel A. J. Brink (G.S.O. 1, 3rd Division) on the 24th seized Mkogwa Hill; but German outlying posts still held the hills of Fulwe and Mkonge. During the 25th the exhaustion of men and animals enforced a day's halt, which was devoted to reconnaissance, in the course of which it was learned that the Germans were evacuating Morogoro. The sound of explosions in that direction tended to confirm this information.

Early on the 26th the 2nd Rhodesia Regiment and two companies of the 130th Baluchis were sent on to take posses-sion of Morogoro. They arrived in the afternoon to find that the last German rear parties had gone some hours earlier, leaving a considerable number of German non-combatants, mostly women and children. Some looting and disorder had taken place, but on the arrival of the Rhodesians order was quickly restored. Lieut.-General Smuts with his advanced G.H.Q. and the headquarters of the 1st Division entered Morogoro on the 27th August.[4]

---

[1] For all practical purposes the force, apart from its attached troops and the two battalions remaining of the 3rd Divn., consisted of the 1st Divn. For details see Note, p. 361.

[2] For example, No. 7 Fd. Bty., ox-drawn, which did not arrive till 7.30 a.m. on 25th, had had no water for 43½ hours.

[3] One considerable fire was started by a motor-cycle skid, the machine bursting into flames as the rider fell.

[4] G.H.Q. went back to Mohale on 28th.

" At Morogoro ", he wrote, " I found many proofs of " the precipitate flight and demoralized condition of the " enemy forces, and I decided to continue the pursuit in " spite of the fact that my forces and animals were worn " out with the exertions of the last three weeks and that my " transport had reached its extreme radius of action ".[1]

Between the Ngerengere river and the Central Railway no German forces of any importance now remained. But south of the railway the outlying heights of Bondwa and Pangawe were believed to be held, and in order to turn them the 1st East African Brigade (Sheppard) and 2nd East African Brigade (Hannyngton) were sent forward across the railway east of Morogoro with orders to converge on Kikundi. Starting on the 26th August from Msungulu, Sheppard, though delayed by a broken bridge near Mohale, crossed the railway on the 27th and pushed on through unknown mountainous country to the Kiroka Pass, encountering only a few snipers. To his left Hannyngton, reaching Mikese unopposed on the 27th, went on through Kikundi on the 28th to the Msumbisi river, where his advanced guard (57th Wilde's Rifles) found the wooden bridge set on fire by a German rearguard and were just in time to save it. Sheppard, meanwhile, had reached Kikundi.

By now it was evident that the whole of the German forces had withdrawn successfully to the southward, but it was still uncertain which routes they had taken.[2] Everything pointed, however, to Kisaki as the most probable rallying-point, and as his next step Lieut.-General Smuts

---

[1] Despatch, op. cit

[2] On 29th August, G.H.Q. Intelligence reported withdrawal of German units as follows (see Sketch 44) :

From Kilosa towards Uleia : two *F.K.*, one *Sch.K.*

From Morogoro :
    (a) via Mlali : six *F.K.*, five *Sch.K.*, one *Res.K.*
    (b) through the mountains : three *F.K.*, " *W* ".*K.*, and detachment.
    (c) via Kiroka Pass (Sketch 45) : ten *F.K.*

It is now known that the German units withdrew as follows :—
    (a) From Kilosa southwards via Uleia : *6., 15., 19., 25.F.K., 2., 5., 7., 8., 9.Sch.K., Abteilungen Arusha* and *Pangani.*
    (b) From Morogoro via Mlali : *1., 4., 9., 11., 13., 16., 17., 21., 23., 24., 27., 30.F.K., 14.Res.K., 1., 6.Sch.K.,* " *W* ".*K.*

Of these, *16.F.K.* left Kisaki on 1st September for Kidodi (7 miles south of Kikumi) to join the units named under (a).
    (c) From Morogoro through the mountains : Baggage, with small detachments.
    (d) From Morogoro via Kiroka Pass and Matombo : *3., 14., 18., 22.F.K.*
    (e) From Kidugalo (on the railway, 22 miles east of Mikese) via Tununguo : *4.Sch.K., Abteilungen Tanga* and *Wilhelmstal.*

planned to envelop them there. The 1st Division was therefore ordered to push on southwards on the eastern side of the Uluguru range, while Major-General Brits with the two battalions of the 2nd South African Infantry Brigade—the skeleton of his 3rd Division—was directed to join the mounted troops at Mlali and thence to hasten round the western side of the mountains.

Thus the physical obstacle presented by the Uluguru range led to the division of the British forces, a part of which, as will be seen in the next chapter, was in consequence subsequently defeated in detail.

NOTE

MAIN BRITISH FORCE, ORDER OF BATTLE, 23RD AUGUST 1916.

1st Division (Maj.-Genl. Hoskins) :

1st E.A. Bde.	2nd E.A. Bde.	1st Divl. Troops
(Br.-Genl. Sheppard)	(Br.-Genl. Hannyngton)	
2/Rhodesia Regt.	57th Wilde's Rifles	25/R. Fusiliers
29th Punjabis	½ Bn. 3/Kashmir	Gold Coast Regt.
130th Baluchis	Rifles	Cape Corps Bn.
2/Kashmir Rifles	3/K.A.R.	
Attached :	Attached :	
Sqdn. 17th Cav.	M.G. Coy., 2/L. N.	
5th Bty., S.A.F.A.	Lancs.	
1 sec. 27th Mtn.	M.G. Sec., 129th	
Bty., R.A.	Baluchis	
	E.A.M.R.	
	M.I., K.A.R.	
	7th Field Bty,	
	27th Mtn. Bty., R.A	
	(less 1 sec)	

3rd Division, less 2nd S.A. Mtd. Bde. (Maj.-Genl. Brits) :

2nd S.A. Inf. Bde.	3rd Divl. Troops
(less 7/, 8/S.A.I.)	
(Br.-Genl. Beves)	
5/S.A.I.	13th (How.) Bty.
6/S.A.I.	
Attached :	
8th Bty., S.A.F.A.	

Army Troops
9th Field Bty.
14th (How.) Bty.
134th (How.) Bty.

Note.—On 30th August the first of the new K.A.R. battalions (1/2nd K.A.R.) reached Morogoro by march route from Korogwe, to join the 1st Division.

CHAPTER XXII
OPERATIONS SOUTH OF THE CENTRAL RAILWAY
September 1916
(Sketches 47, 48, 49, 50, 50a, 51)

OPERATIONS OF THE FIRST DIVISION

Sketch 47 CONTINUING its southward march, the 1st Division was now to encounter somewhat heavier opposition. Early on the 29th August the 2nd East African Brigade (Hannyngton) crossed the Msumbisi. About 10 a.m. its advanced guard, the 3rd Kashmir Rifles, was checked by the well-directed fire of four guns (including one *Königsberg* 4·1-inch) and was only able to proceed after the 3/K.A.R. had been deployed and the 27th Mountain Battery, R.A. brought up in support. The column then made its way forward gradually through difficult country, reaching Pugu at nightfall.[1] Sheppard's brigade, meanwhile, moved up to the Msumbisi crossing, followed by the remainder of the force.

Heavy rain had now set in, which rendered the track impassable for wheeled transport and immobilized the guns and wagons of the division for some days, and a brief halt had to be made. Already exposure, following on the previous hardships, was bringing out latent malaria and dysentery among the troops, whose fighting strength continued to dwindle ;[2] but, with or without vehicles, it was imperative to push on, and on the afternoon of the 31st the movement was resumed.

The 57th Wilde's Rifles (2nd East African Brigade), with the brigade's attached section of the 27th Mountain Battery, R.A., under Colonel T. J. Willans, went forward from Pugu to secure the crossing of the Ruvu river.[3] Their progress through dense tropical forest was delayed by the German rear parties, but by dusk the column reached the river, here closely hemmed in by heights rising to 1,500 feet

---

[1] Casualties : 5 killed, 24 wounded.
[2] The three Indian battalions of the 1st E.A. Bde. now had in all only 15 British officers.
[3] " The distance was said to be four miles, but, owing to an inaccurate " map . . . turned out to be nine." Regimental History, 57th Wilde's Rifles.

or more. It was breast-deep, rapid and unbridged, the only aid to crossing being a single rope stretched across.[1] Using this, one company hauled itself across before nightfall, the remainder following at dawn.

The battalion now (1st September) launched a vigorous attack on the German rear-guards holding the slopes ahead, driving in the defence, and maintained itself under prolonged shelling until, later in the day, the 3/K.A.R. came up in support. The march was resumed next day, the enemy still making a fighting withdrawal.

At the Matombo mission-station, which was reached on the 3rd September, it was ascertained that the Germans had retreated to the heights of Kikarungu, four miles on, which rose some 3,000 feet above the road. Hannyngton's brigade was now reinforced from the divisional reserve by the lately arrived Gold Coast Regiment, which on the 4th September was sent forward to take Kikarungu.[2]

Under continuous artillery fire this battalion succeeded in occupying the foothills before night fell. Next morning (5th), the 3/K.A.R. was ordered to occupy the high hill of Lusangalale and turn the German left ; to the eastward the attenuated 25/Royal Fusiliers,[3] brought up from divisional reserve, moved to the high ridge of Magali, while the 57th came in on the left of the Gold Coast Regiment. During the day the advance, supported by the 27th Mountain Battery, R.A., was gradual. By dawn of the 6th, after much hard climbing, the 3/K.A.R. were on the western spurs of Kikarungu. The roads in rear having dried, the 5th (S.A.F.A.) and 7th Field Batteries came up to give additional support ; and that afternoon the enemy retired from Kikarungu out of touch. Almost all the losses in the

---

[1] The enemy had left all the steelwork for an intended high-level bridge. The material was at once used for road supports and building a temporary bridge.

[2] The Gold Coast Regt., a fine unit 1,428 strong, including 12 m.g., two 2·95-inch mountain guns and 177 specially-enlisted gun-carriers, had landed at Mombasa on 26th July and joined the main British force just after the action on the Wami (17th August). It had already made its name in Togoland and the Cameroons, where on 15th August, 1914, it was the first British unit in the whole war to be in action against the Germans. (See " Military Operations : Togoland and the Cameroons ", pp. 27–9.)

On 27th August, 1916, replying to an enquiry by the C.I.G.S., the C.-in-C. telegraphed : " Both from military and health point of view Gold Coast " Regt. has turned out great success. Any other troops that have been " seasoned in the fighting under Genl. Dobell would be welcome."

[3] The fighting strength of the 25/R.Fus., excluding its 4 m.g. detachments, was at this time down to less than 100.

three days' fighting had fallen on the Gold Coast Regiment ;[1] but in all units the stiff climbing and continual shortage of food, at times half rations or less, had severely taxed the troops engaged.

The next few days were no less arduous. On the 7th September the 3/K.A.R., with a section of the 27th Battery, drove the German rear-guard off the heights of Kasanga, five miles farther south. Meanwhile from Sheppard's brigade the 29th Punjabis, with another section of the 27th Battery, moved (as shown on Sketch 47) without opposition by an easterly route through Tununguo on Tulo, to which place the enemy was then believed to be retiring. Towards Tulo, therefore, Hannyngton's column converged, and after some further minor encounters the leading units of the 1st Division assembled there on the 9th September.

Whilst these operations had been in progress the remainder of the division, including most of the 1st Brigade, had been busily improving the road, the section of which south of the Ruvu needed much work to make it fit for vehicles.[2]

It was soon ascertained by reconnaissance that the enemy had fallen back on Kisaki in accordance with the Commander-in-Chief's expectation. Meanwhile, west of the Uluguru range, the two mounted brigades were moving southwards on that place.

OPERATIONS OF THE MOUNTED TROOPS

Sketch 48   On the 31st August, in compliance with the orders given by the Commander-in-Chief at his recent visit, Enslin with the 2nd South African Mounted Brigade, now reduced by its losses in horses to an effective strength of about 600,

---

[1] Killed, 1 officer (Captain J. F. P. Butler, V.C., D.S.O.), 6 o.r.; wounded, 36 o.r.

[2] Near the Ruvu crossing the road was carried on supports driven into the precipitous sides of the gorge in which the river flowed. Near Bukubuku it ran across steep hillsides descending 2,000 feet to the plain. Here its difficulties, indicated by the relics of former accidents and the beginnings of German work on a fresh alignment, made it for the time being impassable to M.T. ; but the new work begun by the enemy was continued and before long a practicable road—described in the C.-in-C.'s despatch as " a notable " and enduring engineering feat "—was formed. Beyond Bukubuku the road came to be known as " Sheppard's Pass ", Brig.-Genl. Sheppard, himself a Royal Engineer officer, having given much practical assistance with his brigade.

A *Königsberg* gun was found destroyed and abandoned north of the Ruvu crossing.

marched from Mlali to Msongosi, followed at a distance by Major-General Brits with the two South African battalions and two batteries of his exiguous 3rd Division, which on the same day left Morogoro.[1]

At Mahalaka, where it was found that the track leading to Kisaki was impassable for vehicles, all Brits's guns and wheeled transport were turned back to Morogoro, whence they took the easterly route in the wake of the 1st Division.[2] His force had therefore no artillery support. For the next three weeks, moreover, his battalions—the 5/ and 6/South African Infantry—were without greatcoats and blankets, while after the second day's march his units were on half rations or less.

The march south-eastwards from Mahalaka was un-eventful A few German patrols in the passes through the hills at Goma and Mfumbo were easily disposed of, and on the 5th September, when the infantry caught up, Brits's force of perhaps 1,200 rifles in all was assembled at Tyaduma, eight miles north-west of Kisaki.

For several days he had been out of communication with Nussey's mounted brigade to his left, from which no wireless messages came ; nor had he any reliable information as to the enemy's strength ahead of him. His instructions, however, had stressed the importance of seizing Kisaki as soon as possible, and he prepared to press on.

Meanwhile the 1st Mounted Brigade, having left all dismounted men at Mlali, made its way south-westwards through the mountains from Mgeta to Msagara. Reaching the latter place on the 1st September, Nussey found that the route which he had been ordered to take, marked on the map down the left bank of the Mgeta river, did not exist Without his wireless, he could receive no fresh instructions.[3]

Next, therefore, acting on native reports of German troops to the eastward at Chibuka and on Njofu Hill, Nussey secured these localities on the 3rd, driving off small parties of the enemy. He then turned to deal with a hostile force reported to be at Kikeo, six miles south of him on a direct

---

[1] See Order of Battle, p. 361.
[2] One of the C.-in-C.'s difficulties throughout the campaign, notably in the Uluguru operations, was the almost total lack of reliable information as to roads and tracks to be traversed.
[3] See p. 368, f.n. 2.
Runners sent to Mlali to request orders from Major-General Brits arrived after he had left for Mahalaka and were unable to gain touch with him.

route to Kisaki, where he arrived unopposed on the 4th. From the heights German detachments had been seen in retreat, well out of range ; as they went they set fire to dumps of stores and ammunition.[1] But Nussey's men were desperately exhausted and short of food ; many of his horses had foundered in their struggle in the mountains, and it was not until the 7th September that the 1st Mounted Brigade approached the twin hills of Whigu, six miles out from Kisaki and barely five from Brits's force, of whose whereabouts Nussey knew nothing.

Thus, enclosed in the thick bush and unable to communicate, isolated therefore as completely as if separated by a week's march, each column was unaware of the position and intentions of the other.[2] Major-General Brits, who had reached Tyaduma two days before, had not pushed out to the two Whigu Hills from which patrols or possibly even visual signalling might have established contact with Nussey's approaching column, and his plans at this stage do not appear to have taken Nussey into account.

On the 7th September Brits went on towards Kisaki, his infantry under Brig.-General Beves moving with difficulty through the elephant-grass along the Mgeta river (see Sketch 48) while Enslin with the mounted troops made a detour southwards to cut the Kisaki–Iringa road. About 1 p.m. Beves met not only hostile fire but a demoralizing onslaught, as had happened to others at Tanga and Kahe, by wild bees. After some confusion and delay, the transport animals seeming to be specially selected for attack, the march was resumed, progress through the bush being still difficult, and the column crossed to the left bank of the river, driving off a German outpost at the crossing. Towards 4.30 p.m. it came up against strongly-held German defences[3] some two miles short of the boma (3 miles west of Kisaki), and Beves decided to dig in for the night.

---

[1] The enemy's formation of these dumps, which included gun ammunition, suggests that he had intended to make a fighting retirement, but was compelled by Brits's outflanking movement through Mahalaka to retreat in haste to secure the safety of Kisaki.

[2] Their situation was equally unknown at G.H.Q. In the absence of wireless reports the only means of ascertaining their position was from the air, the difficulty of which in bush country has already been mentioned. Air observers who on 6th September reported " our mounted troops " in Kisaki " proved later to have mistaken cattle for the South Africans' horses.

[3] Held by *Abteilung Otto* (*23.*, *24.F.K.*, *6.Sch.K.*, *14.Res.K.*).

Farther south Enslin's brigade, completely out of touch with Beves,[1] had meanwhile been hotly engaged since noon with a considerable force of the enemy,[2] which succeeded in outflanking his right and captured a number of his horses. Unable to make use of their mobility in the bush, his men suffered considerable loss in hand-to-hand fighting before at last they were withdrawn to Tyaduma.[3]

About 10 p.m. a German attack on Brig.-General Beves's force north of the river was easily beaten off. This incident, however, coupled with the repulse of Enslin, decided Major-General Brits to withdraw the two battalions, which accordingly, after an unavailing appeal by both their commanders to the brigadier against any retreat, effected a skilful and unmolested retirement in darkness, rejoining 3rd Division headquarters on the western (or " Big ") Whigu Hill by 4.30 a.m. on the 8th September.

None of the firing during the 7th had been heard by Nussey's troops, only five miles away, which at dawn on the 8th moved against the northern slopes of the eastern (or " Little ") Whigu Hill and occupied them about 8 a.m. Between the hill and the boma, which stood out conspicuously four miles to the south, lay a belt of bush and forest in which opposition was encountered almost at once.[4] Deployed with the 4th Horse to the right, 3rd in the centre, 9th to the left and 2nd Horse in reserve, the brigade was hotly engaged throughout the day, the enemy making repeated and vigorous attempts to envelop both flanks. Between 2 and 3 p.m. the situation on the left flank became serious. The reserve was brought up just in time to deal with a determined bayonet charge by the enemy, which was repulsed in severe hand-to-hand fighting.[5] About 5 p.m. the Germans withdrew, leaving the 1st Mounted Brigade in possession

---

[1] So far as can be ascertained, no arrangements had been made for intercommunication or co-ordination of movement between Beves and Enslin.

[2] *Abteilung Schulz (4., 9., 13., 21.F.K.)* and *Abteilung v. Liebermann (11., 27.F.K., " W ".K.)*, totalling about 1,200, with 14 m.g. According to Lettow (" My Reminiscences ", p. 154) the decisive incident was a counter-attack with the bayonet by *11.F.K.*

[3] Casualties 16 killed, 24 wounded.

[4] Nussey's total effective strength was now about 500, with 4 m.g. The German force here was the *Abteilung Tafel (1., 17., 30.F.K., 1.Sch.K.)*, strength about 700, with 8 m.g.

[5] The charge was made by the *Abteilung v. Liebermann*, the same which had similarly distinguished itself against Enslin on the previous day (see f.n. 2 above).

of the field.[1] Since, however, throughout the day neither men nor horses, already exhausted by their week's march, had had food or water, the brigade could do no more.

That evening Nussey learned that Brits was near Tyaduma, and at nightfall, detaching the 4th Horse to hold Little Whigu, he withdrew the rest of his brigade to Sungomero, where at least there was water. Next day (9th) the 1st Mounted Brigade joined forces with Major-General Brits.

By this time, however, both mounted brigades were so worn out and so depleted in numbers that there could be no question of any immediate further attack by them.[2]

Had Major-General Brits moved to Nussey's assistance the result of the day's fighting would doubtless have been very different. But, in the words of Lieut.-General Smuts's despatch already quoted, " although this action " (Nussey's) " could be heard from Brits's camp, it was found impossible, " owing to the ruggedness of the terrain and the thickness " of the bush, to go to his assistance. If communication " between Brits and Nussey could have been maintained " there is no doubt a joint attack would have led to the " capture of Kisaki, whereas the two isolated efforts led to a " double retirement and a regrettable recovery of enemy " morale ".

It was fortunate that Lettow, whose main concern was obviously to avoid being caught between Hoskins and Brits, did not make use of the three days (8th–10th) in which he might well have inflicted crushing defeat on the latter.[3]

---

[1] British casualties were 4 officers, 19 o.r. killed and about 20 wounded. German losses are not known.

[2] " Nussey's own account of the condition of his brigade before moving " south through the Uluguru " is given in " The South Africans with " General Smuts " (Collyer) as follows : " . . . over 60 per cent. of my " strength were dismounted and their boots and clothing were in an awful " state. I had no pack mules or porters. My battery became hopelessly " immobile at this stage. The only roads . . . were native tracks from " one native town to another . . . all situated on the heights. My greatest " embarrassment . . . was ammunition, so I . . . commandeered 200 porters. " The second night . . . these impressed men escaped during a thunder- " storm and I had to bury 80 cases of ammunition on the top of a mountain. " . . . The mule carrying my wireless set fell over a precipice the second " day after I left Mlali."

[3] Lettow appears to have thought the country about Kisaki too diffi- cult, and to have been more concerned with the threat by the 1st Divn. from the north-east, against which he " considered the opportunity " favourable for achieving a success at Dutumi "—or Nkessa's (see Sketch 47)—" by rapidly moving his main body there from Kisaki." " My Reminiscences ", p. 156.

THE AFFAIR OF THE DUTUMI, 10TH—12TH SEPTEMBER 1916

On the 9th September, hearing of the check to Brits's **Sketches** force west of Kisaki, Lieut.-General Smuts ordered the **47, 49** 1st Division to push on from Tulo to the Dutumi river. The 2nd East African Brigade, with the 3rd Kashmir Rifles as advanced guard, moved off before dawn on the 10th along the Kisaki road and at 10 a.m., after dislodging a well-concealed German outpost, found German troops entrenched some 1,200 yards east of the river.[1] About and beyond Nkessa's the enemy was reported to be in considerable force.

At the same time the 57th Wilde's Rifles, with a section **Sketch 50** of the 27th Mountain Battery, R.A., moved out to the right flank and by noon had seized the high hill of Kitoho which commanded the road, driving a small enemy detachment from the summit and knocking out, with a direct hit, a German gun located near the village beyond the river. During the afternoon the 3/K.A.R. followed the 57th, with orders to pass behind Kitoho and turn the German left. By dusk this battalion had reached without opposition a small stream, of whose water it was badly in need.

In the plain the 3rd Kashmir Rifles, with the machine-gun company of the 2/Loyal North Lancashire on their left and supported by the remaining guns of the 27th Mountain Battery, were strongly opposed and had made but little progress through the tangled elephant grass along the road when night fell.

At dawn on the 11th the 3/K A.R. on the extreme northern flank pushed forward to the Dutumi, which two companies crossed. The movement (not shown on the sketch) of this battalion southwards down both banks of the river was checked at noon by strong enemy opposition which increased until at about 5 p.m. a German counter-attack drove back the two companies that were on the western bank.[2]

Meanwhile during the morning of the 11th, the 5th Battery, S.A.F.A., which had arrived the previous day—the new section of road through Sheppard's Pass having been

---

[1] *Abteilung Stemmermann (3., 14., 18., 22.F.K., 4.Sch.K.),* about 900 in all, with 10 m.g.

[2] The counter-attack was made by the *Abteilung v. Liebermann* already twice so used (see p. 367, f.n. 2, 5) which had just arrived from Kisaki. Four other *F.K.,* with three small units equivalent together to another, had also come up, Lettow himself coming with them. The enemy's total force was now about 2,200, with some 24 m.g.

opened to traffic—came into action on the Kisaki road; the Gold Coast Regiment came up from reserve, sending two companies round Kitoho to reinforce the 3/K.A.R. on the extreme right while the remainder of the battalion extended the left of the attacking line in the plain.

The night of the 11th/12th September was quiet. Daylight of the 12th revealed that on the lower ridge of Kitoho the Germans had abandoned their defences, over which the 57th at once swept down towards Nkessa's, while beyond the 57th the 3/K.A.R. and the two Gold Coast companies, now hampered only by the difficulty of the ground, went forward west of the Dutumi.

South of the road, however, the enemy maintained a stubborn resistance throughout the day. In the late afternoon a German counter-attack was launched on the left of the line against the Gold Coast Regiment, whose flank company had thrust ahead temporarily out of touch. The effort failed ; neither side, in fact, could make headway in the thick vegetation.

Along the road the 3rd Kashmir Rifles had now made progress, inclining right-handed to gain touch with the 57th on ground from which the enemy opposing the North Lancashire machine guns was enfiladed, the 3/K.A.R. meanwhile working forward to gain ridges overlooking the German left and line of retreat. Confused fighting in the bush and plantations north of Nkessa's went on into the afternoon, spreading along the line until 7.30 p.m., when it died away.

Again the night was quiet, and at dawn on the 13th September the all too familiar discovery was made that the enemy had once again withdrawn out of touch.[1]

---

[1] British casualties totalled about 90, including 3 officers, 34 o.r. in the Gold Coast Regt., 22 in the 3/K.A.R. Enemy losses in Europeans are given by Schnee as 2 killed, 12 wounded.

The German movements—an example of operations on interior lines—seem to have been as follows :

On 7th September Otto, with four companies (see p. 366, f.n. 3) was facing Brits ; Tafel, four companies (see p. 367, f.n. 4) was in readiness against Nussey's approach ; Stemmermann, five companies with other detachments (see p. 369, f.n. 1) was retiring on Tulo before the 1st Divn. ; Schulz, four companies and von Liebermann, three companies (see p. 367, f.n. 2) were in reserve at Kisaki.

Against Brits on 7th September Otto was reinforced by Schulz and Liebermann ; next day the two last-named marched north to reinforce Tafel against Nussey.

On 11th September Stemmermann's group, opposing the 1st Divn. at the Dutumi, was reorganized into two groups under Boemcken, while

Continued at foot of next page.

OCCUPATION OF KISAKI

From the 9th to the 12th September Major-General Sketch 49
Brits's famished and worn-out units, still short of supplies,
snatched a breathing-space about Tyaduma. On the 11th,
whilst the fight on the Dutumi was in progress, he was
directed by the Commander-in-Chief to co-operate by moving
on Kisaki from the west and north and by threatening the
enemy's southward line of retreat.

Of information regarding the enemy he had little, and
the plight of his troops precluded all possibility of thrusting
into the trackless and almost impenetrable bush to the
south, a move which in any case the enemy could certainly
have frustrated. On the 12th, therefore, he ordered the
two mounted brigades, now totalling some 1,200, under
Brig.-General Enslin, to move eastwards next day on Mgasi,
thence to strike southwards to Korongo in order to cut the
road east of Kisaki.

Reaching Korongo on the 14th, Enslin learned that the
Germans had evacuated Kisaki and withdrawn eastwards
to hold the south bank of the Mgeta river ; upon which
Brits sent the 5/ and 6/South African Infantry forward into
Kisaki, where they found many German sick and wounded
left behind. In the meantime Hoskins's patrols pushed
forward from Nkessa's through Dakawa to make contact
with Enslin.

Lieut.-General Smuts's two forces were thus once again
in touch, but as before, Colonel von Lettow, with everything in his favour, had eluded his more powerful opponent.

OPERATIONS ON THE MGETA

East of Kisaki the German forces were now well Sketch 49
established along the southern bank of the Mgeta.

Enslin, as yet unaware that Brits's infantry was in
Kisaki, and keeping his two mounted brigades in hand
between Korongo and Dakawa, sent the 7th South African
Horse to cross the river on the 15th September and

Continued from previous page.
on the German right Schulz, and on the left Liebermann with one of Tafel's
companies, were brought in, making a total equivalent to thirteen F.K.
against the 3½ British battalions engaged.

The German troops at this time were probably almost as exhausted
as the British. After referring to their "extraordinary exertions"
(unerhörte Anstrengungen) at the Dutumi, Arning's Vier Jahre Weltkrieg
states (p. 200) that they were so worn out that they fell asleep standing
up (Europäer wie Askari schliesslich im Stehen einschliefen).

reconnoitre eastwards along it and towards Kiderengwe. On this and the following day the regiment met considerable opposition, but successfully made good a crossing five miles east of Kisaki. Meanwhile Major-General Brits moved his infantry eastwards to the crossing and in the face of vigorous resistance established a bridge-head south of the river.

His troops, however, were by this time no longer in fighting condition. Increasingly exhausted by the exertions of the preceding weeks and the continuing shortage of supplies, their numbers depleted by sickness, and almost at the end of their powers, they could do little more than hold their ground. The bush was strongly held by the enemy, who continually sniped the British outposts and from time to time started bush fires which constituted an additional difficulty.[1] For the next two weeks Major-General Brits's troops remained immobile.

All the information now available indicated the enemy's resolve to stand along the Mgeta. In the almost impassable vegetation and network of streams in the malaria-infested Mgeta valley the location and extent of the German positions could not be exactly determined ; but at G.H.Q. it was reasonably assumed that they could hardly extend eastwards as far as Msogera. On this assumption the Commander-in-Chief directed Major-General Hoskins to co-operate with Major-General Brits by threatening the German right flank, sending a battalion across the Mgeta near Msogera, with a second battalion ready in support, but without becoming too deeply committed.[2]

Accordingly on the night of the 18th/19th September the 3/K.A.R., followed at dawn by the Gold Coast Regiment, moved off from Nkessa's down the right bank of the Dutumi, reaching the junction with the Mgeta, which was found in flood but fordable, at 6.30 a.m. on the 19th. The crossing was unopposed, but towards midday, after moving up the farther bank to Msogera and driving in an outlying enemy piquet, the 3/K.A.R. were checked by strongly held German

---

[1] Under cover of one such fire on 20th September, the enemy attempted an attack in considerable strength which was driven off.

On this occasion Brits once more had artillery support from the 3rd Bty., S.A.F.A., which had rejoined after a circuitous march from Mahalaka (see p. 365) via Morogoro and Tulo.

[2] This statement is based on a telegram sent by Major-General Hoskins to the 2nd E.A. Brigade on 18th September which is worded : " Chief wishes you to . . . "

No copy of any G.H.Q. order on the subject can be traced.

defences in the bush.   Here the battalion dug itself in, beating off a heavy attack in the evening, and during the night it consolidated a defensive position resting on the river, with a view to forming a bridgehead.   A company of the Gold Coast Regiment joined it on the 20th, with the remainder of that regiment on the northern bank, and the position was maintained,[1] the K.A.R. bridging the river meanwhile, until the 25th September, when the latter battalion was relieved by the former.

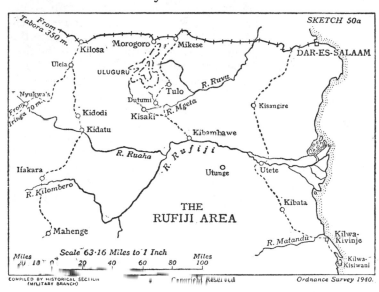

SKETCH 50a

THE RUFIJI AREA

Scale 63·16 Miles to 1 Inch

COMPILED BY HISTORICAL SECTION (MILITARY BRANCH)

Copyright Reserved

Ordnance Survey 1940.

The Germans, however, gave no sign of contemplating withdrawal ; on the contrary, guns and howitzers were brought up and the enemy appeared determined to hold his ground.

Confronted thus by a well-organized defence in very difficult country, and doubting therefore whether an advance from the Dutumi to the crossing of the Rufiji at Kibambawe would be practicable, the Commander-in-Chief decided on the 20th September to launch a strong outflanking column farther to the east, from Tulo towards the lower Rufiji.[2]

---

[1] During the night 20th/21st the Mgeta overflowed its banks and nearly rendered occupation of the position impossible.

[2] War Diary, Advanced G.H.Q.

For this purpose, so long as Kraut's forces south of Kilosa remained to be disposed of and German movements eastward from Tabora were also to be reckoned with, clearly the 2nd Division could not be used. The 1st East African Brigade (Sheppard) had completed its work on the road behind the 1st Division, so that the whole Mgeta front **Sketch 49** could be taken over by that division. Brits's 3rd Division would thus be released to carry out the fresh move now in contemplation.

This plan, however, was short-lived.[1] Heavy rain almost every day during the rest of September again rendered the roads impassable to vehicles and made the supply situation worse than ever.[2] The resulting administrative difficulties delayed the relief of the 3rd Division until the first week in October. In the meantime impending developments on the coast at Kilwa[3] seemed likely to induce a German withdrawal, or at any rate to prevent any hostile counter-offensive on the Mgeta ; and in view of this, and of the imperative necessity of resting his sorely tried troops,[4] Lieut.-General Smuts directed the 1st Division to " refrain " from attacking the enemy "[5] and stand on the defensive. In compliance with these instructions the operations on the Mgeta, apart from minor patrol skirmishes, came to an end.

OPERATIONS BY THE 2ND DIVISION

Sketch 51   It will be remembered that when, after the 2nd Division reached Kilosa (22nd August), the 1st South African Mounted Brigade was sent on to Mlali, the 1st South African Horse remained with the division.[6] This unit, now reduced to a strength of about 300, followed up the retreat southwards of Kraut's companies from Kilosa[7] and at noon on the 25th August overtook and engaged the German rearguard near Uleia, some 18 miles south of Kilosa, losing 2 killed and 4 wounded in the skirmish which ensued. On the following afternoon the Germans continued their retreat, heading south for Mfilisi and Kidodi.

---

[1] The relief of the 3rd Division was postponed on 21st September. (War Diary, Adv. G.H.Q.)

[2] See Chap. XXIII, Note I, p. 393.   [3] See p. 386.

[4] " . . . our men were exhausted and worn out with ceaseless fighting " and marching for several weeks through most difficult country on half " rations or less, and a thorough rest was imperatively necessary, not only " on military, but also on medical grounds." Despatch, op. cit.

[5] Telegram, 26th Sept., B.G.G.S. to 1st Divn.

[6] See p. 356.   [7] See p. 343, f.n. 1.

The Commander-in-Chief now directed Major-General van Deventer to push on the 1st Horse with two infantry battalions towards Kidodi and the crossing of the Ruaha river at Kidatu, and on the 28th August the 10/ and 11/S. African Infantry, with the 2nd Battery, S.A.F.A., joined the 1st Horse at Uleia to form a mixed column under Lieut.-Colonel N. H. M. Burne, of the 11/S.A.I.

During the next four days the column followed up the enemy, meeting no opposition worth mentioning. At dusk on the 2nd September its units, pushing on ahead of their transport, halted at Kikumi, 28 miles from Uleia, in the valley of the Luhembe river down which the Germans were retreating. On moving out from Kikumi next morning, the column at once met with determined resistance by the German rearguard from well-sited and strongly-held positions covering the line of route, and was held up all day. At dawn on the 4th the Germans were found to have withdrawn, and throughout this day the South Africans followed up a slowly and skilfully conducted retreat through difficult bush intersected by rocky ravines. Again, however, they outstripped their transport, and after a hard day the leading companies lay without food or water until long after dark.[1] Although next morning the enemy was found once more to have withdrawn a short distance, both exhaustion of the troops and the increasing difficulty of the country—the track among the rocks needing much work to make it passable for guns and vehicles—prevented an immediate resumption of the pursuit.

Reinforcement, however, was at hand. Leaving Kilosa on the 31st August, the 12/S. African Infantry with the 28th Mountain Battery, R.A., under Lieut.-Colonel L. M. Davies of the latter unit, had come up with Burne's headquarters, some three miles south-east of Kikumi, towards evening of the 4th September.

One squadron of the 1st Horse was already wide on the right flank watching the high hills commanding the track and an enveloping movement against the German left was now planned. On the morning of the 5th Davies, leaving a section of his mountain battery to support Burne until the South African battery could move forward, took his force westwards across the Luhembe at a point some

---

[1] Casualties, 3rd and 4th September : killed, 3 officers, 2 o.r. ; wounded, 1 officer, 11 o.r.

distance in rear of Burne's position, and turned south-east along a rough track parallel to the river. Carrying the detached squadron forward with him over the foothills, he met no appreciable opposition until he reached the tributary Msolwe river late on the 6th.

Here the Germans were found holding the lower spurs of the high ridge of the Bismarckberg which rises steeply to the west of the track beyond the Msolwe. Intending to gain the crest the same evening, Davies disposed his force for attack ; but his progress was hampered by the rough ground, more especially by the deep and rocky·ravine of the Msolwe, and the operation was deferred until the morning. Fitting into this plan came information that Burne, now some distance in rear and, in the words of a subsequent account, " pushing frontally against the complex " of Kraut's machine guns in the bush ", proposed to attack at the same time.

At 5.30 a.m. on the 7th September, without waiting for food,[1] two companies of the 12/S. African Infantry, with two machine guns, went forward, and by 8 a.m. the lower end of the ridge had been occupied by part of these companies. They now came under heavy fire from German guns on a ridge beyond ; these were immediately silenced by the 28th Battery, and little other opposition was met. On the right flank the squadron of the 1st Horse, missing its way, did not reach the final crest ; but in the meantime the remainder of the two attacking companies scaled the almost precipitous hillsides, driving off a German outpost, and after an arduous climb up the lateral spurs of the main ridge gained its dominating key point unopposed. To their left the machine-guns, man-handled when the famished mules gave out, had been carried with equal energy and determination to the crest. By noon the whole ridge had been secured.

An attempted German counter-attack against the lower slopes was promptly beaten off, the machine guns from above, in particular, coming in by surprise with great effect. That afternoon and evening Davies consolidated his position, prepared for further German attack ; but the presence of Davies's force on the heights gained by the fine work of the 12/S. African Infantry, immediately overlooking Kraut's line of retreat, caused a prompt German withdrawal.

---

[1] Many of the men who fought on this day had had no food for 36 hours.

During the night (7th/8th) flames in Kidodi, presumably from stores being destroyed, were seen from the ridge ; and by the morning of the 8th no further opposition remained before either Davies or Burne.[1]

During these operations Major-General van Deventer went from Kilosa to Kadoma and personally took control of the final stage. After a day's rest on the 9th, the two columns converged on Kidodi, dislodging the enemy with little difficulty from the last of his rearguard positions north of that place, and by the evening of the 10th Kidodi was occupied.

Here the southward move came of necessity to an end for the time being. Transport and supply difficulties had become insuperable, and the troops, worn out by incessant hardship, could do no more.[2] The enemy fell back to a strong natural position some five miles south-west of Kidodi and, except that the place was intermittently shelled by a *Königsberg* gun—as at Msiha camp, out of range of the British artillery—hostile activity was suspended.[3]

With the breaking of the " small rains " ten days later the supply situation, here as on the Mgeta, became even more difficult, and for the next three weeks any further effort was out of the question.

---

[1] British casualties, 1 killed, 1 wounded. German losses are not known, but there is no doubt that in the attempted counter-attack on Davies the enemy lost somewhat heavily. Ten boxes of enemy ammunition and much equipment were found abandoned.

[2] " I cannot too strongly emphasize the arduous nature of these " operations, the troops being compelled to climb ridge and mountain " through bush, heavy grass, and dehitu, often without food and without " opportunities of cooking even when rations were issued, at times without " water . . ." (Brig.-General Berrange, operation report.)

On 10th September the war diary of the 3rd S.A. Inf. Bde. records a medical report that 50 per cent. of the troops were unfit for further service through debility due to underfeeding.

On 27th the war diary of the 2nd Divn. gives figures as follows :

		Fit.	Unfit.
3rd S.A. Inf. Bde.	.. ..	1,803	1,065
1st S.A. Mtd. Bde.	..	1,974	590
S.A. Motor Cycle Corps	..	220	48
3rd Div. Troops (att.)	..	755	243
Total..	..	4,752	1,946

[3] Arning (" *Vier Jahre Weltkrieg* ", p. 201) describes how this gun was man-handled across the Msolwe (" a ravine 150 to 180 metres deep " with a 40-degree gradient "). The enemy's continued transportation of these guns in most difficult country was a fine performance.

CHAPTER XXIII

THE COASTAL AREA:

OCCUPATION OF DAR-ES-SALAAM AND THE SOUTHERN PORTS

(Sketches 37, 50a, 52, 53, 53a, 54)

Sketch 37 AT the beginning of August, as a previous chapter has recorded, the area between the sea and Lieut.-General Smuts's line of communication from Msiha Camp back to Korogwe was clear of the enemy. The 40th Pathans, whom it was intended to recall to the main force on the Msiha, were at Manga, some 25 miles north-east of Msiha Camp ; the Royal Navy had landed parties at the minor ports of Mkwaja and Sadani, and had been relieved at the latter place by the 2/West India Regiment, lately brought by sea from Tanga.[1] Reliable local information indicated that the Germans had withdrawn south of the river Wami and were holding in some strength the crossing just south of Mandera.

Approval was now given to plans made by the I.G.C., Brig.-General W. F. S. Edwards, for the seizure of the more important port of Bagamoyo, 30 miles south of Sadani, which was believed not to be held in any strength.[2] For this purpose the available troops were organized in two columns co-operating under the orders of Colonel C. U. Price. Of these, "A" Column, consisting of the 40th Pathans and Jind Infantry, about 800 in all under Lieut.-Colonel W. J. Mitchell, was to move from Manga to seize the crossing of the Wami river near Mandera. "B" Column, the 2/West India Regiment with 50 men each of the Zanzibar Rifles and Intelligence Scouts, totalling about 600, under Lieut.-Colonel C. W. Long, moving first southwards from Sadani to secure the crossing of the river at Wami village, was then to turn westwards along the southern bank of the Wami to join forces with "A" Column. With the two river-crossings in his hands Brig.-General Edwards

---

[1] The 2/W.I.Regt., coming from Sierra Leone, reached Mombasa by way of the Cape on 27th July ; strength 16 B.O., 7 W.O., 492 o.r. The local natives were puzzled by this battalion of negroes, indistinguishable in appearance from themselves, yet treated as white and speaking English. Its men came to be called *Wazungu Waeusi* (black Europeans).

[2] On 5th August a bombardment by H.M.S. *Vengeance* drew no reply.

then proposed, in conjunction with the Royal Navy, to seize Bagamoyo and move down the coast against Dar-es- **End Paper** Salaam.[1] **(N)**

On the 8th August " B " Column duly effected a crossing Sketch 37 at Wami, unopposed, and three days later, having left small garrisons there and at Sadani, it moved on south-westward, passing through Lukambara on the 14th. On the same day " A " Column, now under Major H. S. Tyndall,[2] which had left Manga on the 12th, followed by a bridging-section of the 3rd Sappers & Miners, reached Mandera ; and on the 15th the two columns met south of the river-crossing, where " B " Column had arrived early in the day to find only a small German force which was driven off without difficulty.

The absence of opposition was a surprise to the two columns, for in recently captured German documents great stress had been laid on the importance of defending the crossing. In the meanwhile, however, the I.G.C. had learned that the enemy's units detailed for its defence[3] had been withdrawn to hold the ferry crossing over the Kingani river at Mtoni, four miles west of Bagamoyo.

With a view to forestalling any opposition there, Brig.-General Edwards suggested on the 12th August to the naval Commander-in-Chief, Rear-Admiral Charlton, that Bagamoyo, now reported to have a garrison only 50 strong, should be taken by the Royal Navy. He explained that his troops were at the moment committed to the combined movement on the Mandera crossing, but that he hoped to be able to relieve any naval landing parties within a few days. The suggestion was at once accepted.

THE CAPTURE OF BAGAMOYO, 15TH AUGUST 1916 [4]

Contrary to the military opinion, Rear-Admiral Charlton believed Bagamoyo to be strongly held. Seaplane recon- Sketch 52 naissance had discovered trenches at the northern end of the town covering the best beach for landing, and had located at the southern end two possible centres of resistance screened by trees from the shore, one at the Governor's strongly-built

---

[1] This further move against Dar-es-Salaam was, on 7th August, vetoed temporarily by the C.-in-C.
[2] Lt.-Col. Mitchell fell sick on 12th.
[3] *4.Sch.* and *5.Sch.K.*, with other detachments, under Boemcken.
[4] This operation is not recorded in " Naval Operations ".

house and another at the walled " Old Boma " about 200 yards away. These, enclosed by entrenchments, were selected as the first objectives.

The Admiral decided to land a force just over 300 strong, with four machine guns and six Lewis guns, under Commander R. J. N. Watson, R.N.[1] Of this force one-third, composed of Royal Marines and Zanzibar Rifles, was to attack the Governor's house ; the boma was assigned to the naval party forming the remainder.

Before daylight on the 15th August the squadron, consisting of the battleship *Vengeance*, the cruiser *Challenger*, the monitors *Mersey* and *Severn*, with the armed tug *Helmuth* and other small craft, anchored off Bagamoyo. At 5.30 a.m. six tows started in line abreast from the ships, covered by the fire of the monitors. The fire was answered, unexpectedly, by a *Königsberg* gun outside the southern end of the town and by a fusillade of rifle, machine gun and light artillery fire from the northern beach ; whereupon Commander Watson turned his flotilla towards the heavy gun, zig-zagging, his steam-boats and the *Helmuth* opening with 3-pdrs. as they closed in. The German gun was silenced by the time the tows were within 500 yards of the shore, and by 6 a.m. the parties had landed.

Led by Captain R. H. Thomas, R.M., the Royal Marines rushed the beach, which was not defended, and turned right-handed through the trees to attack the Governor's house. At the same time the main body, under Lieut. E. S. Brooksmith, R.N., advanced against the boma and a detachment under Sub-Lieut. F. G. S. Manning, R.N.R., with a machine gun, turned left to deal with the German gun. This was secured intact, the first *Königsberg* gun to be captured in open fight ; its detachment, sheltering under

---

[1] Composition :
    (a) Royal Navy :
        from *Vengeance*, 8 officers, 50 o.r.
        from *Challenger*, 5 officers, 50 o.r.
        from other ships, 3 officers, 69 o.r.
    (b) Royal Marines :
        from *Vengeance*, 20 o.r.
        from *Challenger*, 11 o.r.
        from *Talbot*, 1 officer, 33 o.r.
    (c) Zanzibar African Rifles :
        1 officer, 54 o.r.
    (d) Intelligence Scouts :
        1 officer, 18 o.r.
    Total : 19 officers, 305 o.r.

cover, fled hastily on being taken by surprise from their right flank.[1] The boma was found unoccupied.

The Royal Marines took possession of the Governor's house without difficulty, but were fired on from the trenches between it and the shore. These were charged with the bayonet and cleared in a brief hand-to-hand fight, in which both Captain Thomas and the German officer in command, Captain Bock von Wülfingen, were killed.

Meanwhile the Admiral received reports, both from the air and by wireless from the landing party, that German troops from the northern end of the town were hurrying southward to meet the British attack. His ships thereupon shelled the town, at about 6,500 yards, and under their fire the Germans melted away into the bush inland.[2] Commander Watson then occupied the town, piqueting the landward side and reassuring the inhabitants. Most of these were found to have taken refuge about the mission church west of the town, where, although that building had been damaged by a shell, no other harm was done.[3] Except for a fire in the native quarter, the town escaped lightly, the European houses for the most part being intact. From midday onwards all was quiet.[4]

THE OCCUPATION OF DAR-ES-SALAAM

The capture of Bagamoyo having cleared the way and Sketch 53 the crossings of the Wami having been secured, Colonel Price withdrew " B " Column to the coast near Sadani, sending 100 men of the 2/West India Regiment by sea to relieve the naval landing party at Bagamoyo.[5] The next objective was Dar-es-Salaam.

[1] One gunner had stayed to relieve the breech block which was later found in a pit near by. About 100 rounds of 4·1 inch ammunition were captured. There is no record of this gun having subsequently been taken into use against the enemy.

[2] It is believed that one shell killed the German commander, Capt. von Boedecker, and that his force then broke up in disorder.

[3] The German bishop steadied the morale of his congregation by celebrating Mass during the shelling by the ships.

[4] Casualties ascertained were : British, 4 killed, 7 wounded ; German, killed, 2 officers, 10 o.r., prisoners, 4 Germans, 15 askari.

The German garrison was found to have consisted of the *Abteilung Boedecker*, including *3.Sch.K.*, total 60 Germans, 350 askari, with 2 m.g., 1 light gun, 1 4·1-inch gun. The heavy gun had arrived from Dar-es-Salaam, drawn by 500 porters, a few days earlier.

[5] The detachment took over the defences of Bagamoyo on 18th August, and was followed two days later by the rest of the 2nd West India Regt., the Jind Infantry, and a mixed detachment of 300 S. African Infantry collected from the L. of C.

During the previous weeks, reconnaissance by the Royal Navy had disclosed elaborate entrenchments a few miles north of Dar-es-Salaam, both round Msasani Bay and near Upanga, while from the latter locality a *Königsberg* gun had fired on the monitors when they made a feint of landing. After Bagamoyo had been secured the attention of the naval squadron was concentrated on the German capital for several days and nights, selected targets of military importance being systematically shelled.[1]

Meanwhile Brig.-General Edwards assembled at Bagamoyo a force totalling about 1,900, with 20 machine guns, under Colonel Price. Included in it was " A " Column, of which the 40th Pathans were to secure the important railway bridge over the Kingani at Ruvu station on the Central Railway, forty miles west of Dar-es-Salaam, while the Jind Infantry was to march on Ngerengere station, forty miles farther west again.[2] Whilst possession of the railway linking Morogoro to Dar-es-Salaam was thus being gained the bulk of Colonel Price's force, following the coast and supported from the sea by the Royal Navy, was to seize Dar-es-Salaam.

On the 31st August these movements began. The coastal force marched in two columns, each about 800 strong ; one along the coast itself, accompanied at sea by an " inshore squadron " composed of the *Mersey* and *Severn*, the gunboat *Thistle* and the *Helmuth*, and one by a parallel route some miles inland.[3]

All available information indicated that the German troops had been withdrawn from Dar-es-Salaam ; it was,

---

[1] On the night of 21st August, H.M.S. *Challenger* fired 50 rounds of 6-inch into the railway station, causing a large fire. It was learned afterwards that this bombardment had had much more moral effect on the inhabitants than any shelling by day.

[2] The 40th Pathans and Jind Infantry had marched from Mandera on 21st August, reaching Bagamoyo on 25th.

[3] The two columns were composed as follows :
   " B " *Column* (inland route) :
      2/L.N. Lancashire Regiment ; 129th Baluchis, 5th Light Infantry, combined as a composite battalion.
   The 2/L.N. Lancashire Regt. had just returned after 5 months' rest in South Africa.
   The 129th Baluchis had marched from Handeni to Korogwe, arriving on 24th August ; went by train to Tanga, thence by sea to Bagamoyo, landing on 29th.
   " C " *Column* (coast route) :
      2nd W. India Regiment ; Details, S. African Infantry (from L. of C.) ; Zanzibar Rifles.
   With this column was a landing party of the Royal Navy with one 3-pdr., 6 m.g., and 6 Lewis guns, under Commander H. D. Bridges, R.N.

indeed, obviously not in the enemy's interest to lock up troops there, nor to subject the large non-combatant German population to a siege.

On the 2nd September, after an unopposed but arduous march in broiling heat through sandy, waterless country, the two columns reached Gunya Peak and Konduchi respectively, establishing outposts that evening on the line Goba-Mbezi. On the following day the naval squadron, taking no chances, shelled the German defences both north and south of the port. The smaller craft, making a feint of landing at Ras Upanga, were fired on with shrapnel, but suffered no damage. Otherwise no resistance was offered and the land columns, together with a few reinforcements landed at Konduchi, converged on Msasani Bay in the course of the day.[1]

Early on the 4th the troops marched on, still unopposed, to the heights near Mabibo, from which they could look down on Dar-es-Salaam, less than three miles away[2]. H.M.S. *Challenger*, flying a white flag, closed in on Makatumbe island and sent the *Echo* into the port with a formal summons to surrender. At 8 a.m. the Deputy Burgomaster came off in the *Echo's* boat to accept the terms laid down, which guaranteed the lives and private property of the inhabitants. The troops, headed by the 129th Baluchis, which had acted as advanced guard throughout the march, then entered and took over the town.

It was found that all the Germans, with the exception of 80 hospital patients and 370 non-combatants, had departed, after clearing the place of all munitions. The various naval bombardments[3] proved to have done little damage, though the railway station was in ruins and the skeleton of the Governor's palace stood as a reminder of 1914. The railway workshops and the electrical plant which served them and lighted the town were still in reasonably good order; but the electric transporter cranes at the harbour had been wrecked,

---

[1] Admiralty papers record that the 2nd W. India Regiment was so desperate with thirst and hunger that it consumed the whole of the 12,000 gallons of water, and also the three days' provisions, landed at Msasani for the needs of the whole force.

[2] In subsequent proceedings in the Admiralty Prize Court, as military testimony that the harbour was in sight of the troops at the time could not be given with certainty, Dar-es-Salaam was adjudged to have been a naval capture and £100,000 prize-money was awarded to the Royal Navy.

[3] See p. 111, f.n. 2.

so that landing facilities were greatly impaired.[1] In the harbour were the steamers *Tabora*, *König* and *Moewe*, all completely wrecked, and the *Feldmarschall*, capable of repair.[2] Sunk in the harbour entrance was the floating dock ; at first it had been hoped to bring this into use, but salvage proved impossible.

Meanwhile the remainder of Colonel Price's force, sent inland in two columns from Bagamoyo, had met with little opposition. The movements of these are shown in Sketch 53. The Jind Infantry, under Major J. A. Phillips, moving westwards across the Kingani river at Mtoni Ferry on the 30th August, and thence through Mbiki and Kisemo, reached Ngerengere station early on the 3rd September. The station was found deserted. The high piers of the railway bridge over the Kingani had been demolished by the Germans, who had then run several trains down the broken line to crash into the river below.[3] There being no sign of the enemy in the neighbourhood, the Jind Infantry left again on the 5th to return to Bagamoyo, whence on the 9th the unit went by sea to Dar-es-Salaam.

It had been hoped that the 40th Pathans under Major Tyndall, which left Bagamoyo at 2 p.m. on the 31st August to march south-westwards up the Kingani, would reach Ruvu station in time to prevent the enemy from demolishing the railway bridge there, in which case the battalion was to remain to protect it. Otherwise Tyndall was to sweep south of the railway to the main Dar-es-Salaam–Morogoro road and turn east along it to Dar-es-Salaam.

After a short halt at Mbwawa, where a German piquet was driven off, the column reached the railway early on the

---

[1] The harbour of Dar-es-Salaam is bounded on all sides by a sandy beach on which, at the customs shed, the Germans had built a wharf accessible to lighters only at half-tide or over. The cranes had been erected to enable lighters to be off-loaded at all states of the tide. The British had therefore to provide floating pontoons connected to the shore to enable stores and personnel to be handled. These were supplemented by sheers to take 15 tons and by a 3-ton crane, erected on the edge of the wharf and therefore only useful during limited hours. With these improvised facilities the whole change of base from Mombasa to Dar-es-Salaam was carried out. Delay in unloading ships was, however, considerable. One cause of this was undoubtedly the shortage of tugs and lighters ; but the need of a deep-water pier was greatly felt, and a pier with a 5-ton steam crane, begun in December, was completed on 23rd January, 1917. (Director of Railways, report, 10th February, 1917.)

[2] See p. 20, f.n. 3.

[3] The girders, four spans 15 metres and one span 30 metres, were practically undamaged by their fall, and were later replaced in their original position.

1st September. Crossing it three miles east of Ruvu station, Tyndall surprised and routed a German party about fifty strong, which proved to be the rear guard of a force of about 50 Germans and 100 askari which had demolished the bridge the day before and was making off southwards.[1]

The hopes of saving the bridge not having been realized, Tyndall continued his march on the 2nd September due south through the bush to strike the Morogoro road near Msenga. Turning east along it through Kola and Kiserawe,[2] he was engaged at various points in a series of small but satisfactory encounters with German detachments and convoys retreating from Dar-es-Salaam, in the course of which the Pathans captured 25 Germans and 20 askari, with baggage and stores, and destroyed 2,000 loads of German rations which they had no means of carrying off. After a trying march the column reached Mtoni village, four miles south of Dar-es-Salaam, on the 5th and entered the capital on the following day.[2]

At long last the possession of the seat of government and principal port of German East Africa, and of the terminal section of the Central Railway—now about to come finally under Allied control throughout its whole length of 780 miles[3]—had given the Commander-in-Chief the new base and shortened line of communication of which he had been so long and so urgently in need.

No immediate benefit could be expected, owing to the destruction of the railway-bridges and of much of the rolling-stock ; but the work of repair was quickly put in hand, and by the 4th October supplies were going forward from the new base.[4]

G.H.Q., which had been at Korogwe up to the 4th September and was at Tanga from the 5th to the 11th, opened

---

[1] The Germans were a detachment of 3.Sch.K. under Lieut. Baldamus, which retreated southwards to Kisangire (see Sketch 50a).

The main bridge at Ruvu, one 40-metre and two 20-metre spans, had been completely destroyed. Two kilometres of line immediately west of the station crossed a valley subject to flooding, and flood openings in the embankment, twenty-one 10-metre spans in all, were also destroyed.

On 13th September the 26th and 27th (Railway) Coys., S. & M., under Maj. L. N. Malan, R.E., reached Ruvu. They completed a diversion on 15th and a further diversion to the westward by 20th.

[2] Casualties during these operations were : killed, 2 o.r. ; wounded, 2 I.O., 2 o.r.

[3] The western section of the line was at this time being taken over by the Belgians, who entered Kigoma on 28th July and Tabora on 19th September. See Chaps. XXV, XXVI.

[4] See Note II, p. 395.

O*

End Paper
(S)

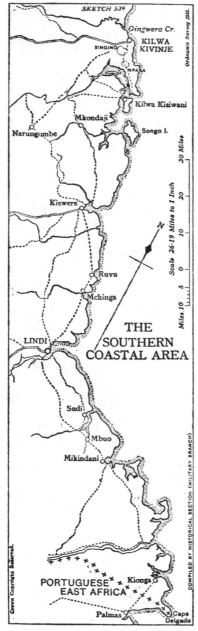

at Dar-es-Salaam on the 12th.[1] Soon afterwards patrols pushing westwards along the railway established contact with the main British force by way of Morogoro.

OCCUPATION OF THE SOUTHERN PORTS

By the first week of September it was becoming increasingly apparent that Lettow intended to fall back on the lower Rufiji with the object of prolonging the campaign by withdrawal towards the Portuguese border. With this in prospect, Lieut.-General Smuts decided to carry out a plan which for some time he had had in mind ; to land a force at Kilwa Kivinje (140 miles south of Dar-es-Salaam), usually known simply as Kilwa, and by operating from that port to confine the enemy to the country north of the Matandu river, the estuary of which is Gingwera creek, just north of the town.

Wild reports, heard at this time, that Lettow had decided to abandon the struggle and escape by sea with his German personnel, obviously called for no

[1] Advanced G.H.Q. was at Morogoro from 31st August onwards.

attention ;[1] but the possibility, however remote, of assistance reaching the enemy from overseas had now to be eliminated. The time had come to occupy effectively the whole of the coast south of Dar-es-Salaam.

In consultation with the naval authorities orders to this end were given on the 6th September. On the same day H.M.Ss. *Vengeance* and *Talbot* sailed southwards, the former carrying Colonel Price with a small landing force of Royal Marines, Zanzibar Rifles and Mafia Rifles destined for Kilwa Kivinje, and the latter escorting the transport *Barjora*, which carried the 2/West India Regiment destined for Kilwa Kisiwani ("Kilwa of the island"), about twenty miles farther south.

At dawn on the 7th the *Talbot* and *Barjora* entered Kilwa Kisiwani harbour. The place was found deserted and the 2/West India Regiment landed without incident. At Kilwa Kivinje, where a party of Mafia Rifles, landing on the north side of Gingwera Creek, had a skirmish with a German detachment, organized resistance had been expected ; but on fire being opened by the 12-inch guns of the *Vengeance* against trenches on Singino Hill, behind the town, white flags were displayed on shore and this place, too, was taken without further opposition. The heights of Singino and Mpara were occupied, the Germans disappearing inland.

For the seizure of the ports farther south a force consisting of a naval detachment, the 40th Pathans, the composite battalion of the 129th Baluchis and 5th Light Infantry, and the Zanzibar Rifles, about 1,100 in all, was organized under the command of Major Tyndall.[2] The Indian units having embarked at Dar-es-Salaam on the 11th September, the force occupied Mikindani, 120 miles south of Kilwa, unopposed on the 13th.

Leaving a garrison there,[3] the column marched northwards through Mbuo to Sudi, which also was occupied without opposition. Again leaving a garrison, the force re-embarked and on the 17th sailed north to Lindi, where the

---

[1] One version even provided a Turkish aeroplane to be sent from Palestine for Lettow himself.
[2] Composition :
Indian units ..	..	..	..	700 all ranks ;
Zanzibar & Mafia Rifles	..	..	200 ,, ,,
Royal Marines	..	..	..	200 ,, ,,
with 2 naval Hotchkiss guns and 12 naval m.g.
[3] 129th Baluchis, 3 officers, 117 o.r.

40th Pathans were landed and stationed.[1] Next day a detachment of the 5th Light Infantry was landed at Kiswere, midway between Lindi and Kilwa. For some time to come no hostile enterprise was to trouble these various garrisons, and from now onwards the whole coast of the German Colony remained in British hands.

OPERATIONS OF THE PORTUGUESE

Sketch 54 At the mouth of the Ruvuma, the line of which inland formed the frontier between the Portuguese colony of Mozambique and German East Africa, the small enclave on the southern bank known as the Kionga Triangle had for many years been the subject of dispute between the Portuguese and German Governments. Taken forcibly by the Portuguese in 1887 from the Sultan of Zanzibar, it had similarly been seized by the Germans in 1894. Portugal had been compelled to recognize this transfer of territory by *force majeure* ; but the memory of it had rankled and had been exacerbated by various minor incidents, chiefly in connection with smuggling raids along the border. In consequence, when Portugal declared war on Germany in March 1916, the recovery of the Kionga Triangle was the first and most obvious aim of the local colonial forces.

These comprised at this time about 1,500 European and 2,800 African troops, the latter consisting of twelve companies of infantry disposed for the most part in small posts End Paper for the defence of the 400 miles of frontier. Of the European (S) troops, most of whom had been sent out as recruits during 1915 and had since suffered seriously from the climate, there was always a considerable percentage in hospital.

Sketch 54 Upon the declaration of war the Portuguese Government had decided to reinforce these troops from home ; but without waiting for the reinforcements the local commander, Major da Silveira, proceeded to take the offensive. Early in April 1916 a force under his command, numbering about 400, was assembled at Palmas, ten miles from the frontier of the Kionga Triangle.[2] The German troops in the Triangle consisted only of a few frontier guards, which made no attempt to resist, and by the 10th April the whole of the

---

[1] At Lindi 3 mines laid by the Germans in the channel were exploded by a party from H.M.S. *Talbot*, and some 40 land-mines along the shore were found and destroyed.

[2] Composition : 3 coys. European infantry, 3 coys. African infantry, 1 bty. mountain artillery, 1 m.g. battery.

Triangle had been occupied by the Portuguese, who established posts along the south bank of the Ruvuma. The opposite bank was held, however, by active German detachments which persistently raided across the shallow estuary, and Major da Silveira decided to drive them off. Towards the end of May the cruiser *Adamastor* and the gunboat *Chaimite* were despatched to support the landing of a force at Mwambo, at the mouth of the river. On the 27th May, covered by the fire of the warships and of a field battery on the southern bank, four groups of lighters filled with native troops were towed across. The enemy, however, undaunted by the covering bombardment, held his fire until the tows were within close range and then opened fire with such effect that the Portuguese were unable to land and did not renew the attempt.[1]

No further operations of any importance occurred for some months, by reason both of administrative difficulties and of continued wastage among the troops from sickness. In the meantime an expeditionary force had been assembled in Portugal under the command of Major-General F. Gil,[2] who with his staff and part of his infantry reached Lourenço Marques on the 27th June. Proceeding up the coast after a conference with the Governor, he disembarked at Palmas on the 5th July. The remainder of the force was to follow.

So far no definite plan of operations had been decided upon. With regard to this Major-General Gil on his arrival was to find his views at variance with those of the British Commander-in-Chief. On the 8th July Lieut.-General Smuts, then halted on the Msiha, telegraphed that the Germans were evidently preparing to withdraw to the south of the Central Railway and that a prompt advance by the Portuguese troops would be of great effect. To this message, and to a cable a week later from the Portuguese Government urging " a rapid offensive in order not to run the risk of " arriving late or of our operations being useless," Major-General Gil could only reply that he was eager to start but

---

[1] No detailed Portuguese account is available. According to the German version (*Der Krieg zur See* : die Kämpfe der kaiserlichen Marine in den deutschen Kolonien, pp. 277–8) the defending force consisted of 3 Germans, 42 askari, under Lieut. Sprockhoff, a naval officer. This account, which claims that the Portuguese suffered heavy loss, gives the date of the affair as 21st May ; the date 27th is deduced from contemporary telegrams.

[2] Composition : 3 infantry bns., 3 mtn. bties., 3 m.g. bties., total rifle strength about 3,000, with 12 guns, 12 m.g.

could not do so until his force was complete, including its transport and stores.

His first plan was to march northwards up the coast from the mouth of the Ruvuma, occupying in succession the ports of Mikindani, Lindi, Kiswere and Kilwa. Lieut.-General Smuts, however, considered that the coastal ports could be occupied without difficulty by British forces from the sea ; whereas a movement into the German food-producing districts about Masasi, 80 miles south-west of Lindi, and Liwale, 70 miles farther north, would be more profitable and could more easily be made from Portuguese territory than from any of the areas then held by British troops. He suggested, therefore, that it was in this direction that Portuguese co-operation would be of most value.

To this Major-General Gil at first demurred, pointing out that his transport was not adequate to supply a large force so far inland, that there were no made roads from the Portuguese frontier towards Masasi, and that the only easy line of approach to that locality was from Lindi.

As a first move, he decided to force the passage of the Ruvuma near its mouth, between Namoto and Nyika. During August his Chief of Staff reconnoitred this area and made plans for the proposed movement up the coast, to be made in concert with that of the British forces then in progress southwards towards Bagamoyo and Dar-es-Salaam.

The force from Portugal, meanwhile, was long on the way. Its transports arrived in slow succession, and not until the 6th September were its principal units all assembled. Even then, moreover, many of the troops were still only partially trained. Added to this, during the period of inaction the young soldiers fell sick in large numbers ; and although additional native troops were recruited, these by no means counterbalanced the dwindling of the European infantry.[1]

Excluding troops in the frontier posts, but including six newly-raised companies of native infantry, Major-General Gil had at his disposal at the beginning of September a fighting strength of about 2,700 rifles, with 14 mountain guns and 10 machine guns. On the 10th he issued preliminary instructions for his force to concentrate about Nakwedanga and march thence northwards on Mikindani.

Three days later came news that Mikindani had been

[1] Within a fortnight of Maj.-General Gil's arrival 300 men had to be shipped back, seriously ill, to Lourenço Marques, followed by 545 more on 29th July.

occupied by the British naval forces. Nevertheless Major-
General Gil decided to proceed with his intended movement.
He wished to avenge the reverse suffered by da Silveira in
May, by driving off the Germans believed to be still holding
the northern bank of the Ruvuma estuary between Mayembe
and the sea, and by planting the Portuguese flag on German
soil.[1] During the night of the 15th/16th September his
main body marched north from Palmas to Kionga, where it
divided into three divergent columns directed respectively on
Namoto, Kambire and Nyika along the south bank of the river.
By the evening of the 18th his dispositions were completed.

At daybreak on the 19th September, the passage of the
estuary was begun at the three selected points ; covered by
the artillery, the right column crossed on rafts, the other
two columns fording the river, which was roughly a thousand
yards wide. They met no opposition, and it was soon learned
from local natives that the German detachment had slipped
away to the westward two days earlier. The Portuguese flag
was duly hoisted, and the troops camped along the river bank.

Since Mikindani to the northward was now in British
hands, there was no object in pushing farther in that direction. To the westward stretched the inhospitable uplands
of the Makonde plateau, where water was scarce. Lack
of transport made it difficult to send any large force south-
westwards towards Newala, seventy miles away on the route
to Masasi. For the time being, therefore, the Portuguese
troops, their further objective uncertain, remained encamped
on the ground they had gained north of the Ruvuma.

SUMMARY : THE SITUATION AT THE END OF
SEPTEMBER 1910

By the end of September 1916 the campaign, disappoint-
ing in its total results so far, and costly beyond all expecta- **End Papers**
tion alike in men and material, had yet made notable **(N), (S)**
progress before coming once more to a standstill. As the
outstanding achievement of the period dealt with in the
present volume, Lieut.-General Smuts had gained full
possession of the Central Railway and acquired the long
needed fresh base at Dar-es-Salaam. The German capital

---

[1] Sprockhoff's detachment (see p. 389, f.n. 1) now consisted of 12 Germans, 113 askari, 59 irregulars, with one 3-pdr. gun and 2 m.g. Its
numbers were estimated by the Portuguese at the time to be 50 Germans,
400 askari.

had been taken, the principal settled areas occupied, the seaports all secured. The German forces still in the field had been driven out of their best territories into the less developed and, on the whole, less healthy regions to the south, where it might be expected that they would find it difficult to maintain themselves.[1]

Nevertheless Lieut.-General Smuts had not yet gained decisive military success in his long duel with the German commander. Faced by a wary and able opponent, he had judged shrewdly and planned skilfully. But in effect his operations, while they had finally wrested from German possession a vast tract of territory, had amounted virtually to a succession of turning movements, resolutely carried through in the face of constant hardship and privation, effectively manoeuvring the Germans into continual retreat at little cost in British battle casualties, but falling short, despite all efforts, of the ultimate aim of defeating the enemy.

Throughout, the Commander-in-Chief had been hampered by the continuously increasing difficulties involved in moving and maintaining his troops on a scale unprecedented, in point of time, numbers and distance, in any previous military operation conducted in similar conditions of climate and terrain. On reaching the Central Railway he might well have paused. Viewing the campaign in retrospect it now seems, indeed, that at that stage he might with great advantage have contented himself with establishing his new base at Dar-es-Salaam ; restoring the railway and organising his supply services on shorter and more manageable lines, meanwhile making his dispositions to end the campaign successfully by the use both of the railway and of the southern ports, with troops reinvigorated by rest.

Lieut.-General Smuts, however, decided otherwise. His reasons for making yet one more call upon the endurance of his troops have been recorded.

His men responded nobly ; but both on the Mgeta and at Kidodi he came, less than a month later, to a point beyond which for a time no force of will could carry him or

---

[1] While the bulk of Lettow's forces was falling back on the Rufiji, the healthier area between Iringa and Mahenge was still open to Kraut retreating southwards from Kilosa and to the units under Wahle in the west when they retired, as they were about to do, south-eastwards from Tabora. Still farther south, however, Br.-General Northey's drive (under Colonial Office control) into the southern areas of German East Africa was co-ordinated with the operations of Lt.-General Smuts. See Chaps. XXVI–XXVIII.

them. He had urged them forward unsparingly, sparing himself still less, and in the despatch already many times quoted he pays richly merited tribute in words which form a fitting conclusion to this volume, to the magnificent devotion and spirit of his army.

Weakened by months of semi-starvation and fever stoically borne, exhausted by endless weeks of marching, climbing and fighting under a tropical sun, the troops, his own South Africans in particular, were falling sick in such numbers that the hospitals were overflowing and the field units reduced to mere cadres. Already, as one of the main lessons of the campaign, it was indisputable that for warfare in tropical Africa troops other than native Africans had proved in general unsuited.

Reluctantly the Commander-in-Chief decided that the bulk of the South African troops must be sent home to the Union to recuperate, that the field army must be reconstituted, and that operations must be suspended whilst other forces were being provided, the new and shorter lines of communication fully established, and the sorely-crippled transport services reorganized. Fresh plans would then be necessary to meet a new situation.

NOTE I

THE SUPPLY AND TRANSPORT SITUATION IN SEPTEMBER 1916

1. The situation with regard to supplies was set down for the C.-in-C. by his A.Q.M.G. in a statement dated 7th September 1916, of which the following is a brief summary, to which approximate distances have been added :

1st Division.—Railhead, Korogwe (to Mkesse's (Dutumi) 225 miles). Refilling-point, Dakawa (90 miles). Division on half rations and entirely dependent on daily supplies. No reserves or margin of safety. Daily lift needed, 17,000 to 20,000 lbs. (Full rations, 30,000).

2nd Division.—Railhead, Moshi (to Kidodi 410 miles). Refilling-point, Cypherkuil (near Chambalo, 260 miles). Division on half rations, but aided by dumps already formed at Cypherkuil and Kilosa, and in no immediate danger of shortage.

3rd Division.—Railhead, Korogwe (to Kisaki, via Mahalaka, 245 miles). Refilling-point, Kangata (180 miles). Division on half rations or less. Daily lift needed 18,000 lbs. This could just be maintained if there were no hitch and only by aid of 30 waggons from 2nd Division. No margin of safety.

Transport vehicles (in terms of carrying capacity) :—

On the road ..	..	132,000 lbs. lift.
In workshops	..	100,000 lbs. lift.
Broken down	..	15,000 lbs. lift.

A reinforcement of 100 Fords was shortly due.[1] On the other hand breakdowns were increasing ; there had been " a steady fall in lift in the last few days " ; and the September rains were about to break.

2. The effect of the rains may be pictured from the following extract :—

" Very heavy rains are reported from all quarters, making
" the situation extremely serious and the supply question
" very acute. Turiani bridge and another . . . . have been
" carried away . . . . All motor transport is at a standstill.
" 1st Division is on half rations and will be able to feed at
" that rate till 26th night, but from then they will be without
" rations at all. Waggons are being pushed out from Mikese
" towards Dutumi with rations for 1st Division, who will
" have to send back porters to meet them. The troops in
" front have been on half rations for some time, and it was
" hoped to give them a rest, and feed them well for the next
" 2 weeks, as they are all very weak from fever, lack of food,
" and continuous fighting. These rains have, however, put
" this out of the question, and the best that can be hoped
" for—provided the rain now holds off—is to prevent them
" from starving for next week or 10 days. The railway
" cannot be repaired . . . . till the beginning of October at
" the earliest." (War Diary, Advanced G.H.Q., 23rd September, 1916.)

3. In an appreciation telegraphed to the C.I.G.S. on 21st September 1916 the C.-in-C. said :—

. . . . " Both man and beast have suffered severely. The
" ox transport has been practically finished by rinderpest and
" fly, while horse sickness and tsetse fly have killed most of
" our horses. About 70 per cent. of van Deventer's division
" are, according to medical report, unfit for work owing to
" the combined effect of malaria, dysentery and debility.
" In the other two divisions the position is not much better,
" though with some weeks' rest and full rations the situation

---

[1] These were the last vehicles to come from England. Sinkings by submarines had already curtailed shipping, and vehicles were subsequently ordered from the U.S.A. via South Africa, whereby quicker and more abundant delivery by a safer sea-route was assured.

It must be remembered that animal transport had been depleted almost to vanishing-point by casualties due to tsetse, disease, and continuous overwork. (See also para. 3.)

" will improve. But as we advance the country is un-
" doubtedly getting much worse for man and beast. Some
" reorganization is inevitable for weeding out unfit troops
" and dismounted members of mounted brigades. . . . .
" The transport situation will improve materially during the
" next fortnight, when the Central Railway between Dar-
" es-Salaam and Dodoma will have been repaired sufficiently
" to carry petrol with supplies for the whole force. Trans-
" port north of Central Railway will then be moved up and
" transferred to south of railway and I trust that it will
" prove sufficient for our requirements. If necessary, I may
" be obliged to supply Northey's force from Kilosa also."

4. Of the transport situation at this time the Commander-in-
Chief later wrote as follows :—

" The Mechanical Transport was in a seriously damaged
" condition in consequence of the strain of continuous work
" over appalling roads or trackless country, and extensive
" repairs, for which there had been no time, were essential.
" The personnel of this transport suffered as did every other
" branch of the forces, from the same diseases as affected the
" fighting troops, and as men dropped out increasing strain
" was thrown on those able to keep going, until the loss of
" men threw scores of vehicles out of work. Animal diseases
" had wiped out horses, mules and oxen by thousands, and
" it was necessary to replace this transport in some way or
" other before movement was possible." (Despatch, op. cit.)

5. The enemy, of course, were likewise in no enviable plight.
But the German forces, smaller in numbers, homogeneous, far
less completely equipped, with far fewer material requirements
and unhampered by a long and lengthening line of communication,
were relatively at an immense advantage in regard to the material
difficulties against which the British had to contend.

NOTE II

THE RESTORATION OF THE CENTRAL RAILWAY

The first troops to reach the Central Railway were, as already
narrated, those of the 2nd Division at the end of July. On their
arrival it was found that, although the enemy had demolished
most of the bridges and had either destroyed or removed much of
the rolling stock, the permanent way had fortunately been left for
the most part intact. It being urgently necessary to get the line
into some sort of working order at the earliest possible moment,
Major-General van Deventer's Pioneers and motor _transport
resorted at once to the expedient already successfully adopted
on the narrow gauge tramway southward from Mombo, on the

Usambara railway, to serve the main force. In June the M.T. workshops at Nairobi, in collaboration with the Uganda Railway, had converted four Ford cars to run on the tram rails, and trials of these quickly led to the conversion of cars and lorries for use as tractors on the railway track. As the first step, therefore, towards re-opening the Central Railway, the bridges were repaired only sufficiently to carry these light vehicles, tractors weighing when loaded 5–6 tons and their trailers, open trucks, carrying 10 tons of supplies.

Major-General van Deventer was thus enabled by the technical skill and inventive ingenuity of his South African Pioneers to make use of the railway almost at once ; whereas to have restored the bridges to carry heavy locomotives would have taken (as in fact it did) several months, during which all his operations would have been at a standstill and—in the words of the C.-in-C.—" an " unbearable strain would be put on our enormously stretched-out " transport lines from Moshi railhead and Korogwe on the Tanga " railway."[1] Only the rail tractors, in short, made it possible for him to supply his division along the 120 miles of railway between Dodoma and Kilosa : " but for this solution of his " transport trouble his [subsequent] advance to the Great " Ruaha river at this stage would have been a physical impossi- " bility."[2]

With the arrival of the main force at Morogoro and the seizure of Dar-es-Salaam the same system was at once adopted on the railway between these places ; " the M.T. workshops at Mombo " and Nairobi made further conversions of lorries which were " shipped to Dar-es-Salaam, until the combined fleet numbered " some 35 tractors ",[3] and the four railway units of Sappers and Miners (25th, 26th, 27th, 28th Coys., forming the Railway Battalion, Lt. Col. C. W. Wilkinson, R.E.) were moved down to deal with the bridges and permanent way[4].

The report by the Director of Railways, Sir William Johns, from which the last quotation is taken, goes on to say : " On the " establishment of through communications for tractors between " the Army and the base at Dar-es-Salaam the second step was " to strengthen the repairs up to heavy engine standard. This " duplication and even triplication of repair work delayed the " advent of the locomotive to some extent, but the proper feeding " of the Army was the first consideration and the rail tractors " were successful in dealing with that. In spite of the delays

---

[1] Despatch, op. cit.
[2] Despatch, op. cit.
[3] Dir. of Railways, Summary of Railway Operations, 9th Feb., 1917.
[4] The 26th and 27th Coys. had marched from Bagamoyo to Ruvu station (see p. 385, f.n. 1) and with a small party of S. African Pioneers began repair of the line in both directions. The 25th and 28th Coys. began working from Dar-es-Salaam westwards on 15th September.

" at the port already referred to,[1] the first engine and train
" reached Ruvu on the 4th October. Simultaneously the first
" tractors reached Dar-es-Salaam from the west and supplies
" began to go forward from the base. After a few days the
" tractors began working from Ruvu westwards, locomotives
" filling the dump from Dar-es-Salaam. On the 21st the locos.
" began forming a dump some 30 miles beyond Ruvu. On the
" 27th the Ngerengere river was crossed and a new dump formed
" on the west bank . . . . The section of line from Ngerengere to
" Morogoro ' [43 miles] ' was an exceptionally heavy one, with
" numerous deep nullahs crossed by high bridges all of which had
" been seriously damaged by the enemy. It was not, therefore,
" till the 24th of the following month [November] that the train
" reached Morogoro. Meanwhile the tractors had done their
" work and the Army was being well fed. The gradual advance
" of the locomotive had enabled military operations to be resumed
" in the Dodoma area, tractors released from the lower section
" being available for transport of supplies farther westward."

On the general subject of railway construction in the field,
Sir William Johns points out the great technical advantages,
" where no break of gauge obscures the issue ", of the metre
gauge,[2] standard in East Africa. Basing himself on these he
re-affirms his view that the construction, in rear of Lieut.-General
Smuts's advance, of a metre-gauge line linking up the Usambara
line with the Central Railway, from Ngombezi to Morogoro,
" would have assisted the prosecution of the campaign even more
" than the tractor service on the Central Railway." With this
view, though it was not accepted at the time, it is difficult to-day
to disagree. It is doubtful, however, whether in the shortage
then prevailing the necessary permanent-way material could
have been obtained.

---

[1] (a) " We had been promised two ships . . . and only obtained one."
(b) Lack of tugs and lighters both at Kilindini (Mombasa) and at
Dar-es-Salaam.
(c) " It should be remembered that ships able to deal with heavy
" lifts, such as . . boilers of engines and large girders, are scarce—there
" were only two on the coast—so had there been any severe stress on the
" railway we should not have been able to meet it for many weeks . . "
" I should recommend . . . several small ships rather than one large
" one, viz.: one for heavy cranes and engines, one for waggons, one for
" rails and sleepers in different holds, one for timber, pumps, etc. It
" is only by some such arrangements that the necessary equipment can
" be brought ashore without delay and as required."
[2] Capable, he says, as the narrower gauges are not, of carrying its own
constructional materials simultaneously with supplies for a large army,
the metre gauge has also in the lightness of its permanent way and rolling
stock a pronounced advantage over the standard European and Indian
gauges of 4' 8½", 5' 6", etc., in any country where landing and similar
difficulties are likely. The experience of the campaign showed that in
easy country—" and much of the alignment is easy "—a metre-guage
line can be laid at the rate of a mile a day and feed an army of 30,000 men.

To sum up, the two points, of course mutually interdependent, which stand out conspicuously are epitomised by Sir William Johns as follows :

" First of all the work of the motor tractors which,
" though to some extent delaying the work of repairs, as all
" work had to be carried out under traffic, nevertheless
" undoubtedly saved the situation.[1]

" Secondly the comparative futility of the German
" demolitions as compared with those executed on the Tanga
" line. The enemy failed to take the one step we feared,
" and the obvious one, of pulling up track and throwing
" miles of fastenings into the bush.[2] Had he done this to any
" extent, the inadequate unloading facilities at the port
" might have led to the withdrawal of our Army from its
" advanced positions and serious delay in military operations."

It remains only to add a reminder that the work of restoration was carried out at high pressure under the same severe stress of tropical climate, sickness and privation, endured by all alike in this campaign, to which reference has been made elsewhere ; and, in noting that within little over 3 months they brought back into efficient service some 300 miles of vital railway, to put on record the fine achievement of all the various technical troops concerned.

NOTE III

GERMAN MISCONCEPTIONS

Colonel von Lettow-Vorbeck, in his account of the campaign, wrote as follows :

" General Smuts realized that his blow had failed. He sent
" me a letter calling upon me to surrender, by which he showed
" that, as far as his force was concerned, he had reached the
" end of his resources ". (" My Reminiscences," p. 158 ; German text, p. 138.)

A more accurate statement is made by Herr Schnee, then Governor of the German colony :

" In a letter addressed to me at the end of September
" 1916 General Smuts, pointing out what in his view was our
" hopeless situation, suggested our surrender under honourable
" conditions and proposed a personal meeting with me and

---

[1] " While the Railway Battalion was working east of Ngerengere, the " S.A. Pioneers had repaired the line to Morogoro sufficiently to take motors " . . . This complicated the strengthening of the line for locomotives, " as work had to be done without hindering traffic, and included the dis- " mantling in almost every case of the Pioneers' work." Report by O.C. Railway Battalion, Feb. 1917.

[2] It has been suggested that the enemy did not attempt this because it seemed useless in view of the speed with which the Usambara line had been repaired ; the British lack of railway material and the landing difficulties possibly did not occur to him.

"Colonel v. Lettow, a proposal which I declined." (*Deutsch-Ost-Afrika im Weltkriege,*" p. 230.)

The fact appears to be that on 30th September 1916 Lieut.-General Smuts wrote to Governor Schnee in connection with certain German allegations of breaches of the Geneva Convention by the British forces at Dar-es-Salaam. After disposing of this matter the Commander-in-Chief went on to " make use of this " opportunity to raise a different and important issue."

Observing that " in spite of the conspicuous ability and " bravery " of the German defence, the end could only be deferred " at the cost of terrible losses and suffering to the population ", he wrote that during the past few months he had had the painful opportunity of witnessing their sad state, which he had done his best to alleviate, and of discussing it with them. " One and all," he said, " while remaining loyal to their people and their Govern-" ment, have expressed their conviction that resistance has gone " far enough and is now only adding to their misery . . . . without " the prospect of any useful result."

Continuing, Lieut.-General Smuts referred to the responsibility of the Governor and of Colonel von Lettow for the welfare of the helpless people of the colony, cut off from succour from abroad and called upon as they had been during two years for efforts and sacrifices which, if continued, must mean untold suffering and could only end in unconditional surrender.

In these circumstances he impressed on the Governor that the time had come for the latter and Colonel von Lettow " to " consider very seriously whether this useless resistance should " not now cease in a manner honourable to themselves ".

" If any discussion with me." the Commander-in-Chief added, " could assist Your Excellency and Colonel v. Lettow in coming " to a conclusion on this question, I am prepared to meet you " and him at a time and place to be agreed upon ".

Lieut.-General Smuts sent a copy of this to Colonel von Lettow, expressing a hope that its subject-matter would also " engage your serious attention ".

This letter, clearly prompted solely by humanitarian considerations, but coming as it did at a moment when the British forces had in fact come temporarily to a standstill, and when Lettow was doubtless unaware of the magnitude of his opponent's resources and preparations for a vigorous resumption of the campaign, may have conveyed an entirely mistaken impression.

In any case, however, it can hardly be disputed that from the German point of view Lettow's practical reaction was the right one. To continue, with his as yet unsubdued force, to contain in East Africa a greatly superior force whose potentialities his surrender would release for use elsewhere was an obviously sound policy which so good a soldier would be the last man to abandon.

CHAPTER XXIV

THE WESTERN AREA 1916

PRELIMINARY OPERATIONS

(Sketches 13, 55, 56, 57, 58, 59, 60)

THE BELGIAN FORCES

Sketch 55 THROUGHOUT the year 1915, as we have seen, the eagerness of the Belgians in the Congo Territory to pass to the offensive on the German western border in co-operation with their Allies in British East Africa had not been gratified.[1] Not only had the British been restricted, of necessity, to the defensive, but—as Major-General Tombeur had had reluctantly to admit in November—the Belgian forces themselves had been unprepared, more especially in regard to transport, supply and communications.

Nevertheless by a notable effort of improvisation, what had formerly been a scattered force of gendarmerie[2] had gradually been organized and trained into an African army whose establishment, first fixed at 10,000, was soon increased to 15,000. The operations of 1914–15 both in East Africa and in the Cameroons[3] had given to a nucleus of these troops some experience of war, and by February 1916, the Belgians, now with complete freedom of movement on Lake Tanganyika, had some 11,000 men along the German border ready to take the field.[4]

---

[1] See Chap. XII.

[2] See p. 29, f.n. 1.

[3] In the Cameroons two Belgian columns, about 600 in all, had co-operated with the French forces.

[4] At the Lutobo conference on 6th February 1916 (see p. 208), Major-General Tombeur gave figures, including the units transferred from Rhodesia (see p. 187), as follows :—
(i) North of Lake Kivu : 5,200 with 32 guns, 32 m.g.
(ii) On the River Russisi : 2,500 with 20 guns, 20 m.g.
(iii) Along Lake Tanganyika : 2,200 with 12 guns, 13 m.g.
(iv) In the (British) Kigezi area (see pp. 50, 198) : 450.
(v) On the Congo, in reserve to (ii) above : 800.
Total : 11,150, with 64 guns, 65 m.g.
During 1915 some 15 to 20 officers and n.c.o.s per month had been sent out from Belgium, eventually bringing the European cadres up to 265 officers, 269 n.c.o.s for an establishment of 15,000 Africans (viz., field force 10,000 ; reserve, 2,000 ; under training, 3,000). By the end of May 1916 the total of African troops trained and under training was given as 11,698. There were no wholly European units.

Munitions received from Belgium between the outbreak of war and the end of 1916 included : 4 batteries, each four 70 mm. hows. ; eight 75 mm. guns ; 16,500 rifles ; 118 m.g. ; 27,000 Mills bombs ; 115,000 rounds gun and how. ammunition.

THE GERMAN FORCES

The German detachments on the frontier of Uganda had been pushed back, as already described, to the general line of the Kagera; but on their western border, except that they retained the Belgian island of Kwijwi on Lake Kivu, seized in September 1914,[1] they were for the most part still in their original frontier positions.

A Belgian estimate in March gave their numbers as about 2,200 in Ruanda and Urundi, more than half of whom were holding the difficult mountainous country about the River Sebea at the northern end of Lake Kivu; about 1,000 along the Kagera; about 600 in the area east of Lake Victoria; and some 200 at Mwanza. It is now known that these figures, somewhere near the mark for the beginning of the year, were much above the actual numbers which eventually opposed the Belgian advance; between January and April, as the result of the growing British pressure elsewhere, the German strength in the western area was considerably reduced.[2] In any case, however, it was certain that the Belgian forces greatly outnumbered the German, and that any difficulties that a Belgian offensive might encounter would be due, as with the British, rather to the nature of the country and to problems of transport and supply than to the strength of the enemy.

Command of all the German troops in the western area as far south as Bismarckburg, designated the "western command", had for some time been exercised by Major-General Wahle, with headquarters at Tabora.[3]

ARRANGEMENTS FOR ANGLO-BELGIAN CO-OPERATION

On the 25th February Lieut.-General Smuts, who had reached Nairobi two days earlier, despatched Brig.-General Sir Charles Crewe, K.C.M.G.,[4] from his staff on a special

[1] See p. 50.

[2] See Note, p. 421.

[3] Major-General Wahle had previously been in charge of the L. of C. (see Chap. III, Note II, p. 53). He assumed command in the west and south in May 1915 (see Chap. XI, Note III, p. 196). He was succeeded on the L. of C. by the naval Captain Looff, late of the *Königsberg*, who at the same time assumed command in the coastal area and became the "eastern commander" (*Ostbefehlshaber*) in June 1916. Wahle, as *Westbefehlshaber*, added the troops at Mwanza and Bukoba to his command on 30th April, 1916.

[4] Sir Charles Crewe, a prominent and forceful figure in South African political life since 1899, had been Colonial Secretary for the Cape Colony 1904–7 and Secretary for Agriculture 1907–8. At the outbreak of war in 1914 he became Director of Recruiting in South Africa.

mission to the Belgian forces, in order to maintain close touch with Major-General Tombeur and in consultation with him to devise the most effective means of Anglo-Belgian co-operation.

With a small staff which included Major E. S. Grogan, Brig.-General Crewe left Nairobi for Uganda on the 6th March. After conferring with the authorities at Entebbe, he proceeded to Mbarara to arrange for the supply and transport services promised to the Belgians at the conference at Lutobo already mentioned, in particular for provision of the stipulated number of 5,000 carriers and 100 ox-wagons.[1]

Sketch 55   Continuing his journey south-westwards through Lutobo, he reached Kabale, in the Kigezi district, at the beginning of April and there made contact with the Belgians.[2]

MINOR OPERATIONS ON THE KAGERA, JANUARY—MARCH 1916

Sketch 55   On the southern Uganda border, under the arrangement made a year earlier,[3] the western sector was held by Belgian troops as far east as Kamwezi. From that point to the

---

[1] Three auxiliary units were formed :
(a) The Congo Carrier Section of the East African Transport Corps (known by its telegraphic address of " Carbel ").
(b) The Bukakata–Lutobo Ox Transport (" Bukalu ").
(c) The Belgian Advance Ox Transport (" Belox ").
The personnel for the two former was furnished by Uganda ; the latter was organized in British East Africa. " Carbel " accompanied the subsequent Belgian advance to Tabora, and thus reached that place before the British forces. (See Chap. XXVI.)
Some difficulty arose from misunderstanding as to the cost involved. The figures agreed to at Lutobo, only six weeks earlier, and ratified by the Belgian Government, had been based solely on the normal rate of wages (Rs.7 per man per month), taking no account of overhead charges for administration, nor of equipment, in regard to which Belgian standards fell short of British. These costs more than doubled the agreed figures, and the danger of a breakdown in the arrangements for co-operation was only averted by the British Government generously consenting to bear the difference.

[2] On 9th and 10th April Brig.-General Crewe conferred in the absence of Major-General Tombeur, with Colonel Molitor, now commanding the recently formed Belgian Northern Brigade, and provisional administrative arrangements for the transport and supply of this brigade were settled.
An important paragraph in the official record of proceedings was as follows :—
" 8. The British will make a demonstration on the Kagera commencing " about the 20th April. It has been explained to Colonel Molitor that " no assistance whatever in the shape of troops can be given him, and that " no promise can be made as to the future.
) " It has further been pointed out to Colonel Molitor that a base on " Lake Victoria [Nyamirembe, near Biharamulo] would appear essential " to maintain his supply service and transport satisfactorily, and he may " eventually desire to base his troops on Lake Victoria." (War Diary, Brig.-General Sir C. Crewe, 11th April, 1916.)
[3] See p. 198.

shores of Lake Victoria 110 miles to the eastward the
British forces, never mustering more than 1,600 in all,[1] were
distributed in some twenty small isolated posts along the
border, mostly in German territory, linked by telegraph
and telephone through Mbarara and Simba respectively to
Entebbe, and maintaining touch by patrols.[2]

End Paper
(N)
Sketch 56

Beyond occasional skirmishes no encounter worth
mentioning occurred until the 18th February, when the
enemy attempted to surprise, at dawn, the British post at
Kachumbe, roughly midway between Dwenkuba and the
Lake. Far from being surprised, the garrison—some 30 of
the Uganda Police Service Battalion, normally under
a n.c.o. (Sergt. C. T. Doran, Uganda Volunteer Reserve),
and commanded during the encounter by Lieut. J. S.
Harmsworth, Intelligence Scouts, who was visiting it at
the time—put up a notable fight. Of the attackers, stated
by prisoners to have been 80 strong, with a machine-gun,
the British detachment, itself suffering no casualties, killed 27
and captured 32, together with the machine-gun and 47 rifles.

A period of quiet for some weeks ensued, marked only
at the western end of the line by patrolling against Batusi
raiders and minor enterprises about Dwenkuba.[3] This lull

---

[1] The numbers fluctuated considerably owing to sickness. On 14th
February 1916, the total effective strength in the "Kagera command"
was as follows :

	Offrs.	O.R.
Headquarters	6	1
2 (single) Coys., 98th Infy.	3	81
4 (single) Coys., 4/K.A.R.	10	296
Uganda Police Service Bn.	10	546
Baganda Rifles (native levies)	8	498
Nandi Scouts (native levies)	—	37
Total	37	1,459

with 4 guns, 0 m.g.

The artillery consisted of one 15-pdr. B.L. gun, 3 small Hotchkiss guns.
The section of the 27th Mtn. Bty. R.A. previously on this front had been
withdrawn. (See p. 226, f.n. 2.)

[2] Telegraph : (i) Entebbe—Masaka—Mbarara—Lutobo—
Kabale—Kigezi (Sketch 57).
(ii) Masaka—Simba.
(iii) Mbara—Ngarama—Nsongezi.
Telephone : (i) Simba—Kiasimbi—Rukuba.
(ii) Simba—Minziro—Kakindu.
(iii) Simba—Nazareth—Gwanda—Sango Bay.
(iv) Nsongezi—Dwenkuba.

[3] On 22nd February a column from Dwenkuba, 170 strong, attacked
and burnt a small German post at Dwakitiku, killing one and capturing
seven wounded German native irregulars.
During the night 3rd/4th March an unsuccessful attempt was made to surprise a new German camp near the same locality. There were no casualties.
A similar skirmish occurred on 6th March.

was due mainly to the raising of carriers for the Belgians, a heavy drain on the resources of the Uganda Protectorate, which made it necessary to reduce the number of carriers along the Kagera to a minimum, thereby seriously affecting both the supply and the medical arrangements of the British troops and thus restricting them to the defensive.

THE EASTERN LAKE AREA

Sketch 13 The frontier area east of Lake Victoria had remained quiet since the minor operations of May 1915 and the affair of Bukoba on the western shore a month later.[1] At the beginning of 1916 the troops in the area, designated the Lake Detachment and administered by the O.C. Troops in Uganda,[2] consisted mainly of the 98th Infantry, Indian Army, under Lieut.-Colonel D. R. Adye, stationed at Karungu, and in camps on the Kuja and Gori rivers, respectively 10 and 25 miles to the south-eastward of that small Lake port.[3] On the 19th February, having in view the prospect of co-operating with a Belgian offensive, Major-General Tighe constituted the Lake Detachment as a separate command, the Lake Force, to comprise also the troops on the Kagera destined to take part in the joint operations. Lieut.-Colonel Adye was appointed in command.

East of the Lake there was a brief period of activity in March. On the 12th some sixty enemy irregulars who had crossed the border, occupying Gurribe and attempting to raid the adjoining villages, were driven off with loss by Intelligence Scouts of the " Skin Corps ".[4] On the

---

[1] See pp. 150–3.

[2] See p. 112, f.n. 2.

[3] Distribution :

H.Q. and 1½ coys. 98th Inf. (3 B.O., 425 o.r.).

Kuja Camp : 1 coy. 98th Inf. (3 B.O., 205 o.r.) ; Intelligence Scouts, H.Q., 150 all ranks.

Gori Camp : 1 coy. 98th Inf. (1 B.O., 150 o.r.).

Small detachments of Intelligence Scouts were also at Niasoku and Taraga.

On 21st March 1½ coys. 98th Inf. embarked at Karungu for Uganda (see p. 406).

[4] See p. 112, f.n. 3. This particular detachment of Intelligence Scouts, under Capt. J. J. Drought, was a troop of warlike local natives who had fled from German territory, all fiercely and with good reason hostile to the Germans. Wearing little clothing beyond a lion's-skin headdress, they came to be known as the " Skin Corps ". At their head was a young chief of great influence, dispossessed by the Germans. He had previously done daring work for Capt. Drought in the E.A.M.R., and had since gathered tribesmen about him, eventually totalling some 200, most of

Continued at foot of next page.

24th March a raiding party of 7 Germans and 100 askari, threatening the Scouts' post at Niasoku, retreated at the approach of a detachment of the 98th. The party made another attempt on the night of the 28th/29th and was driven off by the Skin Corps with a loss of ten wounded.

In the meantime the 98th had been weakened by the despatch of reliefs to Uganda ;[1] but with the exception of a last abortive German attempt against Niasoku on the 21st April there was no further hostile activity. The enemy's attention was now to be engaged by the Belgians farther west.

THE BELGIAN PLAN OF CAMPAIGN

It will be remembered that for a year past the principal Sketch 55 object of the Belgian preparations had been to occupy part of the German territory as a pledge for future peace-terms, the main effort being directed towards Ruanda, with the aim of occupying that province and Urundi and of seeking to extend the occupation to the shores of Lake Victoria.[2]

Ruanda is for the most part a high open plateau, mainly pasture land devoid of trees and bush, presenting little hindrance to movement ; but the frontier from Lake Kivu northwards to Mount Sabinio was protected by the steep ranges about the river Sebea, already mentioned, among which the Germans, under Captain Wintgens, had constructed good defences. From Mount Sabinio eastwards the high volcanic mountains through which runs the frontier of Uganda were equally difficult to cross. Near Lutobo, however, a belt of open country stretched southward into the interior of Ruanda, affording an easy line of advance only lightly watched by the enemy. South of Lake Kivu, the natural obstacles, though considerable, were less Sketch 57 forbidding than those about the Sebea.

Between the Kagera and the Sebea, where no Allied movement in force had so far been attempted, the German border was weakly held. Along the relatively easy road southwards from Lutobo and Kamwezi to Kigali there were

---

Continued from previous page.
whom had armed themselves by stalking German askari, and whose attitude was shown by their eagerness to serve against the Germans for two years without pay. These men were both skilled scouts and fine fighters, and had a variety of successes to their credit besides those here mentioned. See also Fendall, " The East African Force, 1915-1919 ", pp. 217-18.

[1] See p. 406.
[2] See p. 206, f.n. 1.

no defences except a small entrenched position at Kakoma and a blockhouse supporting it at Kasibu. It was therefore decided that the principal Belgian thrust should be made by this route, concurrently with demonstrations to contain the enemy on the Sebea and subsidiary operations south of Lake Kivu.

More than once postponed, the offensive was now planned for the latter half of April. Early in that month, however, as a preliminary, the Belgian detachments on the Kigezi border were relieved by the Uganda Police Service Battalion, part of the latter being in turn relieved on the Kagera by a detachment of the 98th Infantry from the eastern Lake area.[1]

This step not only freed another 500 Belgian troops for the forthcoming operations and restored the defence of a British border to British hands, but was likely also to lead the enemy to expect a Belgian concentration on the Sebea sector.

In outline, the Belgian plan was now as follows. North of Lake Kivu, the Northern Brigade, under Colonel Molitor, was organized in two groups. The first, comprising four battalions, two batteries and the detachments relieved from the Kigezi posts, was to assemble at Lutobo and, under Colonel Molitor himself, strike southwards towards Kigali. The second group, four battalions and 10 guns under Major Rouling, was to demonstrate from Kibati, ten miles north of Lake Kivu, against the Germans on the Sebea. South of Lake Kivu, along the Russisi, stood the Southern Brigade, command of which was assumed on the 23rd April by Lieut.-Colonel Olsen. This brigade was subdivided into three, of which the two smaller southern groups were merely to demonstrate, while the third, three battalions, whose first task was to gain possession of the Russisi crossing near Shangugu, at the southern end of Lake Kivu, was to move on to Nyanza, sixty miles to the eastward, the Batusi capital.[2]

A preliminary demonstration on the lower Russisi by the Southern Brigade, intended to divert the enemy's attention from Lake Kivu, was carried out on the 12th April ;

---

[1] See p. 404, f.n. 4. By 9th April the 5 companies of the Uganda Police Service Bn., under Major E. H. T. Lawrence, with headquarters at Kabale, had taken over the posts between Mt. Sabinio and Kamwezi.

[2] For details of formations see B.O.A., II, pp. 54–5.

a week later the northern group of this brigade, under Major Muller, duly effected a crossing near Shangugu and established a bridgehead.

Meanwhile the initial movements of the remaining Belgian troops had been completed. By the 22nd April Molitor's force had been concentrated at Kamwezi.

THE BELGIAN INVASION OF RUANDA

On the 25th April Colonel Molitor's advanced guard Sketch 57 crossed the German frontier. The few Germans opposing it[1] fell back in some haste to Kigali, after a brief stand on the 30th April at Kasibu. The Belgians followed up, but their movement was hampered by continual rain, and with many of their carriers falling sick their progress was slow. On the 5th May the bulk of the column reached the western end of Lake Mohazi after a minor skirmish, and next day, hearing that the Germans were in general retreat, Molitor pushed on to Kigali unopposed. Meanwhile one battalion, detached from the column at Kasibu, made a trying march south-eastwards to Batangata, arriving on the 3rd May. After sending patrols eastwards as far as the ferry at Kageye on the Kagera, the unit returned, passing south of Lake Mohazi, to rejoin the main column at Kigali.

As a result of Molitor's movement the German posts along the frontier to the west were hurriedly withdrawn. On the 11th May Wintgens abandoned his defences on the Sebea, which were occupied next day by Major Rouling, while from the vicinity of Shangugu the Germans fell back eastwards towards Nyanza, where according to native reports the combined German forces converging from both ends of the lake were to organize a fresh defence.

South of Lake Kivu Major Muller, leaving one battalion at Shangugu for local defence,[2] marched north-eastward with the other two battalions of the 1st Regiment and a battery on the 4th May. Along bad roads and under a continual downpour of rain his column reached Bushekere on the 7th, to find that the direct route thence eastwards across the hills to Nyanza had become impassable. Sending word of this back to Colonel Olsen, Muller continued his march north-eastward, further delayed by numerous

---

[1] It is now known that on 20th April Wintgens reported that along this sector he had only 65 rifles, with no available reserve.

[2] The battalion left at Shangugu rejoined Muller at Nyanza on 29th May.

desertions among his carriers, and on reaching Nyakatala on the 10th learned that the enemy had left that place three days before. Next day, after marching eastwards about six miles, the column came to a halt to await further orders, which by mischance did not arrive until the 16th. On the 17th the march was resumed and two days later, driving out a small German garrison which offered little resistance, Muller occupied Nyanza and received the submission of the Batusi chieftain, Msinga.

Muller's difficulties, unfortunately, had served the enemy well ; for in the meantime the last of Wintgens's troops **Sketch 57** from the Sebea, retreating before Rouling, had passed by way of Lubengera across the front of Muller's column approaching from the south, and went on their way unmolested through Nyanza to Isawi.[1] Wintgens, indeed, owing to Rouling's lack of carriers and consequent delay in starting the pursuit, had had three days' start from the Sebea and was at no time in danger of being overtaken.

By the 21st May, with the arrival of Rouling's troops at Nyanza and the establishment of touch with Molitor[2] at Kigali, the Belgian forces had achieved their first object, the occupation of Ruanda, completely and without opposition.[3] They were now in a position to proceed with the next stage of their intended offensive. Meanwhile preliminary, though restricted, British moves in aid were being made.

DEMONSTRATIONS ON THE KAGERA AND LAKE VICTORIA

Sketch 56 Although, as has been shown, the assistance which enabled Colonel Molitor to invade Ruanda had largely deprived the British detachments on the Kagera of offensive

---

[1] It is now known that by 16th May Wintgens had brought his rearguard from the Sebea to a point some 16 miles north of Nyanza. Langenn, from the Russisi, had retreated eastwards to Iruvura (35 miles south of Nyanza) and had called on Wintgens to join him there. They eventually joined forces at Isawi, midway between the two places, and later withdrew eastwards behind the River Akanjaru.

[2] On 25th May a detachment, sent by Molitor southward from Kigali towards Lake Shohoho, occupied Kaninya, returning north-eastwards to Nsasa on 31st May.

[3] The absence of any serious opposition lends colour to a view since put forward, that the Germans, believing the Belgians would rest content with possession of Ruanda and would go no farther, had never had any intention of opposing them there.

power[1], means were found, nevertheless, both here and on Lake Victoria to contribute further, indirectly, to the Belgian undertaking.

Between the 27th and 29th April British demonstrations were made at several points. Under continual heavy rain, a force from Rukuba, near the centre of the Kagera line, moved southwards against the Germans holding the crossing at Kifumbiro (Kyaka). Farther west a detachment from Dwenkuba, after driving off a German outpost at Busindi, ten miles to the south-east, turned westwards against Dwakitiku to become engaged in three days' intermittent skirmishes there. On Lake Victoria the *Winifred* and *Nyanza*, carrying 150 of the 98th Infantry, staged a feint landing at Bukoba on the 28th April, following this up during the next five days by a similar feint at Nyamirembe, by shelling German signal stations and **Sketch 55** defences along the coast, and by practice landings on the islands. These various operations, carried out successfully and without appreciable loss, duly served their purpose of deterring the Germans in the Bukoba district from moving to the assistance of the weak German forces retreating before the Belgian columns farther west.

But as the Belgians went forward into the enemy's territory, drawing away from their own bases in the Congo, their supply difficulties and the consequent call on British aid inevitably increased. By the middle of May Lieut.-General Smuts had been obliged to say that he could do no more for them " until, if ever, the Belgian force became " based on the south of Lake Victoria ".[2] The British aim, he went on, should rather be " to push the enemy back " from the area between the Kagera and the Lake in " correspondence with their retirement farther west ",[3] a task which would strain his resources to the utmost.

Lieut.-Colonel Adye had himself already proposed, as soon as Belgian progress allowed, to move part of his Kagera force by way of the Lake to land at or near Nyamirembe, after establishing, as a first step, a base on Ukerewe Island, at the entrance to Speke Gulf in the south-eastern corner of

---

[1] See p. 404. It may be added that telegraph communication with Colonel Molitor was provided by the British signal services. Telegraph offices were opened by R.E. Signals at Kasibu (Sketch 57) on the 12th, and at Kigali on 22nd May. A telegraph line to Belgian H.Q. at Kibati was opened on the 23rd.

[2] See p. 402, f.n. 2.

[3] Telegram to Sir C. Crewe, 19th May, 1916.

P

Lake Victoria.   The island, about 25 miles long from east to west and 10 miles wide, was reconnoitred in April with this object in view, and in May a reluctant consent was given by Lieut.-General Smuts to the proposal.   A more definitely aggressive policy, therefore, was now in view, conducive to linking up the Belgian invading force with a base on Lake Victoria served by the British flotilla.

Sketch 56   Notwithstanding the transport and other complications consequent on Belgian requirements, on the 22nd May a British force from Dwenkuba, under Captain E. L. Musson, again took possession of Busindi without difficulty whilst a German attack was being simultaneously beaten off by the weak garrison left behind at Dwenkuba.[1]   On the 29th the Germans were dislodged from their post at Dwakitiku.

By the end of May it was becoming plain that the next move on the Kagera must be, after concentrating about Dwenkuba, to roll up the chain of German posts eastwards along the river as the first step towards the clearing of the district west of Lake Victoria envisaged by Lieut.-General Smuts.[2]   Meanwhile Lieut.-Colonel Adye proceeded to assemble on Lake Victoria the expedition which he was now to lead to Ukerewe Island.

THE OCCUPATION OF UKEREWE ISLAND,
9TH–10TH JUNE 1916

Sketch 55   As an objective Ukerewe Island presented several advantages.   Its possession would facilitate the contemplated landing at Nyamirembe, ninety miles to the south-westward, and the clearing of the Karagwe and Bukoba districts; it would provide, moreover, a suitable base for a subsequent attack on Mwanza, only 30 miles to the south, the principal German port on the Lake and starting-point of the shortest and best route by which to strike at Tabora and the Central Railway.

---

[1] On 21st May a German raiding party had crossed the Kagera west of Kitengule, made an abortive show of attack near the frontier at Kachumbe and Mtugula, and retired across the river, evading pursuit.

[2] At the end of May the distribution of the Kagera troops about Dwenkuba was :

Kagera Camp (Nsongezi crossing)		..	Nandi Scouts 80
Bridgehead	..	..	..	..	4/K.A.R. 60
				U.P.S.B. 60
Dwenkuba	..	..	..	..	4/K.A.R. 30
				U.P.S.B. 90, 1 m.g.
Busindi ..	..	..	..	..	4/K.A.R. 216, 2 m.g.
				Nandi Scouts 20.

The island was known to be rich both in wood fuel needed by the ships and in rice crops, due to ripen towards the end of June, the loss of which would be a serious blow to the enemy.[1] Its present garrison was reported to be probably not more than 60 strong ; the island could, on the other hand, easily be held against recapture. As an intelligence centre it had useful possibilities, while its occupation would have considerable political effect in the whole of the Lake area.

Geographically Ukerewe, although in fact an island, is Sketch 58 for practical purposes a peninsula, being almost joined to the mainland by an isthmus (the " Igongo neck ") which is cut only by the narrow Rugesi channel, passable by nothing larger than a ship's boat. The island is hilly and densely-wooded, with a belt of cultivation along the coast.

On the 4th and 5th June Lieut.-Colonel Adye's force, about 900 in all, embarked in steamers of the Lake Flotilla.[2] These assembled on the 6th some 22 miles E.S.E. of Bukoba in the convenient harbour of Bukerebe Island,[3] where the troops landed and final preparations were made.

It was decided that the principal landing on Ukerewe should be made at the south-eastern end of the island, where Nanso Bay afforded the best available harbour, by the 4/K.A.R., under Lieut.-Colonel W. G. Stonor ; at the same time the Baganda Rifles (Capt. E. T. Bruce) and Skin Corps (Capt. Drought) were to land farther east and seize the Igongo neck.

---

[1] In 1915 a shortage of rice had caused great dissatisfaction among the German native troops in the eastern Lake area ; in consequence the Germans had drafted much additional labour to Ukerewe to extend the planting of rice for 1916. It was reported that they intended to garrison the island very strongly during the harvesting of the crop, and the British expedition was timed to anticipate this by about two weeks. A large rice-mill at Mwanza and a smaller one on Ukerewe were evidence of the importance of the rice crop to the enemy.

[2] Composition :

4/K.A.R. (less 4 (single) coys.)	..	..	.. 450
Baganda Rifles	..	..	.. 200
Intelligence Scouts (Skin Corps)	..	..	.. 140
98th Infantry, M.G. section	..	..	.. 36
		Total..	.. 826

together with medical and supply services and carriers.

A political officer (Captain D. L. Baines) accompanied the expedition.

[3] Bukerebe, just visible on the horizon from Bukoba, was at this time uninhabited. It was selected partly for its sheltered anchorage and partly because assembly there might mislead watchers on the coast as to the intended objective. Shortly before the departure of the expedition the grass on the island was fired to form a smoke-screen which concealed the course taken by the ships.

On the 8th June the expedition sailed from Bukerebe, H.M.Ss. *Winifred* and *Nyanza* carrying the 4/K.A.R. and *Usoga* the remainder of the fighting troops, accompanied by the *Percy Anderson* and preceded by the *Kavirondo* and *Rusinga*. That night the two last-named lay off the northern shore of Ukerewe firing occasional rockets to divert the enemy's attention, the *Kavirondo* proceeding early on the 9th to the northern side of the Igongo neck, and the *Rusinga*, carrying supplies and porters, rejoining the main force. Meanwhile the four remaining ships, showing lights freely, had steamed round the western end of Ukerewe as if making for Mwanza, and finally turned into Speke Gulf in time to land at daylight on the 9th.

Detaching the *Percy Anderson* on patrol to intercept canoes leaving the island, Lieut.-Colonel Adye with the 4/K.A.R. landed unopposed at Peterswerft, a mile west of Nanso Bay, about 6.30 a.m., and during the morning moved on Nanso, his two ships entering harbour in conformity with his movement. At the same time the *Usoga*, farther east, landed the Skin Corps, the Baganda Rifles, and the machine gun section of the 98th Infantry in the bay north of Missuri Point. Making their way through rocky hills and then thick papyrus swamp, Drought's men encountered on the Isthmus a German party some 50 strong, the advanced guard of a force which happened to be in the act of crossing from the mainland to garrison the island. The moment the Germans opened fire the Skin Corps, without waiting for orders, charged with the bayonet and drove them headlong back into the bush, capturing a 1½-inch Krupp gun with its ox-team and 400 rounds of ammunition, at a cost of one man killed. By 9.30 a.m. the neck was cleared of the enemy. The Baganda Rifles and the machine guns of the 98th Infantry came up, unluckily not in time to take part, and in the course of the day the force consolidated the isthmus against attack from the mainland, establishing communication with the *Kavirondo*[1] to the north.

Next morning (10th) the 4/K.A.R. moved from Nanso to Buramba, three miles inland, and later in the day one company, pushing on to the high ground to the westward, hunted out with the bayonet a German detachment which fled into the bush and was not heard of again. For some

---

[1] Unfortunately too late to bring m.g. fire from the ship on the Germans retreating across the Rugesi channel, who were mistaken for Skin Corps.

days patrols scoured the hills, but there was no further fighting and by the 15th June the whole island was firmly in British hands.[1]

Adye's expedition, somewhat unwillingly sanctioned, was thus justified. Not only had the enemy been deprived of the valuable crop of rice, afterwards taken over from the native owners on payment by the British authorities, but Ukerewe became, as had been foreseen, the base for subsequent operations against Mwanza in conjunction with those of the Belgian forces now coming up from the westward.

THE BELGIAN ADVANCE FROM RUANDA

With Ruanda effectively in their possession, the Belgians Sketch 55 proceeded at the end of May, in conformity with their long-standing plan, to extend their occupation southwards and eastwards. Between them and Lake Victoria, the territories of Karagwe and the Bukoba district were still held, though in no great strength, by the enemy ; but the forces of Langenn and Wintgens, considerably inferior in number to the Belgians and now retreating southwards towards Kitega on the Ruvuvu, were in no position to oppose a resumption of the Belgian advance.

By their abandonment of the Kigali–Nyanza area the Germans had, in fact, adopted the course regarded as least probable by Major-General Tombeur.[2] His control over his command as a whole, however, was restricted by the difficulties of communication and the distances involved, and in the subsequent operations Colonels Molitor and Olsen, commanding the Northern and Southern Brigades which went forward from Kigali and Nyanza respectively, exercised a considerable measure of independence. Their subsequent movements can best be followed from sketches 57 and 59.

Colonel Molitor's orders were to continue his advance south-eastwards from Kigali towards Biharamulo, near the south-western end of Lake Victoria. By so doing he would,

---

[1] Eight Germans were captured, together with two 37 mm. field guns, an ingeniously extemporized canoe-torpedo, and a quantity of grenades and other stores. The German askari, about 60 in all, were reported to have deserted, throwing away their arms and uniforms. The local natives needed much reassurance as to their fear of a British withdrawal and subsequent German vengeance.

[2] See B.O.A., II, pp. 189–91.

if he arrived in time, cut off the retreat of the outlying German detachments in Karagwe, and he would in any case be able to link up with the Lake at Nyamirembe and so with the British flotilla, a matter of even greater importance having regard to his supply difficulties.

Sketch 57   To Colonel Olsen, one of whose two regiments (2nd) was still on the Russisi, no specific objective beyond Nyanza had been allotted.   Major-General Tombeur's instructions had laid down in general terms, as the next stage after the occupation of Kigali and Nyanza, a co-ordinated southward advance by Molitor and Olsen spreading fanwise to a line running eastwards from near Luvungi, on the Russisi, past Iruvura to the junction of the Ruvuvu and Kagera rivers (at Ukuswa).[1]   At the end of May the 2nd Regiment was already concentrated at Bugarama, while Olsen, who with his headquarters had followed Muller's march to Sketch 59 Nyanza, had moved south from Nyanza to Nya Luhengere and proposed making for Usumbura, at the head of Lake Tanganyika.   Between Molitor's eastern column, moving from Kigali on Ukuswa, and Olsen to the west, three of Molitor's battalions under Rouling were to maintain touch and to be at call to assist Olsen.

Sketch 55   On the 1st June the *marche en éventail* began.   Two days later Major-General Tombeur gave as a further objective the line Usumbura–Kitega–Biharamulo, at the same time Sketch 59 ordering Olsen to direct his left column from Nya Luhengere on Kitega, the native capital of Urundi, rather than Usumbura.   That column, under Muller, heading at first south-westwards from the Akanjaru river, fought actions at Kokawani on the 6th and at Nyawiogi on the 12th,[2] in each of which the enemy after a brief show of vigorous resistance continued his retreat, and on the 17th Olsen reached Kitega, which had been evacuated by the Germans

---

[1] "*La Marche en Éventail*", B.O.A., II, p. 255.

[2] The German force, with one 3·7 cm. gun and 5 m.g., was about 350 strong at Kokawani and some 700 strong at Nyawiogi.   The casualties ascertained were :
    At Kokawani :
        Belgians, 1 European, 4 askari killed ;   13 askari wounded ; 3 askari missing.
        Germans, 1 European killed ; 4 Europeans, 14 askari wounded.
    At Nyawiogi :
        Belgians, 3 askari killed ; 1 European, 6 askari wounded ; 1 askari missing.
        Germans, 2 Europeans, 2 askari killed ; 2 Europeans, 15 askari wounded ; 15 askari missing.

and occupied during the previous day by one of Rouling's battalions. Here his advance was suspended for about three weeks, while munitions were replenished, fresh carriers enlisted, and the troops reorganized.

Meanwhile Olsen's right column, which had reached Usumbura on the 6th and spent some days in reconnaissance to the south-eastward, marched for Kitega on the 13th June and reached its vicinity on the 19th. On the 27th the young native King, with the regent, his grandmother, made submission to the Belgians.

Farther east Molitor's progress was equally unhindered. On the 2nd June Rouling left Nyanza, two battalions marching north-eastward to cross the Akanjaru at Kionsa and thence southwards round Lake Shohoho to Kaninya, where they were joined by his third battalion (XII) which had crossed at Muyaga.[1] At Kaninya on the 10th he was ordered to detach the last-named battalion southwards, covering Olsen's eastern flank, to Kitega, where it arrived unopposed on the 16th.[2] With his other two battalions he turned eastward towards Biharamulo.

Molitor's left column, commanded by Lieut.-Colonel Sketch 60 Huyghé, was still being assembled between Kigali and Nsasa on the 4th June when Molitor was informed by Major-General Tombeur that a promise had been given to Lieut.-General Smuts that the Belgians would reach Biharamulo by the 15th.[3] Of this there was no real prospect, and the doubts expressed in reply by Colonel Molitor were borne out by events.[4] By the 6th June Huyghé's column was assembled at Nsasa, with small

---

[1] Not to be confused with another place of the same name about 70 miles farther to the S.E. The XII battalion, held up by the enemy at the ford at Muyaga, had tried another ford at Kakoma (8 miles to the north) which was found almost impassable. On its return to Muyaga it found that the enemy had withdrawn, apparently in fear of being turned from Kakoma. (B.O.A., II, p. 291.)

[2] Olsen's arrival at Kitega next day (17th) enabled Rouling to recall this battalion, which marched to Muyaga, 42 miles east of Kitega (see footnote 1). It reached Muyaga on 23rd and left on 29th to rejoin Rouling south of Biharamulo (see p. 418, f.n. 1). (B.O.A., II, pp. 292, 343.)

[3] No mention of such a promise has been found in British contemporary records.

[4] On 5th June, Molitor telegraphed that owing to shortage of ox-transport and possible delay in crossing the Kagera the promise might be difficult to fulfil. On 11th June, however, he telegraphed urgently representing that in view of the distance separating him from Rouling it would not be prudent to march rapidly on Biharamulo. (B.O.A., II., pp. 294–5.)

detachments forward towards the crossings of the Kagera at Rusuma, Mohele and Ishangu (Kageye) ; but its progress was delayed both by increasing difficulties in regard to carriers and supplies and by a shortage of canoes and bridging material. His advanced scouts reached Rusuma on the 10th June, followed by the main body on the 13th, to find the turbulent rapids of the Kagera a serious obstacle and to learn that the crossing at Rusuma was held by Wintgens with some 160 men. He therefore decided to cross both the Kagera and the Ruvuvu, successively, above their point of junction, his detachments to the north crossing independently farther down stream.

After two days of reconnaissance and preparation his main body crossed the Kagera near Ukuswa on the night of the 15th/16th June and the Ruvuvu three nights later, unopposed. By the evening of the 19th the whole force was clear of the river line. Wintgens had meanwhile withdrawn.

On the 21st June Huyghé resumed his march, moving by three parallel routes. His southernmost column gained touch next day with Rouling, whose two battalions, leaving Kaninya on the 11th and 12th and crossing the Ruvuvu at Ruanilo on the 16th and 17th,[1] had come up abreast of Huyghé. The latter entered Biharamulo on the 24th June, and on the following day Colonel Molitor's headquarters were established there.[2]

Such scanty information as existed regarding the enemy, of whom little had been seen, was conflicting ; but it seemed certain that the Belgian movement had, after all, been in time to intercept the German retreat from Karagwe.

With the object, therefore, of closing the gap between Biharamulo and Lake Victoria, Colonel Molitor disposed Huyghé's three battalions to cover Biharamulo, pushing out detachments some 30 miles to the north towards Luapindi[3] and north-east towards Nyamirembe, while

---

[1] One company crossed north of Ruanilo on 14th June. The Belgian official account claims that this crossing caused the Germans to abandon the Karagwe district, their withdrawal dating from that day. (B.O.A., II, p. 307, footnote.)

[2] On 28th June, Molitor reported that his troops and carriers, especially the latter, were in urgent need of 8 to 15 days rest. This does not appear to have been sanctioned. (B.O.A., II, p. 312.)

[3] On 28th June a Belgian company had a lively encounter at Luapindi with some 200 of the enemy, who when darkness fell slipped away into the bush. A German document found in the village confirmed the enemy's southward retreat, passing east of Biharamulo. (B.O.A., II, pp. 316-20.)

Rouling's two battalions extended south-eastwards between Biharamulo and Buzirayombo, with a detached company at Nyamasina, twenty-five miles to the south. On the 30th June the first of Huyghé's troops reached Lake Victoria at Nyamirembe, where they hoisted the Belgian flag.[1]

But the meshes of the Belgian net were too wide. In the difficult hilly country at the southern end of the Lake the Germans, familiar with the ground, had little trouble in making their way southwards unobserved. Their orders to concentrate for an attack on Biharamulo, in which Wintgens was to co-operate,[2] were disregarded, and apart from minor skirmishes here and there only one serious encounter took place.

On the 3rd July a body of some 300 of the enemy under Captain Gudovius, the German commander in Karagwe, which had filtered through the Belgian screen between Biharamulo and Nyamirembe, came up against a Belgian detachment 175 strong under Rouling in person, holding the cross-roads at Kato, midway between Biharamulo and Buzirayombo. From about 1 p.m., when the enemy turned the Belgian left and drove Rouling's men back on to one end of a rocky knoll commanding the Kato-Bwanga road, to about 3.30 p.m., when Rouling himself was badly wounded, fighting went on at close quarters in the bush and the Belgian situation became critical. The firing eventually attracted two more Belgian companies which had been trailing another German party some miles away, and on their arrival Gudovius's force withdrew. As it went it encountered another Belgian company coming up and was dispersed, its field hospital, with Gudovius himself, who had been wounded early in the fight, falling into Belgian hands.[3]

---

[1] Reports of a German column approaching Biharamulo from the N.W. proved eventually to refer to two British columns under Lawrence(see p. 423). (B.O.A., II, p. 320.)

[2] B.O.A., II, p. 315.

[3] The detailed Belgian account is of interest. The two companies which came up had previously, in thick bush, mistaken each other for Germans and opened fire. It is evident that but for this they might have been on the scene sooner.

The Belgian losses were 4 Europeans, 29 askari killed ; 5 Europeans, 25 askari wounded, 5 askari missing. Four Germans who were killed were buried by the Belgians.

Continued at foot of next page.

Meanwhile the remaining Germans from the north had avoided the Belgian posts, and by the 5th July the whole of the Karagwe area, between the Kagera and the Lake, was reported clear of the enemy. This, however, was not the end of the matter, for almost at once it became known that German forces from the south-west, presumably Langenn and Wintgens, were approaching.

After the affair at Kato, which had led to the concentration between that place and Biharamulo of most of his now weary troops, Colonel Molitor redistributed his force in readiness either to deal with this new threat or to co-operate with the British in an attack on Mwanza by way of the Lake. With this object he ordered his right column, two battalions of the 4th Regiment now under Huyghé in succession to Rouling, south-westwards towards Nyatakara, and distributed his left column, the 3rd Regiment, between Biharamulo and Buzirayombo. The remaining battalion (XII) of the 4th Regiment, which had been detached, as will be remembered, in aid of Olsen, was now on its way eastward from Muyaga to Nyatakara, where it arrived somewhat belatedly on the 7th July.[1]

On this day the small detachment at Nyamasina located a much superior German force ten miles to the south-east near Mugando ; this was identified on the 8th as being Langenn's force and was considered too strong to justify an attack by the newly-arrived battalion.

During the next few days Huyghé brought up his other two battalions, the XIIIth to Nyatakara in reinforcement of the XIIth, and the XIth to Bwanga, nearly 40 miles to the north-east. On the 14th July the XIIth and XIIIth, marching eastwards from Nyatakara in pursuit of the Germans, who had meanwhile left Mugando, came up with

---

Continued from previous page.

A curious feature of the affair was that two days earlier, when a small German baggage-party was ambushed, there had been found on a dead German the complete operation order by Captain Gudovius, dated at Luapindi, 27th June, for the retreat of his force in 8 small columns by 6 different routes, bringing his main body through Kato as, in fact, happened. This information appears to have come too late to be acted upon. (B.O.A., II, pp. 332–42.)

[1] The XII Bn. marched east from Muyaga on 29th June and halted from 30th June to 2nd July. On 1st July it received orders to move with all speed to Nyamasina and Nyatakara. Resuming the march on 3rd July, the leading company reached Nyamasina late on 5th July, but the difficulties met with delayed arrival at Nyatakara until the 7th. (B.O.A., II, p. 344.)

them at Djobahika, and for the next 36 hours were engaged in obstinate if intermittent fighting which went largely in the enemy's favour. Touch was not established, as had been expected, with the XIth Battalion which had been summoned from Bwanga, and when, about 5 p.m. on the 15th, a fresh heavy attack was launched by the Germans on Huyghé's right, most of his carriers fled into the bush and were not seen again. As darkness fell a further attack threatened the Belgian left, and the situation remained critical till about midnight (15th/16th), when there was a lull. At 2.45 a.m. Huyghé, now short of ammunition, withdrew his exhausted force to a position some 4 miles back, not without anxiety for the XIth Battalion, now overdue, of which there was still no sign.[1]

Meanwhile the enemy, having once again demonstrated the German aptitude in rearguard action, had likewise withdrawn.

The casualties on both sides had been remarkably few.[2] But the defection of Huyghé's carriers[3] had immobilized his column, now concentrated about Djobahika, and for the next fortnight his troops remained in the area between Nyatakara and Buyombe, reorganizing the carrier and supply services. Colonel Molitor, informed early in July that the idea of a Belgian move against Mwanza by way of Lake Victoria had been abandoned and that Major-General Tombeur proposed to take that place in reverse from the landward side and to move thence against Tabora, had already decided to give his men a much needed rest in the populated and fertile areas round the south-western end of the Lake. For the time being, therefore, the Belgian troops in this area stood fast. The exertions of the past three months had given them, fortunately with little fighting and

---

[1] Apparently not realizing the situation, the XIth Battalion waited for some hours on the 15th in order to recall a detached company and rest the remainder, and did not resume its march until moonrise, about 9 p.m. It arrived to find Djobahika abandoned by both sides and turned north-west to rejoin the other two battalions. (B.O.A., II, p. 393.)

[2] The total Belgian losses are given as 9 killed, 2 Belgians and 8 askari wounded, 2 missing. Enemy sources give the German loss as 2 killed, 5 wounded.

[3] No less than 1,600 carriers are stated to have deserted. (B.O.A., II, p. 431.) The Uganda and local natives serving as carriers were in considerable fear of the Belgian Congo troops, many of whom came of tribes with a propensity for cannibalism. It was freely believed among the carriers that this propensity was indulged whenever supplies ran short.

at almost negligible cost in casualties, possession ot a gratifyingly valuable tract of Africa some three times the size of Belgium.

Sketch 55 The original Belgian objectives in this part of the theatre of war had thus been attained. Meanwhile Major-General Tombeur had for some time been in communication with his Government regarding the further course of the campaign. As early as the 12th June he was directed, first, to maintain contact with the enemy ; secondly, to extend his occupation at least to the general line Usumbura—Lake Victoria, so as to link his force with both the great lakes ; thirdly, to co-ordinate his own with British movements ; but to avoid any merging of the Allied forces and to preserve the independence of the Belgian command. On this basis it was then considered that, once the northern objectives were gained, the only remaining Belgian interest would be the occupation, exclusively by Belgian troops, of Ujiji and the western section of the Central Railway. Major-General Tombeur was authorized, if his situation permitted, to proceed at once with this further plan. Eventually, on the assumption of a British desire for further co-operation, with which he was in agreement, the Belgian commander recommended that his Northern Brigade should march on Mwanza in conjunction with Sir Charles Crewe,[1] while the Sketch 55 Southern Brigade should move on Ujiji with the aid of the British and Belgian vessels on Lake Tanganyika, his two forces then converging on Tabora.[2] On the 12th July these further plans were approved by the Belgian Government ;[3] but in the meantime, as will presently be seen, the British troops had undertaken independently the capture of Mwanza and their commander became committed to a separate line of advance based on that place.

---

[1] See Chaps. XXV, XXVI.

[2] See B.O.A., II, pp. 361-3. According to the B.O.A., Lieut.-General Smuts, in reply to an enquiry by Major-General Tombeur, stated that he considered the continuance of Belgian co-operation indispensable and suggested the plan for attacking Mwanza and Ujiji and thereafter Tabora, as given here. It has not been found possible to confirm this from existing British records.

[3] Subject to the restriction that Belgian forces were not to go south of the Central Railway nor east of the meridian of Tabora, unless subsequent developments justified it. (B.O.A., II, pp. 362-3.)

NOTE

GERMAN FORCES IN THE WEST, JAN.–APRIL 1916.

A captured German return for 1st January 1916 gave details as follows :

District	Units	Ger.	Ask.	Irr.	Guns	m.g.
Ruanda ..	7., 23., 25., 26. F.K.	111	957	279	2	10
Urundi	14. Res.K., Urundi det.	55	450	102	1	2
Bukoba ..	7. Res. K.	48	254	673	2	1
Musoma & Ikoma (Eastern Lake)	" D ", " F " K. ..	23	380	—	—	—
Mwanza ..	" A ", " B ", " E " K. ; one Bty.	79	608	73	6	2
Usuwi (Bihara- mulo)	6. F.K.	16	200	—	—	—
Kigoma ..	.. .. ..	244	180	12	12	1
	Total ..	576	3,029	1,139	23	16

The corresponding figures given in the British Intelligence report for 1st April 1916, totalling 640 Europeans, 7,870 natives, 33 guns, 27 machine guns, were stated to be the maximum estimate and to " include an unknown but large proportion of " levy formations ". By some misapprehension, the Belgian Official account, in quoting these figures, whilst correctly stating that they were regarded as a maximum, incorrectly adds that *toutefois les auxiliaires dont se servaient les Allemands en grand nombre, et particulièrement comme éclaireurs, n'étaient pas compris.*[1]

The distribution of troops in Ruanda and Urundi on the 17th April 1916 is now known to have been as follows :

Based on Kisenyi .. *Abteilung Wintgens* (including " A ", " B ", and *26. F.K.*) 55 Germans, 000 askari, with 3 guns and 5 m.g.

Based on Kitega .. *Abteilung Urundi :* 36 Europeans, 250 askari, 100 auxiliaries, with 2 guns, 3 m.g.

Note.—Not included are *23. F.K.* and *25. F.K.* withdrawn from the *Abteilung Wintgens* to Kondoa Irangi on the 22nd March; *7. F.K.*, withdrawn on the 15th April, which returned to Shangugu three days later ; *14. Res. K.*, from the *Abteilung Urundi*, which proceeded to Kigoma on the 16th April and was eventually withdrawn to Kondoa Irangi.

---

[1] B.O A., I., p. 175.

CHAPTER XXV

THE WESTERN AREA 1916—*(continued)*

ANGLO-BELGIAN CO-OPERATION

(Sketches 13, 55, 58, 59, 60, 61, 62)

THE KARAGWE AREA

Sketch 60 By the first week in June, when Molitor's eastward movement from the Akanjaru had begun and detachments from the British posts on the Kagera, totalling roughly 600, were concentrated south of the river about Dwenkuba, a German withdrawal from the Karagwe area had become inevitable.[1] Consequently, the border posts in the Kigezi district to the westward being no longer needed, between the 8th and 15th the Uganda Police Service Battalion, about 400 in all, was brought in to Kagera Camp, at the crossing near Dwenkuba, and preparations were made for the projected drive eastwards to clear the country south of the Kagera. On the 19th it was ascertained that Mabira, twenty miles southeast of Dwenkuba, a well-fortified German post which was to have been the first objective, had been abandoned by the enemy. Five days later it was learned that Kyaka, at the important crossing forty miles farther east, had also been evacuated.

In the meantime, with combined Allied operations in prospect, Lieut.-General Smuts had decided that the Lake Force, hitherto under Lieut.-Colonel Adye, should be commanded by a more senior officer. The obvious choice was Brig.-General Sir Charles Crewe, who was already responsible for Anglo-Belgian liaison and was familiar with local conditions. Accordingly on the 17th June, after Adye's successful conclusion of the Ukerewe expedition, Brig.-General

---

[1] It is now known that towards the end of May Langenn suggested that Gudovius's troops should be transferred to reinforce Wintgens between the Akanjaru and Ruvuvu rivers. The proposal was rejected by Major-General Wahle, who ordered Gudovius both to maintain his existing positions and to hold the Kagera crossings against the Belgians. By the middle of June, Gudovius, who had meanwhile been refused reinforcements, had been so weakened in the north by detaching troops to meet the Belgians farther south that he began a general withdrawal from Karagwe and the Bukoba district. Wahle's approval of this appears to have been given on 19th June.

Crewe assumed command.[1] His instructions from the Commander-in-Chief, dated 13th June, were that the enemy's retreat from the western shores of the Lake, rendered probable by the seizure of Ukerewe, should immediately be followed up by a British occupation, on the completion of which he was to ask for further instructions. Brig.-General Crewe replied on the 18th that he proposed, first, to use his force on the Kagera to drive the enemy southwards, and secondly, as soon as Kyaka had been End Paper occupied, to seize Bukoba by way of the Lake with troops (N) drawn from the Masaka and lower Kagera areas, moving his whole force eventually to the neighbourhood of Nyamirembe.   Approval of these plans was received on the Sketch 60 27th June, with orders to hasten their execution.[2]

The line of the Kagera being now clear of the enemy, a column 300 strong, under Captain A. F. Carew, was ordered to push rapidly eastwards through Kyaka to Bukoba, the remainder of the Kagera troops moving southwards in two somewhat larger columns under Majors E. H. T. Lawrence and E. L. Musson from Kitengule and Kyaka respectively.[3] At the same time, the additional troops from Masaka and the lower Kagera, 170 of the 98th Infantry and 150 Baganda Rifles, with a machine gun and a 2-pdr.

---

[1] Lieut.-Colonel Adye took over command of the Eastern Lake area under Brig.-General Crewe.

[2] This approval crossed Brig.-Genl. Crewe's further telegram of 26th June suggesting Mariahilf as his next objective.

[3] Composition :

" Flying " Column (Carew)

4/K.A.R.		180
Baganda Rifles		90
Nandi Scouts ..		30

300 with 2 m.g.

" M " Column (Musson)

4/K.A.R.	100
Uganda Police Service Bn.	40
Baganda Rifles	180
Nandi Scouts ..	45

365 with 2 m.g.

Police (" P ") Column (Lawrence)

U.P.S.B.	370
Nandi Scouts ..	25

395 with 3 m.g.

Hotchkiss gun, under Lieut.-Colonel C. R. Burgess, assembled at Sango Bay, whence they sailed on the night of the 27th/28th June for Bukoba.

None of these forces succeeded in overtaking the retreating enemy. Burgess, landing at Bukoba on the 28th, found that Gudovius had abandoned the place five days before, and it was not until two days later that Carew's column joined him there. On the evening of the 1st July their combined forces, less a garrison of 80 Baganda Rifles left at Bukoba, re-embarked to sail for Nyamirembe, where at noon next day a Belgian guard of honour saluted their arrival and contact was established between Brig.-General Crewe and Major-General Tombeur through Lieut.-Colonel Huyghé, the local commander. With a courtesy to which tribute is due,[1] the Belgian troops in occupation were then withdrawn a short distance inland, and in the course of the 3rd July the British force disembarked.

On the same day Musson joined hands with Lawrence's Police at Kamachumu, 32 miles south-west of Bukoba, where it had been hoped that the Germans might be intercepted. But the enemy was already far to the south, being in fact engaged on that day, as we have seen, with the Belgians at Kato. So on the 4th Lawrence and Musson resumed their march southwards, heading for Biharamulo, where the Belgians were known to be. Following parallel routes and rounding up a few enemy stragglers as they went, the two columns on nearing Nyamirembe were diverted by order of Brig.-General Crewe to that place, which they reached on the 9th.

The whole of the Lake Force was thus concentrated at the southern end of Lake Victoria, in close touch for the time being with the Belgian troops about Biharamulo, and ready for the next move.

THE CAPTURE OF MWANZA

End Paper (N)

It will have been noticed that the events of the past few months had gradually brought about a considerable modification of the earlier British policy with regard to the western zone of the theatre of war, where for so long the British attitude had been purely defensive. Lieut.-General Smuts, it is true, in framing his general plan of campaign had

---

[1] It will be remembered that the Belgian flag had already been flying at Nyamirembe for three days. See p. 417.

considered the possibility of combined British and Belgian action in this quarter.[1] But up to April 1916 it had been consistently made clear to the Belgians that British participation in a combined offensive was not likely to be forthcoming on any large scale,[2] and it was not until the Belgian advance through Ruanda and Urundi had with British assistance been successfully carried out, and the Allied forces linked up on Lake Victoria, that a joint movement southwards from the Lake against the western section of the Central Railway came to be accepted as the natural continuation of the operations which have been described.

Brig.-General Crewe's first plan, proposed in a telegram to the Commander-in-Chief on the 26th June, had been to move southwards from an advanced base at Nyamirembe against Tabora, in conjunction with the Belgian Northern Brigade, making Mariahilf (60 miles south of Nyamirembe) his first objective. In reply Lieut.-General Smuts, withholding approval of movement beyond Nyamirembe, directed him to submit fresh proposals after conferring with the Belgian commander, but to afford the latter meanwhile all assistance which would not interfere with his own operations. Sketch 55

Nyamirembe had unfortunately proved at once to be, in Crewe's words, " as a base for any operations, impossible ". There was little water ; local food supplies were scarce ; the surrounding country consisted mostly of rocky hills covered with thick bush, lacking tracks and largely infested with tsetse. The Belgians, moreover, as has been shown, were in need of rest and reorganization, and were still in difficulties with regard to carriers. Clearly the only suitable base for further operations would be Mwanza, against which place it was advisable to strike quickly, before the garrison could be reinforced.

Writing in this sense on the 2nd July to Major-General Tombeur, who had not yet arrived, Brig.-General Crewe proposed that 1,000 Belgian troops should embark at Nyamirembe on the 10th to co-operate next day with his own available 1,200 men[3] in an attack on Mwanza from the Lake, and that a joint Anglo-Belgian base should be established at Mwanza for the projected advance on Tabora.

---

[1] See p. 267.
[2] See Chap. XII, also p. 402, f.n. 2.
[3] Including about 700 on Ukerewe Island, and Burgess's and Carew's forces, roughly 500 ; but excluding Musson and Lawrence marching overland.

In informing the Commander-in-Chief of this, he added that if Lieut.-General Smuts disapproved of a joint attack, or the Belgian commander did not agree, he proposed to capture Mwanza himself, using the whole of his Lake Force.

The British plan was viewed with disfavour by Major-General Tombeur, whose attention was still fixed on the retreating enemy and on the possible arrival of Wintgens and Langenn from the west. He propounded as an alternative a move against Mwanza by land round the southern end of the Lake, aided by the use of British ships to bring stores and supplies to Nyamirembe. This proposal, received on the evening of the 8th July, was unacceptable to Brig.-General Crewe, who therefore decided next day, in the absence of a reply from the Commander-in-Chief, to proceed against Mwanza independently forthwith.

With the timely arrival of the two columns from the Kagera on the 9th, Crewe's force was now some 1,900 strong, with 15 machine guns and a light Hotchkiss gun : ample, in fact, even though deficient in artillery, to deal with the German garrison at Mwanza, whose strength was reported as from 600 to 800.[1]

---

[1] On 9th July the Lake Force was distributed as follows (strengths approximate) :

At Nyamirembe (including Kagera columns) :

	Offrs.	O.R.
98th Infantry	2	170
4/K.A.R.	13	290
Uganda Police S. Bn.	11	400
Baganda Rifles	7	260
Nandi Scouts	3	80
Total	36	1,200 with 7 m.g., 1 Hotchkiss gun.

At Ukerewe :

	Offrs.	O.R.
98th Infantry	1	30
4/K.A.R.	14	440
Baganda Rifles	3	90
Skin Corps	4	150
Total	22	710 with 8 m.g.

The 98th Infantry had suffered so much from sickness that they were at this time unfit for any arduous duty.

The six Lake vessels available were sufficient only to embark the fighting troops, with medical and first line carriers, total about 3,500. Consequently, after landing the troops, two ships had to return to Ukerewe and Nyamirembe for the ammunition and supply columns. As no baggage could be taken, and the two days' cooked rations carried by the troops quickly went bad, considerable hardship was entailed.

Brig.-General Crewe had already, on the 5th July, whilst awaiting Major-General Tombeur's reply, reconnoitred the coast and arranged at Ukerewe for a temporary hospital and for the troops already there to be ready to embark ; it only remained, therefore, to issue his orders.

Mwanza, at the mouth of the gulf of that name, stands Sketch 61 on the western side of a broad promontory some twenty miles across. Of its defences little was known, but from its situation the place would evidently be best attacked from the landward side, and after his reconnaissance Brig.-General Crewe decided to make his landing at Kongoro Point, on the eastern coast of the promontory.

On the 9th July he issued operation orders, dividing his troops into " A " Force (about 800) under Lieut.-Colonel C. R. Burgess and " B " Force (about 600) under Lieut.-Colonel H. B. Towse, with about 400 details in general reserve.[1]

On the evening of the 10th the *Winifred* and *Nyanza*, with the 4/K.A.R. and 98th Infantry from Nyamirembe, reached Nanso harbour, at Ukerewe Island (Sketch 58). Here the 98th were disembarked, to be replaced on board by Drought's Skin Corps. The remaining ships, the *Sybil*, *Usoga* and *Rusinga*, the two latter conveying the troops just

---

[1] Extract from operation order, 9th July, 1916 :

3. Distribution of Troops :

"A" Force, Lieut.-Colonel Burgess.

830 rifles,
7 m.g.
	7 (single) coys. 4/K.A.R.
	African Scouts
	Nandi Scouts
	Det. Fd. Amb.
		H.M.S. *Winifred*
		   ,, *Nyanza*
		   ,, *Sybil*

" B " Force, Lieut.-Colonel Towse.

630 rifles, 4 m.g.	Det. 4/K.A.R. Uganda Police S.Bn. Det. Baganda Rifles Det. Fd. Amb.	H.M.S. *Usoga* ,. *Rusinga*

General Reserve, Captain Tucker, 98th Infantry.

370 rifles, 4 m.g.	Det. Baganda Rifles Det. 98th Infantry	H.M.S. *Sybil* ,, *Kavirondo*

4. Disembarkation :

Troops from *Winifred* and *Nyanza* will disembark at Kongoro Point evening of 11th and during night of 11th/12th July. *Sybil, Usoga,* and *Rusinga* troops will disembark at dawn 12th July in order named.

5. Objectives. First objectives will be as follows :

" A " Force. Mwamba Hill, throwing out scouts to Senga.
" B " Force. Senga.

Further detailed instructions will be issued to Os.C. " A " and " B " Forces.

arrived by land from the Kagera, followed next day, reaching Nanso in the evening.[1]

At 7.30 p.m. on the 11th the *Winifred* and *Nyanza*, carrying " A " Force, moved out from Nanso, and by 9 p.m. the *Winifred*, skilfully handled by Lieut.-Commander F. R. Hemsted, R.N.R., had worked in to within 200 yards of Kongoro Point, where disembarkation began. The sandy beach selected during the reconnaissance was missed in the darkness and the first landing party, of the Skin Corps, came up against a dense belt of papyrus reeds in deep water, through which eventually they found a passage and hauled themselves ashore. " As lightning showed us a " hill in the vicinity," wrote a survivor, " Lieut. F. V. Postma " advanced on it with two sections of Skin Corps and within " five minutes of landing met the enemy advancing to the " shore, their (enemy) leading askaris being shot at two " yards range."

By 10.30 p.m. the Scouts had secured Ugura Hill, overlooking the landing-place, after driving off small parties of the enemy. Whilst the landing was proceeding Lieut.-Colonel Burgess sent the Scouts on to seize the high ground at Mwamba, eight miles inland, and the headland five miles away on the northern flank at Senga Point, both of which were gained by dawn with little opposition.

At daylight on the 12th " B " Force in the *Usoga* and *Rusinga*, together with the rest of " A " Force in the *Sybil*, reached Kongoro, where the *Sybil's* troops disembarked, while Lieut.-Colonel Towse's ships conveyed his force to effect a landing at Senga Point. In the course of the morning the reserve, 98th Infantry and Baganda Rifles from Ukerewe, towed in lighters by the *Kavirondo*, took over at Ugura Hill while Burgess pushed on with " A " Force towards Mwamba, Towse meanwhile moving westwards from Senga Point on Kaienzi. Neither encountered any serious opposition. By the evening disembarkation had been completed and forward reconnaissance made ; " A " Force was firmly established at Mwamba and " B " Force at Kaienzi ; the advance of the latter, turning the

---

[1] Instructions had been given to these three ships to sail on the afternoon of the 11th so as to reach Kongoro Point at daylight on the 12th. Through some misunderstanding they arrived off Nanso at 5 p.m. on 11th, creating considerable dismay by having passed during daylight within sight of the Mwanza promontory and thus given away the concentration of ships at Ukerewe.

right of the German coastal defences, had compelled the enemy to evacuate them. In rear, the 98th and Baganda Rifles had consolidated on Ugura and were watching the Mwanza-Nyanguge road south of the hill. The *Nyanza* and *Rusinga* were now sent back to Ukerewe and Nyamirembe respectively for the ammunition and supply columns and telegraph detachment. On board the *Winifred* Brig.-General Crewe issued orders for next day : " A " Force to push forward to Muhanga, four miles south-east of Mwanza, sending the Skin Corps to cut the Tabora road at the crossing of the river Nyasisi six miles to the southward ; " B " Force to move south-westwards direct on Issenga, with a flank guard following the coast.

On the 13th July, after a personal reconnaissance, Crewe decided to transfer his base from Ugura, where the papyrus belt and absence of tracks inland had hampered landing, to Kaienzi, from which point, in addition to the advantages of a stone pier and a potential motor route to Mwanza, his line of advance would be shortened by some seven miles. This was carried out during the day, the *Nyanza* having returned from Ukerewe at 10 a.m. with carriers, supplies and the telegraph.[1]

That evening Towse, having met little opposition, gained the high ground about Hale, seven miles north-east of Mwanza, while Burgess, after driving off some 150 of the enemy who retreated south-westwards, camped about three miles east of Muhanga.[2]

During the night of the 13th/14th the now deserted German village at Hale was shelled from Mwanza by a *Königsberg* gun, which next day expended some thirty rounds in Towse's direction, inflicting no casualties. Brig. General Crewe with his headquarters had joined Towse on

---

[1] This ship brought also a disturbing report that a German detachment 80 strong, retreating from the Mara river in the Eastern Lake area (Sketch 13), had turned to threaten Ukerewe on learning that the island had been left undefended. 50 Baganda Rifles, to reinforce the 50 of that unit already there, were therefore sent back to Ukerewe. No attack was made.

[2] An interesting episode was Towse's dispersal of a small German patrol, which lost both its Europeans, one killed, one captured. This patrol had been sent to clear up the situation along the coast, and, in the absence of information from it, the German commander in Mwanza appears to have been unaware of the approach of " B " Force. His subsequent tactics in concentrating against Burgess, so that Towse successfully descended on his northern flank, seem to confirm this view. His map was afterwards found, on which Burgess's landing and camping grounds were marked, but no indication was given of Force "B ".

the evening of the 13th ; unfortunately, as the cable laid forward from Kaienzi to him was repeatedly cut by hostile natives, communication with the ships was not maintained and their co-operation suffered in consequence. Efforts to gain touch by runner with Burgess proved equally unsuccessful.[1]

Early on the 14th July the two columns resumed their movement, still meeting little opposition but finding the country broken and difficult. By 1 p.m. Towse was established on the ridges about Issenga and was in helio communication with Burgess some twò miles to the southward. Against the latter, on ground well adapted to defence, the enemy showed every sign of intended resistance ; but the unexpected arrival of Towse behind the German left flank disposed of this at once, and Burgess, debouching from the hills[2] through a narrow defile (" which ", in the words of a survivor " could have been held with one machine gun "), drove off the last of the retreating enemy and at about 3 p.m. entered Mwanza.

Unhappily a detachment of 40 of the 4/K.A.R. and 70 Nandi Scouts, sent by Burgess southwards from Muhanga, had been too late to intercept the retreat.[3]

It was found that the bulk of the German forces had left the place by 1 p.m., the Europeans escaping by water up the Mwanza Gulf while some five hundred askari had taken the Tabora road.[4] The *Königsberg* gun, minus its breech-block, was captured intact.

The only hope of successful pursuit lay in the use of the ships ; but these had remained at Kaienzi, out of touch owing to the field cable having been cut.[5] Consequently it was not until noon on the 15th that the *Winifred* and

---

[1] Runners who were sent out to repeat the orders to Burgess to cut the enemy's line of retreat along the Tabora road returned at dawn with a false report of the rout of "A" Force, presumably to account for their own failure to get through.

[2] As the advanced guard came in sight of the town the aerial mast of the powerful local wireless station, said to be capable of communicating direct with Damascus, and so with Germany, was seen in the act of falling.
   The elimination of this station was of great service to the Allied cause.

[3] The scouts leading the party became scattered in the bush, and their commander, with one other man, reached the road as the last of the German carriers disappeared.

[4] Departure, nevertheless, must have been hurried, for luncheon tables, with the food untouched, were found ready in the German houses.

[5] No orders were given to the ships to move along the coast conjointly with Towse's coastal column and to co-operate so far as their light armament would allow. Contemporary records make no reference to the omission.

Sybil entered Mwanza harbour, where they embarked Brig.-General Crewe with 200 of the 4/K.A.R., 50 Scouts and two machine guns, under Captain R. B. L. Harvey, 4/K.A.R., and proceeded up Mwanza Gulf. Progress was slow, these waters being entirely unknown. At 6.30 p.m., when off 'the headland west of Masua in the eastern arm of the Gulf, orders were given to disembark. Dense reeds and sudd made landing difficult, but by 10.15 p.m. it had been effected, unopposed. Local natives reported that the German craft were at Nyatembe, six miles on, and that 400 of the enemy who had spent the previous night (14th/15th) there were now at Misungi, five miles inland. Pushing on to Nyatembe, where it arrived at 1 a.m. on the 16th, the force duly came upon the German vessels,[1] and made prisoners of four Germans left in charge.

In the meantime the party detached by Burgess on the 14th towards the Tabora road had followed up the German retreat, passing southwards through Usagara at dawn next day, but had been unable to overtake the enemy and had come exhausted to a standstill half way to Misungi. At daylight on the 16th a runner brought word of the movement from Nyatembe to Misungi, and the party resumed its southward march.

At 7 a.m. on the 16th the column from Nyatembe, under Captain Harvey, reached Misungi, drove out a small German piquet, and prepared to rest after its all-night march. Within an hour, however, fire was opened on the village by several field guns and a pom-pom, and soon afterwards the enemy attacked in considerable force. The attack was driven off, but Harvey was not strong enough to pursue, and at 9.30 a.m. he broke off the action and withdrew slowly northwards along the road, the enemy making no attempt to follow.

At noon he met the Nandi Scouts on their way southwards, and with these as rear-guard the combined force made its way back to Mwanza.

The *Winifred* was meanwhile loading up the stores abandoned by the enemy at Nyatembe, and, with Sir Charles Crewe on board, returned to Mwanza the same evening.

---

[1] S.S. *Muansa*, steam launch *Heinrich Otto*, steam pinnace *Schwaben*, and 3 lighters with much baggage, 12 boxes of specie, a Colt automatic gun, a considerable quantity of ammunition, and useful medical stores, and about 100 tons of much-needed native foodstuffs.

With the occupation of Mwanza the first stage of the long march to Tabora had been accomplished. Here, as elsewhere, an important locality had been wrested from the enemy at a negligible cost in casualties,[1] but the enemy's forces had evaded battle and had made good their retreat, unscathed. The map suggests the question whether Burgess, by a swift thrust from Ugura direct on Usagara, might have succeeded in intercepting and defeating the retreating garrison. But this does not appear to have been considered, possibly because the country was unknown and the troops not as yet accustomed to work together.[2]

BELGIAN OPERATIONS EAST OF LAKE TANGANYIKA

Sketch 55   Concurrently with the British and Belgian operations west of Lake Victoria, the territory lying east of Lake Tanganyika and north of the Central Railway was being cleared by our allies in accordance with the general plan already mentioned.[3]

It will be remembered that during the latter half of June the Belgian Southern Brigade, under Colonel Olsen, was concentrated at Kitega, reorganizing, collecting supplies, and preparing for its next move.

On the 19th Major-General Tombeur had instructed his two Brigade Commanders that after reaching the general line Usumbura – Biharamulo all their efforts were to be directed to acquiring the utmost possible extension of their territorial gains.[4] Colonel Olsen therefore planned to march south on a broad front. Again organized in two columns, each comprising three battalions and a battery, his brigade left Kitega on the 8th July, the 2nd Regiment, under Lieut.-Colonel Thomas, heading south-westwards and the 1st Regiment (less one battalion), under Major Muller, together with brigade headquarters, moving south-eastwards towards

---

[1] Killed, 2 o.r.; wounded, 1 offr., 7 o.r. Two Germans, 22 askari were known to have been killed; 10 Germans, 4 askari wounded and captured.

[2] The 4/K.A.R. had never previously, since its formation in 1902, been together as a complete unit. See App. IV.

[3] See p. 420.

[4] See B.O.A., II, Annexe No. 21. As the next objective Major-General Tombeur gave a general line running north-eastward from the vicinity of Kasulu through Kabira (Sketch 59) and Mariahilf to Lake Victoria, with an extension, " if the duration of the War allowed time ", towards Ujiji, St. Michael and Tabora.

the middle reaches of the Mlagarasi river. Preceding their departure, one of Muller's battalions was sent on the 6th Sketch 59 north-eastwards to Muyaga, to march south from there as flank guard and to maintain some touch with Molitor in that direction.

Olsen's information regarding the enemy led him at first to expect opposition both at Nyanza, on Lake Tanganyika, and at Kasulu, forty miles south-east of that place. Later reports indicated that the German commander, Langenn, had moved eastwards, but no sign of the enemy was seen by either column until, as will appear, they converged on Kasulu.[1]

Their progress, impeded in each case by natural difficulties, was somewhat slow. Thomas, moving through hilly and broken country, sent one battalion directly southwards and with the other two reached Rumonge on the 12th and Nyanza on the 15th July. At Nyanza he conferred on the 20th with Lieut.-Colonel Moulaert, commanding the troops on the western shore and the Belgian flotilla, to co-ordinate action against Kigoma. Muller and the left column, obstructed by swamps and rivers, reached Kabira, sixty miles south-east of Kitega, on the 19th, there to be held up for three days by the difficulties of crossing the Mlagarasi river.

Meanwhile Olsen, reaching Nyakasu, thirty miles south of Kitega, on the 16th, was overtaken there by a telegram from Major-General Tombeur directing him to march on Ujiji, whence he was to move eastwards in aid of the Northern Brigade's impending southward advance on Tabora. Thereupon he directed both his columns to converge on Kasulu so as to make a combined attack on that place on the 25th.

No such elaborate operation proved necessary. On the morning of the 24th July Thomas's leading battalion (IV) reached Kasulu and at once attacked the small German

---

[1] Papers found later at Kasulu suggested that Langenn was ordered eastwards on the assumption that Olsen's brigade had been sent to co-operate with Molitor towards Biharamulo and Mwanza. (B.O.A., II, p. 368.)

It is now known that on 18th July Lettow telegraphed to Wahle asking his views as to holding Kigoma and suggesting that, in the event of a threat to the railway east of that place, it would be advisable to withdraw the troops and mobile guns, leaving a *Königsberg* gun and the guns of the armed vessels to cover the withdrawal. On 20th July Wahle reported the evacuation of Kigoma.

garrison, which after a brief resistance abandoned the place and made good its escape.[1] Muller's two battalions arrived from Kabira next day, followed by brigade headquarters on the 26th. Thomas's other two battalions (V. and VII.) had meanwhile turned south for Kigoma, followed from Kasulu on the 28th July by brigade headquarters and the IVth Battalion, while Muller's column diverged again southeastwards from Kasulu in the hope both of cutting off the enemy's retreat along the Central Railway and of barring the approach of any German reinforcements from the east. On neither route was there any sign of opposition until they neared the railway.

On the 27th July the IVth Battalion quickly overcame the half-hearted opposition of a small German force on the railway at Lwiche, where it was learned that Ujiji and Kigoma had been abandoned by the enemy, and the same evening his patrols hoisted the Belgian flag in Ujiji. Next morning Kigoma was occupied. On the 30th Muller reached the railway at Ruchugi, fifty miles east of Kigoma, to find the important railway bridge over the Ruchugi river most efficiently destroyed.

The end of July thus saw the Belgian forces in undisputed possession of the western end of the Central Railway. They had not, unfortunately, arrived in time to deal a blow to the German garrison of Kigoma nor to prevent the enemy from removing all his rolling stock and wrecking such material as was left behind.[2] In the abandoned coastal defences were found the remains of a *Königsberg* gun. On the stocks by the shore a half-erected vessel proved to be the small sea going steamer *Adjutant*, which had been brought up in sections from Dar-es-Salaam, a remarkable effort by the enemy which, had it been made sooner, might well have influenced the situation on the Lake considerably.[3]

On the 28th July another small German craft, which in March had likewise arrived in sections to replace the lost *Kingani*,[4] was sunk a few miles south of Ujiji. It was also

---

[1] Belgian casualties, 3 wounded.   German, 4 killed, 8 wounded.

[2] At Kigoma it was ascertained that the last German train eastwards had passed Lwiche barely two hours before Thomas's battalion arrived.

[3] The *Adjutant*, seized by the British Navy in October 1914, had been recaptured by the Germans on the Rufiji in February 1915, and escaped thence to Dar-es-Salaam.

[4] See p. 193.

found that the steamer *Graf von Götzen* had been scuttled off Kigoma.[1]

With the elimination of the last of the German vessels, **Sketch 55** the troops on the western shore under Lieut.-Colonel Moulaert were free to co-operate with Olsen's brigade in extending the Belgian gains. On the 5th August Moulaert's first detachment left Albertville for Karema and Utinta on the eastern shore, which were occupied on the 7th without opposition. Ten days later his force, now organized as the VIth Belgian battalion, similarly occupied Kibwesa and prepared to march north-eastwards, covering the right flank of Olsen's move on Tabora.

THE BRITISH ADVANCE TO ILOLA

" The rapidity with which the enemy abandoned his **End Paper** " valuable Lake Provinces and Mwanza," wrote Lieut.- **(N)** General Smuts, " was a clear indication that the eventual retreat " [i.e., of the bulk of the German forces in East Africa] " would not be towards Tabora, but farther east " towards Dar-es-Salaam, or south towards Mahenge ".[2] In other words, so far as Brig.-General Crewe's operations were concerned, the enemy was more likely to retreat before an advance southwards from Mwanza than to bring up reinforcements to oppose it. But before Crewe could make any such further move it was necessary to reorganize and concentrate the units of the Lake Force,[3] to establish an advanced supply depot south of Mwanza, and to clear the south-eastern corner of Lake Victoria of any isolated parties of the enemy which might otherwise harass the lengthening lines of communication.

On the 17th July, therefore, Brig.-General Crewe despatched **Sketch 61** patched the Uganda Police Battalion, numbering about 400, to Nyatembe, the most southerly point attainable by steamer, where a supply depot and advanced base were formed.

---

[1] The *Graf von Götzen* was salved and reconditioned by the Tanganyika Government in 1924 and is still in service, re-christened *Liemba*. (Official Handbook of Tanganyika, Sayers, 1930, p. 295.) " It was then found " that the long period of immersion in fresh water had had little effect. " Every steam cock and ' bright part ' in the engine room and elsewhere " had been carefully greased by the Germans who sank her. The result " was that astonishingly little real damage was sustained." (Reid, " Tanganyika without Prejudice ", p. 86.)

[2] Despatch, op. cit.

[3] Notably the 4/K.A.R. (see p. 432, f.n. 2) and the 98th Infantry, part of which latter unit was still at Karungu and Kisumu. (See p. 426, f.n. 1).

Next day the battalion marched inland to Misungi and took up a defensive position covering Nyatembe and the main Mwanza-Tabora road.   At Nyatembe carrier services and ox transport were organized and preparations made for the forward move.   From Karungu and Kisumu the remainder of the 98th Infantry, and from Bukoba the small garrison of Baganda Rifles left there at the end of June, were brought to Mwanza, while a company of the 98th relieved the Baganda Rifles company as garrison on Ukerewe island.   To make good to some extent his lack of artillery Brig.-General Crewe improvised a Naval battery from the guns and personnel of the Lake flotilla.[1]   Other measures taken included the start of telegraph construction to link up Mwanza with the Eastern Lake area, the lack of wireless in the Lake ships and ports being greatly felt.

Sketch 55   On the 25th July 200 men of the recently arrived 98th Infantry, with 80 Nandi Scouts, under Major J. P. Mitford of the 98th, was despatched eastwards in the *Sybil* to the head of the Speke Gulf to deal with the last remnants of the enemy in that direction.   After marching some 40 miles inland and dispersing a German party which made off to the southward, the force returned on the 31st to Mwanza with a captured German and a collection of abandoned rifles and other stores.   This small side-show, together with an earlier reconnaissance on the mainland east of Ukerewe by the Baganda Rifles, finally disposed of the possibility of any threat to the left and rear of the intended advance.[2]

Meanwhile Brig.-General Crewe had left Mwanza on the 17th July to return to Lake Force headquarters at Entebbe, where on the 20th and 21st he and Sir Frederick Jackson, the Governor of Uganda, conferred with Major-General Tombeur regarding the administration of the newly-occupied

---

[1] The battery, under Lieut.-Commander F. R. Hemsted, R.N.R., comprised one 15-pdr. B.L., two 6-pdr., two 3-pdr., with 2 m.g., on extemporised field mountings, drawn by oxen.

[2] Mitford's expedition had, however, also confirmed the indications, already noted at Mwanza, of unrest among the natives.   At Brig.-General Crewe's request the Uganda Government were good enough to lend an officer, Captain Tufnell, who " took over the administration of the Mwanza " district at a very critical time when the local natives were showing " unmistakable signs of unrest, owing to the deportation of the local " sultans by the Germans in their retreat . . . "   It was largely owing to this officer's efforts that " these disquieting signs were quelled and the "troops of the Lake Force had not to be diverted from the pursuit of the " enemy."   (Brig.-General Crewe's report, 20th September, 1916.)   The local " sultans " appear to have been deported and held by the Germans as hostages for the behaviour of their respective tribes.

territory. The subject presented difficulties. On the one hand administration would be greatly facilitated by treating the former German administrative district of Bukoba as a whole; on the other, that district was now occupied partly by British and partly by Belgian troops, and the British claim to administer the whole of it, founded on the occupation of its administrative headquarters at Bukoba, was opposed by the Belgians, for whom a foothold on Lake Victoria had so long been a prized objective, on the incontrovertible ground that they had reached Nyamirembe first.[1] Against the latter contention stood the even more telling fact that the Belgian invasion of the enemy's territory would not have been possible at all without the extensive assistance furnished by the British, not only directly in the way of carriers, supplies, and material in general, but also by the effect of Lieut.-General Smuts's operations in drawing off the German forces and thus eliminating opposition to the Belgian advance.

The outcome of the Entebbe conference was agreement **End Paper** on a joint submission to be made by the respective Com- **(N.)** manders-in-Chief to the British and Belgian Governments of proposals covering all the north-western portion of the German territory. These, " dictated solely by present " convenience . . . without prejudice to any post-bellum " territorial claims," provided that Ruanda, Urundi and the Ujiji district should come under Belgian administration ; that the Mwanza and Mpwapwa districts should be under British administration ; and that the Bukoba and Tabora districts should be " administered in the name of both " Governments by British officials, under the Belgian and " British flags, according to British martial law regulations ".

The subsequent discussion of these proposals, with which neither Government was entirely in agreement, continued for some months, resulting eventually in certain modifications.[2] It will suffice here to say that the policy agreed upon at Entebbe was provisionally adopted.

---

[1] The British suggestion that a Belgian base should be established at Nyamirembe, made at the Kabale conference of 9th–10th April (see p. 402, f.n. 1), was vigorously put forward by the Belgians in support of their claims. (B.O.A., II, p. 410.)

[2] In particular, no joint Anglo-Belgian administration of the Bukoba and Tabora districts was ever set up.

The negotiations, which are dealt with in Vol. II, led early in 1917 to the transfer of Tabora and the eastern portion of the newly-occupied territory to British administration.

Sketch 62   With regard to the continuance of the Anglo-Belgian operations it was further agreed that the Belgian Northern Brigade should march by way of Mariahilf on St. Michael, 50 miles farther east ; the Lake Force from Mwanza moving at the same time by the eastern Tabora route to Iwingo, 100 miles to the south. On reaching these places respectively both forces would stand fast until preparations were complete for a combined advance on Tabora. Both would have the use of Mwanza as a base and of the Lake flotilla for conveyance of their supplies. Major-General Tombeur transferring his headquarters to Mwanza ; the 5,000 carriers supplied by Uganda would remain at Belgian disposal, and Brig.-General Crewe undertook to assist the transport of Belgian loads as far as Pambani, where the westerly route from Mwanza to Tabora through St. Michael diverges from the easterly route.

These points being settled, Sir Charles Crewe re-embarked at Entebbe on the 23rd July for Mwanza, to which place he now transferred his own headquarters.[1] His southward move had meanwhile already begun.

On the 20th July the 4/K.A.R., some 730 strong, were conveyed from Mwanza by steamer to Nyatembe, going forward next day to Misungi to reinforce the Uganda Police Service Battalion. The latter reported that there were German patrols near Mabuki, 13 miles farther along the route to Tabora, and a stronger force of the enemy 8 miles beyond again, near Runere. The 4/K.A.R. on the 22nd reached Mabuki, where a German rear party retreated before its approach, abandoning a light gun. Pushing on through Runere, the 4/K.A.R., followed by the Police battalion, came up on the 25th with the German rearguard, estimated at 1½ companies, at Ilola, 15 miles farther on. The enemy, having made the usual show of opposition, broke and fled, and after being pursued for two miles succeeded in escaping into the bush, losing two Germans and seven askari killed to one man of the 4/K.A.R. wounded.

At Ilola, 62 miles from Mwanza, Brig.-General Crewe decided to pause and concentrate his force, collect supplies and perfect his communications whilst giving the Belgians

---

[1] Among other administrative arrangements, the former headquarters of the Kagera troops (" Kagera Command ") was now closed down.

To a request by Brig.-Genl. Crewe for artillery and for troops in replacement of the 98th Infantry owing to that unit's weakness from fever the C.-in-C. replied with regret that no reinforcements could be spared.

time to come up on the western route. In particular the provision of carriers was a serious problem. The Belgians, crippled by the wholesale desertions after the affair at Djobahika, were still unable to move ; in the British force not only desertion but also sickness had greatly depleted the numbers available, " 580 already being sick at Misungi " with dysentery, pneumonia, and malaria."[1]

There was therefore every reason for a temporary halt. During the next ten days, except for minor operations to clear the flanks and secure the line of communication,[2] the British force stood fast about Malero and Ilola.

---

[1] Brig.-General Crewe's report, 20th September. After stating that 2,000 carriers were brought from Bukoba and 1,000 from Ukerewe, and that " of the latter 1,000 but six remain ", the report adds : " The local " natives of the Mwanza district have also not come forward well ; whether " this is owing to the deportation of the various sultans by the Germans " or owing to the fear of German reprisals at the cessation of hostilities " it is hard to say."

Both the psychological effect of finding themselves far from their own districts and the physical effects, probably enhanced psychologically, of unfamiliar climates, told heavily on native carriers and were ever-present factors in the problems of supply and transport. Recognition is due to the indefatigable and incessant labours of the officers and others responsible for the carrier services under such conditions.

[2] On 31st July the Baganda Rifles were despatched to Kwale, on the western road to Tabora, 22 miles west of Malero, to clear up the situation. There they came in contact with small parties of the enemy, whom they drove southwards for some 10 miles before returning to Malero on 6th August.

On the night of 3rd/4th August a company of the U.P.S. Bn. dispersed a small German post at Ugalo, 14 miles south-east of Ilola.

On 4th August a patrol of 2 Germans, 10 askari, was reported on the L. of C. between Runere and Malero. The 4/K.A.R. sent back 8 men in 2 Ford vans, with 1 motor cyclists, who charged and routed the raiders, capturing both Germans and 2 askari.

CHAPTER XXVI

THE WESTERN AREA, 1916—(*concluded*)

THE OCCUPATION OF TABORA

(Sketches 59, 62, 62a)

THE BELGIAN APPROACH FROM THE WEST

Sketch 59 AT the beginning of August, as we have seen, Thomas's column of the Belgian Southern Brigade was in occupation of Kigoma and Ujiji, while Muller with the left column was established on the railway at Ruchugi, with a flanking battalion to the eastward marching south to rejoin him. Muller's next task was to secure the railway crossing over **Sketch 62** the Mlagarasi river 35 miles east of Ruchugi, Thomas meanwhile following up from Kigoma. Moving off on the 10th August, Muller sent one battalion along the railway and the remainder of his column by a detour through Fumfu, 20 miles south of the railway, to turn the Mlagarasi crossing. On the 14th his turning force crossed the Sindi river about thirty miles east of Fumfu, unopposed, and swung north against the German rearguard under Captain Zimmer, which did not stay to await it.[1] By the evening of that day Muller's battalion on the railway, driving off small German rear parties, had found the Mlagarasi crossing evacuated and established itself on the east bank, where the remainder of his force rejoined it on the 16th and 17th. Here exhaustion of the troops and lack of local supplies compelled Muller to halt for a week.

Meanwhile Thomas, sending one battalion on the 8th **Sketch 59** up the valley of the lower Mlagarasi, and moving off with his main body on the 10th and 12th along the railway, assembled his force at Ruchugi on the 16th and turned **Sketch 62** southwards next day. Passing through Fumfu south-eastwards by parallel routes and reaching Ugombe on the 24th, he detached a company to Kirulumo, twenty miles to the south-east. This unit, joined on the 26th by a patrol from Moulaert's force now approaching from Kibwesa,

---

[1] B.O.A. (II, p. 437) gives the German strength as 150 Germans, 500 askari, with five 10·5 cm. guns, three 3·7 cm. guns, and 10 m.g. The absence of serious enemy opposition suggests that these figures may be too high.

turned eastward and on the 30th, after an 80-mile march, raided successfully a German camp at Simbili. Meanwhile from Ugombe, pushing forward one battalion ahead of his main body, Thomas headed for Katunde, 30 miles south-west of Tabora, where his advanced troops arrived on the 31st August. These, in a bold effort to intercept the enemy's retreat along the railway, on the 30th had detached a platoon which seized the railway station at Usoke, 20 miles north-west of Katunde, driving off its small garrison and consolidating against the arrival of Zimmer's force from the westward. The party made a useful capture of stores and ammunition, and its commander, rightly appreciating the tactical importance of the place, beat off a determined German attack on the 2nd September and held his ground until the arrival of Muller's leading battalion along the railway on the 7th. This came just in time to meet a fresh German attack made from the direction of Tabora. In the sharp engagement which ensued the Belgians put up an excellent defence, eventually driving off the enemy with considerable loss.[1]

Meanwhile two less fortunate encounters had occurred. At Mabama, on the railway 15 miles east of Usoke, to which point Thomas's leading battalion had pushed forward on the 1st September, the enemy was found in strength and the Belgian column, which had hoped to cover Usoke against attack from Tabora, had the worst of a hot fight in which it suffered heavy losses and was obliged to retire southwards on Katunde.[2] Another of Thomas's battalions was ambushed on the 2nd September south of Katunde, and it became apparent that, until the columns approaching from the north were able to co-operate, the Southern Brigade could hardly hope to advance farther.

THE BRITISH ADVANCE RESUMED

On the 5th August Brig.-General Crewe left Mwanza for **Sketch 62** Malero intending to resume his advance. He found at Malero, however, that a German force, estimated to be 1,500 strong, was reported to be holding positions about

---

[1] The Belgians lost 12 killed, and 3 officers, 26 o.r. wounded. They buried 93 of the enemy. (B.O.A., II, pp. 544-9.)

[2] See B.O.A., II, pp. 534-8. Belgian casualties were : killed, 3 Europeans, 82 askari ; wounded, 4 Europeans, 46 askari. Four m.g. were lost (See also p. 445.)

Iwingo, 40 miles to the southward, with posts at Shinyanga and in the Seke hills. His own available fighting strength was about 2,250,[1] of whom half were non-regular troops and many were far from fit. He therefore decided, rather than risk an attack with what might prove to be an inadequate margin of strength, to await the co-operation of Molitor, now approaching the starting-point of the westerly route to Tabora at St. Michael, 55 miles south-west of Malero.

The difficulties of liaison between the two Allied forces, already experienced[2] and due in great part to the dearth of transport and signal facilities, now began to be seriously felt. They persisted throughout the subsequent operations, and contributed not a little to the regrettable absence of any real collaboration in planning and co-ordination of movement. Given also the forceful personalities of the commanders, and the differences on policy which had already arisen, it is hardly surprising that in the outcome their two columns acted virtually as independent forces, engaged in what amounted to be a race for the railway ; a contest, in short, rather than a co-operation. In this it was inevitable, in the circumstances, that the Belgians with their homogeneous forces, better accustomed to living on the country, less dependent than the British on lines of communication, and traversing easier ground on the whole, should have the advantage ; and they profited accordingly. Their difficulties in the matter of inter-communication,[3] on

---

[1] Distribution, 5th August :

At Ilola :	98th Infantry	300	3 m.g.
At Malero :	4/K.A.R. ..	800	7 m.g.
	U.P.S. Bn.	400	3 m.g.
	Baganda Rifles	450	2 m.g.
	Skin Corps	200	
	Nandi Scouts	100	
		2,250	15 m.g.

Naval Battery of one 15-pdr., two 6-pdr., 2 m.g.

[2] For example, although Mwanza had been captured by Crewe on 14th July, Molitor issued orders on the 16th to his left column to "support "if necessary the British attack at Mwanza", but not to do so until the troops had had 8 days' rest prescribed in a previous order (B.O.A., II, Annexe No. 39). See also p. 449, f.n. 1.

[3] The Belgian troops had little in the way of telegraph, signal, despatch-rider, and M.T. resources.

The British signal section which had accompanied Molitor as far as Biharamulo had rejoined the Lake Force after completing the line to that place.

the other hand, made it almost impossible for Major-General Tombeur to exercise any close control over his troops. Such were some of the conditions forming a background to the conjoint southward march which was now to start.

Returning from Malero on the 6th August, Brig.-General Crewe sailed from Mwanza to Nyamirembe to confer on the 7th with Major-General Tombeur, and next day, as already mentioned, the latter transferred his headquarters to Mwanza. It was now agreed that the left column of the Belgian Northern Brigade, 1,200 strong, with a battery, on its arrival at St. Michael should be despatched to Malero. The Allied forces would then make a joint advance in three columns, the Belgians starting southwards from St. Michael and Malero while the British, from the latter point, would make a wide sweep to the eastward so as to turn the right flank of the successive German positions on the Seke ridges and at Shinyanga and Iwingo.

For the moment no date could be fixed for the combined move, it being still uncertain how soon the Belgians, as to whose movements information was somewhat lacking, could reach St. Michael. It was understood, however, that they would be there by the 12th August, and in the meantime the greater part of the British supply, transport and signal organization was busy preparing for their needs. A supply depot was formed at Buwalo, roughly midway between Malero and St. Michael, a telegraph line was run forward from Misungi to that point and 1,000 carriers were collected there These preparations were completed by the 16th August.

Major-General Tombeur's consent to the plan, it must be said, had not been willingly given. In his view Brig.-General Crewe's information regarding the enemy might well prove incorrect ; the Belgian Northern Brigade was already behindhand, and to move one of its columns on from St. Michael to Malero would mean further loss of time ; he would have preferred to march the whole Northern Brigade southwards from St. Michael, and to discover by actual contact the true situation with regard to the enemy. In favour of this policy he argued that, if the British information were well founded, his own force would meet little opposition, and after disposing of any there might be could then turn south-east and take the enemy confronting the British in reverse. Holding strongly to this view, he was nevertheless constrained by his dependence on British help in the matter of supplies ; for Brig.-General Crewe, needing as he did all his transport to serve Malero, was not in a position to extend supply services to St. Michael also.[1]

On the 18th August came news of Molitor, then 20 miles north of St. Michael, and with it an entirely unexpected and disconcerting withdrawal by Major-General Tombeur of the promised Belgian participation in the joint plan to which he had agreed. His latest information, he now said, conflicting with that of Brig.-General Crewe, indicated a concentration of eight or nine German companies with 11 machine guns and at least three guns, some four hours' march south of St. Michael. The enemy being therefore distributed on a 50-mile front, presumably with a wide gap between the forces on either flank, it was desirable, said Major-General Tombeur, to attack simultaneously all along the front, seeking to pierce the centre and turn the inner flanks of the two German groups. The Northern Brigade, which expected to reach St. Michael on the 20th August, and which would then organize its communications to run through Buwalo instead of Mariahilf, would not be ready to move until the 25th. The latter date would, he said, coincide with that on which the British troops would be ready,[2] and since the relative strengths of the enemy's two groups were uncertain, it was desirable that whichever of the Allied forces first overcame the enemy's opposition should go to the assistance of the other by thrusting against the inner flank and rear of the other German group.[3]

Following on Major-General Tombeur's letter came further difficulties arising out of Belgian requests for the use of the Lake Force transport and carriers, without which it was stated that the Belgian forces might not be able to go farther. Molitor's brigade eventually reached St. Michael on the 22nd August, and to give time for the transfer of his line of communications the resumption of his march was postponed until the 30th.

In the meantime the enforced delay in the unhealthy area about Malero had told severely on the British troops and carriers, who were going down in considerable numbers

---

[1] See B.O.A., II, pp. 424–5.

[2] It is not known how this was arrived at. British records indicate that Brig.-General Crewe's force had been ready to move since 8th August.

[3] Major-General Tombeur's letter, dated 17th August 1916, is given in full in the Belgian official account (B.O.A., II, Annexe 54).

with dysentery, malaria, small-pox and, worst of all, cerebro-spinal-meningitis.[1]

Since the Belgian troops were not now to take part, there was no reason to prolong the period of inaction,[2] and Brig.-General Crewe decided to push forward to draw level with them. By the 26th, his carriers having rejoined after serving the Belgians, he was in a position to march.[3]

On that day the 4/K.A.R. were sent out south-eastwards to Ugalo, their movement screened by the Intelligence Scouts between that place and the Seke ridges to the west of it. The remainder of the force, less the Baganda Rifles,[4] left to protect the supply depot and hospital at Malero, moved next day to Ugalo, the 4/K.A.R. and Nandi Scouts pushing on unopposed southwards to Mwasimba to turn the right of the German positions in the Seke hills, which were promptly evacuated. Concentrating at Mwasimba on the 28th and resuming its march next day, the column on the 30th occupied Shinyanga, twenty miles on, driving out the small German garrison. It was now abreast of the Belgian columns fifty miles to the westward, but no direct touch with them was to be had and their exact situation was uncertain. Except for occasional hostile patrols there was no sign of the enemy, who was said by local natives to have fallen back to the Tindo mountains, 25 miles farther south. Pending news of the Belgian movements Brig.-General Crewe stood fast at Shinyanga.

---

[1] By 31st August 425 cases of meningitis had occurred, 185 of them fatal. The Intelligence Scouts and Baganda Rifles suffered most ; at the beginning of September the former unit, having lost over 50 per cent. of its strength, was sent back from Mhuiru to the Tabora area, where the native tribes were out of hand in the absence of any control. Brig.-General Crewe's report records that " this unit . . . had rendered excellent service."

[2] During this period various minor encounters occurred in the course of reconnaissance and patrolling. On 17th August two German guns opened on Malero and Ilola, presumably in order to discover whether the British had artillery ; no reply was made and no casualties were sustained. On 21st August two companies of the 4/K.A.R. with the Nandi Scouts reconnoitred eastwards to Gumali, rejoining at Ugalo on 26th.

[3] By some misunderstanding, 1,000 Lake Force porters, waiting at Buwalo to bring the Belgian column to Malero, had been conveyed by the Belgian staff to St. Michael and did not get back to Malero till the 26th.

[4] The fighting strength was now :

4/K.A.R. ..	..	..	..	785	14 m.g.
98th Inf. (3 coys.)	..	..	..	290	3 m.g.
U.P.S.Bn.	..	..	..	380	3 m.g.
Nandi Scouts	..	..	..	100	
Total	..	..	..	1,555	20 m.g.

with the naval battery (see p. 442, f.n. 1).

On the 3rd September a telegram from the Belgian headquarters, now at Pambani, midway between Nyatembe and Malero, informed him that, according to an intercepted German wireless message of the 1st, the Belgian Southern Brigade (Olsen) had already reached Mabama and Sikonge, respectively 20 miles west and 40 miles south of Tabora, and was being attacked by Wintgens near Mabama. Major-General Tombeur had therefore, it was stated, ordered an immediate advance southwards from St. Michael, to relieve the pressure on the Southern Brigade.[1]

Brig.-General Crewe at once ordered a resumption of his march for the 6th September and moved his headquarters up from Mwanza to Shinyanga. His supply and transport difficulties were now acute : lack of local carriers, sickness among those brought from Uganda,[2] shortage of motor

---

[1] B.O.A., II, pp. 481-4, gives a somewhat different sequence of events. It records that the leading units of the Northern Brigade, under Huyghé (acting for Molitor, who was sick) started south on 1st September ; that at that juncture Major-General Tombeur received British information of the resumption of Crewe's march towards Shinyanga and of the unopposed occupation of " Muatembe " (presumably Mwasimba) ; that the absence of opposition both to Crewe and to Huyghé confirmed Major-General Tombeur's information—which does not appear to have been communicated to Crewe— indicating the withdrawal of the bulk of the enemy towards Tabora to deal with the more serious threat by the Southern Brigade ; that this withdrawal necessitated pushing the Northern Brigade southwards immediately ; and that consequently on 2nd September Major-General Tombeur had ordered the formation by Huyghé of a column to pursue vigorously towards Tabora. On the same day, presumably after issue of this order, the intercepted German telegram came in ; but since Mabama was ahead of the line which the Southern Brigade was to reach by 8th September, the telegram, which reported a Belgian defeat (B.O.A., II, Annexe 73) was doubted. Nevertheless Huyghé was ordered to press on ; guarding against the possibility of Wintgens turning northwards against him, he was to gain touch as quickly as possible with Olsen, making his aim the defeat of the enemy rather than possession of Tabora.

The Belgian account stresses the difficulties of Major-General Tombeur in co-ordinating the operations of his two widely-separated brigades, owing to the telegraph line (constructed by the British signal section which had accompanied Molitor) being frequently broken by giraffes. The British, however, were even less enlightened as to the Belgian operations. The telegram received on 3rd September by Brig.-General Crewe was his first intimation of the progress of the Belgian Southern Brigade in its march eastwards from Ujiji, and his information as to subsequent Belgian movements continued to be of the scantiest.

[2] " The lack of local porters always constituted a serious problem, " and though drafts . . . were regularly sent from Uganda to make good the " large wastage . . . owing to sickness, long delays invariably occurred " in absorbing these . . . owing to (i) the ever-lengthening L. of C., (ii) in- " fectious diseases. For instance, on this date (5th September) . . . " H.M.S. Usoga arrived at Mwanza with 500 Uganda carriers, but owing " to a case of plague breaking out . . . immediately on landing, all this " draft had to be quarantined at Mwanza for over 10 days." Report by Brig.-General Crewe, 18th October 1916.

transport, and the absence of local supplies in the vast barren stretches of bush between Shinyanga and Tabora, all combined to cripple movement.   Unable for these reasons to move the whole force at one time, he subdivided it, sending forward on the 5th the Uganda Police Service Battalion and Nandi Scouts, 450 in all, with 3 machine guns, to secure the Kisumbi Hills, ten miles farther south, from which any enemy in the Tindo Hills could be outflanked. His main body, the 4/K.A.R. and the naval battery, joined the advanced column next day; the 98th Infantry and Baganda Rifles remaining at Shinyanga for want of carriers.

No opposition was encountered.   After a trying 25-mile march in great heat through the fly-infested bush across the lower ridges of the Tindo Hills, Crewe's force, which had left the Kisumbi Hills on the 7th, arrived on the 9th at Kigahumo.   Here a halt was again inevitable in order to organize supply.   Not only had the rough track to be made passable for lorries and ambulance vehicles, but, since ox-transport and pack donkeys could not be used in the fly area, it became necessary to divide the carriers into eight-mile relay teams and to form an advanced base before going farther.[1]

The situation of the force, with an exposed line of communication over 120 miles long, and with but scanty information alike as to its Allies to the west and the enemy (if any) on its open eastern flank, was somewhat precarious. Reports of German detachments at Nzega, 13 miles to the south, and at other points to the south-east led to the despatch on the 10th September of a column which, after a short encounter near Nzega, returned to report that area clear of the enemy.[2]   Other reports were conflicting, but the weight of evidence indicated that the retreating Germans, under Langenn, had divided at Kigahumo, about 500 moving south-westward towards Mambali and 200 southward on Ndala, fifty miles ahead.

---

[1] " This improvised system was most capably handled by Major Scott, " D.A.D.T., and Captain Coote, Political Officer with the force, to whose " indefatigable exertions the possibility and success of a further advance " south were mainly due."   Brig.-General Crewe's report, 18th October.

[2] British column : 300 of the 4/K.A.R., with 6 m.g., under Captain W. J. T. Shorthose, reinforced on 12th September by 1 coy. U.P.S.Bn.

The German force, estimated at about 100, after a show of fight, retreated southwards, leaving 4 prisoners.   The 4/K.A.R. lost 1 killed, 1 wounded.   The column rejoined at Kigahumo on 14th September.

By the 15th, having collected supplies for 20 days at Kigahumo, Brig.-General Crewe was again able to move. He had small hope of being able to overtake Langenn, nor in any case could there be any question of dividing his own force. The Belgians, as he had just learned,[1] were moving south from Mambali ; for his own part he held that his best course was to continue his thrust southwards through Ndala, to strike the Central Railway east of Tabora and thus, given reasonably good fortune, to cut off any German retreat eastwards along the railway.

Accordingly on the 16th September the British column resumed its march, reaching Ngalia's, 25 miles on, two days later. Of the Belgian movements, beyond a confirmation on the 20th of their departure nine days earlier from Mambali, no news came until the 23rd. On this day a Belgian patrol reached Ngalia's with a letter, sent by Huyghé on the 17th, stating that he was 7 miles north of Tabora and in touch with Olsen at Lulanguru (on the railway some 12 miles west of Tabora), and asking for details of the British movements and plans, which were at once sent.

Supply, meanwhile, was still a serious difficulty, rain playing havoc with the road from time to time, and at Ngalia's a further halt became necessary on this account. Advantage was taken of this to bring up the 98th Infantry from Shinyanga. On the 22nd the Nandi Scouts reconnoitred towards Ndala, where they arrived unopposed next morning. In the course of the 23rd Brig.-General Crewe moved his headquarters up from Shinyanga to Ngalia's to direct his final operations, intending now both to cut the railway at Igalula, 20 miles south-east of Tabora, and to gain touch with the Belgians so as to co-operate in a decisive combined attack on Tabora. By midday of the 25th his force and headquarters were concentrated at Ndala and orders had been given for the march next day of the 4/K.A.R. to

---

[1] On 14th September there came by runner a letter sent by Molitor on the 11th from Mambali (47 miles S.W. of Kigahumo) notifying his arrival there on the 9th, reporting gunfire to the south, and stating his intention to march south at once. A previous letter received on the 10th had notified his expectation of reaching Mambali on the 8th ; but on the 12th a telegram (dated 11th) from the British liaison officer at Belgian G.H.Q. had stated that Molitor would probably remain at Ukamwa (13 miles short of Mambali) until the 13th. No other information regarding Belgian plans or movements had so far been received by Brig.-General Crewe since leaving Shinyanga on the 5th.

Igalula. His stage was set ; but there came a dramatic surprise.

At 1.30 p.m. on the 25th September a Belgian motor-cyclist reached Ndala with the news that six days previously —on the 19th, while Crewe's force was halted at Ngalia's— Tabora had been occupied by the Belgian forces.[1]

All question of combined operations against Tabora being thus at an end, it remained only for Sir Charles Crewe to motor in to that place on the 26th September to clear up the situation and discuss future plans with the Belgian commander.

BELGIAN OPERATIONS ABOUT TABORA

From the end of August onwards, as the result of Major- **Sketch 62** General Tombeur's decision to use his Northern Brigade independently of his Allies covering his left flank, the capture of Tabora became from his point of view an all-Belgian enterprise, to be carried through by his two brigades converging on that place from the north and west respectively. Each of them, as the Belgian official account observes, was moving along a well-defined route with a good base behind it, the only difficulty being that of transport. In regard to this the Southern Brigade, using the railway,

---

[1] " No details of previous Tabora fighting nor any mention of strength " nor dispositions of enemy accompanied this report." Lake Force War Diary, 25th September.

The Belgian official account (B.O.A., II, pp. 490–2) after quoting Major-General Tombeur's congratulatory proclamation to his troops, goes on to say that at this juncture Crewe's column, despite all attempts to gain touch with it, was not to be found ; it was supposed to be in the Ndala region. A motor cyclist, it is stated, despatched from Tabora two days after the entry of the Belgian troops, i.e., on 21st September, in search of Crewe towards Ndala, fortunately did not reach (*n'atteignit heureusement pas*) that place, which it is said was then held by one or two German companies opposing Crewe. Another messenger was sent on the 23rd.

The lack of effective liaison has already been mentioned (see p. 442). It is also evident both from the British records and the B.O.A. that Belgian G.H.Q. itself lacked timely information of the situation of the Belgian troops. The dearth of such information produced an unfortunate impression on Brig.-General Crewe and reacted unfavourably on his relations with the Belgian commander.

It should be added that throughout the operations situation reports were regularly sent by Crewe's force, which had no wireless, back to Mwanza for transmission by Belgian wireless, which appears to have been somewhat faulty at times, to Belgian G.H.Q. The latter moved on 9th September from Pambani to St. Michael with a view to following up the Northern Brigade. This important change, entailing much alteration in the channel of communication, was not notified in time by Major-General Tombeur to Lake Force headquarters, then at Kigahumo ; difficulty and confusion resulted.

might hope for early improvement ; the Northern Brigade, on the other hand, with its base in the area of British occupation, felt itself less favourably placed.[1] To co-ordinate the movements of these two widely separated forces, one of which was virtually out of reach of the Belgian G.H.Q., was impracticable ; the utmost that could be done was to urge each to press on, and by closing with the enemy to minimise his advantages of mobility and interior lines.

On the 1st September, when the now re-united Northern Brigade started southwards on its 100-mile march from St. Michael, Olsen was already, as we have seen, within 35 miles of Tabora. It was therefore likely that the Southern Brigade would reach that objective first, and would then, striking northwards, be able to take in reverse the enemy opposing the Northern Brigade. Nevertheless the report of a reverse at Mabama, with the evident corollary that it might be Wintgens rather than Olsen who would turn northwards, was disquieting, and in a succession of urgent telegrams Huyghé, temporarily commanding the Northern Brigade,[2] was directed to concentrate and drive forward to Tabora. His troubles with regard to carriers and the complications due to the change of base to Mwanza were not yet at an end, but by the 2nd September four of his six battalions with part of his artillery were on the move, followed within the next few days by the remainder of his force.[3]

By contrast with the sterile and sparsely populated country traversed by Brig.-General Crewe's force, the relatively populous area between St. Michael and Tabora afforded a sufficiency of local supplies. Thanks to this the Belgian columns, composed of native troops, living on the country, were little retarded by their lack of supply columns and depots and had no need, as had the British columns, to halt periodically to build up rearward services for the

---

[1] See B.O.A., II, p. 481. A passage in the Belgian official account suggests that the difficulties experienced by the British authorities in the maintenance of the joint supply services from Mwanza were not fully appreciated at the Belgian headquarters. The problem of carriers in particular was, as already stated, acute.

[2] Colonel Molitor resumed command on 4th September. (B.O.A., II, p. 505.)

[3] Four companies remained at St. Michael until 9th September, rejoining on 14th September during the affair at Itaga (see pp. 453–4, and B.O.A., II, p. 499).

needs of white and Indian troops.   The Northern Brigade,
therefore, with this advantage and, as it turned out,
meeting no serious opposition,[1] had no difficulty in out-
stripping its Allies, and on the 9th September was assembled
at Mambali, 40 miles north of Tabora.

Meanwhile on the previous day Olsen's left column,
as we have seen, had reached Usoke.   His right column
under Thomas, after the unsuccessful attack on Mabama
on the 1st and the mishap of the 2nd, had fallen back some
20 miles down the Mwhala river, gaining touch with
the remainder of Moulaert's force arriving from Lake
Tanganyika.   From the 3rd to the 9th Thomas reorganized
and rested his troops in the area between Simbili and Ndele,
sending forward one battalion which reinforced Muller at
Usoke on the 8th.

Olsen's information pointed to an intention by the enemy
to cover an early retreat southwards and south-eastwards
from Tabora by a determined resistance in the neighbourhood of Lulanguru.   Although not yet in touch with
Molitor, he determined now to push on to Tabora with his
four battalions from Usoke, his southern flank covered by
Thomas's three battalions directed through Sikonge.   His
resolve was to prove decisive.

On the 10th September, taking personal control of the
operations, Olsen deployed astride the railway and moved
against the German positions about Lulanguru.   The
country, sloping generally downwards from north to south,
was mainly typical open bush, interspersed with rocky
hill and outcrops, well adapted for defence yet presenting
little obstacle to movement, in which the enemy's familiarity
with the ground and the inadequacy of the available maps
placed the Belgians at some disadvantage.

Three days—10th to 12th September—of more or less
continuous and confused fighting ensued, in the course of
which small detachments on both sides, widely scattered
on a broad front, manœuvred constantly against each
other's flanks and the Belgians gained ground.   By the
evening of the 10th Olsen's left battalion was established
on high ground commanding the main Tabora road 4 miles

---

[1] On 2nd September at Kologwe (20 miles south of St. Michael) the
Belgian advanced guard dispersed a German force estimated at three
companies, which abandoned a *Königsberg* gun after using up all its
4·1-in. ammunition.

east of Mabama ; on this as pivot the centre and right swung forward during that day and the 11th. The enemy, falling back gradually to his main defences covering Lulanguru, some three miles farther east, continued to dispute the Belgian advance with all his usual skill in rearguard action, making the fullest use of the superior range of his artillery. On the morning of the 12th an attempted attack by Olsen all along the line was brought to a standstill ; in the afternoon vigorous German counter-attacks, which compelled him to throw in his last reserves, were checked in their turn ; and finally, towards evening, a fresh Belgian thrust restored the situation. Both sides were by now exhausted ; Olsen's ammunition was running short, and wear and tear had put most of his guns out of action ; the main German defence to all appearance still held. For the next two days (13th and 14th) the Belgians stood fast, hurrying forward ammunition and supplies and endeavouring to link up with the Northern Brigade, of whose action at Itaga, mentioned hereafter, news came on the evening of the 14th. They did not discover that the enemy had withdrawn during the night of the 12th/13th.

Meanwhile Thomas had resumed his march, starting eastwards from Ndele. On the 13th, by Olsen's orders, he swung northwards towards Katunde in support of the attack on Lulanguru. Next day his two leading battalions, driving before them a small German rearguard left at Katunde, reached Mabama. His remaining battalion reached Katunde late on the 17th.

On the 15th, with Thomas to supplement his reserves, Olsen resumed his advance, to discover at once that the enemy was gone : the Lulanguru defence had served its purpose.[1] Pushing on during the 17th to the heights of Igange overlooking Tabora from the west, the Southern Brigade dug in to await the arrival of Molitor's force from the north.

The Northern Brigade had remained halted at Mambali during the 10th September to complete its preparations. But on the 11th the sound of gunfire to the south indicated that Olsen was in action, and during the night of the

---

[1] Belgian losses are officially given as 1 European and 16 o.r. killed, 55 wounded, 9 missing (B.O.A., II, p. 565). Contemporary reports made to British G.H.Q. gave considerably higher figures.

11th/12th Molitor marched 20 miles southwards to Utombogo, where he drove off a small German detachment next day. Some four miles ahead the hills at Itaga and Masagola were reported strongly held by the enemy.   He decided to attack.

His men, however, by this time were feeling the effects of the march from St. Michael, suffering especially from the heat, and with the prospect of a stiff fight before him Molitor devoted the 13th to preparation and reconnaissance, deciding to launch his attack that night.   Facing him, in the plain north-west of Tabora, was a series of small rock-strewn hills, that of Itaga confronting him just to the west of his road, while behind that of Masagola three miles to the eastward the Mwanza road converged on Tabora.   On and about these hills, in broken and difficult ground, stood what proved to be a great part of Langenn's and Wintgens's forces.

Molitor's plan comprised a main attack on Itaga from the west, turning the German left, supported by holding attacks from the north towards both Itaga and Masagola. At 12.30 a.m. on the 14th September his guns opened fire, and three hours later his two attacking battalions moved forward from the west.   By daylight the defenders had been driven from the crest of Itaga, leaving two 3·7-cm. guns and two machine guns in Belgian hands ; meanwhile three companies had worked round to the south in rear of the enemy.   But this good start was not matched by corresponding success farther east, where both from Itaga and Masagola the attacking companies met with a hot reception and were forced to withdraw ; and before long the Belgians on the western end of Itaga Hill and in rear of it, under a heavy and well-directed cross and enfilade fire, found themselves unable to hold their ground.

At 1.15 p.m. they were withdrawn, retiring north-westwards and leaving behind the captured German guns and machine guns.   At the mission station a mile to the west of Itaga, to which the companies which had worked round to the enemy's rear had been driven back with considerable loss, a stand was made for a time ; but about 4 p.m. Wintgens, supported by at least two *Königsberg* guns, made a heavy counter-attack, sweeping wide to the south and west from Masagola, which took the mission in rear, enveloped and captured two Belgian guns, and compelled retreat. By the evening of the 14th Molitor's brigade was reassembled north of the Gombe river, where it remained for the next four days.[1]

The severe tactical defeat sustained by Molitor was not too heavy a price to pay for the Belgian strategic gain in diverting Wahle's forces from Olsen. The latter, however, intent on Tabora, doubtless no less exhausted than either Molitor or Wahle after a month of arduous marching, and above all out of touch with Molitor until too late, was unable to turn his advantage to account by going on to take Wahle in rear ; and once again the enemy, centrally placed, skilfully handled and giving away no points, made good a timely withdrawal.

From the 15th to the 18th the German troops remained concentrated about Itaga, shelling Molitor's bivouacs from time to time. But already on the 14th contact had at last been made between the Belgian Northern and Southern Brigades, while the German situation was becoming precarious in view of the weight of the Belgian numbers and the approach of Crewe in support. Huyghé, now commanding the Northern Brigade, wrote on the 17th September to Crewe, giving the Belgian dispositions, and prepared meanwhile to renew the attack on Itaga on the 19th.[2] His plans were needless ; on the night of the 18th/19th the Germans evacuated their ground and retreated south-eastwards through Tabora. Early on the 19th Huyghé's patrols found the Itaga defences abandoned[3] and at 8.45 a.m. two European missionaries reported to a company commander on outpost near Masagola the surrender of Tabora. At 10.30 a.m. this officer entered Tabora, there to join hands with troops of Olsen's brigade

---

[1] The action is described at some length both in the B.O.A. (II, pp. 509–25) and in Arning's *Vier Jahre Weltkrieg* (pp. 240–6), from which latter a translated extract is given in the Belgian work. Belgian casualties are not stated ; Arning gives the German figures as 8 killed, 27 wounded.

The German counter-attack coincided neatly with the arrival of a reserve company sent up from near Lulanguru, which joined in. Arning's account points out with justice the skilful use made by Wahle of his advantage of interior lines, claiming that the German commander boldly depleted the force confronting Olsen, rightly gambling on the latter's impotence from exhaustion.

[2] Col. Huyghé succeeded Col. Molitor in command on 15th September (B.O.A., II, p. 525).

His letter to Crewe was six days on the way. See p. 448.

[3] A 4·1-inch and two 3·4-inch naval guns, duly demolished, were found soon afterwards.

from Igange, to whom in the meanwhile a deputation of the local civil authorities had made a formal surrender.[1] In the course of the 19th September the Belgian troops entered the town and established Belgian authority.[2]

On the 20th September the Northern Brigade occupied the area east of Tabora on either side of the railway, with one battalion to garrison the town ; to the south and south-west Olsen reorganized his brigade with a view to following up the German retreat. Three days later a column of the Southern Brigade marched southwards towards Sikonge and Ipole, which were occupied without opposition by the 27th September. Contact with the retreating enemy was not regained, and the troops were recalled to the southern vicinity of Tabora early in October.

Major-General Tombeur's forces had attained the objectives prescribed by his Government ;[3] indeed, in pushing forward as far as Tabora, they had, in the Belgian view, gone beyond purely Belgian requirements. Tabora and the western end of the railway being in Belgian hands, and the German forces having withdrawn to a distance from which they could no longer effectively threaten the newly-occupied zone, no Belgian interest, it was held, now existed which would justify further Belgian participation in the campaign.[4] At Tabora, therefore, the Belgian operations came to an end for the time being.

---

[1] The deputation, headed by Herr Schoen, secretary to Herr Branders, the District Governor, brought a document signed by the latter, authorizing Herr Schoen, after the evacuation of Tabora by the German troops, to meet the incoming force and make arrangements for Belgian occupation. (B.O.A., II, p. 569.)

[2] Among their first acts the Belgian forces released a considerable number of non-German Europeans—including some 35 missionaries and about 160 other civilians, of whom 100 were British—who had for some time been interned in the local prisons by the German authorities. Many of these white men had been compulsorily employed under native guard on public conservancy and similar work—a degradation which the local natives had not failed to note—and complained bitterly of the callous brutality with which they had been treated.

[3] See pp. 420, 437, and B.O.A., II, pp. 362, 593.

[4] B.O.A., II, pp. 595–6. In justice to our Allies it should be added that, in the words of their official account, they remained faithful to the attitude adopted from the outset, namely, to render any assistance that did not impinge either upon their own interests or their dignity. In particular they recruited 5,000 porters who were sent to Dar-es-Salaam in December 1916, and assisted the subsequent British operations. As will be seen in Vol. II, Belgian forces participated in later operations towards Mahenge.

OPERATIONS BEYOND TABORA

Brig.-General Crewe's visit to Major-General Tombeur at Tabora on the 26th September made it plain that there was little more for the Lake force to do. Tabora and the adjacent area were firmly in Belgian hands ; the Belgians were not prepared to go farther ; the German forces had made good their retreat. The British force, having fulfilled the task of covering the left flank of the Belgian advance from the north, had now no longer any place in the Belgian picture.

After acquainting himself with the recent course of our Ally's operations and dealing with various administrative details,[1] Brig.-General Crewe returned to Ndala on the 27th.

His information showed that the enemy had withdrawn his forces in two separate groups : a main column under Wintgens, 1,400 strong, southwards through Sikonge, and a force of about 400 under Langenn, believed to be accompanied by Major-General Wahle, along the railway towards Malongwe, 70 miles to the eastward. With the

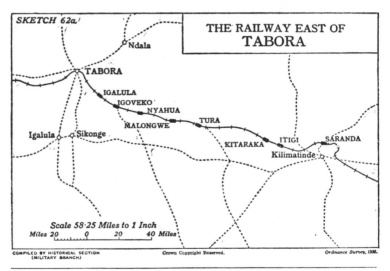

SKETCH 62a.

THE RAILWAY EAST OF TABORA

Scale 58·25 Miles to 1 Inch
Miles 20   0   20   40 Miles

COMPILED BY HISTORICAL SECTION (MILITARY BRANCH)   Crown Copyright Reserved.   Ordnance Survey, 1936.

---

[1] Among these were : (a) Return to Mwanza of the 5,000 Uganda carriers who had served the Belgian Northern Brigade from Kamwezi to Tabora. (b) Evacuation of British subjects and German prisoners of war to Mwanza. (c) Supply of funds for the needs of British subjects in Tabora. (d) Joint examination of documents found. (e) Repair of railway telegraphs eastward from Tabora.

A British officer was left in Tabora to deal with these and any other matters affecting British interests. See also p. 437, f.n. 2.

main group he obviously could not be concerned, and the force retreating eastwards already had at least eight days' start. He decided, nevertheless, to continue his march southwards from Ndala and to clear the railway as far as Malongwe; at the same time he telegraphed to Lieut.-General Smuts a request that van Deventer's detached troops about Kilimatinde,[1] 150 miles away, should co-operate by moving westwards along the railway. By this means the whole of the Central Railway from Dar-es-Salaam to Kigoma would be brought into Allied hands and he would establish direct communication with G.H.Q., the lack of which had been more and more seriously felt as the Lake force drew away from Mwanza.

Brig.-General Crewe therefore sent forward the 4/K.A.R., 450 strong, with 6 machine guns and his 15-pdr. gun, under Major H. A. Lilley, which on the 28th September reached the railway at Igalula unopposed. His supply and transport difficulties, however, continued. Railway rolling stock had either been removed or damaged by the enemy; local supplies had already been depleted by the needs of the Belgian forces; there was a lack of local labour, and scarcity of petrol had immobilized motor transport.

On the 30th September Lilley's column was able to proceed eastwards along the railway, finding on the way a considerable amount of damaged equipment and rolling stock, most of which needed little repair to make it serviceable.[2] No opposition was met until the 4th October, when the vanguard occupied Malongwe station after driving off a German rear party.[3]

On the 6th October an officer's patrol, sent eastwards along the railway, met a patrol of the 4th South African Horse from Kilimatinde, and returned in company with it to Malongwe. The Central Railway in its entirety had passed into Allied keeping.[4]

---

[1] 1 sqdn. 4th S.A. Horse and the 8/S.Afr.Infantry (Taylor's force, see p. 331).

[2] Very little demolition had been carried out on the line : all culverts were intact, and the only serious damage was to pumping machinery for wells at stations. Three damaged engines were found at Igoveko. At Malongwe a quantity of hastily-buried permanent-way material, locomotive parts and other equipment was recovered. Subsequently, 16 engines and much additional material were recovered at Tura station.

[3] 4/K.A.R. casualties, nil. Enemy losses, 4 killed; 2 Germans, 4 askari captured.

[4] Telegraphic communication with Kilimatinde was re-opened on 8th October.

Sketch 62a At this juncture it was learned that Langenn, in his retreat eastwards from Tabora, had quitted the railway at Malongwe and marched southwards, heading for Iringa in concert with Wintgens. All reports pointed to considerable demoralization in the German ranks; desertions were reported to be numerous and transport difficulties serious, confirmation on the latter point being afforded by released Indian prisoners.[1] No Germans, so far as was known, remained north of the railway.[2]

It had now to be decided what further use, if any, was to be made of the Lake force. Whilst Lilley was on his way to Malongwe, Brig.-General Crewe had sent despatches back to Kisumu and had telegraphed a full account of the situation to G.H.Q. His line of communication extended now some 270 miles from Mwanza to Malongwe and, to intensify his transport difficulties, wet weather had already set in as a foretaste of the " small rains " normally due in a month's time. He had supplies to the end of October, after which he would only be able to feed his troops by establishing fresh communications eastwards along the railway—not as yet a practicable proposition; in the Tabora area the Belgian occupation precluded all question either of British administration or of obtaining supplies.

On the 3rd October the Commander-in-Chief telegraphed his decision : " Now that western operations are over it is " unnecessary to keep up your brigade ". He directed, therefore, that the 4/K.A.R. should proceed eastwards along the railway to Saranda, there to join van Deventer ; the 98th Infantry, expected to be required for Egypt,[3] were meanwhile to guard the railway ; the non-regular units remaining would return to Mwanza with a view to disbandment. Brig.-General Crewe himself was eager to return to political life in South Africa, and to this wish Lieut.-General Smuts was prepared to accede.

The dispersal of the Lake force began forthwith. On the 12th October Brig.-General Crewe with his headquarters left Ndala for Mwanza, where on the 17th he handed over

---

[1] 8 I.O., 1 asst. surgeon, 42 o.r., came in at Malongwe on 5th October.

[2] A fine march of 170 miles through unknown country in ten days was made by a patrol of 50 Baganda Rifles under Lieut. W. Newitt, which was despatched on 1st October from Shinyanga to Sekenke (100 miles N.E. of Tabora), and back. It reported the intervening country clear of the enemy.

[3] But see p. 459, f.n. 1.

command to Lieut.-Colonel Adye[1] and left for Entebbe on his way home to South Africa.

By the middle of October the Lake force as a fighting formation had for all practical purposes ceased to exist.

THE TABORA OPERATIONS: SUMMARY

The period of Anglo-Belgian co-operation which ended for the time being with the capture of Tabora by our Ally had, it must be admitted, little military effect on the campaign as a whole. A further broad expanse of the enemy's territory had been seized by invasion, at the cost of much arduous marching and hardship though at relatively little expense in casualties. But in the western zone, as in the principal theatre, military defeat of the enemy had not been achieved. Wahle had, it is true, been forced to retreat by sheer weight of numbers, and the presence of van Deventer to the eastward on the Central Railway had left him no option but to take a direction leading nowhere near the bulk of the German forces. Nevertheless his retreating companies, though outnumbered and, thanks to unremitting British pressure farther east, beyond hope of reinforcement, had made full use of their advantage of interior lines. Displaying determination and aptitude in such rearguard actions as they chose to fight, they had given a good account of themselves before eluding the clutch of the converging British and Belgian columns.

---

[1] See p. 429, f.n. 1. Lt.-Col. Adye reached Ndala on 21st October and after winding up the Lake force organization rejoined his battalion (98th Infantry), on 25th December.

The eventual disposal of the various units of the Lake force was as follows:—

4/K.A.R. Left Malongwe 12th October, arrived Kilimatinde 21st. Came under command of 2nd Divn.

98th Infantry. Left Ndala 9th October for Igalula. Guarding railway Igalula-Tura until 12th December. Reached Dodoma 14th, Morogoro 18th, Dar-es-Salaam 22nd. Embarked for India, 4th January, 1917.

Uganda Police S. Bn. Left Ndala 22nd October: 1 Coy. to Shinyanga, 1 Coy. to Misungi; remainder at Ndala until December. The battalion then returned to Uganda, where it was demobilized on 15th January, 1917, the personnel reverting to civil duty.

Baganda Rifles. Left Ndala 15th October, disbanded at Entebbe 8th November.

Nandi Scouts. Left Ndala 16th–17th October, disbanded at Kisumu 17th November.

Naval Battery. Left Ndala 16th–17th October, disbanded at Kisumu 8th November.

Uganda Carrier Corps. Disbanded in Uganda 31st December.

That these should have failed to corner their opponent is hardly surprising. Only by the most skilful planning and exact timing could they have succeeded in bringing the enemy to bay in the huge quadrilateral north of the Kigoma-Tabora section of the railway. Over distances so great[1] the problems of supply and intercommunication, and the handling of native troops unversed in warfare on such a scale, were reasons enough to prevent any such exactitude. It is due both to our Allies and to the British rearward services to which they were throughout so greatly indebted that tribute should be paid to the magnitude of their achievement, rather than that stress should be laid on its lack of strategic success.[2]

Regret, nevertheless, may well be felt that the Belgian columns, for the reasons already given which the Belgian Government considered decisive, went no farther than Tabora ; for, as later events were to show, the absence of further pursuit left Wahle free eventually to break through Northey's force operating farther south. It may also justly be regretted that in the closing stages of the joint operations matters shaped as they did : for had Olsen come up less rapidly, it seems probable that Molitor's march could have conformed to that of Crewe's slower-moving column, enabling the latter at any rate to intercept the German retreat along the railway and thus to contribute something further to the success obtained.

Brig.-General Crewe had nevertheless the satisfaction of knowing that the Lake force, first under Adye and then under his own command, had served as an effective flank guard to our Allies all the way from the Kagera to the Central Railway. A " scratch " force of necessity, since no troops could be spared from the main operations, it had quickly acquired cohesion and shown its fighting value. From its vigorous offensive on the Kagera it had passed to

---

[1] From Kamwezi to Tabora the Belgian Northern Brigade marched over 400 miles.

[2] To recapitulate : apart from the British naval contribution on Lake Tanganyika, during the whole period of the Belgian operations Belgian material was arriving via Mombasa and Uganda ; British supply services were maintained for the Belgian Northern Brigade, as well as Crewe, across Lake Victoria ; British signal personnel accompanied the Belgian march to Biharamulo ; Uganda carriers served the Belgian Northern Brigade all the way to Tabora. It is not too much to say that without the British contribution, gladly given, in such vital matters, the Belgian invasion could hardly have succeeded.

the successful little amphibious operation at Ukerewe, thence to the seizure of Mwanza, and thence in the face of steadily increasing toil and sickness to its final goal, the Central Railway,[1] reached in circumstances of inevitable disappointment.   Its task had been well fulfilled.

To sum up : by operations predominantly Belgian, with indispensable British support, a great tract of rich territory had been won for Belgium ; the seizure of the enemy's vital lateral railway had been completed ; the German menace to the Belgian Congo had been eliminated ; and for the rest of the campaign the British Commander-in-Chief, whether with or without further Allied co-operation, need have no care as to the northern half of the theatre of war.

There still remained, however, the problem of destroying the German forces in the field.

---

[1] As already suggested in connection with the campaign as a whole (see p. 269, f.n. 2), had the present-day Mwanza–Tabora Railway been in existence, the Anglo-Belgian operations might have gone very differently. In 1916 only some 16 miles of line had been built northwards from Tabora.

CHAPTER XXVII

THE SOUTHERN AREA, 1916 [1]

BRIG.-GENERAL NORTHEY'S ADVANCE TO IRINGA

(Sketches 63, 64, 65, 66)

Sketch 63 WHILST Lieut.-General Smuts was driving the main German forces from Kilimanjaro to the Central Railway and the Belgians were following up the resultant German withdrawal from Ruanda and Urundi, the smaller British forces from the Nyasaland-Rhodesia border, now designated the "Nyasaland-Rhodesia Field Force," were with equal success penetrating north-eastwards into German territory.

By the middle of April 1916 Brig.-General Northey had re-organized his command; his plans had taken shape and his preparations, for which an unusually heavy rainy season had given ample time, were nearing completion.[2] He now had, distributed along the German frontier between Lakes Nyasa and Tanganyika, about 2,600 men (1,100 white, 1,500 native), with 14 guns. His force comprised, in addition to the native troops of the 1/K.A.R. and Northern Rhodesia Police, contingents of the newly raised South African Rifles from the Union and of B.S.A. Police and European volunteers from Southern Rhodesia.

Opposing him the Germans, about 1,500 in all, were known to be holding four frontier posts, said to be strongly defended. These, from east to west, were at Ipiana, near the head of Lake Nyasa; Igamba, 30 miles west of Ipiana, facing Fort Hill; Luwiwa (or Rwiba), 45 miles farther west, facing Ikawa (or Fife); and, at the western end of the border, Namema, 25 miles east of Abercorn.[3]

---

[1] As no operation reports or other contemporary records by units and headquarters of columns are available, it is only possible to narrate the course of operations on very general lines.

[2] In this part of Africa the wet season, in which military operations become almost impossible, normally lasts from December to late April or early May. During the rains of 1915–16 a few minor encounters occurred : e.g., on 28th January, Capt. H. C. Ingles, N.R. Police, with a half-coy. N.R.P., 30 B.S.A. Police, 2 m.g., drove off a German patrol near Ikomba, 70 miles S.E. of Abercorn, killing 7 and capturing 8 of the enemy.

On 28th April, in consequence of reports that the Germans were repairing the *Hermann von Wissmann* (see pp. 180–2) a small force was landed at Sphinxhaven, but found no signs of enemy activity.

[3] For details of the British and German forces see Note, p. 485.

With ample superiority in numbers, Brig.-General Northey decided to attack all four German posts simultaneously with mobile columns based respectively on Karonga, Fort Hill, Fife and Abercorn. On the 15th April he issued preliminary instructions to his prospective column commanders.[1] During the ensuing month final training and preparations were completed; the rains abated; on the 15th May Brig.-General Northey established his headquarters at Fife, and by the 20th his four columns stood ready to move.

THE OPENING ADVANCE

After consulting Lieut.-General Smuts, Brig.-General Northey decided to invest the four German posts on the 25th May. It may be said at once that at none of them did he do more than dislodge the enemy. Sketch 63

His right column, under Lieut.-Colonel G. M. P. Hawthorn, 1/K.A.R., having assembled at Ngaramu, 13 miles north of Karonga, moved off on the afternoon of the 20th, with two broad, rapid and unfordable rivers—Songwe and Kiwira—between it and its objective, Ipiana, 13 miles away. Sending a detachment to demonstrate against one German outpost at Kasimulo, 12 miles up the Songwe, Hawthorn headed for the mouth of that river to deal with another at Nsessi on its farther bank. That evening a company of the 1/K.A.R. crossed by boat, rushed a German piquet of whom 2 were killed, and covered the construction

---

[1] For the benefit of his new and non-regular units Brig.-General Northey went into considerable detail ; the following is an example :
10. *Organisation :*
Every little detail must be thought out beforehand : transport, supply, ammunition, bombs, entrenching tools (every man should carry at least a native hoe), medical stores, stretcher bearers, signallers and their gear ; also means for crossing staked pits or trenches should be considered : leave nothing to chance. You have had ample time to reconnoitre the country and learn every detail about the enemy's positions—how are you going to approach them ? From one, two or more points ? Remember that an accurately timed concentration from exterior points on to a central object is one of the most difficult tasks in war, especially so in a closely intersected bush country. Beware of mines and every sort of trap and ambush. If approaching from one direction only, will you advance with two horns out ? Or will you wait until you get close and then deploy outwards and encircle your victim ? How will you deal with enemy scouts, outposts, piquets, or possible relieving columns ? They must be quickly beaten in or off and nothing must interfere with your carrying out your job, for if you fail this whole project may suffer : your troops will have the confidence of superior numbers, superior artillery, and a better cause.
(" Instructions to Commanders ", 15th April 1916.)

of a pontoon ferry by which the column crossed unmolested during the night. At dawn Hawthorn resumed his march, to find that both Nsessi and Kasimulo had been abandoned by the enemy.

After devoting the 22nd to reconnaissance, he crossed the Kiwira unopposed on the 23rd, reaching Ipiana in the afternoon to find that place, too, abandoned. Natives reported that the garrison had retreated 20 miles north-westwards to Mwasukulu, making for Neu Langenburg some 15 miles beyond, and on the 24th Hawthorn followed.[1]

Forty miles west of Hawthorn's starting-point the next column, under Major R. L. Flindt, 2/South African Rifles, left Fort Hill for Igamba on the night of the 24th/25th, crossed the Songwe unopposed, and next day, like Hawthorn, found its objective evacuated and the garrison reported to have retreated north-eastwards, likewise on Neu Langenburg.

In framing his plans Brig.-General Northey had realized that these withdrawals might frustrate his first intention. With the aid of his next column, however, under Lieut.-Colonel E. Rodger, 2/South African Rifles, which was also to cross the border—from Fife against Luwiwa—he still hoped to corner the enemy at Neu Langenburg, and with this in view he urged on Hawthorn and Flindt to converge on that place from the south-east and south-west respectively.[2] Flindt pushed on from Igamba accordingly ; but the track proved too difficult for his guns, which had to be sent back to follow and overtake Hawthorn.

On the 26th May Hawthorn reached the road junction at Mwasukulu, still meeting no opposition to speak of, and late next day his advanced guard occupied Masoko, five miles to the north, the headquarters of 5.F.K., where stores of enemy ammunition and food were found. Reports that the Ipiana garrison, some 150 against his own 800, was between him and Neu Langenburg proved unfounded ; all indications pointed to the enemy's intention to continue in

---

[1] The attitude of the local natives (Wankondi) is described by an officer who was present as follows :—

" . . . they remained sitting calmly at the doors of their huts, with their " cattle grazing peacefully, . . . as if the war did nòt concern them. They " seemed to have no apprehension as to the behaviour of the soldiers " and regarded the arrival of the British as a welcome change of govern- " ment."

[2] " My object being to shepherd the enemy into Neu Langenburg " until Colonel Rodger was free to make a rapid move to the north side " of that place."

War Diary, Brig.-General Northey, 25th May 1916.

retreat north-eastwards towards Iringa. Heading in that direction from Masoko on the 28th, Hawthorn received orders to co-operate with Flindt and Rodger by blocking the line of retreat eastwards from Neu Langenburg.

He returned at once to Masoko to regain the track to Mwakaleli, 13 miles to the north on the Neu Langenburg-Iringa route. Next day, before starting, he heard that Flindt had reached Neu Langenburg. With a choice of routes thus open, Hawthorn sent half his column direct to Mwakaleli at dawn on the 30th, himself with the remainder, including artillery, marching via Neu Langenburg, where he added to his force a company of the 1/K.A.R. from Flindt's column. On the 31st his whole command, less its guns, was re-united at Mwakaleli.[1]

Meanwhile Flindt, pressing on without his guns and meeting no opposition, had reached Neu Langenburg on the 29th, to find that the last Germans had left during the previous night, abandoning food, ammunition and stores ; whereupon, while Hawthorn went to Mwakaleli, Flindt was sent forward eight miles north-westward to Rungwe, there to come under the command of Rodger, now on the way from Luwiwa.

Rodger's operation against Luwiwa had resulted even more disappointingly than those of the two eastern columns. Leaving Fife on the 24th, by the morning of the 26th he had duly encircled the Germans in a ring of small entrenched posts from which during the 26th and 27th his force gradually closed in. But in its endeavour entirely to surround the German defences, which consisted of two strongly-built works about 1,200 yards apart, Rodger's force was hopelessly strung out.[2] On the morning of the 28th it was found that during the night the Germans, having consumed all their food and water, had slipped away in small parties between Rodger's posts where these were weakest and still some 800 yards from the defences, and made good their escape southwards towards the border.[3]

---

[1] The eastward track from Neu Langenburg proving impracticable for guns, these were sent to join Rodger at Rungwe (see text) and did not rejoin Hawthorn until 3rd July.

[2] " The perimeter held by Colonel Rodger the first night was 8,000 yards, " but even on the third night, when some of his trenches were within " 200 yards of the small boma, he had not less than 4,000 yards to hold " with 500 men." War Diary, Brig.-General Northey, 25th May, 1916.

[3] The garrison appears to have been "L"K., under Lieut. Aumann. From the border it turned north-eastwards into the hills and was not intercepted.

Reassembling his force and leaving a half-company at Luwiwa, Rodger set off next morning (29th) northwards, turning eventually eastward to Rungwe. In the words of Brig.-General Northey, " the escape of the enemy was regret-" table, as Colonel Rodger had a chance such as a com-" mander seldom gets in war. He had four guns, plenty of " ammunition and six machine guns, but the form of warfare " was novel to his troops ."[1] Rodger's operation was in any case a difficult one in which, if the garrison had no intention of making a stand, every advantage lay with the enemy.

The situation at this stage, apart from legitimate disappointment, compelled Brig.-General Northey to re-organize the supply services of his three columns now committed to a pursuit carrying them daily farther from their original bases. He therefore carried out at the end of May what his subsequent despatch described merely as " the most " interesting part of these operations ", a rapid change of base from Karonga to Mwaya, at the head of Lake Nyasa, linked forward to his columns through Neu Langenburg. This was completed by the 31st.[2]

At the western end of the border, meanwhile, the column under Lieut.-Colonel R. E. Murray, B.S.A. Police, which had left Abercorn on the 23rd, moving by the Stevenson Road to cross the Lumi river about 15 miles to the eastward, had by the 25th invested the German post at Namema without meeting opposition. The enemy was strongly emplaced on high ground. His defences being considered too strong for direct assault, Murray's investing force, with its guns on a height to the north-west, closed in round the place to about 400 yards and maintained a siege during the ensuing week.[3] But here, as at Luwiwa, the besiegers were unable to invest closely enough to prevent the enemy's escape ; during the night of the 2nd/3rd June the garrison

---

[1] Despatch, 2nd June 1916. A survivor's comment, pointing out the vital necessity of patrolling by night in such operations, proceeds : " It " is practically useless to . . . hope to keep [a force] surrounded . . . " Continual patrols come very hard on small forces, but from experience . . . " both as surrounder and surrounded, it is the only way to discover a " ' break-away '. Small native patrols with one good European who " understands the country are best."

[2] Unfortunately no administrative details are available.

[3] A bold sortie by the enemy at dawn on the 28th was driven off, the German commander, von Francken, being captured mortally wounded. The B.S.A.Police lost 4 killed, 3 wounded.

trickled out through gaps in Murray's line, losing 3 Germans and 3 askari in so doing, and made off northwards.

Setting out at once in pursuit, Murray reached Mwazye, 30 miles to the north, on the 4th June. Seeing then no hope of overtaking the enemy, who was reported to be making for Tabora, 300 miles away to the north, he turned westwards to deal with the Germans at Bismarckburg, 45 miles off, on Lake Tanganyika.[1] After a minor encounter on the way, at the Kalambo river, he began an investment of Bismarckburg early on the 7th, meeting with a show of resistance during that day.[2] He had not, however, been in a position to co-ordinate his action with that of the British flotilla on the Lake, and so was unable to prevent the enemy from escaping in canoes during the night of the 7th/8th.[3] Next morning Murray took possession of the township, where the flotilla arrived on the following day.

On the 11th Brig.-General Northey, realizing for the first time that the Namema garrison was beyond pursuit, summoned Murray's force to Rungwe to act as reserve to the other three columns, leaving garrisons at Bismarckburg and Namema. The order reached Murray three days later, and on the 15th, his column, less two companies of the Northern Rhodesia Police, set out on its 200-mile march eastwards.[4]

Although the 10-days' investment of Namema had had no better result than the similar efforts farther east, it had at least contained the enemy long enough to dispel any

---

[1] On 4th June Brig.-General Northey telegraphed to Murray : " Push " on for all you are worth after enemy, leaving behind if necessary guns " and least bit mon ; otherwise no rest. Send party to occupy Bismarckburg." It has not been possible to ascertain when this reached Murray. Both on 7th and 8th June Brig.-General Northey sent even more pressing telegrams, urging that the defeat of the enemy was more important than occupation of Bismarckburg, and ordering pursuit. But from the fact that the telegram of the 7th was not answered until the 10th it may be presumed that difficulties of communication prevented these orders from reaching Murray until after his move to Bismarckburg—that place presenting in any case a potential threat on his flank—had put further pursuit out of the question.

[2] Casualties, Lieut. E. L. Ingpen, N.R.P., died of wounds ; 4 wounded. An officer present has recorded that the German commander, Hasslacher, though rejecting a summons to surrender, sent out medical comforts for the British wounded.

[3] The flotilla had reconnoitred Bismarckburg at dawn on 5th June, but saw little and, after firing two shells into the town, withdrew.

[4] Leaving " B " and " D " Coys., N.R.P. and details of B.S.A.P., Murray reached Fife on 23rd and Rungwe on 29th. " E " Coy., N.R.P., from Rodger's column, had remained in the Luwiwa area.

anxiety as to the left flank of Northey's advance from Lake Nyasa. Similarly Rodger's move on Luwiwa had prevented a hostile concentration about Neu Langenburg, where at first it had seemed likely that a stand would be made. Consequently by the first week in June the entire border was clear of the enemy, whose forces were for the most part in hasty and disorganized retreat northwards with the British columns, now no longer dispersed, in pursuit. The two principal German stations, Bismarckburg and Neu Langenburg, were in British hands. Casualties had been light.[1]

CO-ORDINATION OF POLICY

End Paper (S)

On the 4th June Brig.-General Northey had established his headquarters at Neu Langenburg. Throughout his operations, while fulfilling his primary function of ensuring the security of the British border,[2] he had maintained close touch with Lieut.-General Smuts as to the policy to be followed. He had put forward three alternatives, viz. :

(i) to continue the pursuit of the enemy to Iringa, 170 miles north-east of Neu Langenburg ;

(ii) to concentrate about Bismarckburg with a view to marching on Tabora or Kilimatinde, in either case across about 300 miles of barren country, with the added complication of a line of communication 200 miles long between Nyasaland and Bismarckburg ;

(iii) while maintaining the ground already gained, to occupy in addition the Songea district east of Lake Nyasa, a task which he had already suggested for the Portuguese forces, but which had not so far been undertaken.

On the 3rd June Lieut.-General Smuts had telegraphed that, the 1st Division being at Bwiko about to advance on Handeni, the 2nd Division about to push on from Kondoa Irangi, and the enemy's main concentration being round the latter place, he considered Brig.-General Northey would best assist " by an advance to Iringa to block the enemy's " escape in that direction." This was modified by a further

---

[1] On 7th June total British casualties were recorded as : killed, 2 officers, 5 other Europeans, 4 o.r. ; wounded, 11.

Total German casualties are not known : 1 German, 22 askari are known to have been killed ; 14 Germans, 30 askari were captured.

[2] See p. 190.

telegram on the 9th laying down that, in view of indications that the enemy intended to fall back on Iringa if driven from the Central Railway, Northey's advance should not be so rapid as to expose him to the risk of isolated attack.[1]

By this time, as will appear, Hawthorn had broken up Sketch 64 the retreating Germans. Scattered parties of them, however, were reported to be gathering in the mountainous area between Ulongwe, 30 miles east of Neu Langenburg, and Njombe (then also called Ubena)[2], some 45 miles to the north-east, both of which places were said to have been prepared for defence and both of which Brig.-General Northey determined to occupy.

This would extend his force a long way eastwards. But Ulongwe, where 300 of the enemy were reported to be, though accessible only by difficult mountain tracks, was within 20 miles of his base at Mwaya; while Njombe, End Paper through which ran the Neu Langenburg-Iringa telegraph (S) line, was the focus of the tracks linking Neu Langenburg not only with Iringa but also with Mahenge to the east and Songea to the south. His plan moreover maintained " the " principle of striking at a beaten enemy as long as there " was anything left ".[3]

THE PURSUIT FROM NEU LANGENBURG

Beyond Neu Langenburg the pursuing columns were Sketch 63 faced by the Ukinga and Poroto ranges, rising to more than six thousand feet above Lake Nyasa. Up their steep slopes, through a belt of giant bamboo forest, Hawthorn's column climbed from Mwakaleli on the 2nd June to gain the bare Elton Plateau, chrouded in mist and so bitterly cold that despite the exhaustion of the carriers a halt was out of the question. At dusk, after an 18-mile march north-eastwards, it reached the mission station of Magoje, in time to stampede a German rear-party which abandoned its baggage and some 50 rifles. Resuming his march on the 4th and descending into tropical bush, picking up on the way 60 of the German carriers and more abandoned stores, Hawthorn reached the mission at Brandt, 18 miles farther north early on the 5th,

---

[1] As previous chapters have shown, the enemy's eventual retreat southwards from Morogoro was not as yet foreseen.

[2] Now known as Mdandu, about 17 miles N. of the present-day Njombe Boma.

[3] Brig.-General Northey, War Diary, 10th June.

and Buhora, another 18 miles eastward, next morning. Of the retreating enemy, however, there was no sign, and finding that the direct Iringa route eastwards from Buhora had been rendered impassable by heavy rain, Hawthorn returned westwards on the 8th, passing through New Utengule, 16 miles north-west of Brandt, on the 9th and turning north in an endeavour to overtake the Germans retiring before Rodger, who was then 12 miles to his left rear at Ilongo.

The columns of Rodger and Flindt, which, as we have seen, had united under the former at Rungwe on the 2nd June, had pursued the enemy northwards into the Poroto mountains, where on the 6th they had overtaken and attacked a German rearguard, capturing a gun and four Germans. The enemy's force, however, had made off rapidly through New Utengule, heading northwards, before Hawthorn, approaching from the east, could intercept it.

On the afternoon of the 10th Hawthorn overtook and attacked the rearguard of this force near Masanga (otherwise Nyamanga), 20 miles north of New Utengule.[1] Here his pursuit ended, for on the 10th he was ordered to make New Utengule his headquarters, with posts on the Iringa road to the eastward and on his line of communication at Magoje, Mwakaleli, Masoko, and Mwaya. He returned accordingly to New Utengule on the 12th. At the same time Rodger, with headquarters at Rungwe, was directed to gain touch with Hawthorn and establish posts between Rungwe and New Utengule, patrolling to the westward, more especially along the north-western approach to Rungwe through the Igale Pass.

Sketch 64　Meanwhile Northey's eastern flank was watched by a company of the 1/K.A.R., under Captain C. N. Beaumont, in the hills some 10 miles northwest of Ulongwe, and by an advanced post at Neu Wangemannshöhe, midway between Ulongwe and Neu Langenburg, found by a second company under Captain J. E. E. Galbraith at Mwakaleli.

On the 12th June Brig.-General Northey reconstituted a column under Major Flindt, with orders to move eastwards from Masoko on Ulongwe.[2] Next day a detachment of the

---

[1] Casualties : 1/K.A.R., killed, 1 officer, 2 o.r. ; wounded, 5 o.r. ; German, killed, 4 askari ; captured, 4 Germans, 12 askari.

[2] Composition: 2 sqdns. S.A. Rifles ; 2 coys. 1/K.A.R. (Galbraith and Beaumont) ; 1 sect. 12-pdr. Q.F. guns ; four 7-pdr. M.L. guns ; 2 m.g. ; det. S. Afr. Engineers.

1/K.A.R. under Lieut. E. G. Cooper, sent from Mwaya by steamer, occupied Alt Langenburg on the eastern shore of Lake Nyasa. This was the point of departure of the steep track running up to Tandala, 13 miles east of Ulongwe, a route destined to become the line of communication with Njombe.[1] On the 15th, in order to cut off the enemy's retreat from Ulongwe north-eastwards through the hills, Hawthorn was ordered from New Utengule to Njombe.

Flindt's new column reached Neu Wangemannshöhe, much delayed by flooded rivers and steep and difficult tracks, on the 15th, gathering in the two detached companies of the 1/K.A.R. on the way. Leaving his guns to follow, he reached Ulongwe three days later, the enemy departing as he approached. Continuing an arduous though unopposed march eastwards for 13 miles to Mwakete, he turned south to Tandala, another 3 miles, driving off small German rear-parties there on the 22nd.

At Tandala Flindt was held up for some days. His men were exhausted by their march through the hills in biting cold and wet ; his guns had not yet come up ; food was unobtainable locally, and his carriers were deserting.[2] It was not until the 30th that his weary column, fortunately still unopposed on its way north-eastwards across the hills, reached Kidugala and gained touch with Hawthorn, then 12 miles farther east at Njombe.

In the meantime Hawthorn's march south-eastwards from New Utengule was uneventful until on the 20th he reached the Mbarall river near Kidugala, where minor skirmishes occurred with a German force of unknown strength. Next morning the familiar discovery was made that the Germans had withdrawn. On the 22nd Hawthorn entered Kidugala, to learn from native reports that the retreating enemy, about 20 Germans and 220 askari, (irrespective of any that might be retiring from Ulongwe before Flindt) had left Njombe by the route running north to Iringa. By the following evening his force had reached

---

[1] An attempt by the enemy on the night 14th/15th to retake Alt Langenburg was easily repulsed.

[2] On 24th June Flindt telegraphed : " All foraging patrols report " no food in district. Have informed Hawthorn cannot move." Asking for carriers for his guns to be sent up from Alt Langenburg, he added : " These boys must have blankets ; cold intense up here : probable cause " of desertion cold and no food."

its destination at Njombe. Here he was for some days out of touch, his wireless failing to gain communication either with Flindt or with headquarters. As some consolation he found, abandoned by the enemy, 10 tons of wheat and 3 tons of maize to replenish his now nearly exhausted supplies.

On the 24th, shortly after sending a reconnoitring detachment eastwards towards Lupembe in the hope of cutting off parties retreating by that route to Mahenge, he had word from local native headmen of a German con-
Sketch 65 centration near Malangali, about 45 miles north of Njombe. The force was said to be 1,000 strong, and the report strongly suggested the approach of some, at any rate, of the enemy's troops from farther north. The detachment was at once recalled, Njombe was put in a state of defence, and on the 29th, when communication with headquarters was re-established, Hawthorn was ordered to stand fast. Next day Brig.-General Northey telegraphed again : " No general
Sketch 64 " advance will be made beyond line Njombe-Kidugala-
" Brandt until the situation as regards enemy is clearer or " further intimation received from General Smuts. Os.C. " columns will threaten enemy by active patrolling and lose " no opportunity of striking. . . . Meanwhile stores will be " accumulated at Njombe, Kidugala and Brandt preparatory " to further advance."

On the 3rd July Flindt's column, from Tandala, reached Njombe and came under Hawthorn's orders. Meanwhile, to the north-west, Rodger, sent forward from Brandt, reached Buhora on the 1st, with Murray following from Rungwe. Brig.-General Northey's forces were thus, at the beginning of July, disposed in two groups some 40 miles apart, about Njombe and Buhora respectively.

THE ADVANCE TO MALANGALI

Sketch 65 During the first week of July information from various sources confirmed the report, received first by Hawthorn, that a considerable body of German troops was approaching from the north. Said to consist of some 200 Germans, including a detachment of the *Königsberg's* crew, and 700 to 800 askari, including *10.F.K.*, with at least one 10·5-cm. howitzer, the German force was reported to have organized defensive positions at Madibira and Malangali, respectively

45 miles north-east and 40 miles slightly north of east from Buhora on the two alternative routes from that place to Iringa. South of Malangali the enemy was said to have outpost detachments at Emmaberg and Soliwaya on the alternative approaches from Njombe, respectively 20 miles north-east and 25 miles north of that place.[1]

To have diverted these enemy reinforcements from the main theatre of war was in itself a success for Brig.-General Northey, who was now completing supply arrangements for the further move northwards which his columns were now to make.[2]

On the 4th July Hawthorn, now reinforced by Flindt as already described, left Njombe for Soliwaya, 'detaching to his right flank a small force which next day found that the German post at Emmaberg—variously reported as 100 to 300 strong—had been withdrawn two days earlier. The main column, meeting no opposition, camped on the 6th about 3 miles beyond Soliwaya, which had similarly been vacated by the enemy before its arrival. After a day's halt to bring up supplies, Hawthorn reached Idunda, 6 miles south-west of Malangali, on the 8th ; here his flank column rejoined from Emmaberg, having had on the way a successful skirmish on the 6th with a German rearguard.[3] Reconnaissance on the 10th showed that Malangali was strongly held, and for the next fortnight Hawthorn stood fast in his

---

[1] It is now known that on 6th June, Lettow ordered the *Königsberg* detachment (4 officers, 110 o.r.), *10.F.K.*, and a 10·5-cm. howitzer to Iringa, to oppose the British advance from Neu Langenburg, and that on 25th June, Capt. Braunschweig was placed in command of the German troops in the Iringa area. This officer ordered *9.F.K.* from Mufindi (20 m. S.E. of Malangali) to Lupembe, and concentrated the rest of his force at Malangali.

The howitzer was one of four landed at Sudi in March 1916 (see p. 287).

[2] Details are unfortunately lacking. Although the rainy season proper ended in May, heavy rain at times continued to make even carrier transport difficult along the lengthening L. of C.

Well-deserved tribute is paid by Brig.-General Northey in his War Diary to the work of the S. African Engineers and Nyasaland Public Works Dept. on roads and bridges : " Motor-cars can now (5th July) run through " from Mwaya via Neu Langenburg and New Utengule to Brandt . . . " where there were only a month ago only native hoed roads ; this road " starts at 1,500 feet above the sea and crosses the Poroto mountains at " 8,000."

Fortunately most of the country afforded grain and cattle in abundance, while the local natives, as the advance proceeded, welcomed the British and willingly supplied both food and information.

[3] The enemy lost 1 killed, 5 wounded and captured, including a petty officer of the *Königsberg*.

entrenched camp at Idunda, accumulating supplies and reconnoitring in preparation for the combined attack on Malangali which was to follow.

During this period occasional patrol encounters resulted in captures of German seamen[1] and askari whose statements made it plain that the bulk of the German forces was at Malangali and had every intention of standing there.

Meanwhile by the 9th July the columns of both Rodger and Murray were assembled at Buhora, whence they could be moved either to Malangali or to Madibira.

At this juncture reliable reports that the enemy was bridging the Ruaha at Ulema, 20 miles west of Madibira, suggested the possibility that further enemy forces might be approaching from Tabora.[2] Murray was therefore ordered to reconnoitre in that direction,[3] while on the 11th July Brig.-General Northey offered co-operation by Rodger to Hawthorn, should the latter not consider himself strong enough " to attack and capture Malangali position ". Hawthorn's reply—" Think I have enough to attack and " capture position but not the garrison "—went on to suggest that while Rodger's co-operation might make his attack more effective it might alternatively cause the enemy to withdraw from both Malangali and Madibira and concentrate in rear at the junction of the Madibira-Iringa and Malangali-Iringa roads at Wuasa (Sketch 66), 45 miles north-east of Malangali.

This exchange of views was decisive. On the 13th July Brig.-General Northey ordered Rodger, together with Murray's two South African guns, to Igawiro, 26 miles along the Malangali route, where he would come under Hawthorn's orders ; the remainder of Murray's force would remain in reserve at Buhora, patrolling towards Madibira ;[4] and

---

[1] Among others the master-at-arms of the *Königsberg* was captured with a nominal roll of the detachment. The patrols of German seamen, naturally unfamiliar with African warfare, and with a preference for sleeping in villages, were no match for the trained K.A.R. askari in night work in the bush.

[2] As in fact happened a few months later (see Vol. II). This contingency is not mentioned in Brig.-General Northey's war diary until the end of August (see p. 488, f.n. 1).

[3] On 15th Murray reported that construction of a bridge at Ulema had been begun, but had been abandoned.

[4] No details are available as to Murray's movements between 9th July, when he was at Buhora, and 25th July, when he was at Madibira. One of his patrols had the best of a skirmish with a German patrol at Kiwere (15 m. N.E. of Buhora) on 11th July.

Hawthorn, informed to this effect, was ordered to attack Malangali as soon as Rodger could co-operate.

Leaving Buhora on the 14th and passing through Igawiro next day, Rodger's column, unopposed but somewhat hampered by a shortage of carriers, reached the neighbourhood of Malangali on the 20th and gained touch with Hawthorn, now ready to move as soon as Rodger's necessary reconnaissances were completed.[1]

Concurrently with Rodger's move, Murray's column went forward to Madibira to contain whatever German troops might still be there, it being Brig.-General Northey's opinion that the enemy was more likely to call upon Madibira to reinforce Malangali than to withdraw, as Hawthorn had seemed to expect, from both places.

ACTION OF MALANGALI, 24TH JULY 1916

Hawthorn's reconnaissance had located the German Sketch 65 position on a broad ridge some 3 miles long lying roughly east and west between the parallel streams of the Ruaha river and its small southern tributary stream the Mgega.[2] Along the crest, passing through Malangali, runs the main route from Igawiro to Iringa. At the eastern end of the ridge, dominating the undulating bush-clad steppe country to the south and west, and affording perfect observation, stands a rocky outcrop known as the Pakene rocks (now better known as Lihomero) about which the Germans had prepared a well-entrenched defensive system covering the Iringa road, which passes some 500 yards south of the position.

Against an enemy estimated to number not far short of 1,000 thus strongly posted, with a 10·5-cm. howitzer outmatching the light British guns, the combined forces of Hawthorn and Rodger, approaching from the south and

---

[1] The difficulty of controlling these operations at a distance is shown by a telegram on 20th July from Northey to Hawthorn : " Wire date you " propose attack Malangali position as I wish move Murray accordingly." The reply was : " Am waiting till Rodger reports he is satisfied with " reconnaissance. Will wire date as soon as he reports." At 4.20 p.m. on the 21st Hawthorn telegraphed that he proposed leaving Idunda on the 23rd and attacking next day.

[2] The name Ruaha is a local generic term for a river and is given to several different streams in this neighbourhood. The river here referred to eventually runs into the Great Ruaha.

west respectively, totalled about 1,200 : by no means an encouraging superiority.[1]

In his operation orders issued on the 23rd July[2] Hawthorn stated his intention in the first instance to gain a footing on the ridge with a view to enveloping gradually the whole position, and directed that while Rodger approached from the west his own column would move round eastwards across country so as to attack the enemy's left and rear. Both columns were at attack at 8 a.m. on the 24th July.

Moving off on the 23rd, Hawthorn bivouacked for the night in the bush about 10 miles east of Idunda. His route early next morning followed the eastern side of a long valley which runs northward to join that of the Mgega ; into this valley run numerous deep and precipitous rocky lateral ravines, across a series of which with no small difficulty his column made its way. One such ravine in particular caused serious delay in the darkness before dawn. Consequently by the time Rodger's advanced guard—his 1/K.A.R. company, under Captain A. C. Masters, approaching from the west into the eye of the rising sun along the open ridge—came under the enemy's fire, Hawthorn was still moving along high ground a considerable distance east of the German position and separated from it by another deep valley. German carriers could be seen retiring eastwards from the ridge, and Hawthorn's leading troops, a squadron of the 1/South African Rifles and two companies of the 1/K.A.R. under Major Baxter, were hastened across the final ravine and up the steep slopes leading to the Iringa road in the hope of cutting off at least the withdrawal of the enemy's howitzer, which was already in action against Rodger.

---

[1] The composition of the British columns was :

Rodger	Hawthorn
1 Coy.1/K.A.R.	1/K.A.R., 5 coys.
2 sqdns. 2/.Afr. Rifles.	1 sqdn 1/S. Afr. Rifles.
	2 sqdns. 2/S. Afr. Rifles.
4 75-mm. Q.F. guns (5/S. Afr. Md. Rifles).	2 75-mm. Q.F. guns (5/S. Afr. Md. Rifles).
6 m.g.	4 7-pdr. M.L. guns.
	11 m.g.

The German strength appears to have been somewhat over-estimated by Brig.-General Northey. A German account gives it approximately as 550 (*Königsberg* detachment 100 ; three *F.K.* about 150 each) with 6 m.g., one 10·5-cm. howitzer. (*Krieg zur See, Kämpfe d. kais. Marine in d. deutschen Kolonien*, p. 239.)

These figures, however, may be based on peace strengths.

[2] No copy of these orders can be traced. They are referred to in an unofficial record of the 1/K.A.R.

The difficulties of the ground made progress slow. Soon after 11 a.m. Baxter's units gained the road and formed outwards, one company of the 1/K.A.R. north-eastwards to bar the approach from Iringa, with detachments facing north, and the bulk of his force directed westward against the enemy's main position. In close support came another 1/K.A.R. company and two 75-mm. guns, while Flindt with a squadron of the 2/S. African Rifles and a company of the 1/K.A.R. remained in rear, to be followed by the remainder of the column.

Baxter's force on the ridge was soon heavily engaged. Disposed roughly on three sides of a square, some of its units found themselves under enfilade and oblique fire from advanced detachments of the enemy which fell back gradually on the German main position. Meanwhile Rodger's smaller force attacking from the west was held up, unable to advance across relatively open ground in full view of the central rocks ; a situation by which the enemy was quick to profit in order to reinforce resistance to Hawthorn.[1] One attempt by the enemy to counter-attack the latter was effectively broken up ; but hardly had Hawthorn's two 75-mm. guns opened fire when the German howitzer, promptly switching from west to east, put them out of action, knocking out half the detachments and wounding among others Major Barton, Colonel Hawthorn's principal staff officer.[2]

Early in the afternoon Baxter's action in disposing part of his force towards the approaches from Iringa was justified. His company on that flank was now heavily attacked by a force which must have left Malangali earlier to withdraw to Iringa and turned back on hearing the firing." No support to this company appeared possible until the arrival of Flindt with the rest of the column, and its situation

---

[1] The telegraph line to Iringa ran along the ridge and it has been stated by survivors that the Germans had a concealed observer, who tapped into the line, west of their position, reporting Rodger's movements with great accuracy.

[2] The fire of the howitzer, even allowing for the shortness of the range (1,000 to 1,200 yards), was exceedingly accurate. The two guns were disabled, and 10 out of 12 of their detachments hit, by the howitzer's third and fourth shots.

[3] It seems that the Germans had already decided to abandon the Malangali position before the British attack. There is evidence that one of the three F.K. had left for Iringa on the previous day, and that a further detachment withdrew some 3 miles to the northward on Rodger opening fire. The first counter-attack on Hawthorn was presumably made by this latter force.

caused some anxiety.[1] Fortunately, the other companies becoming less heavily engaged, Baxter was presently able to reinforce his eastern flank, and on the arrival of Flindt soon afterwards this flank was cleared and the enemy driven off. Nevertheless in the course of some hours of confused fighting no decisive result was obtained, and when darkness fell the fortunes of the day still seemed uncertain.

In the absence of all contemporary record kept by Rodger's column it is impossible to say how that force fared; but it seems certain that, with all the advantages of ground and observation, the enemy was able to hold Rodger in check with but a small part of his own forces until late in the afternoon. Eventually Rodger's one company of the 1/K.A.R. worked its way forward into the western face of the German position, which the enemy then abandoned. Both the German howitzer and Rodger's guns kept up an intermittent fire until the evening; and by nightfall Hawthorn, still ignorant of Rodger's situation and aware only of indications that some at any rate of the enemy might have moved eastwards along the lower slopes between him and the Ruaha, had no option but to dig in and await events.

The night was bitterly cold, but quiet; and at dawn it was found, as on so many other occasions, that the Germans had slipped away across country under cover of darkness. They left, however, the 10·5-cm. howitzer, of course rendered unserviceable, which its ox-team had not been able to get away.

At first sight the German retreat from Malangali is not easily to be explained; but it may be supposed that the German commander, Braunschweig, over-estimated the numbers opposed to him, and that being attacked on both sides he was apprehensive of envelopment. He had, as Lettow tells us,[2] been sent at the end of June from Dodoma

---

[1] At one moment the Germans contrived to work a machine gun detachment into the K.A.R. position at point-blank range, and were frustrated only by the immediate action of Lieut. E. K. Borthwick, machine gun officer of the 1/K.A.R., who came suddenly upon them in the bush, mounted his own gun and got in first blow, killed the two German gunners and rushed and captured the enemy's gun. For this act he was awarded the M.C.

In this part of the engagement " AR " Coy., 1/K.A.R., suffered heavily, losing its commander, Capt. B. D. Mackintosh, killed, and two of its three subalterns wounded.

[2] " My Reminiscences ", op. cit., pp. 149, 182. It seems also to have been believed that the Wahehe tribe in rear of the Germans was being incited to rise against them. On this point Brig.-General Northey wrote :
Continued at foot of next page.

through Iringa to stay the retreat of the border garrisons; at Malangali he was already far afield, and he was doubtless aware of Murray's move to Madibira in his rear. The direction from which Hawthorn attacked appears to have come as a surprise, and quite probably this threat to the German line of retreat towards Iringa was decisive.

There was at any rate little doubt that the enemy had suffered considerably.[1] Pursuit, though ordered by Brig.-General Northey on the 25th July, was not immediately practicable, since supplies had to be brought up, and it was not until the 29th that Hawthorn, preceded by Rodger, pushed on north-eastwards some 10 miles up the Iringa road. By this time it was known that the German force had fallen back to Wuasa, the road-junction already **Sketch 66** mentioned; and while Brig.-General Northey came in person from Buhora to confer with Hawthorn at Malangali, Murray —who had reached Madibira unopposed on the 25th—was directed to remain at the latter place, patrolling in the direction of Wuasa.[2] On the 30th Rodger reached Bueni, 25 miles from Malangali and 20 miles short of Wuasa, where he too came to a halt.

Brig.-General Northey had now to deal with the situation on his increasingly exposed right flank and rear.

OPERATIONS ROUND LUPEMBE

In the course of his operations so far, which, in addition **End Paper** to assisting Lieut.-General Smuts by drawing away an **(S)** ᴴᴵᴵᴵᴵ ᵐᵛⁱᵃᵇˡᶜ force of the enemy, had secured possession of the

---

Continued from previous page.
"The defeat of the enemy at Malangali and loss of their big gun has had " an enormous effect on the Wahehe tribe, whose territory we are just " penetrating: they would rise at once if they thought they could help " us drive the enemy out, but as they are only armed with spears they " cannot do much." (War Diary, 24th July.)

[1] German losses were reported as: killed, 2 Germans, 8 askari; wounded, 1 German, 10 askari; missing, 10 Germans, 55 askari. Brig.-General Northey's War Diary (24th July 1916) records 13 Germans, 19 askari, buried on the field of battle; 2 Germans, 6 askari taken prisoner; and the enemy's estimated total loss at from 100 to 150.

British casualties were: killed, 3 officers, 3 European o.r., 8 askari; wounded, 7 officers, 29 European o.r., 27 askari; total 14 killed, 63 wounded.

[2] On 28th July, Murray drove the enemy out of Lutego (midway between Madibira and Wuasa), and established himself there. He also sent "A" Coy., N.R.P., 30 miles northwards to the crossing of the Great Ruaha at Kiganga, where it remained for about a week, intercepting the enemy's mails between Iringa and Tabora and gaining much useful information.

southern granary of the German protectorate, Brig.-General
Northey had been fully aware of the risks he ran. " I have
" realized all along ", he wrote, " that at any time the
" bulk of the German forces retiring before General Smuts
" may come on the top of me . . . if so, we will do our
" best to act as a buffer while General Smuts comes down
" after them ".[1] Whilst pushing forward from Njombe he
had hoped that in the wide tract of German territory
between Mahenge and Songea, to the east of his line of
advance, into which the main German forces retreating
before Smuts might fall back, he would have the support of
a parallel movement by Portuguese troops. Our Allies,
however, as we have seen, were not at this time in a position
to render any such aid, and consequently Northey's long,
thin line of communication lay open to attack from the
east.

Soon after the occupation of Njombe information had
begun to come in pointing to the move of German units
Sketch 66 from Iringa and Mahenge towards Lupembe, 40 miles east
of Njombe on the route to Mahenge.[2] Lupembe was of
importance to the enemy, situated as it was in the rice-
growing Masagati district between the Ruhuje and Mnyera
rivers, one of the principal sources of supply for the Mahenge
area, and in it a large crop would soon be ready for
harvesting.

Following on the brief reconnaissance in that direction
already mentioned,[3] a patrol of the 1/K.A.R. under Lieut.
Cooper, sent out from Njombe after Hawthorn's departure
for Malangali, had on the 14th July had a skirmish near
Lupembe in which it captured the German ex-Governor of
the Neu Langenburg district, Dr. Stier,[4] and returned
without casualty.

On the 26th, with the threat from the eastward in mind,
Brig.-General Northey detached the company of the 1/K.A.R.
under Captain Masters, then with Rodger's force at Malangali,
to return with Hawthorn's four 7-pdr. M.L. guns and two
machine guns to Njombe with a view to reconnaissance
towards Lupembe. Moving eastwards from Njombe with

---

[1] War Diary, July 1916.
[2] In particular, *2.F.K.* from Iringa and the small garrison of Songea.
See also Chap. XXVIII, Note, p. 510.
[3] See p. 473.
[4] Later died of wounds. Another German was also captured and
3 askari killed, 2 wounded.

about 150 men, Masters encountered near Lupembe on the
4th August a well-posted force of the enemy whose strength
he estimated at from 300 to 400.   His force suffered somewhat
heavily before being withdrawn, Lieut. Cooper being killed
and he himself wounded.[1]

This confirmation of the enemy's presence on his flank,
coupled with the wishes of Lieut.-General Smuts, which since
the fight at Malangali Brig.-General Northey had been
impatient to learn, led to a change of the latter's dispositions.
The Commander-in-Chief, telegraphing on the 5th, informed
him that until a further advance by van Deventer—then
concentrating in readiness about Nyangalo[2]—on Kilosa
cleared up the situation the enemy's intentions could not
be ascertained ; it could not be said whether any retirement
towards Iringa was taking place.   Lieut.-General Smuts
therefore suggested that Northey should not at present
advance farther towards Iringa, but should make himself
secure at Madibira and Bueni and meanwhile deal with the
enemy in the direction of Lupembe.

Acting on this, on the 7th August Brig.-General Northey
recalled Hawthorn, leaving Rodger and Murray to confront
the Germans then at Wuasa :[3] a decision which meant
weakening his striking force against the enemy's main
concentration, but which was necessary in the absence of
other support on the eastern flank.   Hawthorn began his
return journey next day, was back at Njombe on the 12th
and without delay moved out eastwards towards Lupembe.[4]

No opposition was encountered.   On Hawthorn's approach the Germans retreated, allowing him to occupy the
mission station at Lupembe on the 18th, and next day the
enemy surprisingly evacuated also a commanding natural
position at Mfirika, 5 miles to the south-east, on the edge
of the high plateau of open grass steppe across which the
column had come.

At Mfirika the whole character of the country suddenly
changes.   The ground falls eastwards abruptly, for a

---

[1] Casualties :   killed, 1 officer, 6 o.r. ;   wounded, 1 officer, 21 o.r.
The German strength is given by Arning (op. cit., p. 228) as 250.
[2] See p. 349.
[3] Rodger, with the 2/S. Afr. Rifles, 1 coy. 1/K.A.R. and 2 sections
75-mm. guns, was to remain at Bueni directly under Brig.-General
Northey's orders.
[4] Hawthorn's force now comprised the 1/K.A.R. (5 Coys., about 500
with 12 m.g.), 1/S.Afr.Rifles (reduced by sickness to about 80, with 8 m.g.),
one section 75-mm. guns (5/S. Afr. M.R.), four 7-pdr. M.L. guns.

R *

thousand feet or more, to the densely wooded valleys of the
River Mugwe and other streams draining eventually into the
wide low-lying valley of the Ruhuje and Rufiri rivers,
beyond which rise out of the haze the uplands of Mahenge
over 100 miles away to the north-eastward. Descending
into the bush in the broken ravines beyond Mfirika, patrols
followed up the enemy during the ensuing week, taking a
few prisoners, while the column established itself at
Lupembe and Mfirika.[1]

THE ADVANCE TO IRINGA

**End Paper
(S)**
The uncertainty as to the enemy's intentions which had
led the Commander-in-Chief to suggest, on the 5th August,
that Northey should go no farther towards Iringa, began to
give place to a clearer picture as the main British operations
developed. By the 19th, when Hawthorn's occupation of
Mfirika had reasonably secured Northey's right flank,
Lettow's forces opposing Smuts were in retreat from the
Wami towards Morogoro, while along the Central Railway
Kraut was falling back before van Deventer on Kilosa.
Farther west the Belgians, in possession of the railway
terminus at Kigoma, had begun their convergent march on
Tabora from the west and north with the support of Crewe's
force from Mwanza. From Tabora as yet no danger was to
be expected : between that place and Iringa lay some 250
miles of barren, thinly populated country by no means easy
to traverse even if Wahle's relatively small forces—cut off
from Lettow by van Deventer—should eventually choose to
come that way. From Kilosa, and even from Morogoro,
a German retreat to the healthier area about Iringa was still
a possibility ; but its direction seemed more and more likely
to be towards Mahenge, and in that case Brig.-General
Northey, if he moved to Iringa, would be well placed on the
enemy's flank. For such a move, if it could reasonably be
ventured, he was prepared and eager.

Sketch 66
On the 21st August Rodger, from Bueni, drove the enemy
out of an advanced post at Ngominyi, 12 miles to the northward on the route to Wuasa, and Brig.-General Northey issued
orders preparatory to an attack on the main German position

---

[1] At this time Hawthorn was reinforced at Njombe by a draft for the
1/K.A.R. of about 450 recruits completing training, whose depot was now
brought forward to Lupembe, and who were used to guard his line of
communication when his column subsequently went forward.

at Wuasa six miles beyond. Rodger, leaving a detachment to watch that position, was directed to occupy Rungemba, 10 miles east of Ngominyi, while Murray from the westward was to gain the high ground between Lutego and Wuasa. On the same day Northey telegraphed to Lieut.-General Smuts his readiness to attack Wuasa and advance on Iringa ; and when, on the 22nd, he learned that van Deventer was in Kilosa and Kraut retiring south-eastwards towards Kisaki, it seemed clear that his moment had arrived.

It had also, however, already arrived for the enemy. In the course of the 21st and 22nd the Germans evacuated Wuasa, retiring towards Iringa. This news, together with information that Rodger and Murray had on the 22nd carried out their tasks unopposed, reached Northey on the 23rd, upon which he ordered the former to establish himself strongly between Rungemba and Ngominyi, patrolling eastwards, and Murray to " send strong patrol which will occupy " Iringa if possible ".[1] To both he emphasized the essential need of information as to the direction of the German retirement.

Following up north-eastwards by parallel routes during the 24th and 25th, Rodger established himself some 10 miles north of Rungemba, while Murray, sending forward a strong detachment from Wuasa, on the 26th located the retiring enemy in position at Weru, some 23 miles ahead and 15 miles short of Iringa.[2]

On the 27th August there came, crossing a further enquiry by Northey whether he should push on, a welcome telegram sent two days earlier from G.H.Q. One third of Kraut's force from Kilosa, said the Commander in Chief, which had retired towards Iringa, was likely to diverge towards Mahenge, " giving Iringa a wide berth " ; but, he added, " if you delay too long, enemy may elect to proceed " to Iringa and make your work more difficult." He therefore approved an attempt to reach Iringa at an early date.

No more was needed. Northey's information already tended to show that the Germans about Iringa, if forced to retire, would go south-eastwards towards Mahenge, crossing·

---

[1] The further proviso " only if weakly held ", added on 25th August, had already been fully understood by Murray.

[2] Prisoners and captured documents confirmed that the German units were the *Königsberg* detachment, " L " K., and 2., 5., and 10.F.K., under Captain Braunschweig, totalling about 120 Germans, 640 askari, with 12 m.g.

the Udzungwa range by way of Boma Himbu and Muhanga, respectively 12 and 35 miles from Iringa ; and on the 28th, with this in view, he ordered Rodger and Murray forward to Iringa, the former at the same time to detach a mobile force to move by the most direct route to seize the crossing of the Little Ruaha at Boma Himbu, so as to cut the German line of retreat. He was not to know that in this latter design he had been forestalled by the timely withdrawal of the enemy, and it was not until late on the 29th August that Rodger—apparently not realizing the need for speed—left his camp north of Rungemba, heading north-eastward.[1] Murray, meanwhile, had gone on hotfoot, meeting no opposition, and at 11 a.m. on the 29th his advanced guard, " C " Company, Northern Rhodesia Police, under Captain Dickinson, entered Iringa.[2]

It was quickly verified that the bulk of the enemy's force had retreated south-eastwards, heading for Mahenge as Northey had expected. There can be little doubt that Northey's occupation of Iringa, the northernmost point of his great thrust into the enemy's territory, in the words of his war diary, " decided the Germans in front of van " Deventer to retire direct on Mahenge, and not via Iringa.

---

[1] Brig.-General Northey's orders of 28th August laid down : " Advance " must be immediate and rapid." In the absence of any record, the details of Rodger's movements cannot now be ascertained. But telegrams exchanged between him and Brig.-General Northey show that he waited for information from his reconnoitring patrols, who reported the enemy already across the Little Ruaha moving south-eastwards. On the 29th, Murray being then already in Iringa, Rodger was ordered to pursue eastwards with his whole force, keeping touch by wireless with Murray.

Brig.-General Northey gives his opinion (War Diary, 29th August) that " it was probably the threat of Rodger's column moving on to their line " of retreat which caused [the enemy] to evacuate Iringa without fighting." German sources—which are meagre—suggest as more probable causes the threat of van Deventer from the north-east, and eagerness to join hands with Kraut about Mahenge.

In any case 28th August was probably too late for a coup by Rodger. But it is worth noting that on the 25th, when the C.-in-C.'s telegram on which Northey acted was sent, the German force was still at Weru, on the wrong side of Iringa. Had the telegram not been two days on the way and Northey's orders been given correspondingly earlier, the enemy might well have been intercepted by the " immediate and rapid " move of Rodger to Boma Himbu which Northey ordered but Rodger did not make.

[2] At Iringa Murray freed 16 Indians captured by the enemy, and took over a hospital with a German doctor in charge and several wounded patients. He found some 50 German women and children, and also freed 42 interned British Indians and others. Such food and stores as could not be removed having been destroyed by the enemy, food shortage among the inhabitants gave rise to some anxiety, but was not allowed to delay pursuit.

" Equally van Deventer's advance forced the enemy from
" Iringa to go eastwards and not northwards." In this
fact lies the full strategic justification of Brig.-General
Northey's bold and successful contribution, by his penetration north-eastwards, to the conduct of the campaign as a
whole. More remained, however, for him to do.

NOTE

THE OPPOSING FORCES IN THE SOUTHERN AREA, MAY 1916

(i) *British Forces.* The composition and strengths of Brig.-
General Northey's mobile columns were as follows :
   (*a*) Based on Karonga, under Lieut.-Colonel G. M. P.
Hawthorn, 1/K.A.R.

One sqdn. 1/S. African Rifles ..	..	200 British.
1/K.A.R., H.Q. and 4 coys. ..	..	600 askari.
	Total ..	800 rifles.

2 12-pdr. naval guns (salved from H.M.S. *Pegasus*).
1 7-pdr. M.L. gun.
8 m.g.
Field Wireless Section.

   (*b*) Based on Fort Hill, under Major R. L. Flindt, 2/S.
African Rifles.

One sqdn. 2/S. African Rifles ..	..	170 British.
1/K.A.R., 2 coys.	..	223 askari.
	Total ..	393

2 /5-mmm. Q.F. mountain guns (see below).
2 7 pdr. M.L. guns
2 m.g.
Field Wireless Section.

   (*c*) Based on Fife, under Lieut.-Colonel E. Rodger,
2/S. African Rifles.

2/S. African Rifles (less 1 sqdn.)	..	462 British.
" E " Coy. Northern Rhodesia Police ..		138 askari.
		600

2 75-mm. Q.F. mountain guns (see below).
2 7-pdr. M.L. guns.
6 m.g.
Field Wireless Section.

(*d*) Based on Abercorn, under Lieut.-Colonel R. E. Murray, B.S.A. Police.

2 coys. (" special service ") B.S.A. Police   260 British.
4 coys. (" A," " B," " C," " D "),   540 askari.
N. Rhodesia Police.

                             800

2 75-mm. Q.F. mountain guns (see below).
1 12½-pdr. gun (B.S.A.P.).
1 7-pdr. M.L. gun (from Saisi).
10 m.g.
Total : 2,593 rifles, 14 guns, 26 m.g.

The six 75-mm. Q.F. mountain guns with the force were German guns, captured in German S.W. Africa and brought by the S. African contingent.

Use was made for the first time in this area of transport by pack-oxen, food for which could always be found locally.

It will be noted that there was no general reserve. On this point, forestalling possible criticism, Brig.-General Northey gave his reasons, substantially as follows :

(*a*) The distances involved. There could be no possibility of throwing in a reserve at a point possibly 100 to 200 miles away.

(*b*) The two strong columns were on the flanks, covering the lines of communication back to Zomba and Livingstone respectively.

(*c*) Hawthorn's column had so little in front of it that part of it could at any time be detached if necessary. (Despatch, 2nd June 1916.)

Few details are available as to the administrative side of Brig.-General Northey's operations. Some idea of the amount of organization required is given by the fact that his main base was Durban, his L. of C. forward from that point being as follows :

			Miles
Durban–Beira ..	..	Ocean steamer ..	767
Beira–Chinde ..	..	Coasting steamer ..	141
Chinde–Chindio (up R. Zambezi)		Stern-wheeler ..	120
Chindio–Blantyre	..	Rail	174
Blantyre–Zomba (advanced base)		Lorry	43
Zomba–Fort Johnston		Carriers (cars later) ..	80
Fort Johnston-Karonga		Lake steamer ..	300
Karonga–Mwaya (after 31st May).		do. do. ..	20
			1,645

In addition, the L. of C. in Northern Rhodesia, from Livingstone forward to Fife and Abercorn, was over 750 miles long, more than 500 miles of which lay across barren and almost undeveloped country.

(ii) *German Forces.*—British information on 22nd May 1916 gave the distribution of the German forces as follows :

Station	Germans	Askari	Irregulars	m.g.	Guns
On the border :					
Namema	40	350	—	2	1
Luwiwa	23	250	100	4	1
Igamba	15	200	—	3	1
Ipiana	10	80	—	4	2
Neu Langenburg	12	60	—	2	3
Other small posts	50	150	200	—	—
	150	1,090	300	15	8
Lake Nyasa :					
Wiedhaven ..	4	60	—	—	—
Sphinxhaven ..	—	10	—	—	—
Mtimoni	2	150	—	3	—
	6	220	—	3	—

This estimate was undoubtedly too high. Arning, (*Vier Jahre Weltkrieg*, p. 224) gives the German numbers at this time probably more accurately, as follows :

Station	Principal unit	Germans	Askari	m.g.	guns
Namema ..	'JŁ H K	30	200	3	——
Luwiwa ..	.. " L " Coy.	20	180	3	– –
Ipiana ..	.. 3 F. K.	20	200	2	1
Advanced posts ..	—	7	60	—	—
		77	640	8	1

with about 100 irregulars.

The latter estimate agrees substantially with the figures assumed by Brig.-General Northey in his preliminary instructions to his subordinate commanders, viz., 30 Germans and 300 natives each at Namema and Luwiwa, 10 Germans and 100 natives each at Ipiana and Igamba.

As most of the German carriers had had some military training, casualties could usually be replaced from them.

CHAPTER XXVIII
THE SOUTHERN AREA 1916—(*concluded*)
SUBSIDIARY OPERATIONS, SEPTEMBER 1916
(Sketches 63, 65, 66, 66a, 67, 67a.)

Sketch 66 STRATEGICALLY valuable though his advance to Iringa had been, Brig.-General Northey was increasingly concerned as to the exigencies of supply along a line of communication now extending for 300 miles northwards from his base on Lake Nyasa. His comparatively small force—some 2,000 fighting troops—was split up, moreover, into two halves 100 miles apart, at Lupembe and Iringa respectively. In his view, now that van Deventer, approaching from the north, was within 100 miles of Iringa, with a good route through that place to Mahenge, it was desirable that a part of the main British forces from the north should operate through Iringa, and that he himself should concentrate at Lupembe to co-operate from there.

His suggestion to this effect, made on the 30th August, did not commend itself to Lieut.-General Smuts [1]. It crossed a telegram of the same date in which the Commander-in-Chief urged pursuit and continued pressure on the enemy, suggesting that it might be possible to forestall the retreating main German force by reaching Mahenge first, and that presumably the marshes of the broad Kilombero (otherwise Ulanga) valley and " the mountainous escarpment before " the Mahenge plateau is reached " were the chief obstacles.

Called upon for his views, Brig.-General Northey estimated, somewhat optimistically, that from Lupembe he might reach the Mahenge escarpment in about a fortnight ; adding, however, that the time needed would depend not so much on physical obstacles as on the difficulties of supply, far from his bases, in country impassable for motors and denuded of food by the enemy.

End Paper (S) A further telegram, received on the 3rd September in reply to his suggestion of the 30th August, informed him that van Deventer, now on the way southwards to Kidatu—

---

[1] Brig.-General Northey enquired at the same time as to the likelihood of movement in his direction by the enemy in the western area about Tabora, a possibility now beginning to take shape. In reply (received by Northey 3rd September) the C.-in-C. stated that he did not consider this a serious danger : a view not destined to be confirmed by subsequent events.

the crossing of the Great Ruaha river midway between Kilosa and Mahenge—would detach a mounted squadron to Iringa, proceeding direct with his division so as to approach Mahenge from the north.[1] It was therefore preferable, the message went on, that Northey's force at Lupembe (Hawthorn) should move to Makua (55 miles north-east of **Sketch 66** Lupembe) or thereabouts and his Iringa force to Muhanga, so that these might then converge against Mahenge from the west. Any other plan, said the Commander-in-Chief, would involve loss of time, "which must be avoided, to "anticipate the rainy season ".

There could therefore be no pause after the occupation of Iringa. Earlier reconnaissance had shown that Braunschweig's retreating force was entrenched on rising ground covering the crossing of the Little Ruaha at Boma Himbu (or Ilimbu) ; but by the 2nd September all reports indicated that, although this crossing was still held by a rearguard, the enemy's retreat was continuing.

Leaving a garrison at Iringa, Murray moved out towards Boma Himbu, coming in contact on the 3rd with the German rearguard, which he found strongly posted behind the river with dense thorn bush on either flank. At the same time Rodger, feeling his way across country to strike the Little Ruaha some miles farther south, was preparing to move northwards down the eastern (right) bank so as to turn the Boma Himbu crossing. But the enemy made no stand at Boma Himbu, and when, on the 5th, Rodger crossed the river, he could but continue south-eastwards towards Lukegeta,[2] some 12 miles on, with Murray converging on him along the main route farther north.

Meanwhile, on the previous day, following generally the lines suggested by Lieut.-General Smuts, Brig.-General Northey had ordered the two columns, combined under the command of Rodger, to occupy Muhanga ; after which Rodger was to move south to Makua to co-operate with Hawthorn against Mahenge,[3] and Murray was to move

---

[1] The already exhausted condition of Lieut.-General Smuts's troops (see p. 392) does not seem as yet to have been taken into account.

[2] The name is used to denote generally the high ground just beyond Dabaga.

[3] " General Smuts considers our getting Mahenge before enemy's main " force may cause early surrender. It is therefore of vital importance " quickly to push enemy eastwards and gain footing on Mahenge plateau at " Mtimbira " (midway between Mpanga and Mahenge).
Brig.-General Northey to column commanders, 4th September.

eastwards from Muhanga. Hawthorn at the same time was to occupy Mpanga (otherwise Kiwanga), 45 miles north-east of Lupembe, and thence reconnoitre the river crossings in the Kilombero valley.[1]

The columns of Rodger and Murray were now committed to a pursuit through steep and broken hill country, matted with thick bush and in every way eminently suitable for the enemy's rearguard tactics. Progress was consequently slow and difficult. At Lukegeta (Dabaga) on the 6th September, as previously at Boma Himbu, the German rear-guards were found strongly established, but again were manoeuvred out by dint of laborious flank movement through the bush, Murray digging in within some 400 yards of the northern and western faces of the enemy's position while Rodger hacked a way round to the south-east. On the completion of this movement the enemy's trenches were found evacuated, and early on the 7th Lukegeta was occupied, the enemy falling back on Muhanga with the combined columns in close pursuit.[2]

At this point the difficulty of maintaining supplies along more than 40 miles of makeshift cross-country track running back westwards to Rungemba and Ngominyi had reduced Rodger's column to half rations. As the result of his reports he was ordered by Brig.-General Northey on the 9th to with-draw with three of his squadrons of the 2/S. African Rifles and four guns into reserve near Rungemba, sending his fourth squadron with Major Flindt to relieve Murray's garrison at Iringa and the remainder of his column, including " D " Coy., 1/K.A.R., to reinforce Murray.[3] The order was presently to be modified, as will be seen ; meanwhile before its arrival Rodger and Murray, continuing the same outflanking tactics, had pushed on from Lukegeta across the last high ridge of the Udzungwa ranges to Muhanga, where the hills drop steeply to the plains. Meeting

---

[1] Hawthorn in fact marched to Mkapira, 15 miles S.E. of Mpanga. See p. 447.

[2] Among very few casualties sustained, Lieut. H. J. Marshall, 2/S. African Rifles, was killed.

[3] Informing Murray of this order on 9th September, Brig.-General Northey said : " I have had no information as to enemy's strength and movements " for several days . . . . If you cannot push enemy farther east contain him " where he is and patrol wide to both flanks."

Considerable difficulty was experienced in keeping touch during this period.

occasional slight opposition, they occupied Muhanga on the 11th.[1]

Very evidently it was no part of the German plan to stand and fight, for almost anywhere between Boma Himbu and Muhanga a determined resistance might have been made, at odds by no means unfavourable to the enemy.[2] But no efforts to overtake an enemy bent on retreat could hope to succeed in such difficult country ; and from Muhanga the Germans, after destroying most of what could not be carried away—including over 200 rifles and a quantity of ammunition and native foodstuffs—made good their withdrawal down the precipitous tracks leading to Hange in the foothills nearly 5,000 feet below, and to the open valley beyond.[3]

On arrival at Muhanga Rodger, in accordance with the orders already mentioned, prepared to move with his own units southwards to Makua, while Murray continued the pursuit, toiling on down some 10 miles of tortuous steep descent during the 11th and 12th September. In response, however, to representations by Murray as to the enemy's strength—still estimated at 700—and the difficulty of the country, Brig.-General Northey gave orders on the 12th that two squadrons of the 2/S. African Rifles, with Rodger's four guns and all his machine guns, should be left with Murray ; the other two squadrons, one to garrison Iringa and one in reserve, to remain under the orders of Rodger as commandant on the line of communication forward from Ngominyi. This order in its turn was soon to be modified.

---

[1] A survivor records a difficult and useful move made by Murray's Rhodesians with two squadrons of the 2/S. African Rifles, through the bush wide to the southern flank during the night 7th/8th Sept. The rate " of progress was about 1 mile in 2 hours, but even then the path cleared " was only just sufficient for troops to move in single file . . . . If it did not " rain during the day, a cold nasty rain was almost certain to fall at " night . . . . in the early morning the whole country was shrouded in " mist . . . ."

[2] It was generally felt in Northey's force at this time that the enemy's morale was badly shaken, the Germans themselves being apparently " in " poor health, short of proper food, and mostly thoroughly sick of the war " (War Diary, 11th September). The Germans are, however, also recorded as " fighting obstinate rearguard actions " (*ibid.*). Their withdrawal from Iringa to join forces with Kraut was sound strategy and could hardly in itself be adduced as a sign of lowered morale ; but desertions among German askari are said to have been numerous, and the effects of continued retirement under considerable hardships must have begun to tell.

[3] 13 Germans, 36 German askari, wounded or sick, were left behind at Muhanga.

On the 13th Murray, now within two miles of Hange, but a day's march or more ahead of his guns [1] and unable to get within rifle range of the enemy, reported that the Germans were in rapid retreat into the plains and " in " parlous state for food ".   In view of Kraut's approach from the north he enquired whether he was to pursue farther, volunteering nevertheless to push on to secure the crossing of the Kilombero river south of Ifakara, 40 miles east of Hange.

But the pursuit was now to end.   On the 14th Murray occupied Hange, with an advanced post at Boma Dwangire, 7 miles to the eastward, and Brig.-General Northey, leaving Ifakara to be dealt with by the 2nd Division from the north, issued fresh orders.   Directing Rodger with two squadrons of the 2/S. African Rifles and the guns to watch the Muhanga– Ifakara road, and to screen Murray's departure, he ordered Murray to move with his Rhodesians and " D " Company of the 1/K.A.R., as quickly as supply arrangements would allow, southwards skirting the hills to Makua   There Murray was to gain touch by wireless with Hawthorn, who, it will be remembered, had been ordered to Mpanga, some 18 miles farther south.   These orders, in other words, confirmed the plan laid down a fortnight earlier after the entry into Iringa,[2] but the rôles of Rodger and Murray were now interchanged.

Accordingly on the morning of the 16th Murray's column left Hange, nominally with six days' rations, but in fact exceedingly short of food,[3] and four days later, unopposed, it reached Makua and established communication with

---

[1] Normally ox-drawn, the guns had here to be man-handled.   Some idea of the conditions is given by a survivor : " . . . . oxen were found " quite unequal to the task, and the hauling of the guns was undertaken " by the gunners and ' A ' Coy., N.R. Police (the escort) ;   from the 11th " to the 15th . . . . hauling the guns up the hills and hanging on down the " hills continued from daylight to dark each day . . . . the askari went at it " with light hearts and seldom stopped jesting and singing even when " they were puffing and panting up the steepest of hills . . . ."

[2] See p. 489.

[3] On the 16th Murray reported " am rationed up to and including 22nd." There is evidence, however, that the 1/K.A.R. company was on quarter rations from 16th to 22nd and received no further rations until the 28th.

 A direct track was reported to run from Rungemba to Makua, but the only centre for local purchase of supplies was Iringa, and Murray's supply difficulties up to the point where he came within reach of Hawthorn's base at Lupembe were great and the consequent hardships considerable.   The sudden change of climate, moreover, from the comparatively bracing air of the hills to the fierce heat of the valley, was in itself a trial.

Hawthorn, who was found to be, not at Mpanga, but 15 miles farther south, near Kisingo. On the 23rd Murray was placed under Hawthorn's orders.

During the ensuing week Murray's patrols made their way southwards to the crossings of the Mnyera river east of Mpanga, most of which appeared to be held by the enemy, with whom occasional skirmishing took place. Meanwhile, however, it was becoming daily more certain that in the area to the east of Northey's force the Germans were being reinforced by the arrival of Kraut's companies, and that the idea of forestalling these at Mahenge, although again urged upon Murray and Hawthorn by Northey on the 19th September [1] and still in Lieut.-General Smuts's mind as late as the 22nd, could no longer be maintained. By this time also the possible advent of Wahle's forces, driven out of Tabora, was beginning to loom larger and to cause Brig.-General Northey justifiable uneasiness, of which he did not fail to inform the Commander-in-Chief.

As early as the 9th September the dispersal of his forces **End Paper** and the weakness of his line of communications had led **(S)** Brig.-General Northey to call in as a reinforcement one of the two companies of the Northern Rhodesia Police which had been left in the Bismarckburg district.[2] In that quarter the Belgians had now moved from Karema north-eastwards across the front of the northward retreat of the Bismarckburg garrison, and although it was conceivable that Wahle might attempt to descend past the eastern shores of Lake Rukwa on Fife, such a move seemed most unlikely. A greater threat lay in the possibility of a move by Kraut against Northey's exposed northern outpost at Iringa; and to meet it, rather than reinforce his weak detachment there by depleting the forces directed against Mahenge, Brig.-General Northey eventually renewed his suggestion to the Commander-in-Chief that part of van Deventer's division should take over Iringa.

This, however, as preceding chapters have shown, was out of the question owing to the exhaustion of all Lieut.-General Smuts's troops. Replying on the 22nd September, the Commander-in-Chief telegraphed that van Deventer would push on to hold the important crossing of

---

[1] " Effect on whole campaign might be decisive. You must do your " utmost to reach Mahenge quickly." By this time, however, as Hawthorn and Murray perceived only too clearly, there was no possibility of any such expectation being fulfilled.

[2] See p. 467, f.n. 4, and p. 485.

the Ruaha at Nyukwa's, 70 miles north-east of Iringa, but not beyond.[1] Three days later Lieut.-General Smuts undertook that if necessary the whole 2nd Division should be sent to Nyukwa's. With its present lines of communication running back to Moshi, he said, the division could go no farther; but in a fortnight the situation would be simplified by the opening of the railway from Dar-es-Salaam to Kilosa. He ended by stating the serious plight of van Deventer's exhausted troops, as to which, it would seem, Brig.-General Northey had not previously had much information.

Evidently, therefore, although Northey's force had already been in signal communication with van Deventer's advanced troops,[2] there was no prospect of their early arrival. Meanwhile Rodger with the 2/S. African Rifles, opposed to a superior force of the enemy, would probably be hard put to it to deal with any German counter-thrust round the northern flank, signs of which were seen in a resumption of active German patrolling round Hange and north of Muhanga; while if attack came also from the west the situation at Iringa, already anxious, might become critical.

Notwithstanding, therefore, the continued influx of reinforcements for the enemy, it appeared to Brig.-General Northey that the best hope lay in continued pressure eastwards by Hawthorn and Murray towards Mahenge.

OPERATIONS OF HAWTHORN'S COLUMN

Sketch 66   Although on the 21st August, Hawthorn, after securing the exposed flank of the advance towards Iringa by his

---

[1] The telegram stated that the enemy from the Tabora area, then about Malongwe and Itigi on the Central Railway, had apparently been ordered to retire to the " Itumba mountains ", i.e., the hilly district of that name between Tabora and Iringa, about 150 miles from each. The C.-in-C. went on: " It may be that they do not intend or cannot retire " further east and will await end in those mountains "—an expectation hardly in keeping with the known characteristics of Wahle and Wintgens— adding that he did not consider Iringa in any danger so long as about 200 rifles were there. At the same time van Deventer would send forward his mounted troops as far as Nyukwa's, holding the L. of C. from there to Kilimatinde with infantry ; but it was inadvisable for him to move farther towards Iringa. In conclusion the C.-in-C. said : " Your advance to " Mahenge very important and ably conducted and should,. not be " weakened appreciably. Portuguese forces now across Ruvuma. I shall " ask them to move towards Liwale." [115 miles S.E. of Mahenge].

[2] Helio communication was established on 18th September between a detachment sent out by Flindt some 30 miles N.E. of Iringa and the 1/S. African Horse moving to Nyukwa's.

occupation of Lupembe and Mfirika, had been ordered to
" operate against the enemy retiring through Mahenge "—
presumably the enemy's main forces from the north—he
had first to consolidate Lupembe as an advanced base and
to organise supply. His patrols reported that the country
east of Mfirika was so difficult that movement off the tracks
was almost impossible, and that the Germans, intent
chiefly on getting the Masagati rice crop across the Ruhuje,
were still out of reach. On the 31st his information was that
the Germans were all east of the Ruhuje, in the bend of that
river north of Mkapira. Meanwhile, having replied unfavourably to an optimistic enquiry from headquarters as
to his ability to make a quick raid on Mahenge,[1] he completed his preparations to move eastwards.

The order for this move was given by Brig.-General
Northey on the 4th September. It was interpreted by
Hawthorn as directing him to march to a point 35 miles east of
Lupembe—roughly the junction of the Nyama and Mnyera
rivers—and then turn northwards to Mpanga, whence he
was to reconnoitre the river crossings with a view to
marching on Mahenge [2] in co-operation with Rodger's

---

[1] On 28th August, concurrently with the decision to push on into
Iringa, Brig.-General Northey enquired whether Hawthorn could make a
rapid march to Mahenge, destroy the enemy's supplies there before the
arrival of the German forces from the north—there being " plenty of time
" available "—and return to Lupembe. On receipt of the reply (29th)
that such a raid would take 10 to 12 days—a very low estimate—owing
to the nature of the country and difficulties of supply, the idea was dropped,
and on 30th August Brig.-General Northey put forward the suggestion
already recorded (with which the C.-in-C. did not concur) of a concentration
at Lupembe, leaving Iringa to the Belgians. See pp. 488–4

[2] See above, pp. 489–90. The relevant portion of the telegram of 4th
September addressed to column commanders was as follows. " Hawthorn
" will drive enemy eastwards from Tanganika 35 miles east of Lupembe
" and occupy Kiwanga [Mpanga]. From Kiwanga he will reconnoitre
" crossings of Ulanga river towards Mtimbira."
    A confusion arose here owing to the defects of the very poor maps in
use, on which no place named Tanganika was marked. Sketch 66 shows
the place correctly so known, through which Hawthorn, in fact, passed.
His route via Mfirika was the only good one east of Lupembe, forking
south-eastward from Tanganika to cross the Nyama near Kisingo and
thence following the south bank of the Mnyera.
    But to Hawthorn, before he started, the name Tanganika seems to
have connoted a place 18 miles east of the Sylvester Falls, i.e., at or near
Kisingo. This, at any rate, was the map reference given by him on
4th September in reply to an enquiry by Northey, and accepted by the
latter at least until 10th September.
    Meanwhile on 9th September Hawthorn, on reaching the falls of the
Mugwe river, reported (a) that he was then " at Sylvester Falls " (which
Continued at foot of next page.

column, which was to be sent southwards from Muhanga to Makua.[1]

Accordingly, sending forward an advanced detachment on the 6th September, he moved off from Mfirika with the remainder of his force next day. As had been expected, the obstacles of the ground retarded progress, while the maintenance of supplies was a matter of considerable difficulty.[2] In spite of bad going the column reached the falls of the river Mugwe on the 9th, Tanganika on the 10th, and the junction of the Nyama and Mnyera rivers on the 11th September, meeting no sign of the enemy. From Tanganika onwards the country became somewhat more open, and the overgrown tracks and narrow valleys, in which at almost any point the advance could have been ambushed and easily held up, were left behind.

For the next few days, during which carriers had to be sent back to Lupembe for supplies, Hawthorn was restricted to patrolling north-westwards up the Mnyera and forward to Kisingo, some five miles to the eastward. His patrols, confirming the German withdrawal eastwards, also indicated that the enemy was holding the west bank of the Ruhuje at Mkapira ;[3] on the 15th September, therefore, two companies of the 1/K.A.R. were sent forward to Kisingo, where, by the 17th, the whole column was assembled.

Continued from previous page.

he was not) and (b) that his advanced column " expected to be at Tan- " ganika " (i.e., the real Tanganika) next day ; but without correcting his former map reference.

Northey's small-scale map showed no road past the Sylvester Falls (on the Nyama river), but indicated a direct route north-eastwards from Lupembe to Mpanga. Accordingly on 10th September, referring to the latter route in reply to Hawthorn, he telegraphed : " I expected that " you would use this road and detach force to deal with enemy at Tan- " ganika." It will be observed that the order of 4th September did not say this, and it seems evident that from 4th to 10th September Northey and Hawthorn were at cross purposes, entirely owing to bad maps.

[1] It will be remembered that eventually it was Murray, not Rodger, who went to Makua. See p. 492.

[2] Hitherto on the high open steppe ending at Mfirika it had been practicable for columns to be accompanied by cattle on the hoof, but in the low-lying valleys now to be traversed the presence of tsetse and of a shrub poisonous to all animals except donkeys made this impossible. Fortunately in the game reserve along the Ruhuje and Mnyera valleys elephants were numerous and their meat afforded a welcome substitute. A certain amount of rice was also found still remaining ; but rations became monotonous and were often scanty.

[3] With characteristic vagueness, several adjacent points on the German map then in use are all marked Mkapira. The name is here used to indicate the Ruhuje crossing so marked in Sketch 66, and applies also to the high ground at this point between the Ruhuje and Mnyera rivers.

During this time successive messages received from headquarters, as the situation with regard to the northern columns fluctuated, left Hawthorn in some doubt how best to proceed. Learning on the 14th that Rodger was not to come south, but with no word as to Murray, he decided to march on Mkapira as soon as his carriers returned. Then came an intimation that Murray would move south and " get in touch with Hawthorn who will be about 20 miles " south of Makua " (i.e., at Mpanga, as first ordered).[1] On the 19th, whilst at Kisingo awaiting the return of his carriers, he sent an advanced party eastwards towards Mkapira, and on the same day received orders (dated 17th) which, placed as he was, were puzzling : " Hawthorn and " Murray will co-operate and cross Ulanga, both with " Mtimbira as their objective. If Murray on arrival at " Makua is unable to get touch with Hawthorn he will " move eastwards direct on Mtimbira which will probably " cause enemy at Mkapira to retire." This, which might be taken as implying that Hawthorn should make for Mkapira, was followed by the further telegram of the 19th, already mentioned in connection with Murray,[2] which urged the importance of forestalling Kraut's arrival at Mahenge.

On the 20th September communication with Murray was established ; but between the 17th and 21st the arrival of at least five German units was reported, some of whose patrols and snipers were encountered about Kisingo.[3]

Although, as already stated, it was in the highest degree unlikely that either Hawthorn or Murray could now hope to reach Mahenge, the presence of the enemy at Mkapira left Hawthorn no option but to move in that direction.

Early on the 20th Hawthorn's advanced detachment gained the high ground between the Ruhuje and Mnyera rivers at Mkapira, on which at least a part of the enemy's force was believed to be established, and the next few days were devoted to reconnaissance of the whole area as far as the Ruhuje river. Knowing that Murray had been

---

[1] See p. 490.
[2] See p. 493.
[3] 8.F.K. from the north, 12.F.K. from Mahenge, and Songea detachment reported 17th September ; 26.F.K., 5. and 10.Sch.K. with part of 2.F.K., reported 21st September. These reports are now known to have been inaccurate (8. and 26.F.K., for example, were with Wahle in the west) but there could be no doubt that German units had been brought down towards Mkapira.

ordered eastwards from Makua, Hawthorn determined to attack at Mkapira as soon as Murray was half way to Mtimbira and so in a position to cut off any retreat from Mkapira to Mahenge.

Murray meanwhile continued his march southwards, with patrols wide to his eastern flank, and on the 23rd September—on which day, it will be remembered, he came under Hawthorn's orders—was near Makero, on the Mnyera river, 15 miles to the eastward of Mpanga.[1]

As yet Hawthorn had found no suitable place near Mkapira to cross the Ruhuje—a crocodile-infested river, here some 200 yards wide—and on the 24th, in view of the risk to Murray's column from German reinforcements reported to be still arriving in the bend of the Ruhuje north of Mkapira, he ordered Murray southwards to unite with his own force.

Next day Hawthorn succeeded in getting a patrol across the Ruhuje south of Mkapira, followed by a company of the 1/K.A.R. which established itself, unopposed, on a low ridge covered with dense bush and trees about half a mile east of the river. Whether by reason of this or otherwise, the enemy was now found to have evacuated the west bank, and on the 27th the remainder of Hawthorn's column crossed the Ruhuje, likewise unopposed.

In the afternoon of the 28th, whilst the column was engaged in moving camp from the neighbourhood of the river to the ridge beyond, it was attacked by a considerable force of the enemy, estimated at five companies,[2] with a light field gun, and for about two hours there was a confused and lively exchange of fire in the thick bush, the effects of which were negligible in comparison with its violence. The enemy's gun was knocked out almost at once by short-range machine-gun fire, and attacks on the centre and right of Hawthorn's hastily organized perimeter defence were driven off without difficulty. When darkness fell the enemy withdrew, leaving 8 wounded prisoners and signs of numerous other casualties, and did not renew the attack.[3]

---

[1] Murray's patrols across the Mnyera, east and north-east of Makero, on 24th September successfully ambushed two parties of the enemy and from their prisoners' statements accepted the presence of five German units on Hawthorn's front.

[2] See Note, p. 510.

[3] British casualties were: 1/K.A.R., 1 killed, 2 wounded; 1/S. Afr. Rifles, 2 wounded.   *Continued at foot of next page.*

Meanwhile, in the area between the Ruhuje and the Mnyera, Murray's column was now at hand. Contact with it had, in fact, been established on the 28th, when Murray's staff officer and some of his scouts, having crossed the Ruhuje, passed through the enemy's lines and joined Hawthorn just before the German attack was launched. From Brig.-General Northey had come the news that the 2nd Division, owing to supply difficulties, was unable to move farther south ; [1] Hawthorn's own supply situation, distant as he was some 60 miles from his advanced base at Lupembe, was serious, and no further advance could be made until his stocks had been replenished ; between him and Mahenge the enemy appeared to be in very considerable force. Taking all this into account, and realising that his force was in a somewhat exposed situation, Colonel Hawthorn decided to withdraw again to the west bank of the Ruhuje, there to join forces with Murray and await developments.

Accordingly, on the night of the 29th/30th September his column recrossed the river, joining Murray's force, which had arrived during the previous day. Their combined forces took up a strong position overlooking the Ruhuje on the high ground between the two rivers at Mkapira. Here for the next three weeks they were to remain, establishing posts on the line of communication and building up supplies.[2]

The Occupation of Songea

As the previous chapter has indicated, Brig.-General Northey had hoped, in his drive northward from the Nyasaland border, for Portuguese co-operation in regard to the

End Paper
(S)

Continued from previous page.

It seems probable that the enemy expected only to find the company of 1/K.A.R. which had crossed in advance of the column, not the whole force.

The episode came to be known afterwards as " Donnybrook Fair ", from the great amount of ammunition expended in the long grass and bush with little result.

[1] See p. 377.

[2] Supply difficulties continued for some time. On 7th October (not strictly within the compass of this chapter) Hawthorn telegraphed : " Have been on reduced rations and game for last few days ; have no native " rations for to-morrow ; unless supplies sent up can be increased, carriers " will have to be sent back and force immobilized ; have however two days for Murray's column ".

On 12th October Brig.-General Northey telegraphed, in view of the situation as it had then developed (see Vol. II) : " further move towards Mahenge is impossible ".

Songea area on his extreme south-eastern flank. In its absence he had nevertheless pushed forward, justified in disregarding the risk to his communications from the south-east both by the strategic value of his move on Iringa and by the enemy's weakness round Songea.[1]

But by the end of August, when it was obvious that the Germans retreating before Lieut.-General Smuts would be driven into the southern half of the German territory, the importance of denying them their south-western districts as an ultimate rallying-ground began to be unmistakable. On the 5th September Brig.-General Northey, who now had a newly-raised unit, the Rhodesia Native Regiment, available for the purpose,[2] and perceived that although the Songea district marched with Portuguese territory our Allies there were still unlikely to find themselves able to assist, took up with the Governor of Nyasaland the question of occupying Songea either with the new unit or with Nyasaland volunteers.

The Colonial Office, to whom the Governor referred, at once approved,[3] and when on the 10th, Brig.-General Northey received an enquiry by the Commander-in-Chief whether it would not be possible to send 300 to 400 men from the back areas to Songea, to deter the enemy from a move in that direction, he was able to reply that this had already been arranged.

On the 12th operation orders were issued for the Head-quarters and one of the two companies forming the Rhodesia Native Regiment, leaving Neu Langenburg on the 14th, to embark at Mwaya in H.M.S. *Guendolen* for Wiedhaven whence they would march to Songea, leaving a small base party at Wiedhaven and establishing also a helio station on the opposite shore of Lake Nyasa to tap into the main telegraph line there.

This force, 250 strong, under Lieut.-Colonel A.J.Tomlinson,[4] landed early on the 16th at Wiedhaven, unopposed. The march eastwards was without incident, and at 10 a.m. on the 20th, meeting no opposition worth mentioning, Tom-linson's advanced party entered Songea. On the previous

---

[1] See p. 480, f.n. 2.
[2] See p. 505.
[3] " Inform General Northey . . . . it is desirable he should occupy " Songea as it appears . . . . there is no military difficulty in doing so ". Telegram, 7th September.
[4] Total strength 10 officers, 16 European N.C.O s., 223 askari.

day 4 Germans and 30 askari, the last of the garrison, had left north-eastwards in the direction of Likuyu at Tomlinson's approach, and for several weeks thereafter there was no further sign of the enemy anywhere in the vicinity.

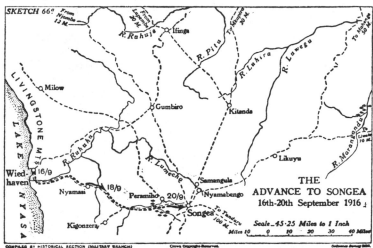

SKETCH 66

THE
ADVANCE TO SONGEA
16th–20th September 1916

Scale_45·25 Miles to 1 Inch

At Songea Tomlinson remained established, collecting supplies and patrolling northwards and eastwards as far as Kitanda and the Mbarangandu river respectively. Here for some months his force was to remain and in due time to take part in events to be narrated in volume II.

OPERATIONS FROM BISMARCKBURG

Turning now to Northey's western flank, it will be readily remembered that in the middle of June, when most of Murray's column after occupying Bismarckburg was brought across to Rungwe to take part in the advance towards Iringa, two companies of the Northern Rhodesia Police, with details of the B.S.A. Police, remained behind to hold the area east and north of Bismarckburg,[1] abandoned by the enemy. In the latter half of that month the fugitive German garrisons of Namema and Bismarckburg were reported to be maintaining themselves, with orders to go no farther, in the wide tract of barren country lying inland to the east of Karema, 120 miles to the northward, known

---

[1] See p. 467

as the Gongwe area.[1] Here they could do no harm and there was no object in following them. If they attempted to come south again the Bismarckburg force, placed on the 29th June under the command of Major W. Baxendale, B.S.A. Police, was ample to deal with them.[2]

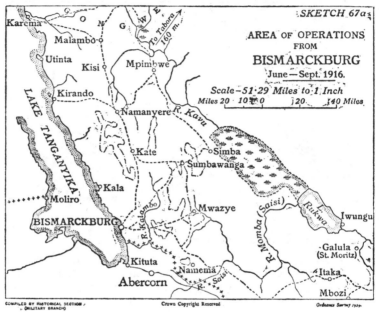

SKETCH 67a

AREA OF OPERATIONS
FROM
BISMARCKBURG
June — Sept. 1916.

Scale—51·29 Miles to 1 Inch
Miles 20   10   0   20   40 Miles

COMPILED BY HISTORICAL SECTION,
MILITARY BRANCH   Crown Copyright Reserved   Ordnance Survey 1937

With this in view Baxendale was given a free hand to use his companies both for patrolling between Bismarckburg and Lake Rukwa and to furnish landing parties which, in co-operation with the naval flotilla, were to work up the eastern shore of Lake Tanganyika.[3]   Throughout July

[1] Erroneously described in the information sent to Brig.-General Northey as the " Gongwe Mountains." The area is in fact part of the undulating plateau lying well to the north of the hills which separate the southern end of Lake Tanganyika from the swamps of Lake Rukwa. " From Gongwe " to Iringa is a journey of six weeks through starvation country from which " the native population have been purposely cleared to prevent an advance " by our troops . . . . on that side ". (Murray, telegram 22nd June.)

[2] Half of " E " Coy., N.R. Police, now on the L. of C. forward from Fife, was also available and during part of August was used in the Bismarckburg area, rejoining early in September.

[3] While Baxendale remained directly under Brig.-General Northey's orders, Lieut.-Colonel H. M. Stennett, N. Rhodesia Police, was placed in administrative charge of the Bismarckburg-Fife area, with instructions to give Baxendale every available man, keeping no garrisons, other than details, at Abercorn and Fife.

a number of such minor expeditions were made, but few signs of the enemy were found. So far as could be ascertained the German force, estimated at about 40 Germans and 300 askari, remained about Mpimbwe, some 85 miles north of Bismarckburg—well placed to continue its retreat on Tabora—with patrols watching the Lake shore.

On the 13th July the mission station of Kala, 25 miles up the coast, was occupied without opposition, and on the same day a detachment which had been sent to Sumbawanga, 50 miles north-east of Bismarckburg, and had then turned westwards towards the Lake, scattered a stray German party at Kate, killing its native sergeant, and capturing also at various places on the way a total of about 30 native irregulars.

As a counter to any German attempt to return southwards, Brig.-General Northey had, as early as the 3rd July, approved in principle of a landing being made at Kirando, 80 miles up the coast, whence the enemy's communications could be threatened. At the end of July it was decided to carry out the plan, and by the 2nd August Kirando had been occupied without opposition.

During the next few days, still with no sign of opposition, a small advanced party from Kirando took possession of Namanyere, 35 miles to the south-eastward, where on the 11th it was joined by Baxendale's column, which had marched unopposed from Bismarckburg.

By this time the Belgian forces of Lieut.-Colonel Moulaert, with Tabora as their objective, had landed on the eastern shore of the Lake[1] and the withdrawal of the Germans became inevitable. From Namanyere Baxendale's patrols, pushed out northwards and north-eastwards to Mpimbwe and the surrounding districts, confirmed the departure of the enemy, and by the 20th he had gained touch with the Belgian column, which was moving on towards Tabora in pursuit.

Little more, therefore, remained to be done. For another fortnight Baxendale continued to patrol forward of the general line Simba–Namanyere–Kirando ;[2] but the area was evidently no longer threatened, and on the 9th September, as has already been said, Brig.-General Northey ordered

---

[1] See p. 435.
[2] It had been proposed, if the enemy came south, to hold posts at these places so as to cover the area south of this line.

Baxendale, with one company, to march to Rungwe as a reinforcement for the main operations, leaving the remaining company for police duties in the Bismarckburg area.[1]

Meanwhile the naval flotilla, which had rendered useful service in the landing operations, and whose further co-operation with the Belgian flotilla had been rendered no longer necessary by the Belgian successes farther north, transferred its base from Lukuga to Bismarckburg and at the suggestion of the Admiralty came under the orders of Colonel Edwards, the Commandant General, Rhodesia.

DRAFTS AND REINFORCEMENTS

In the operations which have been described, Brig.-General Northey's battle casualties had, it is true, been few, and his losses from sickness proportionately less heavy than those among the sorely-tried troops of Lieut.-General Smuts fighting in the unhealthier central areas. His lines of communication, moreover, though lengthened considerably beyond his earlier expectation, had been sufficiently—if at times hazardously—protected by relatively small numbers. Nevertheless his whole force, less than 3,000 strong at the outset, and by the end of September dispersed on a front of 200 miles from Songea to Iringa, had been throughout in need of all the reinforcement obtainable.

The resources of Nyasaland and Rhodesia, however, were limited, while the efforts of the Union of South Africa were of necessity concentrated chiefly on the principal field force under Lieut.-General Smuts.

Brig.-General Northey's contingent from the Union— the 1st and 2nd South African Rifles—had, it will be recalled, been raised at the end of 1915.[2] Drafts for these units continued to arrive in the course of his operations, so that by the end of September 1916 a total of nearly 2,000 South Africans had crossed the German southern border.[3]

In Nyasaland the expansion of the 1/K.A.R., normally recruited in that Protectorate, had, indeed, been actively proceeding, but not for Brig.-General Northey's benefit :

---

[1] Baxendale reached Rungwe on 29th September
[2] See p. 188.
[3] Up to 31st March 1916 : 74 officers, 1,265 o.r. April, May, June : 7 officers, 265 o.r. July, August, September : 18 officers, 242 o.r. Total : 99 officers, 1,772 o.r.

the recruits obtained were required for the 2/K.A.R., now being resurrected at Nairobi, and all this excellent material was destined eventually for the main theatre of war.

No such restriction applied, however, to recruitment in Rhodesia. As has already been recorded, the recommendation by the Commandant General in Rhodesia that a native regiment should be raised in Southern Rhodesia was eventually approved in April 1916. By the end of May a complete unit, 500 strong, known as the Rhodesia Native Regiment, under Lieut.-Colonel A. J. Tomlinson, B.S.A. Police, was in training at Salisbury.[1] Two months later it moved to Zomba, going on at the end of August to Neu Langenburg. Its first task was the occupation of Songea in September, already mentioned. Thereafter it remained in the field throughout the campaign.

In Northern Rhodesia further recruits for the 1/K.A.R., mainly some 300 Awemba, were enlisted by Lieut. A. H. L. Wyatt ; these, with details from Nyasaland, reached Njombe on the 19th August, to go forward to Lupembe as already narrated.[2]

By the end of September Brig.-General Northey's forces, originally about 2,600 strong, had increased to about 3,800.[3]

---

[1] The rank and file included :
    50 transferred from the 100 armed native police forming part of the B.S.A. Police.
    113 Matabele and Mashona.
    219 Awemba and Angoni (natives of N. Rhodesia and Nyasaland enployed in the mines in S. Rhodesia).
  Recruitment was carried out under the Native Affairs Department of Southern Rhodesia

The unit was first armed with Martini-Henry rifles and rearmed with the service Lee-Enfield on reaching Neu Langenburg. Its officers and British N.C.Os. were found partly from the B.S.A. Police and partly from the Native Affairs Department.

[2] See p. 482, f.n. 1.

[3] On 30th September 1916, the strengths of units were returned as follows :

Unit	European Offrs.	R. & F.	Native
1/S. Afr. Rifles	10	138	
2/S. Afr. Rifles	27	506	
Mountain Gun Battery ..	5	101	
B.S.A. Police	13	310	
1/K.A.R.	35	—	1,286 *
N. Rhod. Police	23	24	872
Rhod. Nat. Regt.	17	43	442
	130	1,122	2,600

* Includes 479 recruits.

In the vital matter of carrier services, Brig.-General Northey's needs were naturally heavy. The extension of the lines of communication, along which generally speaking animal transport was out of the question owing to tsetse fly, while only a limited amount of motor transport was available, necessitated a continuous service of carrier convoys requiring numbers far in excess of the fighting troops.[1] These requirements, fortunately, it was found possible to meet; but they involved drawing on almost all the available native man-power.

Lastly, it is due to the British population of the two Rhodesias and Nyasaland to state that practically every available white man had come forward for service, either with the units in the field or in connection with the prosecution of the war.

BRIG.-GENERAL NORTHEY'S OPERATIONS, MAY—SEPTEMBER 1916

SUMMARY

Sketch 63

Between the last week of May and the end of September 1916 the operations of Brig.-General Northey, planned originally with no more than the general object of clearing the Nyasaland–Rhodesia border, had developed almost from the outset into a successful penetration deep into the enemy's territory, with marked effect on the subsequent course of the campaign as a whole.

He had, it is true, been disappointed of his first expectation of rounding up and eliminating the German forces which the previous British weakness had too long allowed to be a menace to the border. Of this it need only be said that the enemy's prompt retreat at the first sign of the British advance was in keeping with the German strategy throughout, a strategy of retreat which here as elsewhere was from the German point of view undoubtedly sound.

Within a few days the direction taken by all except the westernmost German garrison had converted the original advance on a broad front into a pursuit converging on the eastern flank; while in the matter of policy the course of events pointed unmistakably to continuance of the pursuit

---

[1] It is estimated that 17,000 carriers were in service north of the border. A notable tribute to them was paid by Brig.-General Northey in his farewell order in 1918: " I would award the palm of merit to the Tengatenga" (carriers).

northwards towards Iringa and to an eventual endeavour to link up with the main British forces as they moved southward. In this connection it should here be noted that **End Paper (S)** the barren and well-nigh uninhabited waste to the west and north of the general line Neu Langenburg–Iringa–Dodoma was no country for the movement of troops : geography, in short, directed the flow of operations into the narrowing south-eastern areas of the German protectorate.

The occupation of Njombe at the end of June was **Sketch 65** followed by the convergent advance on Malangali during July and the subsequent northward withdrawal of the German forces there, whose diversion from the opposition to Smuts and van Deventer had been one valuable result of Northey's bold northward move.

But already the risk to Northey's almost unprotected communications, and signs of the impending arrival in the Mahenge area of at least a part of Lettow's main forces, made an eastward movement from Njombe to Lupembe a necessity. In consequence by mid-August Northey's **Sketch 66** force was compelled to stand divided into two widely separated groups, one directed northwards on Iringa and one pointed eastwards towards Mahenge ; while as yet he had no safeguard in the Songea area on his distant south-eastern flank.

Nevertheless possession of Iringa, and thereafter a junction with van Deventer, still remained his aims despite the risks involved ; and further, there was even hope that by a quick dash he might cut the only line of German retreat from Iringa. Confirmed in these plans by the approval of Lt. General Smuts in the last week of August, he pushed forward, and at Iringa reached the northern limit of his drive.

By this action he unquestionably diverted the retirement of Kraut's companies opposing van Deventer to the direction of Mahenge, denying them the healthier area about Iringa. But he was not to have the satisfaction of intercepting the timely local German retreat from Iringa, nor—although for nearly another month he remained unaware of the fact— was it within the power of van Deventer's worn-out troops to press on and effect the desired junction.

An unfailing optimism continued throughout September to suggest an endeavour to reach at least the neighbourhood of Mahenge and to forestall the now evident gathering of the German units in the Kilombero valley. But notwithstanding a valiant effort to combine his widely-separated columns in such an attempt—an effort in some measure frustrated by the curious chance of a topographical error [1]— Brig.-General Northey had at no time either the numbers or the supply organization needed for its accomplishment. In the lowlands to the eastward German units continued to arrive from the north; he held Songea, however, though not in any strength. Meanwhile it became evident that the forces of Lieut.-General Smuts could go no farther.

Thus by the end of September Northey's small force, 3,800 in all, opposed to German numbers steadily increasing towards parity if not superiority, stood facing eastwards dispersed along a front of 200 miles from Songea to Iringa, with its far-stretched lines of communication barely protected, with no general reserve and no prospect of further reinforcement : a precarious situation to which only the eventual arrival of van Deventer's troops from the north could bring relief. [2] But before this could come about the anxieties of the situation were to be redoubled by the advent of danger from the direction of Tabora, the threat of which was now clearly perceived.

Brig.-General Northey's operations were conducted with troops who, with the exception of the 1/K.A.R., were all non-regulars with little previous military training. To their persistence and determination in a long and disappointing pursuit, to their steadfastness against constant hardships of climate and frequent shortage of food, and not least to their fighting qualities in the all too rare opportunities of coming to grips with the enemy, high tribute is due.

It is much to be regretted that both lack of space and lack of data have prevented fuller reference being made to

---

[1] See p. 495, f.n. 1.

[2] Brig.-General Northey's war diary for 30th September gives his general situation as follows :

Rodger's column :	1 squadron (S.A.Rifles) at Iringa.
	3 squadrons (S.A. Rifles) east of Muhanga.
Hawthorn and Murray :	at Mkapira and on Ruhuje river.

His information regarding the enemy at this time was :

Opposite Rodger :	2., 5., 10.F.K., Königsberg det., " L." K.
	2 of Kraut's F.K. at Ifakara, 1 at Lofia,
	1 at Mfua.
Opposite Hawthorn :	5. and 10.Sch.K., 12., 15., 26.F.K., Songea
	det. (200), and possibly 8.F.K.

Total equivalent to sixteen F.K. in all, exclusive of Wahle's forces from Tabora. As is now known (see Note, p. 510), this total was not far wrong, although the details of units were somewhat different.

the equally admirable work of the administrative and auxiliary services which, largely organized *ad hoc* by the Union and colonial administrations, enabled the fighting troops to take and keep the field.

Having regard to the great distance separating Northey's troops from the main bulk of the British forces, and to the difficulties of communication between them, the absence of a unified command[1] may perhaps not have been so grave a disadvantage as would at first sight appear. But more probably it is due to Brig.-General Northey's constant care in maintaining touch with Lieut.-General Smuts, and to the ordering of his plans in conformity with the latter's wishes and movements, that so little difficulty was experienced in this respect. The coming of war had taken by surprise an inherently unsound system of divided control, and Brig.-General Northey made the best of it with notable success.

With limited resources and at risks of which he was fully aware, traversing a little-known and undeveloped country very imperfectly mapped, he had in the course of four months carried his columns with unfailing confidence a distance of over two hundred miles from his starting-point, occupying successfully some 25,000 square miles of the enemy's territory.

In so doing he had the advantage throughout of having on his side a friendly native population, for the most part actively willing to supply food and to give information : among them notably the Wahehe about Iringa, with their memories of the German suppression of the Maji-Maji rebellion ten years before,[2] who made no secret of their sympathies.

His operations, moreover, arduous though they were, had involved no such constant and overpowering demands on the health and endurance of his men as had been made on the troops in the principal theatre of operations : the country was less unhealthy, its climate less fierce, the toll of sickness, hunger and exhaustion less devastating. In consequence his force, when of necessity it paused at the end of September, was still in no such grim plight as that of Lieut.-General Smuts's hard-driven men. As events were before long to prove, it was well that it should be so.

---

[1] It will be remembered that during this period **Brig.-General Northey's** command was exercised under the Colonial Office.

[2] See Appendix IV.

NOTE

THE SOUTHERN AREA:

Movements of German Units, August–September 1916

The movements of the various German units are now known to have been as follows :

On 18th August Braunschweig's force (*2., 5., 10.F.K., "L" K., Königsberg det.*), then falling back through Wuasa on Iringa, came under Kraut's orders. On 1st Sept. Falkenstein (half *12.F.K.* and *Songea det.*), previously brought from the south to Tanganika, likewise came under the orders of Kraut, who was directed by Lettow to reinforce him (Falkenstein) with *19.F.K.* and *5.Sch.K.* under Krüger, while *16.F.K.* left Kisaki for Kidodi in replacement of Krüger.

On 10th and 11th Sept. Krüger and Falkenstein joined hands at Mkapira with Krüger in command. Meanwhile on 7th Sept. the *Königsberg det.* as such had been broken up.

On 12th and 13th Sept. Kraut, acting on the news of Braunschweig's further retreat to Muhanga, marched south with *15., 25.F.K., 8.Sch.K.* and *Pangani det.*, followed by *16.F.K.* and *9.Sch.K.*, leaving on the Ruaha Korvetten Kapitän (formerly Lieut. Commdr. retired) Schoenfeld—the officer commanding Kraut's *Königsberg* guns—with *6.F.K., 2.Sch.* and *7.Sch.K.* and *Arusha det.*

On 15th Sept., at Ifakara, Kraut divided his force, detaching *15.F.K.* and *Pangani det.* under Lincke to join Braunschweig, while *25.F.K., 8.Sch.* and *9.Sch.K.*—the two latter formed as a mounted detachment under Meyer—were despatched towards Mtimbira. Two days later (17th) Lincke joined Braunschweig and took over command of their combined forces, *16.F.K.* meanwhile moving to Mtimbira as a reserve.

On 21st Sept. "*L*" *K.* (from Lincke) and *25.F.K.*, both under Aumann, were detailed to block the western approaches to Mtimbira, while Meyer's mounted detachment went forward to Mkapira.

Learning on 26th Sept. that Songea was in British hands, Kraut ordered both Meyer and Falkenstein (taking the latter with half *12.F.K.* and *Songea det.* from Krüger) from Mkapira to march via Kitanda on Songea, and himself on 29th Sept. left Ifakara, with *10.F.K.* taken from Lincke, for Mahenge, where he arrived next day.

At Mahenge Kraut heard of the retreat of the Songea garrison to Likuyu. ¹On this he ordered *5.F.K.* (from Lincke) to Mahenge, and *10.F.K.* to continue southwards towards Songea. These two moves, however, were vetoed by Lettow, who on 1st October directed that the two companies should make for Mkapira, where

Hawthorn and Murray were to be attacked with all available forces. Meantime, in aid of the weak force outside Songea, Kraut ordered *7.Sch.K.*, from Schoenfeld's force on the Ruaha, to proceed via Mahenge towards Songea.

On 6th October Kraut himself, closely followed by *5.* and *10.F.K.*, reached the Ruhuje north of Mkapira. His distribution at this time was thus as follows:

Along the Ruaha: Schoenfeld; *6.F.K., 2.Sch.K., Arusha det.*

Along the Ruipa: Lincke; *2.F.K., 15.F.K., Pangani det.*

Along the Ruhuje: Kraut (H.Q.); *5., 10., 16., 19., 25.F.K., 5.Sch.K.*

Moving on Songea: (at { Falkenstein; $\frac{1}{2}$ *12.F.K., Songea det.*

Kitanda 7th Oct. { Meyer; Mounted det. (formerly *8.Sch.*), *9.Sch.K.*

Ordered to Songea: (at } *7.Sch.K.*
Ifakara 8th Oct.)

Meyer's detachment returned to the Ruhuje on 17th October.

From the foregoing it would appear that the units which attacked Hawthorn at Mkapira on 28th September were *16., 19.F.K., 5.Sch.K.*, and probably *25.F.K.* and " *L* " *K.*

CHAPTER XXIX

SOME GENERAL CONSIDERATIONS

I

THE East African campaign differed fundamentally in several respects from those in any of the other theatres of war.

Neither in Great Britain nor in Germany had any particular thought been given to the situation which the outbreak of a major war in Europe would produce in East Africa. The Berlin Act of 1885 provided, it is true, for an agreed neutrality in the African territories involved ; but the contingency of a lack of agreement on the subject had not been taken into account. In the British and German protectorates alike, as a matter of policy, the local military forces existed only to maintain order and cope with any internal unrest which might occur ; while, so far as Great Britain was concerned, it was taken for granted, as we have seen, that if reinforcement were ever required it would be provided from India. Both sides, therefore, were found unprepared when war broke out, nor was either at first in sufficient strength to embark on any serious offensive. East Africa, in consequence, was from the outset a " sideshow " ; and since the outcome of a conflict there could have no decisive influence on the struggle between the contending Powers, a side-show it remained.

End Papers By contrast with the warfare in the other theatres, where immense and powerful forces operated in relatively small areas of Europe and the Middle East, the campaign in East Africa was one of small forces operating over the vast distances of a tract of the African continent. With numbers amounting to little more than the equivalent of a single corps on the Western Front, Lieut.-General Smuts's operations ranged from Kilimanjaro almost to the Portuguese border five hundred miles away, across German territory nearly twice the size of Germany.

Not only in its vast dimensions but in its physical characteristic—the almost universal and well-nigh trackless bush—lay another peculiarity differentiating the East African from other theatres of war.

512

Tactically, as a survivor has remarked, the campaign might almost " be likened to a huge night operation, a " groping in the obscurity of darkened Africa ".[1] It illustrated, in fact, a military truism : that in such country the ground itself, the difficulties of transport and supply, and the lack of railways and good roads, must operate always against the side which seeks a decision.

There stood out, too, the further distinguishing peculiarity of a climate pitilessly hostile not only to the European but to the Indian soldier ; and in particular, in this connection, the rainy season, which while it lasts not only takes its heavy toll of health, but renders serious military operations a physical impossibility. To this feature, the climate, likewise, but little regard had been paid ; yet here, above all, lay the real reason why, in the end, the valour and steadfast endurance of the troops from the United Kingdom and the British dependencies elsewhere were of no avail to keep them in the field. Only the African soldier could stand the East African climate indefinitely.[2]

II

It is hardly surprising that a campaign of so unusual a character proved long and difficult. Seen as a whole, it comprised four distinct phases, with only the first two of which this volume is concerned.

The first phase, for the reasons already sufficiently indicated in preceding chapters, was mistakenly expected to be decisive. In it, after the expedition from India had failed grievously in November 1914 in an attempt, hopeless from the outset, to conquer the German colony, there ensued throughout 1915 a period of stalemate. This was marked, on the one hand, by the impossibility of further reinforcing the British troops from outside East Africa, until, at the end of the year, South African troops became available ; by the failure to appreciate the possibilities of expanding the K.A.R., the only troops really suited to the country ; and by the consequent restriction to a passive defensive. On the other hand, during this period the Germans built up their force of native troops to a strength which enabled them to maintain a steady, if ultimately unsuccessful, opposition to the subsequent British offensive.

---

[1] Capell, " The 2nd Rhodesia Regiment in East Africa ", p. 71.
[2] See Note, p. 520.

S*

The second phase, which occupied the year 1916, and of which the events are here narrated, consisted of the successful invasion of the German territory from the north by Lieut.-General Smuts, assisted by the simultaneous southward advance in the western area by our Belgian allies and by the lesser operations of Brig.-General Northey striking northwards from the southern German border. By the end of 1916 some two thirds of the German protectorate had passed into Allied possession. Yet the primary object of all war, defeat and elimination of the enemy's forces—forces in this case far smaller than those attacking them, and without hope of reinforcement—was not attained ; while, at immense cost in suffering and hardship, the invaders, dependent on lines of communication of fantastic and ever-increasing length, learned that in tropical Africa neither skilful strategy, nor numbers, nor fortitude and determination beyond all praise, were in themselves sufficient. During this period began that expansion of the African troops which experience had shown to be vital to eventual success.

In the third phase, during 1917, which saw the British field army largely reconstituted with the new African reinforcements, the occupation of the German territory was to be completed, not without hard fighting. Yet still the enemy, in ever-dwindling numbers, but handled with unfailing skill by a master of strategic retreat, remained in being.

The fourth and final phase of the campaign resolved itself into a steady pursuit, first into Portuguese territory and ultimately into Northern Rhodesia ; nor was the rounding-up of the German forces achieved until at long last Colonel von Lettow-Vorbeck, with the exiguous remnant of his troops, surrendered in consequence of the armistice signed on the Western front in November 1918, having successfully contained in Africa for over four years a total force considerably larger than Lord Roberts's whole army in the South African war.

III

As the narrative shows, the East African campaign, starting as it did and conducted as it inevitably was by commanders, staffs and troops for the most part unfamiliar with local conditions, many of them not professional soldiers, and therefore, in general, with everything to learn, could only be one of gradual progression : there could be no prospect of even early, much less of spectacular, success.

Throughout the first dull, defensive phase the ghost of the initial failure at Tanga continued to haunt the theatre of war, sapping morale and undermining confidence to an extent better to be appreciated in retrospect than at the time.

The arrival of the South Africans brought renewed hope ; yet even they, with victory in South-West Africa fresh in their minds, were unprepared for the disillusionments of the very different enterprise which lay before them. The year of Lieut.-General Smuts's command was to prove a period of long, arduous and unsuccessful pursuit of an elusive enemy of a quality and determination no lower than his own, and was to teach lessons in tropical African warfáre such as had certainly not been foreseen. To the characteristic South African strategy of envelopment, steadily maintained despite a succession of disappointments, the German commander opposed a technique of continued skilful retreat, profiting by all his advantages of interior lines, homogeneous troops, mobility and familiarity with the country, and rightly taking no risks which might compromise the continued existence of his forces. The campaign of 1916, in short, became one long rearguard action.

The subsequent phases, with which a later volume will deal, will not be further considered here.

IV

Although the present narrative deals only with the first half of the campaign a few of the lessons already brought out may now perhaps be briefly noted. Some of those, it is hoped, have already been suggested by the preceding chapters.

First in importance would seem to be the vital necessity of good information on which to base plans, both strategic and tactical. To the lack of this may be attributed the unwarranted optimism with which the campaign was begun ; the mistaken belief in the suitability of European and Indian troops ; the use of mounted men[1] and animal transport in country infested by tsetse ; the supply of heavy lorries

---

[1] The case for the employment of mounted infantry in bush warfare will be found argued at some length |from the South African point of view in " The South Africans with General Smuts ", pp. 266–271.

for use in roadless bush ; and in general the conduct of operations on lines unsuited to those peculiarities of the campaign which have already been outlined. The operations had, of course, to be conducted with such resources as were available, and as a side-show the East African campaign could have little claim to special provision ; none the less its history shows plainly how much might have been saved in life and material had good intelligence, collected in peace and wisely applied, been available. The Germans knew their East Africa, and their knowledge served them well.

From a strategic point of view, since the campaign could not affect the ultimate outcome of the war, it may be wondered whether so extensive a commitment in Africa was justified ; whether, indeed, it would not have sufficed to occupy the Kilimanjaro area, as Lieut.-General Smuts did with such success, and thereafter to rest content with ensuring the security of the British territories, both north and south, against such incursions as the Germans, inferior in numbers and cut off from outside help, might attempt. It may at all events be accepted that such would have been Lord Kitchener's view.

It may be doubted, too, whether Lieut.-General Smuts, if he had not been so badly misled by his local weather experts, would have detached van Deventer to Kondoa Irangi as early as he did. That move, whenever it might be made, was bound to have its effect of weakening the opposition to the main British advance ; and it is no disparagement to the successful thrust by van Deventer's mounted troops, under appalling conditions, to say that its effect might well have been far greater had it coincided in point of time more nearly with that of Lieut.-General Smuts's main force down the Pangani.

The course of the subsequent operations, from the Ruvu to the Central Railway, may well be left to speak for itself. It may, however, be remarked that they brought out into harsh relief the fact that mere superiority in numbers, without full ability not only to move them rapidly but to maintain them adequately, was an embarrassment, not an advantage. These operations raise for consideration, too, as has already been suggested, the question whether in 1916—once the occupation of the whole German protectorate came within the range of feasibility—earlier use might not have been made of an undisputed command of the sea ;

establishing bases that would at least have obviated that seemingly endless extension of the communications of the main British force which brought it near to starvation, and to a standstill, successively at the Msiha and the Mgeta.

From the tactical point of view the lessons of bush warfare, familiar to the K.A.R., had to be learned by the rest of the British forces from rude experience. It need only be said that in such fighting, necessarily " blind " and at short range, ambush and surprise were easy and protection difficult. The machine gun especially—" the King of weapons in the bush "—and the mortar were of more value than long-range artillery ; the bayonet, to which the fighting African by nature and upbringing takes kindly, was no less important. In aptitude for bush fighting, as in his imperviousness to the trials of climate, the African soldier stood out pre-eminently above the unaccustomed European and Indian. The African, moreover, is unaffected by that strain on the nerves which long periods in the bush, with its constant sinister suggestion of unseen dangers, tend to produce even in the best of troops of other races.

The moral factor, indeed, must be kept in mind even more constantly in tropical Africa than elsewhere. There can be no doubt that the long spells without recreation, much less leave, and without letters and news,[1] told as heavily on the spirit of the troops as did the privations, sickness and exhaustion, which they so unflinchingly endured, upon their physical health.

With regard to the use of African troops, the figures given in Appendix IV show that there was in fact, contrary to early expectation, no difficulty in finding (though time was required to train) the numbers required. Not all African tribes, however, are of good fighting quality, and as a matter of strategy it will be noted that the safeguarding of the best recruiting areas is in itself of high importance. Had the enemy in the early days succeeded in occupying any of the valuable recruiting grounds in Uganda, British East Africa, Northern Rhodesia and Nyasaland, such a success would have been doubly useful to him, not only in its effect on sources of reinforcement but also from the standpoint of white prestige.

---

[1] For example, the first dismal communiqué on the Battle of Jutland was followed by a period of about 10 days without news, during which the impression persisted that the British fleet had been sunk.

On the African's whole-hearted loyalty and affection for the white leaders whom he has come to know and trust, and on his even deeper and more devoted loyalty to the sovereign and Empire he serves, it is unnecessary to dwell. The corollary to this and to the African's special suitability for warfare in his own country is that the best use of the European soldier is to provide a leaven of individual leaders among African troops. This is not to say that European units might not successfully be employed in special enterprises of brief duration : the clearing of the Kilimanjaro area, already mentioned, for example. But, as an officer of experience has put it, in East Africa an additional hundred white men distributed among the native units might well prove to be worth more than a whole brigade of European troops.[1]

Neither space nor material have been available to deal in any detail with the many administrative problems and difficulties encountered, some of which have been mentioned in preceding chapters. Of one factor, however, vital anywhere and of transcendent importance in East Africa, special mention must be made : water-supply. Throughout the campaign, except in the neighbourhood of the large rivers, water was always scarce and the organization of water-supply an ever-present difficulty. The planning of operations was often conditioned by the necessity of gaining a water-supply, of moving back or forward to the nearest supply,[2] or even of adding water to the loads already carried by the troops.

In this respect, as in others, the enemy was at a considerable advantage, enabled as he was to retreat from one known source of supply to another, his pursuers meanwhile uncertain where water would next be found.

In the matter of transport it will have been realized that the native porter is all-important. To the devoted service given by thousands of these men special tribute is due ; and among the lessons of the campaign the need for their training and organization must not be forgotten. Here, too, the Germans, whose first-line carriers formed an integral part

---

[1] With the proviso that the white personnel need qualities of temperament and leadership above the average, and must have time to learn both their work and the necessary native tongues.

[2] E.g., Longido, 3rd Nov. 1914 (see pp. 97–9) ; Lolkisale, 5th April 1916 (see p. 270) ; Lukigura, 24th June 1916 (see p. 307) ; Fagiri Hill, 7th August 1916 (see p. 338)

of the *F.K.* and were candidates for vacancies in the ranks, have at least pointed the way. Mechanical transport, of course, of which much use was made, affords an alternative : but in a theatre of war in which some thousands of miles of road had to be made to enable wheeled transport to move, and only the lightest of vehicles proved suitable, the carrier alone made military operations possible.[1]

V

The year 1916 saw the transition from a shrewdly-planned and boldly initiated offensive, of which great things had been hoped, to a war of attrition. The situation at the end of September of Lieut.-General Smuts's forces has been summarized in Chapter XXIII, and that of Brig.-General Northey's smaller, separate but collaborating forces in Chapter XXVIII. Coupled with these summaries, the foregoing very general observations may well bring this volume to an end.

It was not until 1917 and 1918 that that great force, the King's African Rifles, was to come fully into its own in concluding the campaign. But of the four years, 1916 was that in which conditions came nearest to those of more normal warfare ; a year in which troops of every denomination—Regulars, New Army, men of the Union, of the British Protectorates and dependencies, of the Indian Army, alike—gave lavishly and of their best in the common cause.

In one other respect 1916 stands out as a landmark. In that year, under their famous leader, the South Africans in East Africa, as on the Western Front, established imperishably in history tho new status of the Union of South Africa as yet one more military nation among the unshakeable brotherhood of the British Commonwealth of Nations.

No words of any later historian can improve upon that leader's own despatch : " . . . in view of the foregoing " statement of the main facts eulogy seems unnecessary " and misplaced. The plain tale of their achievements " bears the most convincing testimony to the spirit, deter- " mination, and prodigious efforts of all ranks. Their work " has been done under tropical conditions which not only " produce bodily weariness and unfitness, but which create " mental languor and depression and finally appal the " stoutest hearts. To march day by day, and week by week,

---

[1] See also p. 140.

" through the African jungle or high grass, in which vision
" is limited to a few yards, in which danger always lurks
" near but seldom becomes visible, even when experienced,
" supplies a test to human nature often in the long run
" beyond the limits of human endurance.

" And what is true of the fighting troops applies in one
" degree or another to all the subsidiary and administrative
" services. The efforts of all have been beyond praise,
" the strain on all has been overwhelming. May the end soon
" crown their labours."

NOTE
EFFECTS OF CLIMATE ON THE TROOPS

The effects of the East African climate on various types of
troops may be judged from the following notes and figures.

(i) *British units.*—The war establishment of the only British
Regular unit engaged in the campaign—the 2/Loyal North
Lancashire Regt., sent from India to Tanga in November 1914,
had been fixed at 832, all ranks, with a view to only seasoned
men being taken. On the 8th March 1915, out of a total strength
of 901, 150 men were in hospital ; by the 10th June the unit
could muster less than 350 ; nine days later the available strength
was 12 officers, 253 o.r. Battle casualties up to the end of 1915
had amounted only to 150, which had been replaced by drafts ;
yet on 31st October the war diary records a total to date of 836
admissions to hospital, only 278 remaining who had so far
escaped becoming hospital cases. At Salaita, on 12th February
1916, the available strength had been brought up to 25 officers,
552 o.r. ; a month later, drafts having been received meanwhile,
the figure was 495 o.r., another 236 being unfit ; and by the
beginning of April it had been decided to send the battalion to
South Africa to recuperate. Having returned in June, strength,
531 all ranks, the unit had dwindled by December, although at no
time seriously engaged, to 345. It was then withdrawn to Egypt.

The 25/Royal Fusiliers, of the " New Army ", landed in
May 1915 1,600 strong. Although sent to a relatively healthy
area, its field strength in March 1916, at the beginning of the
first important operations in which it took part, was about 450.
Three months' operations, during which battle casualties were
about 50, brought the strength down to less than 200 by the
7th July. The remnant remained in the field, but in the following
year (1917), after recuperating in South Africa for some four
months, the unit after its return to East Africa shrank in the
ensuing half year from 450 to 206, these being then reported as
" much debilitated ", and was eventually withdrawn from the
country.

The 2/Rhodesia Regt., which on landing in March 1915 was up
to its establishment of 500, had a total of 111 in hospital three
months later. For the offensive of March 1916 its strength was
16 Officers, 525 o.r. Three weeks' operations, with battle casualties about 60, reduced the total to 333. Brought up to 495 in
May, the unit was reduced to 300 by the end of that month ; in
October the effective strength was 125, of whom only 53 were
doing duty ; and by 21st December only 67 remained, of whom
37 were stated to be unfit. During the period March 1915 to
January 1917 a total of 1,038 of all ranks served with the unit.
Recorded casualties were : killed 36, wounded 84, died of
wounds or disease 32, admissions to hospital 2,272 ; total cases
of sickness 10,626 (including 3,127 malaria, 921 dysentery).

In the South African units the effects of climate, combined
with the hardships of the campaign, were felt even more acutely.
By May 1916 most of the units which had landed three months
earlier had lost half their numbers, and by the end of the year
they were no more than cadres. For example, the 9/S.A.I. landed
on 14th February 1,135 strong. Their subsequent numbers were :
20th March, 804 ; 1st May, 528 ; 25th October, 116. As will be
seen in the text, all the South African units had, after a year of
East Africa, to be sent back to the Union to recuperate.

These figures show that even white men accustomed to life
in the healthier parts of Africa were as readily overpowered by
the East African climate as were those coming both from Great
Britain and from the tropics of India. In the words of a report
by the Director of Medical Services of the East African force,
" The European infantry soldier cannot cope with this climate
" under present active service conditions. The strain of marching
" with heavy equipment, constant exposure to sun and wet,
" general hardship of active service, quickly enfeeble him and
" render him liable to rapid recurrent attacks of malaria, intestinal
" disorders and other diseases incidental to this climate ".[1]

To this may be added that, as the experience of the campaign
showed, the younger men tended to give out more quickly
than the more mature, say of 30 and over.

(ii) *Indian troops.*—The sick rate in the Indian units varied
considerably according to the class composition of units, certain
races with strong caste restrictions as to food, notably the Rajputs,
suffering considerably more than others. All Indian troops,
however, had an average on the sick list of not less than 10 per
cent., and more usually 20 per cent. The percentage increased
during the operations of 1916, by the end of which the Indian
units, like the white troops, were reduced to mere cadres. Things
were no better in 1917. For example, the 129th Baluchis,
although reinforced by drafts, were in March 1917 but 400 strong,

---

[1] Report by D.M.S., 10th August. 1917.

of whom 36 per cent were reported unfit ; by May the strength had fallen to 50 ; built up to 500, the strength again dwindled by November to 250, the loss including 100 battle casualties, and many of those in the ranks being in fact anything but fit.

A special medical commission sent from India in December reported that " generally speaking . . . the climate and other " conditions . . . are most trying to Indian troops on active " service. Their constitutions suffer to such a very serious " degree that this area may be regarded as unsuitable for their " employment, except for short periods, and then only with " considerable precautions for the preservation of health."

The main factors in " the abnormal wastage among Indian " troops in East Africa " were given as : (1) Malaria ; (2) the jigger (" which caused an amount of inefficiency and wastage that " is hardly credible ") ; (3) fevers ; (4) dysentery ; (5) sun fever ; (6) shortage of the special foods required. It was also stated that the transport difficulties of the campaign had necessitated men marching heavy-laden and that this had proved too much for the Indian troops under the African sun.

The Indian troops were all withdrawn at the end of 1917.

(iii) *African troops.*—Except for the fact that personnel recruited in the highlands of the interior suffered considerably in the unhealthy coastal districts, the African troops on the whole, including the contingents from West Africa, had no undue incidence of sickness. Their European officers, moreover, had not only become acclimatized, but " knew the ropes " and in general had the benefit of the amenities and safeguards to health which experience has shown to be necessities for the white man in tropical Africa.

(iv) *Carriers.*—In matters of climate and health the carrier stood naturally on the same footing as the African troops. It has, however, to be remembered that carriers when removed far from their own districts tend to become low-spirited and discontented, a condition predisposing to sickness in any tropical climate, as was found to be the case notably in Crewe's march on Tabora (see Chap. XXVI).

(v) *Requirements of Europeans.*—The point already noted above in connection with the officers of the K.A.R. is of universal application. Conveyance of the European's requirements in the way of equipment and food, however, involves provision of a considerable number of carriers per white man ; a matter to which the Germans, knowing the country, gave considerable attention. The British forces, on the other hand, were never in a position to find enough carriers to provide fully for such needs, and all British personnel suffered accordingly.[1]

---

[1] See Lettow, " My Reminiscences," pp. 113, 117, 176.

TREATIES DEFINING THE BOUNDARIES OF THE BRITISH AND GERMAN PROTECTORATES IN EAST AFRICA.

A.

EXTRACT FROM "AGREEMENT BETWEEN THE BRITISH AND **End Papers** GERMAN GOVERNMENTS, 29TH OCTOBER—1ST NOVEMBER, 1886", AND "ADHESION OF THE SULTAN OF ZANZIBAR, DECEMBER 4, 1886".

Para. 3. Respective Spheres of Influence to be Defined.

Both Powers agree to establish a delimitation of their respective spheres of influence on this portion of the East African Continent of the same character as that to which they have agreed as regards the territories on the Gulf of Guinea.

Territory referred to in Arrangement

The territory to which this arrangement applies is bounded on the south by the Rovuma river, and on the north by a line which, starting from the mouth of the Tana river, follows the course of that river or its affluents to the point of intersection of the Equator and the 38th degree of east longitude, thence strikes direct to the point of inter-section of the 1st degree of north latitude with the 37th degree of east longitude, where the line terminates.

Line of Demarcation.

The line of demarcation starts from the mouth of the River Wanga or Umbe, runs direct to Lake Jipé, passes thence along the eastern side of the lake and crosses the Lumi river.

Taveita and Chagga (Kilimanjaro District).

After which it passes midway between the territories of Taveita and Chagga, skirts the northern base of the Kilimanjaro range, and thence is drawn direct to the point on the eastern side of Lake Victoria Nyanza which is intersected by the 1st degree of south latitude.

B.

Art. I. In East Africa the sphere in which the exercise of influence is reserved to Germany is bounded—

East Africa. German Sphere of Influence

1. To the north by a line which, commencing on the coast at the north bank of the mouth of the River Umba [or Wanga], runs direct to Lake Jipé ; passes thence along the eastern side and round the northern side of the lake, and crosses the River Lumé ; after which it passes midway between the territories of Taveita and Chagga, skirts the northern base of the Kilimanjaro range, and thence is drawn direct to the point on the eastern side of Lake Victoria Nyanza which is intersected by the 1st parallel of south latitude ; thence, crossing the lake on that parallel to the frontier of the Congo Free State, where it terminates.

Mount Mfumbiro

It is, however, understood that, on the west side of the lake, the sphere does not comprise Mount Mfumbiro ; if that mountain shall prove to lie to the south of the selected parallel, the line shall be deflected so as to exclude it, but shall, nevertheless, return so as to terminate at the above-named point.

German Sphere. To the South. Rovuma river to Lake Nyassa and Tanganyika (Stevenson's Road)

2. To the south by a line, which starting on coast at the northern limit of the Province of Mozambique, follows the course of the River Rovuma to the point of confluence of the Msinje ; thence it runs westward along the parallel of that point till it reaches Lake Nyassa ; thence striking northward, it follows the eastern, northern, and western shores of the lake to the northern bank of the mouth of the River Songwe ; it ascends that river to the point of intersection by the 33rd degree of east longitude ; thence it follows the river to the point where it approaches most nearly the boundary of the geographical Congo Basin defined in the 1st Article of the Act of Berlin, as marked in the map attached to the 9th Protocol of the Conference.

From that point it strikes direct to the above-named boundary; and follows it to the point of its intersection by the 32nd degree of east longitude ; from which point it strikes direct to the point of confluence of the northern and southern branches of the River Kilambo, and thence follows that river till it enters Lake Tanganyika.

Map. Nyassa-Tanganyika Plateau

The course of the above boundary is traced in general accordance with a map of the Nyassa-Tanganyika Plateau, officially prepared for the British Government in 1889.

APPENDIX II.

THE NEUTRALITY CLAUSES OF THE BERLIN ACT, 1885

The Berlin Act of 1885, as has been said, made provision for **End Papers** the possibility that the East African territories of the signatory Powers[1] might be kept neutral in the event of war.

It is important that the exact terms of the agreement between the Powers on this subject should be kept in mind.

The following extracts contain the whole of the relevant portions of the Berlin Act in this connection :—

CHAPTER I. DECLARATION RELATIVE TO FREEDOM OF TRADE IN THE BASIN OF THE CONGO, ITS MOUTHS AND CIRCUMJACENT REGIONS, WITH OTHER PROVISIONS CONNECTED THEREWITH.

Freedom of Trade to all Nations

Art. I. The trade of all nations shall enjoy complete freedom :

Basin of the Congo Defined

1. In all the regions forming the basin of the Congo and its outlets. This basin is bounded by the watersheds (or mountain ridges) of the adjacent basins, namely, in particular, those of the Niari, the Ogowé, the Schari, and the Nile, on the north ; by the eastern watershed line of the affluents of Lake Tanganyika on the east ; and by the watersheds of the basins of the Zambeci and the Logé on the south It therefore comprises all the regions watered by the Congo and its affluents, including Lake Tanganyika, with its eastern tributaries.

Maritime Zone Defined

2. In the maritime zone extending along the Atlantic Ocean from the parallel situated in 2° 30′ of south latitude to the mouth of the Logé.

Northern Boundary

The northern boundary will follow the parallel situated in 2° 30′ from the coast to the point where it meets the geographical basin of the Congo, avoiding the basin of the Ogowé, to which the provisions of the present Act do not apply.

---

[1] See p. 4 and Appendix I.

Southern Boundary

The southern boundary will follow the course of the Logé to its source, and thence pass eastwards till it joins the geographical basin of the Congo.

Eastern Boundary

3. In the zone stretching eastwards from the Congo Basin, as above defined, to the Indian Ocean from the 5° of north latitude to the mouth of the Zambesi in the south, from which point the line of demarcation will ascend the Zambesi to 5 miles above its confluence with the Shiré, and then follow the watershed between the affluents of Lake Nyassa and those of the Zambesi, till at last it reaches the watershed between the waters of the Zambesi and the Congo.

Free Trade Principles applied to Signatory Powers, and to such Independent States as may approve the same.

It is expressly recognized that in extending the principle of free trade to this eastern zone, the Conference Powers only undertake engagements for themselves, and that in the territories belonging to an independent Sovereign State this principle shall only be applicable in so far as it is approved by such State. But the Powers agree to use their good offices with the Governments established on the African shore of the Indian Ocean for the purpose of obtaining such approval, and in any case of securing the most favourable conditions to the transit (traffic) of all nations.

CHAPTER III. DECLARATION RELATIVE TO THE NEUTRALITY OF THE TERRITORIES COMPRISED IN THE CONVENTIONAL BASIN OF THE CONGO.

Neutrality of Territories and Territorial Waters

Art. X. In order to give a new guarantee of security to trade and industry, and to encourage, by the maintenance of peace, the development of civilization in the countries mentioned in Article I, and placed under the free trade system, the High Signatory Parties to the present Act, and those who shall hereafter adopt it, bind themselves to respect the neutrality of territories, or portions of territories, belonging to the said countries, comprising therein the territorial waters, so long as the Powers which exercise or shall exercise the rights of sovereignty or Protectorate over those territories, using their option of proclaiming themselves neutral, shall fulfil the duties which neutrality requires.

Hostilities not to extend to Neutralized States

Art. XI. In case a Power exercising rights of sovereignty or Protectorate in the countries mentioned in Article I, and placed under the free trade system, shall be involved in a war then the

High Signatory Parties to the present Act, and those who shall hereafter adopt it, bind themselves to lend their good offices in order that the territories belonging to this Power and comprised in the Conventional free trade zone shall, by the common consent of this Power and the other belligerent or belligerents, be placed during the war under the rule of neutrality, and considered as belonging to a non-belligerent State, the belligerents thenceforth abstaining from extending hostilities to the territories thus neutralized, and from using them as a base for warlike operations.

Serious Disagreements between Signatory Powers to be referred to Mediation

Art. XII.   In case of a serious disagreement originating on the subject of, or in the limits of, the territories mentioned in Article I, and placed under the free trade system, shall arise between any Signatory Powers of the present Act, or the Powers which may become party to it, these Powers bind themselves, before appealing to arms, to have recourse to the mediation of one or more of the friendly Powers.

Or to Arbitration

In a similar case the same Powers reserve to themselves the option of having recourse to arbitration.

As will be seen, the provisions of the Berlin Act made it possible for the Powers concerned to elect beforehand that their respective territories in Central Africa should enjoy neutrality. The Powers had, in the words of Article X, an "option of proclaiming themselves neutral". They were, however, under no obligation to exercise this option, and in actual fact neither Great Britain nor Germany ever did exercise it.[1] The subject was indeed considered in 1898 and again in 1911 by a British Government committee, but in each case the Committee recorded its view that in the event of war it would not be to the advantage of Great Britain that the East African territories should be made neutral.

---

[1] The only state which exercised its power to declare itself neutral was the Independent State of the Congo, which on 1st August 1885 " in " conformity with Article X of the General Act of the Berlin Conference " declared itself perpetually neutral.   This declaration was re-affirmed on 28th December 1894 and remained in force, after the Congo State became a Belgian colony in 1908, up to the outbreak of war in 1914, the neutrality of the Congo being regarded by Belgium as being in many respects a parallel to that of Belgium herself which dated back to 1839.

The Belgian aspect of the matter is dealt with at some length in B.O.A., and in the diplomatic correspondence published as a Belgian Grey Book (Van Oest, 1919).

Thus at the outbreak of war there was no obligation on either the British or the German Government to treat the East African protectorates as neutral, nor was it in the view of the British Government desirable so to treat them.

Under Article XI of the Berlin Act the signatory Powers had, it is true, undertaken in the event of war to lend their good offices with a view to neutrality of these territories by common consent of the belligerents. No steps to this end, however, were taken by any of the signatories on the outbreak of war, and it was not until the 22nd August 1914 that the German Government made proposals, submitted through the Government of the United States, for the neutralization of the African territories. By that time acts of war had been committed on both sides, and the common consent of the belligerents—an essential pre-requisite under the terms of the Berlin Act—was beyond hope of attainment. Nothing came, therefore, not could anything have come, of the German suggestion. Incidentally, the United States, not having ratified their original adherence to the Berlin Act, were in this matter acting solely as an intermediary for transmission of the German proposals ; a position carefully made clear by the United States Government in transmitting them.

It may be further argued that under Article XII of the Berlin Act, a " serious disagreement " having originated " in " the limits of the territories mentioned ", it was incumbent on the disputing Powers, " before appealing to arms, to have recourse " to the mediation of one or more of the friendly Powers ". Against this it may with at least equal force be argued that the " disagreement " in East Africa originated not in Africa but in Europe, so that Article XII was not applicable. Apart, however, from any question of interpretation, the fact remains that in 1914, when at the outset the long-standing neutrality of Belgium itself had been violated by Germany, neither of the disputants concerned, having appealed to arms nearer home, took any action to obtain mediation with regard to East Africa ; nor is it conceivable, in the circumstances, that they should have done so.

There can be little doubt that when War broke out in Europe in 1914 no great amount of consideration was given by any of the signatory Powers, with the possible exception of Belgium, to the situation that would arise in East Africa in regard to the Berlin Act. The wording of the Act was clear. In some quarters there may have been an impression that the East African protectorates would remain neutral[1] and the German Governor, Dr. Schnee, has stated that he hoped this would be the case[2] ; but it is not to be imagined that any responsible authority

---

[1] Schnee, *Deutsch-Ostafrika im Weltkriege*, p. 26.
[2] Schnee, op. cit., p. 38.

acquainted with the terms of the Berlin Act could at any time, either then or now, be under any misapprehension as to the real position.[1]

In short, although the fact may for various reasons be regretted, the British and German protectorates in East Africa never were neutral territory, either juridically or by implication.

APPENDIX III. TANGA

A

INDIAN EXPEDITIONARY FORCE " B "

ORDER OF BATTLE

HEADQUARTERS STAFF

General Officer Commanding	Major-General A. E. Aitken.
A.D.Cs.	Captain D. H. Powell.
	Lieut. Bala Saheb Daphle.
	Lieut. Aga Murtaza Khan.
G.S.O. 1	Bt. Lieut.-Colonel S. H. Sheppard, R.E.
G.S.O. 2 (Intelligence)	Lieut.-Colonel J. D. Mackay.
G.S.O. 3 (Intelligence)	Captain R. Meinertzhagen.
D.A.A. & Q.M.G.	Major C. F. Dobbs.
ᴵ ᴿ ᴴ	Lieut.-Colonel C. B. Collins, R.D.
Assistant Director, Signals	Captain H. C. Howtroy, R.F
Assistant Director, Medical Service	Colonel R. Robertson, I.M.S.
Assistant Director, Supply and Transport	Lieut.-Colonel H. H. Roddy.
Ordnance	Captain G. M. Routh.
Director of Railways	Sir W. Johns.

---

[1] The German military commander, Colonel von Lettow-Vorbeck, was under no such misapprehension. " We were ", he writes, " not " obliged to restrict our operations out of regard for any agreement." Differing, moreover, from the then accepted British opinion, he adds : " From a military point of view it was a disadvantage, not for us, but for " England, if war occurred in East Africa."
Lettow, " My Reminiscences," p. 19.

HEADQUARTERS STAFF—*continued.*

Deputy Director of Railways	Mr. J. Sutherland.
Deputy Assistant Director of Railways	Major G. Lubbock, R.E.
Inspector-General of Communications	Brig.-General W. A. Malleson.
G.S.O. 2.	Major P. C. R. Barclay.
Staff Captain	Captain A. H. W. Elias.
Embarkation Commandant	Lieut.-Colonel C. Bailey.
D.A.A.Q.M.G.	Major G. M. Orr.
Base Supply and Transport	Captain G. E. M. Hogg.

Commandant Base Depot	Lieut.-Colonel R. G. Macpherson.

27th (BANGALORE) BRIGADE :—

G.O.C.	Brig.-General R. Wapshare.
Bde. Major	Major H. De C. O'Grady.
Staff Captain	Captain W. G. Charles.

2 Loyal North Lancashire.
63rd Palamcottah Light Infantry.
98th Infantry.
101st Grenadiers.

IMPERIAL SERVICE BRIGADE :—

G.O.C.	Brig.-General M. J. Tighe.
Bde. Major	Major F. S. Keen.
Staff Captain	Captain R. H. Waller.

13th Rajputs.
2/Kashmir Rifles.
½ 3/Kashmir Rifles.
½ 3/Gwalior Rifles.
61st K.G.O. Pioneers.

B

Unit	British Off.	British O.R.	Indian Off.	Indian O.R.	Total Ration Strength.
Force H.Q.	18	12	1	15	46
27th (Bangalore) Infantry Bde. :					
Brigade H.Q.	3	7	—	6	16
2/Loyal North Lancashire Regt.	28	804	—	—	832
63rd Palamcottah Light Infantry	13	—	17	732a	762a
98th Infantry	13	—	17	732a	762a
101st Grenadiers	13	—	17	732a	762a
Brigade Signal Section	1	12	—	15	28
Imperial Service Infantry Bde. :					
Brigade H.Q.	4	1	—	—	—
13th Rajputs	13	—	17	736	766
2nd Kashmir Rifles	2	—	22	708	732
½ Bn. 3rd Kashmir Rifles	1	—	13	363	377
½ Bn. 3rd Gwalior Infantry	1	—	16	362	379
Brigade Signal Section	1	12	—	15	28
Attached Troops :					
61st K.G.O. Pioneers	13	—	17	736	766
28th Mountain Battery, R.A.	5	—	3	277	285
Gun detachment for Armoured Train (North-Western Railway Volunteers)	3	37	—	—	40
One Coy. Faridkot Sappers and Miners ..	1	—	5	159	165
2 (Railway) Coys., Sappers and Miners Railway Coolie Corps	16	15	33	712	776
Bridging Train..	1	—	1	22	24
Motor Cyclist Signal Section	—	10	—	—	10
Telegraph Section	1	18	—	18	37
Printing Section ⎱ Litho. Section ⎰	—	4	—	8	12
Field Post Office	1	1	1	10	13
½ British Field Ambulance	2	11	—	—	13
1½ Indian Field Ambulance	7	2	—	30	39
Supply and Transport personnel (att'd to various units)	—	—	—	22	22
Lines of Communication :					
L. of C. H.Q.	3	2	—	1	6
H.Q. of Section	2	1	—	1	4
2 Sections Indian Clearing Hospital ..	2	1	—	10	13
1 British Stationary Hospital	1	5	—	—	6
No. 2 Adv. Depot, Medical Stores	—	1	—	—	1
Field Post Office	—	—	1	3	4
Base Depot and Record Office	3	4	—	6	13
Base Ordnance Depot	1	7	—	3	11
Engineer Field Park	1	3	—	14	18
½ Section No. 3 British General Hospital (50 beds)	2	5	—	—	7
3 Sections No. 6 Indian General Hospital (300 beds)	6	1	—	32	39
X-Ray Section..	1	1	—	—	2
No. 38 Sanitary Section	1	10	—	14	35
Field Disbursing Officer	1	2	3	5	11
Base S. & T. Depot	8	14	—	47	69
Supply Coolie Corps	1	1	3	5	10
Base Post Office	—	2	—	6	8
	201	1,019	186	6,566	7,972

(a) *Note.*—Excluding 4 detached to Force H.Q. or Bde. H.Q.
Remarks.—(1) The figures given are approximate only ; contemporary tables vary slightly for certain units.

B

Followers (Indian)		Animals		Tranpsort Vehicles	Guns	Machine Guns	Troopship
Public	Private	Riding Horses	Pack Mules.				
6	26	—	—	—	—	—	Karmala.
1	6	—	—	—	—	—	Karmala.
25	33	—	15	—	—	2	Karmala.
40	18	—	15	—	—	2	Assouan.
40	18	—	15	—	—	2	Nairung.
40	18	—	15	—	—	2	Laisang.
3	1	—	12	—	—	—	Karmala.
—	5	—	—	—	—	—	Karmala.
40	18	—	15	—	—	2	Pentakota.
44	6	—	3	—	—	—	Khosru.
24	7	—	3	—	—	—	⎫Barjora.
36	12	—	2	—	—	—	⎭
3	1	—	12	—	—	—	Karmala.
52	18	—	45	—	—	2	Jeddah.
23	8	—	164	—	6	—	Bharata.
2	3	—	—	—	1	2	⎫Homayun.
18	5	—	18	—	—	—	⎭
700	16	—	—	—	—	—	Muttra.
3	1	—	—	—	—	—	Abbasieh.
—	—	—	—	10	—	—	⎫
12	3	—	—	—	—	—	⎬Karmala.
4	2	—	—	—	—	—	⎭
14	2	—	—	—	—	—	Khosru.
29	5	—	—	—	—	—	⎫Abbasieh.
39	15	—	—	—	—	—	⎭
—	—	—	9	—	—	—	
1	3	—	—	—	—	—	⎫Karmala.
—	2	—	—	—	—	—	⎬
19	1	—	—	—	—	—	⎬Abbasieh.
15	3	—	—	—	—	—	⎭
5	1	—	—	—	—	—	
6	—	—	—	—	—	—	Khosru.
—	3	—	—	—	—	—	Abbasieh.
47	1	—	—	—	—	—	⎫Hoyamun.
17	2	—	—	—	—	—	⎭
22	3	—	—	—	—	—	⎫
55	12	—	—	—	—	—	⎬Abbasieh.
3	2	—	—	—	—	—	⎭
75	1	—	—	—	—	—	
—	2	—	—	—	—	—	Karmala.
182	85	—	—	—	—	—	Abbasieh.
508	3	—	—	—	—	—	Homayun.
9	2	—	—	—	—	—	Khosru.
2,164	386	—	343	—	7	14	

(2) The figures for larger units include medical personnel permanently
attached, but do not include Indian S. & T. personnel temporarily
attached

C

RACIAL COMPOSITION AND STRENGTH OF UNITS.

1. The racial composition of the undermentioned Indian battalions was as follows (single companies) :—

13th Rajputs : 8 Coys. Hindu Rajputs.
61st (K.G.O.) Pioneers : 4 Coys. Tamils.
                       2 ,, Madrasi Musalmans.
                       2 ,, Parayans and Christians.

63rd Palamcottah
    Light Infantry : 4 Coys. Madrasi Musalmans.
                       2 ,, Tamils.
                       2 ,, Parayans and Christians.

98th Infantry : 2 Coys. Hindu Rajputs.
                       3 ,, Hindustani Musalmans.
                       2 ,, Ahirs (E. Punjab.)

101st Grenadiers : 2 Coys. Dekhani Mahrattas.
                       2 ,, Konkani Mahrattas.
                       2 ,, Rajputana Musalmans.
                       2 ,, Punjabi Musalmans.

2. Actual numbers at Tanga cannot be ascertained exactly, but a rough probable estimate is given in the following table. These figures have been calculated by subdividing the total of Indian officers and men (see Appendix B.) in proportion to percentages ascertained from the " Annual Class Composition Return " of units of the Indian Army for 1st January, 1914

Approximate Strengths.

	Musalmans				Dogras	Gurkhas	Hindu Rajputs	Ahirs	Parayans	Tamils	Mahrattas	Brahmins	Others, various.	Total, Indian troops (all ranks), as in App. VI, B.
	Punjabi.	Hindustani.	Rajputana.	Madrasi.										
13th Rajputs	23	15	—	—	—	23	—	—	—	—	—	—	7	753
61st (K.G.O.) Pioneers	—	—	—	218	—	—	685	—	173	362	—	—	—	753
63rd P.I. Inf.	—	240	172	315	—	—	—	—	82	210	—	—	142	749
98th Infantry	202	—	—	—	—	—	255	172	—	—	—	—	82	749
101st Grenadiers	255	—	—	—	102	358	—	—	—	—	337	—	38	749
2/Kashmir Rifles	—	—	—	—	192	184	—	—	—	—	—	—	15	730
⅓/Kashmir Rif.	23	4	60	—	—	—	—	—	—	—	—	—	—	376
⅓/Gwalior Rif.	—	—	—	—	—	—	164	11	—	—	26	60	30	378
Total..	503	259	232	533	294	565	1104	183	255	572	363	60	314	5,237

PREPARATORY ORDERS FOR DISEMBARKATION

1. The Force will probably disembark at TANGA.

2. Covering party, Naval Brigade and Imperial Service Brigade, all under Brig.-General M. J. Tighe, C.B., C.I.E., D.S.O.

3. Military Landing Officer, Lieut.-Colonel C. Bailey, 1st Skinners' Horse. Staff Officer, Major G. M. Orr, 11th Lancers.
61st Pioneers will provide Beach parties, and guards and fatigues on or near Beach.

4. Each unit will leave a guard of 2 N.C.O.s and 6 men with the Military Landing Officer on Beach to guard regimental Kits and Stores when disembarked.

5. Provost police to land with their units and report to Captain P. L. Coleridge, 63rd Light Infantry (Asst. Provost Marshal) at the Military Landing Officer's station on Beach.

6. Unexpended portion of day's ration, and one day's cooked or tinned ration in addition, to be taken ashore on the person by all troops and followers, including both Coolie Corps. Also one day's uncooked ration, in regimental charge, by 27th Brigade, Imperial Service Brigade and No. 28 Mountain Battery. 4 days' rations, in addition, are being carried by Imperial Service Brigade ashore, and stacked there. 3 days' grain and 2 days' fodder for all animals to be taken ashore by units. Also filled water chagals, as water may be scarce ; and mosquito nets.

7. 200 rounds per man on person, 50 rounds as regimental reserve. Blanket stretchers to be carried.

8. Pioneers to wear full field service kit.

9. One Regimental Military Transport Officer to be told off, for each transport from units, or details on board.

Fatigues. Each troop-ship—One double company.

HOMAYUN 1 Section Faridkot Sappers.
MUTTRA 1 Section Railway Company (or 80 coolies).
ABASSIEH } Fatigue parties will be sent later.
BHARATA }
RHEINFELS Stevedores.

10. Detailed orders, and order of disembarkation will be issued later.

30/X/14.   (*Signed*) S. H. Sheppard, Lieut.-Colonel.
                        General Staff, I.E.F. " B ".

APPENDIX III

E

(i)

OPERATION ORDER No. 1

by

Major-General A. E. AITKEN

Commanding Expeditionary Force " B "

Mombasa,
November 1st, 1914

1. From reliable information received it appears improbable that the enemy will actively oppose our landing.

Opposition may, however, be met with anywhere inland, and a considerable force of the enemy is reported to be in the vicinity of Vanga.

2. It is the intention of the G.O.C. to land at Tanga, and establish a base there, preparatory to an advance up the Tanga-Moshi Railway.

3. The landing will commence on November 2nd. The time of commencement of disembarkation depends upon whether minesweeping operations are necessary or not.

4. Brigadier-General M. J. Tighe, C.B., C.I.E., D.S.O., (Imperial Service Brigade), will form the covering party and will take up a position covering the town and port of Tanga. Post, telegraph and telephone offices and the railway station, to be occupied as soon as possible.

The telegraph lines to Bagamoyo and Vanga (if any) to be cut, and the roads to these places watched. Exits from the town to be blocked, to prevent the despatch of native information. Captain Carr-Harris, R.E., to accompany the Imperial Service Brigade, to inspect culverts, etc., for possible mines.

5. The order of landing is given in the attached table, Appendix " B " ; and distribution of duties at Base immediately on landing in Appendix " A ".

6. Unexpended portion of day's ration for day of landing, and one day's cooked or tinned ration in addition, to be taken ashore on the person by all troops and followers, including both Coolie Corps. Also one day's uncooked ration, in regimental charge, by 27th Brigade, Imperial Service Brigade and No. 28 Mountain Battery.

4 days' rations, in addition, to be carried ashore by Imperial Service Brigade and stacked there. 3 days' grain and 2 days' fodder for all animals to be taken ashore by units. Also filled water chagals, as water is scarce ; and mosquito nets.

7. 200 rounds per man on person, 50 rounds as regimental reserve. Blanket stretchers to be carried. Pioneers to wear full field service kit. Kits and tents to be taken ashore by units, and stacked on beach until transport is available to remove them.

Lighters must be loaded, and cleared, with the utmost despatch. Men must be prepared to wade ashore, through two or three feet of water, if necessary.

8. One regimental Military Transport Officer to be told off for each transport, from units or details on board ; he will remain on board until the transport is completely unloaded, unless otherwise ordered. Fatigues as under, will be under his orders, to work holds, etc., as may be required :—

Each troopship   One Double-Company.

Homayun   1 Section Faridkot Sappers.

Abbassieh   Fatigue parties will be sent for complete unloading, probably on sixth day.

Rheinfels   Military Transport Officer, Stevedores, and men of Railway companies as may be arranged by Director of Railways.

9. The Native town and all Bazaars in Tanga are placed out of bounds.

10. Normal hours of unloading transports—6 a.m. to 6 p.m. but every endeavour will be made to land the troops, etc., assigned to First day, on the 2nd November, even if the normal hours are exceeded.

11. Four signallers with visual equipment, to remain on each ship till unloaded. Visual stations will be established on shore by A.D.A.S., for communication with transports.

12. Reports to S.S. *Karmala* till further orders.

(*Signed*] S H Sheppard, Lieut.-Colonel,
General Staff, I.E.F. " B ".

(with attached)

APPENDIX " A "

Immediate arrangements on shore at Tanga, after the landing has been effected by the Covering Force.

APPENDIX " B "
Order of Landing.

E

(ii)

APPENDIX " A " TO OPERATION ORDER No. 1

Immediate arrangements on shore at TANGA, after a landing has been effected by the Covering Force.

---

1. The I.G.C. will be responsible for local protection, and will be in general charge of all arrangements affecting Line of Communication and Base units.

He will have under his orders :—
(a) The Military Landing Officer,
   Lieut.-Colonel C. Bailey, 1st Skinner's Horse.
   Staff Officer—Major G. M. Orr, 11th Lancers.

Their duty will be to work the beaches, in conjunction with the Royal Navy.

(b) The Base Depot Commandant and his Staff :—
   Lieut.-Colonel R. G. Macpherson, 37th Dogras.
   Captain J. S. Marshall, 35th Sikhs.
   Captain J. M. C. Wemyss, Royal Scots.

Their duty will be :—
(i) Detailed distribution of camping areas or buildings for Line of Communications and Base units.

N.B.—The D.A.A. and Q.M.G. will, in co-operation with Base Depot Commandant, tell off camping areas, etc., for other units of the Force, and for porters ; and both must work in with I.G.C.'s, G.S.O. II, and Administrative officers concerned (A.D.M.S., A.D.S and T., C.R.E., and D.A.D.M.S. Sanitary).

(ii) Internal police arrangements, with I.G.C.'s, G.S.O. II.

(iii) Arrangements for collection of all undesirable characters, preparatory to deportation.

(c) The Sanitary Section (see (b) (i) above). One Double Company of 61st Pioneers will be placed at the disposal of the I.G.C. for work connected with (b) above.

2. The C.R.E. and Field Engineers will, in co-operation with the I.G.C., arrange :—
   Water Supply
   Landing Stages
   Letters for wharves
   Flares and lamps for beaches.
   Blocks and tackle for derricks, etc.

The Faridkot Sappers (less 1 Section) will be placed at the disposal of the C.R.E.

3. The Supply Coolie Corps, and Railway Coolie Corps, will be placed at the disposal of the A.D.S. & T.

Notes Regarding Areas and Buildings

Buildings.

(i) Hospitals, British and Indian, to have first choice of houses.

(ii) Base Commandant's Office (permanent).

(iii) I.G.C.'s Office.

(iv) A good house, or set of houses, for valuable stores such as Treasure. Ordnance Field Park.

(v) S. & T. Offices and Storehouses.

(vi) Engineer Field Park ; most of stores are not perishable, but are heavy—so Park should not be too far from shore.

(vii) Field Disbursing Officer's Office.

(viii) Post and Telegraph Offices.

(ix) Railway Offices and Storehouses.

Areas.

Troops, British or Indian, should not be billeted in native quarters, because of the Jigger flea.

So note carefully the native and European divisions of the place.

E (iii)

APPENDIX "B" TO OPERATION NO. 1.

Order of Landing.

Units.	Ship.	Probable Lighters, etc.	Day.	Remarks.
1. 13th Rajputs (less 2 Double Coys.) and Imperial Service Bgde. Scouts.	Pentakota	Two lighters	First	Order of mooring :— 1. Pentakota. 2. Jeddah. 3. Homayun. 4. Khosru. 5. Barjora. 6. Karmala. 7. Abbassieh. 8. Assouan. 9. Nairung. 10. Laisang. 11. Muttra. 12. Bharata. 13. Rheinfels (to take up No. 2 billet when Jeddah is cleared).
2. (a) Beach party, 1 Double Company 61st Pioneers. (b) For use of I.G.C.—61st Pioneers (less 3 Double Coys.).	Jeddah	Two lighters	do.	(a) 5 officers to be sent as Assistant Beach masters. The 1 Double Company Beach party includes sufficient men for reliefs. (b) To rendezvous clear of beach, and await orders of I.G.C. Permanent guard of 1 and 6, for G.O.C. Forces, to be told off from this Double Coy. *N.B.*—Naval Beach Master— Lieut. Petrie, R.N. 4 seamen and 1 signalman to each Beach party. 2 seamen in each lighter.
3. Military Landing Officer and staff, and his signal units, and A.D.A.S. G.O.C. Imp. Service Bgde. and Brigade Signal Section and mules. I.G.C. and Staff, C.R.E., A.D.M.S., D.A.A. & Q.M.S. and A.D.S. & T. Rockets and flares and lamps for beach	Karmala	S.S. Barjun and 2 boats from Karmala.	do.	S.S. Barjun to pick up O.C. Base Depot and Staff, Major Tilbury-Brown and Captain Carr-Harris from Abassieh, with their kits.

No.	Unit	Ship	Craft		Remarks
4.	1 Double Company, 13th Rajputs	Penrakota	One lighter	do.	Porters from S.S. Cupid, and from lighters, will commence to arrive at beach about this time. Probable numbers, 3,000.
5.	2nd Kashmir Rifles and Base Supply Depot.	Khosru	Four lighters in two trips.	do.	Must be ready to carry loads for Imperial Service Brigade shortly after they land.
6.	Punjab Coolie Corps	Homayun	Two lighters	do.	
7.	Composite Battalion, Imperial Service Brigade.	Barjora	Four lighters in two trips.	do.	
8.	Sanitary Section Base Supply Depot Base Depot Establishment Field Engineers	Anassieh	S.S. Barjun	do.	Pontoon personnel to go to Rheinfels on S.S. Barjun and, if sea is calm enough, get pontoons and superstructure afloat, ready to be towed ashore, when tug is available.
9.	Faridkot Sappers Landing Stage Pumps Letters for wharves and beaches	Homayun	One lighter	do.	
10.	Force Headquarters, Staff baggage, messes, etc. not taken in No. 3 above. Motor Cyclist Section Telegraph Section (no mules)	Karmala	S.S. Barjun and 2 boats from Karmala.	do.	

N.B.—(*a*) Each unit to leave a guard of 2 and 6, with Lieut.-Colonel Bailey, Military Landing Officer, to look after regimental kits and stores.

(*b*) All empty ammunition boxes to be brought ashore by units, and collected on the beach under orders of the Military Landing Officer.

(*c*) It is impossible to give exact hours for lighters, etc. Military Transport Officers on board transports must keep a sharp look-out for returning lighters, so as to avoid any waste of time in loading and towing.

Units.	Ship.	Probable Lighters, etc.	Day.	Remarks.
11. Loyal North Lancs., G.O.C. 27th Brigade and Signal Section. All mules on board.	Karmala	Four lighters	Second	The Provost Marshal, Captain Coleridge, 63rd Light Infantry, to collect his provost police ashore from these units and report to the Military Landing Officer.
12. 63rd Palamcottah Light Infantry ..	Assouan	do	do.	
13. 98th Infantry	Nairung	do.	do.	
14. 101st Grenadiers	Laisang	do.	do.	
15. 1 Double Coy. 61st Pioneers	Jeddah	S.S. Cupid	do.	To rendezvous clear of beach and await orders from G.O.C. Force.
16. Railway Coolie Corps	Muttra	Four lighters	do.	To be at disposal of A.D.S. & T. until further orders.
17. ½ British Field Ambulance	Abassieh	One lighter	do.	
½ Indian Field Ambulance	Bharata	Four lighters	do.	
18. No. 28 Mountain Battery				
19. No. 25 and 26 Railway Coys.	Muttra	Four lighters	do.	

Thereafter complete unloading of transports, in order of mooring. About 2 ships per diem.

N.B.—(a) Each unit to leave a guard of 2 and 6 with Lieut.-Colonel Bailey, Military Landing Officer, to look after regimental kits and stores.

(b) All empty ammunition boxes to be brought ashore by units, and collected on the beach under orders of the Military Landing Officer.

(c) It is impossible to give exact hours for lighters, etc. Military transport Officers on board transports must keep a sharp look-out for returning lighters, so as to avoid any waste of time in loading and towing.

E

(iv)

ADDENDUM TO OPERATION ORDER No. 1

All military transport afloat, i.e., hired transports, tugs, lighters, etc., are under the orders of Commander E. J. Headlam, Royal Indian Marine, Marine Transport Officer, I. E. F. East Africa.

During the disembarkation of troops or stores no orders are to be given to any steamers, tugs, launches, lighters, etc., except by the following:

On Shore.—The Senior Naval Officer, the Military Landing Officer and his Staff Officer, the Marine Transport Officer and his assistant, and the Naval Beach Master.

Afloat.—The Senior Naval Officer, the Marine Transport Officer, the Assistant Marine Transport Officer, or the Overseer of Transport labour and craft.

F

OPERATION ORDER No. 2

by

Major-General A. E. Aitken

Commanding Indian Expeditionary Force " B "

November 2nd 1914   H.T. *Karmala*

1. Owing to the necessity for sweeping for mines in Tanga Bay the convoy (or part of it) will anchor to-night 2-3 miles east of Tanga.

2. The covering party will now consist of the 13th Rajputs and 61st Pioneers, all under the command of Brigadier-General M. J. Tighe, C.B., C.I.E., D.S.O.

The town of Tanga is to be seized to-night.

3. 300 porters will be landed for the carriage of 1st Line equipment, telegraph stores, etc.

4. A visual station will be established on the shore, west of the anchored convoy, and a cable run to Tanga.

5. Reports to *Karmala*.

(*Signed*) S. H. *Sheppard*,
Lieut.-Colonel.
G.S.O. 1., I.E.F. " B."

(Issued at 5 p.m.)

G

OPERATION ORDER No. 3
by
Major-General Aitken
Commanding I.E.F. " B "

near Tanga
4.11.14.

1. The enemy is reported to be in considerable force west of the German hospital.

2. The G.O.C. intends to attack them, and occupy Tanga to-night.

3. The Imperial Service Brigade (less 3 Coys. Gwalior Infantry) under General Tighe, will advance on a front of about 600′, with their right on Tanga Bay.

The 27th Brigade, under General Wapshare, will continue the line to the left—his left flank battalion being echeloned to the left rear.

The right of the 27th Brigade will direct.

4. General Reserve, 61st Pioneers, under G.O.C. Force.

5. Three Companies Gwalior Infantry will be placed at the disposal of Colonel Malleson, to cover the Red House, Western landing beach, and Signal Tower.

6. Bayonets will be fixed, as the country to be operated in is thick.

7. The advance will commence at 12 noon, and will be covered, as far as possible, by the guns of H.M.S. *Fox*, and No. 28 Mountain Battery on S.S. *Bharata*.

8. Reports to Reserve.

9. Central Signal Station—Signal Tower.

(*Signed*) S. H. Sheppard, Lieut.-Colonel,
G.S.O. 1, I.E.F. " B ".

(Dictated to representatives
of units at 10.15 a.m.)

H
OPERATION ORDER No. 4
by
Major-General A. E. Aitken, Commanding I.E.F. " B ",
Sent as Field Message.

Ras Kasone
4.11.14.

1. The Force will re-embark to-day as follows :—
   (a) By 12 noon, the L.N. Lancs. and 1½ Bns. Kash. Inf.
       will have taken up and entrenched a position covering
       the RED HOUSE and embarkation beach, under
       Brig.-General TIGHE.
   (b) The first units to embark will be the 61st and 63rd,
       and 500 porters, in the KHALIFA* group.
   (c) Next, the 98th and 101st, and 500 porters, in the
       CUPID* group.
   (d) The 13th Rajputs, and all details, in the MVITA*
       group.
   All the above to be formed up, north of the RED HOUSE,
by 11 a.m., when routes to the beach will be pointed out to them.
   (e) The Gwalior Inf. and ½ Kashmir Rifles will form the
       BAJUNE* group—the former to be formed up, north
       of the RED HOUSE, at 12 noon.
   (f) The 2nd Kashmir Rifles and L.N. Lancs. will form the
       TANGA* and HELMUTH* groups.

2. The C.R.E. will at once take steps to have at least five
routes to the beach prepared by 10.30 a.m.   The 61st Pioneers
are placed at his disposal for the purpose.

3. Kits will not be taken.

4. Reports to the Cliff due East of the RED HOUSE.

(*Signed*) S. H. Sheppard, Lieut.-Colonel
G.S. " B ".

Verbally to representatives, between 7.0 and 8.30 a.m.
All details of defensive position, forming-up places, and ship
groups, explained personally to all.

* Name of Tug.

APPENDIX III

K

STANDING ORDERS

by

Major-General A. B. Aitken
Commanding Indian Expeditionary Force " A "

1. (a) Seniority roll of Field Officers is attached as Appendix " A ".
(b) Station calls is attached as Appendix " B."

Marches. 2. (a) Military police, camp colours, Sanitary Section and water guards will normally march in rear of the leading Battalion of the main body.
(b) Followers will march in formed bodies with the baggage of their respective units, and commanding officers of units will issue strict orders to their respective baggage guards to see that this order is enforced, and no straggling is allowed.
(c) Baggage guards must not straggle, they must march in groups of suitable size distributed along the line of baggage.

Camps. 3. (a) Attention is invited to Field Service Regulations, Part I, Sections 55–63, and Standing Order No. 13 " Medical."
(b) Working parties when proceeding outside camp will be fully armed, and proper precautions taken for their protection.
(c) All jungle should be cut down for 30 or 40 yards round a camp.

Duties. 4. (a) Duties will mount daily at 5 p.m. when in camp. If on the march, one hour after arrival of main body in camp.
(b) Permanent duties are as follows :—

Force Headquarters—1 N.C.O., 6 men	.. 61st Pioneers.
2 Orderlies per brigade	27th Brigade.
	I.S. Brigade.
1 Motor cyclist.	.. Signal Section.
Assistant Provost Marshal—Captain Coleridge,	63rd L. Infy.
Provost Establishment—1 N.C.O., 6 men	.. Loyal N. Lancs.
2 men ..	.. 63rd P.L.I.
2 men ..	.. 98th Infantry.
2 men ..	.. 101st Grenadiers.
Ambulance Guard—1 N.C.O., 3 men...	.. By Brigades. To be changed weekly.

Discipline. 5. (a) *Treatment of inhabitants.*—As the complete success of our operations for the pacification of the country will very largely depend on the attitude adopted by us to the native tribes, the G.O.C. Force desires to impress on all ranks the vital importance of kind and even generous treatment, especially as it is understood that the existing Administration has not been particularly noted for these qualities. It is most desirable to show the tribes that they have nothing to fear from us provided they behave themselves in accordance with any orders which may be issued from time to time.
(b) *Prisoners of war.*—These will invariably be kindly but firmly treated. They will be handed over as early as possible after their capture under Brigade arrangements, to the Assistant Provost Marshal, or the nearest quarter guard.
(c) No inhabitant will on any account be allowed to enter or leave the precincts of a camp without a pass signed by the Assistant Provost Marshal or by a staff officer. All persons found without a pass will be handed over to the Assistant Provost Marshal or nearest guard.
All ranks are particularly requested to see that this is enforced rigidly, so as to eliminate the danger of hostile native spies.

(*d*) All private followers will be registered and furnished with passes under brigade arrangements. Officers Commanding units in Force troops will apply to the Assistant Provost Marshal for passes. All officers commanding units will forward a roll of registered followers to the Assistant Provost Marshal as early as possible, and notify any alterations or changes as may occur from time to time.

A nominal roll of all registered followers will also be forwarded to the Base Commandant for information.

(*e*) All native villages are out of bounds, except where necessary to enter them under orders, during operations, etc.

6. The attention of all concerned is invited to Indian Supplement Reports and to Field Service Regulations, Part II, Chapter 16, and Appendix 12 ; Returns. and to the Field Service Regulations, Part II, Sections 129–132 :—

    (i) Field states will be rendered on Sundays at 5 p.m., and after an action.

    (ii) War diaries will be submitted on the last day of the month.

    (iii) Reports on actions :—As soon after the action as possible.

    (iv) All correspondence, reports, and returns, which under Field Service Regulations, Part II, quoted above, laid down to be sent to the " Adjutant General's office," at the Base, will be addressed to, and dealt with by, the Commandant, Base Depot and Record Section.

7. All private letters will be censored :—   Correspon-
    (i) Post-cards mentioned in Field Service Regulations, Part II, dence and Chapter XII, Section 100, provided the stipulations laid down Censorship. are strictly followed, will be subject to no delay.

    (ii) All ranks are reminded that any reference to military operations, *e.g.* composition, numbers of force, movements, detail of localities, supplies, moral of troops, etc., will be treated as a breach of discipline. Subject to these restrictions, private letters will be forwarded as expeditiously as the Censor's staff can deal with the correspondence passing through their hands.

    (iii) (*a*) As a general rule, during the first phase of operations, private telegrams will not be accepted at the Field Telegraph office except under very exceptional and urgent circumstances, and then only after being approved of by Brigade Commanders or the I.G.C.

        (*b*) Should officers or others wish to cable home or elsewhere, they may *post* their telegram to the Base Telegraph Office, where it will be dealt with as quickly as circumstances permit. These should be addressed " Officer in charge Base Telegraph Office." And endorsed in the corner " Telegrams from. . . . ." (Rank and name and Corps). All telegrams will be censored before despatch.

Besides the local censorship referred to above, telegrams will be subject to a further censorship at Zanzibar and at other terminal stations in the Empire.

Telegrams :—(*a*) Must be in plain English.
           (*b*) Name of sender must be in body of message.
           (*c*) Address must be in full.

    (iv) The charges due for any such cablegrams sent, will be debited to the officer concerned, and be deducted monthly by the Field Disbursing Officer at the Base.

        Intimation of the amount due for telegrams must be sent to the Disbursing Officer before the 25th of every month by the telegraph department.

    (v) Officers are reminded that all communications to the press, including photographs, sketches, etc., are forbidden unless passed by the censor.

Intelligence.   8. The G.O.C. wishes to impress on all the importance of taking all possible steps to prevent information of our movements or strength reaching the enemy.

Great care should be taken that no papers or returns which might, if they fell into the hands of the enemy, be of use to him, are unnecessarily carried on the person.

Wireless.   9. All officers should be warned that if they have occasion to use Wireless Telegraphy, every message sent by it must be in cipher until further orders.

Postal.   10. Postal arrangements will be notified later.

Telegraph and Signalling.   11. (i) Attention of all Officers is drawn to Field Service Regulations, Part II, Indian Supplement, Chapter XVIII.

(ii) Messages to any of the Force Headquarters Staff should simply be addressed " H.Q."

(iii) A list of the station calls has been issued to all regimental signalling officers (see Appendix B) and the letters of these calls are to be used in addressing messages :—

Thus a message to an officer on the Brigade Staff of the 27th Brigade would be addressed " Staff B "; a message to the G.O.C. or Staff of the Imperial Service Brigade would be addressed " Staff C."

While Commanding K.—Officer Comdg. 2nd Kashmir Rifles,

and Commanding Q.B.—Officer Comdg. " B " Company, 63rd Light Infantry.

A typical message is attached as Appendix " C."

(iv) The following officers only are allowed to send " Clear the Line " messages :—

(1) G.O.C.	Major-General A. E. Aitken.
(2) G.S.O. (I.)	Lieut.-Colonel S. H. Sheppard, D.S.O., R.E.
(3) Brigade Comdr., 27th Infy Brigade.	Brigadier-General R. Wapshare.
(4) Brigade Comdr. Imp. Service Brigade.	Brigadier-General M. J. Tighe, C.B., C.I.E., D.S.O.
(5) I.G.C.	Colonel W. Malleson, C.I.E.
(6) Base Commandant ..	Lieut.-Colonel C. Bailey,1st Lancers.
(7) The Assistant Director Telegraphs and Signals.	Captain H. C. Hawtrey, R.E.
(8) Officers Commanding detached forces as in Indian Supplement to F.S.R. II, para. 89, 1 (i) over their own field lines.	

(v) " Priority Messages " may be sent by the above, and in addition by all Staff Officers of Force Head-Quarters, Brigade Head-Quarters, Line of Communication Head-Quarters, and Base Staff, and by " Commanders " on the spot," in case of necessity.

Ammunition.   12. Reserve Ammunition loads should be made into boxes of 60 lbs. weight.

Medical.   13. A pamphlet, entitled " Medical Notes," will be issued to all units in sufficient numbers to ensure all ranks and followers knowing its contents. Officers Commanding units and departments are requested to impress on all under their command that the *prevention of disease* in Force " B " is of more importance than anything else. This is especially necessary in the low-lying maritime (malarial) belts of country. It is only *by individual effort* that the prevention of disease can be thoroughly carried out.

Supplies.   14. Local supplies will only be collected under orders of the A.D.S. and T., or in his absence by the senior officer present.

15. With reference to Field Service Regulations, Part II, Sections 13, Base. 25 (9), 56 (3), and 137, Lieut.-Colonel C. Bailey, Base Commandant, is also the Military Landing Officer.

16. As thunderstorms in the area of operations are usually very Miscellan-severe, Officers and N.C.Os. commanding piquets or guards may use eous. their discretion during them as regards sentries fixing bayonets.

(Not reproduced : Appendix A.   Seniority Roll of Officers.
                   Appendix B.   Station calls allotted to " B " force.
                   Appendix C.   Specimen message.)

APPENDIX IV

THE KING'S AFRICAN RIFLES

THE KING'S AFRICAN RIFLES.

The King's African Rifles played so outstanding a part in the East African campaign of 1914-18, in the course of which they were expanded to no less than fourteen times the strength at which they mobilized, it has been thought desirable to give here in some detail an account of the origins and development of that great Corps. During the period dealt with in the present volume the only K.A.R. units engaged were those existing in August 1914 ; but, as the narrative shows, within eighteen months the necessity of a large-scale expansion had come to be fully appreciated. From October 1916 onwards, as a later volume will record, the burden of the campaign was borne increasingly by the new units, which, if inevitably to some extent less fully trained, none the less fully upheld the fine standard of conduct in the field set by the original battalions and maintained ever since.

I.

Local Forces in East Africa up to 1902.

The diverse origins of the King's African Rifles in the four British protectorates of East Africa were as follows :

(i) *Uganda*.[1] The military forces of Uganda, and to some extent also those of British East Africa, trace their origin back to the force of Sudanese troops originally under Emin Pasha.[2] These troops, isolated in the Equatorial Province of the Upper Nile by the revolt of the Mahdi in 1883, moved southwards in 1885 after the fall of Khartoum and eventually settled along the Albert Nile and about Lake Albert, there to remain under many vicissitudes, cut off from civilization, until in April 1888 a relief expedition under the explorer H. M. Stanley gained touch with them. A year later Emin, whose authority had by that time virtually disappeared, departed with Stanley to the east coast. The remains of his former command, with their households, a vast assemblage estimated at 12,000 in all, were settled partly under a loyal Sudanese officer, Selim Bey, round the southern end of Lake Albert and partly under one Fadl el Mula, a disaffected officer who had mutinied in the previous year, about Wadelai.

---

[1] For a fuller historical survey of the earlier years of the Uganda Protectorate see Thomas and Scott, " Uganda."

[2] This remarkable character was one Eduard Schnitzer, a German of Jewish descent, who after a varied career as a doctor of medicine in the near East embraced Muhammadanism, adopted the name Emin, and in 1876 took service under Gordon in the Sudan, where he eventually became Governor of the Equatorial Province. In 1889 he passed for a time into German service, in which in 1890 he founded a post at Bukoba. His melancholy history ended in 1892, when, whilst making an independent expedition westwards towards the Congo, he was murdered in tragic circumstances by Arabs to whose escort he had entrusted himself.

Meanwhile for some years past the country west and north of Lake Victoria had been riven by continual internecine struggles arising out of the varied activities of European missionaries, Arabs and rival native chiefs. At the end of 1890 Captain Frederick Lugard (now Lord Lugard), from Nyasaland, reached Uganda in the interests of the Imperial British East Africa Company, on whose behalf he undertook the restoration of order. To strengthen the Company's meagre forces Lugard determined to draw on the relics of Emin's Sudanese. With this in view he visited Lake Albert and in September 1891 persuaded Selim, who had some 600 armed men in his following of about 8,000, to move south into the Toro district, whence two years later they were all moved eastwards and brought under control.[1]

From the Company's original force some 600 strong—about half of it Sudanese recruited in Cairo, with some natives of Zanzibar, and the remainder armed Swahili carriers—to which another 100 had been added from Selim's men, the forces of the newly formed Protectorate grew by 1893 to a total of 600 regulars with 300 reservists. To these were added in 1894 some of Fadl el Mula's followers, and on the 1st September 1895 the force, now organized in companies of locally-recruited Sudanese under British officers, was officially constituted as the Uganda Rifles.

By 1897, in which year a mutiny[2] occurred the strength had risen to 1,600. As the result of the mutiny the establishment of British officers was considerably increased and the loyal remnant was reinforced from India. Forming the nucleus of what was to be designated the 1st Battalion, Uganda Rifles, 200 Sikhs and 200 Punjabi Mussulmans raised in India were organized in four companies, to which were added, on their arrival at Mombasa in May, 1898, two companies of Swahilis and two of Somalis. The latter were subsequently replaced by two companies formed from the Sudanese soldiers who had remained loyal.[3]

---

[1] " By conducting them into Toro " Lugard " made accessible for " recruiting some of the finest material for native troops in Africa." Thomas and Scott, op. cit., p. 263.

[2] " During the years 1894 to 1897 these incomparably hardy soldiers " put in an astonishing amount of service on punitive expeditions, patrols " and escorts. But under the financial limitations imposed by the Home " Exchequer, too much was demanded of them. They were over-worked, " under- and often unpaid, and not very understandingly handled, and the " impartial inquirer cannot, at this distance of time, fasten upon them " more than a share of the blame for the outbreak of the Sudanese mutiny " in 1897 . . . . Of the total force 510 were in mutiny at Luba's Fort." Thomas and Scott, op. cit., p. 264.

[3] A colony of these loyal Sudanese was afterwards founded at Bombo, where they and their descendants still remain.

Subsequent recruiting brought the Africans of the Uganda Rifles by 1901 to a strength of 1,364 ; the Indian contingent still numbered 387 ; total 1,751.

(ii) *British East Africa* : Between 1888 and 1895 the local forces of the Imperial British East Africa Company, consisting of Zanzibaris, Sudanese, Swahilis and Somalis, fluctuated in numbers between 200 and 1,000 men. They were organized and trained, so far as circumstances permitted, under British Army officers placed at the Company's disposal. A part of these forces accompanied Lugard to Uganda in 1890 and rendered useful service in the operations of the two following years.

In 1895, on the transfer of the Company's territory to the Government of the United Kingdom, the best men, including 250 of Selim Bey's troops, were formed into a new force designated the East African Rifles. A contingent of 300 men raised in India brought the total strength to 4 British officers and about 1,000 men. Detachments of this force co-operated usefully with Indian troops in suppressing Mubarak's rebellion of 1895–6, and the Uganda mutiny of 1897–8, and on two later occasions served against the Ogaden Somalis.

After the Uganda mutiny the East African Rifles were re-organized into five companies of Sudanese and three of Swahilis, with an establishment of 19 British officers and 880 men. In 1900 the Indian contingent, then 560 strong, returned to India, and an additional company of Swahilis was enrolled in its place. In 1901 the Sudanese companies were reduced to four, with an increased establishment, and furnished a camel corps of 100 men for service in Jubaland. The total strength in 1901 was 1,080.

(iii) *Nyasaland.* The clashes with Arab slave-traders and warlike native tribes which resulted from the activities of the African Lakes Corporation led to the employment by the Corporation of armed natives under British leaders. In 1891, when the extended British protectorate was proclaimed, a force of 50 Sikh volunteers was brought from India. Its strength was gradually increased until in 1894 it amounted to 3 British officers, 200 Sikhs 150 native regulars and a varying number of irregulars. During the first year of British administration the force was frequently employed in punitive expeditions and the suppression of the slave-trade and between 1893 and 1895 it had further hard fighting against the slave-raiding Yao chiefs.

In 1896 the force developed into a regiment designated the British Central African Rifles, renamed in 1898 the 1st Bn. Central Africa Regiment.[1]

---

[1] In 1897 the establishment of the B.C.A. Rifles was 738 Africans, together with an Indian contingent of 175 Sikhs.

In 1897 and 1898 the unit took part in successful expeditions under Lieut.-Colonel (afterwards Brig.-General Sir William) Manning, against the Ngoni and the Nguru.[1]

It was composed in 1898 of six companies ; subsequently three more companies were raised for service in North Eastern Rhodesia, where they continued to serve until 1901, when they were relieved by a locally-raised civil police force.

The 1st Bn., including 135 Sikhs, was actively employed in 1899 in co-operation with the Portuguese against the Yao chief Mataka, and in the same year 100 men took part in a punitive expedition in North Eastern Rhodesia, in the course of which they marched 1,000 miles in two months.

A second battalion of the Central Africa Regiment[2] was raised in 1899 for garrison duty at Mauritius, in substitution for a British infantry battalion. This measure, however, proved unpopular with the inhabitants of Mauritius, and early in 1900 the 2nd Bn. was withdrawn and sent to Somaliland.

In July 1900, half the 2nd Bn. moved from Somaliland to the West Coast of Africa where, together with the Headquarters and some 200 Africans and 70 Sikhs of the 1st Battalion it took part in the Ashanti Campaign of 1900-1901.[3]

The remaining half of the 2nd Battalion left Somaliland in December 1900 for Gambia, taking part in the punitive expedition of 1901.

(iv) *Somaliland.* The British Protectorate over the Somali coast, established in 1887 and at first administered as a dependency of India, was taken over in 1898 by the Foreign Office. The local forces originally consisted of a small police levy (subsequently divided into military and civil police) and camel corps, under the command of an officer of the Indian Army.

At the end of 1900 Somali levies were temporarily raised for an expedition against the Mullah. These numbered 100 camelry, 400 mounted infantry, and 1,000 infantry, commanded by officers of the British Army In the latter half of 1901 their strength was reduced ; but a recrudescence of the Mullah's activity at the end of that year led to their being restored to their former numbers. They were then designated as militia.

(v) *Formation of the K.A.R.* In March 1901 the War Office took up with the Foreign Office, which then administered the British protectorates in East and Central Africa, the general

---

[1] In his despatch on these operations Lieut.-Colonel Manning wrote that " the Sikhs and native troops have most cheerfully borne the great " discomfort and hardship of a campaign in the rainy season, and their " gallantry in the face of the enemy is worthy of all praise."

[2] Establishment 20 officers, 1,080 Africans.

[3] This detachment made a complete circuit of Africa, proceeding via the Cape and returning via the Mediterranean.

question of the organization of the local forces so far maintained as separate corps. Pointing out that the existing forces of any one protectorate were not adequate to ensure internal security without recourse to outside aid and that, while in the past recourse had been made to reinforcements from India, this might not be possible in the future, the War Office proposed that the several forces should be linked into one organization, as had been done a few years previously on the West Coast of Africa,[1] so as to permit of reinforcement of one protectorate from another in emergency. The proposal was agreed to. With effect from the 1st January 1902 the various East African forces were incorporated to form a new regiment, on which H.M. King Edward VII was graciously pleased to confer the title " The King's African " Rifles ".

The King's African Rifles, as now constituted, comprised the following :

1st Bn. (8 coys.)
    formerly 1st Bn. Central Africa Regiment.
2nd Bn. (6 coys.)
    formerly 2nd Bn. Central Africa Regiment.
Indian Contingent (2 coys.)

British East Africa :
    3rd Bn. (7 coys., camel coy.)
        formerly East African Rifles.

Uganda :
    4th Bn. (9 coys.)
        formerly Uganda Rifles.
    5th Bn. (Indian) (4 coys.)
        formerly Uganda Rifles.

British Somaliland :
    6th Bn. (3 coys., camel corps, militia infantry, mounted infantry)
        formerly local forces in the Protectorate.

The total strength of the regiment on its formation was 104 officers, 4,579 native officers and men.[2]

---

[1] In 1898, after investigation by an inter-Departmental Committee, the local military forces of Nigeria, the Gold Coast, Sierra Leone and the Gambia had been reorganized and linked together under the designation of the West African Frontier Force.

[2] See Command Paper Cd. 1635, " Africa No. 9." It was decided that all battalions though " Rifles " in name, should drill as infantry of the line. This was due to the facts that only a relatively small number of officers was drawn from rifle regiments and that the personnel of the 5th (Indian) Battalion would have had to learn " Rifle " drill whilst in Africa and return to the normal infantry drill in India.

To co-ordinate administration and training, an Inspector-General of the King's African Rifles was appointed, with a small staff and an office in London. His duties included periodical visits of inspection to the various battalions.[1]

II

The K.A.R. up to the outbreak of war : 1902–14.

The following is a summary of the numerous and somewhat confusing changes made in the constitution of the various battalions during the twelve years preceding the outbreak of war. It is necessary to keep in mind throughout that each battalion is associated directly with its own particular East African protectorate, from which alone its rank and file were drawn.

(i) *1st and 2nd Battalions* (British Central Africa, now Nyasaland). The 1st and 2nd Bns. were formed from the Central Africa Regiment, of the British Central Africa Protectorate. Under the initial organization the 1st Bn. constituted the garrison of that protectorate, while the 2nd Bn., until 1904, was held available as a general reserve for all the four protectorates (Central Africa, East Africa, Uganda, Somaliland).[2]

Both battalions served with distinction in the Somaliland operations of 1902–04.[3] From Somaliland the 1st Bn. returned direct to British Central Africa ; the 2nd Bn. followed, after three months' duty at Nairobi.

The establishment of both battalions was then (1904) fixed at six companies, together with a depot company, each 100 rank and file. The battalions were made interchangeable for " foreign " service in British East Africa alternating with " home "

---

[1] Between 1902 and 1014 the appointment of Inspector-General of the K.A.R. was held by :—
Brig.-General Sir William M. Manning, K C.M.G., C.B. (January 1902 to October 1907)
Colonel T. F. Gough, V.C., U.M.G., A.D.C. (October 1907 to December 1909).
Colonel G. H. Thesiger, C.B., C.M.G. (December 1909 to September 1913).
Colonel A. R. Hoskins, D.S.O. (September 1913 to December 1914).
[2] The Sikhs of the former Central Africa Regt. remained as an " Indian contingent " (strength in 1902, 2 B.O., 160 o.r.) attached to the battalion serving in the B.C.A. Protectorate. They consisted of specially selected volunteers, with not less than 3 and not more than 9 years' service, from the Indian Army. The contingent was reduced in 1906 from two coys. to one, strength 2 B.O., 102 o.r.
[3] The 2nd Bn. took part in the action at Erego, 6th October 1902. At Gumburru, April 1903, most of the detachment, which was overwhelmed after inflicting heavy loss on the Mullah, belonged to the 2nd Bn., which lost 7 officers killed. Both battalions were at Jidballi, January 1904, when a loss of over 1,000 was inflicted on the enemy.

service in British Central Africa. " Foreign " service was for three years. Under this arrangement the 1st Bn. went to British East Africa in 1905.[1]

Early in 1906 the two depot companies were merged in one, reduced to 100 rank and file, and the " foreign " service battalion, though it remained in British East Africa, was made available for duty in any of the four protectorates.

In March 1906 the Government of British East Africa decided that the total strength of the K.A.R. in that protectorate— 3rd (B.E.A.) Bn. (eight companies), with the 1st Bn. (six companies) as a reserve—might safely be reduced by four companies. Reductions ensued both in British East and British Central Africa. In the course of the year, with the approval of the British Central Africa Government, the 2nd Bn. was reduced from six to four companies and the combined depot company was abolished. The 1st Bn. not having completed its tour of " foreign " service, the view was taken that it would be a breach of faith with the African troops to reduce its strength before its relief, due in June 1908 ; meanwhile casualties were not replaced.

At the same time, however (September 1906), two of the 1st Bn.'s six companies were transferred from British East Africa to garrison Zanzibar, the Sultan's armed forces having been disbanded. British East Africa was thus relieved of the expense of these two companies by the Sultan of Zanzibar, without imposing an immediate reduction on the 1st Bn. In January 1907 the Central Africa battalion in British East Africa ceased to be regarded as a reserve and became liable for detachment duties both at Zanzibar and elsewhere, hitherto restricted to the 3rd Bn.[2]

The 1st Bn. was relieved in British East Africa and Zanzibar in June 1908 by the 2nd Bn., and on return to its home protector-ate (henceforward called Nyasaland) was reduced, like the 2nd Bn., to four companies each 100 strong. Five months later, headquarters and three companies were despatched to Somaliland, taking part in the subsequent operations and leaving in Nyasaland only one company, together with the Indian contingent, until their return in January 1910.

In January 1911, as the result of representations made by the Governor of British East Africa with a view mainly to saving the

---

[1] The 1st Bn. was engaged in the expedition of 1905 against the Nandi tribe, 1905–06.

[2] In September 1907 the Governors of Uganda and British East Africa, on the ground of reducing their military expenditure, put forward a proposal to disband all the K.A.R. units in their protectorates and to replace them by police. This unpractical proposal was not agreed to either by the Committee of Imperial Defence or by the War Office, and was dropped.

cost of transporting Nyasaland troops to and from that protectorate every three years, it was decided to disband the 2nd Bn., then serving there.[1] Headquarters and two companies of the battalion returned to Zomba in June, followed in September by the two companies from Zanzibar, and on the 31st December 1911 the 2nd Bn. was officially disbanded.[2]

Meanwhile the 1st Bn. had been reduced in April to two companies. In July, to meet the needs of British East Africa and Zanzibar, two additional companies, one for each, had hurriedly to be re-raised.[3] An additional company raised in 1912 brought the 1st Bn. to five companies in all, one more of which was sent to British East Africa.[4]

Early in 1913 the Indian contingent in Nyasaland was disbanded and a sixth company was raised for the 1st Bn., enabling it to send yet another company to British East Africa.[5] During the first half of 1914 the 1st Bn. was again re-organized, consisting finally of the four companies (each 100 strong) then in British East Africa and four companies (each 75 strong) in Nyasaland.[6]

(ii) *3rd Battalion* (British East Africa). The 3rd Bn. was formed from the former East African Rifles, with an establishment of seven companies of infantry, one of camelry (for service in Jubaland), each 125 rank and file.

A detachment, numbering about 300, took part with the 1st and 2nd Bns. in the Somaliland operations, 1902-04, and in 1905-06 the 3rd Bn., with the 1st and 4th Bns., was engaged in the expedition against the Nandi tribe.

Among the reductions made in March 1906, already mentioned,[7] two companies of the 3rd Bn. were disbanded. No

---

[1] The two coys. at Zanzibar had been found by the 2nd Bn. from June 1908 to February 1910, then by the 3rd Bn. until October 1910, then again by the 2nd Bn. until September 1911.

[2] It is believed that almost all the rank and file then must over to the Defence Force in German East Africa, and fought against us in 1014-18.

[3] In 1911 the Overseas Defence Committee agreed to the reduction of the Zanzibar garrison to one coy., and to the raising of one coy. of local armed constabulary. The arrangement, started in September 1911, did not work well and in October 1913 it was decided to revert to the former garrison, two coys. K.A.R.

The second coy. was found by the 1/K.A.R. until February 1914, when the garrison dropped again to one coy., 3/K.A.R.

[4] Of the three coys., 1/K.A.R., in B.E.A. one was employed early in 1912 on the Turkana and Maraquet patrols; the other two, including one from Zanzibar relieved by the 3/K.A.R. in May 1912, were detached to Jubaland.

[5] All the four coys., 1/K.A.R., then in B.E.A. took part in the Jubaland operations which ended in May 1914. One of them was relieved two months later by a coy. from Nyasaland.

[6] For distribution, see p. 560 f.n.

[7] See p. 554.

further change of composition occurred until May 1911, when an additional company was formed, making the total (including camel company) seven companies.[1]

Throughout 1911 the unfortunate decision of that year to disband the 2nd Bn., to which reference has already been made, had its repercussions on the 3rd Bn., which experienced much difficulty in obtaining recruits and fell steadily below establishment, while a heavy strain was thrown on its capacity for training.[2] To make matters worse, a severe outbreak of beri-beri between December 1911 and May 1912 resulted in deaths equivalent to the strength of a company, leaving " C " Coy. non-existent, thus reducing the battalion to six companies.[3]

In May 1912 one company relieved the company of the 1st Bn. then at Zanzibar. Three companies took part in the Jubaland operations between December 1913 and May 1914. The outbreak of war found the 3rd Bn. still deficient of one company, with the remaining six (including the camel company) dispersed on the northern border and the Juba river.[4]

(iii) *4th and 5th Battalions* (Uganda). The 4th Bn. was formed from the Africans, and the 5th Bn. from the Indian contingent, comprised in the former Uganda Rifles.[5]

The 5th (Indian) Bn. as such was disbanded in 1904, when the term of service of most of its rank and file, all Indian, expired. At the same time the 4th Bn., hitherto nine African companies, each 125 strong, was re-organized to consist of seven African companies at that strength together with an " Indian " contingent " of two companies, each 100 rank and file.

Thus re-organized the 4th Bn., with the 1st and 3rd, took part in the operations of 1905–06 against the Nandi tribe.

Up to 1906 the battalion was normally dispersed among a number of isolated stations. In 1907 the battalion headquarters and four companies were concentrated at Bombo, some 25 miles north of Kampala, within easy march of Lake Victoria and in an area free from sleeping sickness ; one company was disbanded, and two were stationed respectively at Hoima and Mbarara, while the two companies of the Indian contingent continued to garrison Entebbe and Kampala.

---

[1] In the meantime three infantry companies and the camel company had taken part, with the 1st Bn., in the Somaliland operations from February 1909 to January 1910. From November 1911 to January 1912 two coys., with a coy. of the 1/K.A.R., were employed on the Maraquet patrol.

[2] The establishment in 1910 was 20 officers, 1 W.O., 789 o.r. At the beginning of 1912 the battalion had fewer trained men than at any time in its history.

[3] " C " Coy. was not re-formed, owing to the superstitious fears of the men.

[4] For distribution see p. 560 f.n.

[5] Total strengths on 31st March 1902 were : 4th Bn., 1,054 ; 5th Bn., 398.

Between February 1909 and January 1910 headquarters and four companies took part in the Somaliland operations; a patrol was maintained in the Turkana territory in 1910–11. Incidentally, throughout the period 1902–11 the 4th Bn. was constantly called upon for escorts to successive Boundary Commissions delimiting the frontiers of Uganda.

In March 1913 the Indian contingent was disbanded, its personnel returning to India and being replaced by a seventh African company. No further change of organization took place up to the outbreak of war.

Two companies were engaged in a brief and successful expedition against the Dodinga tribe on the northern border which ended in August 1913; in September one company was despatched for the operations against the Merehan Somalis, from which it returned in July 1914, three other companies being employed on the L. of C. from February to May 1914.

The distribution of the battalion in July 1914, when an expedition against the Turkana was on the point of being undertaken, is given in Part III.

(iv) *6th Battalion* (Somaliland). On the formation of the K.A.R. in 1902 it had been intended that the existing levies in Somaliland should be organized as a 6th Battalion, to consist of three infantry companies, a camel company, with additional levy companies. The operations in Somaliland, however, delayed matters and it was not until 1904 that the 6th Bn. was formed. In the following year, as the result of a decision to recruit the 6th Bn. entirely from India, the battalion was re-constituted, to consist now of four companies of Punjabi Mussulmans, each 100 rank and file, including one camel company.

In 1908 the Indian contingent was reduced to one infantry and one camel company, while four and a half companies of Somali militia, part of the permanent forces of the Somaliland Protectorate, were incorporated in the 6th Bn.

The British withdrawal to the coastal area in 1909 led to the disbandment of the 6th Bn. in March 1910 and to its replacement by the Somaliland Camel Constabulary, now the Somaliland Camel Corps.

(v) *The K.A.R. as a whole.* It will be noted that although the normal function of the K.A.R. was the maintenance of internal security, all the battalions were also at various times engaged in punitive expeditions.[1]

Between 1910 and 1912 the responsibilities both of Uganda and of the East Africa Protectorate were greatly increased: in Uganda the administration of the Nile Province and the

---

[1] In 1909 no fewer than 1,200 of the K.A.R. were on active service in Somaliland; on 1st April 1914 the numbers engaged in the Jubaland operations were over 1,000 of the K.A.R., with 250 irregulars.

districts along the northern border were undertaken, while in British East Africa the administered area was extended northwards to the Abyssinian border. Notwithstanding this, in 1911, as we have seen, the twenty companies of the K.A.R. were reduced by three, the loss of four by disbandment of the 2nd Bn. being compensated only by the addition of one newly-raised company to the 3rd Bn. Even the further additions to the 1st Bn., one company in 1912 and one in 1913, did not make good the loss of the whole homogeneous 2nd Bn.[1]

In July 1914 a re-organization of the K.A.R., proposed by the Inspector-General (Colonel A. R. Hoskins) was approved. Under this scheme, which was abandoned owing to the outbreak of war, it was intended to maintain in British East Africa the 3rd Bn., at five companies (total 500), a new battalion from Nyasaland, relieved triennially, at four companies (total 400), with two " flying columns ", each 250.[2]

The strengths in East Africa would then have been :

E.A. Protectorate	3rd Bn. ..	..	..	500
	New Nyasaland bn.	..	..	400
	Flying columns		..	500
Uganda	4th Bn. ..	..	..	875
Nyasaland	1st Bn. (3 coys.) ..	..	..	300
Zanzibar	1st Bn. (2 coys.) ..	..	..	200
		Total	..	2,775

Comparing these figures with the actual strengths on the outbreak of war, viz., 150 below a total establishment of 2,325, it will be seen that Col. Hoskins's scheme—had time allowed of its adoption—would have provided 600 additional trained African soldiers who would have been invaluable in the difficult situation which confronted the African dependencies in the opening phase of the campaign.

---

[1] Strengths (excluding Indian contingents) :—

				Jan. 1911.	Jan. 1912.
1st Bn.	..	..	..	4 coys.	4 coys. (a)
2nd Bn.	..	..	..	4 ,,	—
3rd Bn.	..	..	..	6 ,,	7 coys. (b)
4th Bn.	..	..	..	6 ,,	6 ,,
		Total	..	20 coys.	17 coys.

Notes.—(a) Reduced to 2 coys., April 1911 ; restored to 4 coys., July 1911.

(b) One additional coy. raised, May 1911.

[2] At this time the sanctioned strength in the B.E.A. Protectorate was : 3rd Bn. (6 coys.), 750 ; 1st Bn. (4 coys.), 400. These normally furnished 2 coys. for Zanzibar. Col. Hoskins proposed alternatively that a garrison for Zanzibar be found from India, or that the 1/K.A.R. detachment be increased to 5 coys. (500) of which 2 coys. would serve at Zanzibar and be relieved annually.

To sum up. The details which have been given indicate clearly the absence of any uniformity or continuity of policy in regard to the East African native force up to the outbreak of war. Throughout the period in question, moreover, the subject was considered solely from the point of view of internal security and punitive expeditions. There is no indication that the possibility of a European war, entailing serious large-scale operations against the organized armed forces of the neighbouring German protectorate, ever entered into the calculations either of the Government of the United Kingdom or of the local British Colonial administrations. At all events no preparations for such an eventuality appear ever to have been considered. No troops were stationed near the German borders, and in so far as any requirements beyond the scope of the K.A.R. were envisaged at all it seems always to have been assumed that troops from India would be available.

III.

The K.A.R. at the outbreak of war, August 1914

At the outbreak of war in 1914 the K.A.R., as we have seen, consisted of three infantry battalions, comprising twenty companies varying in strength from 75 to 125, together with one camel company, on a total establishment of 70 officers, 3 British N.C.Os., 2,325 other ranks.[1] Each company had one machine

---

[1] Establishment :—

	Offrs.	B.N.C.O.	O.R.
1st Bn. Headquarters, Zomba. Nyasaland, 4 coys. (75) E. Afr. Protectorate 4 coys. (100)	24	1	700
3rd Bn. H.Q., Nairobi. E.A. Protectorate, 5 coys. (125), 1 camel coy. (125)	24	1	750
4th Bn. H.Q., Bombo. Uganda and E.A. Protectorate, 7 coys. (125)	22	1	875
Total	70(a)	3(b)	2,345

(a) Includes 3 Bn. Comdrs, 0 Occonds-in-Command, 2 Adjutant-and-Quartermasters, 1 Adjutant, 1 Quartermaster, 25 Coy. Comdrs., 35 Subalterns. Four of the Coy. Comdrs. were employed on special duties.
(b) Regl. Serjt. Majors.

Racial Composition.

1st Bn., and (up to its disbandment in 1911)
2nd Bn. : Principally Yao, with smaller proportions of Nyanja, Ngoni, Nguru, Atonga.
3rd Bn. : The Bn. from its formation had a high proportion of Sudanese. In 1907 an attempt made to raise 1 Coy. of Masai proved unsuccessful. After 1908 three of the six companies were respectively Abyssinians (with Sudanese N.C.Os.), Nandi, and a mixed company including Swahili, Nyamwezi and Manyema.
4th Bn. : Mainly Sudanese, with 1 Coy. Baganda and one mixed "Swahili" company of Nyamwezi, Sukuma, Kavirondo, and a few Swahilis.

Continued at foot of next page.

gun. The force had no artillery. No organized reserve was maintained.

Between the three battalions of the King's African Rifles there was no close connection. They had, however, certain features in common, viz.,

(i) All were administered under the K.A.R. Regulations and local K.A.R. ordinances, the latter being virtually identical in all three protectorates.

(ii) The terms of service for British personnel were practically the same throughout.

(iii) The Inspector General of the K.A.R. formed a connecting link. This officer, although exercising no executive functions, spent some six months of each year in inspecting the various units of the K.A.R. During the remainder of the year he was at the Colonial Office, where he acted as military adviser to the Secretary of State.

In East Africa each unit, whether battalion or company, came under the authority of the Governor of the protectorate in which it served, forming as it did the local garrison. The Governor was thus invested with the status of a local Commander-in-Chief, which, while it did not entitle him to assume the actual direction of any military operations, imposed on him the

---

Continued from previous page

Distribution.—At the end of July 1914 sub-units of the K.A.R. were stationed as follows (" A/1 " means " A " Coy., 1st Bn., etc.) :—

Jubaland	Serenli	A/1, C/1, E/3.
	Yonti	B/1, E/1.
	Gobwen	F/3 (camels).
Northern Garrisons, B.E.A.	Moyale	½D/3
	Kulal	½B/3
	Marich	½B/3
Northern Garrisons, Uganda.	Morongole	E/4
	Maroto	D/4
	On march to Maroto ..	C/4
Uganda	Bombo	A/4
	Entebbe	G/4
E.A. Protectorate ..	Baringo	F/4 ⎫ moving to
	Mumia's	B/4 ⎭ Turkana
	On march, Marich to Kisumu on relief	½A/3
	Nairobi	½D/3, ¼A/3 (M.I. recruits)
Zanzibar		G/3
Nyasaland	Zomba	H/1
	Mangoche	G/1
	Furlough, ordered E.A.P. ..	F/1
	do., on return from E.A.P.	D/1

Sketch No. 1 shows this distribution, but with certain changes which were ordered between 30th July and 2nd Aug. 1915.

obligation of deciding the extent to which military force should be used and of issuing instructions accordingly to the local commander.

While co-operation between the Governors and the military commanders, as was to be expected, was in general close and active, the disadvantages of this system of command became apparent from the outset of the operations in East Africa, and there can be little doubt that the undue prolongation of the early stages of the campaign was to some extent attributable to this cause.

IV.

The Expansion of the K.A.R. during the campaign, 1914–18.

(i) *General Course of Events.* When war broke out there existed, as stated in the text, no organized reserve for the K.A.R. Nevertheless at the three headquarters, Nairobi, Bombo and Zomba, numbers of ex-K.A.R. askari came eagerly forward to rejoin. Some of these, formed into so-called " Reserve " Companies, went into action in the early days of the war and showed themselves fully up to the high standard of their earlier training,[1] while older " reservists " were employed on internal security duties. At this time, however, K.A.R. officers being in general averse from enlisting men of tribes other than those of proved fighting ability, and the number of such tribes being limited, the intake of recruits was slow. As the campaign went on, tribes of less-known military value were drawn upon, providing eventually a valuable accession of strength.

In January 1915 the War Office proposed a substantial increase in the K.A.R., and late in February the Colonial Office sanctioned the enlistment of 600 additional recruits. But matters went no farther, partly in consequence of the adverse report made by Colonel Kitchener in March and partly because the local administrations, hardly appreciating as yet the full needs of the situation, viewed with disfavour the prospect of large numbers of natives, trained to arms, returning to their villages at the conclusion of hostilities. For some months, therefore, no action was taken beyond efforts to keep existing companies up to strength.

Meanwhile the K.A.R. units in the field began to be depleted by casualties. Their numbers were further diminished when in July 1915 two companies of the 1st Bn. serving in British East Africa were sent back to Nyasaland, having exceeded their normal period of such " foreign " service by over a year. Those of their men who so wished were discharged, the remainder being given leave on re-engagement.

---

[1] Notably at Karonga and Kisii.

Towards the end of 1915 an appeal in Nyasaland, originally for 500 recruits for the 1st Bn., for service in British East Africa, proved so popular that by March 1916 no less than 984 recruits and 180 old soldiers had been sent to that protectorate. The additional numbers threw too great a strain on the administrative resources of the 3rd Bn. headquarters. In consequence, a proposal made in February by Major-General Tighe, that the detached companies of the 1st Battalion should be organized as a new battalion, was approved by the War Office on the 4th March, and on the 1st April 1916 the formation of a new 2nd Bn. was begun at Nairobi.[1]

The re-raising of the 2nd Bn. had hardly begun when Lieut.-General Smuts—newly arrived and as yet unfamiliar with East African conditions, but having as his expert adviser Brig.-General A. R. Hoskins, recently Inspector-General of the K.A.R.—proposed the immediate raising of a further three battalions, " in view of the tried and proved value of African troops in this " country ".[2]

These, he expected, would take from six to nine months to raise and train, by which time it was hoped that the campaign would have been concluded ; but the proposed new units would be of value " during the unsettled period which may be expected " to ensue ", while the rainy season now at hand offered a good opportunity for the existing trained battalions to train the new recruits.

On the 6th April Brig.-General Hoskins called a conference of K.A.R. officers at Nairobi, at which measures were decided upon for the necessary recruiting. Four days later the Commander-in-Chief supplemented the proposals for an increase by transmitting a recommendation from the Governor of British East Africa that the whole of the K.A.R. should be treated as Imperial troops for the duration of the War. Viewing the matter in retrospect, it is clear that great advantage would have accrued had this fairly obvious suggestion been advanced by the War Office either in November 1914, when assuming control of this theatre of war, or in January 1915, when proposing an expansion, or even in August of the same year, when urgent and well-considered representations to the same end had been made by the military commanders in the field.

On the 15th April the Colonial Secretary telegraphed his agreement in principle to the proposed increase of the African troops, and the requisite measures were put in hand. In order to leaven the new recruits with seasoned soldiers, the 2nd, 3rd and 4th Bns. were each sub-divided into two units during April

---

[1] The former 2nd Bn. had, it will be remembered, been disbanded from motives of economy in 1911.

[2] Telegram, C.-in-C. to War Office, 3rd April 1916.

and May ; at the same time the 2½ companies of the 3rd Bn., still on the northern frontier of British East Africa, were re-organized, together with companies of armed police and other details, into a new 5th Bn., to garrison Jubaland and guard the Abyssinian border.

Thus by the 1st June 1916 the K.A.R. had become five regiments, viz., Nos. 2, 3 and 4, each consisting of two battalions and a depot, and Nos. 1 and 5, each one battalion and a depot.

In July and August a further recruiting drive in Nyasaland, extended to include North-Eastern Rhodesia, where sufficient Awemba tribesmen were recruited for one double-company, brought in a total of some 1,750 recruits and 90 old soldiers as an addition to the 2nd K.A.R.

Of the new battalions the 1/2nd and 2/2nd were alone ready for the field when, in October, the Colonial Office authorized a further increase, in view of the possibility that the campaign might be prolonged. Between October 1916 and January 1917 the battalions already in process of being raised were therefore augmented by the addition of a third battalion to each of the 2nd, 3rd and 4th K.A.R., and of a second and third battalion to the 1st K.A.R., making the total strength thirteen battalions and five depots, organized thus :—

1st K.A.R.
2nd K.A.R.
3rd K.A.R. } each comprising 1st, 2nd, 3rd Bns. and Depot.
4th K.A.R.

5th K.A.R.   1st Bn. and Depot.

In February 1917 it was decided further to increase the strength from thirteen to twenty battalions.[1] By this time, apart from employment in the East Africa campaign and for the purpose of garrisoning occupied territory, the possibility was also in view that the K.A.R. might eventually provide a force for service in another theatre of war, as will presently be seen.

This expansion included the formation in April 1917 of two additional battalions for training purposes. In the new scheme two new regiments were also raised, viz., the 6th (German East Africa) and the 7th (Zanzibar). Two further training battalions were raised early in 1918.

The final establishment was, therefore, twenty-two battalions, made up as follows :—

1st K.A.R. (recruited in and based on Nyasaland) ;
     Depot and four battalions, viz., 1/1st, 2/1st, 3/1st, 4/1st.

2nd K.A.R. (recruited in Nyasaland, based on British East Africa):
     Depot and four battalions, viz., 1/2nd, 2/2nd, 3/2nd, 4/2nd.

---

[1] See Vol. II.

3rd K.A.R. (recruited in and based on British East Africa) :
Depot and four battalions, viz., 1/3rd, 2/3rd, 3/3rd, 4/3rd.

4th K.A.R. (recruited in Uganda, based on British East Africa) :
Depot and six battalions, viz., 1/4th, 2/4th, 3/4th, 4/4th, 5/4th, 6/4th.

5th K.A.R. (Jubaland garrison) :
Depot and one battalion, viz., 1/5th.

6th (German East Africa) K.A.R. :
Depot and two battalions, viz., 1/6th, 2/6th.

7th (Zanzibar and Coastal) K.A.R. :
Depot and one battalion, viz., 1/7th.

By November 1918 the experience of the campaign had made abundantly clear what the Staff at G.H.Q. in 1916 had only just begun to realize : that for practical reasons of climate, health and diet requirements neither European nor Indian units are suitable for large-scale operations in tropical Africa and that highly trained African troops, expanded to war requirements, and under white leadership, afford the only satisfactory material for such warfare.[1]

Unhappily the belated and hasty war-time expansion of the four K.A.R. battalions of April 1916 into the twenty-two battalions of 1917 and 1918 proved also that it was no easy matter to improvise African troops,[2] since their training takes more time than that of white recruits and they need officers and non-commissioned officers able to speak their language. During the operations in 1918 certain K.A.R. units, consisting largely of recruits with only a few months' training, proved markedly inferior to the veteran askari on the German side ; and it was

---

[1] In the past a similar lesson had already been taught by the campaigns in the West Indies between 1739 and 1814, in the earlier of which British troops were employed, who died in great numbers from tropical diseases. Eventually these were replaced by a large force of native troops locally recruited (the twelve battalions of the West India Regiment), who achieved the final conquest of the French islands. The lesson had to be re-learned in East Africa in 1914–1918.

[2] It was found that, while the fully-trained askari of the K.A.R. made extremely good soldiers, some 30 per cent. of the recruits had to be weeded out as being unlikely to become efficient. In the words of an officer with long experience of the K.A.R. both before and during the campaign, " troops hastily raised during the war from material not much " better than carriers and trained by officers with no experience of African " natives could not be depended upon as those fully trained before " hostilities began."

With regard to musketry in particular the pre-war standard was difficult to keep up. The trained askari becomes a good shot and his fire control is excellent, but this takes time to achieve ; the partially-trained native soldier blazes away ammunition regardless of a target. It was very noticeable in 1917–18 that the newer askari of the K.A.R. were inferior to the old in this respect. The pre-war askari, moreover, had in general some previous experience of active service.

then a matter for regret that a large number of potential officers among the white settlers in the East African protectorates had been wasted in the ranks in local white volunteer units at the beginning of the campaign[1].

(ii) *Details regarding units.*

1st *K.A.R.*

Owing to the need for all available Nyasaland recruits to join the battalions of the 2nd K.A.R. it was not possible to expand the 1st K.A.R. during 1916. Indeed, to stimulate recruiting, the 2nd K.A.R. was given a higher rate of pay.[2] As the natural result recruiting for the 1st K.A.R. came to a standstill. Early in 1917, however, this anomaly was remedied and both the 1st and the 2nd K.A.R. received the higher rate.

On the 22nd January 1917 the original 1st Bn., then in the Lupembe-Pangrasi area, was divided into two battalions. The recruit companies were broken up and drafted to the other companies ; the four-company system was introduced and two battalions of three companies each were formed in the field, each of which was to be brought up to strength with a recruit company from the depot.

The 1st K.A.R. battalions were composed as follows :—

1/1*st :* " AR " and " H " Coys., amalgamated into " A " (Atonga) Company ; " BR " Coy. and recruits became " B " Coy. ; " D " Coy. with recruits became the new " D " Coy. The 1/1st remained in the Lupembe-Pangrasi area.

2/1*st :* " A " (recruit Awemba) Coy. ; the former " F " Coy. and recruits became " B " (Angoni) Coy. ; the former " CR " Coy. and recruits became " C " (Yao) Coy. " D " Coy., raised at Zomba in April 1917 with a mixed composition of Yao, Awemba, Ngoni and Nguru, eventually joined the 2/1st at Luambala

---

[1] At the outbreak of war the 1st Bn., in Nyasaland, obtained additional officers and specialists from the Nyasaland Volunteer Reserve, who displayed great gallantry and suffered heavy casualties in the earlier engagements.

Similarly, early in 1916, when the second battalions of the 2nd, 3rd and 4th K.A.R. were formed, the additional officers needed were obtained almost entirely from the ranks of the East Africa Mounted Rifles, 2/Rhodesia Regt., and, to a lesser extent, the S. African infantry units. These likewise showed high military qualities and proved of the utmost value by reason of their knowledge of the African native and mastery of native languages.

As time went on and the supply of potential officers and N.C.Os. with local African knowledge dwindled, more and more of the European personnel, much of it unversed in the handling of African troops, came from overseas. In consequence, as will be seen from the table on p. 575, the proportion of Europeans to natives increased rapidly in the latter half of 1917 and continued to increase until the end of the campaign.

[2] £1 1s. 4d. per month as against 15s. for the 1st K.A.R.

(Portuguese E.A.) in December 1917. The 2/1st moved to the Songea area.

3/1st : Raised at Zomba in January 1917 ; took the field in Portuguese East Africa in March 1918. (See Vol II).

4/1st : Formed as a training battalion at Zomba on 1st November 1917.

2nd K.A.R.

Formation of a new 2nd Bn. K.A.R. began as stated above at Nairobi on 1st April 1916. On 12th April, a draft of 1,115 N.C.Os. and men (including 131 old soldiers) arrived from Nyasaland. In May orders were received to form two battalions ; this re-organization was completed about 15th July.

The 1/2nd K.A.R. consisted mainly of Yaos ; the 2/2nd received all Atonga and Ngoni, with some Yao and Nyanja. These battalions were the first of the new K.A.R. units to take the field.

Details as to 2nd K.A.R. battalions :

1/2nd : Left Nairobi 4th August 1916, strength 21 officers, 2 British W.O., 511 o.r., for Handeni via Voi-Moshi-Korogwe to join the 1st Divn. At Handeni 13th-17th August. Marched to Morogoro, arriving 30th August. Return march to Korogwe, 10th-23rd September.[1] Embarked at Tanga 4th October for Kilwa Kisiwani, arriving 6th.

2/2nd : Left Nairobi 31st August 1916, strength 19 officers, 590 o.r., for Handeni via Korogwe to join the 1st Divn. Arrived Korogwe 3rd, Handeni 8th September.

Returned to Korogwe, preceding 1/2nd K.A.R., and thence to Tanga, arriving 16th. Embarked 22nd September for Kilwa Kisiwani, arriving 29th.

In August 1916 the recruiting drive already mentioned raised some 1,800 men, of whom a part brought the 1/2nd and 2/2nd up to establishment, the remainder being taken for a new battalion.

3/2nd : Formed at Mbagathi, near Nairobi, 10th January 1917. Engaged at Lindi, June 1917.

4/2nd : Raised at Mbagathi as a training battalion, 1st April 1918.

3rd K.A.R.

The original 3rd Bn., of which " A ", " B ", " D ", " E " Coys. were in the field in April 1916 when expansion of the K.A.R. began, eventually became the 1/3rd K.A.R. It remained in the field, while recruits were trained at Nairobi. Of its other companies, " C " Coy., as already mentioned, had ceased to exist in 1912 ; in June 1916 " F " (Camel) and half of " G "

---

[1] The long march to Morogoro and back, under conditions of considerable hardship, afforded excellent training.

Coys. were incorporated in the new 5th K.A.R. (q.v.), the. remainder being absorbed in the 3rd Bn. On 28th November 1916 both the original 3rd Bn. and a large draft from Nairobi reached Kilwa, where reorganization into the new 1/3rd and 2/3rd at once began.[1]

Details as to 3rd K.A.R. battalions:

1/3rd : Formed from " B " and " D " Coys., with recruits. Moved to Matandu 8th December 1916.

2/3rd : Formed from " A " and " E " Coys., with recruits. Remained at Kilwa in reserve.

3/3rd : Raised at the depot at Nairobi, 15th March 1917; took the field at Kilwa in June 1917.

4/3rd : Originally designated 3/6th; raised at Nairobi as a training battalion, October 1917.

4th K.A.R.

From the time of its first formation in 1902 until it took part in the capture of Mwanza in July 1916 (see Chap. XXV) the 4th K.A.R. had never been assembled as a battalion, its companies having formed detachments dispersed from the Belgian Congo to the coast of British East Africa. Up to the end of the subsequent advance on Tabora (see Chap. XXVI) it retained its pre-war organization in eight companies lettered " A " to " H ". In October and November 1916, whilst on the Central Railway these were re-organized as four numbered companies, the intention being that in due time the 1/4th should be formed by expanding Nos. 1 (" A ", " C ", " F ") and 2 (" D ") Coys., while the 2/4th, raised in Uganda in June 1916 and training at Mbagathi, was to incorporate Nos. 3 (" B ", " E ") and 4 (" G ", " H ") Coys.

Details as to 4th K.A.R. battalions:

1/4th and 2/4th : Nos. 1 to 4 Coys., still designated the 1/4th K.A.R., took part in the Iringa operations of December 1916.

On 1st February 1917 the 2/4th disembarked at Dar-es-Salaam. The original allocation of companies had meanwhile been altered as follows: 1/4th to consist of Nos. 2, 3, half No. 4 (" G ") Coys. 2/4th, on reaching Iringa, to incorporate Nos. 1, half No. 4 (" H ") Coys. with the newly-raised companies. The incoming portion (including Bn. H.Q.) of the 2/4th remained about Dodoma until May 1917, incidentally taking part on 24th February in the ceremonial handing-over of Tabora by the Belgians to the British.

Early in March 1917, H.Q. with 2½ Coys., 1/4th, were moved south from Iringa to reinforce Brig.-General Northey (see Vol. II), leaving 1½ Coys. still with the " Iringa column ". The companies

---

[1] Prior to this there had been no opportunity of training the 3/K.A.R. in the then comparatively recent formations of the four-company battalion organization.

thus left, already destined for the 2/4th, were now transferred to the latter battalion and remained about Iringa as a detachment from it until the H.Q. and remainder of the 2/4th reached Iringa on 18th May 1917.

The 1/4th was completed at Njombe on 1st May 1917 by a draft of 10 officers, 384 o.r., with 4 m.g.

3/4th: Raised 23rd January 1917; trained at Mbagathi; arrived at Lindi 21st July.

4/4th: Raised 1st May 1917; trained at Mbagathi until 9th August. On 10th August training was interrupted to send 480 recruits with 4 m.g., at two hours' notice to take part in the pursuit of Naumann. After Naumann's surrender on 1st October, training was resumed at Dodoma. Early in November the unit moved to Lindi, completing assembly there by the 16th. On 23rd January 1918 it moved to Portuguese East Africa.

5/4th: Raised 1st August 1917; trained at Mbagathi; moved to Portuguese East Africa August 1918.

6/4th: Raised 21st January 1918; became a training battalion at Mbagathi.

5th K.A.R.

Raised as one battalion (1/5th), 1st June 1916, with a depot based on Jubaland. Formed, in order to guard the northern frontier, from " F " (Camel), and half " G " Coys., of the original 3rd Bn. (q.v.), with companies of armed police and other details. Not further expanded.

6th K.A.R.

Raised April and May 1917 from recruits previously intended to form 4/ 5/ and 6/ battalions, 3rd K.A.R., with a considerable proportion of surrendered ex-German askari. In June 1917 a depot was formed at Tabora.

Details as to 6th K.A.R. battalions:

1/6th: Raised 1st June 1917; in general reserve July 1917. Moved to northern border early in 1918.

2/6th: Raised 1st August 1917; on garrison duties in occupied German territory.

7th K.A.R.

One battalion (1/7th) raised 1st May 1917 from the Zanzibar and Mafia Rifles, with recruits from coastal towns, to provide coastal garrisons, with a depot at Zanzibar.

In July 1917 moved from Zanzibar to Voi. From 1st August, employed as L. of C. and coastal garrison troops.

(iii) *Changes in Organization,* 1914-18.

The principal changes in organization made in the course of the campaign were as follows:

(1) The appointment of Inspector-General, K.A.R., ceased to exist in December 1914.

(2) Early in 1916 the K.A.R. units were removed from the control of the Protectorate governments (except to some extent in the case of Nyasaland, where conditions were exceptional) and became for all practical purposes a single force.

(3) During 1917 sanction was given to the appointment of a Commandant of the K.A.R. to control and supervise the whole force.[1] His duties included those of inspection formerly held by the Inspector-General, but, unlike the Inspector-General, he was also directly responsible to the Secretary of State for the Colonies for the administration of the force. With headquarters at Nairobi, he corresponded with the Secretary of State through the officer administering the Government of the East African Protectorate, and subsequently direct.

(4) A central K.A.R. headquarters staff was formed under the Commandant, consisting of an Assistant Commandant,[2] an A.A. & Q.M.G., D.A.A.G., and D.A.Q.M.G.

(5) Late in 1916 a large central training depot for officers and men was formed at Mbagathi, near Nairobi, where training of K.A.R. recruits had been carried out on a small scale since April of that year.

(6) Conditions of service throughout the K.A.R. were made uniform. Before the war the rates of pay of native soldiers had been different in the three battalions ; a universal rate was now fixed throughout the K.A.R. A scheme of disability compensation for native ranks was also instituted.

(7) The financial arrangements of the force were placed on a centralised basis. A separate account was established for the K.A.R., the Protectorate governments were relieved of the financial administration of their former units, and a new K.A.R. Pay Department was set up under a Chief Paymaster, K.A.R.

(8) The establishments of regiments and battalions were completely reorganised. The double-company system was introduced into each battalion, and considerable numbers of British N.C.Os. were appointed, who made excellent platoon sergeants and platoon commanders. Formerly there had been hardly any British N.C.Os. serving in the K.A.R.

---

[1] Colonel E. H. Llewellyn. This officer had been appointed to the C.-in-C's. staff in June 1916 to supervise the raising of the three new battalions then being recruited, with the status of a Commandant of a K.A.R. battalion. The rapid further expansion which followed was all effected under his supervision, and he came to be known by the unofficial title " Commandant of the K.A.R." given to him by Lieut.-General Smuts. In May 1917 representations by Lieut.-General Hoskins, then C.-in-C., led to recognition of Colonel Llewellyn's greatly increased responsibilities, as the result of which he was officially appointed as Commandant of the K.A.R. with the rank of Brig.-General, antedated to 1st Jan. 1917.

[2] Colonel G. F. Phillips.

U

(9) Special units and departments common to the whole force were either set up or their formation contemplated. Among these were :

Units raised :
   Signal Company . . . 3rd August 1917.
   Mounted Infantry Company . . . expanded from the original M.I. recruits of the 3rd Bn.

Units proposed :
   Intelligence Department.
   Artillery units.
   Sapper Company.
   Transport Service.
   Medical Department.
   Military Police.

(10) Recruiting for the K.A.R. was carried out throughout East and Central Africa on a centralised basis under a Chief Recruiting Officer, K.A.R., with a staff of K.A.R. recruiting officers.

(11) The conquest of German East Africa went far to centralize the force, since it opened up land connection between Uganda, the British East Africa Protectorate and Nyasaland, and threw open German East Africa itself as a recruiting and training ground. The 6th K.A.R., in particular, included many surrendered German askari.

(12) As will be seen below, the possibility of employing the K.A.R. in other theatres of war was under consideration at various stages of the campaign, and a definite scheme for the despatch of a K.A.R. contingent to Palestine was well in hand when hostilities came to an end.

(iv) *Proposed employment of the K.A.R. overseas*

The question whether formations of the K.A.R. might suitably be employed in theatres of war other than East Africa was first raised in a telegram from the C.I.G.S. to Lieut.-General Smuts on the 31st July 1916, in which information was requested under a comprehensive series of headings. Replying on the 12th September the Commander-in-Chief gave his views as follows :

As to numbers, although the native population was large, the great majority of the tribes were unwarlike and physically unfit for the hardships of the field. The warlike tribes in the interior about the great lakes had already been largely tapped by the Germans and to a lesser degree by the British.

Although the Germans had made great efforts to recruit and train large bodies of native troops for two years, not more than half their forces had attained a degree of efficiency which would fit them to face good European troops.

Lieut.-General Smuts considered it just possible to raise a maximum of three infantry brigades by voluntary enlistment. They would require one year's continuous hard training to be fit to take the field. The climate of Egypt and possibly Mesopotamia would suit them, and in fighting alongside white troops they would do well. At the same time it had to be borne in mind, he said, that German askari in the East African campaign had never ventured to face white troops in open terrain and their fine fighting qualities were displayed only in the bush. They might be useful in trenches, although their shooting had remained bad in spite of long training. He was doubtful whether even three brigades could be induced to volunteer for service outside East Africa, the natives generally having a horror of going overseas.[1]

The officer problem, as he saw it, presented great difficulties on linguistic and other grounds, and it would probably be necessary to obtain as many officers and non-commissioned officers as possible from East Africa.

With regard to rations, native food was very simple, consisting of meat, rice, fruit and mealies. The cost of the force would be low, although for overseas service rates of pay would have to be somewhat higher than in East Africa.

The C.-in-C. had no fear of political difficulties resulting from the raising of additional native troops, since only comparatively small numbers could be recruited and the absence of cohesion among the tribes minimised any risk from this source in the immediate future.

Lieut.-General Smuts ended with the suggestion that, if the Army Council considered a limited scheme on the above lines worth trying, at the conclusion of the East African campaign one brigade should be raised from trained ex-German askari, who in his view would impartially serve any master who fed and paid them ; another brigade from surplus Belgian askari, and a third from recruits then being trained for post-War service in East Africa. Those three brigades could take the field in reasonable time and could be maintained by drafts of fresh recruits.

Nothing further came of these proposals. During the ensuing twelve months the expansion of the King's African Rifles continued apace, and a year later the subject was re-opened by the C.I.G.S., who on the 5th October 1917 called for a report as to the value of the new battalions, to enable him to consider the

---

[1] This is hardly the case. The objection is not to going overseas but to cold climates, from which the natives have a great aversion. At the present day there is no difficulty in getting volunteers from Nyasaland troops for service with the Somaliland Camel Corps, travelling by sea to join.

possibility of using a contingent from them in another theatre of war.

Lieut.-General van Deventer, now Commander-in-Chief, in a prompt reply, said tersely that the K A R. would be of no use in Europe. " In East African warfare the best K.A.R. battalions " are equal to the best Indian regiments ". But to meet unfamiliar conditions in Egypt or Mesopotamia they would need six to eight months training. Most of the units were below strength and contained a large proportion of recruits, while a major difficulty (as Lieut.-General Smuts had also said) was the dearth of officers and N.C.Os. with experience and a knowledge of native languages. Recruiting on the whole was satisfactory and at the end of the campaign a good supply of recruits might be expected from the former German protectorate. Meanwhile he recommended that the K.A.R. should draw on the police of British East Africa and Uganda for veteran askari to serve as N.C.Os., replacing the police vacancies with K.A.R. recruits.

Here the matter rested until on the 16th January 1918 the C.I.G.S., wishing to form an East African overseas contingent without further delay, called for a detailed statement showing what could be provided towards two brigades with their ancillary units for this purpose.

Three days later Lieut.-General van Deventer replied that thirteen battalions were in the field, each about 600 strong ; that five more, each about 1,000, formed the garrison of German East Africa and held the northern frontier of British East Africa ; and that there were two training battalions.[1] On the cessation of local hostilities he proposed to re-organise the K.A.R. to provide two brigades, each of four battalions at full war establishment, for service overseas. Six battalions would form the local garrison in East Africa, and there would be four training battalions, with depots for each regiment. It was proposed, in view of the difficulties of shipping, that first re-inforcements of 30 (later 20) per cent. should accompany the overseas contingent. Lieut.-General van Deventer also emphasized that the necessary number of men would not be available earlier than eight months after the end of local hostilities, and even then not without difficulty, for the troops needed leave owing to war-weariness, and it was essential that they should be thoroughly trained before going overseas.

The C.I.G.S. expressed his concurrence generally with these views on the 31st January, directing that for the moment only such preliminary action should be taken as would not interfere with local operations. On the 23rd March the British Military Representative to the Supreme War Council at Versailles was

---

[1] The 4/2nd K.A.R. and the 6/4th K.A.R. had not yet been raised.

informed that, as soon as the situation in East Africa allowed, a force of K.A.R. would be formed for service in Palestine. Between July and September 1918 details were worked out between the G.O.C.-in-C., East Africa, the Colonial Office and the War Office. The scheme received final approval on the 26th September.

The detailed proposals were as follows :—

(1) *Overseas Contingent :*

(a) The first and second battalions of the 1st, 2nd, 3rd and 4th K.A.R. to form the King's African Rifles Expeditionary Force, organised as two infantry brigades, each of four battalions, viz.:

Central Africa Brigade   1/1st, 2/1st, 1/2nd, 2/2nd K.A.R.

East Africa Brigade   1/3rd, 2/3rd, 1/4th, 2/4th K.A.R.

(b) The third battalions of each of the first four regiments to become training battalions for the battalions of their respective regiments which were included in the contingent.

(c) The 4/1st, 4/2nd, 4/3rd and 6/4th K.A.R. to be incorporated in their respective regiments in order to bring the Overseas Contingent up to strength immediately.

(d) The Overseas Contingent and four training battalions to be concentrated at Mbagathi.

(e) Depots, for the collection of recruits and elementary training only, for the first four regiments to be at Zomba (1st and 2nd), Mbagathi (3rd) and Bombo (4th) respectively.

(f) Two machine gun companies to form part of the Overseas Contingent and a first re-inforcement of 20 per cent. to accompany the brigades when they left East Africa.

(2) *Garrisons :*

(i) It was considered desirable that for convenience of administration the garrison battalions and regiments which they formed should be kept separate, as far as possible, from the Overseas Contingent, owing to their different functions. They were to have separate depots, and probably different establishments.

(ii) It was therefore proposed :

    (a) The 1/5th and 1/6th K.A.R. to garrison the B.E.A. Protectorate and Uganda (including the Northern Frontier District and Turkana country).

    (b) The garrison of German East Africa and Zanzibar to be the 2/6th, 1/7th and 5/4th K.A.R., with the 4/4th K.A.R. stationed in German East Africa as a reserve.

In view of (i) above, it was proposed to re-number the 4/4th and 5/4th K.A.R. as the 1/8th and 2/8th K.A.R. respectively and to form a separate depot for the 8th K.A.R.

The advantage of this proposal was that the first four regiments would thus be entirely for overseas units and that the last four would be entirely for garrison units. The depots of the former would be for elementary training and the depots of the latter would be full depots.

The 1918 proposals, like those of 1916, were thus contingent on the cessation of hostilities in East Africa ; but they were not designed to come to fruition until some eight months after that event.[1] The collapse of the Central Powers which became apparent in October 1918 swept away all need to consider these plans further. At noon on the 31st October 1918 the Armistice with Turkey came into force, and on the 5th November Lieut.-General van Deventer was informed that the two brigades of the King's African Rifles were no longer required for service overseas.

V.

The K.A.R. after the Armistice

After the surrender of Colonel von Lettow-Vorbeck, which followed on the Armistice in Europe, it was decided that ten of the twenty-two battalions should be disbanded immediately, the establishment of the force being fixed provisionally at twelve battalions.[2]

Subsequently, as the result of discussion with the local Governments and the Commandant of the K.A.R., it was decided that the garrison of East Africa should, as from the 1st April 1919, consist of six battalions.

As a temporary measure, pending the settlement of trouble on the Abyssinian frontier, the 2/3rd K.A.R., 2/6th K.A.R. and K.A.R. Mounted Infantry were retained. By the end of April 1919 the local situation in British East Africa allowed of the disbandment of the 2/6th and of two of the four companies of the 2/3rd K.A.R. The disbandment of the remainder was approved in August 1919. The post-war garrison thus eventually came down to the 1st, 2nd, 3rd, 4th, 5th and 6th Battalions, K.A.R.

The appointments of Commandant of the K.A.R. and of his staff remained in being until the 1st October 1919, when they

---

[1] The fact that they were approved in these terms throws light on the expectations held in September 1918 as to the probable further duration of the War on the various fronts.

[2] A matter of some importance in connection with the disbandment of the K.A.R. units has been pointed out by a survivor. On demobilization the men had very large balances of pay to come to them, as they very rarely drew pay in the field. These balances were paid out in paper money instead of silver currency, owing to shortage of the latter. This the men were unable to understand, with the result that they felt that the Government had cheated them. The matter was aggravated by the fact that the Indian traders in the villages took advantage of these fears, demanding higher prices, showing an increase in some cases of as much as 50 per cent., if payment were made in paper currency. Eventually officers were sent into the districts to protect the discharged men's interests ; but not before considerable harm had been done.

were abolished, and that of Inspector-General of the K.A.R. was restored. The first holder of the new appointment was Brig.-General G. M. P. Hawthorn.

VI.

Tables

(i) Strength of the King's African Rifles at various periods from 1914 to 1919.[1]

Date	Officers	British N.C.Os.	Natives.	Proportion Europn. to Native, 1 in
			5	
Aug. 4, 1914	70	2	2,177	30
Jan. 1, 1915	100	2	3,325	33
July 1, 1915	129	2	3,883	30
Jan. 1, 1916	133	2	4,209	31
July 1, 1916	243	10	$8,15_4$	32
Jan. 1, 1917	380	50	$15,30^4$	$35\frac{1}{2}$
July 1, 1917	535	118	23,325	$35\frac{1}{2}$
Jan. 1, 1918	951	776	27,269	16
July 1, 1918	1,193	1,497	30,658	$11\frac{1}{2}$
Nov. 1, 1918	1,423	2,046	31,955	$9\frac{1}{4}$
Jan. 1, 1919	1,297	1,916	29,137	9

(ii) Casualties in the King's African Rifles during the East Africa campaign, 1914-18.[1]

	Killed.	Wounded.	Died of disease.	Total.
Officers	66	194	34	294
British N.C.Os.	47	50	30	100
Natives	1,195	3,553	3,039	7,795

(iii) Distribution of K.A.R. battalions, November 1918.

In the field :

With Western Force :
   1/1st, 2/1st and 3/1st K.A.R.
   1/4th and 2/4th K.A.R.

With Eastern Force :
   1/2nd, 2/2nd and 3/2nd K.A.R.
   1/3rd and 2/3rd K.A.R.
   3/4th and 4/4th K.A.R.

[1] Tables (i) and (ii) are based on a telegram dated 14 Feb., 1919 from Commandant K.A.R., to Secretary of State for the Colonies.

<table>
<tr><td>On garrison duties :</td><td>Training battalions :</td></tr>
</table>

On garrison duties :	*Training battalions :*
German East Africa :	4/1st K.A.R...Zomba
3/3rd K.A.R.	4/2nd K.A.R...Mbagathi
5/4th K.A.R.	4/3rd K.A.R...Nairobi
2/6th K.A.R.	6/4th K.A.R...Mbagathi
1/7th K.A.R.	
British East Africa :	
(Northern Fronti :)	
1/5th K.A.R.	
1/6th K.A.R.	

APPENDIX V

THE GERMAN DEFENCE FORCE IN EAST AFRICA

The Defence Force (*Schutztruppe*) of the German Protectorate, like the King's African Rifles, originated from disbanded Sudanese soldiers of the Egyptian Army. In 1888-9, when as the result of the so-called Arab revolt[1] the German Chartered Company had lost its hold of the entire territory except the ports of Bagamoyo and Dar-es-Salaam, Captain Hermann von Wissmann, already celebrated as an explorer, was commissioned by the German Government to raise a force to put down the Arabs. It being manifestly impossible to recruit any such force locally, Wissmann had recourse to Egypt, where the British withdrawal from the Sudan in 1886 had led to the disbandment of several Sudanese units of the Egyptian Army. Some of the disbanded Sudanese, fine fighting men, enlisted willingly in Cairo for the new service, and arrived at Bagamoyo in May 1889.[2] There they were organized into six companies of infantry, together with an additional company formed of 100 Ngoni of Zulu origin recruited in Portuguese East Africa, at a total strength of about 850, with 25 officers and 63 German non-commissioned officers.

With this force Wissmann attacked the " Arab " force blockading Bagamoyo, stormed its camp with slight loss, and scattered it in all directions. An advance along the coast followed. Sadani, Pangani and Tanga were captured, and the coast occupied as far as the Umba river. The Arab leader, Bushiri, who had been guilty of many atrocities, was eventually caught and hanged. In the following year (1890) the southern coast and the Kilimanjaro area were occupied after some minor engagements.

---

[1] The Arab revolt was so termed because it was instigated and aided by the Arabs, although the " Arab " force, about 800 in all, seems to have included many coastal Africans, now generally termed " Swahilis."

[2] Their enlistment was facilitated by the British Government, which permitted the recruitment of these Sudanese in Egypt, and allowed them to camp for four weeks at Aden while awaiting transport to East Africa.

In 1891 the Defence Force was formally recognised by the Imperial government and designated *Kaiserliche Schutztruppe*. It was now re-organised in ten companies, viz., four mobile, four for the coastal garrisons of Tanga, Bagamoyo, Dar-es-Salaam, Kilwa and Lindi,[1] and two recruit companies.

A beginning was made of the enrolment of local recruits, who were also employed in the armed police force which was formed in the following year at a strength of 10 Europeans, 6 native officers and 415 African ranks. Later (1894–95) the Defence Force was increased to twelve companies by absorbing the native officers and 252 other ranks of the police.

Meanwhile the new troops had been taught a stern lesson in bush warfare by the warlike Wahehe, who had adopted the weapons and tactics of the conquering Zulus farther south. A German column about 400 strong under Kommandeur von Zelewski, moving from Kilwa towards Iringa, was surprised on the march, rushed from the flank by a horde of spearmen many times its number, and virtually annihilated. Only a small rear-guard with one white officer succeeded in disengaging from the fight and withdrawing in good order.[2]

Taught by this disaster, the German troops evolved a suitable system of bush tactics, and their subsequent operations were uniformly successful. Some sharp actions round Moshi and Tabora[3] were followed by a campaign which broke the forces of the Wahehe, whose chief village, Kuirenga (Old Iringa), was stormed by a German force of five companies, with three guns, in October 1894.

In the southern area of the German sphere of influence the Arab slave-trade was still active, and it was decided to place an armed vessel on Lake Nyasa to put it down. The necessary funds were raised by the German Anti-Slavery Society by public subscription in Germany, and a small steamer, named " Hermann von Wissmann " after the German commander, was placed on

---

[1] The inland garrisons of the German Force at this period were Mpwapwa and Tabora, Masindi and Moshi in the Kilimanjaro district, Mwanza and Bukoba on Lake Victoria.

[2] The German column consisted of three companies (two Sudanese, one Ngoni Zulu) with one gun and two m.g. The Wahehe were stated to be more than 3,000 strong. Apparently the German column was marching in single file along a bush track with no flank-guard out, the men's rifles were not loaded, and the Wahehe, lying in ambush, charged so quickly that no effective defence was possible. The rear-guard, when it reached safety, mustered only 4 Europeans and 62 askari out of a previous total of 14 Europeans, 362 askari. This fight was officially recorded as the worst defeat suffered by German troops in East Africa prior to the War of 1914–18. An imposing memorial was afterwards erected on the scene of the affair, at Rugaro, near Iringa.

[3] Also operations against the Wagogo tribe near Dodoma, in which Lieutenant (afterwards Captain) Tom von Prince first made his reputation. Prince was killed on 4th November 1914, in the action at Tanga.

Lake Nyasa in September 1893[1]. In the course of operations against tribes in the Songea area between 1891 and 1895 tactics and organization suitable to the country were gradually perfected, and in the light of this experience it was decided to retain an organization of separate independent companies. As the occupation proceeded, it became possible to recruit among the tribes which had submitted, notably the Wanyamwezi round Tabora, the Ngoni of the south, the Wasukuma and Manyema. These gradually replaced the Sudanese in the ranks, the latter becoming N.C.Os.

From 1895 onwards for about ten years ensued a period of comparative peace, during which German authority was extended to the fullest limits of the prescribed sphere of influence, garrisons being established at Ujiji in 1896, at Usumbura in 1897, at Bismarckburg in 1898 and at Kisenyi in 1899. The slow but steady progress made during these years was sharply interrupted in 1905 by a revolt, known as the Maji-Maji rebellion, which broke out among the tribes in the hinterland of Kilwa and spread rapidly over the whole southern area of the German Protectorate. The Defence Force, numbering at the outset about 1,700, backed by about 650 armed police, was hard put to it to stem the rising, which spread northward until Dar-es-Salaam, Morogoro and Kilosa were all seriously threatened. The rebels' main concentration was in the valley of the Ruaha about Kidatu, whence they were eventually driven south, but the isolated German garrison of Mahenge was blockaded for several weeks before being relieved. Fighting continued during 1906 ; but by the end of that year the revolt had been crushed, except in the vicinity of Songea, where the last bands of rebels were hunted down early in 1907.[2]

During this rebellion more troops had been raised, partly from tribes in the north of the protectorate, partly in Italian Somaliland, and the field forces were increased from 12 companies

[1] The German flag had appeared on Lake Nyasa for the first time when it was hoisted at Lumbira Bay (Alt Langenburg) on the Kaiser's birthday in January 1892.

[2] The Maji-Maji rebellion was so named from the Swahili word *maji*, meaning water. The tribes were incited by medicine-men to believe that possession of a certain medicine rendered a warrior invulnerable by bullets, which would turn to water. The revolt was in several respects an astonishing example of fanatical native mass-psychology, successfully worked up against Europeans on the basis of this belief. Contrary to expectation, many normally peaceable tribes rose in concerted action, while the more warlike tribes remained quiet. The revolt was finally quelled by extensive and merciless destruction of crops and villages, with consequent famine and disease, the number who died in the rising and as a result of it being estimated at over 100,000.

The German casualties during the 18 months' operations are said to have been 73 killed, 98 wounded, 70 missing. See Sayers, " Handbook " of Tanganyika ", pp. 72–5.

to 15, the establishment of officers being raised from 47 to 79. The years which followed, however, were peaceful, and in 1909 the Defence Force was reduced by one unit to the total of 14 companies at which it stood until the outbreak of war, with a corresponding increase in the native police. This measure was viewed with disfavour by the military authorities ; for, although the police force was armed, its military training was rudimentary and its administration was entirely under civil control.[1]

In 1914 the establishment of the German Defence Force was 68 German combatant officers,[2] 60 warrant officers and N.C.Os., 132 German medical and non-combatant officers and officials, 2 African officers, 184 African N.C.Os. and 2,286 askari ; total 260 Germans, 2,472 Africans. This somewhat exceeded the establishment of the King's African Rifles[3] ; but there is no evidence that the size of either force was based on any other considerations than those of internal security.

In its organization the German Defence Force resembled the King's African Rifles in that it was administered by authorities at the German Colonial Office and was directly under the control of the civil Governor of the protectorate. The two forces differed, however, in that the King's African Rifles had no centralized command and no headquarters in Africa, their three battalions being administered by different Protectorates, with an Inspector-General in London ; whereas the German Defence Force had at its head a commander permanently in the country.

His powers, it is true, were not in theory extensive, and he was subordinate to the civil Governor in all questions of defence ; but his rank made it possible, nevertheless, for his advice to carry weight.

In January 1914 this appointment was taken over by Lieut.-Colonel von Lettow-Vorbeck, a Prussian officer of varied

---

[1] " There prevailed a constant tendency to increase this police force " more and more, to the detriment of the Defence Force. In this manner " alongside the latter a second force of the same strength had come into " being which was in its very nature a travesty of a military organiza- " tion . . . . The Police askari often became slack and lacked the strict " discipline necessary . . . . To this was added a further defect which " ought to have been avoided. The police were partly recruited from " the native N.C.Os. of the Defence Force. The latter was thereby " deprived of its best elements, who, after joining the police, lost their " good military qualities ". Lettow, " My Reminiscences ", pp. 6–7.

[2] A commandant with one staff officer, 17 captains, 49 subalterns. Officers were selected from the German regular forces at home and were appointed for 2½ years ; but in practice this term was repeatedly extended. Thus of the officers who subsequently distinguished themselves in the war, Captain Kornatski had served continuously with the force since 1902, Schulz since 1903, Otto since 1904, Wintgens since 1905, Langenn-Steinkeller and Stemmermann since 1908.

[3] 2,397 in all ; see Appendix IV. The K.A.R., however, was spread over three territories.

experience, who had qualified at the Staff College, had served both in China during the " Boxer " revolt of 1900 and in South-West Africa in the Herero campaign, and had subsequently commanded the 2nd Marine Battalion at Wilhelmshafen after employment on the staff of a corps. From the moment of his arrival this officer, a commander of outstanding military capacity and personality, devoted himself to an active study of the potentialities of the armed forces of the protectorate. As a soldier he quickly formed views in which he did not, as he puts it, " succeed in interesting the authorities " ; holding to them nevertheless, he spent the first months of his command in extensive reconnaissance and inspection throughout the protectorate, took in hand the reorganisation and re-armament[1] of units, and busied himself, notwithstanding a dearth of official encouragement, in increasing the efficiency of his men. Their performance under his command during the campaign of 1914-18 bore ample testimony to his abilities alike as a trainer of troops and a determined leader in war.

APPENDIX VI

GERMAN UNITS AND FORMATIONS: ORGANIZA-
TION AND DESIGNATIONS

The organization of the units of the German Defence Force after mobilization was peculiar to this campaign and calls for brief explanation.

The independent regular companies in which the German Defence Force was organized were usually sub-divided into 3 " platoons " (Züge) each about 60 strong, with a total per company of about 16 to 20 German officers and N.C.Os., about 200 askari, with 2 or more machine guns. They acted as self-contained mobile tactical units, each with its own supply and transport organization, including as a rule some 250 carriers. When in the field they included, besides their regular personnel, a fluctuating number of irregular native auxiliaries (ruga-ruga) armed with firearms or spears. A proportion also of the enlisted carriers, notably those selected for the machine guns, were uniformed and armed. The total ration strength of such a unit, complete with irregulars and carriers, was usually well over 400 of all ranks and at times much higher.

---

[1] Up to the time of Lettow's first inspection only three units had modern rifles ; three more were then re-armed. " It subsequently " became a factor of the greatest importance that at any rate these arms, " with the necessary ammunition, reached the Colony just in time for " the outbreak of war ". Lettow, op. cit., p. 13.

The term adopted by the Germans shortly before 1914 for this type of unit was *Feldkompagnie* (abbreviated *F.K.*). In order to avoid confusion with the normal " Field Company " (abbreviated " Fd. Coy.") of the British Army—a unit of the Royal Engineers—the German term and abbreviation have been used unchanged in the text wherever this has been conveniently possible.

A second type of unit raised by the Germans after mobilization was termed *Schützenkompagnie* (" Sharpshooter Company "). The term *Schützen* was derived from the German regular army, in which certain regiments and battalions so designated[1] corresponded more or less with the " Rifle " corps of the British Army ; but to translate *Schützenkompagnie* by " Rifle Company " would be likewise confusing, since the latter term has now a definite technical significance. The German designation and its abbreviation—*Sch. K.*—have therefore been retained in the text.

In a few instances a third type of unit, the " Reserve Company ", will be found mentioned. For this the German abbreviation *Res. K.* has been used.

The miscellaneous artillery of the Defence Force, for the most part light 3.7 cm. field guns, was as a rule allotted to companies and had no separate organization.

As the campaign progressed and the German units increased in number, it became usual for several companies to be grouped for operations under one named commander, the group, or *Abteilung*,[2] being designated for the time being by his name : e.g., *Abteilung Schulz*, *Abteilung Kraut*, etc. These were, however, only temporary formations, companies being transferred from one *Abteilung* to another as required. The term therefore corresponded in practice to the British term " Force "—as in " Northey's Force ". The German term has been retained in the text whenever possible.

---

[1] For example, the Guard *Schützen Battalion*, which was heavily engaged against the British 3rd Division in the Battle of the Marne, 1914. the " Military Operations : France & Belgium 1914 ", Vol. I.

[2] In the German regular army this term is used in two different senses : (*a*) a detachment, (*b*) a subdivision of a large unit ; for example an *Abteilung* of an Artillery Regiment is equivalent to a British regiment (formerly " brigade ") of artillery, a German Regiment of Artillery being equivalent to the Divisional Artillery group of the British organization.

GENERAL INDEX

A.

Abdul Rahman, Jemadar, 86
Abercorn, defence of, 176–8
Adamaster (Portuguese cr.), 389
Adjutant (German S.S.), 434
Adler, Capt., 104, 250, 257, 262
Admiralty, refuses to ratify local naval truce, 21 ; institutes blockade, 135 ; organization of naval flotillas, L. Victoria, 149, L. Tanganyika, **192** ; 101, 162, 163, 504
Adye, Lieut.-Col. D. R., in command of Lake Force, 404 ; Ukerewe Island operations, 409–13 ; in command Eastern Lake area, 422–3, 459
Aga Khan, 131
Air, arrival of R.N.A.S. squadron, 216 ; reconnaissances, 230, 240, 255, 291, 295, 300, 303, 328, 346, 351, 381 ; reinforcements, 266, 285 ; bombing, 295 ; defective machines, 311
Aitken, Major-Gen. A. E., appointed to command I.E.F. " B ", 61–2, 63 ; instructions to, 61, 65–7, 97 ; 69, 71 ; assumes command in B.E.A., 73 ; protests against local naval truce, 74 ; orders for attack on Tanga, 74 ; arrival 75 ; baulked of surprise, 76, 77 ; action at Tanga, 83, 84–103 ; diverts attack, 90 ; efforts to rally troops, 91 ; decides against night attack, 92 ; orders withdrawal, 92 ; report to Government, 100, 108, 111 ; exonerated by Parliament, 101 ; 110 ; succeeded in command, 117.
Alexandre Delcommune (Belgian S.S.), disabled, 28, 55–6, 192
Alt Langenberg, occupied, 471
Ames, Major C. G., 89
Ammunition, German replenishment, 154, 162 ; Belgian lack of, 201 ; reserves and supply, 217 ; expended at Kahe, 257, at Kondea Irangi, 280, at Mkalamo, 297

Animals, effects of climate on, *see* Climate
Arabs, early settlement in East Africa, 1 ; use of, by British and Germans, 19, 33
Armoured cars, 217, 230, 277, 285, 329, 351
Artillery, non-existent in Aug. 1914, 19 ; reinforcements from India, 31, 47, 68 ; naval, 72, 220–1, 436, 442, 445, 459 ; at Tanga, 84, 88–9, 94 ; reinforcements from S. Africa, 164, 215 ; position in Jan. 1916, 219–21
Asquith, Rt. Hon. H. H. (Prime Minister), 30
Assouan (Brit. troopship), 72
Astraea (Brit. L. Cr.), raid on Dar-es-Salaam, 20, 55 ; 74
Athi river, German secret camp on, 148
Attenborough, Commander F. L., R.N., 19
Augar, Capt., 261
Aumann, Lieut., 174, 465
Auracher, Dr., 76, 103–5

B.

Bagamoyo, capture of, 378, 379–81
Bailey, Lieut.-Col C., 71
Baldamus, Lieut., 385
Ball, Capt., L. P, 313
Barjora (Brit. troopship), 94–5, 121, 124–5, 387
Barrow, Gen. Sir Edmund (Mil. Sec., India Office), 30, 64, 100
Barton, Capt. C. W., 168, 171–4
Batusi tribe, 26 ; revolt, 49 ; 403, 408
Baumstark, Major, 47–8, 56, 59, 73, 103–6, 261
Baxendale, Major W., 502–4
Baxter, Major, 476–8
Bayonet, actions, 244, 245, 305, 367 ; importance of, 517
Beaumont, Capt. C. N., 470
Bees attack troops, 87, 252, 366
Belfield, Sir Henry (Gov. B.E.A.), 18, 29, 66, 73, 100, 109, 130, 210

583

INDEX TO ARMS, FORMATIONS, AND UNITS

(53912) Wt. 2639 1,500 8/41 Hw. G.34   S.O. Code No. 70-378-1

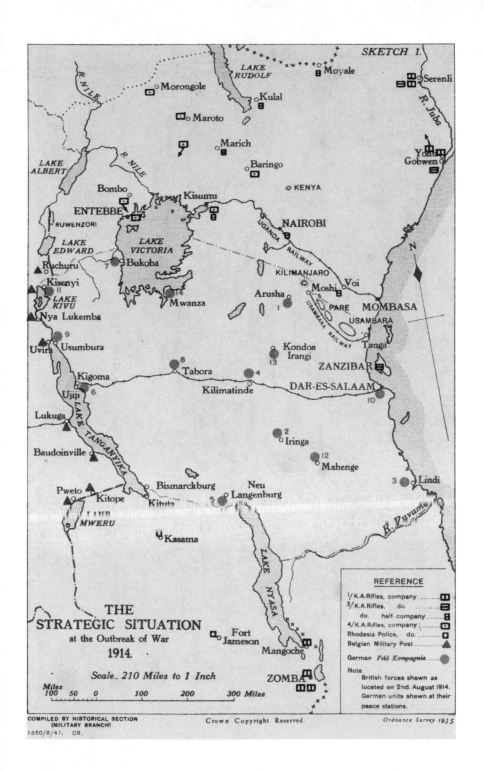

SKETCH 1.

R. NILE

LAKE RUDOLF

○ Morongole

○ Moyale

□□ Serenli

R. JUBA

○ Kulal

○ Maroto

○ Marich

□

□ Yonte
□ Gobwen

□ Baringo

LAKE ALBERT

R. NILE

Bombo

ENTEBBE

RUWENZORI

LAKE EDWARD

○ Kisumu

□

✧ KENYA

LAKE VICTORIA

○ Bukoba

NAIROBI

UGANDA RAILWAY

KILIMANJARO

N

▲ Ruchuru

▲ Kisenyi 11

LAKE KIVU

7

Mwanza

14

Arusha

1

☀ Moshi

PARE

○ Voi

USAMBARA RAILWAY

MOMBASA

USAMBARA

▲ Nya Lukemba

9

Tanga

▲ Uvira Usumbura

Kigoma

8 Tabora

Kilimatinde 4

Kondoa Irangi

13

ZANZIBAR

DAR-ES-SALAAM

▲ Ujiji 6

LAKE TANGANYIKA

10

▲ Lukuga

2
Iringa

▲ Baudoinville

12
Mahenge

Bismarckburg

Neu
Langenburg

3 ○ Lindi

▲ Pweto Kitope
Kituta

LAKE MWERU

R. RUVUMA

○ Kasama

LAKE NYASA

THE
STRATEGIC SITUATION
at the Outbreak of War
1914.

Scale_ 210 Miles to 1 Inch

□ Fort
Jameson

Mangoche

ZOMBA

Miles
100 50 0   100   200   300 Miles

REFERENCE

¹/K.A.Rifles, company .... □□
³/K.A.Rifles, do. .... □
    do. half-company.... □
⁴/K.A.Rifles, company.... □
Rhodesia Police, do. .... □
Belgian Military Post .... ▲
German *Feld Kompagnie*..... ●

Note.
    British forces shewn as
    located on 2nd. August 1914.
    German units shewn at their
    peace stations.

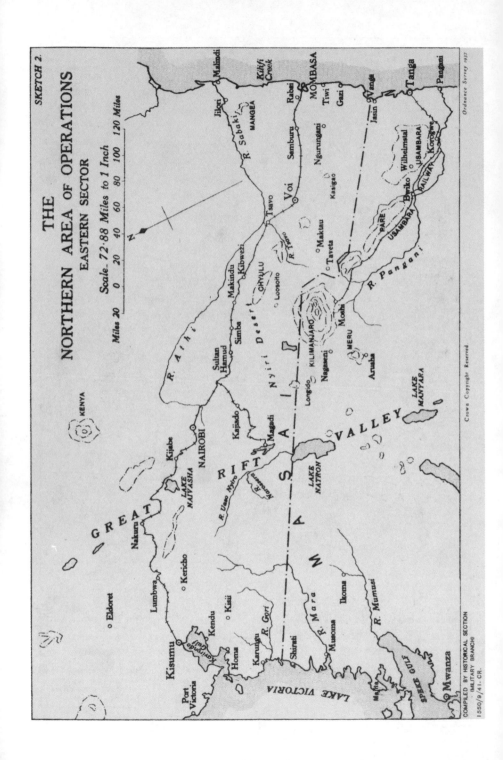

SKETCH 2.

THE
NORTHERN AREA OF OPERATIONS
EASTERN SECTOR

Scale_ 72·88 Miles to 1 Inch

Miles 20   0   20   40   60   80   100   120 Miles

Ordnance Survey 1937

Crown Copyright Reserved

COMPILED BY HISTORICAL SECTION
(MILITARY BRANCH)
1550/9/41. CR.

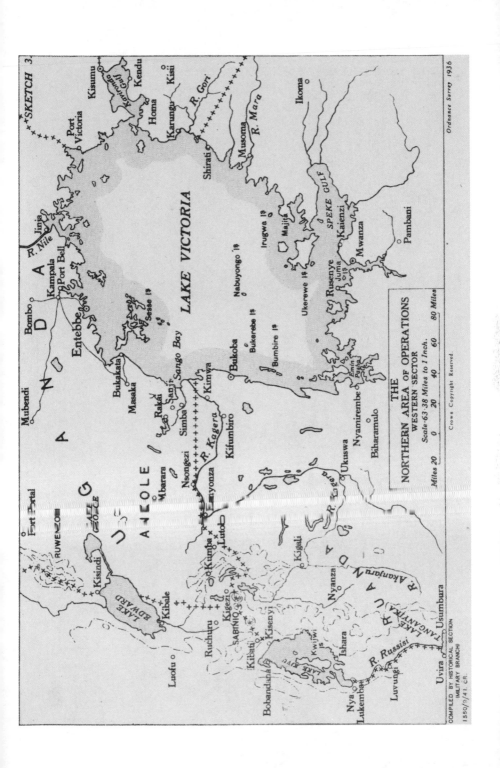

SKETCH 3.

THE
NORTHERN AREA OF OPERATIONS
WESTERN SECTOR
Scale—63.38 Miles to 1 Inch.

Miles 20   0   20   40   60   80 Miles

Crown Copyright Reserved.

Ordnance Survey 1936

COMPILED BY HISTORICAL SECTION
(MILITARY BRANCH)
1550/9/41. CR.

LAKE VICTORIA

UGANDA

ANKOLE

RUANDA

Fort Portal
Mubendi
Bombo
Kampala
Port Bell
Entebbe
Jinja
R. Nile
Port Victoria
Kisumu
Kendu
Homa
Karungu
Kisii
R. Gori
R. Mara
Musoma
Shirati
Ikoma
Bukakata
Masaka
Sango Bay
Sesse I?
Rakai
Sanjir
Simba
Kifumbiro
Nsongezi
Mbarara
Nyonza
R. Kagera
Kimwa
Bukoba
Nabuyongo I?
Bukerebe I?
Bumbire I?
Irugwe I?
Majita
Ukerewe I?
Rusenye
Juma
Emin Pasha
Nyamirembe
Biharamlo
Ukuswa
Nyanza
R. Engeo
Akanyaru
Kigali
Luto
Kiumba
Kigezi
SABINIO
Kisenyi
Ruchuru
Kibale
Kibati
Kwijwi I?
Ishara
Nya Lukemba
Luvungi
Uvira
Usumbura
R. Russisi
LAKE EDWARD
LAKE KIVU
LAKE TANGANYIKA
RUWENZORI
RU-GE-GE
SPEKE GULF
Mwanza
Kaienzi
Pambani
Kisindi
Luofu
Bobandiaha
Kavirondo Gulf
Port Victoria

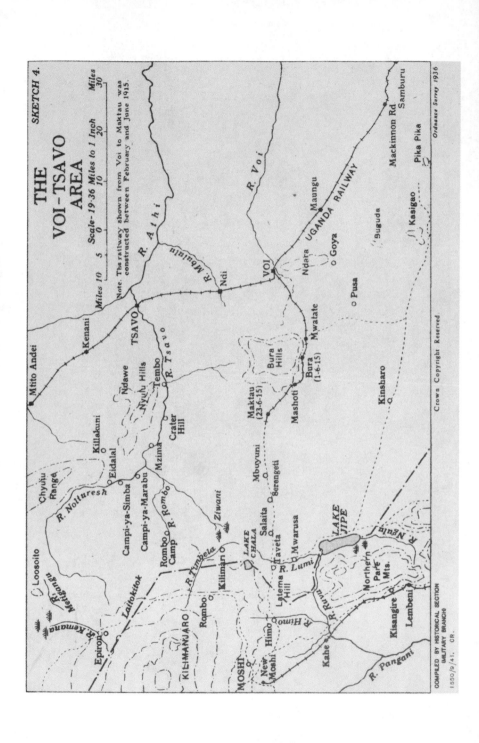

SKETCH 4.

THE
VOI-TSAVO
AREA

Scale-19·36 Miles to 1 Inch

Miles 10 5 0 10 20 30 Miles

Note. The railway shown from Voi to Maktau was
constructed between February and June 1915.

Ordnance Survey 1936

COMPILED BY HISTORICAL SECTION
(MILITARY BRANCH)

1850/9/41. OR.

Loosoito
R. Kemana
R. Metianga
Epirori
Chyulu Ranga
R. Nolturesh
Laitokitok
KILIMANJARO
Rombo
R. Timbela
Kilimani
R. Himo
New Moshi
MOSHI
Kahe
R. Himo
R. Ruvu
LAKE CHALA
Taveta
R. Lumi
Latema Hill
Mwarusa
LAKE JIPE
R. Njuru
Northern Pare Mts.
Kisangire
Lembeni
R. Pangani

Mtito Andei
Kenani
Killakuni
Eidalal
Campi-ya-Simba
Campi-ya-Marabu
Rombo Camp
R. Rombo
Ziwani
Mzima
Crater Hill
Tembo
Nyuhu Hills
Ndawe
TSAVO
R. Tsavo
Mbuyuni
Serengeti
Salaita
Ndi
R. Athi
R. Mbulutu
R. Voi
VOI
Ndara
Goya
Suguda
Kasigao
UGANDA RAILWAY
Mackinnon Rd
Pika Pika
Samburu
Maungu
Pusa
Mwatate
Bura Hills
Bura (1-6-15)
Maktau (23-6-15)
Mashoti
Kinsharo

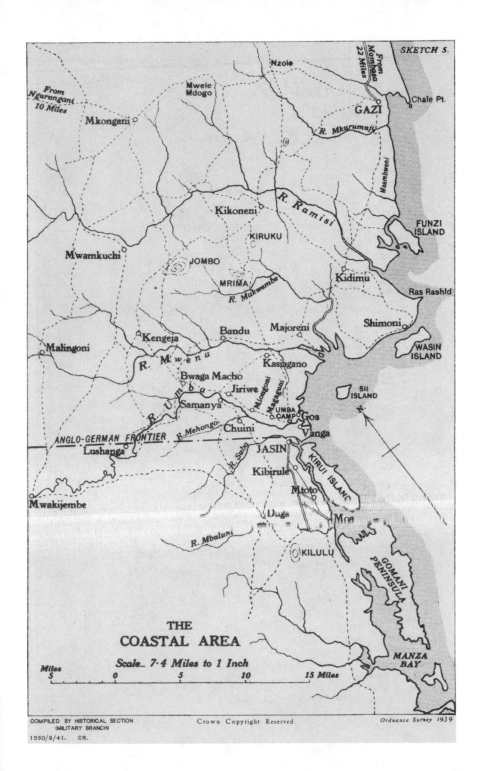

From Mombasa 22 Miles

Chale Pt.

GAZI

R. Mkurumuji

Nzole

Mwele Mdogo

From Ngurungani 10 Miles

Mkongani

Maambweni

R. Ramisi

FUNZI ISLAND

Kikoneni

KIRUKU

Mwamkuchi

JOMBO

Kidimu

Ras Rashid

MRIMA

R. Makwambe

Malingoni

Kengeja

Bandu

Majoreni

Shimoni

WASIN ISLAND

R. Mwena

Kasiagano

Bwaga Macho

Jiriwe

SII ISLAND

U m b a

Mloogoni

Mageani

Samanya

UMBA CAMP

Goa

N.

ANGLO-GERMAN FRONTIER

R. Mehongo

Chuini

Vanga

R. Umba

Lushanga

JASIN

KIRUI ISLAND

R. Sabo

Kibirule

Mwakijembe

Mtoto

GOMANI PENINSULA

Duga

Moa

R. Mbuluni

KILULU

MANZA BAY

THE
COASTAL AREA

Scale_ 7·4 Miles to 1 Inch

Miles
5   0   5   10   15 Miles

COMPILED BY HISTORICAL SECTION
(MILITARY BRANCH)
1550/9/41.   CR.

Ordnance Survey 1939

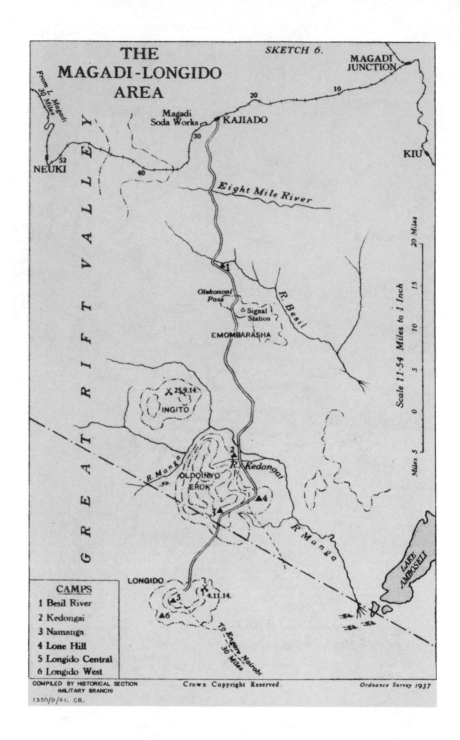

THE
MAGADI-LONGIDO
AREA

SKETCH 6.

MAGADI
JUNCTION

From L. Magadi
30 Miles

20

10

Magadi
Soda Works   KAJIADO

30

KIU

52
NEUKI   40

Eight Mile River

20 Miles

15

Scale 11·54 Miles to 1 Inch

10

5

Miles 5   0

●1

*Olokononi
Pass*

△ Signal
Station

R. Besil

EMOMBARASHA

✕ 25.9.14

INGITO

2

▲

R. Kedongai

R. Manga

OLDOINYO
EROK

▲4

3 ▲

R. Manga

LONGIDO

▲5   4.11.14.

▲6

*To Engera Nairobi
30 Miles*

LAKE
AMBOSELI

CAMPS
1 Besil River
2 Kedongai
3 Namanga
4 Lone Hill
5 Longido Central
6 Longido West

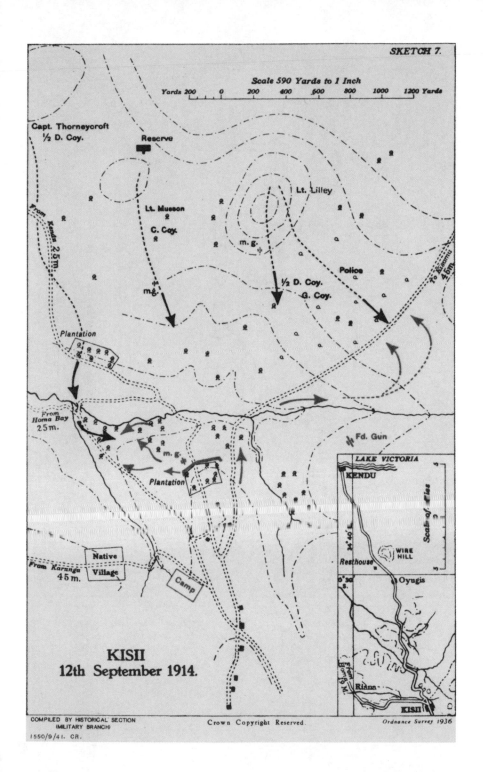

SKETCH 7.

Scale 590 Yards to 1 Inch

Yards 200   0   200   400   600   800   1000   1200 Yards

Capt. Thorneycroft
½ D. Coy.

Reserve

Lt. Lilley

Lt. Musson
C. Coy.

m. g.

½ D. Coy.
G. Coy.

Police

From Kendu 25 m.

To Kisumu 46 m.

m. g.

Plantation

From Homa Bay
25 m.

Fd. Gun

m. g.

Plantation

Native
Village

Camp

From Karungu
45 m.

KISII
12th September 1914.

LAKE VICTORIA

KENDU

WIRE
HILL

Resthouse

Scale of Files

Oyugis

34° 40' E.

0° 30' S.

Riana

KISII

COMPILED BY HISTORICAL SECTION
(MILITARY BRANCH)

1550/9/41. CR.

Crown Copyright Reserved.

Ordnance Survey 1936

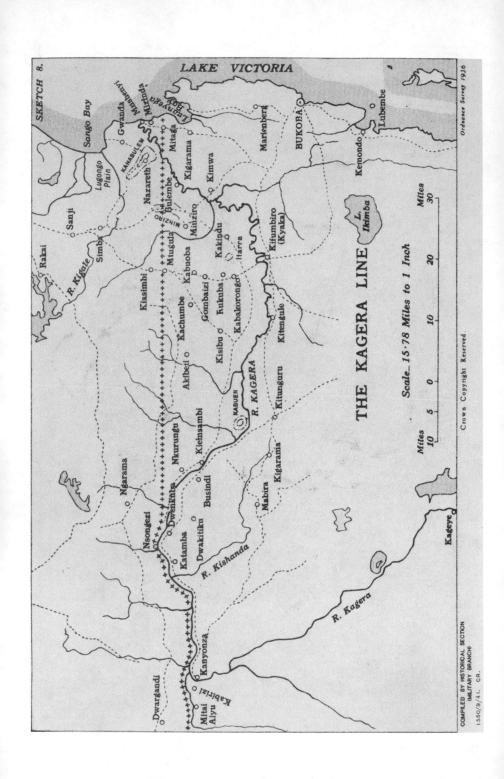

SKETCH 8.

LAKE VICTORIA

THE KAGERA LINE

Scale — 15·78 Miles to 1 Inch

Mites 10 5 0 10 20 30 Miles

COMPILED BY HISTORICAL SECTION
(MILITARY BRANCH)
1.550/9/41. GR.

Ordnance Survey 1936

Crown Copyright Reserved

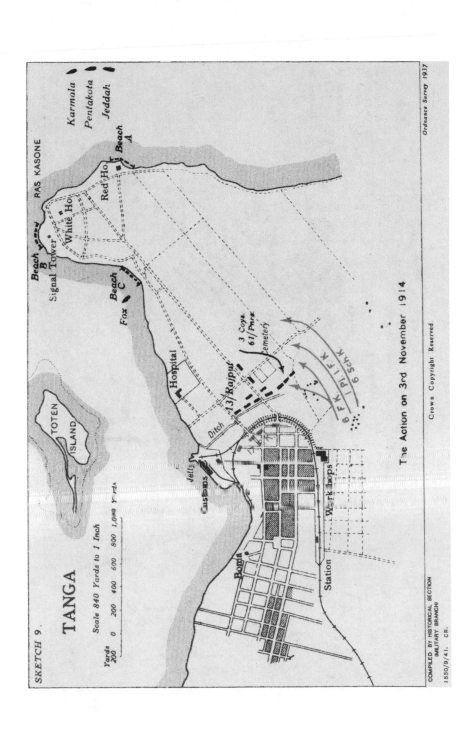

SKETCH 9.

TANGA

Scale 840 Yards to 1 Inch

Yards 200 0 200 400 600 800 1,000 Yards

RAS KASONE

Karmala
Pentakota
Jeddah

Beach A

Red Ho

White Ho

Signal Tower

Beach B

Beach C

Fox

TOTEN ISLAND

Hospital

Ditch

13/Rajput

3 Coys. 61/Pion.

Cemetery

6 F.K. 1 Pl. F.K.
6 Sch.K.

Jetty

Customs

Boma

Station

Workshops

The Action on 3rd November 1914

Ordnance Survey 1937

Crown Copyright Reserved

COMPILED BY HISTORICAL SECTION
(MILITARY BRANCH)

1850/9/41. CR.

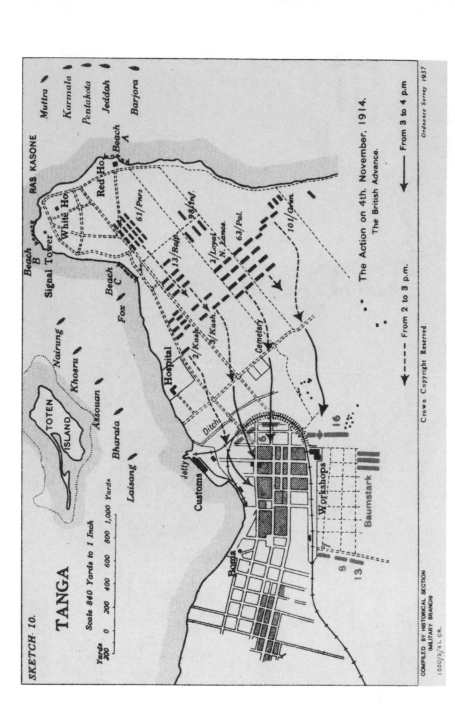

SKETCH. 10.

TANGA

Scale 840 Yards to 1 Inch

Yards
200 0 200 400 600 800 1,000 Yards

RAS KASONE

Beach B
Signal Tower
White Ho
Red Ho
Beach A

Muttra
Karmala
Pentakota
Jeddah
Barjora

Nairung
Khosru

TOTEN
ISLAND

Assouan
Bharata
Laisang

61/Pns
98/Inf.
13/Rajp.
2/Loyal.
N. Lanca.
63/Pal.
101/Gren.

Beach C
Fox

Hospital
2/Kash.
3/Kash.
2/Kash.

Cemetery

Ditch

Jetty
Customs

Bomu

Workshops
Baumstark

16
6
7
8
13

The Action on 4th. November, 1914.
The British Advance.

● ● ● From 2 to 3 p.m.   From 3 to 4 p.m.

━━━━ From 3 to 4 p.m

Ordnance Survey 1937

COMPILED BY HISTORICAL SECTION
(MILITARY BRANCH)

1550/9/41. CR.

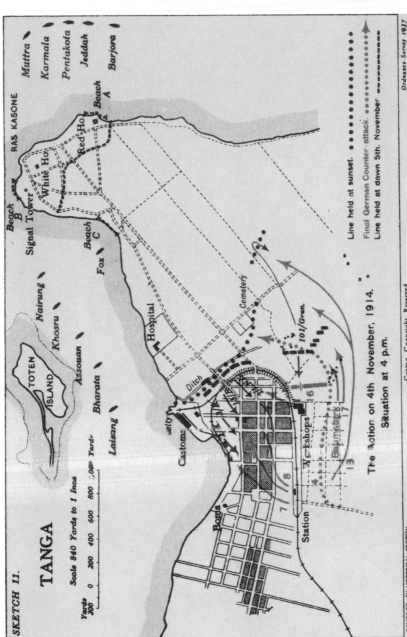

SKETCH 11.

TANGA

Scale 880 Yards to 1 Inch

Yards
200 0   200 400 600 800 ...0 Yards

Muttra
Karnala
Pentakota
Jeddah
Barjora

RAS KASONE

Beach B
Signal Tower
White Ho.
Red Ho.
Beach A

Beach C
Fox

Nairung
Khosru
Assouan
Bharata
Laisang

TOTEN ISLAND

Hospital

Cemetery

101/Gren.

Ditch

Customs

Boma

Workshops

Station

Line held at sunset. •••••••••

Final German Counter-attack. ••••••••••

Line held at dawn 5th. November. ▬▬▬▬▬

The Action on 4th November, 1914.
Situation at 4 p.m.

Crown Copyright Reserved.

Ordnance Survey 1937.

COMPILED BY HISTORICAL SECTION
(MILITARY BRANCH)
1550/2/44. GR.

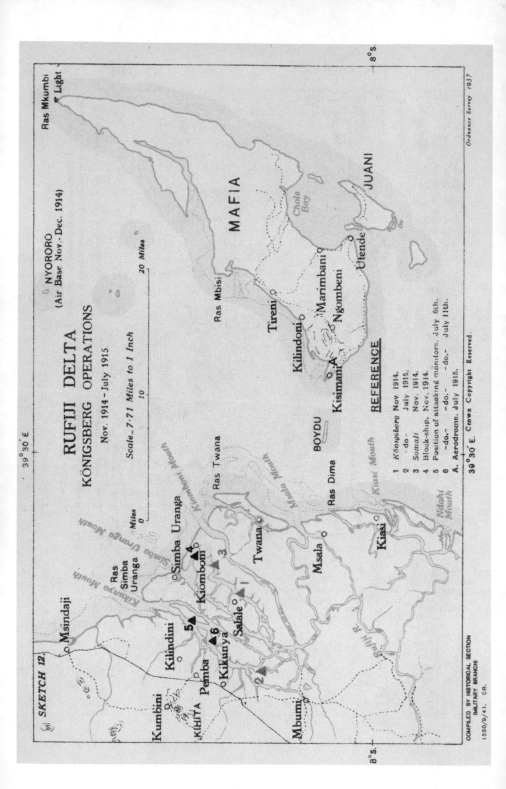

(o) SKETCH 12.

39°30′E.

RUFIJI DELTA
KÖNIGSBERG OPERATIONS
Nov. 1914—July 1915.

Scale—7·71 Miles to 1 Inch

○ NYORORO
(Air Base Nov.-Dec. 1914)

Ras Mkumbi
⚓ Light

8°S.

MAFIA

Chole Bay

JUANI

Utende

Marimbani
Ngombeni

Tireni

Kilindoni
A
Kisimani

Ras Mbisi

BOYDU

Kiasi Mouth

Ndahi
Mouth

Msala Mouth

Ras Dima

Kiasi

Msala

Twana

Ras Twana

Kiombni Mouth

Simba Uranga Mouth

Simba Uranga

4
Kiomboni
3

Twana

Salale
1

Ras
Simba
Uranga

Kikunya Mouth

Msindaji

Kumbini

KIHTA
Pemba

Kilindini

Kikunya
6
5

2

Mbumi

Rufiji R.

REFERENCE

1   Königsberg Nov 1914.
2   -do-   July 1915.
3   Somali Nov. 1914.
4   Block-ship, Nov. 1914.
5   Position of attacking monitors, July 6th.
6   -do-   -do-   -do.-   July 11th.
A   Aerodrome, July 1915.

39°30′E. Crown Copyright Reserved.

Miles
0   Miles

0   10   20 Miles

Ordnance Survey 1937

COMPILED BY HISTORICAL SECTION
(MILITARY BRANCH)

1550/9/41. CR.

8°S.

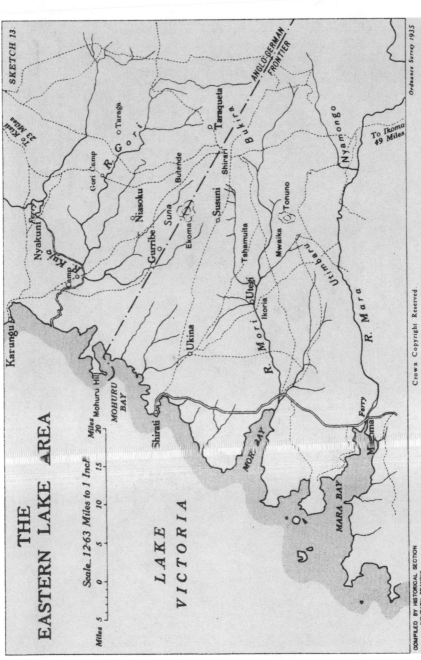

SKETCH 13.

THE
EASTERN LAKE AREA

Scale 1·63 Miles to 1 Inch

Miles 5   0   5   10   15   20   Miles

LAKE
VICTORIA

MOHURU
BAY

Mohuru Hill

Shirati

MORI BAY

MARA BAY

Ferry

Musoma

Karungu

Nyakuni Ferry

To Kisii 20 Miles
To Kisii 23 Miles

R. Gori

Gori Camp

oTaraga

Kanji Camp

Niasoku

Gurribe

Suna

Ekoma

Butehde

Susuni

Ukina

Utegi

Ikoria

R. Mori

Tshamuita

Mwaika

Tonuno

R. Mara

Utimanga

Nyamongo

To Ikoma
49 Miles

Shirati

Tareqweta

Bukira

ANGLO-GERMAN FRONTIER

Ordnance Survey 1935

COMPILED BY HISTORICAL SECTION
(MILITARY BRANCH)
1550/9/41. CR.

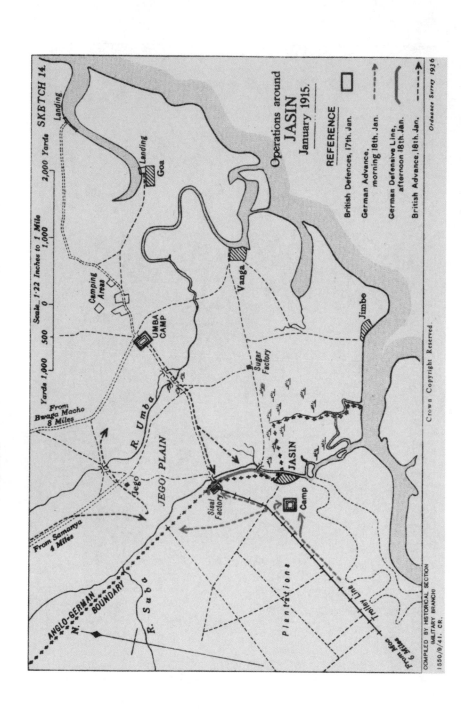

SKETCH 14.

Operations around
JASIN
January 1915.

REFERENCE

☐ British Defences, 17th. Jan.

–––––→ German Advance,
      morning 18th. Jan.

⌐––––→ German Defensive Line,
      afternoon 18th. Jan.

⌐–––→ British Advance, 18th. Jan.

Ordnance Survey 1936

COMPILED BY HISTORICAL SECTION
(MILITARY BRANCH)
1550/9/41. CR.

Scale 1·22 Inches to 1 Mile

Yards 1,000   500   0   1,000   2,000 Yards

Landing

Goa

Landing

Camping
Areas

UMBA
CAMP

R. Umba

Vanga

Jimbe

Sugar
Factory

From
Bwaga Macho
8 Miles

Jego

JEGO PLAIN

JASIN

Sisal
Factory

Camp

From Samanya
4 Miles

ANGLO-GERMAN
BOUNDARY

R. Suba

N.

Plantations

Trolley Line

From Moa
6 Miles

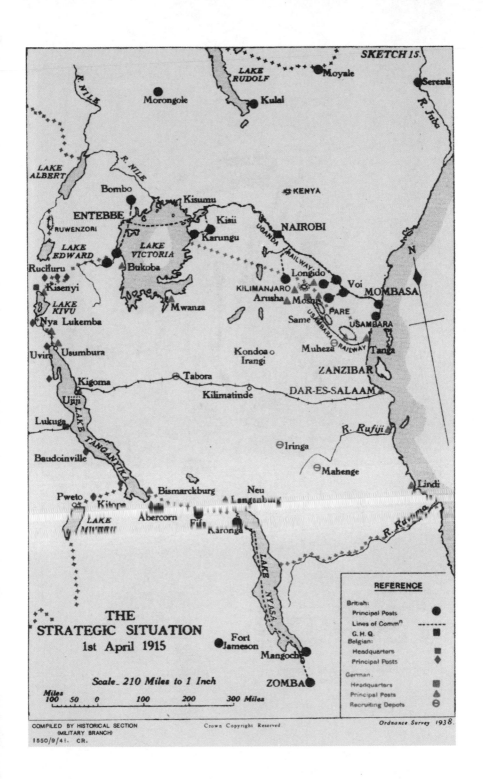

SKETCH 15.

THE
STRATEGIC SITUATION
1st April 1915

Scale — 210 Miles to 1 Inch

Miles
100 50 0   100   200   300 Miles

REFERENCE

British:
Principal Posts   ●
Lines of Comm^n   ------
G.H.Q.   ■
Belgian:
Headquarters
Principal Posts   ◆
German:
Headquarters
Principal Posts   ▲
Recruiting Depots   ⊖

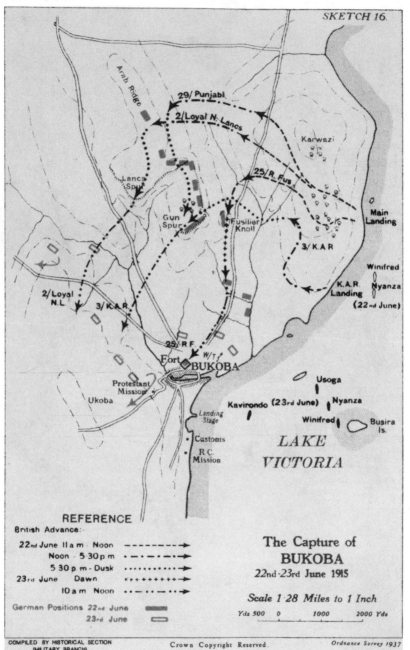

SKETCH 16.

Arab Ridge

29/ Punjabi
2/ Loyal N. Lancs

Karwazi

Lancs Spur

25/ R. Fus.

Main Landing

Gun Spur

Fusilier Knoll

3/ K.A.R.

Winifred

2/ Loyal N.L.

3/ K.A.R.

K.A.R. Landing (22nd June)

Nyanza

25/ R.F.

W/T

Fort BUKOBA

Usoga

Protestant Mission

Kavirondo (23rd June)

Nyanza

Ukoba

Landing Stage

Winifred

Busira Is.

Customs

R.C. Mission

LAKE VICTORIA

REFERENCE
British Advance:-

22nd June 11 a.m - Noon	- - - - - →
Noon - 5·30 p.m	- · - · - · →
5·30 p.m - Dusk	· · · · · · · →
23rd June Dawn	+ + + + + + + →
10 a.m - Noon	- · · - · · — →

German Positions 22nd June ▬▬▬
23rd June ▭

The Capture of
BUKOBA
22nd-23rd June 1915

Scale 1·28 Miles to 1 Inch

Yds 500   0   1000   2000 Yds

COMPILED BY HISTORICAL SECTION
(MILITARY BRANCH)
1550/9/41. CR.

Crown Copyright Reserved.

Ordnance Survey 1937

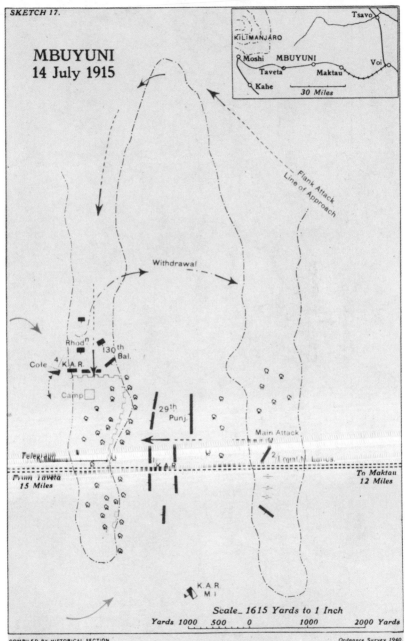

SKETCH 17.

MBUYUNI
14 July 1915

KILIMANJARO

Tsavo

Moshi MBUYUNI

Taveta Maktau Voi

Kahe 30 Miles

Flank Attack
Line of Approach

Withdrawal

Rhodⁿ

Cole 4/K.A.R. 130th Bal.

Camp

29th Punj.

Main Attack

Telegraph

K.A.R.

2 Light M.G. Batts.

From Taveta
15 Miles

To Maktau
12 Miles

K.A.R.
M.I.

Scale_ 1615 Yards to 1 Inch

Yards 1000   500   0   1000   2000 Yards

COMPILED BY HISTORICAL SECTION
(MILITARY BRANCH)

Ordnance Survey 1940

1550/9/41. CR.

Crown Copyright Reserved

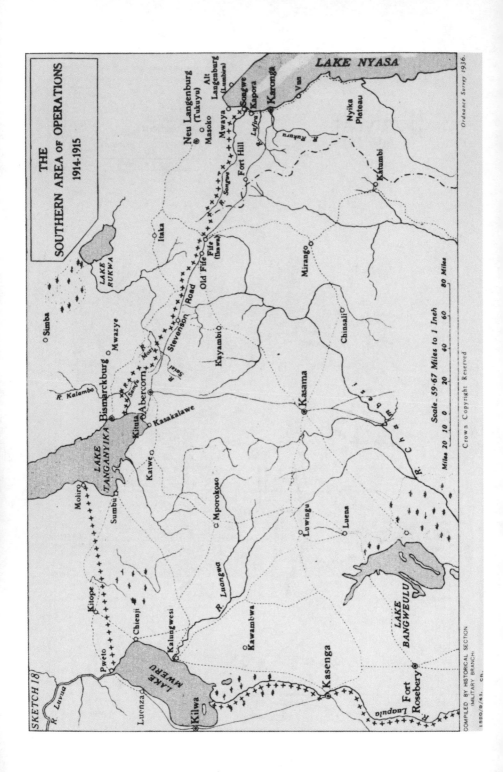

SKETCH 18

THE
SOUTHERN AREA of OPERATIONS
1914-1915

LAKE NYASA

R. Luvua

R. Luvua

LAKE
TANGANYIKA

Moliro

Kitope

Pweto

Chienji

Kalungwesi

Sumbu

Kilwa

LAKE
MWERU

Lucnza

Kasenga

Fort
Rosebery

R. Luapula

LAKE
BANGWEULU

Kawambwa

Luwingu

Luena

Kasama

Mporokoso

Katwe

Kasakalawe

Kiluta

Abercorn

Bismarckburg

R. Kalembo

Simba

LAKE
RUKWA

Mwazye

R. Saisi

R. Saisi

R. Msizi

R. Mosi

Stevenson Road

Itaka

Old Fife

Fife
(Ikawa)

Kayambi

Kayambi

Mirango

Chinsali

R. Chambezi

R. Chambezi

R. Chambezi

Neu Langenburg
(Tukuyu)

Masoko

Alt
Langenburg
(Lumburu)

Songwe

Kapora

Karonga

R. Songwe

Fort Hill

Mwaya

Lufira

Vua

Nyika
Plateau

Katumbi

R. Ruhuhu

Scale. 59·67 *Miles to 1 Inch*

Miles 20 10 0   20   40   60   80 Miles

Luangwa

R. Luangwa

Ordnance Survey 1936.

COMPILED BY HISTORICAL SECTION
(MILITARY BRANCH).
1550/9/41.   GS.

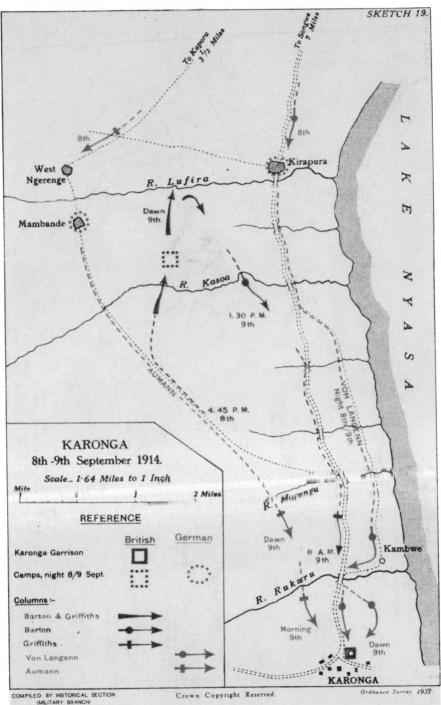

SKETCH 19.

To Kapora 3½ Miles

To Songwe 7 Miles

L A K E   N Y A S A

8th

8th

West Ngerenge

Kirapura

R. Lufira

Dawn 9th.

Mambande

R. Kasoa

1. 30 P. M. 9th

AUMANN

4. 45 P. M. 8th

VON LANGENN Night 8th/9th

KARONGA
8th -9th September 1914.

Scale _ 1·64 Miles to 1 Inch

Mile   2 Miles

R. Murungu

Dawn 9th

11 A. M. 9th

Kambwe

REFERENCE

British   German

Karonga Garrison

Camps, night 8/9 Sept.

Columns :-

Barton & Griffiths

Barton

Griffiths

Von Langenn

Aumann

R. Rukuru

Morning 9th

Dawn 9th

KARONGA

COMPILED BY HISTORICAL SECTION
(MILITARY BRANCH)
1550/9/41. CR.

Ordnance Survey 1937.

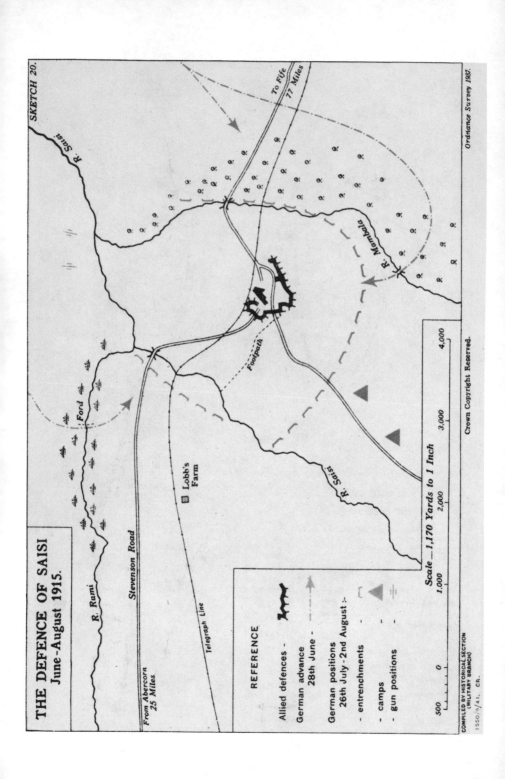

THE DEFENCE OF SAISI
June–August 1915.

SKETCH 20.

R. Saisi

R. Rumi

From Abercorn 25 Miles

Stevenson Road

Telegraph Line

Ford

Lobb's Farm

Footpath

To Fife 77 Miles

R. Mambala

R. Saisi

REFERENCE

Allied defences -

German advance 28th June -

German positions 26th July - 2nd August :—
- entrenchments -
- camps -
- gun positions -

Scale _ 1,170 Yards to 1 Inch

500   0   1,000   2,000   3,000   4,000

COMPILED BY HISTORICAL SECTION (MILITARY BRANCH)

1550/9/41. CR.

Crown Copyright Reserved.

Ordnance Survey 1937.

SALAITA
12th February 1916.

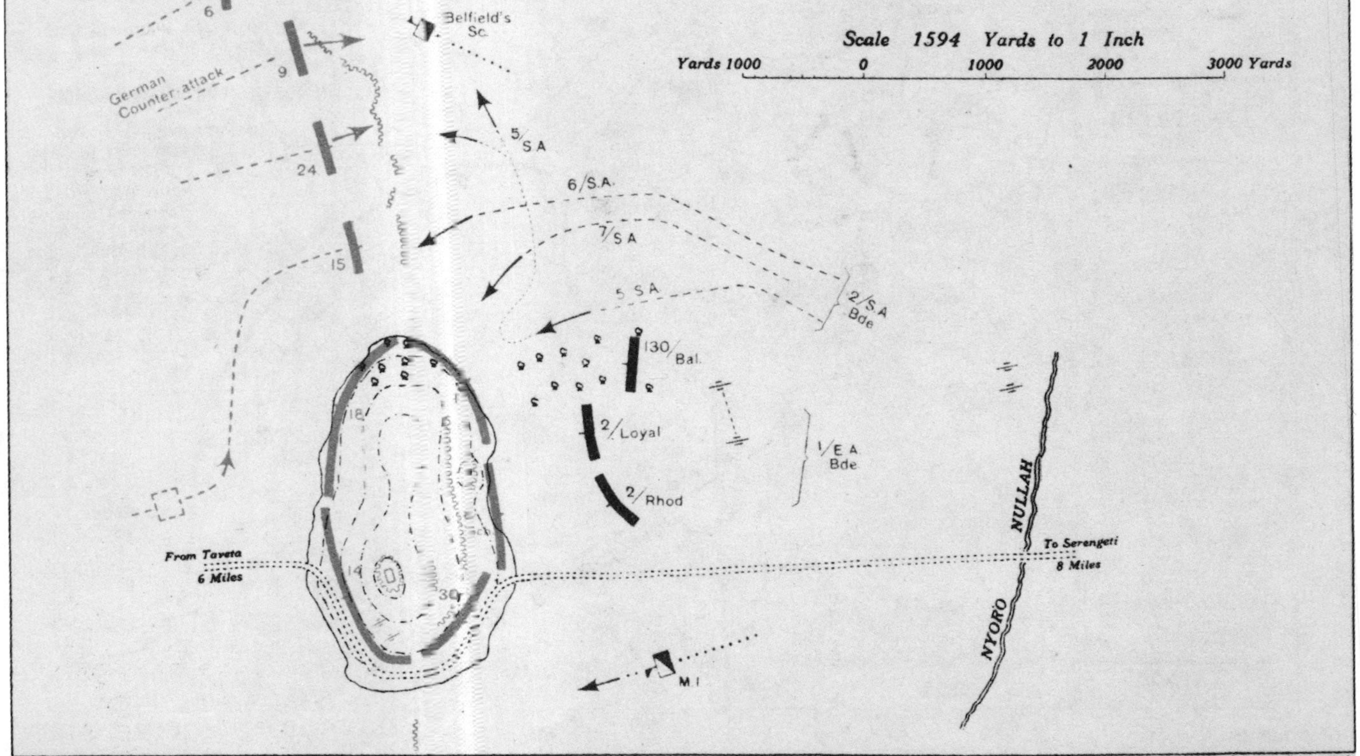

Scale 1594 *Yards to 1 Inch*

Yards 1000   0   1000   2000   3000 Yards

2/S.A Bde

1/E.A Bde

30/Bat.

2/Loyal

2/Rhod

M.I

5/S.A

6/S.A

7/S.A

5.S.A

Belfield's Sc.

6

9

24

15

German attack

Counter attack

NYORO NULLAH

To Serengeti 8 Miles

From Taveta 6 Miles

Ordnance Survey 1937.

COMPILED BY HISTORICAL SECTION (MILITARY BRANCH)
1550/9/41. CR.

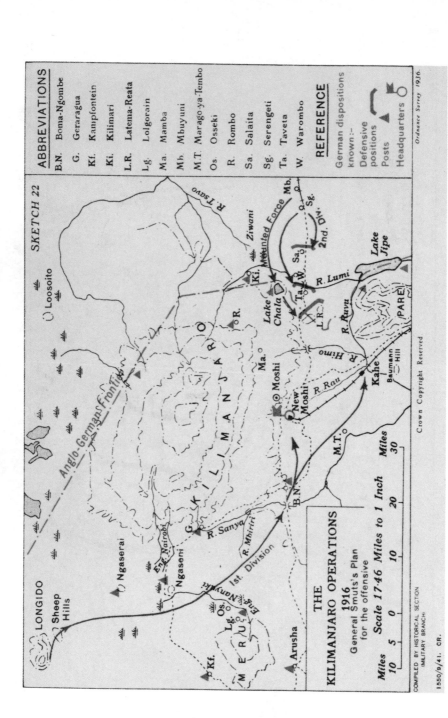

SKETCH 22

ABBREVIATIONS

B.N. Boma-Ngombe
G. Geraragua
Kf. Kanplontein
Ki. Kilimari
L.R. Latema-Reata
Lg. Lolgorain
Ma. Mamba
Mb. Mbuyuni
M.T. Marago-ya-Tembo
Os. Osseki
R. Rombo
Sa. Salaita
Sg. Serengeti
Ta. Taveta
W. Warombo

REFERENCE

German dispositions
known:-
Defensive
positions
Posts
Headquarters

Ordnance Survey 1936.

THE
KILIMANJARO OPERATIONS
1916
General Smuts's Plan
for the offensive

Scale 17·46 Miles to 1 Inch

Miles 10 5 0 10 20 30 Miles

COMPILED BY HISTORICAL SECTION
IMILITARY BRANCH

1550/9/41. CR.

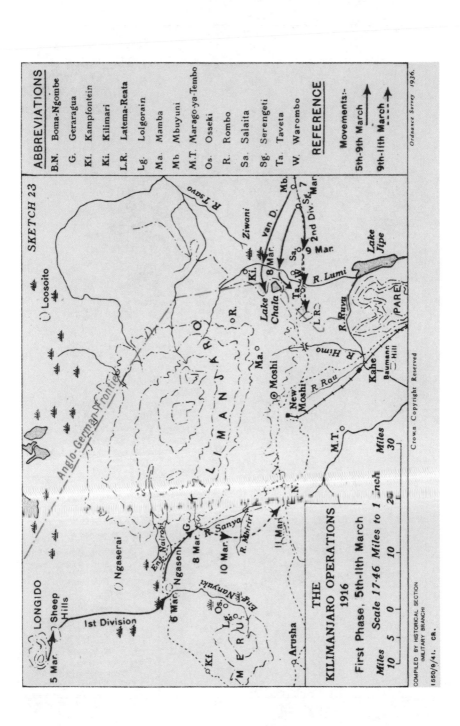

SKETCH 23

ABBREVIATIONS

B.N. Boma-Ngombe
G. Gerarágua
Kf. Kampfontein
Ki. Kilimari
L.R. Latema-Reata
Lg. Lolgorain
Ma. Mamba
Mb. Mbuyuni
M.T. Marago-ya-Tembo
Os. Osseki
R. Rombo
Sa. Salaita
Sg. Serengeti
Ta. Taveta
W. Warombo

REFERENCE

Movements:-

5th-9th March

9th-11th March

LONGIDO

Sheep Hills

1st Division

5 Mar.

Loosoito

Anglo-German Frontier

R. Tsavo

Ngaserai

6 Mar. Ngaseni

Eng. Nairobi

8 Mar.

R. Sanya

10 Mar.

R. Mbiriri

11 Mar.

K I L I M A N J A R O

Ma.

R.

Ziwani

Ki.

8 Mar.

Lake Chala

van D.

Mb.

Sg.

7 Mar.

Sa.

Ta.

9 Mar.

2nd Div.

L.R.

Moshi

New Moshi

R. Rau

R. Himo

R. Lumi

R. Ruvu

Kahe

Baumann Hill

Lake Jipe

(PARE)

M.T.

Lg.
Os.
Eng. Nanyuki

Kf.

M E R U

Arusha

THE KILIMANJARO OPERATIONS 1916

First Phase, 5th-11th March

Scale 17·46 Miles to 1 inch

Miles 10 5 0 10 20 30 Miles

COMPILED BY HISTORICAL SECTION
(MILITARY BRANCH)
1550/9/41. G.B.

Ordnance Survey 1936.

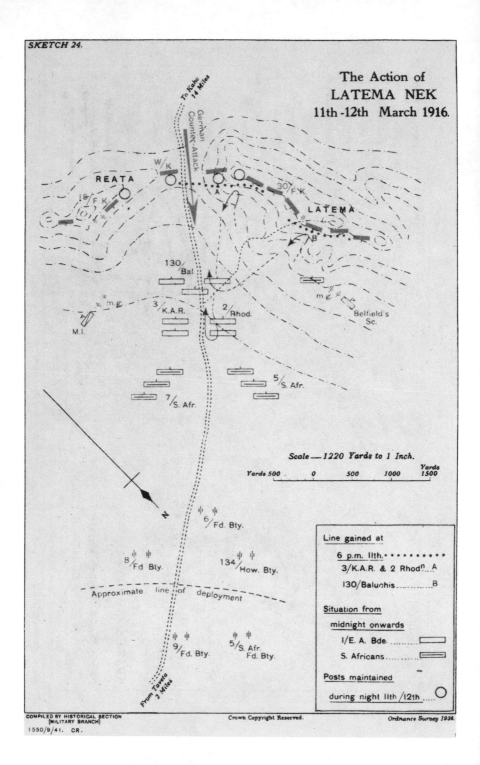

SKETCH 24.

The Action of
LATEMA NEK
11th-12th March 1916.

To Kahe
14 Miles

German Counter-Attack

REATA

W/K

18/F.K.

A

30/F.K.

LATEMA

B

130/Bal

m.g.

M.I.

3/K.A.R.

2/Rhod.

m.g.

Belfield's
Sc.

7/S. Afr.

5/S. Afr.

Scale — 1220 Yards to 1 Inch.

Yards 500   0   500   1000   Yards 1500

N

6/Fd. Bty.

8/Fd. Bty.

134/How. Bty.

Approximate line of deployment

9/Fd. Bty.

5/S. Afr. Fd. Bty.

From Taveta
2 Miles

Line gained at

6 p.m. 11th. · · · · · · · · · ·
3/K.A.R. & 2 Rhodⁿ A
130/Baluchis . . . . B

Situation from
midnight onwards
I/E. A. Bde. . . . .
S. Africans . . . .

Posts maintained
during night 11th/12th

COMPILED BY HISTORICAL SECTION
(MILITARY BRANCH)
1550/9/41. CR.

Crown Copyright Reserved.

Ordnance Survey 1936.

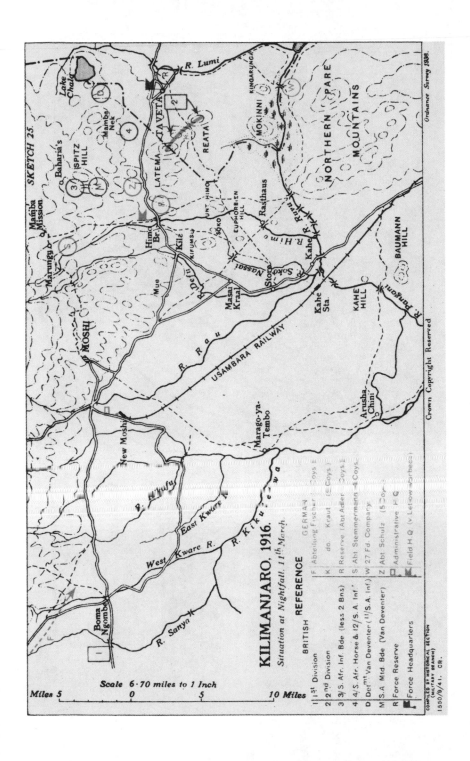

KILIMANJARO, 1916.

Situation at Nightfall, 11th March.

REFERENCE

BRITISH

1. 1st Division
2. 2nd Division
3. 3/S. Afr. Inf. Bde (less 2 Bns)
4. 4/S. Afr. Horse & 12/S.A. Inf.
   D. Det.nt Van Deventer (11/S.A. Inf.)
   M.S.A Mtd. Bde (Van Deventer)
   R. Force Reserve
   ■. Force Headquarters

GERMAN

F. Abteilung Fischer (3 Coys)
K. do. Kraut (3 Coys)
R. Reserve (Abt Adler 2 Coys)
S. Abt Stemmermann (4 Coys)
W. 27 Fd. Company
Z. Abt Schulz (5 Coys)
□. Administrative HQ
■. Field HQ (v.Lettow-Vorbeck)

SKETCH 25.

Scale 6·70 miles to 1 Inch

Miles 5   0   5   10 Miles

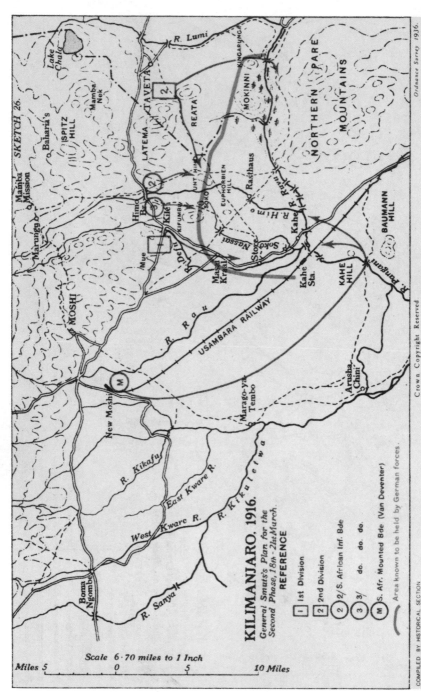

SKETCH 26.

KILIMANJARO. 1916.

General Smuts's Plan for the
Second Phase, 18th–21st March.

REFERENCE

1	1st Division
2	2nd Division
②	2/ S. African Inf. Bde
③	3/ do. do. do.
Ⓜ	S. Afr. Mounted Bde (Van Deventer)

⌒ Area known to be held by German forces.

Scale 6·70 miles to 1 Inch

Miles 5   0   5   10 Miles

COMPILED BY HISTORICAL SECTION
(MILITARY BRANCH)
1550/8/41.   CR.

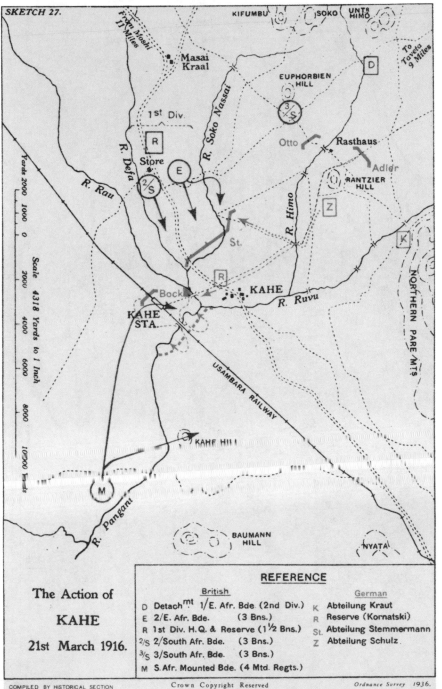

SKETCH 27.

KIFUMBU   SOKO   UNT&
              HIMO

From Moshi
11 Miles

To Taveta 9 Miles

Masai Kraal

EUPHORBIEN HILL

D

1st Div.

R. Soko Nassai

Otto

Rasthaus

R. Defa

R

Store

Adler

2/S

E

RANTZIER HILL

R. Rau

St.

R. Himo

Z

K

NORTHERN PARE M?S

R

KAHE

Bock

R. Ruvu

KAHE STA.

USAMBARA RAILWAY

KAHE HILL

M

R. Pangani

BAUMANN HILL

NYATA

Yards 2000 1000 0
Scale 4318 Yards to 1 Inch
2000 4000 6000 8000 10?000 Yards

REFERENCE

The Action of

KAHE

21st March 1916.

British

D   Detach^mt 1/E. Afr. Bde. (2nd Div.)
E   2/E. Afr. Bde.   (3 Bns.)
R   1st Div. H.Q. & Reserve (1½ Bns.)
2/S   2/South Afr. Bde.   (3 Bns.)
3/S   3/South Afr. Bde.   (3 Bns.)
M   S.Afr. Mounted Bde. (4 Mtd. Regts.)

German

K   Abteilung Kraut
R   Reserve (Kornatski)
St.   Abteilung Stemmermann
Z   Abteilung Schulz

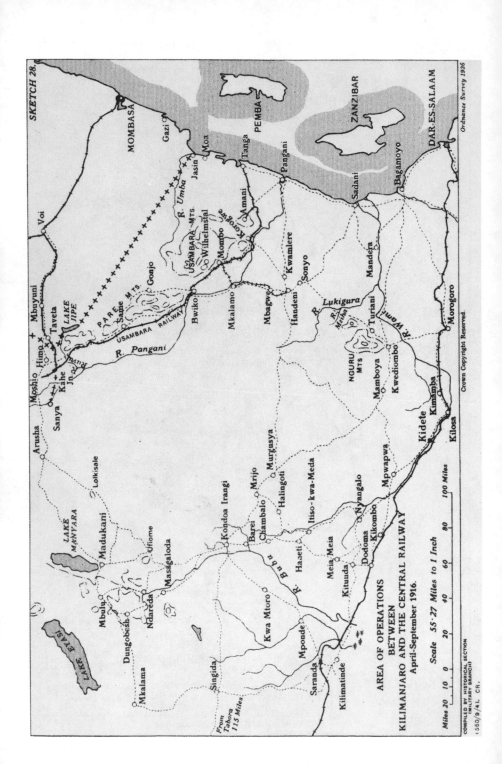

SKETCH 28.

AREA OF OPERATIONS
BETWEEN
KILIMANJARO AND THE CENTRAL RAILWAY
April-September 1916.

Scale 55·27 Miles to 1 Inch

Miles 20 10 0   20   40   60   80   100 Miles

COMPILED BY HISTORICAL SECTION
(MILITARY BRANCH)
1550/9/41. CR.

Ordnance Survey 1936

Crown Copyright Reserved.

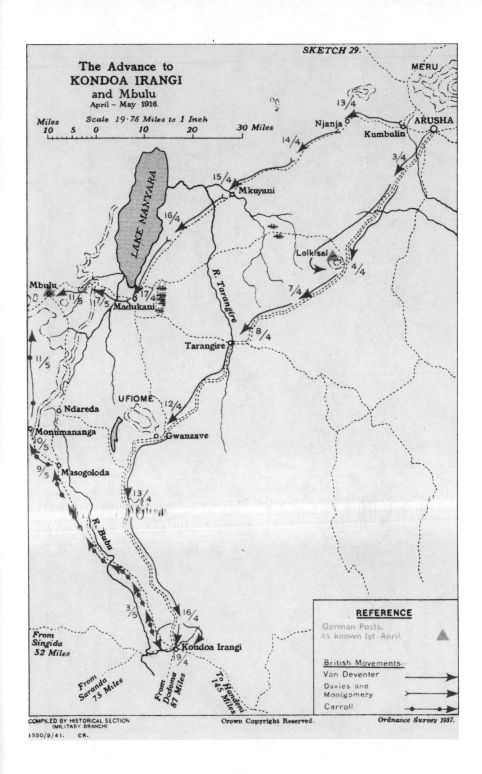

SKETCH 29.

The Advance to
KONDOA IRANGI
and Mbulu
April – May 1916.

Miles
10   5   0   Scale 19·75 Miles to 1 Inch
                10   20   30 Miles

MERU

13/4

Njanja   ARUSHA
          Kumbulin

14/4

3/4

LAKE MANYARA

15/4   Mkuyuni

16/4

Lolkisal

4/4

7/4

Mbulu

11/5   17/5   Madukani   R. Tarangire

8/4

Tarangire

11/5

12/4

UFIOME

Ndareda

Monumananga   Gwanzave

10/5

9/5   Masogoloda

13/4

R. Buba

3/5   16/4

From
Singida
52 Miles   Kondoa Irangi

19/4

From
Saranda
75 Miles   From
              Dodoma
              87 Miles   To Handeni
                            145 Miles

REFERENCE

German Posts.
as known 1st April.

British Movements:—
Van Deventer
Davies and
Montgomery
Carroll

COMPILED BY HISTORICAL SECTION
(MILITARY BRANCH)   Crown Copyright Reserved.   Ordnance Survey 1937.

1550/9/41.   CR.

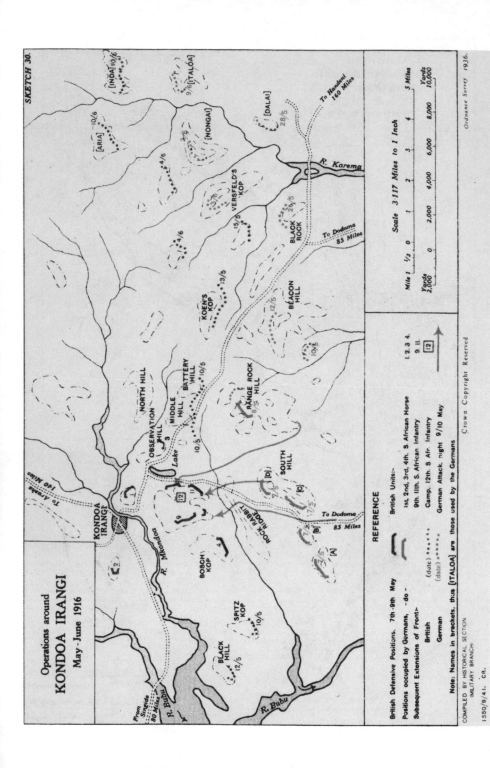

SKETCH 30.

Operations around
KONDOA IRANGI
May-June 1916

REFERENCE

British Defensive Positions, 7th-9th May

Positions occupied by Germans, –do –

Subsequent Extensions of Front—
British   (date) ••••••
German   (date) •••••••

British Units:—
1st, 2nd, 3rd, 4th. S. African Horse
9th. 11th. S. African Infantry
Camp. 12th. S Afr. Infantry
German Attack, night 9/10 May

1. 2. 3. 4.
9. II.
[12]

Note: Names in brackets, thus [TALOA] are those used by the Germans.

Scale 3·117 Miles to 1 Inch

Mile 1   ½   0   1   2   3   4   5 Miles

Yards 2,000 0   2,000   4,000   6,000   8,000   10,000 Yards

Crown Copyright Reserved

Ordnance Survey 1936.

COMPILED BY HISTORICAL SECTION
(MILITARY BRANCH)

1550/9/41. C.R.

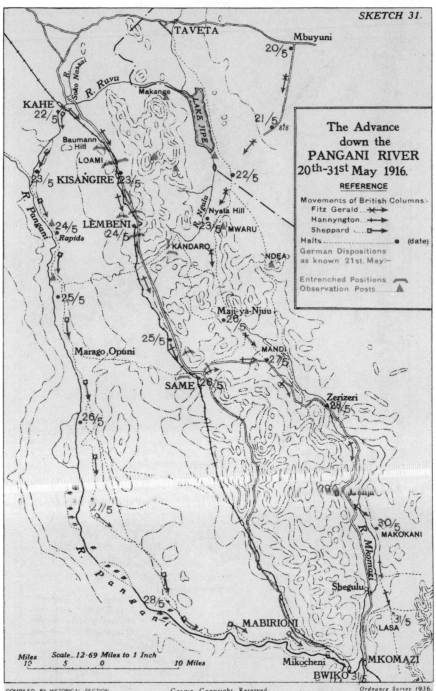

SKETCH 31.

TAVETA

Mbuyuni

20/5

R. Soko Nassai

R. Ruvu

Makange

LAKE JIPE

21/5 878

KAHE
22/5

Baumann Hill

LOAMI

23/5 KISANGIRE 23/5

R. Pangani

24/5 LEMBENI
Rapids 24/5

KANDARO

Njuu

22/5

Nyata Hill

23/5 MWARU

NDEA

The Advance
down the
PANGANI RIVER
20th-31st May 1916.

REFERENCE

Movements of British Columns:-
Fitz Gerald...⤬→
Hannyngton...←→
Sheppard ...□→
Halts..........● (date)

German Dispositions
as known 21st. May:-

Entrenched Positions
Observation Posts ▲

25/5

Maji-ya-Njuu
26/5

Marago, Opuni

25/5

MANDI
27/5

SAME 26/5

Zerizeri
28/5

26/5

R. Mkomazi

Lenju

30/5
MAKOKANI

27/5

Shegulu

28/5

MABIRIONI

LASA

31/5

Miles
10   Scale 12·69 Miles to 1 Inch
    5   0   10 Miles

Mikocheni

MKOMAZI

BWIKO 31/5

R. Pangani

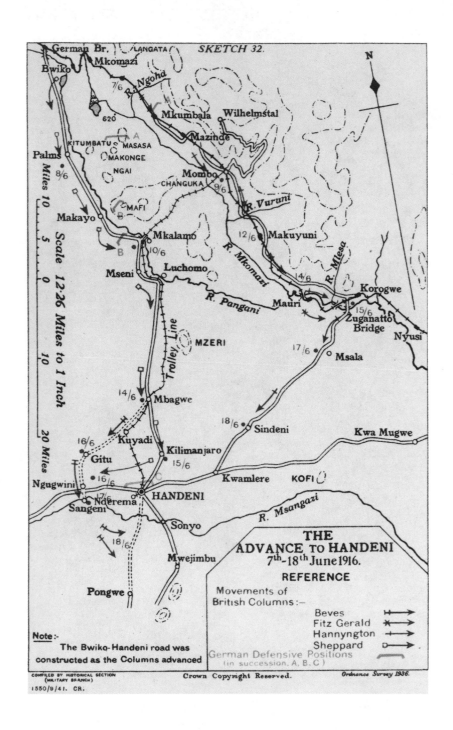

SKETCH 32.

THE
ADVANCE TO HANDENI
7th-18th June 1916.

REFERENCE

Movements of
British Columns:—

Beves	⊢——→
Fitz Gerald	✕——→
Hannyngton	+——→
Sheppard	◻——→

German Defensive Positions
(in succession, A, B, C)

Note:-
    The Bwiko-Handeni road was
constructed as the Columns advanced

COMPILED BY HISTORICAL SECTION
(MILITARY BRANCH)
1550/9/41. CR.

Crown Copyright Reserved.

Ordnance Survey 1936.

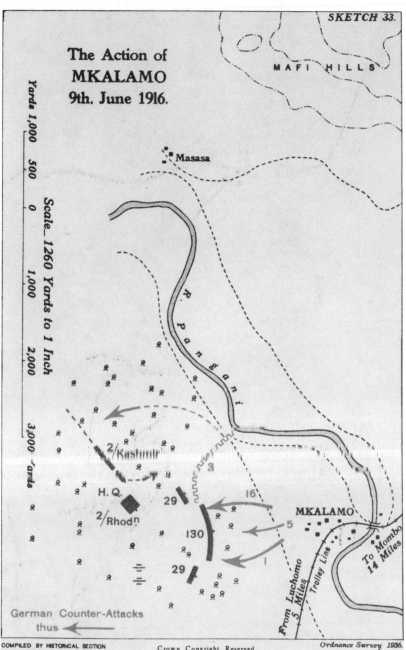

SKETCH 33.

The Action of
MKALAMO
9th. June 1916.

MAFI HILLS

Yards 1,000   500   0   1,000   2,000   3,000 Yards

Scale 1260 Yards to 1 Inch

Masasa

R. Pangani

2/Kashmir

3

H.Q.   29   16

MKALAMO

2/Rhodⁿ   130   5

29   1

To Mombo
14 Miles

From Luchomo
5 Miles

Trolley Line

German Counter-Attacks
thus

COMPILED BY HISTORICAL SECTION
(MILITARY BRANCH)

Crown Copyright Reserved.

Ordnance Survey 1936.

1550/9/41. CR.

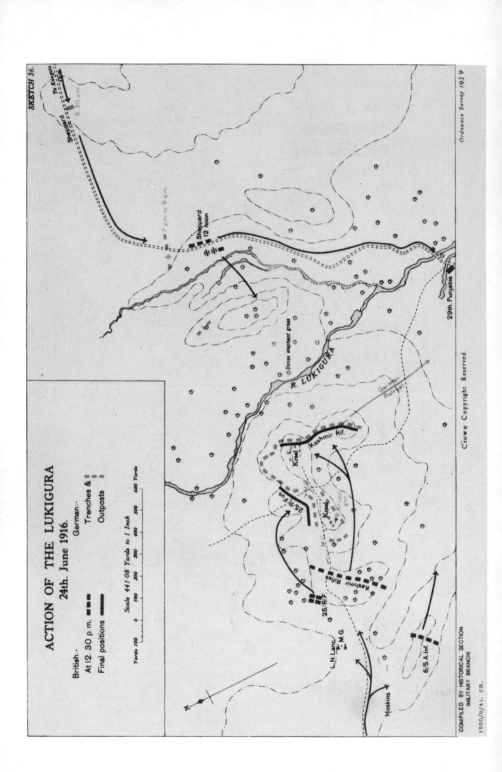

SKETCH 36.

ACTION OF THE LUKIGURA
24th. June 1916.

British:-   German:-
At 12.30 p.m. ▬▬▬▮ Trenches & ▮▮
Final positions ▬▬▬ Outposts ▮

Scale 44·1·08 Yards to 1 Inch
Yards 100   0   100   200   300   400   500   600 Yards

R. LUKIGURA

Dense elephant grass

German Retreat

Kraal

Kashmir Rif.

25/R.Fus.

Kraal

Krupp

M.G.

Kashmir Rifles

25/R.F.

L.N.Lanc.

M.G.

6/S.A.Inf.

Hoskins

N

Sheppard
6.30 a.m.
To Kangata
To Dar

7 a.m. to 9 a.m.

Sheppard
12 noon

29th Punjabis

COMPILED BY HISTORICAL SECTION
(MILITARY BRANCH)

1550/9/41. CR.

Ordnance Survey 1939

Crown Copyright Reserved.

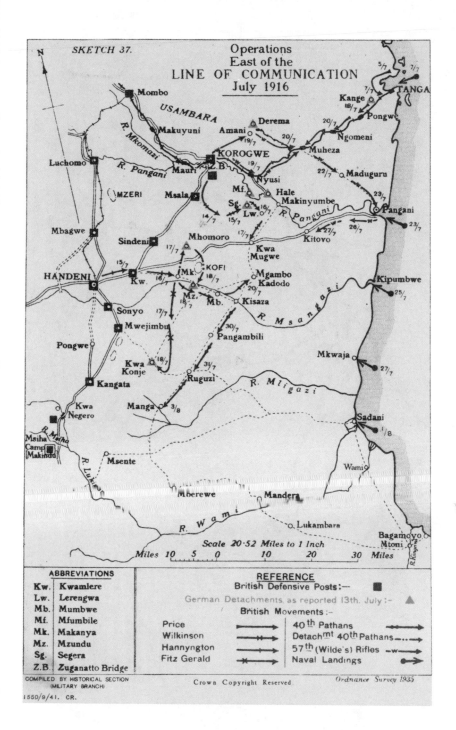

SKETCH 37.

Operations
East of the
LINE OF COMMUNICATION
July 1916

Scale 20·52 Miles to 1 Inch

Miles 10   5   0   10   20   30   Miles

ABBREVIATIONS	
Kw.	Kwamlere
Lw.	Lerengwa
Mb.	Mumbwe
Mf.	Mfumbile
Mk.	Makanya
Mz.	Mzundu
Sg.	Segera
Z.B.	Zuganatto Bridge

REFERENCE
British Defensive Posts:— ■
German Detachments, as reported 13th. July :- ▲
British Movements :-

Price	───▶	40th Pathans	───▶
Wilkinson	──×──▶	Detachmt 40th Pathans	···▶
Hannyngton	──×──▶	57th (Wilde's) Rifles	-w-▶
Fitz Gerald	──×──▶	Naval Landings	●──▶

COMPILED BY HISTORICAL SECTION
(MILITARY BRANCH)

1550/9/41. CR.

Ordnance Survey 1935

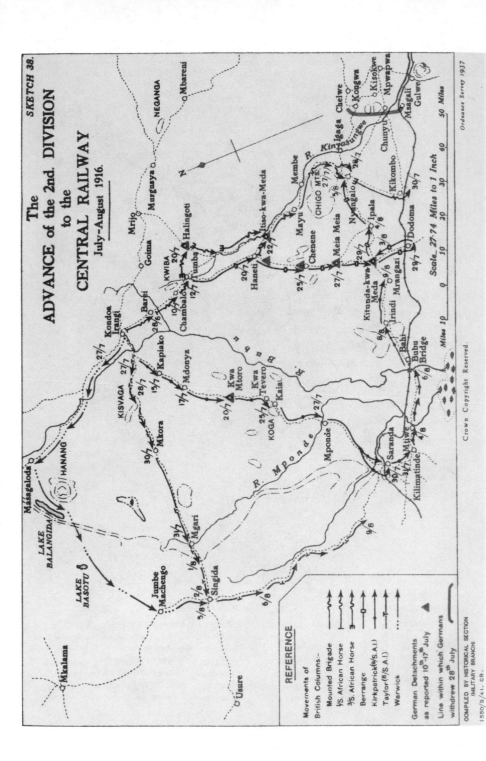

SKETCH 38.

The
ADVANCE of the 2nd. DIVISION
to the
CENTRAL RAILWAY
July–August 1916.

REFERENCE

Movements of
British Columns:—

Mounted Brigade
1/S. African Horse
3/S. African Horse
Berrange
Kirkpatrick(6/S.A.I.)
Taylor(8/S.A.I.)
Warwick

German Detachments
as reported 10th-17th July

Line within which Germans
withdrew 28th July

Scale, 27·74 Miles to 1 Inch

Crown Copyright Reserved

Ordnance Survey 1937

COMPILED BY HISTORICAL SECTION
(MILITARY BRANCH)
1550/8/41. CR.

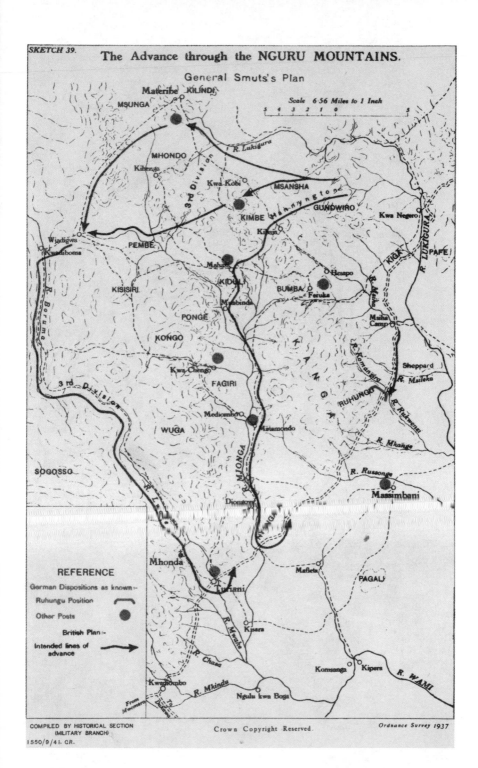

SKETCH 39.

The Advance through the NGURU MOUNTAINS.

General Smuts's Plan

Scale 6·56 Miles to 1 Inch

5 · 4 · 3 · 2 · 1 · 0 · · · · · 5

Materibe · KILINDI

MSUNGA

R. Lukigura

MHONDO

Kibenga

Kwa-Kobi · MSANSHA

2nd Division

Hannyngton

KIMBE · GUNDWIRO · Kwa Negro

Kihaja

Wiadigwa · PEMBE

Kwadiboma

Mahar

Hesapo

KISISIRI · KIDUL · BUMBA · Feruka

Myabinda

R. Boruma · PONGE

KONGO

Msiha Camp

R. Komanging

Sheppard

3rd Division · Kwa-Chengo · R. Maileko

FAGIRI · RUHUNGO · R. Rutwenti

Mediombo

WUGA · Matamondo

R. Mkange

SOGOSSO

R. Russonge

Dionson · Massimbani

R. Lut

NJONGA

NTUGA

Mhonda

Mafleta · PAGALI

REFERENCE · Turiani

German Dispositions as known :-

Ruhungu Position

Other Posts · ●

British Plan :-

Intended lines of advance · →

R. Mvake · Kisara

R. Chasa · R. Mkindu

Komsanga · Kipera · R. WAMI

Kwagorombo

From Msomero · R. Mkindu · Ngulu kwa Boga

COMPILED BY HISTORICAL SECTION
(MILITARY BRANCH)
1550/9/41. GR.

Ordnance Survey 1937

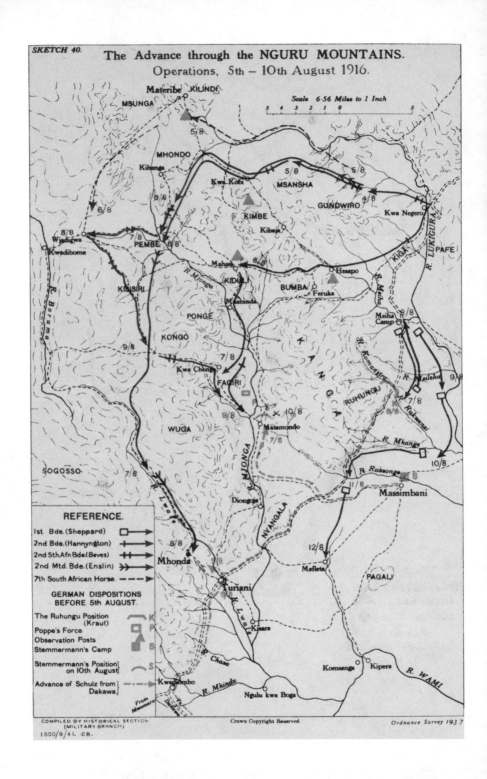

SKETCH 40.

The Advance through the NGURU MOUNTAINS.
Operations, 5th – 10th August 1916.

Scale 6·56 Miles to 1 Inch

REFERENCE.

1st Bde.(Sheppard)
2nd Bde.(Hannyngton)
2nd Sth.Afn.Bde.(Beves)
2nd Mtd. Bde.(Enslin)
7th South African Horse.

GERMAN DISPOSITIONS
BEFORE 5th AUGUST.

The Ruhungu Position
(Kraut)
Poppe's Force
Observation Posts
Stemmermann's Camp

Stemmermann's Position
on 10th August
Advance of Schulz from
Dakawa.

COMPILED BY HISTORICAL SECTION
(MILITARY BRANCH)
1550/9/41. ·CR·

Crown Copyright Reserved

Ordnance Survey 1937

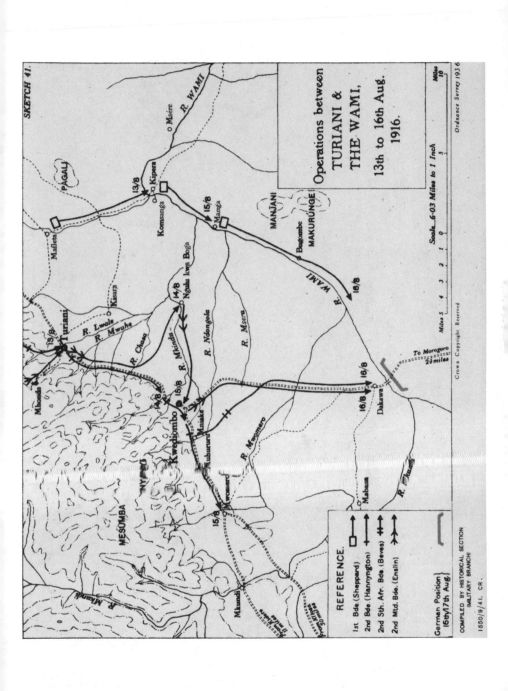

SKETCH 41.

Operations between
TURIANI &
THE WAMI,
13th to 16th Aug.
1916.

Scale 6·03 Miles to 1 Inch

Ordnance Survey 1936

Crown Copyright Reserved

REFERENCE.

1st Bde. (Sheppard)
2nd Bde. (Hannyngton)
2nd Sth. Afr. Bde. (Beves)
2nd Mtd. Bde. (Enslin)

German Position
16th/17th Aug.

COMPILED BY HISTORICAL SECTION
(MILITARY BRANCH)

1550/9/41. CR.

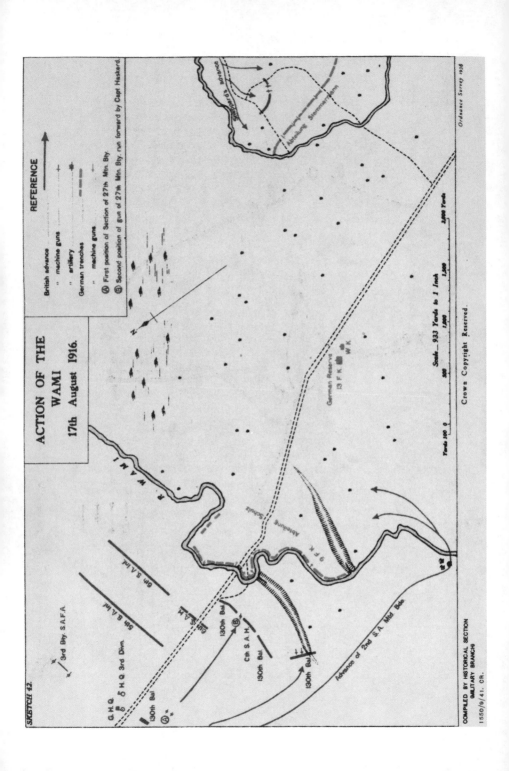

SKETCH 42.

ACTION OF THE
WAMI
17th August 1916.

REFERENCE

British advance ....
" machine guns ——+——
" artillery ——·—·—
German trenches ━━━━━
" machine guns ↓

Ⓐ First position of Section of 27th Mtn. Bty.
Ⓑ Second position of gun of 27th Mtn. Bty. run forward by Capt Haskard.

N

R. WAMI

3rd Bty. S.A.F.A.

G.H.Q.
H.Q. 3rd Divn.

130th Bat.

6th S.A. Inf.

5th S.A. Inf.

7th S.A.M.

130th Bat.

Cth S.A.H.

130th Bat.

130th Bat.

Advance of 2nd S.A. Mtd. Bde.

Abteilung Schultz

9 F.K.

St 2

Abteilung Stemmermann

Schulberg's advance

German Reserve
13 F.K.
W.K.

Yards 100 0   500   1,000   1,500   2,000 Yards

Scale—933 Yards to 1 inch

Crown Copyright Reserved.

Ordnance Survey 1916

COMPILED BY HISTORICAL SECTION
MILITARY BRANCH
1550/9/41. OR.

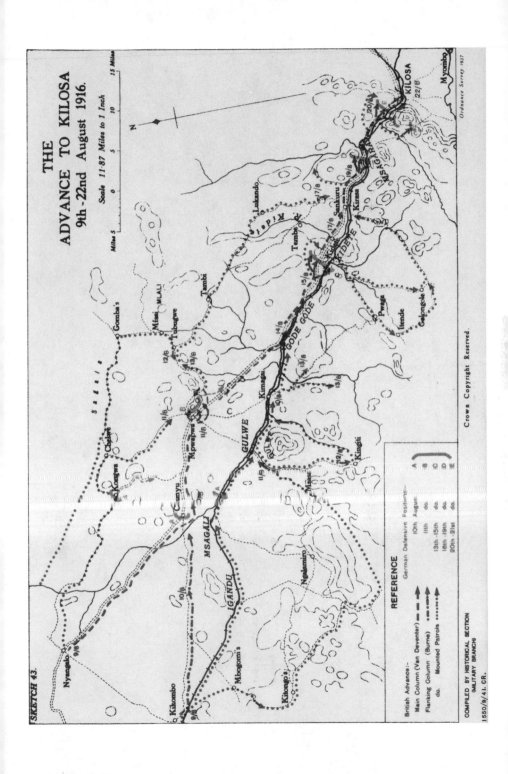

SKETCH 43.

THE
ADVANCE TO KILOSA
9th - 22nd August 1916.

Scale 11·87 Miles to 1 Inch

Miles 5   0   5   10   15 Miles

N

Ordnance Survey 1937

Crown Copyright Reserved.

REFERENCE

British Advance :—

German Defensive Positions		
	10th August	A
	11th do.	B
	13th -15th do.	C
	16th -19th do.	D
	20th -21st do.	E

Main Column (Van Deventer) — — —

Flanking Column (Burne) — · —

do.   Mounted Patrols · · · · ·

COMPILED BY HISTORICAL SECTION
(MILITARY BRANCH)

1550/8/41. CR.

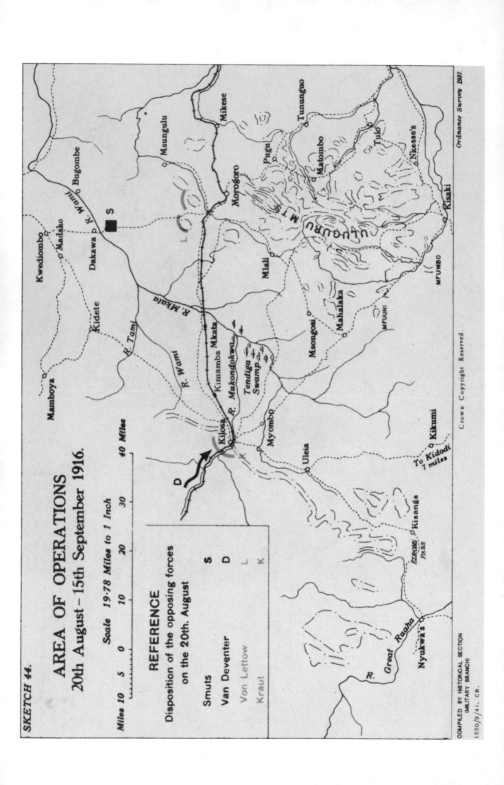

SKETCH 44.

AREA OF OPERATIONS
20th August – 15th September 1916.

Scale 19·78 Miles to 1 Inch

Miles 10   5   0   10   20   30   40 Miles

REFERENCE

Disposition of the opposing forces
on the 20th. August

Smuts   S
Van Deventer   D
Von Lettow   L
Kraut   K

Crown Copyright Reserved.

COMPILED BY HISTORICAL SECTION
(MILITARY BRANCH)
1550/9/41. CR.

Ordnance Survey 1937.

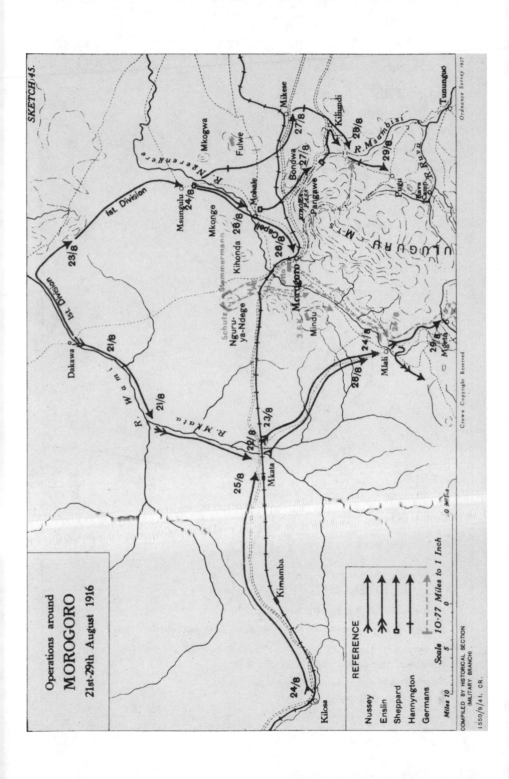

SKETCH.45.

Operations around
MOROGORO
21st-29th August 1916

REFERENCE

Nussey
Enslin
Sheppard
Hannyngton
Germans

Scale 10·77 Miles to 1 Inch

Miles 10   5   0

COMPILED BY HISTORICAL SECTION
(MILITARY BRANCH)

1550/9/41. CR.

Ordnance Survey 1937

Crown Copyright Reserved

0 Miles

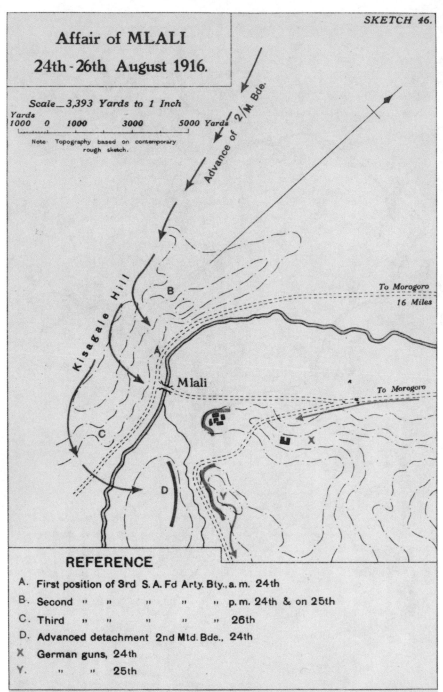

Affair of MLALI

24th-26th August 1916.

SKETCH 46.

Scale _ 3,393 Yards to 1 Inch

Yards
1000   0   1000   3000   5000 Yards

Note: Topography based on contemporary rough sketch.

Advance of 2/M. Bde.

Kisagale Hill

To Morogoro
16 Miles

Mlali

To Morogoro

REFERENCE

A. First position of 3rd S.A. Fd Arty. Bty., a.m. 24th

B. Second "   "   "   "   " p.m. 24th & on 25th

C. Third "   "   "   "   " 26th

D. Advanced detachment 2nd Mtd. Bde., 24th

X German guns, 24th

Y.   "   "   25th

COMPILED BY HISTORICAL SECTION
(MILITARY BRANCH)
1550/9/41. CR.

Ordnance Survey 1937

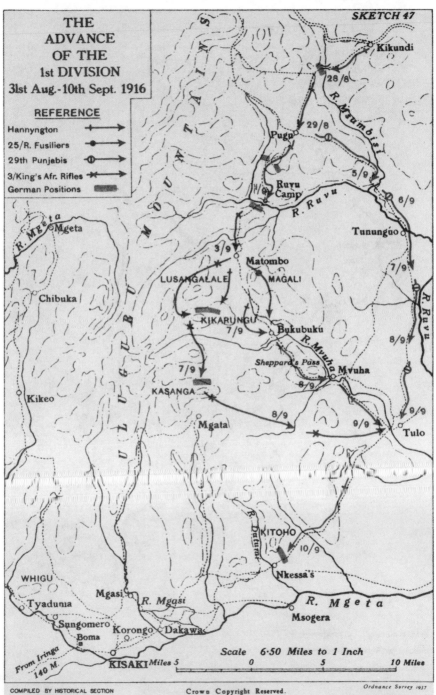

SKETCH 47

THE
ADVANCE
OF THE
1st DIVISION
31st Aug.-10th Sept. 1916

REFERENCE

Hannyngton ━━▶

25/R. Fusiliers ●━━▶

29th Punjabis ⦶━━▶

3/King's Afr. Rifles ×━━▶

German Positions ▬▬

Kikundi

28/8

R. Msumbisi

29/8

Pugu

5/9

6/9

Ruvu
Camp

R. Ruvu

Tununguo

R. Mgeta

Mgeta

7/9

R. Ruvu

3/9

Matombo

LUSANGALALE

MAGALI

Chibuka

KIKARUNGU

7/9

Bukubuku

R. Mvuha

8/9

Sheppard's Pass

Mvuha

7/9

8/9

KASANGA

9/9

Kikeo

Mgata

8/9

Tulo

9/9

R. Duturai

KITOHO

10/9

Nkessa's

WHIGU

Tyadunia

Mgasi

R. Mgasi

R. Mgeta

Sungomero

Korongo

Dakawa

Boma

Msogera

From Iringa
140 M.

KISAKI

Miles 5   0   5   10 Miles

Scale   6·50 Miles to 1 Inch

COMPILED BY HISTORICAL SECTION
(MILITARY BRANCH)

1550/9/41. C.R.

Crown Copyright Reserved.

Ordnance Survey 1937

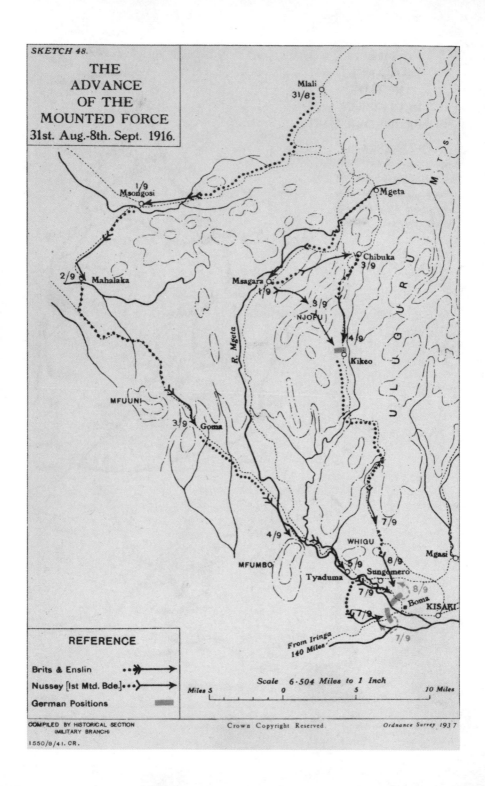

SKETCH 48.

THE
ADVANCE
OF THE
MOUNTED FORCE
31st. Aug.-8th. Sept. 1916.

Mlali
31/8

1/9
Msongosi

Mgeta

Chibuka
3/9

2/9 Mahalaka

Msagara
1/9

3/9
NJOFU

4/9
Kikeo

R. Mgeta

U L U G U R U

MTS.

MFUUNI

3/9 Goma

4/9

WHIGU

Mgasi

MFUMBO

5/9

8/9

Sungomero

Tyaduma

7/9

8/9

Boma
KISAKI

7/9

7/9

From Iringa
140 Miles

7/9

REFERENCE

Brits & Enslin ●●➤➤➤

Nussey [1st Mtd. Bde.] ●●➤➤

German Positions ▬▬

Scale   6·504 Miles to 1 Inch
Miles 5   0   5   10 Miles

COMPILED BY HISTORICAL SECTION
(MILITARY BRANCH)

Crown Copyright Reserved.

Ordnance Survey 1937

1550/9/41. CR.

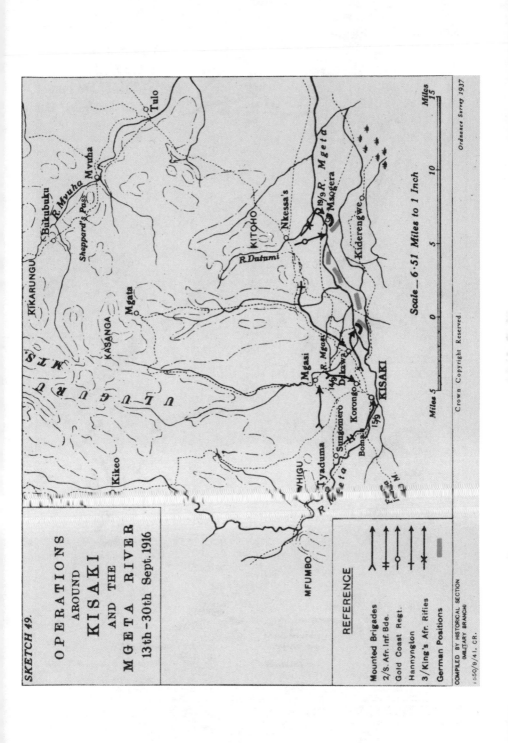

SKETCH 49.

OPERATIONS
AROUND
KISAKI
AND THE
MGETA RIVER
13th–30th Sept.1916

REFERENCE

Mounted Brigades
2/S. Afr. Inf. Bde.
Gold Coast Regt.
Hannyngton
3/King's Afr. Rifles
German Positions

Scale—6·51 Miles to 1 Inch

Crown Copyright Reserved

Ordnance Survey 1937

COMPILED BY HISTORICAL SECTION
(MILITARY BRANCH)
1550/9/41. CR.

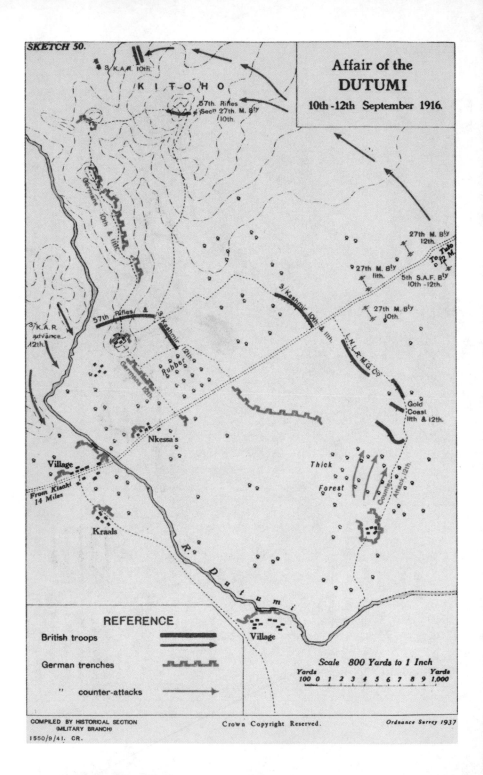

SKETCH 50.

Affair of the
DUTUMI
10th -12th September 1916.

K I T O H O

3 K.A.R. 10th.
57th. Rifles
Secⁿ 27th. M. B⁺ʸ
10th.

Germans 10th & 11th.

27th. M. B⁺ʸ
12th.
To Tulo
17 M.

27th. M. B⁺ʸ
11th.
5th S.A.F. B⁺ʸ
10th -12th.

3/ Kashmir 10th & 11th.

27th. M. B⁺ʸ
10th.

57th Rifles &
3 Kashmir 12th.

L.N.L.R. M.G. C⁰

3/K.A.R.
advance
12th.

Germans 12th.

Rubber

Gold
Coast
11th & 12th.

Nkessa's

Village

Thick

From Kisaki
14 Miles

Forest

Counter Attack, 12th.

Kraals

R. Dutumi

REFERENCE

British troops

German trenches

"   counter-attacks

Village

Scale   800 Yards to 1 Inch
Yards   Yards
100 0 1 2 3 4 5 6 7 8 9 1,000

COMPILED BY HISTORICAL SECTION
(MILITARY BRANCH)
1550/9/41. CR.

Ordnance Survey 1937

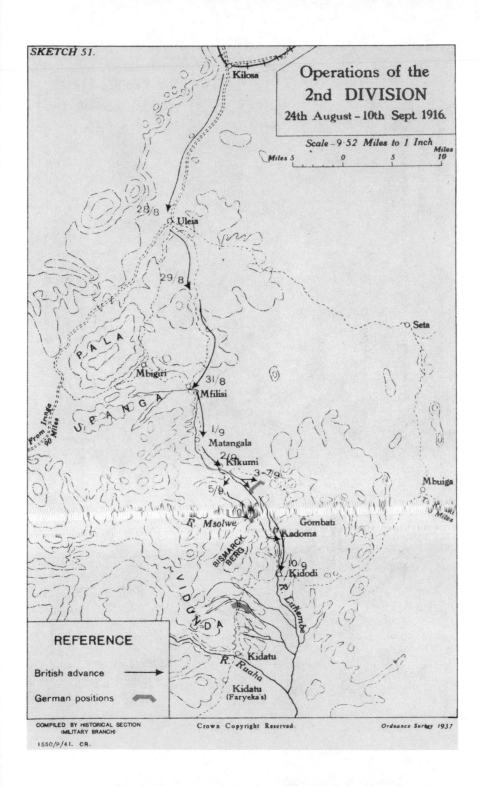

SKETCH 51.

Kilosa

Operations of the
2nd DIVISION
24th August – 10th Sept. 1916.

Scale – 9·52 Miles to 1 Inch

Miles 5   0   5   Miles 10

28/8

Uleia

29/8

Seta

PALA

Mbigiri

31/8

Mfilisi

UPANGA

From Iringa 90 Miles

1/9
Matangala

2/9 Kikumi

3–7/9

5/9

Mbuiga

R. Msolwe

Gombatı

Kadoma

BISMARCK BERG

10/9
Kidodi

VIDUNDA

R. Luhembe

Kidatu

R. Ruaha

Kidatu
(Faryeka's)

REFERENCE

British advance ⟶

German positions

COMPILED BY HISTORICAL SECTION
(MILITARY BRANCH)

Crown Copyright Reserved.

Ordnance Survey 1937

1550/9/41. CR.

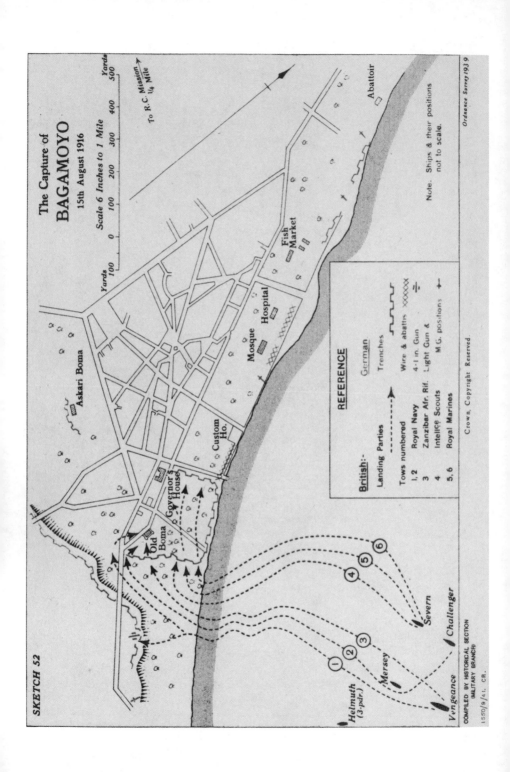

SKETCH 52

The Capture of
BAGAMOYO
15th August 1916

Scale 6 Inches to 1 Mile
0   100   200   300   400   500
Yards   Yards

To R.C. Mission
¼ Mile

Yards
100   0

Askari Boma

Old Boma

Governor's House

Custom Ho.

Mosque

Hospital

Fish Market

Abattoir

Helmuth
(3-pdr.)

Mersey

Vengeance

Severn

Challenger

1

2

3

4

5

6

REFERENCE

British:-   German

Landing Parties ═══▶   Trenches ﻌﻌﻌﻌ

Tows numbered   Wire & abattis ⬚⬚⬚⬚

1, 2   Royal Navy   4·1 in. Gun ⚓

3   Zanzibar Afr. Rif.   Light Gun ⚓

4   Intellce Scouts   M.G. positions ✛

5, 6   Royal Marines

Note. Ships & their positions
not to scale.

Crown, Copyright Reserved

Ordnance Survey 1939

COMPILED BY HISTORICAL SECTION
(MILITARY BRANCH)

1550/9/41. CR.

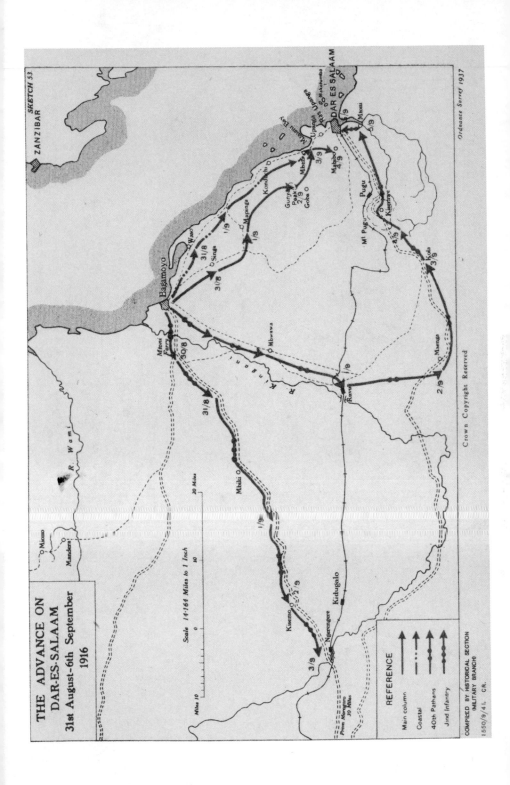

THE ADVANCE ON DAR-ES-SALAAM

31st August–6th September 1916

ZANZIBAR *SKETCH 53*

Scale 1:4:164 Miles to 1 Inch

REFERENCE

Main column
Coastal
40th Pathans
Jind Infantry

COMPILED BY HISTORICAL SECTION
(MILITARY BRANCH)

1550/9/41. CR.

Crown Copyright Reserved

Ordnance Survey 1937

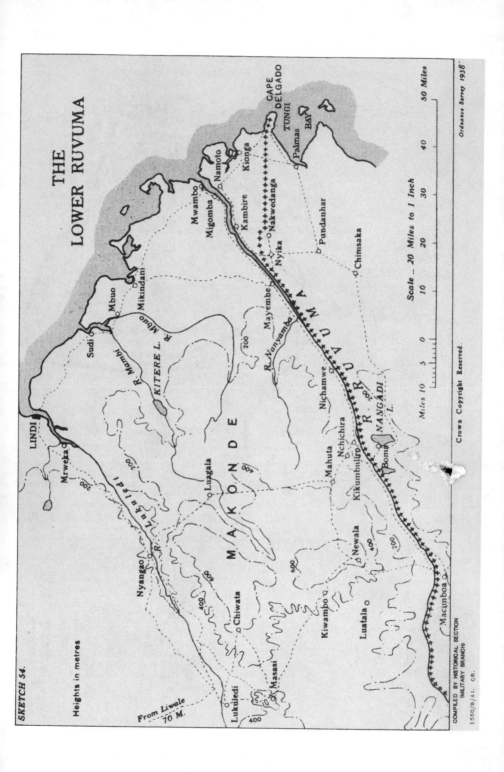

SKETCH 54.

THE
LOWER RUVUMA

Heights in metres

Scale – 20 Miles to 1 Inch

Miles 10   5   0   10   20   30   40   50 Miles

Crown Copyright Reserved.

Ordnance Survey 1938

COMPILED BY HISTORICAL SECTION
(MILITARY BRANCH)

1550/8/41. C.R.

LINDI

Mrweka

Nyangao

Chiwata

Masasi

Lukuledi

From Liwale
70 M.

Sudi

Mbuo

Mikindani

Luagala

M A K O N D E

Kiwambo

Newala

Luatala

Macumboa

KITERE L.

R. Mbuo

R. Mambi

R. Lukuledi

Mwambo

Migomba

Namoto

Namoto

Kambire

Kionga

CAPE
DELGADO

TUNGI
BAY

C. Palmas

Nakwedanga

Nyika

Pundanhar

Chimsaka

Mayembe

R. Nanyamba

R U V U M A

Nichamwe

Mahuta

Nchichira

Kikumbuliro

Somi

NANGADI
L.

700

200

400

600

200

400

600

400

800

600

400

200

200

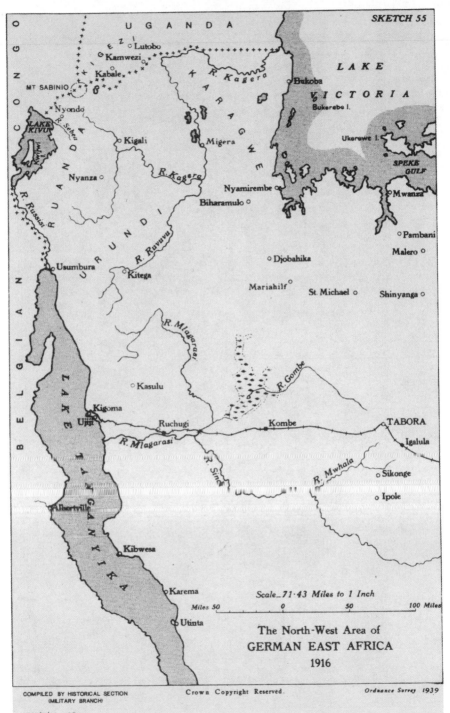

CONGO

UGANDA

E Z I o Lutobo
o Kamwezi
Kabale
MT SABINIO
Nyondo
R. Sebui

LAKE KIVU

RUANDA

Kigali

Nyanza o

R. Russissi

R. Kagera

KARAGWE

Migera

R. Kagera

URUNDI

Usumbura
Kitega

R. Ruvuvu

LAKE VICTORIA

o Bukoba

Bukerebe I.

Ukerewe I.

SPEKE GULF

Nyamirembe o
Biharamulo o

Mwanza

o Pambani

Malero o

o Djobahika

Mariahilf o
St. Michael o
Shinyanga o

R. Mlagarasi

BELGIAN

LAKE

TANGANYIKA

Kasulu o

Kigoma
Ujiji

Ruchugi

R. Mlagarasi

R. Sindi

R. Gombe

Kombe o

TABORA

Igalula o

R. Mwhala

o Sikonge

o Ipole

Albertville

Kibwesa

Karema o

Utinta o

Scale_71·43 Miles to 1 Inch

Miles 50   0   50   100 Miles

The North-West Area of
GERMAN EAST AFRICA
1916

COMPILED BY HISTORICAL SECTION
(MILITARY BRANCH)

Crown Copyright Reserved.

Ordnance Survey 1939

1550/9/41. CR.

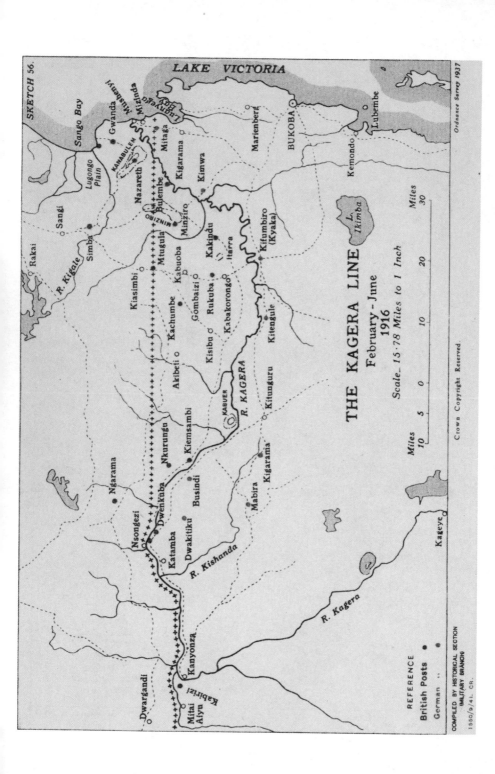

SKETCH 56.

LAKE VICTORIA

THE KAGERA LINE
February – June
1916
Scale_ 15·78 Miles to 1 Inch

Miles   Miles
10   5   0   10   20   30

Crown Copyright Reserved.

REFERENCE
British Posts   ●
German   "   ○

COMPILED BY HISTORICAL SECTION
(MILITARY BRANCH)

1550/9/41. CR.

Ordnance Survey 1937

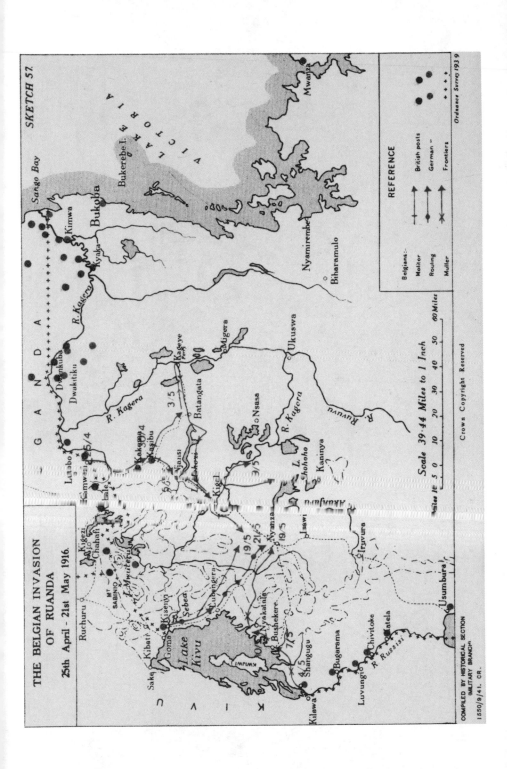

SKETCH 57.

THE BELGIAN INVASION
OF RUANDA
25th April - 21st May 1916.

REFERENCE

Belgians:—
Moulaert
Rouling
Muller

British posts
German "
Frontiers

Scale 39·44 Miles to 1 Inch
Miles 10   5   0   10   20   30   40   50   60 Miles

Crown Copyright Reserved

Ordnance Survey 1939

COMPILED BY HISTORICAL SECTION
(MILITARY BRANCH)
1550/9/41. CR.

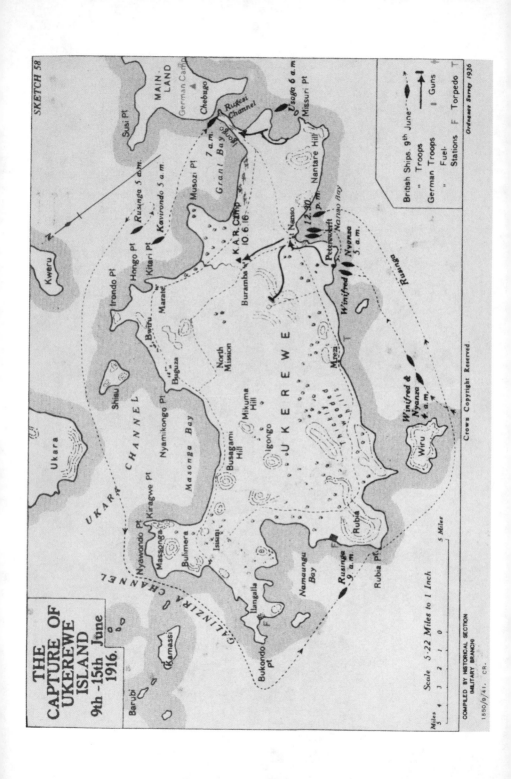

SKETCH 58

THE
CAPTURE OF
UKEREWE
ISLAND
9th–15th June
1916.

Scale 5·22 Miles to 1 Inch

Miles 5 4 3 2 1 0   5 Miles

COMPILED BY HISTORICAL SECTION
(MILITARY BRANCH)

1550/9/41. CR.

Crown Copyright Reserved

Ordnance Survey 1936

British Ships. 9th June
   "   Troops
German Troops
   "   Fuel-
   "   Stations   F Torpedo

Guns

MAIN-
LAND

German Camp

Chebugo

Rugesi
Channel

Grant Bay

Usoga 6 a.m.

Missuri Pt

Nantare Hill

Nanso

Peterwerft

Winifred

Nyanza
5. a.m.

Nansio Bay

Rusinga

Winifred &
Nyanza
4 a.m.

Wiru

Rubia

Rubia Pt.

Rusinga
9. a.m.

Namaungu
Bay

Ilangalla

Bukondo
Pt.

Kamassi

Barubi

Ukara

Kweru

Susi Pt

Rusinga 5 a.m.

Kavirondo 5 a.m.

Hongo Pt

Kitari Pt

Irondo Pt

Marate

Bwiru

Buguza

Musozi Pt

K.A.R. Camp
10.6.16

Buramba

North
Mission

Mikuma
Hill

Igongo

Mwazi

Thickets
Woods

U K E R E W E

Busagami
Hill

Masonga Bay

Nyamikongo Pt

Kiragwe Pt

Massonga

Nyawondo Pt

Bulimera

Issiny

Shisu

U K A R A   C H A N N E L

G A L I N Z I R A   C H A N N E L

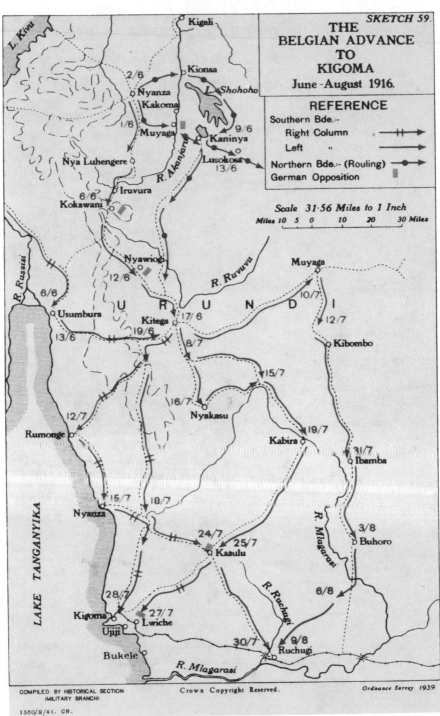

SKETCH 59.

THE BELGIAN ADVANCE TO KIGOMA
June - August 1916.

REFERENCE
Southern Bde.:-
Right Column
Left "
Northern Bde.:- (Rouling)
German Opposition

Scale 31·56 Miles to 1 Inch

Miles 10 5 0 10 20 30 Miles

L. Kivu

Kigali

2/6
Kionsa
Nyanza
Kakoma
L. Shohoho
1/6
Muyaga
9/6
Kaninya
Nya Luhengere
Lusokosa
13/6
R. Akanjaru
6/6
Iruvura
Kokawani

R. Russisi
6/8
Nyawiogi
12/6
Muyaga
R. Ruvuvu
10/7
U   R   U   N   D   I
Usumbura
Kitega
17/6
12/7
13/6
19/6
8/7
Kibombo
15/7
16/7
Nyakasu
19/7
Rumonge
12/7
Kabira
31/7
Ibamba
15/7   10/7
Nyanza
3/8
24/7
25/7   Buhoro
Kasulu
R. Mlagarasi
28/7
6/8
Kigoma
27/7
Lwiche
R. Ruchugi
Ujiji
30/7
9/8
Ruchugi
Bukele
R. Mlagarasi

LAKE TANGANYIKA

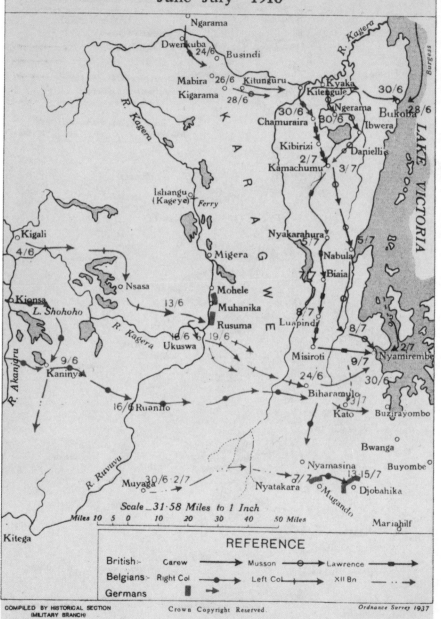

SKETCH 60.

BRITISH & BELGIAN OPERATIONS
WEST OF LAKE VICTORIA
June - July 1916

Ngarama

Dwenkuba 24/6 Busindi

Mabira 26/6 Kitunguru
Kigarama 28/6

R. Kagera

Chamuraira 30/6 30/6

Kyaka
Kitengule
30/6
28/6
Ngerama Bukoba
Ibwera

Burgess

LAKE VICTORIA

Kibirizi
2/7
Kamachumu 3/7

Daniell's

Ishangu (Kageye) Ferry

Nyakarahura 5/7 Nabula 5/7
Biaia

Kigali
4/6

Migera

Nsasa

Kiensa
L. Shohoho
13/6

Mohele
Muhanika
Rusuma 18/6 19/6
Ukuswa

Luapindi 8/7 8/7

R. Akanjru
9/6
Kaninya

R. Kagera

Misiroti 9/7

Nyamirembe 2/7

24/6
30/6

16/6 Ruanflo

Biharamulo 3/7
Kato Buzirayombo

Bwanga
Buyombe

Muyaga 30/6 2/7
Nyatakara 3/7
Nyamasina
Djobahika 13 15/7
Mugando

R. Ruvuvu

Scale - 31.58 Miles to 1 Inch
Miles 10 5 0 10 20 30 40 50 Miles

Kitega

Mariahilf

REFERENCE

British:-	Carew	→	Musson	⊖→	Lawrence	■→
Belgians:-	Right Col	●→	Left Col	┼→	XII Bn	—··→
Germans	▮→					

COMPILED BY HISTORICAL SECTION
(MILITARY BRANCH)
1550/9/41. CR.

Ordnance Survey 1937

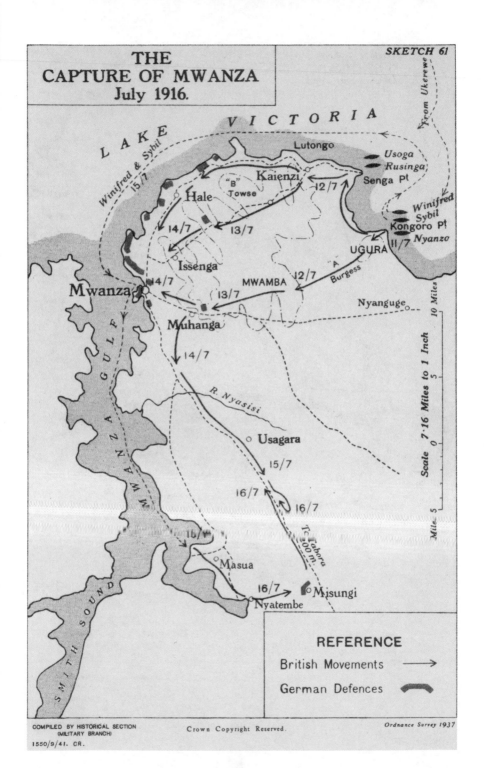

THE
CAPTURE OF MWANZA
July 1916.

SKETCH 61

REFERENCE

British Movements →

German Defences

COMPILED BY HISTORICAL SECTION
(MILITARY BRANCH)
1550/9/41. CR.

Ordnance Survey 1937

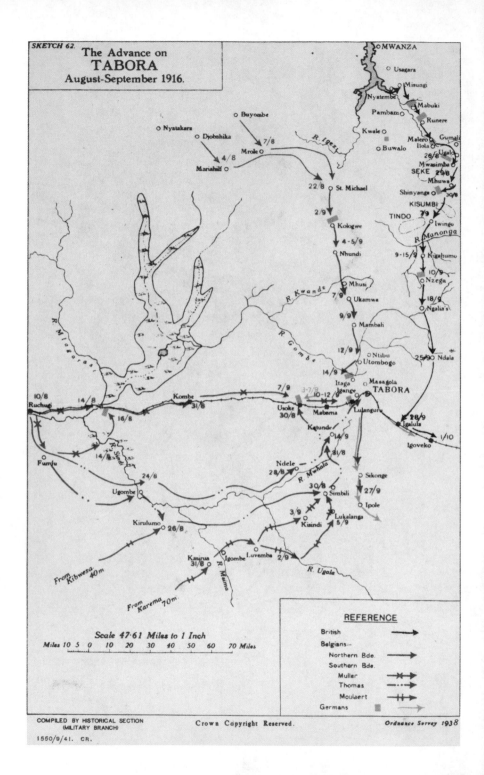

SKETCH 62.
The Advance on
TABORA
August-September 1916.

MWANZA
Usagara
Misungi
Nyatembe
Mabuki
Pambani
Runere
Kwale
Buyombe
Malero
Gumali
Nyatakara
Djobahika
Mrole
7/8
Itola
Ugala
26/8
Mariahilf
4/8
Buwalo
Mwasimba
SEKE 29/8
Mhuwa
Shinyanga
30/8
22/8
St. Michael
KISUMBI
TINDO
7/9
2/9
Iwingu
Kologwe
R. Manonga
4-5/9
9-15/9
Kigahumo
Nhundi
10/9
Nzega
Mhusi
7/9
Ukamwa
18/9
9/9
Ngalia's
Mambali
25/9 Ndala
12/9
Ntibu
Utombogo
14/9
Masagola
Itaga TABORA
Igange
7/9
3-7/9
10-12/9
Kombe
31/8
Usoke
Mabema
Lulanguru
10/8
14/8
30/8
28/9
Ruchugi
16/8
Katunde
Igalula
14/9
1/10
Fumfu
14/8
31/8
Igoveko
24/8
Ndele
Sikonge
Ugombe
28/8
30/8
27/9
Simbili
Ipole
Kirulumo
26/8
3/9
Lukalanga
Kisindi
5/9
Kasirua
Igombe
Luvemba
31/8
2/9
From Kibwesa 40m
R. Ugala
From Karema 70m.

REFERENCE
British
Belgians:—
  Northern Bde.
  Southern Bde.
  Muller
  Thomas
  Moulaert
Germans

Scale 47.61 Miles to 1 Inch
Miles 10 5 0   10   20   30   40   50   60   70 Miles

R. Igesi
R. Kwande
R. Gombe
R. Mkarara
R. Sindi
R. Mania
R. Mwhala

COMPILED BY HISTORICAL SECTION
(MILITARY BRANCH)

1550/9/41. CR.

Ordnance Survey 1938

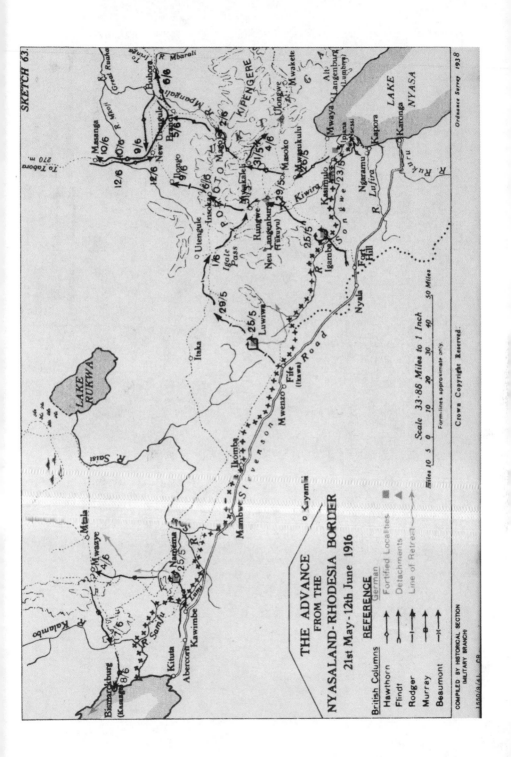

SKETCH 63.

THE ADVANCE
FROM THE
NYASALAND-RHODESIA BORDER
21st May - 12th June 1916

REFERENCE

British Columns   German
Hawthorn   ⟶   ▨ Fortified Localities
Flindt   ⟶   ▲ Detachments
Rodger   ⊢—⟶   Line of Retreat
Murray   ⊶⟶
Beaumont   ⤙⟶

Miles 10 5 0   10   20   30   40   50 Miles
Scale 33·86 Miles to 1 Inch
Form-lines approximate only

COMPILED BY HISTORICAL SECTION
(MILITARY BRANCH)

Ordnance Survey 1938

Crown Copyright Reserved.

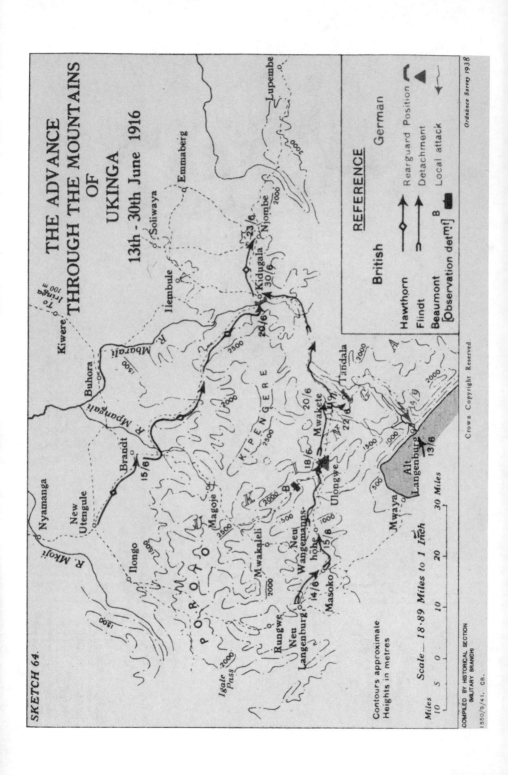

SKETCH 64.

THE ADVANCE
THROUGH THE MOUNTAINS
OF
UKINGA
13th - 30th June 1916

REFERENCE

British   German

Hawthorn ➤➤➤   Rearguard Position
Flindt ➤➤➤   Detachment
Beaumont ⬛ᴮ   Local attack
[Observation det.ⁿ]

Contours approximate
Heights in metres

Scale — 18·89 Miles to 1 Inch

Miles 10 5 0   10   20   30 Miles

COMPILED BY HISTORICAL SECTION
(MILITARY BRANCH)

1550/9/41. CR.

Crown Copyright Reserved.

Ordnance Survey 1938

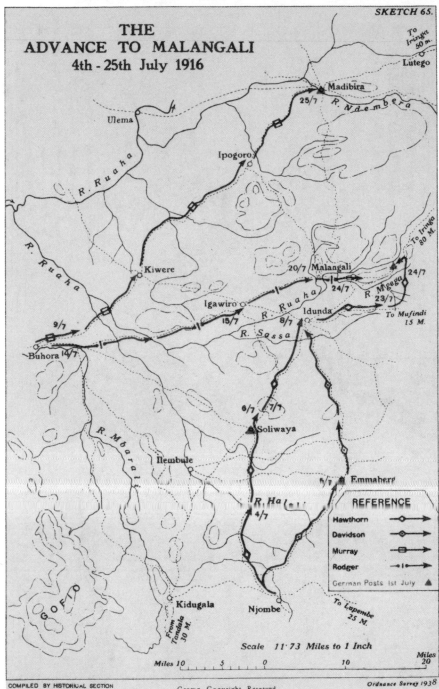

SKETCH 65.

THE
ADVANCE TO MALANGALI
4th - 25th July 1916

To Iringa 50 m.

Lutego

Madibira

25/7

R. Ndembera

Ulema

Ipogoro

R. Ruaha

Kiwere

To Iringa 80 M.

20/7 Malangali

24/7

24/7 R. Mgega

23/7

9/7

Igawiro

R. Ruaha

Idunda

To Mufindi 15 M.

13/7

8/7

R. Sassa

Buhora 14/7

R. Mbarali

6/7 7/7

Soliwaya

Ilembule

5/7 Emmabere

R. Hal...

4/7

GOFI

REFERENCE

Hawthorn	→◇→
Davidson	→◆→
Murray	◫→
Rodger	◂ꜜ→
German Posts 1st July	▲

From Tandala 30 M.

Kidugala

Njombe

To Lupembe 25 M.

Scale 11·73 Miles to 1 Inch

Miles 10   5   0   10   Miles 20

COMPILED BY HISTORICAL SECTION
(MILITARY BRANCH)

Crown Copyright Reserved.

Ordnance Survey 1938

1550/9/41. CR.

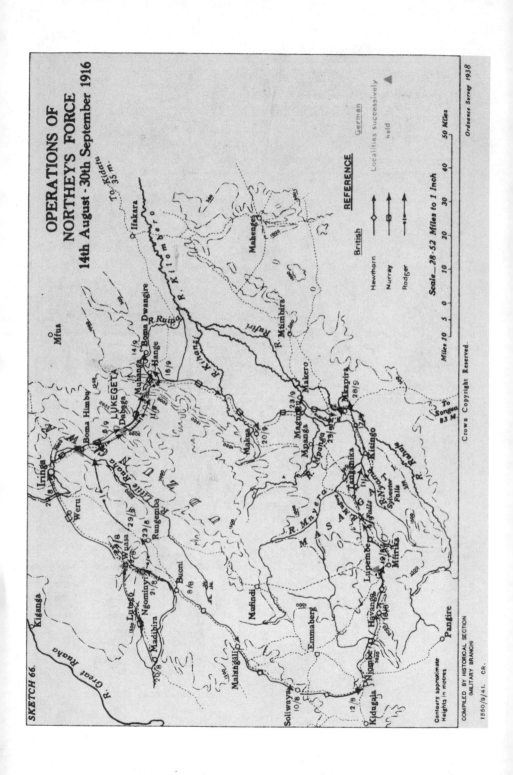

SKETCH 66.

OPERATIONS OF
NORTHEY'S FORCE
14th August - 30th September 1916

REFERENCE

British

Hawthorn
Nurray
Rodger

German

Localities successively
held

Scale—28·52 Miles to 1 Inch

Miles 10   5   0   10   20   30   40   50 Miles

Contours approximate
Heights in metres

Ordnance Survey 1938

COMPILED BY HISTORICAL SECTION
(MILITARY BRANCH)

1550/9/41.   CR.